The Elements of International Law

THE DORSEY SERIES IN POLITICAL SCIENCE

EDITOR **NORTON E. LONG** *Brandeis University*

The Elements of
International Law

GERARD J. MANGONE

Professor of Political Science and Associate Dean
The Maxwell School of Citizenship and Public Affairs
Syracuse University

REVISED EDITION · 1967

THE DORSEY PRESS

HOMEWOOD, ILLINOIS

Revised Edition

First Printing, March, 1967

Library of Congress Catalog Card No. 67–15797

Printed in the United States of America

Preface

THE SECOND EDITION of this book, like the first, has been designed as a fundamental introduction to the study of international law by the use of text, cases, and documents. Certain descriptive and historical information, easily available in other books on international law, has been omitted in the interest of emphasizing contemporary issues and helping the student to perceive the dynamic development of a world legal order with its promises and its faults.

At the outset the reader should be clear that the study of international law forms only a part of an analysis of international relations. Essentially the discipline of international law is a systematic way of looking at the juridical relations of states as they seek to work out their national interests in a world community by resort to legal argument, binding agreements, arbitration, or adjudication. The formulation and practice of law between states can be seen every day in the negotiations of national and international officials, as well as in issues placed before national or international courts, while virtually all the public pronouncements on world politics and world order refer to rights and duties within the international system.

The law of nations has a respectable history. Like other systems of law, it depends heavily upon tradition, analogy, and deduction. But as Justice Oliver Wendell Holmes, Jr., once pointed out, "We do not realize how large a part of our law is open to reconsideration upon a slight change in the habit of the public mind." The eye of the student, scholar, and statesman, therefore, should be fixed on ways to make the current practice of international law contribute to a desirable future for mankind. Put another way, they should be prepared to engage in a battle for values.

To claim that legal rules can answer all the problems of the peoples on this planet would be fatuous, for human behavior is just too spontaneous, irrational, and free-willed ever to be completely harnessed by the conservative bridle of law. Life is much larger than legalities. But to ignore the necessity of fashioning legal authority for an ideal of justice that may transcend the petty passions of the moment is only begging for bestiality.

Among others who have given constructive ideas and suggestions to the outline and text of this book in its first and second editions I wish to thank Leo Gross of the Fletcher School of Law and Diplomacy; Oliver J. Lissitzyn of Columbia University; Oscar Schacter of the United Nations Institute for Training and Research; Quincy Wright, professor emeritus of the University of Chicago and scholar of the world; Edward D. Re, Chairman of the U.S. Foreign Claims Settlement Commission; George Manner of the University of Illinois; and Stanley V. Anderson of the California Bar and the University of California at Santa Barbara. The completion of the manuscript for the second edition was enormously facilitated by the devoted research of my assistant, Robert S. Peckham, who tracked down data and documents, and the nimble, painstaking typing of my efficient secretary, Lelia Letherland. To both of them I am sincerely grateful. All errors of fact or deficiencies of judgment are mine.

I also wish to thank the following publishers: Cambridge University Press, for permission to quote from Lord McNair's *International Law Opinions* (1956); Macmillan Company for permission to quote from Philip C. Jessup, *A Modern Law of Nations* (1948); Manchester University Press, for permission to quote from Quincy Wright, *The Role of International Law in the Elimination of War* (1961); Stevens and Sons, for permission to quote from Paul Weiss, *Nationality and Statelessness in International Law* (1956); and *Washington Law Review*, for permission to reprint part of the article of Peter E. Herzog on *The Court of Justice of the European Communities* (Volume 4, No. 3, June, 1966).

GERARD J. MANGONE

Syracuse, New York
January, 1967

List of Cases Edited or Cited

Bibliographical Notes

Beyond the introduction of this book the advanced study of international law will require a reference to primary or source materials. These include treaties and other international agreements, court reports or decisions, collections of cases, commentaries, diplomatic correspondence and state papers, opinions of the attorneys general, and specialized periodicals or yearbooks that treat international legal problems. For convenience a brief guide to some sources is listed below.

I. TREATIES AND OTHER INTERNATIONAL AGREEMENTS

A. International Collections

DUMONT, JEAN. *Corps universel diplomatique du droit des gens,* 8 vols., Amsterdam, 1726–31. Covers treaties of alliance, peace, neutrality, commerce, etc. from the time of Charlemagne (800) to time of publication.

VON MARTENS, G. F. *Recueil des principaux traités d'alliance de paix . . .* (1761–1801), 7 vols., Göttingen, 1791–1801; 2d ed., 8 vols. (1761–1808), Vols. 5–8 ed. by K. von Martens, Göttingen, 1817–35.

VON MARTENS, G. F. *Supplément au Recueil . . .* (1494–1807), 8 vols., Göttingen, 1802–8.

VON MARTENS, G. F. *Nouveau recueil des traites . . .* (1808–39), 16 vols., Vols. 5–16 ed. by K. von Martens and others, Göttingen, 1817–42. *Nouveau Supplements* (1761–1839), 3 vols.

VON MARTENS, G. F. *Nouveau recueil general de traites . . .* (1840–74), 20 vols., Göttingen, 1843–75; 2d series (1876–1908), 35 vols., Göttingen and Leipzig, 1876–1908; 3rd series (1907–42), Leipzig, 1909–42.

HUDSON, MANLEY O. *International Legislation,* 9 vols. Collection of texts of all multilateral treaties of general interest beginning with the Covenant of the League and continuing to 1945. Each document is supplemented by editor's notes and pertinent bibliography.

LEAGUE OF NATIONS. *Treaty Series.* Contains treaties registered with the Secretariat of the League. 205 volumes covering the period 1920–46.

UNITED NATIONS. *Treaty Series.* Contains treaties registered with U.N. Series contains 524 volumes up to 1965.

B. National Collections

1. UNITED STATES

MILLER, DAVID H. *Treaties and Other International Acts of the United States of America.* 8 volumes, covering the period 1776–1863. Washington, D.C.: U.S. Government Printing Office, 1931–48.

MALLOY, WILLIAM M. *Treaties, Conventions, International Acts, Protocols, and Agreements between the United States of America and Other Powers.* Vols. I–II, 1776–1909, edited by Malloy; Vol. III, 1910–23, by C. F. Redmond; Vol. IV, 1923–37, by E. J. Trenwith. Washington, D.C.: U.S. Government Printing Office, 1910–38.

Treaty Series. Individual prints of treaties numbered serially from 1908 onwards, including some executive orders and agreements, published until 1945.

Executive Agreements Series. Individual prints of executive agreements, numbered serially from 1929 to 1945.

Treaties and Other International Acts Series. After 1945, U.S. Treaty Series and Executive Agreement Series are incorporated in this series beginning with number 1501. Issued in individual prints.

Treaties and Other International Agreements. Bound volumes issued annually, beginning in 1950, containing treaties and executive agreements for year in question, which have been previously issued in individual prints noted above. Before 1950, all treaties were bound in the *United States Statutes at Large.* Executive agreements were also included from 1931 to 1950.

Treaties in Force. Annual publication listing by countries and subjects the international agreements of the United States currently in force.

2. GREAT BRITAIN

HERTSLET. *Hertslet's Commercial Treaties.* London, 31 vols., containing collection of treaties and conventions between Great Britain and foreign powers, and of laws, decrees, orders in council, etc. so far as they relate to commerce, navigation, slavery, extradition, nationality. Vols. 1–19 published by Butterworth, 1827–95 and Vols. 20–31 published by H.M. Stationery Office.

British and Foreign State Papers. Series began in 1812. After 1922, Hertslet is included in this series.

Treaty Series, including ratified treaties and other agreements or exchanges of note, numbered each year since 1892.

II. INTERNATIONAL COURT DECISIONS

A. Permanent Court of International Justice (PCIJ)

Official publications of the PCIJ are broken down into six series:
1. Judgments, Orders, and Advisory Opinions.
2. Opinions.
3. Acts and Documents Relating to Judgments and Advisory Opinions.
4. Texts Governing the Jurisdiction.
5. Annual Report.
6. General Index.

An unofficial collection is found in:

HUDSON, MANLEY O. *World Court Reports: A Collection of the Judgments, Orders and Opinions of the Permanent Court of International Justice,* 4 volumes, Carnegie Endowment for International Peace, 1934–43.

GUGGENHEIM, PAUL. *Répertoire des décisions et des documents de la procédure écrite et orale de la Cour permanente de justice internationale et de la Cour internationale de justice.* Geneva: Librairie E. Droz, 1961.

B. International Court of Justice (ICJ)

Official publications of the ICJ are broken down into four series:
1. Reports of Judgments, Advisory Opinions, and Orders ("ICJ Reports").
2. Pleadings, Oral Arguments, Documents.
3. Acts and Documents concerning organization of the Court.
4. International Court of Justice Yearbook ("ICJ Yearbook").

Two books of special interest dealing with the Permanent Court of International Justice and the International Court of Justice are:

HAMBRO, EDVARD ISAK. *The Case Law of the International Court: A Repertoire of the Judgments, Advisory Opinions and Orders of the Permanent Court of International Justice and of the International Court of Justice,* 3 vols. Series contents are: I, Until 1951; II, 1952–1958; III, Individual and Dissenting Opinions, 1947–1958. Leiden: A. W. Sijthoff, 1960–1963.

LAUTERPACHT, H. *The Development of International Law by the International Court.* London: Stevens & Sons, 1958. This is a revised edition of the 1934 volume entitled, *The Development of International Law by the Permanent Court of International Justice.*

C. Permanent Court of Arbitration

SCOTT, J. B. *The Hague Court Reports,* 2 vols. New York: Oxford University Press, 1916 and 1932. Contains awards, agreements for arbitration and other documents in cases submitted to court.

D. Court of Justice of the European Communities

Reports of the Decisions of the Court of Justice of the European Communities, 10 volumes published up to 1964 containing the decisions rendered from 1954 onward, in four official languages. Paris, Recueil Sirey; Luxembourg, Services des Publications des Communautés Européenes.

Common Market Reporter, published by the Commerce Clearing House, Inc., Chicago, contains contemporary decisions of the Court as well as national court decisions involving Common Market treaty questions.

E. European Court of Human Rights

Publications. Series A: *Judgments and Decisions;* Series B: *Pleadings, Oral Arguments, and Documents.*

F. Other Collections of Cases and Claims before International Tribunals or Commissions

UNITED NATIONS. *Reports of International Arbitral Awards,* 14 volumes published to 1964. Contain decisions of various claims commissions since 1910 to present, arranged by commissions and parties.

MOORE, J. B. *History and Digest of the International Arbitrations to which the United States has been a Party,* 6 vols. Washington, D.C.: U.S. Government Printing Office, 1898. Covers period from colonial times to 1890.

MOORE, J. B. *International Adjudications, Ancient and Modern,* 6 vols. New York: Oxford University Press, 1929–33.

LAUTERPACHT, H. *International Law Reports.* Before 1950, titled *Annual Digest and Reports of Public International Law Cases.* Annual publications from 1919 containing summaries of cases relating to international law arising in international courts and tribunals and national courts for year in question. Usually published 3–4 years after cases recorded.

III. NATIONAL COURT DECISIONS

United States Reports contains nearly all written decisions of the United States Supreme Court from the first reported case of the Court in 1791. The first ninety volumes are cited by the names of the official reporters, i.e., Dallas, Cranch, etc. under the former title of *Reports of Cases Argued and Adjudged in the Supreme Court of the United States.* In 1875 the title was changed to *United States Reports.* There is also an unofficial *Lawyer's Edition of the Supreme Court Reports* and the *Supreme Court Reporter,* from 1882.

Federal Reporter, since 1880, reports decisions of the United States Courts of Appeal, the District of Columbia Court of Appeals, and, up until 1931, the United States district courts.

Federal Supplement, since 1932, reports selected decisions of United States district courts.

The United States Court of Claims, Customs Court, and Court of Customs and Patent Appeals also have their official reports.

Foreign Claims Settlement Commission, semiannual reports to the United States Congress from 1954 onward. "Settlement of Claims," published in 1955, covers the activities of predecessor national claims commissions from 1949 to 1955.

English *Law Reports* from 1865 are published in different series: i.e., Appeal Cases (House of Lords and Judicial Committee of the Privy Council), Queens Bench Division, Chancery Division, and Probate, Divorce and Admiralty Division—and others prior to 1926. Not all cases are reported in these semiofficial *Law Reports.* Other cases can be found in the *All-England Law Reports,* the *Law Times Reports,* and *Weekly Law Reports.*

IV. SELECTED CASE BOOKS

HUDSON, MANLEY O. *Cases on International Law.* 3d ed. St. Paul: West Publishing Company, 1951.

BRIGGS, HERBERT W. *The Law of Nations: Cases, Documents, and Notes.* 2d ed. New York: Appleton-Century-Crofts, 1952.

GREEN, LESLIE C. *International Law through the Cases.* 2d ed. New York: Praeger, 1955.

JAEGER, WALTER, H. E., and WILLIAM V. O'BRIEN. *International Law: Cases, Text-notes, and other Materials.* Rev. ed. Washington, D.C.: Georgetown University Press, 1959–60.

KATZ, MILTON, and KINGMAN BREWSTER, JR. *The Law of International Transactions and Relations.* Brooklyn: Foundation Press, 1960.

BISHOP, WILLIAM W., JR. *International Law: Cases and Materials.* 2d ed. New York: Prentice-Hall, 1962.

KISS, ALEXANDRE CHARLES. *Répertoire de la pratique française en matière de droit international public.* Paris: Editions du Centre national de la recherche scientifique. Beginning in 1962.

SOHN, LOUIS B. *Cases on United Nations Law.* Brooklyn: The Foundation Press, 1956. Supplemented by SOHN, LOUIS B., *Recent Cases on United Nations Law.* Brooklyn: The Foundation Press, 1963.

British International Law Cases: A Collection of Decisions of Courts in the British Isles on Points of International Law. New York: Oceana Publications, 1964– . Beginning in 1964, this series was prepared under the auspices of the International Law Fund and the British Institute of International and Comparative Law. Two volumes had appeared by the end of 1965 dealing with states as international persons.

V. COMMENTARIES OR DIGESTS

SYATAUW, J. J. G. *Decisions of the International Court of Justice; A Digest.* Leiden: A. W. Sijthoff, 1962. Kept up to date by periodical supplements.

WHITEMAN, MARJORIE MILLACE. *Digest of International Law,* 5 vols. Washington, D.C.: Government Printing Office, 1963–65. Covers documents and files, accumulated in the Department of State primarily during the last two decades. Earlier digests were edited by Green Haywood Hackworth (1940–44), John Bassett Moore (1906), and Francis Wharton (1886).

LAUTERPACHT, E. *International Law Reports.* London: Butterworth. 29 volumes by mid-1966.

A British Digest of International Law. London: Stevens, 1965. 10 volumes of Phase I covering 1860–1914 had been produced by mid-1966.

VI. PRINTED DIPLOMATIC CORRESPONDENCE AND STATE PAPERS

A. United States

MANNING, WILLIAM R. *Diplomatic Correspondence of the United States: Canadian Relations 1784–1860,* 3 vols. Washington, D.C.: Carnegie Endowment for International Peace, 1940–43.

MANNING, WILLIAM R. *Diplomatic Correspondence of the United States Concerning the Independence of the Latin-American Nations,* 3 vols. New York: Oxford University Press, 1925.

B. Great Britain

Documents on British Foreign Policy, 1919–1939, 23 vols. (selected documents).

British and Foreign State Papers. Series began in 1812.

VII. OPINIONS OF ATTORNEYS GENERAL

McNAIR, ARNOLD D. *International Law Opinions selected and annotated,* 3 vols. (I–II, Peace; III, War and Neutrality). Cambridge University Press, 1956.

DEENER, DAVID R. *The United States Attorneys General and International Law.* The Hague: Martinus Nijhoff, 1957.

VIII. SELECTED PERIODICALS AND YEARBOOKS

The American Journal of International Law. Published quarterly since 1907.

The British Yearbook of International Law. Published annually since 1920.

The International and Comparative Law Quarterly. Quarterly published by (British) Society of Comparative Legislation since 1952. Supersedes *International Law Quarterly* (1947–51) and *Journal of Comparative Legislation and International Law* (1896–1951).

Recueil des Cours. Published by the Academy of International Law at The Hague. An "encyclopedia" of international law, since 1923. Contains lectures and articles on various subjects by noted jurists and legal scholars.

Annuaire français de droit international. Published by the National Center for Scientific Research, Paris, for the Academy of International Law, The Hague, since 1955.

Journal du droit international. Published in Paris by the Librarie générale de droit et de jurisprudence since 1874.

UNITED NATIONS. *Yearbook of the International Law Commission.* Published annually from 1949.

International Legal Materials. Published bi-monthly by the American Society of International Law since 1962.

Table of Contents

SECTION III

THE EFFECT OF TREATIES AND OTHER INTERNATIONAL AGREEMENTS   87

SECTION IV

JURISDICTION: TITLE AND TRANSFER OF SOVEREIGNTY   131

SECTION V

JURISDICTION: THE SEAS, VESSELS, SPACE, AND CARRIERS   161

SECTION VI

NATIONALITY: JURISDICTION OVER PERSONS   199

SECTION IX

INTERNATIONAL CLAIMS: PERSONAL INJURIES AND WAR DAMAGES 343

SECTION X

INTERNATIONAL CLAIMS: BREACH OF CONTRACT AND EXPROPRIATION OF PROPERTY 365

SECTION XI

THE LEGAL REGULATION OF INTERNATIONAL FORCE 417

SECTION XII

THE DEVELOPMENT OF INTERNATIONAL LAW   470

INDEX

I

Nature, Sources, and Application of International Law

The functions of international law, as in any system of law, are to assist in the maintenance of order and in the administration of justice.
—QUINCY WRIGHT[1]

THE study of international relations, embracing the interaction of states and their peoples with one another in a world community, may be conveniently divided into topics or subjects that are: (*a*) essentially *political;* (*b*) essentially *organizational,* including the administrative process; and (*c*) essentially *legal.* As a discipline, international law cannot be divorced from a sound knowledge of international politics and international organization. In both domestic and foreign affairs, law depends on power and persuasion—the stuff of politics; politics depends on organization and administration for effectiveness; and organized society cannot function without rules, regulations, and reasonable expectations—the very fabric of law.

The law of nations or among nations, or international law—a term first used in 1780 by Jeremy Bentham, the English philosopher[2]—has a long history dating back to diplomatic practices among ancient kingdoms and

---

[1] *The Role of International Law in the Elimination of War* (Manchester: Manchester University Press, 1961), p. 1.

[2] *An Introduction to the Principles of Morals and Legislation* (n.p., 1780) (Edinburgh: Stevenson & Co., 1789), p. 149.

the earliest philosophical inquiries into the nature of moral imperatives for princes and peoples. Beginning in the 17th century, the emergence of the modern nation-state system in Western Europe led to systematic speculation about the rules of behavior to be followed by states in both their peaceful and bellicose relations with one another and the obligations to be observed by them in the conduct of their international affairs.[3] Down to the present day, however, scholars and statesmen have debated the reality of international law, questioning whether a legal order truly exists among states and whether the practices of international relations reflect any "law" other than the transient wills of individual states.

An analysis of the nature of international law must come to grips with three salient issues. First, how do the practices between strong and weak states, generally subsumed under international law, differ from orders backed by threats, since in a society not all orders backed by threats are legal? Second, how do the obligations imposed on states differ from etiquette, courtesy, or moral duty, since not all obligations in a community are legal? Third, are there international rules, defined and widely recognized as legal rules, for without such rules a legal system would be unworkable?

At the outset of a study of the elements of international law it must be admitted that in world society no supernational king, president, or legislature exists to pass laws or issue orders binding on all states. It must also be noted that sanctions by a supernational police in the form of fines, arrest, or imprisonment for allegedly illegal acts do not occur. Finally, it must be acknowledged that the rules of international law are rarely tested in an international court; they can be tested only when states choose to submit to the court's jurisdiction. What, then, is the nature of international law?

Nature

In 1927, the Permanent Court of International Justice declared:

> . . . the words, "principles of international law" as ordinarily used can only mean international law as it is applied between all nations belonging to the community of States. . . .

International law governs relations between independent States. The rules of law binding upon States, therefore, emanate from their own free will as expressed in conventions or by usages generally accepted as expressing principles of law and established in order to regulate the relations between these coexisting independent communities or with a view to the achievement of

---

[3] See Arthur Nussbaum, *A Concise History of the Law of Nations* (New York: Macmillan Co., 1954), for perspective on the development of international jurisprudence and the work of such authors as Vitoria, Suarez, Gentilis, Grotius, Pufendorf, and Vattel.

common aims. Restrictions upon the independence of States cannot therefore be presumed.[4]

However, this narrow definition of international law will no longer suffice, for states by their own free will have created a large number of international organizations and agencies that are themselves juridical bodies. Such legal entities may negotiate and contract with states, approve international recommendation and regulations, and appear in or utilize courts under international norms. Furthermore, through international agreements and international agencies individuals may also have a legal status not dictated by national law but by international law. Thus, public international law[5] today consists of those principles, understandings, agreements, and rules that prescribe the legal conduct of one state toward another in the world community, and comprehends the actions, rights, and responsibilities of organizations or individuals subject to public international norms.

Much ink could be spilled over a further definition of international law, but the important point is that where a society exists, law will be found; where regular communication and commerce have been established, rules and regulations must follow. All men require some peaceful pursuit of their livelihoods, some enjoyment of their labor and their beliefs, some reasonable expectations about tomorrow and the next day. Law attempts to preserve order while pursuing justice.

The novice in the field of international law may be stumped by the absence of any hierarchy of command in the relations of states and by the lack of any sovereign legislature able to pass statutes that apply to all peoples. He may be frustrated in not finding for the world community, by analogy, an executive that can police the breaches of international law, or an international court that can compel miscreant states to appear before it. Yet, states and international agencies act as though there were international law, and refer to it voluminously in countless negotiations, agreements, and litigations. Philip C. Jessup, a distinguished scholar of international law and a judge of the International Court of Justice, wrote: "The significant question to ask about international law is whether the use of that term is in accordance with an accurate observation and study of the conduct of states in the world community."[6]

Therefore, one should ask: Are treaties ordinarily observed as law by contracting states? Have international customs among states received such

---

[4] *The Lotus Case*, P.C.I.J. Series A, No. 10.

[5] Private international law or conflict of laws involves questions about which law a national court should apply in reaching a decision because the status or capacity of the parties in the action before it may depend upon rules or occurrences outside the "forum." For example, the determination of the marital status of a person in a case before an American court might depend upon the application of French, or British, or Indian law, not the laws of the United States.

[6] *A Modern Law of Nations* (New York: Macmillan Co., 1948), p. 6.

sanction over the years that states would rarely violate their practice? Do states and their governments acknowledge some international responsibilities, and do they, in principle or fact, make restitution for wrongs done to aliens, other states, or international agencies? Have the hundreds of administrative rulings by international organizations been regularly admitted and effectively carried out by the states of the world, even contrary to their vote? And when a case is heard on points of international law by either a national or international tribunal, is the judgment or award ordinarily accepted by the litigants?

In their range of principles, concepts, methods, and function, international law and national or municipal law have much in common; in their actual forms and application, they do not. But it would be misleading to say that international law is not law because it is not completely analogous to municipal law.

Sources

Any legal system requires a body of law. To find the federal law of the United States, for example, demands a detailed study of the Constitution and an examination of the statutes of Congress. Then, the decisions of the federal courts must be analyzed, the executive orders of the President must be perused, and the rulings of administrative agencies weighed. Such a search takes great effort, but at least as much perseverance is needed to expose the body of international law.

International law can be found in an exhaustive variety of documents, digests, and decisions. No single code exists. And no single legislature empowered to make law for all nations exists. Instead, international law derives from the host of treaties and conventions made by states, as well as many other types of international agreements. Such law is to be found in the customs and practices of states in their dealings with one another. And it can be witnessed in the thousands of decisions that have been made by national courts, arbitral tribunals, claims commissions, and international courts, which often refer to the general principles of law recognized by civilized nations or the writings of eminent authorities on international law. At the cutting edge of the development of international law, the United Nations has sought by resolutions and recommendations to propose, confirm, or declare certain norms of international relations.

The rudimentary system of international law once depended largely on custom, for the mores of a community, when recognized as compulsory on individuals, are the very genesis of law. In the beginning of the modern nation-state system about the 16th century, few treaties existed to supply the definition of international obligations, and reliance had to be placed on what princes and jurists considered to be the right practice of states. Sometimes, judgments were derived from an actual observation of customs or the few treaties as a "positive" indication of law; at other times, opinions were based on recourse to higher principles of justice that any right-thinking human being, endowed with reason, would find "natural."

Today, many thousands of bilateral treaties between two states and multilateral treaties among three or more states are in force. Moreover, the treaties themselves can create organizations able to make international agreements and international rulings. Virtually all these instruments that mold legal obligations are written, recorded, authenticated, or registered. Although custom has gradually receded as a source of international law, the underlying mores of the world community, not yet translated into compulsory obedience but felt by judges before whom cases are brought, will continue to be translated into judgments. Thus, the ambiguities and generalizations of words or phrases in treaties, no matter how carefully drawn, will be reinterpreted by men in the light of prevailing principles or rules of conduct. Similarly, the extent and application of custom—of the usual practice of governments across frontiers and toward aliens and with foreign powers—will be reexamined and invigorated with the ever-changing ideas of right and wrong in the community.

The infusion of morality into international law—whether morality stems from the general principles of law recognized by nations or from the reasoning of scholars, statesmen, and judges—makes its study dynamic. Moreover, although multilateral treaties, conventions, and other international agreements, ever increasing in number, have been described as "international legislation," they still leave large areas of international relations uncharted by rules other than a few well-defined customs. In this stage of the development of international law, therefore, courts and the opinions of judges play an extraordinary role. Only at infrequent intervals and before different types of judicial or quasi-judicial bodies can it be said that international law is decided. Treaties and custom, of course, gird the framework of legal relations in the world of nations, but cases yield the detailed mosaic of human problems that transcend political borders.

In the first document that follows, Articles 38 and 59 of the *Statute of the International Court of Justice,* the evidence of international law to be considered by the Court is clearly indicated. It is also possible for the Court to decide a case *ex aequo et bono,* on just and fair grounds, but any decision of the Court applies only to the case and to the parties actually before it. The second document, the *Asylum Case,* involves the states of Colombia and Peru. Colombia had given political asylum to Víctor Raúl Haya de la Torre in its embassy in Lima and wished to have him safely escorted out of Peru, since the government of Peru had posted police around the embassy walls to arrest Haya de la Torre. The Court in this case had to face the problem of when constant and uniform usage in international relations becomes customary international law. In the third document, *Customary Law and Treaty Law*, a United States senator, Albert Gore, presents an American view of customary international law before the Legal Committee (VI) of the United Nations General Assembly.

STATUTE OF THE INTERNATIONAL COURT OF JUSTICE, 1945

Article 38

(1) The Court, whose function is to decide in accordance with international law such disputes as are submitted to it, shall apply:

(a) international conventions, whether general or particular, establishing rules expressly recognized by the contesting states;

(b) international custom, as evidence of a general practice accepted as law;

(c) the general principles of law recognized by civilized nations;

(d) subject to the provisions of Article 59, judicial decisions and the teachings of the most highly qualified publicists of the various nations, as subsidiary means for the determination of rules of law.

(2) This provision shall not prejudice the power of the Court to decide a case *ex aequo et bono*, if the parties agree thereto.

Article 59

The decision of the Court has no binding force except between the parties and in respect of that particular case.

ASYLUM CASE (COLOMBIA v. PERU)
International Court of Justice, 1950
1950 I.C.J. Reports 271

*   *   *

On behalf of Colombia:

May it please the Court
to adjudge and declare:

I.—That the Republic of Colombia, as the country granting asylum, is competent to qualify the offence for the purpose of the said asylum, within the limits of the obligations resulting in particular from the Bolivarian Agreement on Extradition of July 18th, 1911, and the Havana Convention on Asylum of February 20th, 1928, and of American international law in general;

II.—That the Republic of Peru, as the territorial State, is bound in the case now before the Court to give the guarantees necessary for the departure of M. Víctor Raúl Haya de la Torre from the country, with due regard to the inviolability of his person.

*   *   *

On behalf of Peru:

May it please the Court

To set aside submissions I and II of the Colombian Memorial.

*   *   .   *

To adjudge and declare,

As a counter-claim, under Article 63 of the Rules of Court and in the same decision, that the grant of asylum by the Colombian Ambassador at Lima to Víctor Raúl Haya de la Torre was made in violation of Article 1, paragraph 1, and of Article 2, paragraph 2, item 1 (*inciso primero*), of the Convention on Asylum signed in 1928, and that in any case the maintenance of the asylum constitutes at the present time a violation of that treaty.

*   *   *

The Colombian Government has referred to the Bolivarian Agreement of 1911, Article 18, which is framed in the following terms:

Aside from the stipulations of the present Agreement, the signatory States recognize the institution of asylum in conformity with the principles of international law.

In recognizing "the institution of asylum," this article merely refers to the principles of international law. But the principles of international law do not recognize any rule of unilateral and definitive qualification by the State granting diplomatic asylum.

*   *   *

The Colombian Government further relies on the Havana Convention on Asylum of 1928. This Convention lays down certain rules relating to diplomatic asylum, but does not contain any provision conferring on the State granting asylum a unilateral competence to qualify the offence with definitive and binding force for the territorial State. . . .

*   *   *

The Colombian Government has finally invoked "American international law in general." In addition to the rules arising from agreements which have already been considered, it has relied on an alleged regional or local custom peculiar to Latin-American States.

The Party which relies on a custom of this kind must prove that this custom is established in such a manner that it has become binding on the other Party. The Colombian Government must prove that the rule invoked by it is in accordance with a constant and uniform usage practised by the States in question, and that this usage is the expression of a right appertaining to the State granting asylum and a duty incumbent on the territorial State. This follows from Article 38 of the Statute of the Court, which refers to international custom "as evidence of a general practice accepted as law."

In support of its contention concerning the existence of such a custom, the Colombian Government has referred to a large number of extradition treaties which, as already explained, can have no bearing on the question now under consideration. It has cited conventions and agreements which do not contain any provision concerning the alleged rule of unilateral and definitive qualification such as the Montevideo Convention of 1889 on international penal law, the Bolivarian Agreement of 1911 and the Havana Convention of 1928. It has invoked conventions which have not been ratified by Peru, such as the Montevideo Conventions of 1933 and 1939. The Convention of 1933 has, in fact, been ratified by not more than eleven States and the Convention of 1939 by two States only.

It is particularly the Montevideo Convention of 1933 which Counsel for the Colombian Government has also relied on in this connexion. It is contended that this Convention has merely codified principles which were already recognized by Latin-American custom, and that it is valid against Peru as a proof of customary law. The limited number of States which have ratified this Convention reveals the weakness of this argument, and furthermore, it is invalidated by the preamble which states that this Convention modifies the Havana Convention.

Finally, the Colombian Government has referred to a large number of particular cases in which diplomatic asylum was in fact granted and respected. But it has not shown that the alleged rule of unilateral and definitive qualification was invoked or—if in some cases it was in fact invoked—that it was, apart from conventional stipulations, exercised by the States granting asylum as a right appertaining to them and respected by the territorial States as a duty incumbent on them and not merely for reasons of political expediency. The facts brought to the knowledge of the Court disclose so much uncertainty and contradiction, so much fluctuation and discrepancy in the exercise of diplomatic asylum and in the official views expressed on various occasions, there has been so much inconsistency in the rapid succession of conventions on asylum, ratified by some States and rejected by others, and the practice has been so much influenced by considerations of political expediency in the various cases, that it is not possible to discern in all this any constant and uniform usage, accepted as law, with regard to the alleged rule of unilateral and definitive qualification of the offence.

The Court cannot therefore find that the Colombian Government has proved the existence of such a custom. But even if it could be supposed that such a custom existed between certain Latin-American States only, it could not be invoked against Peru which, far from having by its attitude adhered to it, has, on the contrary, repudiated it by refraining from ratifying the Montevideo Conventions of 1933 and 1939, which were the first to include a rule concerning the qualification of the offence in matters of diplomatic asylum.

CUSTOMARY LAW AND TREATY LAW
Statement of United States Representative (Senator Gore) to the United Nations General Assembly Legal Committee, 21 November 1962
47 Department of State Bulletin 972–979

Until very recently, Communist writings on international law seemed to take the position that only international law flowing from treaties is worthy of respect. The expressly consensual element in the formation of international law was stressed to the exclusion of other lawmaking processes. This approach derived from an extreme and archaic view of the sovereignty of the state, a view which, reduced to simple terms, taught that only the specific, articulated consent of the state could operate to subject the state to international law. Thus, at our 717th meeting on November 21st last year, the distinguished representative of the Soviet Union, Professor Tunkin, said:

"The transformation which took place in the human society and, above all, the changes in its economic structure led to alterations in international law. Those alterations were effected by *agreement between States* which constituted *the only means of creating and changing the norms of international law.*"

This extreme doctrinal emphasis on treaty law at the same time attempted to portray the great body of customary international law as outmoded, obsolete, colonialist; as bourgeois, creditor-oriented, and—in some sinister sense—"Western."

*   *   *

Surely we all recognize that a part of what was international law, now irrevocably dead, could not today be justified. The nineteenth century capitulations between certain European and certain Asian and African states cannot be defended. However, not only have these capitulations long since ceased to exist, they represented international law not flowing from custom but from international agreements. They were, in fact, treaties.

*   *   *

This is not to say that customary international law has carried forward no elements that require pruning, no aspects that require revision. On the contrary, the very concept of the progressive development of international law imports change. My delegation recognizes that existing international law, whether springing from custom or from treaty, or other source, needs to be strengthened; that the rule of law in international affairs is far from realized. International law must grow, it must change, and it must change for the better. In the process of change, the new states of the world can make a contribution of particular importance.

*   *   *

At the same time, as we jointly undertake the progressive development of international law, we must take care not to depreciate and discard that which is of value in existing international law. Today's international law, whether stemming from treaty or custom, or general principles of law, is a valuable law, responsive to the needs of states the world over, whether new or old, whether of the East or of the West. The fact that older states of Europe and the Americas have played a predominant role in the creation of customary international law does not mean that that law is not of universal validity and appeal. There is much in international law that flows from the mere existence of states; the content of the law has not been determined by the region of the world in which those states happen to have been located. Moreover, to the extent that international law does have a specifically Western content—a content which can easily be exaggerated—that is not necessarily occasion for apology. There is much in the tradition of Western legal thought and practice of which every man, whatever the geographical accident of his birth, can be proud. . . .

Application

No legal system endures without interpretation and enforcement. Courts are not the sole evidence or even the main evidence of a working legal system. Diplomats and administrators both in national governments and in international agencies constantly interpret and apply international law. Their daily behavior reflects well-established customs and specific agreements among states. They follow such norms as regularly as law-abiding people observe municipal law. Moreover, as in municipal law, most international controversies are settled out of court or without trial.

In general, men obey law by their conduct, not by command; individuals respond to custom, to the ordinary day-to-day practices of their community, with few challenges or doubts, and thus follow rules as law-abiding creatures without the need for constant orders and outright coercion. Most people most of the time obey law by habit and acquiescence rather than an imminent fear of the police. International law exists because most states conduct themselves most of the time in accordance with their treaty obligations and customary international practices. Nevertheless, there must be some judicial process and authority to insure a definition of and a compliance with international law in those cases where diplomatic remedies are unavailing, inappropriate, or nonexistent.

National Power to Adjudicate

Lacking an international sheriff or marshal to haul either states or individuals before an international bar of justice, the system of international law is largely maintained by the national power of states to adjudicate cases that involve foreign relations, treaties, and other subjects recognized by states to be justiciable under the law of nations. The constitutions of many modern states expressly testify to the existence of international law, and they establish the customs and practices of nations, including treaties, as a part of national law. Therefore, national courts with the power of the state behind them hear and decide the overwhelming number of cases that involve issues of international law, thus affording an open discussion of the facts, rules, and judicial reasoning that lead to a decision as well as a reasonable certainty of performance by the litigants.

The states of the world, however, have by no means solved the dilemma of reconciling their sovereign will and prejudices with universal

11

norms that might be prescribed by a disinterested international legislature or tribunal. National judges faced with choices of principle in enunciating rules of international law enter the realm of philosophy and inescapably bring to their judgments something of their national culture and their national politics. However, in the United Kingdom or Italy, in Japan or India, in the United States and elsewhere, hundreds of national courts regularly interpret and decide international law as faithfully as possible, providing beyond the great pillars of custom and treaty the detailed legal mosaic of foreign affairs and international relations.

The following documents include: (*a*) articles of the *Constitution of the United States* to illustrate the national power of the United States to adjudicate international law issues; (*b*) a ruling of the Supreme Court in the *Paquete Habana* case against an action of the United States under the law of nations, which again raises the question of when usage becomes an established international rule; and (*c*) excerpts from the *constitutions of Japan, Italy, and the Federal Republic of Germany*, which are more recent expressions of the relation between national and international law in the post-World War II constitutions.

CONSTITUTION OF THE UNITED STATES, 1789

Article I, Section 8

The Congress shall have power . . . to define and punish piracies and felonies committed on the high seas, and offences against the law of nations; to declare war, grant letters of marque and reprisal, and make rules concerning captures on land and water; . . .

Article III, Section 2

The judicial power shall extend to all cases, in law and equity, arising under this Constitution, the laws of the United States, and treaties made, or which shall be made, under their authority;—to all cases affecting ambassadors, other public ministers and consuls;—to all cases of admiralty and maritime jurisdiction;—to controversies to which the United States shall be a party. . . .

Article VI

. . . This Constitution, and the laws of the United States which shall be made in pursuance thereof; and all treaties made, or which shall be made, under the authority of the United States, shall be the supreme law of the land; and the judges of every state shall be bound thereby, anything in the constitution or laws of any state to the contrary notwithstanding. . . .

THE PAQUETE HABANA and THE LOLA
United States Supreme Court, 1900
175 U.S. 677

Mr. Justice Gray Delivered the Opinion of the Court

These are two appeals from decrees of the district court of the United States for the southern district of Florida condemning two fishing vessels and their cargoes as prize of war.

Each vessel was a fishing smack, running in and out of Havana, and regularly engaged in fishing on the coast of Cuba; sailed under the Spanish flag; was owned by a Spanish subject of Cuban birth, living in the city of Havana; was commanded by a subject of Spain, also residing in Havana; and her master and crew had no interest in the vessel, but were entitled to shares, amounting in all to two thirds, of her catch, the other third belonging to her owner. Her cargo consisted of fresh fish, caught by her crew from the sea, put on board as they were caught, and kept and sold alive. Until stopped by the blockading squadron she had no knowledge of the existence of the war or of any blockade. She had no arms or ammunition on board, and made no attempt to run the blockade after she knew of its existence, nor any resistance at the time of the capture.

*   *   *

Both the fishing vessels were brought by their captors into Key West. A libel for the condemnation of each vessel and her cargo as prize of war was there filed on April 27, 1898; a claim was interposed by her master on behalf of himself and the other members of the crew, and of her owner; evidence was taken, showing the facts above stated; and on May 30, 1898, a final decree of condemnation and sale was entered, "the court not being satisfied that, as a matter of law, without any ordinance, treaty, or proclamation, fishing vessels of this class are exempt from seizure."

Each vessel was thereupon sold by auction; the Paquete Habana for the sum of $490; and the Lola for the sum of $800. There was no other evidence in the record of the value of either vessel or of her cargo.

*   *   *

By an ancient usage among civilized nations, beginning centuries ago, and gradually ripening into a rule of international law, coast fishing vessels, pursuing their vocation of catching and bringing in fresh fish, have been recognized as exempt, with their cargoes and crews, from capture as prize of war.

This doctrine, however, has been earnestly contested at the bar; and no complete collection of the instances illustrating it is to be found, so far as we are aware, in a single published work, although many are referred to and discussed by the writers on international law, . . . It is therefore worth the while to trace the history of the rule, from the earliest accessible sources, through the increasing recognition of it, with occasional setbacks, to what we may now justly consider as its final establishment in our own country and generally throughout the civilized world.

*   *   *

International law is part of our law, and must be ascertained and administered by the courts of justice of appropriate jurisdiction as often as questions of right depending upon it are duly presented for their determination. For this purpose, where there is no treaty and no controlling executive or legislative act or judicial decision, resort must be had to the customs and usages of civilized nations, and, as evidence of these, to the works of jurists and commentators who by years of labor, research, and experience have made themselves peculiarly well acquainted with the subjects of which they treat. Such works are resorted to by judicial tribunals, not for the speculations of their authors concerning what the law ought to be, but for trustworthy evidence of what the law really is. . . .

*   *   *

This review of the precedents and authorities on the subject appears to us abundantly to demonstrate that at the present day, by the general consent of the civilized nations of the world, and independently of any express treaty or other public act, it is an established rule of international law, founded on considerations of humanity to a poor and industrious order of men, and of the mutual convenience of belligerent states, that coast fishing vessels, with their implements and supplies, cargoes and crews, unarmed and honestly pursuing their peaceful calling of catching and bringing in fresh fish, are exempt from capture as prize of war.

*   *   *

Upon the facts proved in either case, it is the duty of this court, sitting as the highest prize court of the United States, and administering the law of nations, to declare and adjudge that the capture was unlawful and without probable cause; and it is therefore, in each case,—

Ordered, that the decree of the District Court be reversed, and the proceeds of the sale of the vessel, together with the proceeds of any sale of her cargo, be restored to the claimant, with damages and costs.

Mr. Justice Fuller, with Whom Concurred Mr. Justice Harlan and Mr. Justice McKenna, Dissenting

The district court held these vessels and their cargoes liable because not "satisfied that as a matter of law, without any ordinance, treaty, or proclamation, fishing vessels of this class are exempt from seizure."

This court holds otherwise, not because such exemption is to be found in any treaty, legislation, proclamation, or instruction granting it, but on the ground that the vessels were exempt by reason of an established rule of international law applicable to them, which it is the duty of the court to enforce.

I am unable to conclude that there is any such established international rule, or that this court can properly revise action which must be treated as having been taken in the ordinary exercise of discretion in the conduct of war.

*   *   *

These records show that the Spanish sloop Paquete Habana "was captured as a prize of war by the U.S.S. Castine" on April 25, and "was delivered" by the Castine's commander "to Rear Admiral Wm. T. Sampson (commanding the North Atlantic Squadron)," and thereupon "turned over" to a prize master with instructions to proceed to Key West.

That the vessels were accordingly taken to Key West and there libeled, and that the decrees of condemnation were entered against them May 30.

It is impossible to concede that the Admiral ratified these captures in disregard of established international law and the proclamation, or that the President, if he had been of opinion that there was any infraction of law or proclamation, would not have intervened prior to condemnation.

*   *   *

All this was in accordance with the rules and usages of international law, with which, whether in peace or war, the naval service has always been necessarily familiar.

I come then to examine the proposition "that at the present day, by the general consent of the civilized nations of the world, and independently of any express treaty or other public act, it is an established rule of international law, founded on considerations of humanity to a poor and industrious order of men, and of the mutual convenience of belligerent states, that coast fishing vessels, with their implements and supplies, cargoes and crews, unarmed, and honestly pursuing their peaceful calling of catching and bringing in of fresh fish, are exempt from capture as prize of war."

*   *   *

In truth, the exemption of fishing craft is essentially an act of grace, and not a matter of right, and it is extended or denied as the exigency is believed to demand.

"It is," said Sir William Scott, "a rule of comity only, and not of legal decision."

*   *   *

It is needless to review the speculations and repetitions of the writers on international law. Ortolan, De Boeck, and others admit that the custom relied on as consecrating the immunity is not so general as to create an absolute international rule; Heffter, Calvo, and others are to the contrary. Their lucubrations may be persuasive, but not authoritative.

In my judgment, the rule is that exemption from the rigors of war is in the control of the Executive. He is bound by no immutable rule on the subject. It is for him to apply, or to modify, or to deny altogether such immunity as may have been usually extended.

*　　　*　　　*

CONSTITUTION OF JAPAN, 1946

*　　　*　　　*

We believe that no nation is responsible to itself alone, but that laws of political morality are universal; and that obedience to such laws is incumbent upon all nations which would sustain their own sovereignty and justify their sovereign relationship with other nations.

Article 98

This Constitution shall be the supreme law of the nation and no law, ordinance, imperial rescript or other act of government, or part thereof, contrary to the provisions hereof, shall have legal force or validity.

The treaties concluded by Japan and established laws of nations shall be faithfully observed.

CONSTITUTION OF THE ITALIAN REPUBLIC, 1948

Article 10

Italy's juridical organization conforms with the generally recognized principles of international law. The legal status of foreigners is regulated by law in conformity with international rules and treaties. A foreigner to whom the practical exercise in his own country of democratic liberties, such as are guaranteed by the Italian Constitution, is precluded, is entitled to the right of asylum within the territory of the Republic, under conditions laid down by law. The extradition of a foreigner for political offenses is not admitted.

Article 11

Italy condemns war as an instrument of aggression against the liberties of other peoples and as a means for settling international controversies; it agrees in conditions of equality with other States, to such limitation of sovereignty as may be necessary for a system calculated to ensure peace and justice between Nations; it promotes and encourages international organizations having such ends in view.

BASIC LAW OF THE FEDERAL REPUBLIC OF GERMANY, 1949

Article 24

(1) The Federation may, by legislation, transfer sovereign powers to international institutions.

(2) For the maintenance of peace, the Federation may join a system of mutual collective security; in doing so it will consent to those limitations of its sovereign powers which will bring about and secure a peaceful and lasting order in Europe and among the nations of the world.

(3) For the settlement of disputes between nations the Federation will accede to conventions concerning a general, comprehensive obligatory system of international arbitration.

Article 25

The general rules of international law form part of Federal law. They take precedence over the laws and directly create rights and duties for the inhabitants of the federal territory.

International Power to Adjudicate

The nation-state system originated in Europe with personal sovereigns—kings and princes who recognized no external law other than God as superior to their command within their domains. As personal rule was consolidated and developed into popular rule in the 19th and 20th centuries, and as the number of states increased, the sovereign "will of the people" still balked at transferring lawmaking or law-interpreting powers to an authority beyond the control of the state. Nevertheless, two states could agree to arbitrate an issue—that is, establish an umpire or panel, selected by mutual agreement, to settle a rather specific issue. Although not a judicial procedure, international arbitrations contributed much to the definition of the law of nations and the spirit of adjudication between nations.

During the 19th century, the number of successful international arbitrations gradually increased to the point where a Permanent Court of Arbitration was established by a multilateral convention at the Hague Peace Conference in 1899, further amended at the second Hague Peace Conference in 1907. The Permanent Court of Arbitration, which still exists, really ought to be called the international panel of arbitrators, for it has consisted of a group of men, known for their probity and competence in international law, who have been nominated by states and who are readily available for arbitration work if requested by the parties to a dispute. Similarly, several international claims commissions have been set up by two states to hear the complaints of their nationals over alleged wrongs done to them as aliens. But again, like arbitral boards, such commissions do not function as courts, with permanent, qualified, disinterested judges and all the other procedures and practices that mark controversial cases in a modern court.

The record of international courts is brief. After World War I, Article 14 of the League of Nations called for the establishment of a Permanent Court of International Justice to hear and determine any dispute of an international character submitted to it by the parties thereto, and to give advisory opinions to the Council or Assembly of the League. In 1920, the Statute of the Permanent Court of International Justice was approved by the Assembly of the League and later ratified by 51 states. From 1922 to 1939, the Court considered 66 cases. The court rendered 32 judgments, none of which was disregarded, and it gave 27 advisory opinions.

At the end of World War II in 1945, the International Court of Justice, consisting of 15 judges elected to 9-year terms by both the Security Council and the General Assembly, acting independently, was established as the principal juridical organ of the United Nations. The new Court came into existence with the ratification of the United Nations Charter, and succeeded to virtually the same structure and the same jurisdiction as the Permanent Court. The Court consists of 15 judges, no two of whom may be nationals of the same state. They are elected to nine-year terms by absolute majorities of the Security Council and the General Assembly, each organ voting independently. States parties to the Statute of the Court, but not members of the United Nations also vote. Five judges retire every three years, and new elections are held for the vacancies. Candidates are nominated, regardless of nationality, by "national groups" in each state which ideally select persons of high moral character with the best professional competence for such an eminent jurisprudential appointment. In practice, nationals of the five great powers of the United Nations have always been elected to the Court, while there have been tacit political understandings and coalitions to ensure a reasonable distribution of judges from the principal legal systems or regions of the world. Where a party to a litigation does not have one of its nationals sitting on the Court, it may designate a judge to sit *ad hoc* and take part in the decision. The Court meets in the Hague. The members of the Court receive an annual salary of $25,000, generally tax-free, and appropriate pensions after nine years of service. Today, every member of the United Nations as well as Liechtenstein, San Marino, Switzerland, West Germany, Vietnam, and Monaco— virtually every state in the world—is a party to the Statute of the International Court of Justice. Between 1946 and 1966, the International Court of Justice considered 49 cases, rendered 29 judgments and gave 13 advisory opinions.

The International Court of Justice, therefore, is the World Court, but it has not been the only court empowered by international agreement to hear cases of an international character. A Central American Court of Justice had a brief, harried existence for a few years prior to 1917. After World War II, the International Military Tribunals at Nuremberg and at Tokyo were empowered by international agreement to try war criminals whose offenses had no particular geographical location. Although properly hedged by legal procedures, the tribunals were unique, with judges selected from the victorious states and constituted only to hear the special charges against the planning and conduct of war by Germany and Japan. Finally, since 1952 certain states of Europe have established the Court of Justice of the European Communities and the European Court of Human Rights. The first is concerned with the European coal, iron, and steel community, the common market, and the atomic energy community; the second is concerned with the European Convention on Human Rights. Here the list of "international" courts abruptly ends.

The International Court of Justice cannot hear a case between private parties, or a state and a private party, or between an international organization and a state or another international organization; it can try only cases between states, and then only by their agreement. In the courts of states, no question exists about "compulsory jurisdiction," for the essence of sovereignty is to compel obedience to the laws. Individuals and other legal persons have few escapes from suits or public prosecution when instituted. Virtually any dispute between two states can be tried before the International Court of Justice if the two consent to it, but little can be done when a state has deliberately refused litigation. Some states have consented in advance to "compulsory jurisdiction" by means of a declaration recognizing the competence of the Court to adjudicate certain issues between them and other states that have made the same declaration. Such "compulsory jurisdiction" refers only to the interpretation of a treaty, a question of international law, a fact constituting a breach of international obligation, and the nature or extent of reparations due for such a breach of international obligation.

It has been customary for states that accept the "compulsory jurisdiction" of the Court to note that disputes essentially within their domestic jurisdiction are excluded; but in 1946 the United States, through a reservation proposed by Senator Tom Connally on the floor of the Senate, added to its declaration the phrase, "as determined by the United States." The effect of this reservation is that the state rather than the Court determines for itself whether anything up for litigation is essentially within its domestic jurisdiction, thus nullifying the whole idea of "compulsory jurisdiction."

Despite the outcry of many scholars and jurists, the United States reservation to the jurisdiction of the Court still obtains, and many states have added similar reservations to their declarations of submission to the Court's jurisdiction on certain issues. In 1957, the Court was compelled to find that it lacked jurisdiction in a dispute between France and Norway when Norway invoked the French reservation to compulsory jurisdiction on matters "essentially within the national jurisdiction" as understood by France.[7] Although Norway had not originally put this limit on her declaration accepting the compulsory jurisdiction of the Court, the principle of reciprocity operated, and France was left without further recourse before the Court. It is an apt commentary on the application of international law that in 1966 only 21 states had accepted the compulsory jurisdiction of the Court without significant reservations.

Technically speaking, the authority of any decision by the International Court of Justice is limited to the case actually before it. Precedents and previous judicial decisions by the Court do not bind its future. Nevertheless, Sir Hersh Lauterpacht, a judge of the Court until his death in 1960, pointed out that the Court's practice of invoking its own decisions over a period of years has resulted in the formulation or clarification of a substantial body of rules of international law. For example, Vice President Alfaro, giving a separate opinion in 1962,[8] dealt with the principle that a

---

[7] *Norwegian Loans Case (France* v. *Norway)*, 1957 I.C.J. Reports 9, 26–27.

[8] *Case Concerning the Temple of Preah Vihear (Cambodia* v. *Thailand)*, I.C.J. Reports, 1962, 39–51.

state party to an international litigation is bound by its previous acts or attitudes when they are in contradiction to its claims in the litigation. He cited no fewer than nine previous judgments or opinions of the Court as well as half a dozen findings by arbitral tribunals or claims commissions that applied or recognized the principle. Lauterpacht wrote:

> International tribunals, when giving a decision on a point of international law, do not necessarily choose between two conflicting views advanced by the parties. They state what the law is. Their decisions are evidence of the existing rule of law. That does not mean that they do not in fact constitute a source of international law. For the distinction between the evidence and the source of many a law is more speculative and less rigid than is commonly supposed. . . . It is of little import whether the pronouncements of the Court are in the nature of evidence or of a source of international law so long as it is clear that in so far as they show what are the rules of international law they are largely identical with it.[9]

The documents that follow illustrate the international power to adjudicate through: (*a*) Articles 36 and 37 of the *Statute of the International Court of Justice;* (*b*) the *Anglo-Iranian Oil Company Case,* in which the Court had to determine its own jurisdiction, (*c*) the international agreement establishing the *International Military Tribunal* of 1945—the first such tribunal ever established by a number of Great Powers—with its particular jurisdiction; (*d*) the organization and jurisdiction of the *European Community Court of Justice,* with the cases of (*e*) *Humblet* v. *Belgium* and (*f*) *Costa* v. *E.N.E.L.:* and finally (*g*) the jurisdictional articles of the *European Court of Human Rights.*

STATUTE OF THE INTERNATIONAL COURT OF JUSTICE, 1945

Article 36

1. The jurisdiction of the Court comprises all cases which the parties refer to it and all matters specially provided for in the Charter of the United Nations or in treaties and conventions in force.

2. The states parties to the present Statute may at any time declare that they recognize as compulsory *ipso facto* and without special agreement, in relation to any other state accepting the same obligation, the jurisdiction of the Court in all legal disputes concerning:

a. the interpretation of a treaty;
b. any question of international law;
c the existence of any fact which, if established, would constitute a breach of an international obligation;
d. the nature or extent of the reparation to be made for the breach of an international obligation.

---

[9] Sir Hersh Lauterpacht, *The Development of International Law by the International Court* (New York: Frederick A. Praeger, Inc., 1958), p. 21.

3. The declarations referred to above may be made unconditionally or on condition of reciprocity on the part of several or certain states, or for a certain time.

4. Such declarations shall be deposited with the Secretary-General of the United Nations, who shall transmit copies thereof to the parties to the Statute and to the Registrar of the Court.

5. Declarations made under Article 36 of the Statute of the Permanent Court of International Justice and which are still in force shall be deemed, as between the parties to the present Statute, to be acceptances of the compulsory jurisdiction of the International Court of Justice for the period which they still have to run and in accordance with their terms.

6. In the event of a dispute as to whether the Court has jurisdiction, the matter shall be settled by the decision of the Court.

Article 37

Whenever a treaty or convention in force provides for reference of a matter to a tribunal to have been instituted by the League of Nations, or to the Permanent Court of International Justice, the matter shall, as between the parties to the present Statute, be referred to the International Court of Justice.

ANGLO-IRANIAN OIL COMPANY CASE (UNITED KINGDOM v. IRAN)
International Court of Justice, 1952
1952 I.C.J. Reports 93

*   *   *

On April 29th, 1933, an agreement was concluded between the Imperial Government of Persia (now the Imperial Government of Iran, which name the Court will use hereinafter) and the Anglo-Persian Oil Company, Limited (later the Anglo-Iranian Oil Company, Limited), a company incorporated in the United Kingdom. This agreement was ratified by the Iranian Majlis on May 28th, 1933, and came into force on the following day after having received the Imperial assent.

On March 15th and 20th, 1951, the Iranian Majlis and Senate, respectively, passed a law enunciating the principle of nationalization of the oil industry in Iran. On April 28th and 30th, 1951, they passed another law "concerning the procedure for enforcement of the law concerning the nationalization of the oil industry throughout the country." These two laws received the Imperial assent on May 1st, 1951.

As a consequence of these laws, a dispute arose between the Government of Iran and the Anglo-Iranian Oil Company, Limited. The Government of the United Kingdom adopted the cause of this British Company and submitted, in virtue of the right of diplomatic protection, an Application to the Court on May 26th, 1951, instituting proceedings in the name of the Government of the United Kingdom of Great Britain and Northern Ireland against the Imperial Government or Iran.

*   *   *

In the present case the jurisdiction of the Court depends on the Declarations made by the Parties under Article 36, paragraph 2, on condition of reciprocity, which were, in the case of the United Kingdom, signed on February 28th, 1940, and, in the case of Iran, signed on October 2nd, 1930, and ratified on September 19th, 1932. By these Declarations, jurisdiction is conferred on the Court only to the extent to which the two Declarations coincide in conferring it. As the Iranian Declaration is more limited in scope than the United Kingdom Declaration, it is the Iranian Declaration on which the Court must base itself. . . .

*   *   *

According to the first clause of this Declaration, the Court has jurisdiction only when a dispute relates to the application of a treaty or convention accepted by Iran. The Parties are in agreement on this point. But they disagree on the question whether this jurisdiction is limited to the application of treaties or conventions accepted by Iran after the ratification of the Declaration, or whether it comprises the application of treaties or conventions accepted by Iran at any time.

The Government of Iran contends that the jurisdiction of the Court is limited to the application of treaties or conventions accepted by Iran after the ratification of the Declaration. It refers to the fact that the words "*et postérieurs à la ratification de cette déclaration*" follow immediately after the expression "*traités ou conventions acceptés par la Perse.*"

The Government of the United Kingdom contends that the words "*et postérieurs à la ratification de cette déclaration*" refer to the expression "*au sujet de situations ou de faits.*" Consequently, the Government of the United Kingdom maintains that the Declaration relates to the application of treaties or conventions accepted by Iran at any time.

If the Declaration is considered from a purely grammatical point of view, both contentions might be regarded as compatible with the text. . . .

But the Court cannot base itself on a purely grammatical interpretation of the text. It must seek the interpretation which is in harmony with a natural and reasonable way of reading the text, having due regard to the intention of the Government of Iran at the time when it accepted the compulsory jurisdiction of the Court.

*   *   *

. . . the text of the Iranian Declaration is not a treaty text resulting from negotiations between two or more States. It is the result of unilateral drafting by the Government of Iran, which appears to have shown a particular degree of caution when drafting the text of the Declaration. . . .

On May 10th, 1927, the Government of Iran denounced all treaties with other States relating to the regime of capitulations, the denunciation to take effect one year thereafter, and it had commenced negotiations with these States with a view to replacing the denounced treaties by new treaties based on the principle of equality. At the time when the Declaration was signed in October 1930, these negotiations had been brought to an end with some States, but not with all. The Government of Iran considered all capitulatory treaties as no longer binding, but was uncertain as to the legal effect of its unilateral denunciations. It is unlikely that the Government of Iran, in such circumstances, should have been willing, on its own initiative, to agree that disputes relating to such treaties might be submitted for adjudication to an international court of justice by virtue of a general clause in the Declaration.

*　　　*　　　*

Having regard to the foregoing considerations, the Court concludes that the Declaration is limited to disputes relating to the application of treaties or conventions accepted by Iran after the ratification of the Declaration.

The United Kingdom contends, however, that even if the Court were to hold that the Declaration applies only to disputes relating to the application of treaties or conventions accepted by Iran after the ratification of the Declaration, it would still have jurisdiction in the present case. The contention of the United Kingdom is that the acts of which it complains constitute a violation by Iran of certain of its obligations to the United Kingdom resulting from treaties or conventions accepted by Iran after the ratification of the Declaration. The treaties and conventions relied upon in this connection are:

(i) The Treaty of Friendship, Establishment and Commerce concluded between Iran and Denmark on February 20th, 1934; the Establishment Convention concluded between Iran and Switzerland on April 25th, 1934; and the Establishment Convention concluded between Iran and Turkey on March 14th, 1937.

*　　　*　　　*

The United Kingdom relies on these three treaties by virtue of the most-favoured-nation clause contained in Article IX of the Treaty concluded between the United Kingdom and Iran on March 4th, 1857, and in Article 2 of the Commercial Convention concluded between the United Kingdom and Iran on February 9th, 1903.

*　　　*　　　*

It is argued by the United Kingdom Government that the conduct of the Iranian Government towards the Anglo-Iranian Oil Company constitutes a breach of the principles and practice of international law which, by her treaty with Denmark, Iran promised to observe towards Danish nationals, and which, by the operation of the most-favoured-nation clause contained in the treaties between Iran and the United Kingdom, Iran became bound to observe towards British nationals. Consequently, the argument continues, the dispute which the United Kingdom has brought before the Court concerns situations or facts relating directly or indirectly to the application of a treaty—the Treaty of 1934 between Denmark and Iran—accepted by Iran after the ratification of her Declaration.

The Court cannot accept this contention. It is obvious that the term *traités ou conventions* used in the Iranian Declaration refers to treaties or conventions which the Party bringing the dispute before the Court has the right to invoke against Iran, and does not mean any of those which Iran may have concluded with any State. But in order that the United Kingdom may enjoy the benefit of any treaty concluded by Iran with a third party by virtue of a most-favoured-nation clause contained in a treaty concluded by the United Kingdom with Iran, the United Kingdom must be in a position to invoke the latter treaty. The treaty containing the most-favoured-nation clause is the basic treaty upon which the United Kingdom must rely. It is this treaty which establishes the juridical link between the United Kingdom and a third-party treaty and confers upon that State the rights enjoyed by the third party. . . .

*　　*　　*

The United Kingdom argued that the question which the Court had to consider was not "what are the treaties which confer on Great Britain the rights in question," but "what are the treaties whose application is in dispute." But from the legal point of view, what is in dispute is not the application of the Treaty of 1934 between Iran and Denmark, but the application of the Treaty of 1857 or the Convention of 1903 between Iran and the United Kingdom in conjunction with the Treaty of 1934 between Iran and Denmark. There could be no dispute between Iran and the United Kingdom upon the Iranian-Danish Treaty alone.

*　　*　　*

The Court must, therefore, find in regard to the Iranian-Danish Treaty of 1934, that the United Kingdom is not entitled, for the purpose of bringing its present dispute with Iran under the terms of the Iranian Declaration, to invoke its Treaties of 1857 and 1903 with Iran, since those Treaties were concluded before the ratification of the Declaration; that the most-favoured-nation clause contained in those Treaties cannot thus be brought into operation; and that, consequently, no treaty concluded by Iran with any third party can be relied upon by the United Kingdom in the present case.

The Court will now consider whether the settlement in 1933 of the dispute between the Government of the United Kingdom and the Government of Iran relating to the D'Arcy Concession, through the mediation of the Council of the League of Nations, resulted, as is claimed by the United Kingdom, in any agreement between the two Governments which may be regarded as a treaty or convention within the meaning of this expression in the Iranian Declaration.

*   *   *

In November 1932 the Iranian Government decided to cancel the D'Arcy Concession. On December 19th, 1932, the United Kingdom Government, having protested to the Iranian Government without avail, submitted the case to the Council of the League of Nations. The Council placed the question on the agenda and appointed a Rapporteur. On February 3rd, 1933, the Rapporteur informed the Council that the Governments of Iran and the United Kingdom had agreed to suspend all proceedings before the Council; that they agreed that the Company should immediately enter into negotiations with the Iranian Government, the respective legal points of view being entirely reserved; and that, in the event that the negotiations should fail, the question should go back to the Council. After prolonged discussion between the representatives of the Iranian Government and the representatives of the Company, an agreement—the Concession Contract—was signed by them at Tehran on April 29th. It was subsequently ratified by the Iranian Government. On October 12th, the Rapporteur submitted his report, together with the text of the new concession, to the Council, declaring that "the dispute between His Majesty's Government in the United Kingdom and the Imperial Government of Persia is now finally settled." Thereupon the representatives of Iran and the United Kingdom at the Council each expressed their satisfaction at the settlement thus reached. The question was removed from the agenda of the Council.

The United Kingdom maintains that, as a result of these proceedings, the Government of Iran undertook certain treaty obligations towards the Government of the United Kingdom. It endeavours to establish those obligations by contending that the agreement signed by the Iranian Government with the Anglo-Persian Oil Company on April 29th, 1933, has a double character, the character of being at once a concessionary contract between the Iranian Government and the Company and a treaty between the two Governments. It is further argued by the United Kingdom that even if the settlement reached in 1933 only amounted to a tacit or an implied agreement, it must be considered to be within the meaning of the term "treaties or conventions" contained in the Iranian Declaration.

The Court cannot accept the view that the contract signed between the Iranian Government and the Anglo-Persian Oil Company has a double character. It is nothing more than a concessionary contract between a government and a foreign corporation. The United Kingdom Government is not a party to the contract; there is no privity of contract between the Government of Iran and the Government of the United Kingdom. Under the contract the Iranian Government cannot claim from the United Kingdom Government any rights which it may claim from the Company, nor can it be called upon to perform towards the United Kingdom Government any obligations which it is bound to perform towards the Company. The document bearing the signatures of the representatives of the Iranian Government and the Company has a single purpose: the purpose of regulating the relations between that Government and the Company in regard to the concession. It does not regulate in any way the relations between the two Governments.

*   *   *

The Court has found that the United Kingdom is not entitled to invoke any of the treaties concluded by Iran with Denmark and Switzerland in 1934 and with Turkey in 1937 and that no treaty or convention was concluded in 1933 between Iran and the United Kingdom. No other treaties having been relied upon by the United Kingdom as treaties or conventions subsequent to the ratification of the Iranian Declaration, the Court must conclude that the dispute brought before it by the United Kingdom is not one of those disputes arising "in regard to situations or facts relating directly or indirectly to the application of treaties or conventions accepted by Persia and subsequent to the ratification of this Declaration." Consequently, the Court cannot derive jurisdiction in the present case from the terms of the Declaration ratified by Iran on September 19th, 1932.

*   *   *

The principle of *forum prorogatum*, if it could be applied to the present case, would have to be based on some conduct or statement of the Government of Iran which involves an element of consent regarding the jurisdiction of the Court. But that Government has consistently denied the jurisdiction of the Court. Having filed a Preliminary Objection for the purpose of disputing the jurisdiction, it has throughout the proceedings maintained that Objection. It is true that it has submitted other Objections which have no direct bearing on the question of jurisdiction. But they are clearly designed as measures of defence which it would be necessary to examine only if Iran's Objection to the jurisdiction were rejected. No element of consent can be deduced from such conduct on the part of the Government of Iran. Consequently, the Submission of the United Kingdom on this point cannot be accepted.

Accordingly, the Court has arrived at the conclusion that it has no jurisdiction to deal with the case submitted to it by the Application of the Government of the United Kingdom dated May 26th, 1951. . . .

*   *   *

For these reasons,

The Court,

by nine votes to five,
finds that it has no jurisdiction in the present case.

*   *   *

Dissenting Opinion of Judge Hackworth

I agree with the conclusion of the Court that the Declaration applies only to treaties and conventions accepted by Iran subsequent to the ratification of its Declaration. I do not, however, consider that, in reaching this conclusion, it was necessary or even permissible for the Court to rely upon the Iranian Parliamentary Act of approval as evidence of the intention of the Iranian Government, since that was a unilateral act of a legislative body of which other nations had not been apprised. National courts may, as a matter of course, draw upon such acts for municipal purposes, but this Court must look to the public declarations by States made for international purposes, and cannot resort to municipal legislative enactments to explain ambiguities in international acts. The fact that this was a public law which was available after 1933 to people who might have had the foresight and the facilities to examine it, is no answer. When a State deposits with an international organ a document, such as a declaration accepting compulsory jurisdiction of the Court, upon which other States are expected to rely, those States are entitled to accept that document at face value; they are not required to go back to the municipal law of that State for explanations of the meaning or significance of the international instrument. . . .

*   *   *

I also agree with the Court that the Concession Agreement between Iran and the Anglo-Iranian Oil Company, Limited, of 1933, cannot be regarded as a treaty or convention in the international law sense, and consequently cannot be regarded as coming within the purview of the Iranian Declaration.

*   *   *

I regret that I cannot agree with the conclusion of the Court that the United Kingdom is not entitled for jurisdictional purposes, to invoke, by virtue of the most-favoured-nation clauses in earlier treaties between that country and Iran, provisions of treaties concluded by Iran with other countries subsequent to the ratification of its Declaration accepting jurisdiction of the Court.

The conclusion that the treaty containing the most-favoured-nation clause is the *basic* treaty upon which the United Kingdom must rely amounts, in my judgment, to placing the emphasis on the wrong treaty, and losing sight of the principal issue. . . .

* * *

I find nothing in the Iranian Declaration to suggest that it is necessary that action under it shall be premised exclusively on a single treaty. I find nothing to suggest that it is necessary that such an action shall be based on a treaty between the plaintiff State and the defendant State. The Declaration, though drafted with meticulous safeguards, does not specify any such condition, nor does it specify that in considering a dispute as to the application of a treaty or convention accepted by Iran subsequent to the ratification of the Declaration, an earlier treaty may not be drawn upon. This would indeed have been a strange limitation. All that the Declaration requires in order that the dispute shall fall within the competence of the Court, is that it shall relate to the application of treaties or conventions accepted by Iran subsequent to the ratification of the Declaration, and nothing more.

The Danish Treaty answers this description. It is in that Treaty and not in the most-favoured-nation clause that the substantive rights of British nationals are to be found. Until that Treaty was concluded, the most-favoured-nation clauses in the British-Persian treaties were but promises, in effect, of non-discrimination, albeit binding promises. They related to rights *in futuro*. There was a right to claim something but it was an inchoate right. There was nothing to which it could attach itself unless and until favours should be granted to nationals of another country. But when Iran conferred upon Danish nationals by the Treaty of 1934 the right to claim treatment "in accordance with the principles and practice of ordinary international law," the right thereupon *ipso facto* became available to British nationals. This new right—based on international law concepts—came into existence not by virtue of the earlier treaties alone or even primarily, but by them plus the new treaties which gave them vitality. The new treaty is, in law and in fact, the fountain-head of the newly-acquired rights.

* * *

THE INTERNATIONAL MILITARY TRIBUNAL, 1945
13 Department of State Bulletin 222

WHEREAS the United Nations have from time to time made declarations of their intention that War Criminals shall be brought to justice;

AND WHEREAS the Moscow Declaration of the 30th October 1943 on German atrocities in Occupied Europe stated that those German

Officers and men and members of the Nazi Party who have been responsible for or have taken a consenting part in atrocities and crimes will be sent back to the countries in which their abominable deeds were done in order that they may be judged and punished according to the laws of these liberated countries and of the free Governments that will be created therein;

AND WHEREAS this Declaration was stated to be without prejudice to the case of major criminals whose offenses have no particular geographic location and who will be punished by the joint decision of the Governments of the Allies;

NOW THEREFORE the Government of the United States of America, the Provisional Government of the French Republic, the Government of the United Kingdom of Great Britain and Northern Ireland and the Government of the Union of Soviet Socialist Republics (hereinafter called "the Signatories") acting in the interests of all the United Nations and by their representatives duly authorized thereto have concluded this Agreement.

Article 1

There shall be established after consultation with the Control Council for Germany an International Military Tribunal for the trial of war criminals whose offenses have no particular geographical location whether they be accused individually or in their capacity as members of organizations or groups or in both capacities.

Article 2

The constitution, jurisdiction and functions of the International Military Tribunal shall be those set out in the Charter annexed to this Agreement, which Charter shall form an integral part of this Agreement.

*   *   *

I. Constitution of the Tribunal

Article 1

In pursuance of the Agreement signed on the 8th day of August 1945 by the Government of the United States of America, the Provisional Government of the French Republic, the Government of the United Kingdom of Great Britain and Northern Ireland and the Government of the Union of Soviet Socialist Republics, there shall be established an International Military Tribunal (hereinafter called "the Tribunal") for the just and prompt trial and punishment of the major war criminals of the European Axis.

*   *   *

II. Jurisdiction and General Principles

Article 6

The Tribunal established by the Agreement referred to in Article 1 hereof for the trial and punishment of the major war criminals of the European Axis countries shall have the power to try and punish persons who, acting in the interests of the European Axis countries, whether as individuals or as members of organizations, committed any of the following crimes.

The following acts, or any of them, are crimes coming within the jurisdiction of the Tribunal for which there shall be individual responsibility:

(a) *Crimes Against Peace:* namely, planning, preparation, initiation or waging of a war of aggression, or a war in violation of international treaties, agreements, or assurances, or participation in a common plan or conspiracy for the accomplishment of any of the foregoing;

(b) *War Crimes:* namely, violations of the laws or customs of war. Such violations shall include, but not be limited to, murder, ill-treatment or deportation to slave labor or for any other purpose of civilian population of or in occupied territory, murder or ill-treatment of prisoners of war or persons on the seas, killing of hostages, plunder of public or private property, wanton destruction of cities, towns or villages, or devastation not justified by military necessity;

(c) *Crimes Against Humanity:* namely, murder, extermination, enslavement, deportation, and other inhuman acts committed against any civilian population, before or during the war; or persecutions on political, racial or religious grounds in execution of or in connection with any crime within the jurisdiction of the Tribunal, whether or not in violation of domestic law of the country where perpetrated.

*   *   *

COURT OF JUSTICE OF THE EUROPEAN COMMUNITIES
Article by Peter E. Herzog
Washington Law Review, Vol. 41, No. 3, June, 1966

*   *   *

The Court of Justice of the European Communities is the successor of the Court of Justice of the European Coal and Steel Community created by the Treaty of Paris of 1951. The basic rules concerning that court's jurisdiction were laid down in the treaty. An annexed protocol contained the statute of the court with additional provisions relating to its organization and procedure. These were not very detailed. Instead, the court was authorized and directed to promulgate rules of procedure. The new court opened officially on December 4, 1952, in Luxemburg with the swearing in of its seven judges. Its first business was the drafting of rules of procedure, which were promulgated on March 4, 1953. The court was then ready to begin its judicial functions. About a year later, the court published additional rules concerning the rights and duties of attorneys and agents appearing before the court, recusant witnesses and letters rogatory. The original rules had ignored costs, and this matter was taken care of in a further set of rules promulgated shortly thereafter.

In 1957, the nations which had participated in the European Coal and Steel Community signed the two treaties creating the European Economic Community ("Common Market") and the European Atomic Energy Community ("Euratom"). Each treaty provided for the creation of a court of justice to serve as judicial arm of its community. Annexed to each treaty was a protocol containing the statute of the court. A further convention on certain institutions common to the European Communities provided that a single court should perform the functions of the separate courts mentioned in the various treaties. It did not give that court a distinctive name, however. In accordance with the convention, the Court of Justice of the European Coal and Steel Community came to an end in 1958 and was replaced by, or rather continued as, the Court of Justice for the three communities. There was some change in judicial personnel. Pending cases were continued.

One of the first activities of the new Court following the appointment of its members seems to have been the selection of a name. It chose the name "Court of Justice of the European Communities," though no official announcement to that effect was ever published in the Official Gazette of the European Communities. The Court then prepared a new set of rules, which were promulgated on March 3, 1959. The rules of the old Coal and Steel court were abrogated. The new rules had to be submitted to the Council of Ministers for approval; the Rome treaties of 1957 did not continue the Court's power to make rules without outside supervision. The rules did not deal with three matters for which, in the nature of things, the cooperation of the member states of the communities was particularily necessary, namely letters rogatory, legal aid and the punishment of perjurious witnesses and experts. After consultation with the governments of the member states and council approval, supplemental rules concerning these matters were enacted on March 9, 1962. Hence, the legal provisions relating to the procedure of the Court of Justice of the European Communities must be gleaned from a rather multifarious array of texts: the Coal and Steel, Common Market and Euratom treaties, the statutes annexed to them the protocol on common institutions of the three communities, and the Court's rules of 1959 as well as the supplemental rules of 1962. . . .

The Court of Justice of the European Communities consists of seven judges appointed for terms of six years by unanimous agreement of the member states. In practice, each member nation has the right to propose one judge (one nation can propose two judges), and the proposals made by a member state concerning the appointment of "its" judge are not seriously challenged by the other nations. The membership of the Court is subject to partial renewal every three years. The members of the Court elect one of their colleagues as presiding judge for a period of three years. All judges of the Court must now be law-trained and qualified to hold highest judicial office in their home state, or be otherwise possessed of outstanding qualifications. The rules for the appointment of judges have been criticized on the ground that the short, but renewable terms give the member states too much power over "their" judges. In fact, however, no complaints about improper conduct by judges seem to have been voiced. Furthermore, rather substantial salaries (at least by European standards) and sizable severance benefits payable to a judge not reappointed at the end of his term may tend to increase judicial self-reliance. The rule prohibiting the disclosure of opinions voiced by judges in conference and the absence of dissenting opinions makes it difficult for outsiders to blame any particular member of the Court for a decision reached by the Court and is an additional guarantee of judicial independence.

Also on the staff of the Court are two so-called advocates-general (*avocats généraux, Generalanwaelte*). Their role is similar to that of the *commissaires du gouvernement* before the highest French administrative tribunal, the *Conseil d'Etat:* one of them prepares an elaborate submission (*conclusions, Schlussantraege*) for each case; in it he surveys the facts of the case and the applicable law and suggests a judgment to the Court. The advocate-general represents only the law as such and his own conscience. He is by no means the representative of the interests of the European Communities. The Court is not bound to decide in accordance with the advocate-general's submission, but frequently does so.

Each judge and advocate-general is assisted by one *attaché*, who performs functions quite similar to those performed by the law clerk of an American judge. However, the *attachés* enjoy permanent appointments.

The Registrar of the Court is in charge of the Court records and must be present at each hearing. In addition, he is the chief administrative officer of the Court: unlike national courts in Europe, which are administratively part of an executive department, the Ministry of Justice, the Court of Justice of the European Communities administers itself. Since the Court must conduct its proceedings in all the four official languages of the Communities, Dutch, French, German, and Italian, it has a language department which translates all documents received or issued by the Court and operates the simultaneous translation service which makes it possible to follow oral proceedings of the Court in any of the Community languages. . . .

*   *   *

. . . . The basic function of the Court is the review of decisions, both individual (quasi-judicial) and general (quasi-legislative) issued by the executive organs of the European Communities: High Authority of the Coal and Steel Community, Commissions of the Economic Community and Euratom, and Councils of Ministers of the Communities. Individual (quasi-judicial) decisions can be attacked on four grounds: lack of jurisdiction on the part of the community organ having issued the decision, violation of substantial procedural requirements, violation of one of the treaties or of an implementing rule, and *détournement de pouvoir* (use of a granted power for an improper purpose). Review can be sought by Community organs (other than the one having issued the decision), member states and individuals or corporations. Under the Coal and Steel Treaty, however, private individuals and corporations may seek a review of decisions only if they are enterprises engaged either in coal or steel production (or, to some extent wholesaling), or associations of such enterprises. Community institutions and member states can bring direct proceedings to have general (quasi-legislative) decisions declared invalid. Others may do so only to a very limited extent. Under the Coal and Steel treaty they must show that there has been *détournement de pouvoir* concerning them, under the Common Market and Euratom treaties they must show that what appears to be a general decision in fact concerns them directly and individually.

The Court may also hear proceedings against Community organs based on their failure to act where they had a duty to do so.

The Court of Justice is competent in tort actions against the Communities. It has no general contractual competence, unless such a competence is conferred upon it by an appropriate clause in a contract entered into by one of the Community organs.

Most important in terms of the numbers of cases brought has been the Court's right to hear disputes involving community organs and their employees.

In a sense, the Court is also an international tribunal. It may hear disputes between member states of the European Communities concerning the Community treaties. It is likewise competent to hear suits through which member states are to be compelled to abide by their treaty obligations.

Increasingly significant, national courts before which cases involving the meaning of the European treaties or of regulations enacted by Community organs are pending may, and sometimes must, stay their proceedings and certify the question raised to the Court in Luxemburg for a preliminary ruling.

In some cases the Court must render what is more or less an advisory opinion. It also has a number of very specialized duties in connection with the Euratom treaty and some auxiliary Community institutions such as the European Investment Bank. Finally, it must authorize acts of execution (such as attachments) affecting Community property.

*   *   *

The powers of the Court are not the same in all the types of proceedings mentioned. Particularly in suits by employees, damage actions and suits to review fines imposed by Community organs it has a so-called *pleine juridiction*. This means that it may change or modify the decision of the Community organ involved, can review the exercise of discretion of such an organ and will feel less bound by the parties' pleadings. In most other cases . . . the Court may only approve the administrative decision under attack, or declare it void and remit the matter to the Community organ which issued it for further proceedings. Deference will be paid to the Community organs' discretionary findings, though the Court is not ordinarily prevented from examining the evidence relied on by the Community body. . . .

*   *   *

CASES HANDLED BY COURT OF JUSTICE OF EUROPEAN COMMUNITIES AND
COURT OF JUSTICE OF EUROPEAN COAL AND STEEL COMMUNITY

Year	New Cases Introduced	Cases Decided	Cases Settled	Cases Pending
1953	4	0	4	0
1954	10	9	1	0
1955	10	5	5	0
1956	11	6	5	0
1957	19	17	2	0
1958	43	37	6	0
1959	47	41	6	0
1960	25	24	1	0
1961	26	20	6	0
1962	36	32	4	0
1963	111	63	21	27
1964	58	33	4	48
1965 (Jan.–July)	46			

HUMBLET v. BELGIUM
Court of Justice of the European Communities, 1960
6 Recueil de la Jurisprudence de la Cour 1125

The plaintiff, a Belgian citizen and official of the European Coal and Steel Community, lodged this appeal against Belgium in the Court of Justice of the European Communities, alleging that Belgium had violated the Protocol on the Privileges and Immunities of the E.C.S.C. by considering his Community salary in determining the Belgian supplementary tax rate. Under Belgian revenue laws the supplementary tax (*impôt complémentaire*) is imposed in addition to various taxes on specific income. It is a progressively graduated tax assessed against the joint income of the spouses, irrespective of their individual earnings. The Belgian tax authorities took the position that, while plaintiff's salary was tax exempt, it had to be considered in determining the tax rate upon "other taxable income" subject to the supplementary tax. In the plaintiff's case, the "other taxable income" referred to income received by his wife, who was not an official of the Community.

While the plaintiff, in express reliance on the Protocol on Privileges and Immunities, refused to declare his Community earnings, the Belgian tax authorities determined the supplementary tax rate on the basis of their own estimate of the plaintiff's Community salary. Having exhausted all Belgian administrative, but not judicial, remedies, the plaintiff appealed to the Community Court. He requested the Court to declare that Belgium had violated Article 11 (b) of the Protocol. In addition, he sought an annulment of the tax assessment and an order compelling Belgium to pay him all sums with interest and cost on the amounts paid or to be paid by him to the Belgian tax authorities.

Under Article 16 of the Protocol on the Privileges and Immunities of the European Coal and Steel Community in conjunction with Article 43 of E.C.S.C. Treaty, the Court has jurisdiction over all disputes concerning the interpretation or application of the Protocol. The defendant asserts, however, that the Court lacks jurisdiction in this case, since the dispute does not involve the interpretation of the Protocol but rather the proper application of Belgian law to the income of plaintiff's wife who herself is not an official of the Community.

The E.C.S.C. Treaty is governed by the principle of strict separation of powers between the institutions of the Community and of the member States. Community law does not grant to the institutions of the Community the power to annul legislative or administrative acts of member States. Thus, if the High Authority believes, for example, that a member State has violated the Treaty by passing or retaining legislation in conflict with the Treaty, it lacks the power to annul or void these provisions. Instead, the High Authority can only proceed in accordance with Article 88 of the Treaty by noting its violation and in conjunction therewith instituting the proceedings therein provided for, in order that the State involved repeal the acts in question.

The same is true of the Court which, as the guardian of Community law under Article 31 of the Treaty, has jurisdiction based upon Article 16 of the Protocol to decide any dispute involving its interpretation or application. It cannot, however, by its own authority void or annul laws or administrative acts of member States. . . .

*   *   *

If the Court declares in its judgment that an administrative or legislative act of a member State violates Community law, then this State is required under Article 86 of the E.C.S.C. Treaty to repeal this act and possibly to remedy the illegal consequences caused by it. This obligation follows from the Treaty and the Protocol, which have the force of law within the territories of the member States as a result of their ratification and precedence over national law. If the Court should in this case declare the tax assessment to be illegal, the Belgian government would be required to take the necessary steps to bring about its annulment and to compensate the plaintiff for such sums as may have been improperly collected.

*   *   *

While the privileges and immunities were granted "solely in the interest of the Community," it should not be overlooked that they were expressly granted "to officials of the institutions of the Community." The fact that the privileges, immunities and conveniences are designed to serve the public interest of the Community, clearly justifies the powers vested in the High Authority to determine the classes of officials to which the Protocol shall apply (Article 12), or, if necessary, to waive the immunity of an official (Article 13 (b)). But this does not mean that these privileges were granted to the Community rather than to the officials. This construction is, furthermore, justified by the wording of the above-mentioned provisions.

It follows that the Protocol grants to the persons therein mentioned a personal right (*subjektives Recht*) protected by the right of appeal provided for in Article 16 of the Protocol.

*   *   *

Article 16 of the Protocol, according to which "any dispute concerning the interpretation or application of the . . . Protocol shall be submitted to the Court," contains no reference to any procedure, which might have to be instituted prior to the filing of an appeal with the Community Court. Anyone who believes himself aggrieved by an improper interpretation or application of this Protocol may, according to the wording of this Article, submit the dispute to the Court. It follows that officials of the Community are authorized under Article 16 to appeal to the Court against their national government without having previously proceeded in accordance with any other procedure provided for under provisions of Community or domestic law.

*   *   *

It could surely not have escaped the authors of the Treaty that the "disputes," which would arise from the "interpretation or application" of the Protocol would consist mainly of differences of opinion between the persons to whom the Protocol grants certain privileges and immunities on the one hand, and the authorities who have an interest in a narrow interpretation of these privileges and immunities on the other. Viewed in this light, the parties to the instant litigation would certainly seem to represent the typical parties to the "dispute" within the meaning of Article 16.

*   *   *

In addition, it must be determined whether the appeal is inadmissible, because the plaintiff may not have exhausted the administrative and judicial remedies available to him under the law of his home country.

*   *   *

The Treaties establishing the European Communities have not placed the Community Court above national judicial tribunals in the sense that the decisions of these courts can be appealed to the Community Court. The Community Court, on the other hand, has exclusive jurisdiction as far as the interpretation of the Protocol is concerned. As already indicated, the Treaties are based on the principle of strict separation of jurisdiction between the Community Court on the one hand, and national judicial tribunals on the other. It follows therefrom that any overlapping of these separate jurisdictions is precluded. Once the Court has jurisdiction, there can be no talk of prior "exhaustion" of local remedies, since this would amount to the submission for resolution of one and the same legal dispute first to national courts and subsequently to the Community Court.

Since the Court has jurisdiction to decide the instant case within the limits indicated above, the plaintiff's failure to exhaust his country's judicial remedies cannot be a bar to the admissibility of this appeal.

Accordingly, the plaintiff's right to appeal has been clearly established. The appeal is, therefore, admissible insofar as the Court has jurisdiction to grant the relief requested.

*   *   *

a. The Protocol on the Privileges and Immunities of the E.C.S.C. prohibits member States from imposing any tax on an official of the Community, if this tax is based in whole or in part on his compensation received from the Community.

b. The Protocol also prohibits consideration of this compensation in determining the tax rate on income from other sources.

c. The same is true as far as taxes are concerned which are owed by a spouse of such official, if the tax is assessed jointly against the spouses.

COSTA v. E.N.E.L.
Court of Justice of the European Communities, 1964
2 Common Market Reporter 7384

*   *   *

Under the provisions of Law No. 1643 of December 6, 1962, and of subsequent decrees, the Italian Government nationalized the production and distribution of electrical energy and created an organization known as E.N.E.L., to which were transferred the assets of electrical enterprises.

Engaged in litigation with the E.N.E.L. with regard to payment of a bill for use of electricity, Maître Costa, in his capacity as consumer and shareholder in the Edison-Volta Company, which was affected by the nationalization in question, requested during the proceedings before the Giudice Conciliatore of Milan that Article 177 of the EEC Treaty be applied in order to obtain an interpretation of Articles 102, 93, 53 and 37 of the Treaty which, he claimed, had been violated by the above-mentioned Italian law.

*   *   *

This request for a preliminary ruling was submitted to the Court by the registrar of the Giudice Conciliatore and recorded by the registry of the Court on February 20, 1964.

*   *   *

Unlike ordinary international treaties, the EEC Treaty established its own legal order, which was incorporated into the legal systems of the Member States at the time the Treaty came into force and to which the courts of the Member States are bound. In fact, by establishing a Community of unlimited duration, having its own institutions, personality and legal capacity, the ability to be represented on the international level and, particularly, real powers resulting from a limitation of the jurisdiction of the States or from a transfer of their powers to the Community, the States relinquished, albeit in limited areas, their sovereign rights and thus created a body of law applicable to their nationals and to themselves.

This incorporation into the law of each member country of provisions of a Community origin, and the letter and spirit of the Treaty in general, have as a corollary the impossibility for the States to assert as against a legal order accepted by them on a reciprocal basis a subsequent unilateral measure which could not be challenged by it. The executory power of Community law cannot, in fact, vary from one State to another because of subsequent internal laws without jeopardizing fulfillment of the Treaty objectives set forth in Article 5, paragraph 2, and without bringing about a discrimination prohibited by Article 7. The obligations agreed to in the Treaty establishing the EEC would not be unconditional, only contingent, if they could be challenged by future legislative acts of the signatories.

The preeminence of Community law is confirmed by Article 189, under which regulations are "binding" and "directly applicable in each Member State." This provision, which contains no reservation, would be meaningless if a Member State could unilaterally nullify its effects through a legislative act that could be asserted as against the Community texts.

As a result of all these factors, it would be impossible legally to assert any internal text whatsoever against the law created by the Treaty and originating from an independent source, considering the specific original nature of that law, without robbing it of its Community nature and without jeopardizing the legal foundation of the Community itself. The transfer by the States from their internal legal systems over to the Community legal order, of rights and obligations to reflect those set forth in the Treaty, therefore entails a definitive limitation of their sovereign rights, against which a subsequent unilateral act that would be incompatible with the Community concept cannot be asserted.

*   *   *

The Court, ruling on the plea of inadmissibility based on Article 177, declares and decrees:

The questions submitted by the Giudice Conciliatore of Milan by virtue of Article 177 are admissible in so far as they concern, in this case, an interpretation of the provisions of the EEC Treaty, since no subsequent unilateral act can be asserted against the rules of the Community; rules as follows:

*   *   *

(3) Article 53 constitutes a Community rule capable of entailing for those subject to the law rights which the domestic courts must safeguard.

These provisions prohibit any new measure whose object is to make the establishment of nationals of other Member States subject to stricter rules than those reserved for those subject to the law, regardless of the legal make-up of the enterprises.

(4) All of the provisions of Article 37, paragraph 2, constitute a Community rule capable of entailing for those subject to the law rights which the domestic courts must safeguard.

Within the framework of the question presented, the object of these provisions is to prohibit any new measure that is contrary to the principles of Article 37, paragraph 1, i.e., any measure, the object or effect of which is a new discrimination between the nationals of the Member States as to supply and marketing, through monopolies or organizations that must, on the one hand, have as their object transactions in a commercial product that can involve competition and trade between Member States and, on the other hand, play an active part in such trade.

* * *

International Adjudication of Human Rights

At the Hague Congress of 1948 attended by 713 European delegates from 16 countries, a proposal was adopted to guarantee human rights through a court of justice. A year later the Council of Europe was officially created by 10 western European States, with one of its aims being the maintenance and further realization of human rights. In 1950, the European Convention on Human Rights was signed and since then ratified by 15 states (but not by France, Malta, or Switzerland), leading to the establishment of the European Commission on Human Rights and the European Court of Human Rights.

The Commission has consisted of 15 members, no two of whom may be nationals of the same state, and they are elected by the Committee of Ministers for a six-year term, with a possibility of reelection.

The Court of Human Rights consists of a number equal to the membership of the Council of Europe, which was 18 in 1966, and members are elected by the Consultative Assembly (which is the parliamentary body of the Council of Europe) from a list submitted by the Council members. A chamber of seven may hear cases, with each state party to a case entitled to have one judge of its nationality sitting on the bench, and may relinquish jurisdiction to the full court in certain instances.

* * *

EUROPEAN COURT OF HUMAN RIGHTS
European Convention for the Protection of Human Rights and Fundamental Freedoms, 1950*
45 A.J.I.L. Supp. 24

* * *

Article 19

To ensure the observance of the engagements undertaken by the High Contracting Parties in the present Convention, there shall be set up:

(1) A European Commission of Human Rights hereinafter referred to as "the Commission";

(2) A European Court of Human Rights, hereinafter referred to as "the Court."

* * *

---

* In force 3 September 1953.

Article 44

Only the High Contracting Parties and the Commission shall have the right to bring a case before the Court.

Article 45

The jurisdiction of the Court shall extend to all cases concerning the interpretation and application of the present Convention which the High Contracting Parties or the Commission shall refer to it in accordance with Article 48.

Article 46

(1) Any of the High Contracting Parties may at any time declare that it recognises as compulsory *ipso facto* and without special agreement the jurisdiction of the Court in all matters concerning the interpretation and application of the present Convention.

(2) The declarations referred to above may be made unconditionally or on condition of reciprocity on the part of several or certain other High Contracting Parties or for a specified period.

(3) These declarations shall be deposited with the Secretary-General of the Council of Europe who shall transmit copies thereof to the High Contracting Parties.

Article 47

The Court may only deal with a case after the Commission has acknowledged the failure of efforts for a friendly settlement and within the period of three months provided for in Article 32.

Article 48

The following may bring a case before the Court, provided that the High Contracting Party concerned, if there is only one, or the High Contracting Parties concerned, if there is more than one, are subject to the compulsory jurisdiction of the Court or, failing that, with the consent of the High Contracting Party concerned, if there is only one, or of the High Contracting Parties concerned if there is more than one:

- (a) the Commission;
- (b) a High Contracting Party whose national is alleged to be a victim;
- (c) a High Contracting Party which referred the case to the Commission;
- (d) a High Contracting Party against which the complaint has been lodged.

Article 49

In the event of dispute as to whether the Court has jurisdiction, the matter shall be settled by the decision of the Court.

Article 50

If the Court finds that a decision of a measure taken by a legal authority or any other authority of a High Contracting Party, is completely or partially in conflict with the obligations arising from the present Convention, and if the internal law of the said Party allows only partial reparation to be made for the consequences of this decision or measure, the decision of the Court shall, if necessary, afford just satisfaction to the injured party.

*　　*　　*

Article 52

The judgment of the Court shall be final.

Article 53

The High Contracting Parties undertake to abide by the decision of the Court in any case to which they are parties.

*　　*　　*

FOR FURTHER STUDY

RICHARD A. FALK. *The Role of Domestic Courts in the International Legal Order.* Syracuse, N.Y.: Syracuse University Press, 1964.

WERNER FELD. *The Court of the European Communities.* The Hague: Martinus Nijhoff, 1964.

WOLFGANG FRIEDMAN. *The Changing Structure of International Law.* New York: Columbia University Press, 1964.

SHABTAI ROSENNE. *The World Court, What It Is and How It Works.* New York: Oceana Publications, 1962.

H. L. A. HART. *The Concept of Law.* Oxford: Clarendon Press, 1961.

ARTHUR NUSSBAUM. *A Concise History of the Law of Nations.* Rev. ed. New York: Macmillan Co., 1954.

II

The Legal Personality of States and International Organizations

I N any legal system, certain persons endowed with a legal personality, such as a corporation in municipal law, may have rights and duties. Until quite recently, states were considered the only legal persons under the law of nations. Today, states are still by far the main actors and subjects of international law, and, in fact, only states may be parties to contentious cases before the International Court of Justice. But what is a *state?*

States can vary in size as from Malta to Canada, in population as from Gambia to China, or in wealth or power as from Somalia to the United States of America. What counts legally, however, is the existence of a political community for people living in a particular area, where the law of a government is widely recognized and generally enforceable, and which is independent of the control of any other state. But how does a political community become a state?

By the legal instrument of a treaty, states may be created by other states, such as Switzerland by the Treaty of Westphalia in 1648, or Poland and Czechoslovakia by the Treaty of Versailles in 1919. States may also be proclaimed, as Vietnam and Cambodia were in 1942, Laos in 1945, or Israel in 1948. Two or more states may unite, as in the formation of a new and larger state like Italy and Germany in the 19th century, or the short-lived Syrian-Egyptian United Arab Republic in 1958. Political communities may achieve a sovereign status from a ruling government and become independent states, as did the several colonies and territories of

Great Britain, such as Nigeria in 1960 or Guyana in 1966. Moreover, from being a ward of a great state a mandate or a trust territory may become an independent state, as did Tanganyika in 1961. Other political arrangements in achieving statehood are possible.

Recognition of States

However states seek or obtain existence, they may not always gain the recognition of other states. For example, although proclaimed as a state in 1960, Katanga was never recognized by any other state; Israel has not yet been recognized as a state by Arab states; and although in 1954 the Soviet Union recognized the German Democratic Republic as a sovereign state, its statehood has not been acknowledged by most other states in the world.

States, as legal entities, ought not to be confused with *governments*. By internal political changes within states, governments come and go. Governments may assert their claims to speak for a state, and sometimes two governments at the same time maintain claims to speak for the same state. But the legal personality of the state continues. In the international legal system, states, not governments, have rights that may be defended and obligations that must be fulfilled with respect to other states.

Only by assuming a continuous legal personality for the state would international agreements between, let us say, Canada and Brazil have any meaning, for their governments may be changed at any time by internal politics. All international obligations would be uncertain if governments were the legal parties to a treaty. A most cogent opinion on this matter was given as early as 1764 to the King of Great Britain by his Advocate:

First, that all treaties whatsoever . . . concluded between Sovereigns of respective States are not Personal but National and therefore like all other national rights and obligations, inseparable from each other, are valid in Succession.

Were it otherwise, doubtless the Law of Nations would have required and established a Custom that all Treaties should be renewed and republished upon every Change of the Sovereign Person or Mode of Government. . . .[1]

Similarly, property of India, France, Mexico, or Ethiopia that is situated abroad does not belong to their governments, whatever their forms may take at the moment, but to the state itself. Governments may determine the use of the state's assets for a while, but the assets—land,

---

[1] Lord McNair, *International Law Opinions* (3 vols.; Cambridge: Cambridge University Press, 1956), Vol. 1, p. 4.

gold, commodities, vessels, and so forth—are owned by the state. Governments may be elected by the people, or hold the reins of public order and discipline with the mute acquiescence of the people, or even seize the machinery of the state and forcibly subdue all opposition; but their claims for recognition, to speak for the foreign affairs of the state, to commit its personality to new international legal obligations, or to possess its property abroad will depend on the acknowledgment of other states.

The *Kasendorf* case, which follows, illustrates the continuance of the state of Estonia as a legal personality in United States law.

State Personality

DAMARA MULLART v. OREGON
In Matter of Estate of August Kasendorf
Supreme Court of Oregon, 1961
353 Pac. 2d 531

Warrenton, Justice

*   *   *

August Kasendorf died testate in Multnomah county, November 21, 1943, leaving his entire estate, consisting of real and personal property, to his brother and four sisters, who were residents and nationals of Estonia. No contact having been established with these legatees, proceedings were instituted in 1951 for the determination of heirship pursuant to paragraphs 19–1301, 19–1906, OCLA, as amended by ch. 184, Oregon Laws 1945 (now ORS 117.510, 117.560).

*   *   *

The questions presented for our determination are: Who were the legatees, if any, that survived the testator, and if they were residents of Estonia on November 21, 1943, did the laws of that country as of that date meet the requirements of par. 61–107, OCLA, supra, so as to entitle such Estonian legatees, or their survivors, to receive a distributive share of August Kasendorf's estate?

*   *   *

The testimony of claimant's witnesses, all of whom are former nationals of Estonia, and the majority of whom are refugees, must be read with some consideration and understanding of the catastrophic events which occurred in that small republic during the year 1941 to 1943 and resulted in its complete subjugation to the Soviet authority.

Estonia is one of the three Baltic states which suffered the same tragic experiences of that period. It is a relatively small area, 18,357 square miles, slightly less than the combined areas of Lake and Harney counties of our own state, and with a population in 1940 of only 1,126,415. The Russians, in June, 1941, without the formalities of war or warning, moved in and overwhelmed it with its military might. At the same time the Soviet hastily and cruelly deported about 60,000 of its people to Russia and Siberia and, in addition, exterminated many of its elderly residents. This policy of destroying or decimating families and rendering normal economic life chaotic continued long afterward.

*   *   *

Sometime after 1941, the Germans overran Estonia and for the time forced Soviet retirement. But the Russians attacked again in 1943 and compelled the Germans to evacuate. Ever since the Russians have remained in complete control. As a result of the ebb and flow of this tide of invasion, and particularly the expulsion of the Germans by the Russians in 1943, their warring armies by bombing raids and consequent fires, destoyed large segments of the metropolitan and suburban areas of Estonia and with it went the destruction of many public buildings and valuable records which ordinarily might be expected to supply records of vital statistics and pedigree.

These conditions account in large measure for the want of more satisfactory records concerning the Kasendorf family tree and the dependence of the claimant upon hearsay to establish relationship to the decedent, August Kasendorf.

The case for the claimant is dependent primarily on the testimony of Damara and Paul Janes in establishing the relationship of Anna and Damara to August Kasendorf and the nonexistence of any other relatives surviving the testator. It was testimony admitted without objection and to which no rebuttal was offered. It stands uncontradicted.

*   *   *

Unless the testimony of Damara Mullart and Paul Janes is absolutely false, Anna Mikli and her daughter have established their place in the genealogy of the Kasendorf family and Anna's sole heirship in the August Kasendorf estate.

*   *   *

Having concluded that Anna Mikli was the sole legatee surviving at the time of the death of her brother August and entitled to his entire estate, we now turn to the matter of her entitlement to take her inheritance, being, as she was, a resident and national of Estonia at the time of the death of the testator.

Section 61–107, OCLA, supra, requires of a nonresident heir two phases of proof as a condition precedent to taking and receiving any personal property by descent or inheritance: (1) proof of a reciprocal right of

American citizens by descent or inheritance, or its proceeds, from a foreign estate (in this case from an Estonian estate) and in like manner as aliens (Estonians) are permitted to take in Oregon; and (2) proof of the right of American citizens to receive by payment to them in the United States or its territories moneys originating from estates of persons dying in such foreign countries. . . .

But before giving answer to the foregoing questions concerning these two conditions precedent, we deem it important to take notice that notwithstanding the turbulent and chaotic conditions which have prevailed in Estonia since 1940, the claims of Russia to sovereignty over what once was the peaceful Republic of Estonia have never been recognized by the United States. This is not only a matter of common knowledge, but has documented attestation as exhibits in this proceeding and, ineffective as they may be in many fields of consular activity, the Department of State continues to recognize Estonian consuls, which would include Mr. Johannes Kaiv, the Acting Consul General, with offices in New York.

Consul Kaiv . . . represented that the law of Estonia relating to the inheritance rights of foreigners was promulgated on September 13, 1938, and is as published in the State Gazette No. 79 of September 16, 1938, a certified copy of which appears in the record. As it appears there, it provides:

"*Section 1.*
"A foreigner has the right to inherit in Estonia only if an Estonian citizen in a corresponding degree of relationship and under the same conditions has the right to inherit according to the laws of the state of which the said foreigner is a citizen.
"A foreigner cannot receive a larger share of the inheritance than an Estonian citizen would receive of a similar inheritance in the said foreign country.
"*Section 2.*
"This law applies also to all such estates which are in process at the time this law becomes effective and in regard to which a court's decision confirming the inheritance rights has not yet taken legal effect."

He also asserted that it was in effect at the time of the forcible occupation of Estonia by the Russians in 1940 and still continues in effect. . . .

*   *   *

. . . In answer to the first question arising under par. 61–107, OCLA, supra, it is apparent to us from the foregoing and particularly from the law as found in State Gazette No. 79 that an American citizen under the Estonian law had the same "right to take" or inherit as did its own nationals enjoy and "in like manner" to the laws of this state without restriction to nationality, religion or political affiliation. . . .

But in so saying, we limit our conclusion to the proposition that the Estonian law meets the condition of the "right to take." It does not include a provision to insure "the right to receive" as required by par. 61–107, OCLA, supra. All parties are cognizant of its insufficiency in this respect. The state points to the exchange laws of Estonia as rendering the

"right to receive" uncertain by reason of the discretionary powers reserved to Estonian officials who are appointed to administer those laws
and the Consul General confirmed this by saying: "According to these
laws and regulations [relating to foreign exchange] a license from the
Bank of Estonia was necessary for export of foreign currency from
Estonia."

*   *   *

If the American heirs had to depend upon the uncertainties of the
exchange laws to receive payment of their inheritance in the United
States, we would feel compelled, as were we in the Christoff and Stoich
estates, to deny claimant's right to take from the Kasendorf estate. But we
find that an American's right to receive payment of an Estonian legacy in
the United States is not dependent alone on the whims of Estonian
officialdom under the exchange regulations of that country. Such an
American heir could, if he had been disappointed in that direction, invoke
the aid of a United States Consul, resident in Estonia, as provided by Art.
XXIV of the Treaty of 1925, and have that official demand receipt for
and transmit to him through appropriate agencies of this government such
heir's share of an Estonian estate.

Art. XXIV of the Treaty of Friendship, Commerce and Consular
Rights, signed by the United States and Estonia on December 23, 1925 (44
Stat. 2379) reads:

"A consular officer of either High Contracting Party may in behalf of his
non-resident countryman receipt for their distributive shares derived from
estates in the process of probate or accruing under the provisions of so-called
Workman's Compensation Laws or other like statutes provided he remit any
funds so received through the appropriate agencies of his Government to the
proper distributees, and provided further that he furnish to the authority or
agency making distribution through him reasonable evidence of such
remission."

The state concedes that this treaty has not been abrogated.

Treaties may be considered as evidence of foreign law . . . We have
no doubt that Estonia treats its treaty obligations, as does the United
States, as the supreme law of the land. . . .

We, therefore, hold:

1. That Jaan Kasendorf, Miina Kasendorf, Leena Suurthal and Liisa
Kasendorf, respectively, the brother and three sisters of August Kasendorf, deceased, predeceased the testator without leaving lineal descendants
surviving;

2. That August's sister Anna Mikli died sometime subsequent to the
forepart of December, 1943;

3. That, as shown by the record in this proceeding, Damara Mullart is
the daughter and only child of Anna Mikli;

4. That the laws of Estonia, as they were on November 21, 1943,

supplemented by the provisions of the Treaty of 1925 between the United States and Estonia, meet the requirements of par. 61–107, OCLA, supra, with respect to the rights of American citizens to take and receive inheritances in Estonian estate; and

5. That the property of the estate of August Kasendorf, when available for distribution, should be delivered to the duly appointed, qualified and acting administrator of the estate of Anna Mikli, deceased, acting pursuant to appointment of the circuit court in that estate.

*　　*　　*

Recognition of Governments

The recognition of governments should always be distinguished from the recognition of states. In 1927, a United States Circuit Court of Appeals put the doctrine succinctly:

The granting or refusal of recognition of a government has nothing to do with the recognition of the state itself. If a foreign state refused the recognition of a change in the form of government of an old state, this latter does not thereby lose its recognition as an international person.[2]

In 1967, some states recognized the government at Peking as the government of China, while other states recognized the government at Taipei on the island of Taiwan as the government of China, even though the Taipei government exercised no physical control over the mainland. But the state of China continued to exist, with each government claiming to represent its international legal personality. Moreover, where a state withholds or withdraws recognition from a foreign government, or breaks diplomatic relations, the legal obligations of both states toward each other under international law do not cease. For instance, the 1961 rupture of diplomatic relations between Havana and Washington did not end the obligations of Cuba and the United States toward each other as states—obligations either sanctioned by treaties and other international agreements in force, or by the usages of the law of nations.

The legal personality of a state can continue even during military occupation or the peaceful assumption of governing powers by a foreign state. For example, the Netherlands government-in-exile in London during World War II could legislate in certain areas of municipal law for the state of the Netherlands under occupation by Adolph Hitler's German army. In 1952, the International Court of Justice held that the treaties concluded by Morocco before the 1912 Treaty of Fez, which established France as a "protecting" power, were valid and binding on France.[3]

The creation, division, amalgamation, or annihilation of states necessarily raises difficult questions of succession to various rights and obligations under international law. Similarly, changes in the government of a state, by violent or peaceful means, and the unwillingness of some states to recognize new governments as legally enpowered to act for a state raise additional problems of international legal as well as political relations. Compounding the difficulty have been situations in which a government has been recognized as in fact (*de facto*) in control of a state, but not by

---

[2] *Lehigh Valley Railroad Co.* v. *State of Russia*, 21 F. 2d 396 (1927).
[3] *United States Nationals in Morocco Case*, 1952, I.C.J. Report 6.

law (*de jure*) of the recognizing state, or in which some states recognize one government as the agent for a state while other states recognize another government as the agent of the same state.

A special interest in the problem of international recognition of governments as the legal agents for states arises in conjunction with membership in international organizations. As long as interstate relations were bilateral, one state's refusal to recognize the government of another, or its decision to recognize one government over another in the face of a political struggle for control of that state, had consequences for only two or three parties. Today, however, legal anomalies may arise from the presence within an international organization of a state whose representatives are recognized as the government by some member states but not by others. Within the compass of their basic treaties or statutes, international organizations can approve resolutions and votes that will create obligations for all the states of the organization. A nice legal question, therefore, is whether the officials of a government not recognized by a member state can help create obligations for that state through the medium of an international organization—for example, the budget assessments approved by the General Assembly of the United Nations or the rule-making power invested in certain U.N. specialized agencies over its members.

It can always be argued, of course, that state and government recognition and representation are political issues, but that rationale hardly eliminates the legal procedures and the legal rules likely to be followed in specific cases affecting state and personal property that are brought before courts for adjudication. And legal points themselves frequently are used to bolster the dubious political arguments of states.

The documents that follow illustrate (*a*) the status and power of an unrecognized *de facto* government by the *Salimoff* case; (*b*) the problem of two governments claiming to act for one state by *Bank of China* v. *Wells Fargo;* the United Nations problem of the recognition and representation of the Peking government of China by (*c*) *Memorandum by the United Nations Secretary-General,* (*d*) *Letter of the Permanent Representative of China to the United Nations,* and (*f*) *Statement of United States Policy with Respect to Mainland China.*

De Facto and *De Jure* Government

SALIMOFF & COMPANY v. STANDARD OIL COMPANY
New York Court of Appeals, 1933
262 N.Y. 220

Pound, Chief Justice

*   *   *

. . . The Soviet government, by a nationalization decree, confiscated all oil lands in Russia and sold oil extracted therefrom to defendants. The former owners of the property, Russian nationals, join in an equitable action for an accounting on the ground that the confiscatory decrees of the unrecognized Soviet government and the seizure of oil lands thereunder have no other effect in law on the rights of the parties than seizure by bandits. (*Luther* v. *Sagor & Co.*, (1921) 1 K.B. 456; s. c., 3 K.B. 532; cited in *Sokoloff* v. *National City Bank*, 239 N.Y. 158, 164.) The complaints have been dismissed.

The question is as to the effect on the title of a purchaser from the unrecognized confiscating Soviet Russian government. Does title pass or is the Soviet government no better than a thief, stealing the property of its nationals and giving only a robber's title to stolen property? Plaintiffs contend that the Soviet decrees of confiscation did not divest them of title.

When a government which originates in revolution is recognized by the political department of our government as the *de jure* government of the country in which it is established, such recognition is retroactive in effect and validates all the actions of the government so recognized from the commencement of its existence. (*Oetjen* v. *Central Leather Co.*, 246 U.S. 297; *Terrazas* v. *Holmes*, 115 Tex. 32.) The courts of one independent government will not sit in judgment upon the validity of the acts of another done within its own territory, even when such government seizes and sells the property of an American citizen within its boundaries. If the Soviet government were a *de jure* government, it would follow that title to the property in this case must be determined by the result of the confiscatory Soviet decrees.

The status of the Soviet government is defined by the Secretary of State's office as follows:

"1. The Government of the United States accorded recognition to the Provisional Government of Russia as the successor of the Russian Imperial Government, and has not accorded recognition to any government in Russia since the overthrow of the Provisional Government of Russia.

"2. The Department of State is cognizant of the fact that the Soviet regime is exercising control and power in territory of the former Russian Empire and the Department of State has no disposition to ignore that fact.

"3. The refusal of the Government of the United States to accord recognition to the Soviet regime is not based on the ground that that regime does not exercise control and authority in territory of the former Russian Empire, but on other fact."

It follows that the question as to the validity of acts and decrees of a regime, not the subject of diplomatic recognition, becomes a matter to be decided by the courts in an appropriate case. Thus it was held that out of respect for the political departments of the United States government only a recognized government may be a plaintiff in the courts of this State. (*Russian Socialist Federated Soviet Republic* v. *Cibrario*, 235 N.Y. 255.)

It has been held by the Appellate Division:

"Whatever may be said of the propriety of justice of the nationalizing decrees promulgated by the Soviet government of Russia, those decrees were made by the *de facto* government of that country and are there in full force and effect and binding upon all Russian nationals. . . .

"Under well-established principles of international law and in accordance with the decisions of our courts, the Soviet law and decrees must be given internal effect in that country." (237 App. Div. 686, 689, 690.)

Writers have been inclined to the view that where a *de facto* government reigns supreme within its own territory, the courts should give full effect to its decrees, in so far as they affect private rights. . . .

The courts of this State have not gone so far. The question with us is whether, within Russia, the Soviet decrees have actually attained such effects as to alter the rights and obligations of parties in a manner we may not in justice disregard, even though they do not emanate from a lawfully established authority, recognized politically by the government of the United States. (*Russian Reinsurance Co.* v. *Stoddard*, 240 N.Y. 149, 157.) We have considered the extraterritorial effect of Soviet decrees which liquidated Russian banks (*Petrogradsky M.K. Bank* v. *National City Bank*, 253 N.Y. 23) and insurance companies (*First Russian Ins. Co.* v. *Beha*, 240 N.Y. 601). We have reached the conclusion in those and similar cases that such decrees had no extraterritorial effect and that the continued existence of such companies, wherever they were found to function outside of Russia, would be recognized. The consequence has been that corporations non-existent in Soviet Russia have been, like fugitive ghosts endowed with extraterritorial immortality, recognized as existing outside its boundaries. . . .

In this case another situation is presented. The oil property confiscated was taken in Russia from Russian nationals. A recovery in conversion is dependent upon the laws of Russia. (*Riley* v. *Pierce Oil Corp.*, 245 N.Y. 152, 154.) When no right of action is created at the place of wrong, no recovery in tort can be had in any other State on account of the wrong. The United States government recognizes that the Soviet government has functioned as a *de facto* or *quasi* government since 1917, ruling within its borders. It has recognized its existence as a fact although it has refused diplomatic recognition as one might refuse to recognize an objectionable relative although his actual existence could not be denied. It tells us that it has no disposition to ignore the fact that such government is exercising control and power in territory of the former Russian empire. . . .

As a juristic conception, what is Soviet Russia? A band of robbers or a government? We all know that it is a government. The State Department knows it, the courts, the nations and the man on the street. If it is a government in fact, its decrees have force within its borders and over its nationals. "Recognition does not create the state." (*Wulfsohn* v. *Russian S.F.S. Republic*, 234 N.Y. 372, 375.) It simply gives to a *de facto* state international status. Must the courts say that Soviet Russia is an outlaw and that the Provisional government of Russia as the successor of the Russian Imperial government is still the lawful government of Russia although it is long since dead? (See *Nankivel* v. *Omsk All Russian Government*, 237 N.Y. 150, 156.) The courts may not recognize the Soviet government as the *de jure* government until the State Department gives the word. They may, however, say that it is a government, maintaining internal peace and order, providing for national defense and the general welfare, carrying on relations with our own government and others. To refuse to recognize that Soviet Russia is a government regulating the internal affairs of the country, is to give to fictions an air of reality which they do not deserve.

The courts cannot create a foreign wrong contrary to the law of the place of the act. (*Slater* v. *Mexican Nat. R.R. Co.*, 194 U.S. 120; *American Banana Co.* v. *United Fruit Co.* 213 U.S. 347.) The cause of action herein arose where the act of confiscation occurred and it must be governed by the law of Soviet Russia. According to the law of nations it did no legal wrong when it confiscated the oil of its own nationals and sold it in Russia to the defendants. Such conduct may lead to governmental refusal to recognize Russia as a country with which the United States may have diplomatic dealings. The confiscation is none the less effective. The government may be objectionable in a political sense. It is not unrecognizable as a real governmental power which can give title to property within its limits.

*　　　*　　　*

The legitimate conclusion is that the existing government cannot be ignored by the courts of this State, so far as the validity of its acts in Russia is concerned, although the attempt is here made to nullify such acts and create a cause of action in tort in favor of Russian nationals against American corporations, purchasers for value from the Soviet government of property in Russia in accordance with Soviet law.

*　　　*　　　*

Non-recognition is no answer to defendant's contention, no reason for regarding as of no legal effect the laws of an unrecognized government ruling by force, as the Soviet government in Russia concededly was. "Within its own territory the Soviet was a sovereign power." (W. S. Andrews, J., in 12 Cornell Law Quarterly, 441.)

The order in each case should be affirmed, with costs; . . .

*   *   *

Two Governments of One State

BANK OF CHINA v. WELLS FARGO BANK & UNION TRUST COMPANY
United States District Court, 1952
104 F. Supp. 59

Goodman, District Judge

*   *   *

Plaintiff, a Chinese corporation, filed these actions to recover the total sum of $798,584.64 on deposit in the defendant Bank. Defendant Bank filed answers asserting its willingness to pay the sum, but alleging that it was unable to do so because of conflicting claims of corporate authority to receive payment. Thereafter the attorneys for the plaintiff moved for summary judgment in plaintiff's favor. Later, a second group of attorneys, claiming that they were the only attorneys empowered to represent the plaintiff Bank of China, filed a motion to dismiss these actions or in the alternative to substitute themselves as the attorneys for the plaintiff . . .

*   *   *

The question now presented is essentially one of law. The attorneys who initiated this action contend that the controlling corporate authority of the Bank of China is vested by its Articles of Association in the Nationalist Government of China. They note that the Bank of China was directed by representatives of that Government when the deposit in suit was made. The Nationalist Government, they point out, not only still exists, but is the only government of China recognized by the United States. The Bank of China, they assert, still functions under the control of the Nationalist Government at its present seat on the Island of Formosa and at branch offices in various parts of the world. The Bank of China, so functioning, is the plaintiff in this action, they say, and the rightful claimant to the deposit in suit.

The intervening attorneys contend that the Peoples Government of China, as the successor in fact to the Nationalist Government in continen-

tal China, has succeeded to the corporate rights of the Chinese State in the
Bank of China. They allege that the operations of the Bank of China
throughout the Chinese Mainland and in certain branch offices abroad are
now conducted by new Government directors appointed by the Peoples
Government in conjunction with the directors representing private stockholders. It is only through these banking operations, they argue, that the
corporate purposes of the Bank of China are now being realized. Only
through operations so conducted, they say, can the rights of the Chinese
State as majority stockholder and those of the private investors be given
any substance. Such corporate operations, the intervening attorneys urge,
are the true indicia of rightful ownership of the deposit.

The issue before the Court has therefore been reduced to a comparatively narrow one. It appears from the record, that there are two Banks of
China now functioning. The question is: Which Bank of China is legally
entitled to the deposit in suit? For convenience, the plaintiff will hereafter
be referred to as the "Nationalist" Bank of China, and the Bank of China
represented by the intervening attorneys as the "Peoples" Bank of China.

At the outset, the Court must determine whether these causes may
finally be disposed of by summary judgment. Rule 56(c), F.R.C.P., 28
U.S.C. If there is "a genuine issue as to a material fact," summary disposition of the causes cannot be made. This does not mean that *any* factual
dispute bars summary judgment. The dispute must be as to *material* facts;
and the issue thus resulting must be "genuine."

Fairly summarized, the showings made for and against the motion for
summary judgment follow:

For the "Nationalist" Bank of China:

The Articles of Association of the Bank of China show that it was
established in 1912. It was reorganized in 1928 as an international exchange
bank under special charter of the Nationalist Government, and its status
was revised in 1935 by order of the Ministry of Finance. At that time one
half of the Bank's capital stock was held by the Government and one half
by private investors of Chinese nationality. In 1942 the status of the Bank
was again revised by Government decree whereupon the Government
invested additional funds and became the holder of two thirds of the
capital stock. Since the 1942 revision, 13 of the 25 authorized directors
have been appointed by the Minister of Finance on behalf of the Government, and the remaining 12 have been elected by the private stockholders.
Thirteen directors constitute a quorum. In addition to the power to
conduct ordinary domestic and foreign banking, the Articles of Association entrust the Bank with the authority to issue government bonds in
foreign markets and to handle public funds deposited abroad as well as
government treasury funds. The Minister of Finance is authorized by the
Articles to restrain any action of the Bank in violation of the Articles or
detrimental to the Government. Duly authenticated certificates of the
Minister of Finance of the Nationalist Government and the Secretary of
the Bank of China set forth the governmental decrees and directors'

resolutions by which, during the year 1949, the head office of the Bank was moved from Shanghai respectively to Canton, Chungking, and finally to Taipeh, Formosa, as the armies of the Nationalist Government retreated before revolutionary forces. Other certificates of the Secretary of the Bank and the Nationalist Minister of Finance attest to the ratification of these suits on behalf of the Nationalist Bank of China by the Board of Directors and the Nationalist Government, as majority stockholder.

For the "Peoples" Bank of China:

By affidavits, several of the intervening attorneys and one Frederick Field, a United States citizen resident in New York City who claims to be the attorney-in-fact for the Peoples Bank of China, attest to the following facts: In May of 1949, the Chinese Peoples' Liberation Army took possession of the physical plant of the Head Office of the Bank of China in Shanghai. The powers of the Board of Directors of the Bank in respect to its operations in the area controlled by the Peoples' Army were then vested in an organization denominated "East China Finance and Economic Administration." By October of 1949, the so-called "Peoples Government" had supplanted the Nationalist Government in dominion over the Chinese Mainland. The Peoples Government, claiming to have succeeded to the ownership of the Government stock in the Bank of China, then appointed new Government directors and officers for the Bank and moved the Head Office from Shanghai to Peiping. The corporate authority of ten of the twelve directors, who, since 1948, have represented the private shareholders, has been recognized by the Peoples Government. On April 9, 1950, seven of these directors, in person or by proxy, met with the new government directors to conduct the operations of the Bank. Since then the recognized private directors, in person or by proxy, and the new government directors have continued to administer the affairs of the Bank of China on the Chinese Mainland and in areas abroad where the Peoples Government is recognized. Copies of the minutes of certain of the meetings of these directors duly certified by the Secretary of the Peoples Bank of China are appended to the affidavits of the intervening attorneys.

The affidavits, certificates, and other documents proffered by the plaintiff and the intervening attorneys are in conflict only in the sense that they allege facts in support of adverse claims to the funds deposited with the defendant Bank. The events and transactions set forth by both sides are not reciprocally denied. Only the legal effect of the factual occurrences and the conclusions to be drawn from them are in dispute. Thus the Court may assume the truth of the facts set forth by both sides and be required to decide only the legal effect. Consequently there is no genuine issue of material fact requiring a further hearing or trial.

*   *   *

Consequently, we now reach the question: Which Bank of China is legally entitled to the funds deposited with the defendant Bank?

The controlling corporate authority of the Bank of China is effectively vested in the Government of China by virtue of its majority stock ownership, its dominant voice in the managing directorate, and the supervisory powers accorded by the Articles of Association to the Minister of Finance. A determination of what government, if any, should be recognized by this court as now entitled to exercise this corporate authority over the deposit in suit, will govern the disposition of these causes.

The issue thus posed focuses attention at the outset on the fact that of the two governments asserting corporate authority, one is recognized by the United States while the other is not. If this fact, per se, is determinative, the issue is resolved. If whenever this court is called upon to determine whether there is a government justly entitled to act on behalf of a foreign state in respect to a particular matter, the court is bound to say, without regard to the facts before it, that the government recognized by our executive is that government, then nothing more need be said here. To permit this expression of executive policy to usurp entirely the judicial judgment would relieve the court of a burdensome duty, but it is doubtful that the ends of justice would thus be met. It has been argued that such is the accepted practice. But the authorities do not support this view.

There is, of course, the long line of New York decisions arising out of the nationalization of Russian corporations by the Soviet Government at a time when it was unrecognized by the United States. In those decisions, the New York courts stated time and again that no effect would be given to the acts of the unrecognized Soviet Government, in so far as property situated in this country was concerned. But in every instance, the governmental acts, which the courts chose to ignore, were acts of confiscation. Confiscatory acts were held to be repugnant to the public policy of the forum. Public policy, rather than the unrecognized status of the Soviet Government, shaped the decisions in the Russian nationalization cases. This, the Court of Appeals of New York has expressly stated. Such decisions do not bar the way to giving effect to acts of non-recognized governments even in respect to property within our borders, if justice so requires.

Some more recent decisions of the federal courts, involving Soviet nationalization of corporations of the Baltic states, give great weight to the executive policy of non-recognition. But it cannot be said that these decisions establish an all-embracing rule that no extra-territorial effect may ever be given the acts of an unrecognized government.

Nor, as has been argued, does the decision of the Supreme Court in *United States* v. *Pink*, 1942, 315 U.S. 203, 62 S.Ct. 552, 86 L.Ed. 796, impose upon this court a duty to give conclusive effect to every act of a recognized government. Pink requires that full faith and credit be accorded those acts which our executive has expressly sanctioned. But such executive sanction is not expressed by governmental recognition per se.

The decisions just set forth, as well as others in this field, reveal no rule of law obliging the courts to give conclusive effect to the acts of a recognized government to the exclusion of all consideration of the acts of an opposing unrecognized government. Nor does it appear that such a sweeping rule would be a sound one.

Even were the court solely concerned with the implementation of our executive foreign policy, it would be presumptuous to blindly effectuate every act of a recognized government or to treat every act of an unrecognized government as entirely fictional. Early in our national history, our recognition policy was generally based on the executive's view of the stability and effectiveness of the government in question. More recently recognition has been granted and withheld at the diplomatic bargaining table. Our policy has thus become equivocal. Conflicting considerations are balanced in the exeutive decision. Moreover, an act of recognition does not necessarily mark a sudden reversal in executive policy. It may come as a culmination of a gradual change in attitude. Thus the import of recognition or non-recognition may vary with time and circumstance.

Recognition is not intended to sanctify every act, past and future, of a foreign government. The withholding of recognition may cast a mantle of disfavor over a government. But it does not necessarily stamp all of its acts with disapproval or brand them unworthy of judicial notice. Our executive, on occasion, has even entered into a treaty with an unrecognized government.

This is not to suggest that the courts should regard executive policy in respect to recognition and non-recognition of foreign governments as meaningless or of little consequence. In any particular situation, executive policy may be crucial, as indeed it appears to be in the present case. But, it is a fact which properly should be considered and weighed along with the other facts before the court.

Turning to the record in this case, it appears that two governments are governments in fact of portions of the territory of the State of China. The "Peoples" Government has supplanted the "Nationalist" Government in dominion over the entire Chinese Mainland with an area of more than 3,700,000 square miles, and a population of more than 460,000,000. The "Nationalist" Government controls one of the 35 provinces of China, the Island of Formosa, which has an area of 13,885 square miles and a population in excess of 6,000,000. It is obvious that the "Peoples" Government is now the government in fact of by far the greater part of the territory of the Chinese State. Nevertheless the "Nationalist" Government controls substantial territory, exceeding in area that of either Belgium or the Netherlands, and in population that of Denmark or Switzerland.

Each government, in its respective sphere, functions effectively. Each is recognized by a significant number of the nations of the world. Each maintains normal diplomatic intercourse with those nations which extend recognition. This has been the status quo for more than two years.

Each government is in a position to exercise corporate authority in behalf of the Bank of China. That is, each government is capable of utilizing the corporate structure and certain corporate assets to promote the corporate purposes. . . . Each government is in a position to act through the corporate structure of the Bank of China to carry on these international functions in the areas abroad where such Government is recognized and these domestic functions within the territory such Government controls. Each government is in fact doing so. The Bank of China, as controlled by the Nationalist Government, continues to function on the Island of Formosa and through its foreign branches in the United States, Cuba, Australia, Japan, Indo-China, and elsewhere where the Nationalist Government is recognized.

The Peoples Government as successor in fact to the Nationalist Government on the Chinese Mainland is exercising the prerogatives of the Government in respect to the Bank of China there. The Peoples Government has not nationalized the Bank of China, nor confiscated its assets, nor denied the rights of private stockholders. It exercises the authority vested in the Government of China as majority stockholder. The Bank of China continues to function in accordance with its Articles of Association under the guidance of the appointees of the Peoples Government and the majority of the directors previously elected by private stockholders on the Chinese Mainland and through branches in London, Hong Kong, Singapore, Penang, Kuala, Lumpar, Batavia, Calcutta, Bombay, Karachi, Chittagong, and Rangoon.

This factual situation is without analogous precedent in any reported case. The resulting legal problem, arising as it does out of sweeping historical changes and the claims of rival governments, cannot be met by the application of technical rules of corporation law.

A year and a half ago, this Court felt that the best course was to withhold judgment. At that time the Nationalist forces had only recently retreated to their last stronghold; their ability to consolidate this position was doubtful. The Peoples Government which had assumed control of the Chinese Mainland had not yet demonstrated its stability. Our executive policy had not assumed definite outlines in the wake of these events. The emigré directors of the Bank who sought control of the deposit in suit could not demonstrate their authority to do so or their ability to apply the funds to corporate purposes. The Bank of China, under new management on the Chinese Mainland, was not yet functioning normally in accordance with its Articles of Association. Whether its assets there would be employed for corporate purposes or diverted to other ends was not known.

Now time has clarified the picture. Both the Nationalist and Peoples Governments have maintained and strengthened their positions. Our national policy toward these governments is now definite. We have taken a stand adverse to the aims and ambitions of the Peoples Government. The armed forces of that Government are now engaged in conflict with our forces in Korea. We recognize only the Nationalist Government as the representative of the State of China, and are actively assisting in developing its military forces in Formosa. The Bank of China now operates as two corporate entities, each performing within the area of its operations the functions bestowed upon the Bank of China by its Articles of Association. Each Bank of China is in a position to employ the deposit in suit for corporate purposes.

From a practical standpoint, neither of the rival Banks of China is a true embodiment of the corporate entity which made the deposit in the Wells Fargo Bank. The present Nationalist Bank of China is more nearly equivalent in the sense of continuity of management. The Peoples Bank is more representative in ability to deal with the greater number of private stockholders and established depositors and creditors. Were the Court to adopt a strictly pragmatic approach, it might attempt a division of the deposit between these two banks in the degree that each now exercises the functions of the Bank of China. Or the Court might award the entire deposit to the bank it deems to be the closest counterpart of the corporation contemplated by the Articles of Association.

But this, the Court could not do merely by balancing interests of a private nature. Such a course would ultimately entail determining which bank best serves the corporate interests of the State of China. That determination could not be made, while the State, itself, remains divided, except by an excursion into the realm of political philosophy. Were there only one government, in fact, of the Chinese State, or only one government in a position to act effectively for the State in respect to the matter before the Court, the Court might be justified in accepting such a government as the proper representative of the State, even though our executive declined to deal with it. Here, there co-exist two governments, in fact, each attempting to further, in its own way, the interests of the State of China, in the Bank of China. It is not a proper function of a domestic court of the United States to attempt to judge which government best represents the interests of the Chinese State in the Bank of China. In this situation, the Court should justly accept, as the representative of the Chinese State, that government which our executive deems best able to further the mutual interests of China and the United States.

Since the Court is of the opinion that it should recognize the Nationalist Government of China as legally entitled to exercise the controlling corporate authority of the Bank of China in respect to the deposit in suit, the motion for summary judgment in favor of the Bank of China, as controlled by the Nationalist Government, is granted. The motion of the intervening attorneys to dismiss, or, in the alternative, for their substitution as attorneys for the plaintiff, is denied.

*   *   *

Recognition and Representation

LEGAL ASPECTS OF REPRESENTATION IN THE UNITED NATIONS (1)
Memorandum by the United Nations Secretary-General
U.N. Doc. S/1466, 8 March 1950

The primary difficulty in the current question of the representation of Member States in the United Nations is that this question of representation has been linked up with the question of recognition by Member Governments.

It will be shown here that this linkage is unfortunate from the practical standpoint, and wrong from the standpoint of legal theory.

From a practical standpoint, the present position is that representation depends entirely on a numerical count of the number of Members in a particular organ which recognize one government or the other. It is quite possible for the majority of the Members in one organ to recognize one government, and for the majority of Members in another organ to recognize the rival government. If the principle of individual recognition is adhered to, then the representatives of different governments could sit in different organs. Moreover in organs like the Security Council, of limited membership, the question of representation may be determined by the purely arbitrary fact of the particular governments which happen to have been elected to serve at a given time.

From the standpoint of legal theory, the linkage of representation in an international organization and recognition of a government is a confusion of two institutions which have superficial similarities but are essentially different.

The recognition of a new State, or of a new government of an existing State, is a unilateral act which the recognizing government can grant or withhold. It is true that some legal writers have argued forcibly that when a new government, which comes into power through revolutionary means, enjoys, with a reasonable prospect of permanency, the habitual obedience of the bulk of the population, other States are under a legal duty to recognize it. However, while States may regard it as desirable to follow certain legal principles in according or withholding recognition, the practise of States shows that the act of recognition is still regarded as essentially a political decision, which each State decides in accordance with its own free appreciation of the situation.

A recent expression of this doctrine occurred during the consideration of the Palestine question in the Security Council, when the representative of Syria questioned the United States recognition of the Provisional Government of Israel. The representative of the United States (Mr. Austin) replied:

"I should regard it as highly improper for me to admit that any country on earth can question the sovereignty of the United States of America in the exercise of that high political act of recognition of the *de facto* status of a State.

"Moreover, I would not admit here, by implication or by direct answer, that there exists a tribunal of justice or of any other kind, anywhere, that can pass judgment upon the legality or the validity of that act of my country.

"There were certain powers and certain rights of a sovereign State which were not yielded by any of the Members who signed the United Nations Charter and in particular this power to recognize the *de facto* authority of a provisional Government was not yielded. When it was exercised by my Government, it was done as a practical step, in recognition of realities: the existence of things, and the recognition of a change that had actually taken place. I am certain that no nation on earth has any right to question that, or to lay down a proposition that a certain length of time of the exercise of *de facto* authority must elapse before that authority can be recognized."

Various legal scholars have argued that this rule of individual recognition through the free choice of States should be replaced by collective recognition through an international organization such as the United Nations (e.g. Lauterpacht, *Recognition in International Law*). If this were now the rule then the present impasse would not exist, since there would be no individual recognition of the new Chinese Government, but only action by the appropriate United Nations organ. The fact remains, however, that the States have refused to accept any such rule and the United Nations does not possess any authority to recognize either a new State or a new government of an existing State. To establish the rule of collective recognition by the United Nations would require either an amendment of the Charter or a treaty to which all Members would adhere.

On the other hand *membership* of a State in the United Nations and *representation* of a State in the organs is clearly determined by a collective act of the appropriate organs; in the case of membership, by vote of the General Assembly on recommendation of the Security Council, in the case of representation, by vote of each competent organ on the credentials of the purported representatives. Since, therefore, recognition of either State or government is an individual act, and either admission to membership or acceptance of representation in the Organization are collective acts, it would appear to be legally inadmissible to condition the latter acts by a requirement that they be preceded by individual recognition.

This conclusion is clearly borne out by the practise in the case of admission to membership in both the League of Nations and in the United Nations.

In the practise of the League of Nations, there were a number of cases in which Members of the League stated expressly that the admission of another State to membership did not mean that they recognized such new Member as a State (e.g. Great Britain in the case of Lithuania, Belgium and Switzerland in the case of the Soviet Union; Colombia in the case of Panama).

In the practise of the United Nations there are, of course, several instances of admission to membership of States which had not been recognized by all other Members, and other instances of States for whose admission votes were cast by Members which had not recognized the candidates as States. For example, Yemen and Burma were admitted by a unanimous vote of the General Assembly at a time when they had been recognized by only a minority of Members. A number of the Members who, in the Security Council, voted for the admission of Transjordan [Jordan] and Nepal, had not recognized these candidates as States. Indeed, the declarations made by the delegation of the Soviet Union and its neighbours that they would not vote for the admission of certain States (e.g., Ireland, Portugal and Transjordan [Jordan]), because they were not in diplomatic relations with these applicants, were vigourously disputed by most other Members, and led to the request for an advisory opinion of the International Court of Justice by the General Assembly.

The Court was requested to answer the question whether a Member, in its vote on the admission to membership of another State, was "juridically entitled to make its consent to the admission dependent on conditions not expressly provided" by paragraph 1 of Article 4 of the Charter. One of the conditions which had been stated by Members had been the lack of diplomatic relations with the applicant State. The Court answered the question in the negative. At its fourth session the General Assembly recommended that each Member act in accordance with the opinion of the Court.

The practise as regards representation of Member States in the United Nations organs has, until the Chinese question arose, been uniformly to the effect that representation is distinctly separate from the issue of recognition of a government. It is a remarkable fact that, despite the fairly large number of revolutionary changes of government and the larger number of instances of breach of diplomatic relations among Members, *there was not one single instance of a challenge of credentials of a representative* in the many thousands of meetings which were held during four years. On the contrary, whenever the reports of credentials committees were voted on (as in the sessions of the General Assembly), they were always adopted unanimously and without reservation by any Members.

The Members have therefore made clear by an unbroken practise that

(1) a Member could properly vote to accept a representative of a government which it did not recognize, or with which it had no diplomatic relations, and

(2) that such a vote did not imply recognition or a readiness to assume diplomatic relations.

In two instances involving non-members, the question was explicitly raised—the cases of granting the Republic of Indonesia and Israel the right to participate in the deliberations of the Security Council. In both cases, objections were raised on the grounds that these entities were not States; in both cases the Security Council voted to permit representation after explicit statements were made by members of the Council that the vote did not imply recognition of the State or government concerned.

The practise which has been thus followed in the United Nations is not only legally correct but conforms to the basic character of the Organization. The United Nations is not an association limited to like-minded States and governments of similar ideological persuasion (as is the case in certain regional associations). As an Organization which aspires to universality, it must of necessity include States of varying and even conflicting ideologies.

The Chinese case is unique in the history of the United Nations, not because it involves a revolutionary change of government, but because it is the first in which two rival governments exist. It is quite possible that such a situation will occur again in the future and it is highly desirable to see what principles can be followed in choosing between the rivals. It has been demonstrated that the principle of numerical preponderance of recognition is inappropriate and legally incorrect. Is any other principle possible?

It is submitted that the proper principles can be derived by analogy from Article 4 of the Charter. This Article requires that an applicant for membership must be able and willing to carry out the obligations of membership. The obligations of membership can be carried out only by governments which in fact possess the power to do so. Where a revolutionary government presents itself as representing a State, in rivalry to an existing government, the question at issue should be which of these two governments in fact is in a position to employ the resources and direct the people of the State in fulfilment of the obligations of membership. In essence, this means an inquiry as to whether the new government exercises effective authority within the territory of the State and is habitually obeyed by the bulk of the population.

If so, it would seem to be appropriate for the United Nations organs, through their collective action, to accord it the right to represent the State in the Organization, even though individual Members of the Organization refuse, and may continue to refuse, to accord it recognition as the lawful government for reasons which are valid under their national policies.

LEGAL ASPECTS OF REPRESENTATION IN THE UNITED NATIONS (2)
Letter of the Permanent Representative of China to the Secretary-General
U.N. Doc. S/1470, 13 March 1950

*   *   *

Since the beginning of the United Nations, the Soviet delegation has not made a single constructive contribution to the work of the Organization. The Soviet Union has already a rival organization in the Cominform. It uses the United Nations only for the purposes of obstruction and propaganda. Nevertheless, you published a memorandum with the purpose of appeasing the Soviet delegation by sacrificing the delegation of the National Government of China.

It is for these reasons that I have ventured to characterize your memorandum as bad politics.

On the technical side your memorandum asserts that it is wrong to link the question of representation with the question of recognition by Member Governments. International law has nothing direct to say for or against this linkage. As practised in the League of Nations as well as in the United Nations, this linkage is the general rule; the few cases of non-operation of linkage which your memorandum cited, have been the exceptions. The Soviet delegation, in voting on admission of new Members, specifically stressed the linkage between admission and recognition. In spite of the advisory opinion of the International Court of Justice, the Soviet veto on a number of applications for membership holds today. The deputy representative of the United States to the United Nations, in his press statement of 8 March, made it clear that the American Government would continue to support my delegation and to vote against admission of a Communist delegation for the specific reason that the United States continued to recognize the National Government of China.

Your memorandum proposes a new criterion, namely, "whether the new Government exercises effective authority within the territory of the State and is habitually obeyed by the bulk of the population." The individual governments, in deciding to accord recognition to, or withhold recognition from, a new Government, must take into consideration the very criterion that you suggest for deciding on representation. In fact, recognition and representation are based on similar considerations. The linkage between recognition and representation is only natural and inevitable.

If you wish to institute "an inquiry as to whether the new Government exercises effective authority within the territory of the State and is habitually obeyed by the bulk of the population," the only possible procedure, consistent with the principles of the Charter, is a fair and free election. In spite of appearances, the Communist regime in China does not have the support of the Chinese people. Its ideology and programme are un-Chinese. Internationally, the Communist regime is regarded by the Chinese people as a puppet regime. Today, the opposition to the Communist regime is stronger than it was a year ago. . . .

* * *

The question in which you have intervened was originally raised by the Soviet delegation in the various organs of the United Nations, beginning with the Security Council in January of this year. In every instance a positive decision was made in accordance with the rules of procedure. As Secretary-General, your duty is to execute and administer the decisions of the Councils and Commissions. It is not your duty to call into question the wisdom of the decisions of the organs of the United Nations.

* * *

My Government does not wish to put a narrow interpretation to Article 99 of the Charter, which is the only Article that assigns a sphere of political action to the Secretary-General. That Article authorizes the Secretary-General to "bring to the attention of the Security Council any matter which in his opinion may threaten the maintenance of international peace and security." Nobody can believe that the question of Chinese representation "may threaten the maintenance of international peace and security." Even if it were such a matter, you should not have circulated a secret memorandum to a limited number of the delegates to the Security Council, excluding the delegation which is most directly concerned.

For these reasons, your memorandum and the mode of its circulation constitute bad law.

* * *

UNITED STATES POLICY WITH RESPECT TO MAINLAND CHINA
Statement of Assistant Secretary of State for Far Eastern Affairs
1966 Senate Foreign Relations Committee Hearings 641–649

This brings me to the whole question of how we deal specifically with Communist China. Let me briefly review and analyze some of the things we have done or might do.

As far as contacts through diplomatic channels are concerned, we have had 128 meetings at the ambassadorial level with Peking's representatives, first in Geneva and now Warsaw. I think it is fair to say that we have had the longest and most direct dialog of any major Western nation with Communist China.

I am bound to say at the same time, however, that the dialog so far has not been very productive and founders on the fundamental issue of Peking's demand for Taiwan and by its stated conviction that the United States is by historical necessity Peking's prime antagonist on the world scene. But it is fair to say that it is more of a dialog than we could expect to have if we were ever to recognize Communist China, if the experience of Western diplomats in Peking is representative. And it is an opportunity to try directly to make them understand that we have no hostile designs on mainland China or its leaders but that we fully intend to maintain our commitments to defend our friends and allies against Communist aggression and that the United States seeks peace, freedom, and stability for the countries of Asia.

In addition to these direct contacts, we have of course been prepared to deal with Communist China in multilateral forums where its interests are directly involved. This was true of the Geneva conferences of 1954 and 1961–62, and we have made clear our willingness to participate in a Geneva conference type of format to resolve the present Vietnam problem or to have Communist China appear at the United Nations if Hanoi or Peking were ever ready to let the United Nations deal with the Vietnam issue.

*   *   *

Some nations at the U.N. hope that Communist China's seating would have a moderating effect on its policies. They advance the thesis that, not being included in the U.N., Peking feels rejected and acts with considerably less restraint than if it were a member with a member's obligations.

We respect those who hold this view, but we cannot agree with it. It seems to us a rationalistic view that ignores the deep-seated historic and ideologic reasons for Peking's current attitudes. Nor does this theory—the "neurosis" theory if you will—explain Peking's behavior toward other Communist nations or its behavior in Afro-Asian groupings to which Communist China has been fully welcomed. . . . Moreover, we must consider Peking's price for entering the U.N. On September 29, 1965, Chen Yi, the Chinese Communist Premier, made the following demands:

1. The expulsion of the Republic of China from the U.N.
2. The complete reorganization of the U.N.
3. The withdrawal of the General Assembly resolution condemning Peking as an aggressor in the Korean conflict.
4. The branding of the United States as an aggressor in that conflict.

These are obviously unacceptable conditions.

The Republic of China, for example, is one of the original signatories of the United Nations Charter and has lived up to its obligations as a U.N. member in good faith. More than 13 million people live on the Island of Taiwan. This is a larger population than that of 83 members of the United Nations. The United States for many years has had close and friendly relations with the Republic of China, and since 1954 we have been bound by treaty to join with it in the defense of Taiwan. It would be unthinkable and morally wrong to expel the Government of the Republic of China from the U.N. to meet this demand of Peking's.

One must also consider the attitude of Communist China toward conflict, not only where its own interests are directly concerned but even in cases where they are not. Had Communist China been in the United Nations, could there have been a cease-fire resolution of the India-Pakistan conflict in September and could Secretary General U Thant have received any mandate to bring that conflict to a halt? Peking's critical comment on the Tashkent proceedings is a clear answer. We are dealing with a nation that, at least as far as we can now see, will attempt as a matter of principle to put a monkey wrench into every peacemaking effort which may be made in the world.

Finally, there is the psychological factor: whether the admission to the U.N. of a nation that is dedicated to violent revolution and currently supporting North Vietnam's aggression against South Vietnam and threatening India in seeking to exacerbate and extend the Indo-Pakistan conflict would, in fact, not encourage Peking to think it is on the right track while deeply discouraging other nations which are resisting Peking's pressures and seeking to maintain their own independence.

It continues, therefore, to be U.S. policy to support the position of the

Republic of China in the U.N. For our part, we will also continue to oppose the admission of Communist China.

*   *   *

Many people do not realize that it is Communist China which has prevented any movement toward bilateral contacts. The United States over the past several years has tried to promote a variety of contacts, but the Chinese have kept the door tightly barred.

Since 1958, for example, we have validated passports of over 80 representatives of newspapers and other media for travel to Communist China. Only two have been admitted. We have tried unsuccessfully to arrange with the Chinese either a formal or an informal exchange of newsmen and more recently we have indicated to them our willingness unilaterally and without reciprocity to see Communist Chinese newsmen enter the United States.

In addition, we have a short time ago amended our travel regulations to permit doctors and scientists in the field of public health and medicine to travel to Communist China. . . .

We have discussed with various scientific and other organizations their interests in arranging people-to-people exchange with the Chinese. We have encouraged the exchange of publications between various universities and institutions in the United States with Peking. There is a free flow of mail to and from Communist China. All of these efforts have been consistent with our worldwide concern for a freedom of information and for the exchange of knowledge and views in humanitarian fields. Yet they have been consistently rejected by Communist China. . . .

*   *   *

These are samples of what we are up against. We are Peking's great enemy because our power is a crucial element in the total balance of power and in the resistance by Asian states to Chinese Communist expansionist designs in Asia . . . the problem must be considered basically in the same way we did that of the Soviet Union. We must, on the one hand, seek to curtail Peking's ambitions and build up the free nations of Asia and of contiguous areas; on the other hand, while maintaining firm resistance to their expansionist ambitions, we can, over time, open the possibility of increased contacts with Communist China, weighing very carefully any steps we take in these general areas lest we impair the essential first aim of our policy, including our clear commitments.

*   *   *

International Organizations

The full legal personality of the League of Nations was never quite clear. Nevertheless, the first general international organization for the maintenance of peace exercised from 1919 to 1946 the power to contract, making agreements with Switzerland for its headquarters in Geneva as well as corporate agreements, while it administered property and supervised international mandates.

The Charter of the United Nations goes further in authorizing the organization through its competent organs to enter into agreements with member states as well as nonmember states, and with other international organizations.[4] Under this authority, to give a few examples, the United Nations has concluded agreements with such specialized agencies as the Food and Agriculture Organization and the International Civil Aviation Organization; it has made trusteeship agreements for dependent territories with states like Great Britain and France; it is a party to the multilateral convention on immunities and privileges for representatives and officials of the organization; and it concluded the Headquarters Agreement between the United States and the United Nations at New York. Moreover, in 1948 the United Nations exercised its authority to borrow money when it received a loan of $65 million to finance construction of its headquarters; no legal question was raised by the organization's members, who were thereafter assessed to repay the loan.

Thus, a certain type of international legal personality was created by the international agreement of states to the Covenant of the League of Nations, the Charter of the United Nations, and the constitutions of several other public international agencies. Such organizations are not states with all the rights and duties of states under international law. But they are legal persons that can negotiate and contract with states or other international organizations, and there are frequently provisions for the judicial settlement of controversies arising from such international agreements. Plainly, these arrangements go beyond any single municipal law and represent a further development in the scope and functions of international law, with new legal persons, practices, and agreements evolving from the recent needs of a world society.

The increase in international organization responsibilities for peacekeeping through the United Nations after 1945 led to an important question about the organization's legal capacity to bring international claims against a state whose government was allegedly responsible for in-

---

[4] See, particularly, Articles 43, 63, 77, 83, 104 and 105.

juries suffered by United Nations agents in the performance of their duties.

Altogether, seven agents of the United Nations had been killed in Palestine during their official observations of the troubled armistice between the Arabs and the Jews. The culmination, on 17 September 1948, was the deaths of Count Folke Bernadotte, the United Nations Mediator and a national of Sweden, and Colonel Serot, a United Nations Observer and a national of France. Under international law, states had the right to bring claims on behalf of their nationals, but could the United Nations bring a claim for injury to one of its agents? If so, how could such an action by the United Nations for its agent be reconciled with the right of a state on behalf of the same individual as one of its nationals?

The *Reparations for Injuries Suffered in the Service of the United Nations* advisory opinion, which follows, further illuminates the legal personality of the United Nations. The right to bring a claim, of course, does not provide the remedies. The United Nations cannot appear as a litigant before the International Court of Justice, but it may negotiate with states for its rights. In fact, on 14 June 1950, through diplomacy, Israel sent to the United Nations $54,628 as an indemnity for the death of Count Bernadotte, acknowledging only laxity and errors in the investigation that followed the event. To maintain its rights, the United Nations may also be able to sue in a national court, where most international law cases are heard. The *Balfour Guthrie & Company* case, which also follows, illustrates a suit for nonperformance of contract, with the United Nations as a plaintiff.

REPARATIONS FOR INJURIES SUFFERED IN THE SERVICE OF THE UNITED NATIONS
International Court of Justice (Advisory Opinion), 1949
1949 I.C.J. Reports 174

On December 3rd, 1948, the General Assembly of the United Nations adopted the following Resolution:

"Whereas the series of tragic events which have lately befallen agents of the United Nations engaged in the performance of their duties raises, with greater urgency than ever, the question of the arrangements to be made by the United Nations with a view to ensuring to its agents the fullest measure of protection in the future and ensuring that reparation be made for the injuries suffered; and

"Whereas it is highly desirable that the Secretary-General should be able to act without question as efficaciously as possible with a view to obtaining any reparation due; therefore

"The General Assembly

"Decides to submit the following legal questions to the International Court of Justice for an advisory opinion:

" 'I. In the event of an agent of the United Nations in the performance of his duties suffering injury in circumstances involving the responsibility of a State, has the United Nations, as an Organization, the capacity to bring an international claim against the responsible *de jure* or *de facto* government with a view to obtaining the reparation due in respect of the damage caused (a) to the United Nations, (b) to the victim or to persons entitled through him?

" 'II. In the event of an affirmative reply on point I(b), how is action by the United Nations to be reconciled with such rights as may be possessed by the State of which the victim is a national?' " . . .

*   *   *

The questions asked of the Court relate to the "capacity to bring an international claim"; accordingly, we must begin by defining what is meant by that capacity, and consider the characteristics of the Organization, so as to determine whether, in general, these characteristics do, or do not, include for the Organization a right to present an international claim.

Competence to bring an international claim is, for those possessing it, the capacity to resort to the customary methods recognized by international law for the establishment, the presentation and the settlement of claims. Among these methods may be mentioned protest, request for an enquiry, negotiation, and request for submission to an arbitral tribunal or to the Court in so far as this may be authorized by the Statute.

This capacity certainly belongs to the State; a State can bring an international claim against another State. Such a claim takes the form of a claim between two political entities, equal in law, similar in form, and both the direct subjects of international law. It is dealt with by means of negotiation, and cannot, in the present state of the law as to international jurisdiction, be submitted to a tribunal, except with the consent of the States concerned. . . .

But, in the international sphere, has the Organization such a nature as involves the capacity to bring an international claim? In order to answer this question, the Court must first enquire whether the Charter has given the Organization such a position that it possesses, in regard to its Members, rights which it is entitled to ask them to respect. In other words, does the Organization possess international personality? This is no doubt a doctrinal expression, which has sometimes given rise to controversy. But it will be used here to mean that if the Organization is recognized as having that personality, it is an entity capable of availing itself of obligations incumbent upon its Members.

To answer this question, which is not settled by the actual terms of the Charter, we must consider what characteristics it was intended thereby to give to the Organization.

The subjects of law in any legal system are not necessarily identical in their nature or in the extent of their rights, and their nature depends upon the needs of the community. Throughout its history, the development of international law has been influenced by the requirements of international life, and the progressive increase in the collective activities of States has already given rise to instances of action upon the international plane by certain entities which are not States. This development culminated in the establishment in June 1945 of an international organization whose purposes and principles are specified in the Charter of the United Nations. But to achieve these ends the attribution of international personality is indispensable.

The Charter has not been content to make the Organization created by it merely a centre "for harmonizing the actions of nations in the attainment of these common ends" (Article I, para. 4). It has equipped that centre with organs, and has given it special tasks. It has defined the position of the Members in relation to the Organization by requiring them to give it every assistance in any action undertaken by it (Article 2, para. 5), and to accept and carry out the decisions of the Security Council; by authorizing the General Assembly to make recommendations to the Members; by giving the organization legal capacity and privileges and immunities in the territory of each of its Members; and by providing for the conclusion of agreements between the Organization and its Members. Practice—in particular the conclusion of conventions to which the Organization is a party—has confirmed this character of the Organization, which occupies a position in certain respects in detachment from its Members, and which is under a duty to remind them, if need be, of certain obligations. It must be added that the Organization is a political body, charged with political tasks of an important character, and covering a wide field namely, the maintenance of international peace and security, the development of friendly relations among nations, and the achievement of international co-operation in the solution of problems of an economic, social, cultural or humanitarian character (Article I); and in dealing with its Members it employs political means. The "Convention on the Privileges and Immunities of the United Nations" of 1946 creates rights and duties between each of the signatories and the Organization (see, in particular, Section 35). It is difficult to see how such a convention could operate except upon the international plane and as between parties possessing international personality.

In the opinion of the Court, the Organization was intended to exercise and enjoy, and is in fact exercising and enjoying, functions and rights which can only be explained on the basis of the possession of a large measure of international personality and the capacity to operate upon an international plane. It is at present the supreme type of international organization, and it could not carry out the intentions of its founders if it was devoid of international personality. It must be acknowledged that its Members, by entrusting certain functions to it, with the attendant duties and responsibilities, have clothed it with the competence required to enable those functions to be effectively discharged.

Accordingly, the Court has come to the conclusion that the Organization is an international person. That is not the same thing as saying that it is a State, which it certainly is not, or that its legal personality and rights and duties are the same as those of a State. Still less is it the same thing as saying that it is "a super-State," whatever that expression may mean. It does not even imply that all its rights and duties must be upon the international plane, any more than all the rights and duties of a subject of international law and capable of possessing international rights and duties, and that it has capacity to maintain its rights by bringing international claims. . . .

Question I(a) is as follows:

"In the event of an agent of the United Nations in the performance of his duties suffering injury in circumstances involving the responsibility of a State, has the United Nations, as an Organization, the capacity to bring an international claim against the reponsible *de jure* or *de facto* government with a view to obtaining the reparation due in respect of the damage caused (a) to the United Nations . . . ?"

The question is concerned solely with the reparation of damage caused to the Organization when one of its agents suffers injury at the same time. It cannot be doubted that the Organization has the capacity to bring an international claim against one of its Members which has caused injury to it by a breach of its international obligations towards it. The damage specified in Question I(a) means exclusively damage caused to the interests of the Organization itself, to its administrative machine, to its property and assets, and to the interests of which it is the guardian. It is clear that the Organization has the capacity to bring a claim for this damage. As the claim is based on the breach of an international obligation on the part of the Member held responsible by the Organization, the Member cannot contend that this obligation is governed by municipal law, and the Organization is justified in giving its claim the character of an international claim.

When the Organization has sustained damage resulting from a breach by a Member of its international obligations, it is impossible to see how it can obtain reparation unless it possesses capacity to bring an international claim. It cannot be supposed that in such an event all the Members of the Organization, save the defendant State, must combine to bring a claim against the defendant for the damage suffered by the Organization.

*   *   *

Question I(b) is as follows:

". . . has the United Nations, as an Organization, the capacity to bring an international claim . . . in respect of the damage caused . . . (b) to the victim or to persons entitled through him?"

The traditional rule that diplomatic protection is exercised by the national State does not involve the giving of a negative answer to Question I(b).

In the first place, this rule applies to claims brought by a State. But here we have the different and new case of a claim that would be brought by the Organization.

In the second place, even in inter-State relations, there are important exceptions to the rule, for there are cases in which protection may be exercised by a State on behalf of persons not having its nationality.

In the third place, the rule rests on two bases. The first is that the defendant State has broken an obligation towards the national State in respect of its nationals. The second is that only the party to whom an international obligation is due can bring a claim in respect of its breach. This is precisely what happens when the Organization, in bringing a claim for damage suffered by its agent, does so by involving the breach of an obligation towards itself. Thus, the rule of the nationality of claims affords no reason against recognizing that the Organization has the right to bring a claim for the damage referred to in Question I(b). On the contrary, the principle underlying this rule leads to the recognition of this capacity as belonging to the Organization, when the Organization invokes, as the ground of its claim, a breach of an obligation towards itself. . . .

The Court is here faced with a new situation. The questions to which it gives rise can only be solved by realizing that the situation is dominated by the provisions of the Charter considered in the light of the principles of international law.

The question lies within the limits already established; that is to say it presupposes that the injury for which the reparation is demanded arises from a breach of an obligation designed to help an agent of the Organization in the performance of his duties. It is not a case in which the wrongful act or omission would merely constitute a breach of the general obligations of a State concerning the position of aliens; claims made under this head would be within the competence of the national State and not, as a general rule, within that of the Organization.

The Charter does not expressly confer upon the Organization the capacity to include, in its claim for reparation, damage caused to the victim or to persons entitled through him. The Court must therefore begin by enquiring whether the provisions of the Charter concerning the functions of the Organization, and the part played by its agents in the performance of those functions, imply for the Organization power to afford its agents the limited protection that would consist in the bringing of a claim on their behalf for reparation for damage suffered in such circumstances. Under international law, the Organization must be deemed to have those powers which, though not expressly provided in the Charter, are conferred upon it by necessary implication as being essential to the performance of its duties. . . .

Having regard to its purposes and functions already referred to, the Organization may find it necessary, and has in fact found it necessary, to entrust its agents with important missions to be performed in disturbed parts of the world. Many missions, from their very nature, involve the agents in unusual dangers to which ordinary persons are not exposed. For the same reason, the injuries suffered by its agents in these circumstances will sometimes have occurred in such a manner that their national State would not be justified in bringing a claim for reparation on the ground of diplomatic protection, or, at any rate, would not feel disposed to do so. Both to ensure the efficient and independent performance of these missions and to afford effective support to its agents, the Organization must provide them with adequate protection.

*   *   *

For this purpose, the Members of the Organization have entered into certain undertakings, some of which are in the Charter and others in complementary agreements . . . It must be noted that the effective working of the Organization—the accomplishment of its task, and the independence and effectiveness of the work of its agents—require that these undertakings should be strictly observed. For that purpose, it is necessary that, when an infringement occurs, the Organization should be able to call upon the responsible State to remedy its default, and, in particular, to obtain from the State reparation for the damage that the default may have caused to its agent.

In order that the agent may perform his duties satisfactorily, he must feel that this protection is assured to him by the Organization, and that he may count on it. To ensure the independence of the agent, and, consequently, the independent action of the Organization itself, it is essential that in performing his duties he need not have to rely on any other protection than that of the Organization (save of course for the more direct and immediate protection due from the State in whose territory he may be). In particular, he should not have to rely on the protection of his own State. If he had to rely on that State, his independence might well be compromised, contrary to the principle applied by Article 100 of the Charter. . . .

Upon examination of the character of the functions entrusted to the Organization and of the nature of the missions of its agents, it becomes clear that the capacity of the Organization to exercise a measure of functional protection of its agents arises by necessary intendment out of the Charter.

The obligations entered into by States to enable the agents of the Organization to perform their duties are undertaken not in the interest of the agents, but in that of the Organization. When it claims redress for a breach of these obligations, the Organization is invoking its own right, the right that the obligations due to it should be respected. On this ground, it asks for reparation of the injury suffered, for "it is a principle of international law that the breach of an engagement involves an obligation to make reparation in an adequate form"; as was stated by the Permanent Court in its Judgment No. 8 of July 26th, 1927 (Series A., No. 9, p. 21). In claiming reparation based on the injury suffered by its agent, the Organization does not represent the agent, but is asserting its own right, the right to secure respect for undertakings entered into towards the Organization.

Having regard to the foregoing considerations, and to the undeniable right of the Organization to demand that its Members shall fulfill the obligations entered into by them in the interest of the good working of the Organization, the Court is of the opinion that, in the case of a breach of these obligations, the Organization has the capacity to claim adequate reparation, and that in assessing this reparation it is authorized to include the damage suffered by the victim or by persons entitled through him.

*　　*　　*

The question remains whether the Organization has "the capacity to bring an international claim against the responsible *de jure* or *de facto* government with a view to obtaining the reparation due in respect of the damage caused (a) to the United Nations, (b) to the victim or to persons entitled through him" when the defendant State is not a member of the Organization.

In considering this aspect of Question I (a) and (b), it is necessary to keep in mind the reasons which have led the Court to give an affirmative answer to it when the defendant State is a Member of the Organization. It has now been established that the Organization has capacity to bring claims on the international plane, and that it possesses a right of functional protection in respect of its agents. Here again the Court is authorized to assume that the damage suffered involves the responsibility of a State, and it is not called upon to express an opinion upon the various ways in which that responsibility might be engaged. Accordingly the question is whether the Organization has capacity to bring a claim against the defendant State to recover reparation in respect of that damage or whether, on the contrary, the defendant State, not being a member, is justified in raising the objection that the Organization lacks the capacity to bring an international claim. On this point, the Court's opinion is that fifty States, representing the vast majority of the members of the international community, had the power, in conformity with international law, to bring into being an entity possessing objective international personality, and not merely personality recognized by them alone, together with capacity to bring international claims.

*　　*　　*

Question II is as follows:

"In the event of an affirmative reply on point I(b), how is action by the United Nations to be reconciled with such rights as may be possessed by the State of which the victim is a national?"

The affirmative reply given by the Court on point I(b) obliges it now to examine Question II. When the victim has a nationality, cases can clearly occur in which the injury suffered by him may engage the interest both of his national State and of the Organization. In such an event, competition between the State's right of diplomatic protection and the Organization's right of functional protection might arise, and this is the only case with which the Court is invited to deal.

In such a case, there is no rule of law which assigns priority to the one or to the other, or which compels either the State or the Organization to refrain from bringing an international claim. . . .

*   *   *

The question of reconciling action by the Organization with the rights of a national State may arise in another way; that is to say, when the agent bears the nationality of the defendant State.

The ordinary practice whereby a State does not exercise protection on behalf of one of its nationals against a State which regards him as its own national, does not constitute a precedent which is relevant here. The action of the Organization is in fact based not upon the nationality of the victim but upon his status as agent of the Organization. Therefore it does not matter whether or not the State to which the claim is addressed regards him as its own national, because the question of nationality is not pertinent to the admissibility of the claim.

In law, therefore, it does not seem that the fact of the possession of the nationality of the defendant State by the agent constitutes any obstacle to a claim brought by the Organization for a breach of obligations towards it occurring in relation to the performance of his mission by that agent.

*   *   *

For these reasons,

The court is of opinion *On Question I(a):* . . . unanimously . . . *On Question I(b):* . . . by eleven votes against four . . . *On Question II:* by ten votes against five . . .

Dissenting Opinion by Judge Krylov

I agree with the Court's Opinion to the effect that the United Nations Organization has the right to bring an international claim with a view to obtaining reparation for damage caused to the Organization itself; i.e., I reply in the affirmative to Question I(a) put to the Court by the General Assembly. It is beyond doubt that the Organization is entitled to defend its patrimony; in particular, to claim compensation for direct damage caused to itself, including disbursements in cases where an official of the Organization has suffered injury in the performance of his duties: for example, funeral expenses, medical expenses, insurance premiums, etc. In my opinion an affirmative reply to Question 1(a) fully meets the practical requirements referred to by the Secretary-General of the United Nations.

I agree in a large measure with the arguments used in the dissenting opinions of Judges Hackworth and Badawi Pasha, and I believe that the United Nations Organization is not entitled, according to the international law in force, to claim compensation for injuries suffered by its agents.

The majority of the Court has founded this right to bring a claim on the right of functional protection exercised by the Organization in regard to its officials and—more generally—its agents.

I entirely associate myself with the desire unanimously expressed by the General Assembly of the United Nations in the recital clauses of its Resolution of December 3rd, 1948, of "ensuring to its agents the fullest measure of protection. . . ."

But I consider that this aim should be attained *proprio modo*, i.e., by the elaboration and conclusion of a general convention. I think that the problem should be approached in the same way as in the Convention concerning the Privileges and Immunities of the Organization, of representatives of governments and of the officials of the Organization.

To affirm, in the Court's Opinion, a right of the Organization to afford international protection to its agents as an already existing right, would be to introduce a new rule into international law and—what is more—a rule which would be concurrent with that of diplomatic protection which appertains to every State vis-à-vis its nationals.

The alleged new rule of functional protection will give rise to conflicts or collisions with the international law in force. The Court is not entitled to create a right of functional protection which is unknown in existing international law.

The Court itself states that it is confronted with a "new situation," but it considers itself authorized to reason—if I may so express it—*de lege ferenda*.

*   *   *

The conflict between the existing rules of international law (diplomatic protection of nationals) and the rules declared by the Court to be in existence—i.e., the rules of functional protection—is still further intensified by the fact that the majority of the Court even declares that the protection afforded by the United Nations Organization to its agent may be exercised against the State of which the agent is a national. We are thus far outside the limits of the international law in force.

*   *   *

It should also be observed that the relations between a State and its nationals are matters which belong essentially to the national competence of the State. The functional protection proclaimed by the Court is in contradiction with that well-established rule.

I therefore feel justified in asserting that the protection by the United Nations Organization of its agents could not be well founded from the standpoint of the international law in force, even if we are considering the relations between the United Nations and its Members.

Still less is it possible to assert this right of the United Nations Organization vis-à-vis non-member States . . .

It is true that the non-member States cannot fail to recognize the existence of the United Nations as an objective fact. But, in order that they may be bound by a legal obligation to the Organization, it is necessary that the latter should conclude a special agreement with these States.

I associate myself with the concern of the majority of the Court to find appropriate legal means whereby the United Nations may attain its objects—i.e., in the present case, protect its agents. But as I have already said, we must found the right of the Organization to bring an international claim in order to promote its agent on the express consent of the States, either by the preparation and conclusion of a general convention, or by agreements concluded between the Organization and the respective States in each individual case.

The Court can only interpret and develop the international law in force; it can only adjudicate in conformity with international law. In the present case, the Court cannot found an affirmative reply to Question I(b) either on the existing international convention or on international custom (as evidence of a general practice), or again, on any general principle of law (recognized by the nations).

Such are the reasons for my negative answer to Question I(b) put by the General Assembly, and they render it unnecessary for me to give an answer to Question II.

BALFOUR GUTHRIE & COMPANY v. UNITED STATES
United States District Court, 1950
90 F. Supp. 831

Goodman, District Judge

* * *

The competency of the United Nations to sue the United States in Federal Court under the Suits in Admiralty Act, 46 U.S.C.A. sec. 741 et seq., is the principal and unique question tendered by the exceptions to the libel of the United Nations and other joint libelants. As well do the exceptions question the right of the United Nations to maintain the libel against American Pacific Steamship Co., a co-respondent.

The libel alleges that in the autumn of 1947, the United Nations International Children's Emergency Fund shipped from the ports of Tacoma and Oakland aboard the SS Abraham Rosenberg a large quantity of powdered milk destined for Italy and Greece. A portion of the shipment, it is alleged, was never delivered to the consignee and another portion arrived in a damaged condition. The Abraham Rosenberg was owned by the United States and was operated under a bareboat charter by respondent American Pacific Steamship Company. The United Nations and six other shippers, whose merchandise allegedly suffered a similar fate, have joined in the libel against the United States and the American Pacific Steamship Company

Whether the United Nations may maintain these proceedings against respondent American Pacific Steamship Company can be first and more easily answered.

The International Court of Justice has held that the United Nations is a legal entity separate and distinct from the member States. While it is not a state nor a super-State, it is an international person, clothed by its Members with the competence necessary to discharge its functions.

Article 104 of the Charter of the United Nations, 59 Stat. 1053, provides that "the Organization shall enjoy in the territory of each of its Members such legal capacity as may be necessary for the exercise of its functions and the fulfillment of its purposes." As a treaty ratified by the United States, the Charter is part of the supreme law of the land. No implemental legislation would appear to be necessary to endow the United Nations with legal capacity in the United States. But the President has removed any possible doubt by designating the United Nations as one of the organizations entitled to enjoy the privileges conferred by the International Organizations Immunities Act, 59 Stat. 669, 22 U.S.C.A. secs. 288–288f. Section 2(a) of that Act, 22 U.S.C.A. sec. 228a (a), states that "international organizations shall, to the extent consistent with the instrument creating them, possess the capacity—(i) to contract; (ii) to acquire and dispose of real and personal property; (iii) to institute legal proceedings."

The capacity of the United Nations to maintain the libel against the American Pacific Steamship Company is completely consistent with its charter. The libel asserts rights flowing from a contract made by a specialized agency of the United Nations in the performance of its duties. The agency, the International Children's Emergency Fund, was created by resolution of the General Assembly of the United Nations on December 11, 1946. (Resolution 57(1), United Nations Yearbook 1946–47, 162). Its function is to promote child health generally and in particular to assist the governments of countries, that were the victims of aggression, to rehabilitate their children. The solution of international health problems is one of the responsibilities assumed by the United Nations in Article 55 of its Charter, 59 Stat. 1045.

Whether the United Nations may sue the United States is a more difficult question. It is apparent that Article 104 of the Charter of the United Nations was never intended to provide a method for settling differences between the United Nations and its members. It is equally clear that the International Organizations Immunities Act does not amount to a waiver of the United States' sovereign immunity from suit. The precise question posed is whether the capacity to institute legal proceedings conferred on the United Nations by that Act includes the competence to sue the United States in cases in which the United States has consented to suits by other litigants.

The broad purpose of the International Organizations Immunities Act was to vitalize the status of international organizations of which the United States is a member and to facilitate their activities. A liberal interpretation of the Act is in harmony with this purpose.

The considerations which might prompt a restrictive interpretation are not persuasive. It is true that history has recorded few, if any, instances in which international entities have submitted their disputes to the courts of one of the disputing parties. But international organizations on a grand scale are a modern phenomena. The wide variety of activities in which they engage is likely to give rise to claims against their members that can most readily be disposed of in national courts. The present claim is such a claim. No political overtones surround it. No possible embarrassment to the United States in the conduct of its international affairs could result from such a decree as this court might enter. A claim for cargo loss and damage is clearly susceptible of judicial settlement. Particularly is this so in this litigation inasmuch as the United Nations' claim is one of several of the same nature arising out of the same transaction or occurrence.

International organizations, such as the United Nations and its agencies, of which the United States is a member, are not alien bodies. The interests of the United States are served when the United Nations' interests are protected. A prompt and equitable settlement of any claim it may have against the United States will be the settlement most advantageous to both parties. The courts of the United States afford a most appropriate forum for accomplishing such a settlement.

It may be contended that since international organizations are granted immunity from suit by the International Organizations Immunities Act, an equitable and complete judicial settlement of claims asserted against the United States may not be had. But this possible objection is more fancied than real. For the United Nations submits to our courts when it urges its claim and cannot consequently shut off any proper defenses of the United States.

Finally, it cannot be denied that when the Congress conferred the privileges specified in the International Organizations Immunities Act, it neither explicitly or implicitly limited the kind or type of legal proceedings that might be instituted by the United Nations. There appears to be no good reason for the judicial imposition of such limitations.

The exceptions of the respondents are severally overruled.

FOR FURTHER STUDY

P. H. KOOIJMANS. *The Doctrine of the Legal Equality of States.* Leyden: A. W. Sythoff, 1964.

C. WILFRED JENKS. *The Proper Law of International Organizations.* Dobbs Ferry, New York: Oceana Publications, 1962.

GUENTER WEISSBERG. *The International Status of the United Nations.* New York: Oceana Publications, 1961.

J. W. SCHNEIDER. *Treaty-Making Power of International Organizations.* Geneva: Librairie E. Droz, 1959.

D. P. O'CONNELL. *The Law of State Succession.* Cambridge: Cambridge University Press, 1956.

K. MAREK. *Identity and Continuity of States in Public International Law.* Geneva: Librairie E. Droz, 1954.

J. C. CHEN. *The International Law of Recognition.* New York: Frederick A. Praeger, Inc., 1951.

III

The Effect of Treaties and Other International Agreements

THE essence of law is obligation. On the international scene, engagement of the faith and credit of states and international organizations to perform acts of one kind or another can be accomplished through a variety of instruments known as treaties, agreements, conventions, protocols, pacts, declarations, exchange of notes, and other names. Agreements concluded by international organizations have borne such titles as "memorandum," "exchange of letters," even "note of understanding," but the vast majority contain the word "agreement." The League of Nations "covenant" was a multilateral treaty; so, too, is the United Nations "charter."

All these instruments have the same effect under international law, namely, a commitment for which there is international liability. Without the expectation of performance by its parties, contracts in any community would be useless and social order impossible. And without some sanctions for violation of promises, injustice would be the reward of the faithful.

Treaties or other public international agreements between states and international organizations should be distinguished from contracts between states and alien individuals or corporations. Such contracts or concessions can raise questions of international law in respect to the diplomatic protection of states afforded to their own citizens and the prosecution of claims, but they are not governed by the rules of international law on treaties. For example, if the United States sought compensation for a petroleum company or an engineering firm, incorporated in Delaware and owned by American nationals, whose concession had been canceled or whose contract had been abrogated by another state's municipal law, it would proceed on its right to extend protection to its nationals, not as a remedy for a breach of an international agreement.

The gravity of international obligations through treaties has traditionally been underscored by procedure, consisting of: signature by a person with "full powers," a plenipotentiary; then ratification by the constitutional processes of the contracting states; then an exchange of ratifications between states, or a deposit of the ratification with a state or an international organization. Modern treaties ordinarily require the ratification of a state after its representative has signed the document to make the agreement binding. Other conditions to give legal effect to a treaty may be specified, and in the case of multilateral agreements a minimum number of ratifications may be necessary before the treaty has any binding force.

Under Articles 102 and 103 of the United Nations Charter, every treaty and international agreement entered into by the members of the organization shall be registered with and published by the Secretariat as soon as possible. No treaty in force after establishment of the United Nations may be invoked before any organ of the organization by any party unless the treaty has been registered. Reservations to a treaty may be expressed by a state (*a*) at the time of signature, (*b*) at ratification, or (*c*) when adhering to a multilateral convention. In bipartite agreements, such reservations may be quickly and clearly accepted or rejected by the other contracting party. However, considerable legal confusion exists about the limit of reservations that each state in a multipartite convention can be allowed before all the reciprocal obligations in the instrument are diluted and the agreement becomes nugatory. Signed letters and agreements have the same legal effect as treaties. A large amount of national business today among states and international organizations is transacted by such instruments, often through officials of relatively minor rank in a government.

A fundamental norm of international law is that treaties must be observed (*pacta sunt servanda*). Yet, how and when is a binding international obligation on the state recognizable in international law? Responsible agents ordinarily commit their states by agreements to international obligations. For treaties, the act of ratification after signature is the most frequent way a state assumes a liability. Suppose, however, a chief of state had obtained power in violation of the national constitution, or an ambassador plenipotentiary had been appointed by fraud, or a legislature had ratified a treaty contrary to its own rules of procedure. The violation of municipal law may not by itself invalidate an international agreement, especially if consent to the obligation was given by an agent or organ empowered to do so under international law. In only a few instances have treaty negotiators exceeded their authority, and then their work was subject to ratification; international executive agreements, backed only by the authority of the office, are more likely to create legal problems.

Moreover, in 1933 the Permanent Court of International Justice held that a 1919 oral declaration made by the Foreign Minister of Norway to the Danish Minister created an international obligation. The Foreign Minister, M. Ihlen, had said that the Norwegian government "would not make any difficulties" in settling the question of the Danish government's desire to have its sovereignty over the whole of Greenland recognized by all interested powers.

The Court considers it beyond all dispute that a reply of this nature given by the Minister for Foreign Affairs on behalf of his Government in response to a request by the diplomatic representative of a foreign Power, in regard to a question falling within his province, is binding upon the country to which the Minister belongs.[1]

Other questions about the validity of international agreements may arise in connection with fraud, error, or the individual coercion of representatives of states, but the most important issue is the legitimacy of treaties that states have signed and ratified under duress, such as all the peace treaties of World War I and World War II. Prior to the League of Nations, the validity of a peace treaty could not be doubted merely because it resulted from war or a threat of force by one state against another. Coercion itself was regarded as a remedy for the rights of states under existing international law from the 17th to the 20th century. But beginning with the League of Nations, and especially since the United Nations, the threat of use of force in international relations has been abjured by the organization's member states. Therefore, the conclusion of a treaty by member or nonmember states processed by threat or use of force in violation of the principles of the United Nations charter may be judged illegal.

Furthermore, in the development of peacekeeping through international organization, states may be required by their pledges under the Charter to take actions inconsistent with their treaty obligations. For example, the Security Council might call on a state to impose a trade embargo against another state as part of a collective sanctions measure by the United Nations, although a commercial trade agreement between the two states is still in force. In such cases, Article 103 of the Charter specifies that obligations under the Charter shall prevail over any other international agreement in the event of conflict between them.

From these observations it should be clear that the agency and circumstances leading to an international agreement may indicate the extent of the international obligation. *The South West Africa Cases* (preliminary objections), which follow, are of special interest. The plaintiffs, Liberia and Ethiopia, alleged that South West Africa was a territory under a League of Nations mandate to be exercised by South Africa, that the mandate was a treaty in force, that South Africa was subject to the international obligations of Article 22 of the Covenant of the League of

---

[1] *Eastern Greenland Case*, Series A/B, No. 53, p. 71.

Nations, including the obligations to submit to the supervision and control of the General Assembly of the United Nations with respect to the exercise of the mandate, and that South Africa, through its policy of *apartheid* and other acts, was violating its international obligations for the supervision of the mandate and the promotion of the welfare and social progress of the inhabitants. Before the trial of the merits of the case, South Africa raised four preliminary objections to the jurisdiction of the International Court of Justice.

The Nature of Treaties

SOUTH WEST AFRICA CASES, Preliminary Objections
International Court of Justice
1962 I.C.J. Reports 319

*   *   *

The issue of the jurisdiction of the Court was raised by the Respondent in the form of four Preliminary Objections. Its submissions at the end of its written and oral statements are substantially the same, except that on the latter occasion the grounds on which the respective objections are based were summarized under each Objection, and, with reference to the submissions in the first Preliminary Objection, the Respondent introduced a modification on 22 October 1962, as a consequence of its replies to questions put to the Parties by Members of the Court. The Court will deal first with this modification.

The amended text of the First Objection reads:

"Firstly, the Mandate for South West Africa *has never been, or at any rate* is since the dissolution of the League of Nations no longer, a 'treaty or convention in force' within the meaning of Article 37 of the Statute of the Court, this Submission being advanced

(a) with respect to the Mandate as a whole, including Article 7 thereof, and

(b) in any event, with respect to Article 7 itself."

The amendment consists in the addition of the italicized words. . . .

In the Court's opinion, this modified view is not well-founded for the following reasons . . . the Mandate for South West Africa took the form of a resolution of the Council of the League but obviously it was of a different character. It cannot be correctly regarded as embodying only an executive action in pursuance of the Covenant. The Mandate, in fact and in law, is an international agreement having the character of a treaty or convention. The Preamble of the Mandate itself shows this character.

The agreement referred to therein was effected by a decision of the Principal Allied and Associated Powers including Great Britain taken on 7 May 1919 to confer a Mandate for the Territory on His Britannic Majesty and by the confirmation of its acceptance on 9 May 1919 by the Union of South Africa. The second and third paragraphs of the Preamble record these facts. It is further stated therein that "His Britannic Majesty, for and on behalf of the Government of the Union of South Africa . . . has undertaken to exercise it on behalf of the League of Nations in accordance with the following provisions." These "provisions" were formulated "in the following terms."

The draft Mandate containing the explicit terms was presented to the Council of the League in December 1920 and, with a few changes, was confirmed on 17 December 1920. The fourth and final paragraph of the Preamble recites the provisions of Article 22, paragraph 8 of the Covenant, and then "confirming the said Mandate, defines its terms as follows: . . ."

Thus it can be seen from what has been stated above that this Mandate, like practically all other similar Mandates, is a special type of instrument composite in nature and instituting a novel international regime. It incorporates a definite agreement consisting in the conferment and acceptance of a Mandate for South West Africa, a provisional or tentative agreement on the terms of this Mandate between the Principal Allied and Associated Powers to be proposed to the Council of the League of Nations and a formal confirmation agreement on the terms therein explicitly defined by the Council and agreed to between the Mandatory and the Council representing the League and its Members. It is an instrument having the character of a treaty or convention and embodying international engagements for the Mandatory as defined by the Council and accepted by the Mandatory.

The fact that the Mandate is described in its last paragraph as a Declaration (*exemplaire* in the French text) is of no legal significance. The Mandates confirmed by the Council of the League of Nations in the course of 1922 are all called instruments (*actes* in the French text), such as the French Mandate for Togoland, the British Mandate for the Cameroons, the Belgian Mandate for East Africa (Ruanda-Urundi), etc. Terminology is not a determinant factor as to the character of an international agreement or undertaking. In the practice of States and of international organizations and in the jurisprudence of international courts, there exists a great variety of usage; there are many different types to which the character of treaty stipulations has been attached.

Moreover, the fact that the Mandate confirmed by the Council of the League embodies a provision that it "shall be deposited in the archives of the League of Nations" and that "certified copies shall be forwarded by the Secretary-General of the League of Nations to all Powers Signatories of the Treaty of Peace with Germany," clearly implies that it was intended and understood to be an international treaty or convention embodying international engagements of general interest to the Signatory Powers of the German Peace Treaty.

It has been argued that the Mandate in question was not registered in accordance with Article 18 of the Covenant which provided: "No such treaty or international engagement shall be binding until so registered." If the Mandate was *ab initio* null and void on the ground of non-registration it would follow that the Respondent has not and has never had a legal title for its administration of the territory of South West Africa; it would therefore be impossible for it to maintain that it has had such a title up to the discovery of this ground of nullity. The fact is that Article 18 provided for registration of "Every treaty or international engagement entered into *hereafter* by any Member of the League," and the word "hereafter" meant after 10 January 1920 when the Covenant took effect, whereas the Mandate for South West Africa, as stated in the preamble of the instrument, had actually been conferred on and accepted by the Union of South Africa more than seven months earlier on 7–9 May 1919; and its terms had been provisionally agreed upon between the Principal Allied and Associated Powers and the Mandatory, in August 1919. Moreover, Article 18, designed to secure publicity and avoid secret treaties, could not apply in the same way in respect of treaties to which the League of Nations itself was one of the Parties as in respect of treaties concluded among individual Member States. The Mandate for South West Africa, like all the other Mandates, is an international instrument of an institutional character, to which the League of Nations, represented by the Council, was itself a Party. It is the implementation of an institution in which all the Member States are interested as such. The procedure to give the necessary publicity to the Mandates including the one under consideration was applied in view of their special character, and in any event they were published in the *Official Journal* of the League of Nations.

Since the Mandate in question had the character of a treaty or convention at its start, the next relevant question to consider is whether this treaty or convention, with respect to the Mandate as a whole including Article 7 thereof, or with respect to Article 7 itself, is still in force. The Respondent contends that it is not in force, and this contention constitutes the essence of the First Preliminary Objection. It is argued that the rights and obligations under the Mandate in relation to the administration of the territory of South West Africa being of an objective character still exist, while those rights and obligations relating to administrative supervision by the League and submission to the Permanent Court of International Justice, being of a contractual character have necessarily become extinct on the dissolution of the League of Nations which involved as a consequence the ending of membership of the League, leaving only one party to the contract and resulting in the total extinction of the contractual relationship.

Similar contentions were advanced by the Respondent in 1950, and the Court in its Advisory Opinion ruled:

"The authority which the Union Government exercises over the Territory is based on the Mandate. If the Mandate lapsed, as the Union Government contends, the latter's authority would equally have lapsed. To retain the rights derived from the Mandate and to deny the obligations thereunder could not be justified." (I.C.J. Reports 1950, page 133.)

*   *   *

The unanimous holding of the Court in 1950 on the survival and continuing effect of Article 7 of the Mandate, continues to reflect the Court's opinion today. Nothing has since occurred which would warrant the Court reconsidering it. All important facts were stated or referred to in the proceedings before the Court in 1950.

The Court finds that, though the League of Nations and the Permanent Court of International Justice have both ceased to exist, the obligation of the Respondent to submit to the compulsory jurisdiction of that Court was effectively transferred to this Court before the dissolution of the League of Nations. . . .

*   *   *

The Court concludes that Article 7 of the Mandate is a treaty or convention still in force within the meaning of Article 37 of the Statute of the Court and that the dispute is one which is envisaged in the said Article 7 and cannot be settled by negotiation. Consequently the Court is competent to hear the dispute on the merits.

For these reasons,

THE COURT,

by eight votes to seven,

finds that it has jurisdiction to adjudicate upon the merits of the dispute.

Joint Dissenting Opinion of Sir Percy Spender and Sir Gerald Fitzmaurice

*   *   *

We are not unmindful of, nor are we insensible to, the various considerations of a non-juridical character, social, humanitarian and other, which underlie this case; but these are matters for the political rather than for the legal arena. They cannot be allowed to deflect us from our duty of reaching a conclusion strictly on the basis of what we believe to be the correct legal view. They do however lead us to draw attention to another aspect of the matter.

A Court called upon to consider objections to its jurisdiction must exclude from consideration all questions relating to the merits of the dispute, unless the jurisdictional issues are so intertwined with the merits that they cannot be considered separately, and must be joined to the merits. It is nevertheless legitimate for a Court, in considering the jurisdictional aspects of any case, to take into account a factor which is fundamental to the jurisdiction of any tribunal, namely whether the issues arising on the merits are such as to be capable of objective legal determination.

*   *   *

We are most reluctant to devote any space to the 1950 Opinion, as we shall call it. We believe that Opinion was wrong in one or two important aspects, but by no means in all. But this belief has not affected our views in the present case, because we think that different issues are now involved. We are compelled to make this clear because, in the first place, the Judgment of the Court is partly founded on the 1950 Opinion; and secondly, the relevance of that Opinion was much debated in the arguments of the Parties to the present proceedings. . . .

*   *   *

As regards one of the central issues arising in 1950, namely that of the status of the Mandate as an international institution, the Court in 1950 did little more than find, on various grounds, that the dissolution of the League of Nations had not caused the Mandate to lapse, and that despite this dissolution, the Mandate was still in force. But the Court did not specifically address itself to the question of the basis upon which the Mandate was in force nor, in particular, to whether it was still in force as a treaty or convention. In the dispositive of its 1950 Opinion, the Court did no more, in relation to the present context, than state that by reason of Article 37 of the Statue, the present Court was substituted for the former Permanent Court; but both there, and in the very brief references to Article 37, and to Article 7 of the Mandate, made in the body of the Opinion, the Court seems to have assumed the existence of the necessary conditions without going into that matter . . . no jurisdictional issue of any kind was before the Court in 1950. . . .

In the same way we think that the 1950 finding of the Court, to the effect that the Assembly of the United Nations was entitled to exercise the supervisory functions of the former League Council under Article 6 of the Mandate, is equally irrelevant to the present proceedings, which do not involve any specific issue of "devolution," "inheritance" or "carry over"—much as these matters have been discussed in the arguments of the parties . . . the issue now before the Court is a purely jurisdictional one. The jurisdiction of the Court could not be presumed on any merely devolutionary basis. . . .

*   *   *

. . . since the burden of establishing the jurisdiction of the Court lies on the party asserting it, and this must be established conclusively, it follows that it is for the Applicants to show that the Mandate is beyond reasonable doubt a "treaty or convention in force" for the purposes of Articles 36 and 37 of the Statute . . . a duty lies upon the Court, before it may assume jurisdiction, to be conclusively satisfied—satisfied beyond a reasonable doubt—that jurisdiction does exist. . . .

*   *   *

. . . while international law takes, and rightly takes, a liberal view of what constitutes a treaty, convention or other forms of international agreement, the notion is not an unlimited one. It is not synonymous, as the Judgment of the Court might almost lead one to suppose, with international acts and instruments generally. Thus, in its final draft on the "Conclusion, Entry into Force and Registration of Treaties" completed earlier this year (Document (A/CN. 4/148 of 3 July 1962), the International Law Commission of the United Nations adopted the following definition of a treaty, with which we associate ourselves:

" 'Treaty' means any international agreement in written form, whether embodied in a single instrument or in two or more related instruments and whatever its particular designation [here follows a list of some dozen possible appelations including of course 'convention', 'agreement' and 'declaration'], concluded between two or more States or other subjects of international law and governed by international law."

It will be seen that this concept of what constitutes a treaty, though wide, is not a limitless one. We draw attention in particular, in the context, to the phrases "in written form" and "concluded between two or more States or other subjects of international law." Thus a verbal agreement, while it might be held binding . . . would not be a treaty or convention. Nor would a statement (e.g. of intention) made, or an assurance given, in the course of, say, a speech at an international conference or assembly, be a treaty or convention. A declaration containing a unilateral assumption of obligations would not be an international agreement at all, since an international agreement must be concluded between "two or more" parties.

The quasi-treaty character which "optional clause" declarations made under paragraph 2 of Article 36 of the Statute are sometimes said to possess, would arise solely from the multiplicity of these declarations and their interlocking character, which gives them a bilateral or multilateral aspect. A single such declaration, if it stood quite alone, could not be an international agreement. . . .

. . . The Judgment of the Court in effect identifies the idea of an international agreement with any act or instrument embodying, or giving rise to, international obligations, or which contains or involves an international "engagement." This we believe to be a fallacy, as the above examples show, and others could be adduced. . . .

*   *   *

. . . it may be tempting to regard an instrument containing an adjudication clause (particularly one worded like Article 7—"The Mandatory agrees . . . ,") as being *pro tanto* of a conventional character. We do not however think it possible or legitimate to detach and isolate one provision of an instrument, ascribe a treaty character to it and then, on that basis, deem a similar character to be thereby imparted to the whole instrument . . .

*   *   *

The actual transfer of the territories to the various Mandatories, in their capacity as such, was provided for by Article 257 of the Treaty of Versailles; but already before that Treaty was signed on June 28, 1919, a decision of the Supreme War Council, made and published by it early in May of that year, had designated the various Mandatories, and amongst them the Union of South Africa in respect of South West Africa; in point of fact the Respondent accepted the Mandate the same month. This decision of the Supreme War Council was confirmed in August of the same year. But even before that, most of the mandated territories (including South West Africa) were being administered by the future mandatories on a basis of military occupation resulting from the operations of the War. . . .

*   *   *

The Treaty of Versailles (and with it the League Covenant which formed part of it) came into force on January 10, 1920, and it was therefore not until then that, by virtue of Article 257, the actual transfer of the mandated territories to the Mandatories, in their capacity as such, formally took effect. On the same date, the Mandates System came into being under Article 22 of the Covenant; but the actual Mandates did not appear until much later—in the case of South West Africa, not until December 17, 1920. . . .

*   *   *

On the face of it, the Mandate as set out in the League Council's resolution of December 17, 1920, does not look like a treaty, convention or other form of international agreement . . . it looks like what it purported to be—a Declaration promulgated by a resolution of the Council of the League in the exercise of a power conferred upon it by paragraph 8 of Article 22 of the Covenant, exercisable precisely if the terms of the Mandate had not been "previously agreed upon by the Members of the League." To all appearance therefore, the Mandate was a quasi-legislative act of the League Council, carried out in the exercise of a power given to it by the Covenant to meet a stated contingency. . . .

*   *   *

Since, in our view, the Mandate has not, and never did have the intrinsic character of an international agreement, it is strictly unnecessary to consider whether it is still in force, regarded as a "treaty or convention." Nevertheless we propose to do so, because the Mandate, if not itself an international agreement, had certain aspects on the basis of which it may be argued that it had some conventional character. This being so, we would not wish to rest our view on the sole conclusion that it had not—correct though we believe this conclusion to be.

* * *

It is, or should be, common ground that assuming the Mandate to have been a treaty or convention, there must have been parties to it . . . We do not accept the view that a treaty can be "partyless". . . .

* * *

. . . It has been suggested that the Principal Allied and Associated Powers were the parties, together with the Mandatory. If such was the case, these Powers appear to have been totally unaware of it for upwards of forty years. It has already been seen that the original idea of casting the Mandate into the form of an ordinary treaty or convention was abandoned, and in our view no contractual nexus was established or intended to be established with or between the Principal Allied and Associated Powers on the basis, or in consequence, of the Mandate instrument. . . .

* * *

. . . If the Members of the League were parties to the Mandate in their capacity as such, there would be no problem, for the League being dissolved, its former Members have lost that capacity and could no longer be parties to the Mandate as Members of the League. The question is therefore, and must be, if they were parties, were they so in their individual capacity as separate sovereign States, still extant (as States) today?

* * *

We think this question can only be answered in the negative. . . . The whole form and method of issue of the Mandate is hostile to the notion of the individual Members as separate parties to it, or as having any status in regard to it, other than as Members of the League and through their participation in its activities.

* * *

. . . the inevitable conclusion must be drawn that, all other candidates having been eliminated the only party to the Mandate, apart from the Mandatory (and if the Mandate was a treaty or convention at all) was the League itself or the Council acting for it. . . . The only doubt . . . is whether, at that date, an international organization such as the League, and still more . . . the League Council, would have been regarded as having separate international personality and treaty-making capacity. . . .

*　　　*　　　*

These can only be speculations. What is quite clear is that if the Mandate was a treaty or convention, the parties, and only parties to it, were the Mandatory and the League or its Council. Since neither League nor Council exist now, the number of parties is less than two, and therefore, as a treaty or convention, the Mandate is no longer in force.

*　　　*　　　*

. . . the conditions requisite to give the Court jurisdiction under Articles 36 and 37 of its Statute are not fulfilled, inasmuch as the Mandate was the act of the League Council and is not and never was a "treaty or convention" (or other form of international agreement); or alternatively, if it was, it is no longer in force as such, as there would now remain only one party—the Mandatory.

Treaties and Municipal Law

Judges in every country who interpret and apply international law within their national courts can run into a conflict between international obligation and municipal law. In British courts, when questions involving treaties arise the judge is likely to inquire whether the actions expected from the executive officers or courts as a result of the treaty have been authorized by the existing law of the land and, more particularly, by statutes of Parliament. In American courts, no easy road of rationalization lies ahead for a judge who finds that the laws of the United States made pursuant to the Constitution and treaties made under the authority of the United States shall *both* be the supreme law of the land.

A United States court may have to determine, first of all, whether a treaty alleged to control the facts of the case is self-executing or not. Put another way, does the treaty itself legislate for the United States, or does it merely pledge the good faith of the United States to legislate through its constitutional processes? Much depends on the construction of the language and import of the parties. No absolutely certain answer can be given—that is the reason for litigation.

Under international law, when a state plainly agrees to transfer land or to pay sums of money to named parties little doubt exists about the character of the act, even though an additional legislative act may be needed for national authority and appropriations. But when broad pledges to promote commerce and trade or to protect human rights and fundamental freedoms are made by states, courts may be inclined to regard them as the contractual stipulations of sovereigns with each other, never intended to stand alone as rules enforceable in their national courts without further implementing legislation.

A far more troubling problem, touching the very essence of international obligation, is the dilemma of reconciling national will expressed internally through legislation with national will expressed externally through treaties. By political confusion, they may contradict each other and require the most judicious reconciliation. During the highly nationalistic period of American government in the 19th century, United States federal courts approved the alleged contraventions of treaties by congressional acts partly on grounds of the compact's non-self-executing nature,[2]

---

[2] *Foster* v. *Neilson*, 27 U.S. 253 (1829), but the doctrine was not followed in several other cases. In *Chae Chan Ping* v. *United States*, 130 U.S. 851 (1889), the Supreme Court held that if a treaty operates by its own force and relates to a subject within the power of Congress, it can be considered in that respect equivalent to a legislative act to be repealed or modified at the pleasure of Congress.

partly by escaping judicial responsibility in holding that the breach of faith touched national law and addressed itself to the political branches of the government,[3] and partly by stating that if a statute and treaty were inconsistent, the one later in date would control the other.[4]

The Supreme Court took another tack in 1933 when it held that a section of the Tariff Act of 1922, which Congress reenacted in identical terms in 1930, did not abrogate a 1924 treaty between the United States and Great Britain. The Court said, "A treaty will not be deemed to have been abrogated or modified by a later statute unless such purpose on the part of Congress has been clearly expressed. . . . [5]

Peculiar problems in international law on treaties reach the United States because of its federal system and its separation of powers in the national government; but in every state, even where the treaty-making powers are perfectly blended with legislation within the government or where no powers are reserved to local governments, a choice must be made between national and international norms of conduct. The future issues of international law will depend very largely on argument concerning how far international obligations transcend and supersede national enactments in an ever-widening field of human activity.

Treaties and the U.S. Constitution

Ever since 1796, when the Supreme Court found a peace treaty with England to prevail over a Virginia statute,[6] the courts in the United States have not hesitated to give a superior place to treaties over the acts of the states of the Union. Such judgments stemmed partly from a sense of duty to international obligations, but mainly from the intent of Article VI of the Constitution: the Constitution, laws of the United States in pursuance of the Constitution, and treaties made under the authority of the United States shall be the supreme law of the land. Yet, suppose a treaty seems to contradict the Constitution?

In 1918, the State of Missouri argued that an act of Congress after a treaty with Great Britain regulating migratory birds was unconstitutional by interfering with the rights reserved to the states by the Tenth Amendment. Indeed, the same kind of act, passed by Congress without a treaty, had been held unconstitutional by a United States District Court. Nevertheless, the Supreme Court denied Missouri. There are situations in which acts of Congress, when made in pursuance of the Constitution, are the supreme law of the land and others in which treaties, when made under the authority of the United States, are the supreme law of the land. The Court said, "It is obvious that there may be matters of the sharpest

---

[3] *Taylor* v. *Morton*, 23 FC 784 (1885) and 67 U.S. 481 (1863), and *Head Money* cases (*Edye* v. *Robertson, Cunard Steamship* v. *Robertson*) 112 U.S. 580 (1884).

[4] *Whitney* v. *Robertson*, 124 U.S. 190 (1888).

[5] *Cook* v. *United States* (The Mazel Tov), 288 U.S. 102 (1933).

[6] *Ware* v. *Hylton*, 3 Dallas 199.

exigency for the national well-being that an act of Congress could not deal with but that a treaty followed by such an act could . . .".[7]

The Supreme Court has never maintained that no limits can be set to the treaty-making power of the federal government, but no treaty has ever been held to be unconstitutional. And, incidentally, Congress has never refused to appropriate the money necessary to execute a treaty.

Even more controversial than an apparent conflict between treaties made under the authority of the United States and the enumerated powers of the federal government under the Constitution has been the extent to which the President, acting only on the authority of his office as Chief Executive or Commander in Chief, may by international executive agreements commit the United States to actions that should be legalized by acts of Congress or that tend to override local laws of the individual states. The Supreme Court decision in the *Pink* case in 1942 and subsequent acts of the President during World War II stirred up a political tempest with allegations that the Chief Executive, through international executive agreements, was thwarting both the legislative powers of Congress and the reserved rights of the states, thereby subverting the Constitution.

Although the decision in (*a*) the *Sei Fujii* case, which follows, was based upon American constitutional law, the Supreme Court of California commented on the nature of self-executing and non-self-executing treaties, particularly since a lower court had held the land law invalid under the United Nations Charter; (*b*) the *John T. Bill* case illustrates the problem of a conflict between a treaty and a United States statute; while (*c*) *U.S.* v. *Pink* opens difficult questions about the effect on New York State law of diplomatic recognition and international agreements undertaken by the President on his own authority.

Non Self-Executing Treaty

SEI FUJII v. CALIFORNIA
Supreme Court of California, 1952
242 P. 2d 617

Gibson, Chief Justice

*   *   *

Plaintiff, an alien Japanese who is ineligible to citizenship under our naturalization laws, appeals from a judgment declaring that certain land purchased by him in 1948 had escheated to the state. There is no treaty between this country and Japan which confers upon plaintiff the right to

---

[7] *Missouri* v. *Holland*, 252 U.S. 416.

own land, and the sole question presented on this appeal is the validity of the California alien land law.

*   *   *

It is first contended that the land law has been invalidated and super-seded by the provisions of the United Nations Charter pledging the member nations to promote the observance of human rights and funda-mental freedoms without distinction as to race. Plaintiff relies on state-ments in the preamble and in Articles 1, 55 and 56 of the Charter, 59 Stat. 1035.

It is not disputed that the charter is a treaty, and our federal Constitu-tion provides that treaties made under the authority of the United States are part of the supreme law of the land . . . and that the judges in every state are bound thereby. U.S. Const., art. VI. A treaty, however, does not automatically supersede local laws which are inconsistent with it unless the treaty provisions are self-executing In the words of Chief Justice Marshall: A treaty is "to be regarded in courts of justice as equivalent to an act of the Legislature, whenever it operates of itself, without the aid of any legislative provision. But when the terms of the stipulation import a contract—when either of the parties engages to perform a particular act, the treaty addresses itself to the political, not the judicial department; and the Legislature must execute the contract, before it can become a rule for the court." *Foster* v. *Neilson,* 1829, 2 Pet. 253, 7 L.Ed. 415.

In determining whether a treaty is self-executing courts look to the in-tent of the signatory parties as manifested by the language of the instru-ment, and, if the instrument is uncertain, recourse may be had to the circumstances surrounding its execution.

*   *   *

It is clear that the provisions of the preamble and of Article 1 of the charter which are claimed to be in conflict with the alien land law are not self-executing. They state general purposes and objectives of the United Nations Organization and do not purport to impose legal obligations on the individual member nations or to create rights in private persons. It is equally clear that none of the other provisions relied on by plaintiff is self-executing. Article 55 declares that the United Nations "shall promote: . . . universal respect for, and observance of, human rights and funda-mental freedoms for all without distinction as to race, sex, language, or religion," and in Article 56, the member nations "pledge themselves to take joint and separate action in cooperation with the Organization for the achievement of the purposes set forth in Article 55." Although the member nations have obligated themselves to cooperate with the interna-tional organization in promoting respect for, and observance of, human rights, it is plain that it was contemplated that future legislative action by the several nations would be required to accomplish the declared objectives, and there is nothing to indicate that these provisions were intended to become rules of law for the courts of this country upon the ratification of the charter.

The language used in Articles 55 and 56 is not the type customarily employed in treaties which have been held to be self-executing and to create rights and duties in individuals.

*   *   *

The provisions in the charter pledging cooperation in promoting observance of fundamental freedoms lack the mandatory quality and definiteness which would indicate an intent to create justiciable rights in private persons immediately upon ratification. Instead, they are framed as a promise of future action by the member nations. Secretary of State Stettinius, Chairman of the United States delegation at the San Francisco Conference where the charter was drafted, stated in his report to President Truman that Article 56 "pledges the various countries to cooperate with the organization by joint and separate action in the achievement of the economic and social objectives of the organization without infringing upon their right to order their national affairs according to their own best ability, in their own way, and in accordance with their own political and economic institutions and processes."

*   *   *

The humane and enlightened objectives of the United Nations Charter are, of course, entitled to respectful consideration by the courts and Legislatures of every member nation, since that document expresses the universal desire of thinking men for peace and for equality of rights and opportunities. The charter represents a moral commitment of foremost importance, and we must not permit the spirit of our pledge to be compromised or disparaged in either our domestic or foreign affairs. We are satisfied, however, that the charter provisions relied on by plaintiff were not intended to supersede existing domestic legislation, and we cannot hold that they operate to invalidate the alien land law.

*   *   *

The next question is whether the alien land law violates the due process and equal protection clauses of the Fourteenth Amendment. . . .
. . . we hold that the alien land law is invalid as in violation of the Fourteenth Amendment.

Conflict of Treaty and National Statute

JOHN T. BILL COMPANY v. UNITED STATES
Court of Customs and Patent Appeals, 1939
104 F. 2d 67

Garrett, Presiding Judge

*   *   *

In this appeal from the judgment of the United States Customs Court, Third Division, there are involved two protests of importers (the cases having been consolidated for trial) by which they seek to recover such duties as were assessed as countervailing duties upon merchandise described as bicycle parts imported from Germany . . .

The merchandise was classified under paragraph 371 of the Tariff Act of 1930, 46 Stat. 625, which reads:

"Par. 371. Bicycles, and parts thereof, not including tires, 30 per centum ad valorem: Provided, That if any country, dependency, province, or other subdivision of government imposes a duty on any article specified in this paragraph, when imported from the United States, in excess of the duty herein provided, there shall be imposed upon such article, when imported either directly or indirectly from such country, dependency, province, or other subdivision of government, a duty equal to that imposed by such country, dependency, province, or other subdivision of government on such article imported from the United States, but in no case shall such duty exceed 50 per centum ad valorem."

The first importation was assessed with duty at 50 per centum ad valorem, the collector citing as authority T.D. 42382, which is a Treasury Decision published October 5, 1927, wherein the Secretary of the Treasury advised "for . . . information in connection with the assessment of duty under paragraphs . . . 371 . . ." that Germany exacted a duty of 100 marks per 100 kilos on bicycle parts of worked iron when imported from the United States. The second importation was likewise assessed. . . .

It will be observed that paragraph 371, supra, provides a normal duty rate of 30 per centum ad valorem. The duties resulting from that rate are not here in question, it being claimed in both protests that the assessments should be at that rate. . . .

The protests are predicated upon the treaty between the United States and Germany proclaimed October 14, 1925, 44 Stat. 2132, particularly upon Article VII thereof which, so far as here pertinent, reads:

"Each of the High Contracting Parties binds itself unconditionally to impose no higher or other duties or conditions and no prohibition on the importation of any article, the growth, produce or manufacture, of the territories of the other than are or shall be imposed on the importation of any like article, the growth, produce or manufacture of any other foreign country.

* * *

"With respect to the amount and collection of duties on imports and exports of every kind, each of the two High Contracting Parties binds itself to give to the nationals, vessels and goods of the other the advantage of every favor, privilege or immunity which it shall have accorded to the nationals, vessels and goods of a third State, and regardless of whether such favored State shall have been accorded such treatment gratuitously or in return for reciprocal compensatory treatment . . . .

* * *

That Article VII of the treaty was in full force at the time of the respective importations here involved is not in question and various Treasury Decisions are cited which show that at those times merchandise of the kind involved was admissible from other foreign countries at a duty rate of only 30 per centum ad valorem.

Stated briefly, it is the contention of appellants that the action of the collector in exacting a duty of 50 per centum ad valorem was in violation of the unconditional grant of most-favored-nation treatment accorded Germany in the above treaty in view of the fact that bicycle parts of worked iron were then admissible from other countries at a lower rate of duty. The entire contention rests upon the *unconditional* character of the treaty, it, in effect, being conceded that, upon the authority of a long line of decisions by both the executive and judicial branches of the Government, the most-favored-nation doctrine would not apply in this case were the treaty of the conditional type, such, for example, as the treaty with Belgium which was involved in the case of *Minerva Automobiles, Inc.* v. *United States* (1938), 96 F.2d 836, 25 C.C.P.A., Customs, 324, T.D. 49424. . . .

* * *

That the treaty with Germany was a departure from former practice is a matter of history. It was consciously intended to be such. On the part of the United States the negotiations were conducted under the direction and supervision of the Secretary of State, Honorable Charles E. Hughes. After the treaty had been completed and submitted to the Senate of the United States for its action elaborate hearings were had before that body's Committee on Foreign Relations, beginning January 25, 1924. As a part of the hearings there appears a communication from Mr. Hughes to the Chairman of the Senate Committee on Foreign Relations, from which we quote the following excerpts:

* * *

". . . The question which has arisen with respect to the most-favored-nation clauses in the pending treaty with Germany grows out of the fact that these clauses provide reciprocally for most-favored-nation treatment without regard to the question whether a favored third State shall have been accorded the favor gratuitously or in return for special compensation. In other words, the pending treaty applies what is termed the 'unconditional' most-favored-nation principle. This is indeed a departure from our former practice, but it is believed to be a wise departure.

"The traditional policy of the United States in respect to most-favored-nation treatment was developed on the theory that privileges and concessions in the field of duties on imports or exports should be granted only in return for privileges and concessions reciprocally accorded. . . .

"In practice, the application of the principle of granting special concessions in return for special concessions involved the upsetting of the equilibrium of conditions which it was in the interest of this country to maintain. It was the interest and fundamental aim of this country to secure equality of treatment, but the conditional most-favored-nation clause was not in fact productive of equality of treatment and could not guarantee it. It merely promised an opportunity to bargain for such treatment. Moreover, the ascertaining of what might be equivalent compensation in the application of the conditional most-favored-nation principle was found to be difficult or impracticable. Reciprocal commercial arrangements were but temporary makeshifts; they caused constant negotiation and created uncertainty. Under present conditions, the expanding foreign commerce of the United States needs a guarantee of equality of treatment which can not be furnished by the conditional form of the most-favored-nation clause."

*   *   *

From the language of the treaty, particularly in the light of the foregoing elaborate construction of it by Mr. Hughes, it seems clear to us that the levy of duties at the rate of 50 per centum ad valorem while similar merchandise was being admitted, or was subject to admission, from other countries at the rate of 30 per centum ad valorem, was in contravention of the treaty's provisions.

*   *   *

The treaty was reciprocal and it was self-executing, requiring no legislation other than its own enactment, so far as any matter here involved was concerned. There is no claim that the rate of duty which Germany was then assessing upon bicycle parts imported from the United States was any higher than the rate imposed upon those parts when imported from other countries, and the fact that such rate was higher than the basic rate imposed by the United States is not of legal moment.

There remains to be considered the contention made by counsel for the Government that the most-favored-nation clause of the treaty with Germany was superseded by the Tariff Act of 1930. . . .

*   *   *

. . . At the time of the enactment of the 1930 tariff act the German Treaty was the only one of its type which had been ratified and embodied in the statutes at large, and we find no history connected with the passage of the tariff act which indicates any intention on the part of Congress to abrogate or supersede that treaty. It is well established, of course, that where a treaty and an act of Congress are in conflict, the latest in date must prevail. *United States* v. *Lee Yen Tai* (1902), 185 U.S. 213, 22 S.Ct. 629, 46 L.Ed. 878. It is equally as well established that repeals by implication are not favored and that in the case of treaties, as in the case of statutes, where provisions "cover, in whole or in part, the same matter, and are not absolutely irreconcilable, the duty of the court—no purpose to repeal being clearly expressed or indicated—is, if possible, to give effect to both." This principle was so stated as to statutes in the case of *Frost* v. *Wenie* (1895), 157 U.S. 46, 58, 15 S.Ct. 532, 39 L.Ed. 614, and the Supreme Court definitely applied it in the case of a treaty in the Lee Yen Tai case, supra.

Obviously the treaty with Germany marked the adoption of a new policy on the part of the United States. The history of the period is replete with statements to that effect, and, as was indicated in the letter of Mr. Hughes, supra, it was contemplated that such new policy would be followed in the negotiation of additional treaties with other countries. We feel justified in concluding that these facts and the expressed intent must have been in the mind of Congress at the time of the enactment of the Tariff Act of 1930, and that had the Congress intended to alter such policy it would have been expressed in the act.

* * *

In view of the foregoing, we are of the opinion that paragraph 371 of the Tariff Act of 1930, supra, did not repeal or supersede the unconditional most-favored-nation provisions of the treaty with Germany with respect to the merchandise involved, and, since we are of the opinion that the assessment of the duties here complained of was contrary to such provisions, we disagree with the conclusion reached by the Third Division.

Accordingly, the judgment of the United States Customs Court is reversed and the cause remanded for further proceedings in conformity with the views herein expressed.

Reversed and remanded.

* * *

Conflict of Executive Agreement and State Law

UNITED STATES v. PINK
United States Supreme Court, 1942
315 U.S. 203

Douglas, Justice

*   *   *

This action was brought by the United States to recover the assets of the New York branch of the First Russian Insurance Co. which remained in the hands of respondent after the payment of all domestic creditors. The material allegations of the complaint were in brief as follows:

The First Russian Insurance Co., organized under the laws of the former Empire of Russia, established a New York branch in 1907. It deposited with the Superintendent of Insurance, pursuant to the laws of New York, certain assets to secure payment of claims resulting from transactions of its New York branch. By certain laws, decrees, enactments and orders in 1918 and 1919 the Russian Government nationalized the business of insurance and all of the property, wherever situated, of all Russian insurance companies (including the First Russian Insurance Co.), and discharged and cancelled all the debts of such companies and the rights of all shareholders in all such property. The New York branch of the First Russian Insurance Co. continued to do business in New York until 1925. At that time respondent, pursuant to an order of the Supreme Court of New York, took possession of its assets for a determination and report upon the claims of the policyholders and creditors in the United States. Thereafter all claims of domestic creditors, i.e., all claims arising out of the business of the New York branch, were paid by respondent, leaving a balance in his hands of more than $1,000,000. In 1931 the New York Court of Appeals (255 NY 415, 175 NE 114) directed respondent to dispose of that balance as follows: first, to pay claims of foreign creditors who had filed attachment prior to the commencement of the liquidation proceeding and also such claims as were filed prior to the entry of the order on remittitur of that court; and second, to pay any surplus to a quorum of the board of directors of the company. Pursuant to that mandate, respondent proceeded with the liquidation of the claims of the foreign creditors. Some payments were made thereon. The major portion of the allowed claims, however, were not paid, a stay having been granted pending disposition of the claim of the United States. On November 16, 1933, the United States recognized the Union of Soviet Socialist Republics as the de jure Government of Russia and as an incident to that recognition accepted an assignment (known as the Litvinov Assignment) of certain claims. The Litvinov Assignment was in the form of a letter, dated November 16, 1933, to the President of the United States from Maxim Litvinov, People's Commissar for Foreign Affairs, reading as follows:

"Following our conversations I have the honor to inform you that the Government of the Union of Soviet Socialist Republics agrees that preparatory to a final settlement of the claims and counterclaims between the Government of the Union of Soviet Socialist Republics and the United States of America and the claims of their nationals, the Government of the Union of Soviet Socialist Republics will not take any steps to enforce any decisions of courts or initiate any new litigations for the amounts admitted to be due or that may be found to be due it, as the successor of prior Governments of Russia, or otherwise, from American nationals, including corporations, companies, partnerships, or associations, and also the claim against the United States of the Russian Volunteer Fleet, now in litigation in the United States Court of Claims, and will not object to such amounts being assigned and does hereby release and assign all such amounts to the Government of the United States, the Government of the Union of Soviet Socialist Republics to be duly notified in each case of any amount realized by the Government of the United States from such release and assignment.

"The Government of the Union of Soviet Socialist Republics further agrees, preparatory to the settlement referred to above not to make any claims with respect to:

"(a) judgment rendered or that may be rendered by American courts in so far as they relate to property, or rights, or interests therein, in which the Union of Soviet Socialist Republics or its nationals may have had or may claim to have an interest; or,

"(b) acts done or settlements made by or with the Government of the United States, or public officials in the United States, or its nationals, relating to property, credits, or obligations of any Government of Russia or nationals thereof."

This was acknowledged by the President on the same date. The acknowledgment, after setting forth the terms of the assignment, concluded:

"I am glad to have these undertakings by your Government and I shall be pleased to notify your Government in each case of any amount realized by the Government of the United States from the release and assignment to it of the amounts admitted to be due, or that may be found to be due, the Government of the Union of Soviet Socialist Republics, and of the amount that may be found to be due on the claim of the Russian Volunteer Fleet."

On November 14, 1934, the United States brought an action in the federal District Court for the Southern District of New York, seeking to recover the assets in the hands of respondents. This Court held in *United States v. Bank of New York & T. Co.* (1936), 296 US 463, 80 L ed 331, 56 S Ct 343, that the well settled "principles governing the convenient and orderly administration of justice require that the jurisdiction of the state court should be respected" (p. 480); and that whatever might be "the effect of recognition" of the Russian Government, it did not terminate the state proceedings (p. 479). The United States was remitted to the state court for determination of its claim, no opinion being intimated on the merits (p. 481). The United States then moved for leave to intervene in the liquidation proceedings. Its motion was denied "without prejudice to the institution of the time-honored form of action." That order was affirmed on appeal.

Thereafter the present suit was instituted in the Supreme Court of New York. The defendants, other than respondent, were certain designated policyholders and other creditors who had presented in the liquidation proceedings claims against the corporation. The complaint prayed, inter alia, that the United States be adjudged to be the sole and exclusive owner entitled to immediate possession of the entire surplus fund in the hands of the respondent.

Respondent's answer denied the allegations of the complaint that title to the funds in question passed to the United States and that the Russian decrees had the effect claimed. It also set forth various affirmative defenses —that the order of distribution pursuant to the decree in 255 NY 415, 175 NE 114, could not be affected by the Litvinov Assignment; that the Litvinov Assignment was unenforceable because it was conditioned upon a final settlement of claims and counterclaims which had not been accomplished; that under Russian law the nationalization decrees in question had no effect on property not factually taken into possession by the Russian Government prior to May 22, 1922; that the Russian decrees had no extraterritorial effect, according to Russian law, that if the decrees were given extraterritorial effect, they were confiscatory and their recognition would be unconstitutional and contrary to the public policy of the United States and of the State of New York; and that the United States under the Litvinov Assignment acted merely as a collection agency for the Russian Government and hence was foreclosed from asserting any title to the property in question.

. . . Subsequently the Appellate Division of the Supreme Court of New York affirmed, without opinion, the order of dismissal in the instant case. The Court of Appeals affirmed with a per curiam opinion. . . .

*   *   *

We granted the petition for certiorari because of the nature and public importance of the questions raised.

*   *   *

The New York Court of Appeals held in the Moscow F. Ins. Co. Case that the Russian decrees in question had no extraterritorial effect. If that is true, it is decisive of the present controversy. For the United States acquired under the Litvinov Assignment only such rights as Russia had.

. . . If the Russian decrees left the New York assets of the Russian insurance companies unaffected, then Russia had nothing here to assign. But that question of foreign law is not to be determined exclusively by the state court. . . . Here title obtained under the Litvinov Assignment depends on a correct interpretation of Russian Law . . . questions of foreign law on which the asserted federal right is based are not peculiarly within the cognizance of the local courts. While deference will be given to the determination of the state court, its conclusion is not accepted as final.

We do not stop to review all the evidence in the voluminous record of the Moscow F. Ins. Co. Case bearing on the question of the extraterritorial effect of the Russian decrees of nationalization. . . . Subsequently to the hearings in that case, however, the United States, through diplomatic channels requested the Commissariat for Foreign Affairs of the Russian Government to obtain an official declaration by the Commissariat for Justice of the R.S.F.S.R. which would make clear, as a matter of Russian law, the intended effect of the Russian decree nationalizing insurance companies upon the funds of such companies outside of Russia.

*   *   *

We hold that so far as its intended effect is concerned the Russian decree embraced the New York assets of the First Russian Insurance Co.

The question of whether the decree should be given extraterritorial effect is of course a distinct matter. One primary issue raised in that connection is whether under our constitutional system New York law can be allowed to stand in the way.

The decision of the New York Court of Appeals in the Moscow F. Ins. Co. Case is unequivocal. It held that "under the law of this State such confiscatory decrees do not affect the property claimed here" (280 NY 314, 20 NE (2d) 758); that the property of the New York branch acquired a "character of its own" which was "dependent" on the law of New York . . . ; that no "rule of comity and no act of the United States government constrains this State to abandon any part of its control or to share it with a foreign State". . . ; that although the Russian decree affected the death of the parent company, the situs of the property of the New York branch was in New York; and that no principle of law forces New York to forsake the method of distribution authorized in the earlier appeal . . . and to hold that "the method which in 1931 conformed to the exactions of justice and equity must be rejected because retroactively it has become unlawful.". . .

It is one thing to hold as was done in *Guaranty Trust Co. v. United States* (1938) . . . that under the Litvinov Assignment the United States did not acquire "a right free of a preexisting infirmity" such as the running of the statute of limitations against the Russian Government, its assignor. Unlike the problem presented here and in the Moscow F. Ins.

Co. Case, that holding in no way sanctions the asserted power of New York to deny enforcement of a claim under the Litvinov Assignment because of an overriding policy of the State which denies validity in New York of the Russian decrees on which the assigned claims rest. That power was denied New York in *United States* v. *Belmont* (1937). . . . With one qualification to be noted, the Belmont Case is determinative of the present controversy.

That case involved the right of the United States under the Litvinov Assignment to recover from a custodian or stakeholder in New York funds which had been nationalized and appropriated by the Russian decrees.

This Court, speaking through Mr. Justice Sutherland, held that the conduct of foreign relations is committed by the Constitution to the political departments of the Federal Government; that the propriety of the exercise of that power is not open to judicial inquiry; and that recognition of a foreign sovereign conclusively binds the courts and "is retroactive and validates all actions and conduct of the government so recognized from the commencement of its existence.". . . It further held . . . that recognition of the Soviet Government, the establishment of diplomatic relations with it, and the Litvinov Assignment were "all parts of one transaction, resulting in an international compact between the two governments." After stating that "in respect of what was done here, the Executive had authority to speak as the sole organ" of the national government, it added . . . : "The assignment and the agreements in connection therewith did not, as in the case of treaties, as that term is used in the treaty making clause of the Constitution (Art. 2, sec. 2), require the advice and consent of the Senate." It held . . . that the "external powers of the United States are to be exercised without regard to state laws or policies. The supremacy of a treaty in this respect has been recognized from the beginning." And it added that "all international compacts and agreements" are to be treated with similar dignity for the reason that "complete power over international affairs is in the national government and is not and cannot be subject to any curtailment or interference on the part of the several states.". . . This Court did not stop to inquire whether in fact there was any policy of New York which enforcement of the Litvinov Assignment would infringe since "no state policy can prevail against the international compact here involved.". . .

*　　　*　　　*

The holding in the Belmont Case is therefore determinative of the present controversy [and] . . . forecloses any relief to the Russian corporation. For this Court held in that case . . . : ". . . our Constitution, laws and policies have no extraterritorial operation, unless in respect of our own citizens. . . . What another country has done in the way of taking over property of its nationals, and especially of its corporations, is not a matter for judicial consideration here. Such nationals must look to their own government for any redress to which they may be entitled."

But it is urged that different considerations apply in case of the foreign creditors to whom the New York Court of Appeals . . . ordered distribution of these funds. The argument is that their rights in these funds have vested by virtue of the New York decree; that to deprive them of the property would violate the Fifth Amendment which extends its protection to aliens as well as to citizens; and that the Litvinov Assignment cannot deprive New York of its power to administer the balance of the fund in accordance with its laws for the benefit of these creditors.

* * *

If the President had the power to determine the policy which was to govern the question of recognition, then the Fifth Amendment does not stand in the way of giving full force and effect to the Litvinov Assignment. To be sure, aliens as well as citizens are entitled to the protection of the Fifth Amendment. . . . A State is not precluded, however, by the Fourteenth Amendment from according priority to local creditors as against creditors who are nationals of foreign countries and whose claims arose abroad. . . . By the same token, the Federal Government is not barred by the Fifth Amendment from securing for itself and our nationals priority against such creditors. And it matters not that the procedure adopted by the Federal Government is globular and involves a regrouping of assets. There is no Constitutional reason why this Government need act as the collection agent for nationals of other countries when it takes steps to protect itself or its own nationals on external debts. There is no reason why it may not through such devices as the Litvinov Assignment make itself and its nationals whole from assets here before it permits such assets to go abroad in satisfaction of claims of aliens made elsewhere and not incurred in connection with business conducted in this country. The fact that New York has marshaled the claims of the foreign creditors here involved and authorized their payment does not give them immunity from that general rule.

. . . The powers of the President in the conduct of foreign relations included the power, without consent of the Senate, to determine the public policy of the United States with respect to the Russian nationalization decrees. "What government is to be regarded here as representative of a foreign sovereign state is a political rather than a judicial question, and is to be determined by the political department of the government." *Guaranty Trust Co.* v. *United States* . . . That authority is not limited to a determination of the government to be recognized. It includes the power to determine the policy which is to govern the question of recognition. Objections to the underlying policy as well as objections to recognition are to be addressed to the political department and not to the courts. . . . Power to remove such obstacles to full recognition as settlement of claims of our nationals . . . certainly is a modest implied power of the President who is the "sole organ of the federal government in the field of international relations." *United States* v. *Curtiss-Wright Export Corp.* . . . Effectiveness in handling the delicate problems of foreign relations requires no less. Unless such a power exists, the power of recognition might be thwarted or seriously diluted. No such obstacle can be placed in the way of rehabilitation of relations between this country and another nation, unless the historic conception of the powers and responsibilities of the President in the conduct of foreign affairs . . . is to be drastically revised. It was the judgment of the political department that full recognition of the Soviet Government required the settlement of all outstanding problems including the claims of our nationals. Recognition and the Litvinov Assignment were interdependent. We would usurp the executive function if we held that that decision was not final and conclusive in the courts.

"All constitutional acts of power, whether in the executive or in the judicial department, have as much legal validity and obligation as if they proceeded from the legislature, . . ." The Federalist, No. 64. A treaty is a "Law of the Land" under the supremacy clause (Art. 6, Cl. 2) of the Constitution. Such international compacts and agreements as the Litvinov Assignment have a similar dignity. . . .

. . . state law must yield when it is inconsistent with or impairs the policy or provisions of a treaty or of an international compact or agreement. . . .

*   *   *

The action of New York in this case amounts in substance to a rejection of a part of the policy underlying recognition by this nation of Soviet Russia. Such power is not accorded a State in our constitutional system. To permit it would be to sanction a dangerous invasion of Federal authority. For it would "imperil the amicable relations between governments and vex the peace of nations.". . . It would tend to disturb that equilibrium in our foreign relations which the political departments of our national government had diligently endeavored to establish.

We repeat that there are limitations on the sovereignty of the States. No state can require our foreign policy to conform to its own domestic policies. Power over external affairs is not shared by the States; it is vested in the national government exclusively. It need not be so exercised as to conform to state laws or state policies whether they be expressed in constitutions, statutes, or judicial decrees. And the policies of the States become wholly irrelevant to judicial inquiry, when the United States, acting within its constitutional sphere, seeks enforcement of its foreign policy in the courts. For such reasons, Mr. Justice Sutherland stated in *United States* v. *Belmont*, . . . "In respect of all international negotiations and compacts, and in respect of our foreign relations generally, state lines disappear. As to such purposes the State of New York does not exist."

We hold that the right to the funds or property in question became vested in the Soviet Government as the successor to the First Russian Insurance Co.; that this right has passed to the United States under the Litvinov Assignment; and that the United States is entitled to the property as against the corporation and the foreign creditors.

The judgment is reversed and the Cause is remanded to the Supreme Court of New York for proceedings not inconsistent with this opinion.

Reversed.

*   *   *

(Reed, J. and Jackson, J. did not participate in the consideration or decision of this case; Frankfurter, J. wrote a concurring opinion; Stone, J. and Roberts, J. dissented.)

Dissenting Opinion of Chief Justice Stone

I think the judgment should be affirmed.

*   *   *

We have no concern here with the wisdom of the rules of law which the New York courts have adopted in this case or their consonance with the most enlightened principles of jurisprudence. State questions do not become federal questions because they are difficult or because we may think that the state courts have given wrong answers to them. The only questions before us are whether New York has constitutional authority to adopt its own rules of law defining rights in property located in the state, and if so whether that authority has been curtailed by the exercise of a superior federal power by recognition of the Soviet Government and acceptance of its assignment to the United States of claims against American nationals, including the New York property.

I shall state my grounds for thinking that the pronouncements in the Belmont Case, on which the Court relies for the answer to these questions, are without the support of reason or accepted principles of law. No one doubts that the Soviet decrees are the acts of the government of the Russian state which is sovereign in its own territory, and that in consequence of our recognition of that government they will be so treated by our State Department. As such, when they affect property which was located in Russia at the time of their promulgation, they are subject to inquiry if at all only through our State Department and not in our courts . . . But the property to which the New York judgment relates has at all relevant times been in New York in the custody of the Superintendent of Insurance as security for the policies of the insurance company, and is now in the Superintendent's custody as Liquidator acting under the direction of the New York courts. . . . In administering and distributing the property thus within their control, the New York courts are free to apply their own rules of law including their own doctrines of conflict of laws . . . except in so far as they are subject to the requirements of the full faith and credit clause—a clause applicable only to the judgments and public acts of states of the Union and not those of foreign states. . . .

This Court has repeatedly decided that the extent to which a state court will follow the rules of law of a recognized foreign country in preference to its own is wholly a matter of comity, and that in the absence of relevant treaty obligations the application in the courts of a state of its own rules of law rather than those of a foreign country raises no federal question. . . .

*   *   *

Recognition, like treaty making, is a political act and both may be upon terms and conditions. But that fact no more forecloses this Court, where it is called upon to adjudicate private rights, from inquiry as to what those terms and conditions are than it precludes, in like circumstances, a court's ascertaining the true scope and meaning of a treaty. Of course the national power may by appropriate constitutional means override the power of states and the rights of individuals. But without collision between them there is no such loss of power or impairment of rights, and it cannot be known whether state law and private rights collide with political acts expressed in treaties or executive agreements until their respective boundaries are defined.

It would seem therefore that in deciding this case some inquiry should have been made to ascertain what public policy or binding rule of conduct with respect to state power and individual rights has been proclaimed by the recognition of the Soviet Government and the assignment of its claims to the United States. The mere act of recognition and the bare transfer of the claims of the Soviet Government to the United States can of themselves hardly be taken to have any such effect, and they can be regarded as intended to do so only if that purpose is made evident by their terms, read in the light of diplomatic exchanges between the two countries and of the surrounding circumstances. Even when courts deal with the language of diplomacy, some foundation must be laid for inferring an obligation where previously there was none, and some expression must be found in the conduct of foreign relations which fairly indicates an intention to assume it. Otherwise courts rather than the executive may shape and define foreign policy which the executive has not adopted.

We are not pointed to anything on the face of the documents or in the diplomatic correspondence which even suggests that the United States was to be placed in a better position with respect to the claim which it now asserts, than was the Soviet Government and nationals. Nor is there any intimation in them that recognition was to give to prior public acts of the Soviet Government any greater extraterritorial effect than attaches to such acts occurring after recognition—acts which by the common understanding of English and American courts are ordinarily deemed to be without extraterritorial force, and which in any event have never before rules of law to foreign-owned property within their territory. . . .

Recognition opens our courts to the recognized government and its nationals, . . . It accepts the acts of that government within its own territory as the acts of the sovereign, including its acts as a de facto government before recognition, . . . But until now recognition of a foreign government by this Government has never been thought to serve as a full faith and credit clause compelling obedience here to the laws and public acts of the recognized government with respect to property and transactions in this country. One could as well argue that by the Soviet Government's recognition of our own government, which accompanied the transactions now under consideration, it had undertaken to apply in Russia the New York law applicable to Russian property in New York. . . .

*   *   *

By transferring claims of every kind, against American nationals, to the United States and leaving to it their collection, the parties necessarily remitted to the courts of this country the determination of the amounts due upon this Government's undertaking to report the amounts collected as "preparatory to a final settlement of the claims and counterclaims" asserted by the two governments. They thus ended the necessity of diplomatic discussion of the validity of the claims, and so removed a probable source of friction between the two countries. In all this I can find no hint that the rules of decision in American courts were not to be those afforded by the law customarily applied in those courts. But if it was the purpose of either government to override local law and policy of the states and to prescribe a different rule of decision from that hitherto recognized by any court, it would seem to have been both natural and needful to have expressed it in some form of undertaking indicating such an intention. . . . Treaties, to say nothing of executive agreements and assignments which are mere transfers of rights, have hitherto been construed not to override state law or policy unless it is reasonably evident from their language that such was the intention. . . .

Under our dual system of government there are many circumstances in which the legislative and executive branches of the national government may, by affirmative action expressing its policy, enlarge the exercise of federal authority and thus diminish the power which otherwise might be exercised by the states. It is indispensable to the orderly administration of the system that such alteration of powers and the consequent impairment of state and private rights should not turn on conceptions of policy which if ever entertained by the only branch of the government authorized to adopt it, has been left unexpressed. It is not for this Court to adopt policy, the makings of which has been by the Constitution committed to other branches of the government. It is not its function to supply a policy where none has been declared or defined and none can be inferred.

Mr. Justice Roberts joins in this opinion.

Revision and Renunciation of Treaties

Breaches of contract, of course, give grounds for legal action. The unilateral denunciation of a treaty, usually on allegations of bad faith by the other party or on materially changed circumstances, must face political and legal consequences. Part of the cause of breaches of international obligations, however, has been the difficulty of revising treaties between nations when the circumstances of their agreements are no longer what they were (*rebus non sic stantibus*). Assuming that treaties were binding and that no adjustments could be made without the consent of the contracting parties, international law has labored under the burden of a dynamic world community tied to rigid legal instruments. Article 19 of the League of Nations Covenant recognized the problem by stating that the Assembly might from time to time advise League members to reconsider treaties that had become inapplicable, but the article was never acted on. The United Nations Charter does not deal with the revision of treaties.

The improved drafting of treaty documents, which increasingly provide time limits for a renewal or denunciation of the terms, has given some flexibility to the awkward problem of the revision of international arrangements. But the phenomenal appearance of hundreds upon hundreds of multilateral international conventions from the end of the 19th century onward and the concomitant establishment of permanent international organizations and agencies have cast doubt on the customary rule of international law that a treaty may not be revised or terminated unless all parties consent to it.

If every technical modification of a basic multilateral treaty, such as the one that governs the International Telecommunications Union, required the express consent of each and every one of the contracting states, rules to meet changing circumstances would be awkward and slow, paralyzing the functions of the organizations. Thus, in a limited area of international relations the parties to a treaty have consented in advance to be bound by qualified majorities on certain activities.

Rule making on technical matters in the specialized agencies is one illustration. The Security Council of the United Nations, by the vote of nine states including the five permanent members, may legally call on states to support peacekeeping activities; the General Assembly, by a two-third vote, may assess member states of the United Nations for the budget. Nevertheless, the right of a state to withdraw from any of these international organizations or agencies to which the state has voluntarily committed itself has never been legally challenged, and would be a course open to any state unwilling to accept any revision of the international convention.

The unilateral denunciation or breach of a treaty can lead to grave international consequences. States have frequently alleged that they would no longer be bound by a previous engagement due to changed circumstances, bad faith of the other contracting power, incapacity to perform the obligations by reason of municipal law, and so forth. The burden of justifying the denial of an international obligation rests on the denunciatory state. Furthermore, as the Permanent Court of International Justice observed,

> It is a principle of international law that the breach of an engagement involves an obligation to make reparation in an adequate form. Reparation therefore is the indispensable complement of the failure to apply a convention and there is no necessity for this to be stated in the convention itself.[8]

Case law in this highly politicized area of international relations remains scant. Too often in the past, force or threats of force have been used by stronger states against weaker ones to redress alleged breaches of international obligations. Even with the United Nations Charter, diplomatic or economic retaliation by states for allegedly broken agreements cannot be ruled out, while the United Nations itself provides for sanctions against those who fail to honor their Charter obligations.

Suspension and Termination

Whether a treaty that has been denounced by one party is still in force poses a ticklish question for judges. Another enigma is whether a multilateral convention governing a particular subject retains its legal force when a later multilateral convention governing the same subject fails to receive all the accessions of the original parties.

As already indicated, states may claim that circumstances have so completely changed since a treaty was consummated that its legal effect has been nullified. In 1941, for example, the Attorney General believed that an International Load Line Convention no longer bound the United States. Of the 36 states that had ratified or acceded to the convention, 10 were at war and 16 were under military occupation. He wrote:

> . . . the implicit assumption of normal peacetime international trade, which is at the foundation of the International Load Line Convention, no longer exists. . . . It is a well-established principle of international law, rebus sic stantibus, that a treaty ceases to be binding when the basic conditions upon

---

[8] *Chorzow Factory (Jurisdiction) Case,* 1927 P.C.I.J., Series A, No. 9, p. 21.

which it was founded have essentially changed. Suspension of the convention is the unquestioned right of a state adversely affected by such essential change.[9]

But the allegation of changed circumstances remains a double-edged sword, always ready to cut both ways and destroy the bonds of obligation. This is particularly true when issues and interpretation rest before national tribunals, and states hesitate to resolve the test of rational determination before an international court.

No clearer mark of changed circumstances exists than the outbreak of war between contracting states. Historically, there has been a presumption, but not a conclusion, that war abrogated all bilateral treaties between belligerent states. As recently as 1949, the French Court of Cassation held that all ordinary bilateral treaties between Italy and France had been terminated by the outbreak of World War II.[10]

American courts have taken a different view. "International law today does not preserve treaties or annul them regardless of the effect produced. It deals with such problems pragmatically, preserving or annulling as the necessities of war exact."[11]

The United States apparently regarded virtually all its bilateral treaties with enemy states of World War II as at least suspended, although a few had provisions that remained in force throughout the world.

Treaties of alliance would obviously be nullified by a state of war, while treaties of cession or boundaries, as completed acts or regulating the conduct of hostilities, surely would survive. But in between is a large area of doubt that can only be put to the judgment of a court, with the expectation that treaties compatible with a state of war will be enforced, while treaties incompatible with hostilities will not. On extradition, in particular, the Department of State regarded its treaty with Spain abrogated after war in 1898, while apparently its treaty with Germany was suspended and not revived during and after World War I.

The modern trend is for peace settlements to specify what treaties shall be revived between former enemy states. Nevertheless, important distinctions between termination and suspension still exist for the affected parties, and words have ways of being interpreted differently by different people. Today, a general belief exists that, under international law, multilateral treaties are only suspended by war or, in the case of conventions on the conduct of war, continued. Yet, the same caution must be exercised in generalizing about such a "principle" as about any other until an adequate number of cases have been heard by both national and international

---

[9] 4 Opinions of the Attorney General 119.

[10] Actually, two sections of this Supreme Court of France held different opinions, but the full court held that war abrogates any kind of treaty, other than those expressly designed to regulate warfare or to continue during warfare. "If the question comes before the International Court of Justice, it is likely that it would be decided in the manner followed by the French Courts." See J. G. Castel, "Comments on Effect of War on Bilateral Treaties," *Michigan Law Review*, Vol. 566 (1953), p. 571.

[11] *Techt* v. *Hughes*, 254 U.S. 643 (1920).

tribunals. Even more to the point in the future of this dynamic world community will be the clarification of terms like "war" and "belligerents" under the United Nations Charter.

In the following cases, *Argento* v. *Horn* illustrates the effect of war on a treaty of extradition between Italy and the United States; *Zschernig* v. *Miller* deals with a treaty between the United States and Germany that not only survived a war between them and a new treaty but also remained in force for an area over which Germany could not exercise sovereignty.

ARGENTO v. HORN
United States Court of Appeals, 1957
241 F. 2d 258

Stewart, Circuit Judge

*   *   *

Appellant's primary demand for freedom is based upon a most fundamental contention. It is his claim that there exists no valid extradition treaty between the United States of America and the Republic of Italy, and that in the absence of such a treaty, there is no legal authority for the surrender to Italy of a fugitive in the United States. The appellant also contends that several items of evidence were improperly admitted by the Commissioner, and that if they had been excluded, there would have been no evidence to connect him with any crime committed in Italy.

Without question the appellant is on sound ground in asserting that he cannot be extradited to Italy in the absence of a valid treaty so providing. That the Executive is without inherent power to seize a fugitive criminal and surrender him to a foreign nation has long been settled. . . .

While Congress might conceivably have authorized extradition in the absence of a treaty, it has not done so. . . .

*   *   *

A treaty of extradition was concluded between the two nations in 1868, 15 Stat. 629. Valid amendments were made to the treaty in 1869 and 1885, 16 Stat. 767 and 24 Stat. 1001. Murder was one of the crimes made extraditable by the treaty.

On December 11, 1941, 55 Stat. 797, the Congress of the United States declared that a state of war existed between the United States and Italy. At the conclusion of the war a treaty of peace was concluded, effective September 15, 1947. 61 Stat. 1245. This peace treaty, which was duly ratified by the United States Senate, provided in Article 44 as follows:

"1. Each Allied or Associated Power will notify Italy, within a period of six months from the coming into force of the present Treaty, which of its pre-war bilateral treaties with Italy it desires to keep in force or revive. Any provisions not in conformity with the present Treaty shall, however, be deleted from the above-mentioned treaties."

*   *   *

On February 6, 1948, the Secretary of State of the United States notified the Republic of Italy that the United States desired to keep in force or revive, among others, the Extradition Treaty of 1868, as amended.

It is the appellant's position that under established principles of international law the outbreak of war between Italy and the United States in 1941 operated to abrogate completely the extradition treaty previously existing between the two nations. That being so, the appellant argues that in order to revive the extradition treaty it was necessary to make a new treaty, and that a new treaty under the Constitution of the United States could have been made only by the President, with the explicit concurrence of the Senate by a two-thirds vote. U.S. Const. Article II, Section 2. The appellees concede in their brief, as they obviously must, "that it would . . . require the concurring action of the President and the Senate to re-enact a treaty once dead as distinguished from one which is dormant or held in abeyance. . . ."

Whether the war between Italy and the United States completely annulled the previous extradition treaty is thus the central question before us. If the war did have that effect, the appellant is correct in his position that there is now no treaty of extradition between the two nations, since it is conceded that the "notification" of February 6, 1948, was not submitted to the United States Senate for its advice and consent.

Early publicists adopted the view that war *ipso facto* abrogates all treaties between the belligerent nations. In more recent times, however, this theory has been rejected by the textwriters in international law, and it seems never to have been espoused by courts in the United States.

*   *   *

While it is therefore settled, at least in this country, that all treaties are not automatically abrogated by the outbreak of war between the parties, it is not easy to postulate an applicable standard to determine whether a particular treaty has survived a war. The difficulty was stated more definitely than was the solution in *Karnuth v. United States*, 1929, 279 U.S. 231, at page 236, 49 S.Ct. 274, at page 276, 73 L.Ed. 677:

"The effect of war upon treaties is a subject in respect of which there are widely divergent opinions. The doctrine sometimes asserted, especially by the older writers, that war *ipso facto* annuls treaties of every kind between the warring nations, is repudiated by the great weight of modern authority; and the view now commonly accepted is that 'whether the stipulations of a treaty are annulled by war depends upon their intrinsic character.' 5 Moore's Digest of International Law, sec. 779, p. 383. But as to precisely what treaties fall and what survive, under this designation, there is lack of accord. The authorities, as well as the practice of nations, present a great contrariety of views. The law of the subject is still in the making, and, in attempting to formulate principles at all approaching generality, courts must proceed with a good deal of caution. But there seems to be fairly common agreement that at least the following treaty obligations remain in force: Stipulations in respect of what shall be done in a state of war; treaties of cession, boundary, and the like; provisions giving the right to citizens or subjects of one of the high contracting powers to continue to hold and transmit land in the territory of the other; and, generally, provisions which represent completed acts. On the other hand, treaties of amity, of alliance, and the like, having a political character, the object of which 'is to promote relations of harmony between nation and nation,' are generally regarded as belonging to the class of treaty stipulations that are absolutely annulled by war. Id., p. 385, quoting Calvo, Droit Int. (4th Ed.) IV. 65, sec. 1931."

Counsel have cited to us no decision, and we have found none, specifically relating to the effect of war upon a treaty of extradition. Such a treaty does not conveniently fit into either of the alternative classifications set out in the Karnuth opinion quoted above. If the question were to be decided in a vacuum, the conclusion could only be that it is extremely doubtful that war *ipso facto* abrogates a treaty of extradition. Fortunately, however, the question need not be so decided, but can and must be decided against the background of the actual conduct of the two nations involved, acting through the political branches of their governments.

*   *   *

The consummation of the treaty of peace with Italy in 1947 containing Article 44 providing for "notification" by the United States of each prewar bilateral treaty it desired to keep in force or revive, the ratification of that treaty by the United States Senate, the subsequent notification by our State Department with regard to the extradition treaty, and the conduct of the political departments of the two nations in the ensuing nine years, evidencing their unqualified understanding that the extradition treaty is in full force and effect, all make it obvious that the political departments of the two governments considered the extradition treaty not abrogated but merely suspended during hostilities. There is, to be sure, a certain circuity of reasoning in deciding that the parties did not need to make a new treaty of extradition for the reason that they did not in fact make one. Yet it is exactly that pragmatic and cautious approach that, if the question is doubtful, the authorities enjoin. *Terlinden* v. *Ames*, 184, U.S. 270, 22 S.ct. 484, supra. "A construction of a treaty by the political department of the Government, while not conclusive upon a court called upon to construe such a treaty in a matter involving personal rights, is nevertheless of much weight.". . .

It is our conclusion that the treaty of extradition between the United States and Italy was not terminated but merely suspended during the war, and that it is now in effect.

*   *   *

ZSCHERNIG v. MILLER
Supreme Court of Oregon, 1966
412 P. 2d 781

Holman, Justice

Pauline Schrader, a resident of Oregon, died intestate on September 30, 1962. She left an estate comprised of both real and personal property. Her next of kin were a brother and sister, two nieces and two nephews, all of whom are nonresident aliens residing in the Soviet-occupied zone of Germany, hereinafter referred to as East Germany. These relatives as plaintiffs, brought a proceeding for a determination of heirship in their favor. This was contested by the State of Oregon, through its State Land Board, which requested that the property be escheated to the state.

ORS 111.070 provides that the right of nonresident aliens to take property from Oregon estates is dependent upon (1) the reciprocal right of the citizens of the United States similarly to take property from estates in the country of which the alien is an inhabitant or citizen; (2) the right of citizens of the United States to receive in this country money originating from estates in such foreign country; and (3) proof that such aliens will receive the benefit of money or property from estates in this state without confiscation in whole or in part by such foreign country. The statute further provides that if these three prerequisites are not found to exist and there are no other heirs, the property will escheat to the State of Oregon. . . .

The trial court found that the evidence did not establish the existence of reciprocal rights to take property from or to receive the proceeds of East German estates at the date of decedent's death, that ORS 111.070 was valid and controlling, and that the proceeds of the estate escheated to the State of Oregon. Plaintiffs appealed.

*   *   *

Plaintiffs refer this court to Article IX, paragraph 3 of the Treaty of Friendship, Commerce and Navigation with the Federal Republic of Germany, October 29, 1954 . . . (effective July 14, 1956), hereinafter referred to as the 1954 Treaty, which was negotiated by the United States with the government having jurisdiction over that territory known popularly as West Germany. They contend that it extends to them, as East German residents, reciprocal rights of inheritance.

*   *   *

This raises the question whether East German residents are entitled to the benefits of the treaty. Plaintiffs contend that all citizens of Germany,

East and West, are encompassed by the terms of the treaty because the state of Germany and its nationals continue to exist despite Germany's defeat and occupation by the allied forces. . . . The plaintiffs correctly contend that the West German government is the only legally constituted government of the state of Germany recognized by the United States. . . . From this line of reasoning they deduce that the 1954 Treaty entered into with the United States by the West German government was for the benefit of all Germans.

* * *

. . . The "territories" referred to are delineated by Article XXVI of the treaty, which provides, in part:

"1. The territories to which the present Treaty extends shall comprise all areas of land and water under the sovereignty or authority of each Party, other than the Panama Canal Zone and the Trust Territory of the Pacific Islands.

2. The present Treaty shall also apply . . . to Land Berlin which for the purposes of the present Treaty comprises those areas over which the Berlin Senate exercises jurisdiction."

This language seems to say that the 1954 Treaty was meant to apply only to that geographic area of Germany over which the government of West Germany exercises its jurisdiction.

* * *

. . . The State Department of the United States has declared the position of our government with respect to Article XXVI of the 1954 Treaty as follows:

"Pursuant to that provision in Article XXVI, therefore, the treaty applies with respect to all territory under United States jurisdiction other than that specifically excluded and to all territory under the sovereignty or authority of the Federal Republic of Germany. Consequently, the 1954 treaty does not apply with respect to the territory commonly referred to as East Germany." . . .

To the contrary, however, the position of the West German government, as contained in a Foreign Office certificate issued at Bonn on September 30, 1963, and introduced into evidence, is as follows:

"It is the position of the Government of the Federal Republic of Germany that rights granted by Article IX, Paragraph 3 of the Treaty of Friendship, Commerce and Navigation . . . are due and accorded to all German citizens. A citizenship of the Federal Republic of Germany as distinct from a citizenship of the Soviet occupied zone which might possibly give rise to a different application of Article IX, Paragraph 3 of the said treaty does not exist."

It is the belief of this court that neither German citizenship nor nationality has real bearing on this issue because territorial application of the 1954 Treaty, by the terms of Article XXVI, is governed by sovereignty. The West German government has no sovereign authority over that geographical area known as East Germany. . . . We believe it was not the intent of the United States and West Germany, at the time of making the 1954 Treaty, to extend its provisions to residents of East Germany.

*   *   *

Plaintiffs contend that if the 1954 Treaty is inapplicable Articles IV and XXV of the Treaty of Friendship, Commerce and Consular Rights with Germany, December 8, 1923 . . . (effective October 14, 1925) amended June 3, 1935 . . . hereinafter referred to as the 1923 Treaty, are applicable.

The state of Oregon contends that the 1923 Treaty has been abrogated by virtue of subsequent events. Article XXVIII of the 1954 Treaty with the West German government provides as follows:

"The present Treaty shall replace and terminate provisions in force in Articles I through V . . . of the treaty of friendship, commerce and consular rights between the United States of America and Germany, signed at Washington December 8, 1923. . . ."

The 1954 Treaty thus purports to abrogate Article IV of the 1923 Treaty dealing with the rights of individuals to take property. However, the 1954 Treaty, as previously pointed out, explicitly extends only to those areas over which West Germany has sovereignty. This does not include East Germany. Its provisions would therefore not affect the application of the 1923 Treaty to East Germany. This conclusion has also been reached by the United States State Department. . . .

*   *   *

Since the enactment of the 1923 Treaty, World War II has ensued, Germany has been defeated and occupied, and the Soviet government has created a regime in East Germany which is not recognized by the United States as a legal government. The United States government still treats East Germany as Soviet-occupied territory of Germany. No treaty of peace has ever been consummated. What then is the status of the 1923 Treaty as it relates to East Germany?

In considering whether the many changes in Germany's status would abrogate the treaty, the case of Clark v. Allen, 331 U.S. 503, 67 S.Ct. 1431, 91 L.Ed. 1963 (1947), must be considered. . . .

*   *   *

The court there held that the 1923 Treaty between the United States and Germany was not entirely abrogated by the outbreak of World War II and the enactment of the Trading with the Enemy Act. It held that the treaty provisions regarding descent and distribution of property were still in effect. The court said as follows:

"We start from the premise that the outbreak of war does not necessarily suspend or abrogate treaty provisions. Society for the Propagation of the Gospel in Foreign Parts v. Town of New Haven, 8 Wheat. 464. . . . There may of course be such an incompatibility between a particular treaty provision and the maintenance of a state of war as to make clear that it should not be enforced. Karnuth v. United States, 279 U.S. 231. . . . Or the Chief Executive or the Congress may have formulated a national policy quite inconsistent with the enforcement of a treaty in whole or in part. This was the view stated in Techt v. Hughes, supra, and we believe it to be the correct one. . . . 331 U.S. 508–509. . . .

*   *   *

Concerning the continued applicability of the 1923 Treaty, Mr. Justice Douglas said . . .

". . . We have no reliable evidence of the intention of the high contracting parties outside the words of the present treaty. The attitude and conduct under earlier treaties, reflecting as they did numerous contingencies and conditions, leave no sure guide to the construction of the present treaty. Where the relevant historical sources and the instrument itself give no plain indication that it is to become inoperative in whole or in part on the outbreak of war, we are left to determine, as Techt v. Hughes, supra, indicates, whether the provision under which rights are asserted is incompatible with national policy in time of war. So far as the right of inheritance of realty under Article IV of the present treaty is concerned, we find no incompatibility with national policy, for reasons already given."

What of the effect of the events subsequent to the termination of World War II? Is the provision of the treaty under which the right to inherit is asserted incompatible with present national policy? At the time Clark v. Allen, supra, was decided the war was over and Germany had been occupied by the Allies. The court said as follows:

"It is argued, however, that the Treaty of 1923 with Germany must be held to have failed to survive the war, since Germany, as a result of its defeat and the occupation by the Allies, has ceased to exist as an independent national or international community. *But the question whether a state is in a position to perform its treaty obligations is essentially a political question.* Terlinden v. Ames, 184 U.S. 270. . . . We find no evidence that the political departments have considered the collapse and surrender of Germany as putting an end to such provisions of the treaty as survived the outbreak of the war or the obligation of either party in respect to them. . . . 331 U.S. at 514 . . . (emphasis ours).

The world political situation has vastly changed in the nearly twenty years since the decision in Clark v. Allen, supra. As previously pointed out, the Soviet government has purported to turn over power in East Germany to a regime which is not recognized by the United States. However, the executive branch of the United States government, which is charged with the negotiation and interpretation of treaties, has recently indicated publicly its attitude concerning the continued effectiveness of Article IV of the 1923 Treaty and its application to East Germany.

"[The 1954] Treaty is applicable to the area of Germany constituting the Federal Republic and Land Berlin. It appears that Article IV of the treaty of friendship, commerce, and consular rights between the United States and Germany signed on December 8, 1923 (44 Stat. 2132), which contains provisions relating to rights of inheritance of and succession to property, continues in force with respect to areas of Germany not presently included in the territory of the Federal Republic and Land Berlin. The entry into force of the 1954 treaty between the United States and the Federal Republic, which replaced and terminated Article IV of the 1923 treaty with respect to the area of Germany constituting the Federal Republic and Land Berlin, had no effect on the 1923 treaty with respect to the area of Germany not included in the Federal Republic and Land Berlin. . . .

This indicates that the United States government still considers Article IV of the 1923 Treaty in effect with relation to East Germany. While that attitude of the United States government is not binding upon this court in an adjudication of title to private property, the State Department document is entitled to great weight. . . . In the case of Estate of Nepogodin, 134 Cal. App. 2d 161, 285 P. 2d 672 (1955), the court considered whether communist control of Manchuria, the part of China where decedent's heirs resided, was such to invalidate a treaty with Nationalist China which was used as evidence of reciprocal rights of inheritance. The court there said . . .

". . . The ratification exchange shows that the United States Government did not then consider the conditions existing in China an unsurmountable obstacle to the effectiveness of the Treaty . . .

*   *   *

Terlinder v. Ames, Clark v. Allen, and Estate of Nepogodin all say that the ability of a foreign country to comply with its treaty obligations is essentially a political question. In view of these cases and the present attitude of the State Department, we apply the principle of judicial abstention to the question of whether a foreign state is able to carry out its treaty obligations and therefore whether the United States is still bound. The political department of the federal government particularly charged with the negotiation and enforcement of the treaty in question has determined that the United States is still obligated. We therefore hold Articles IV and XXV of the 1923 Treaty to be still in effect as they apply to the territory of East Germany.

The court realizes there is the practical problem of delivery of any benefits of the real property to the heirs at law in East Germany. The United States government does not recognize the regime established there and has no diplomatic relations with it. . . .

*   *   *

. . . Plaintiffs, therefore, claim the West German Consul is authorized to receive funds for them to be invested for their benefit by the West German government until such time as they may receive the funds.

Although Article XXV of the 1923 Treaty was incorporated into and made a part of the 1954 Treaty, we have, in this opinion, held that the 1954 Treaty does not extend to those persons who reside in that area over which West Germany does not have sovereignty. For that reason West German consular officers have no authority under the 1954 Treaty to act for and receive property for persons residing in East Germany.

*   *   *

The fact that plaintiffs cannot immediately receive the benefit of decedent's real property does not mean that they cannot inherit or own it because we have determined that ORS 111.070 (1) (c), which makes their ability to receive the benefits of the property in East Germany a prerequisite to vesting of title, must yield to Article IV of the 1923 Treaty with Germany. . . . The German heirs at law are now the owners of real property in this state.

*   *   *

FOR FURTHER STUDY

LORD McNAIR. *The Law of Treaties.* Oxford: Clarendon Press, 1961.

HANS BLIX. *Treaty-Making Power.* New York: Frederick A. Praeger, Inc., 1960.

ELBERT M. BYRD, JR. *Treaties and Executive Agreements in the United States.* The Hague: Martinus Nijhoff, 1960.

EDWIN C. HOYT. *The Unanimity Rule in the Revision of Treaties.* The Hague: Martinus Nijhoff, 1959.

J. W. SCHNEIDER. *Treaty-Making Power of International Organizations.* Geneva: Librairie E. Droz, 1959.

STUART HULL McINTYRE. *Legal Effect of World War II on Treaties of the United States.* The Hague: Martinus Nijhoff, 1958.

ROBERT R. WILSON. *The International Law Standard of Treaties of the United States.* Cambridge, Mass.: Harvard University Press, 1953.

IV

Jurisdiction: Title and Transfer of Sovereignty

W HO owns the moon? The question is no longer academic, for space travel has now put this luminous satellite of earth, inspiration of dreams and poetry for so many centuries, within the physical grasp of states on this planet.

International law has just begun to address itself to the problem of jurisdiction over the moon and the planets of the solar system, but for centuries the acquisition and transfer of title to land on earth has been an important element of international law. Discovery and possession may be the beginning of a state's right to sovereignty over an area, but it is not legally conclusive.

In the 15th and 16th centuries, when European states first sent their sailing vessels over the seas to conquer or colonize sparsely inhabited or uninhabited lands, discovery, usually followed by a symbolic act such as planting a cross or a coat of arms, gave a putative right of territorial sovereignty. This was especially true if no other state disputed the claim. Where substantial communities of American Indians, Asians, or Africans had been established, the Europeans employed treaties of cession or purchase, if not outright conquest, to gain the title from the indigenous population. Although the legal concepts of sovereignty hardly matched the understanding of the dominated peoples and fraud often played a role in these transactions, the European states and their colonies maintained and gradually perfected their rights over the succeeding centuries. In due course, such titles have been transmitted to other states by gift, purchase, annexation, revolution, and war—all generally confirmed by treaty or other international agreements.

By the 20th century, however, the idea that discovery alone could gain title received no credence, especially since the technical resources available to states made it possible to explore, exploit, and administer almost any area on earth. In 1928, the Permanent Court of Arbitration held in the *Island of Palmas* case that discovery without occupation gave little evidence of the right to sovereignty. In the Court's words:

> . . . occupation, to constitute a claim to territorial sovereignty, must be effective, that is offer certain guarantees to other states and their nationals. It seems, therefore, incompatible with this rule of positive law that there should be regions which are neither under the effective sovereignty of a state nor without master, but which are reserved for the exclusive influence of one state, in virtue solely of a title of acquisition which is no longer recognized by existing law. . . . For these reasons, discovery alone, without any subsequent act, cannot at the present time suffice to prove sovereignty over the Island of Palmas. . . .[1]

Yet, "effective occupation" itself is a concept much discussed in diplomatic and judicial circles. It is generally understood to mean that occupation by a state in a territory must be: (*a*) peaceful, that is, not an immediately contestable act subject to dispute; (*b*) actual and practical occupation, that is, not merely an assertion or decree of occupation, but physical, political, and legal acts sufficient to show that the state was acting as a sovereign over the area; and (*c*) continuous.

In the *Minquiers and Ecrehos* case, both the United Kingdom and France claimed sovereignty over two groups of islands and rocks off the coast of France in the English Channel. Concerning the Ecrehos area, the International Court of Justice found that:

> . . . the Ecrehos group in the beginning of the thirteenth century was considered and treated as an integral part of the fief of the Channel Isands which were held by the English King, and that the group continued to be under the dominion of that King, who in the beginning of the fourteenth century exercised jurisdiction in respect thereof. The Court further finds that British authorities during the greater part of the nineteenth century and in the twentieth century have exercised State functions in respect of the group. The French Government, on the other hand, has not produced evidence showing that it has any valid title to the group. In such circumstances it must be concluded that the sovereignty over the Ecrehos belongs to the United Kingdom.

With respect to the Minquiers, the Court stated that France did not have valid title because various acts, such as the application of a French national to French authorities for a concession, some official visits, and buoying outside the reefs of the group

> can hardly be considered as sufficient evidence of the intention of that Government to act as sovereign over the islets; nor are those acts of such a character that they can be considered as involving a manifestation of State authority in respect of the islets.

*   *   *

---

[1] U.N. Reports of International Arbitral Awards 829.

. . . sovereignty over the Minquiers belongs to the United Kingdom.[2]

States have also laid claims to territory on the principle of contiguity. Such claims may be not only to accretions along the shores due to river deposits, or deliberate filling as practiced by the Netherlands, but also to islands beyond a state's territorial waters, yet closer to its shores than to any other state. An extension of this assertion is the sector principle for Arctic and Antarctic lands. States such as Canada and the Soviet Union, or Chile and Argentina, have drawn lines from their eastern and western borders to intersect at the north or south pole, respectively. They then assert sovereignty over all the land encompassed by the wedge. Other states that have made claims to the polar regions by discovery and exploration, especially in Antarctica, do not recognize the sector principle as confirming title on adjacent states.

States also claim sovereignty over the seas that fringe their land areas, over the bays that cut into their coastline, over portions of rivers and lakes that form their frontiers with other states, and over the airspace above their surfaces. The distance from the land area of such claims to marginal waters or airspace raises questions of international law and problems of jurisdiction, which will be analyzed in Section V.

The best evidence of the transfer of territorial sovereignty from one state to another is, of course, a treaty detailing the area, the terms of purchase or cession, and so forth. But often treaties yield inadequate evidence. In the *Minquiers and Ecrehos* case, the International Court of Justice examined, without success, treaties dating back to the 13th and 14th centuries in trying to determine whether the United Kingdom or France had acquired title to two small channel islands. Eventually, the Court's judgment had to fall back on the stronger evidence of the United Kingdom's exercise of jurisdiction over these islands.

Moreover, some of the difficulties of drafting and transcribing documents can be seen in the *Case of Sovereignty over Certain Frontier Land*, when Belgium and the Netherlands disputed title to several plots of land at their border.[3] Belgium claimed title by virtue of a Boundary Convention of 1843 and a Descriptive Minute ascribing the plots to Belgium. The Netherlands claimed that an error in the Descriptive Minute vitiated the convention, for a Communal Minute signed in 1841 by burgomasters and officials of both countries had ascribed the plots to the Netherlands. The Court found that not only was the treaty valid and binding on the determination of title for Belgium in 1843, but also that despite various acts of the Netherlands, alleged to be acts of sovereignty, Belgium neither acquiesced to such acts as sovereign acts nor lost its sovereignty by nonassertion of rights. However, the vote was ten to four; Judge Lauterpacht was convinced that the confusion of minutes made the convention void and inapplicable with respect to the determination of title to these

---

[2] Unanimous judgment, with two individual opinions, 1953 I.C.J. Reports 47.
[3] 1959 I.C.J. Reports 209.

plots. Other errors creep into treaty definition. In 1962, the boundary line between Cambodia and Thailand was supposedly governed under a treaty of 1904 by the watershed between the Pnom Dang Rek and Pnom Padang chain of mountains, but the subsequent frontier map placed the temple at Preah Vihear contrarily on the Cambodian side.[4]

Treaties, therefore, will not always be conclusive determinants of title under international law. Where no pertinent treaty exists, effective occupation and the exercise of jurisdiction over a long period of time without contestation by another state can confirm title under international law. Remote islands and areas inhospitable to man, such as Greenland, cannot be occupied very effectively, of course. Until 1921, no state had disputed Denmark's sovereignty over that great frigid island, and until 1931 no other state had even put forth a claim of sovereignty. When settling the dispute between Denmark and Norway, the Permanent Court of International Justice observed that in unsettled or thinly populated areas, "provided that the other state could not make out a superior claim," international tribunals have been satisfied with very little in the exercise of sovereign rights as a justification for title.[5]

In the future, boundary disputes and controversies over title may give additional tests to international law, especially after the recent momentous transfers from European colonial holdings to independent states in Asia and Africa. For example, lines of the Chinese–Indian border are still uncertain, while Pakistan claims Kashmir against India's assertion of sovereignty. In 1962, the Indonesians and Dutch finally settled by negotiation the long disputed status of West Irian (New Guinea). When the Council of Foreign Ministers after World War II was unable to agree on the status of the former Italian colonies of Libya and Somalia, the United Nations itself proved to be the midwife to their creation as independent states. But other maps of American, Asian, or African territories, drawn hastily or inaccurately under earlier European dominance and with doubtful international sanctions, may give rise to controversies.

Most of the disputes will probably be settled by political means, for states naturally display great reluctance to try a case before a dispassionate court when their legal arguments are weak. Guatemala, for example, has claimed for decades that the title to British Honduras (Belize), allegedly ceded to Great Britain by a convention of 1859, has reverted to Guatemala due to annulment of that convention. Although from 1946 to 1951 Great Britain offered to accept the jurisdiction of the International Court of Justice on the claim, Guatemala would only accept the Court's jurisdiction provided the case was decided *ex aequo et bono*, out of fair and good considerations beyond legal norms.

---

[4] *Case Concerning the Temple of Preah Vihear* (*Cambodia* v. *Thailand*), 1962 I.C.J. Reports 6.

[5] *Legal Status of Eastern Greenland Case* (*Denmark* v. *Norway*), P.C.I.J., Series A/B, No. 53, 1933.

Exercise of Sovereignty

In 1955 the International Court of Justice was faced with a challenge to the titles of Portugal over the two enclaves in Indian territory and the right of passage from Portuguese Daman on the coast to the enclaves, which Portugal required to exercise its sovereignty. The Court gave a divided opinion, upholding the title but constraining its exercise through the right of passage. On 18 December 1961, Indian military forces took over the Portuguese territories of Goa, Daman, and Diu. Seven members of the United Nations Security Council called for a cease-fire and withdrawal of the Indian forces from the territories, but the Soviet Union vetoed the resolution with the support of three other members of the Council.

RIGHT OF PASSAGE OVER INDIAN TERRITORY (PORTUGAL v. INDIA)
International Court of Justice, 1960
1960 I.C.J. Reports 4

*   *   *

The present dispute was referred to the Court by an Application filed on 22 December 1955.

In that Application the Government of the Portuguese Republic states that the territory of Portugal in the Indian Peninsula is made up of the three districts of Goa, Daman and Diu. It adds that the district of Daman comprises, in addition to its littoral territory, two parcels of territory completely surrounded by the territory of India which constitute enclaves: Dadra and Nagar-Aveli. It is in respect of the communications between these enclaves and Daman and between each other that the question arises of a right of passage in favour of Portugal through Indian territory, and of a correlative obligation binding upon India. The Application states that in July 1954, contrary to the practice hitherto followed, the Government of India, in pursuance of what the Application calls "the open campaign which it has been carrying on since 1950 for the annexation of Portuguese territories," prevented Portugal from exercising this right of passage. This denial by India having been maintained, it has followed, according to the Application, that the enclaves of Dadra and Nagar-Aveli have been completely cut off from the rest of the Portuguese territory, the Portuguese authorities thus being placed in a position in which it became impossible for them to exercise Portuguese rights of sovereignty there.

It is in that situation, and in order to secure a remedy therefor, that Portugal has referred the matter to the Court.

*   *   *

Accordingly the first question with regard to which the submissions of Portugal call upon the Court to decide is whether, on the eve of the events which occurred at Dadra and at Nagar-Aveli in 1954, Portugal had a right of passage over the territory of India to the extent necessary for the exercise of Portuguese sovereignty over the enclaves, which right was subject to the regulation and control of India.

Portugal asks the Court to hold that it had this right. India asks it to hold that the claim is unfounded.

*   *   *

The Court will now proceed to consider the merits.

It follows from what has been indicated above, that the Court has only three questions to consider on the merits:

(1) The existence in 1954 of a right of passage in Portugal's favour to the extent necessary for the exercise of its sovereignty over the enclaves, exercise of that right being regulated and controlled by India;

(2) Failure by India in 1954 to fulfil its obligation in regard to that right of passage;

(3) In the event of a finding of such failure, the remedy for the resulting unlawful situation.

Portugal claims a right of passage between Daman and the enclaves, and between the enclaves, across intervening Indian territory, to the extent necessary for the exercise of its sovereignty over the enclaves, subject to India's right of regulation and control of the passage claimed, and without any immunity in Portugal's favour. It claims further that India is under obligation so to exercise its power of regulation and control as not to prevent the passage necessary for the exercise of Portugal's sovereignty over the enclaves.

India contends that the right claimed by Portugal is too vague and contradictory to enable the Court to pass judgment upon it by the application of the legal rules enumerated in Article 38 (1) of the Statute. Portugal answers that the right which it claims is definite enough for determination on the basis of international law, and that all that the Court is called upon to do is to declare the existence of the right in favour of Portugal, leaving its actual exercise to be regulated and adjusted between the Parties as the exigencies of the day-to-day situation might require.

India argues that the vague and contradictory character of the right claimed by Portugal is proved by Portugal's admission that on the one hand the exercise of the right is subject to India's regulation and control as the territorial sovereign, and that on the other hand the right is not accompanied by any immunity, even in the case of the passage of armed forces.

*   *   *

In support of its claim, Portugal relies on the Treaty of Poona of 1779 and on *sanads* (decrees), issued by the Maratha ruler in 1783 and 1785, as having conferred sovereignty on Portugal over the enclaves with the right of passage to them.

India objects on various grounds that what is alleged to be the Treaty of 1779 was not validly entered into and never became in law a treaty binding upon the Marathas. The Court's attention has, in this connection, been drawn *inter alia* to the divergence between the different texts of the Treaty placed before the Court and to the absence of any text accepted as authentic by both parties and attested by them or by their duly authorized representatives. The Court does not consider it necessary to deal with these and other objections raised by India to the form of the Treaty and the procedure by means of which agreement upon its terms was reached. It is sufficient to state that the validity of a treaty concluded as long ago as the last quarter of the eighteenth century, in the conditions then prevailing in the Indian Peninsula, should not be judged upon the basis of practices and procedures which have since developed only gradually. The Marathas themselves regarded the Treaty of 1779 as valid and binding upon them, and gave effect to its provisions. The Treaty is frequently referred to as such in subsequent formal Maratha documents, including the two *sanads* 1783 and 1785, which purport to have been issued in pursuance of the Treaty. The Marathas did not at any time cast any doubt upon the validity or binding character of the Treaty.

India contends further that the Treaty and the two *sanads* of 1783 and 1785 taken together did not operate to transfer sovereignty over the assigned villages to Portugal, but only conferred upon it, with respect to the villages, a revenue grant of the value of 12,000 rupees per annum called a *jagir* or *saranjam*.

Article 17 of the Treaty is relied upon by Portugal as constituting a transfer of sovereignty. From an examination of the various texts of that article placed before it, the Court is unable to conclude that the language employed therein was intended to transfer sovereignty over the villages to the Portuguese. There are several instances on the record of treaties concluded by the Marathas which show that, where a transfer of sovereignty was intended, appropriate and adequate expressions like cession "in perpetuity" or "in perpetual sovereignty" were used. The expressions used in the two *sanads* and connected relevant documents establish, on the other hand, that what was granted to the Portuguese was only a revenue tenure called a *jagir* or *saranjam* of the value of 12,000 rupees a year. This was a very common form of grant in India and not a single instance has been brought to the notice of the Court in which such a grant has been construed as amounting to a cession of territory in sovereignty.

It is argued that the Portuguese were granted authority to put down revolt or rebellion in the assigned villages and that this is an indication that they were granted sovereignty over the villages. The Court does not consider that this conclusion is well-founded. If the intention of the Marathas had been to grant sovereignty over the villages to the Portuguese, it would have been unnecessary for the grant to recite that the future sovereign would have authority to quell a revolt or rebellion in his own territory. In the context in which this authorization occurs, it would appear that the intention was that the Portuguese would have authority on behalf of the Maratha ruler and would owe a duty to him to put down any revolt or rebellion in the villages against his authority.

It therefore appears that the Treaty of 1779 and the *sanads* of 1783 and 1785 were intended by the Marathas to effect in favour of the Portuguese only a grant of a *jagir* or *saranjam*, and not to transfer sovereignty over the villages to them.

*   *   *

It is clear from a study of the material placed before the Court that the situation underwent a change with the advent of the British as sovereign of that part of the country in place of the Marathas. The British found the Portuguese in occupation of the villages and exercising full and exclusive administrative authority over them. They accepted the situation as they found it and left the Portuguese in occupation of, and in exercise of exclusive authority over, the villages. The Portuguese held themselves out as sovereign over the villages. The British did not, as successors of the Marathas, themselves claim sovereignty, nor did they accord express recognition of Portuguese sovereignty, over them. The exclusive authority of the Portuguese over the villages was never brought in question. Thus Portuguese sovereignty over the villages was recognized by the British in fact and by implication and was subsequently tacitly recognized by India. As a consequence the villages comprised in the Maratha grant acquired the character of Portuguese enclaves within Indian territory.

*   *   *

It is common ground between the Parties that the passage of private persons and civil officials was not subject to any restrictions, beyond routine control, during these periods. There is nothing on the record to indicate the contrary.

*   *   *

The Court, therefore, concludes that, with regard to private persons, civil officials and goods in general there existed during the British and post-British periods a constant and uniform practice allowing free passage between Daman and the enclaves. This practice having continued over a period extending beyond a century and a quarter unaffected by the change of regime in respect of the intervening territory which occurred when India became independent, the Court is, in view of all the circumstances of the case, satisfied that that practice was accepted as law by the Parties and has given rise to a right and a correlative obligation.

The Court therefore holds that Portugal had in 1954 a right of passage over intervening Indian territory between coastal Daman and the enclaves and between the enclaves, in respect of private persons, civil officials and goods in general, to the extent necessary, as claimed by Portugal, for the exercise of its sovereignty over the enclaves, and subject to the regulation and control of India.

As regards armed forces, armed police and arms and ammunition, the position is different.

It appears that during the British period up to 1878 passage of armed forces and armed police between British and Portuguese possessions was regulated on a basis of reciprocity. No distinction appears to have been made in this respect with regard to passage between Daman and the enclaves. There is nothing to show that passage of armed forces and armed police between Daman and the enclaves or between the enclaves was permitted or exercised as of right.

Paragraph 3 of Article XVIII of the Treaty of Commerce and Extradition of 26 December 1878 between Great Britain and Portugal laid down that the armed forces of the two Governments should not enter the Indian dominions of the other, except for the purposes specified in former Treaties, or for the rendering of mutual assistance as provided for in the Treaty itself, or in consequence of a formal request made by the Party desiring such entry. Subsequent correspondence between the British and Portuguese authorities in India has shown that this provision was applicable to passage between Daman and the enclaves.

* * *

The requirement of a formal request before passage of armed forces could take place was repeated in an agreement of 1913.

* * *

Both with regard to armed forces and armed policy, no change took place during the post-British period after India became independent.

It would thus appear that, during the British and post-British periods, Portuguese armed forces and armed police did not pass between Daman and the enclaves as of right and that, after 1878, such passage could only take place with previous authorization by the British and later by India, accorded either under a reciprocal arrangement already agreed to, or in individual cases. . . .

* * *

The Court is, therefore, of the view that no right of passage in favour of Portugal involving a correlative obligation on India has been established in respect of armed forces, armed policy, and arms and ammunition. . . .

*　　*　　*

Having found that Portugal had in 1954 a right of passage over intervening Indian territory between Daman and the enclaves in respect of private persons, civil officials and goods in general, the Court will proceed to consider whether India has acted contrary to its obligation resulting from Portugal's right of passage in respect of any of these categories.

*　　*　　*

It may be observed that the Governor of Daman was granted the necessary visas for a journey to and back from Dadra as late as 21 July 1954.

The events that took place in Dadra on 21–22 July 1954 resulted in the overthrow of Portuguese authority in that enclave. This created tension in the surrounding Indian territory. Thereafter all passage was suspended by India. India contends that this became necessary in view of the abnormal situation which had arisen in Dadra and the tension created in surrounding Indian territory.

*　　*　　*

In view of the tension then prevailing in intervening Indian territory, the Court is unable to hold that India's refusal of passage to the proposed delegation and its refusal of visas to Portuguese nationals of European origin and to native Indian Portuguese in the employ of the Portuguese Government was action contrary to its obligation resulting from Portugal's right of passage. Portugal's claim of a right of passage is subject to full recognition and exercise of Indian sovereignty over the intervening territory and without any immunity in favour of Portugal. The Court is of the view that India's refusal of passage in those cases was, in the circumstances, covered by its power of regulation and control of the right of passage of Portugal.

For these reasons

THE COURT

*　　*　　*

by eleven votes to four,

finds that Portugal had in 1954 a right of passage over intervening Indian territory between the enclaves of Dadra and Nagar-Aveli and the coastal district of Daman and between these enclaves, to the extent necessary for the exercise of Portuguese sovereignty over the enclaves and subject to the regulation and control of India, in respect of private persons, civil officials and goods in general;

by eight votes to seven,

finds that Portugal did not have in 1954 such a right of passage in respect of armed forces, armed police, and arms and ammunition;

by nine votes to six,

finds that India has not acted contrary to its obligations resulting from Portugal's right of passage in respect of private persons, civil officials and goods in general.

*   *   *

Trusteeship

Until the creation of the League of Nations Covenant in 1919, the General Treaty for the Renunciation of War in 1929, and the Charter of the United Nations in 1945, the acquisition of title by conquest and subjugation was widely recognized. Most titles owe their origins to intimidation or forceful occupation and annexation, gradually recognized by time, peaceful transfer, and general acquiescence. The presumption under the Charter of the United Nations is that member states will respect one another's territory, that they will not use force in their international relations, and that state conquest, in the old sense, is an illegal basis for a claim to sovereignty. For the present, however, the world is still full of challenged titles, whether by nonrecognition, as in the Soviet Union's assertion of sovereignty over Latvia, Lithuania, and Estonia, or by various aspersions, as those made by African statesmen against Portuguese possession of Angola and Mozambique.

The transfer of whole territories in Asia and Africa without the consent of their inhabitants, as spoils of war from the vanquished to the victor, led to a new legal concept of the mandate or, under the Charter of the United Nations, trust, in which title over a territory does not pass from one state to another. At the Berlin Conference of 1885 and the Brussels Conference of 1890, the Great Powers of Europe had already taken account of their rapid exploitation of Africa and exchanged promises to suppress the slave trade and set other standards of civilized conduct for the welfare of the inhabitants of their possessions. But sovereignty over these possessions remained with the European states. Their responsibilities were to their own national consciences. At the end of World War I, the Allied Powers had no intention of returning remote German colonies like Tanganyika and the Cameroons, or Turkish possessions like Syria, which was agitating for national independence, to their former masters. However, a considerable public opinion in both Europe and the United States was repelled by the idea of transferring whole countries and groups of islands, with their peoples, like pieces of real estate from the domain of the defeated empires to the victorious states.

Jan Christian Smuts of South Africa first suggested that the detached possessions be given self-government under the administration of the new League of Nations. A substantial modification of this idea, which had to face the weakness of international administration then and the political strength of the Great Powers, was embodied in a new mandate system. Article 22 of the Covenant of the League of Nations provided that "the tutelage of such peoples," not yet able to stand by themselves under the strenuous conditions of the modern world, "should be entrusted to advanced nations . . . and that this tutelage should be exercised by them as Mandatories on behalf of the League."

The mandate system has been called a sham for the political designs of the mandatory powers, ignoring the wishes of the inhabitants and, in some cases, tantamount to annexation. Nevertheless, while the mandated territories ceased to be under the sovereignty of Germany or Turkey—a fact confirmed by the peace treaties—sovereignty over them did not pass to the mandatory powers.

Following World War II, the League's mandate system was transformed into the trusteeship system of the United Nations. Japan, as a mandatory power for the Marianas, Marshall, and Caroline Islands in the Pacific, was replaced by the United States as a trustee, while Italy became a temporary trustee for Somalia prior to its independence. All the remaining mandates of the League, with the exception of South-West Africa, were brought voluntarily under the trusteeship system by special agreement between the trustees and the United Nations. In the fall of 1966, only three United Nations trust territories—the Pacific Islands (Micronesia), Nauru, and New Guinea—still existed; all the others had achieved a self-governing status by independence or integration with a neighboring state.

In *Brunell* v. *United States*, which follows, the legal status of Saipan in the U.S. Trust Territory of the Pacific Islands was defined with respect to the Federal Tort Claims Act of the United States; in the advisory opinion on the *Status of South-West Africa*, the International Court of Justice stated its view of the international status of that territory and the obligations of South Africa as a League mandatory power with respect to the new United Nations system.

BRUNELL v. UNITED STATES
United States District Court, 1948
77 F Supp. 68

Ryan, District Judge

*   *   *

Plaintiff, a professional entertainer and a citizen of the State of New York residing in this district, alleges that on October 16, 1945 she was lawfully touring in Saipan with a U.S.O. Camp Show, and that while being transported in an army jeep, operated and controlled by a member of the armed forces, the jeep through the negligence and carelessness of the operator ran off the road and struck a tree, as a result of which, and without any negligence on her part, she sustained serious bodily injuries. The complaint contains the following allegations:

"11. That on the 16th day of October, 1945, Saipan was not a foreign country.

"12. That prior to the 16th day of October 1945, Saipan was conquered by the United States Armed Forces and that on the 16th day of October 1945, and ever since, Saipan has been owned, occupied, managed, controlled and administered by the United States of America."

Plaintiff seeks judgment in the sum of $75,000, as compensation for her injuries and necessary expenses.

* * *

Beginning with Vattel, in the middle of the Eighteenth Century (*Droit des Gens,* liv.iii. sections 197, 198), it has been recognized that sovereignty does not arise until the invading belligerent has completely ousted the enemy and has definitely acquired the territory by conquest or by treaty of cession. Wheaton, *International Law,* 6th Ed., points to the line of demarcation existing between mere military occupation and conquest, and complete subjugation, writing (at pp. 780, 781):

"Conquest or complete subjugation implies the permanent subjection of the occupied country to the sovereign of the occupying forces, with the intention that this territory shall be annexed to the dominions of the new sovereign and shall henceforth be considered as a constituent portion thereof; that is, conquest depends on 'firm possession' together with the intention and the capacity to hold the territory so acquired.

"The rights of occupancy, then, cannot be co-extensive with those of sovereignty. They are due to the military exigencies of the invader, and consequently are only provisional. The local inhabitants do not owe the occupant even temporary allegiance; and the national character of the locality is not legally changed."

The status of foreign territory when occupied by the armed forces of the United States was defined in *Fleming* v. *Page* [1850], 9 How. 603, 13 L.Ed. 276, it being held there that although such territory comes under the sovereignty of the United States and that foreign nations are bound to regard it as such, it does not in fact become a part of the United States. And, it was also held that goods imported from Mexican territory occupied by the United States were liable to duties, as coming from a foreign country. The opinion of the Court in *Fleming* v. *Page,* supra, was quoted with approval in *De Lima* v. *Bidwell,* 1900, 182 U.S. 1, at 182, 21 S.Ct. 743, at page 747, 45 L.Ed. 1041:

"In delivering the opinion of the court Mr. Chief Justice Taney observed: 'The United States, it is true, may extend its boundaries by conquest or treaty, and may demand the cession of territory as the condition of peace, in order to indemnify its citizens for the injuries they have suffered, or to reimburse the government for the expenses of the war. But this can be done only by the treaty-making power or the legislative authority, and is not a part of the power conferred upon the President by the declaration of war . . . While it was occupied by our troops, they were in an enemy's country, and not in their own; the inhabitants were still foreigners and enemies, and owed to the United States nothing more than the submission and obedience, sometimes called temporary allegiance, which is due from a conquered enemy when he surrenders to a force which he is unable to resist.' "

And, the Court further said at page 194 of 182 U.S., at page 752 of 21 S.Ct.: "Possession is not alone sufficient as was held in *Fleming* v. *Page;* nor is a treaty ceding such territory sufficient without a surrender of possession."

In the De Lima case, supra, the Supreme Court adopted and approved the principles enunciated by Vattel in the Eighteenth Century. . . . Mr. Chief Justice Marshall in *American Ins. Co.* v. *356 Bales of Cotton,* [1828] 1 Pet. 511, 7 L.Ed. 242, said: "The usage of the world is, if a nation be not entirely subdued, to consider the holding of conquered territory as a mere military occupation until its fate shall be determined at the treaty of peace. If it be ceded by the treaty the acquisition is confirmed, and the ceded territory becomes a part of the nation to which it is annexed, either on the terms stipulated in the treaty of cession or on such as its new master shall impose.". . .

*   *   *

The fact that some twenty-one months after the date of the alleged accident—in July, 1947 the United States became the trustee of Saipan by designation of the United Nations does not change the status of Saipan of October 16, 1945; under the trusteeship, Saipan still remains a foreign country. The United States has only undertaken for an indefinite period to act as trustee of it on behalf and for the benefit of the United Nations.

*   *   *

Congress by the term "foreign country" in the Federal Tort Claims Act, limited the operation of the Act to areas which were actually a component part of political subdivision of the United States. Although, on October 16, 1945, Saipan was in the possession and under the control of the United States by reason of military conquest and occupation, it cannot in any sense be deemed to have been either a component part or a political subdivision of this nation. . . .

*   *   *

We reluctantly come to the conclusion that the Island of Saipan is a foreign country within the exception of the Federal Tort Claims Act. Although plaintiff's claim seems to be both just and meritorious, the court is without power to entertain her action or grant her relief. The claim of plaintiff for the serious injuries she allegedly sustained while performing work of importance to the morale of our armed forces, can be recognized only by special legislation of Congress. Properly presented to the appropriate Congressional Committee, plaintiff's claim will receive just and sympathetic consideration.

Motion granted; complaint dismissed.

STATUS OF SOUTH-WEST AFRICA
International Court of Justice, Advisory Opinion, 1950
1950 I.C.J. Reports 129

*   *   *

On December 6th, 1949, the General Assembly of the United Nations adopted the following resolution:

"The General Assembly,

Recalling its previous resolutions 65 (I) of 14 December 1946, 141 (II) of 1 November 1947 and 227 (III) of 26 November 1948 concerning the Territory of South-West Africa,

Considering that it is desirable that the General Assembly, for its further consideration of the question, should obtain an advisory opinion on its legal aspects,

I. *Decides* to submit the following questions to the International Court of Justice with a request for an advisory opinion which shall be transmitted to the General Assembly before its fifth regular session, if possible:

'What is the international status of the Territory of South-West Africa and what are the international obligations of the Union of South Africa arising therefrom, in particular:

(a) Does the Union of South Africa continue to have international obligations under the Mandate for South-West Africa and, if so, what are those obligations?

(b) Are the provisions of Chapter XII of the Charter applicable and, if so, in what manner, to the Territory of South-West Africa?

(c) Has the Union of South Africa the competence to modify the international status of the Territory of South-West Africa, or, in the event of a negative reply, where does competence rest to determine and modify the international status of the Territory?' "

*   *   *

The Court is of opinion that an examination of the three particular questions submitted to it will furnish a sufficient answer to this general question and that it is not necessary to consider the general question separately. It will therefore begin at once with an examination of the particular questions.

QUESTION (a): *"Does the Union of South Africa continue to have international obligations under the Mandate for South-West Africa and, if so, what are those obligations?"*

The Territory of South-West Africa was one of the German overseas possessions in respect of which Germany, by Article 119 of the Treaty of Versailles, renounced all her rights and titles in favour of the Principal Allied and Associated Powers. When a decision was to be taken with regard to the future of these possessions as well as of other territories which, as a consequence of the war of 1914–1918, had ceased to be under the sovereignty of the States which formerly governed them, and which were inhabited by peoples not yet able to assume a full measure of self-government, two principles were considered to be of paramount importance: the principle of non-annexation and the principle that the well-being and development of such peoples form "a sacred trust of civilization."

With a view to giving practical effect to these principles, an international régime, the Mandates System, was created by Article 22 of the Covenant of the League of Nations. A "tutelage" was to be established for these peoples, and this tutelage was to be entrusted to certain advanced nations and exercised by them "as mandatories on behalf of the League."

Accordingly, the Principal Allied and Associated Powers agreed that a Mandate for the Territory of South-West Africa should be conferred upon His Britannic Majesty to be exercised on his behalf by the Government of the Union of South Africa and proposed the terms of this Mandate. His Britannic Majesty, for and on behalf of the Government of the Union of South Africa, agreed to accept the Mandate and undertook to exercise it on behalf of the League of Nations in accordance with the proposed terms. On December 17th, 1920, the Council of the League of Nations, confirming the Mandate, defined its terms.

In accordance with these terms, the Union of South Africa (the "Mandatory") was to have full power of administration and legislation over the Territory as an integral portion of the Union and could apply the laws of the Union of the Territory subject to such local modifications as circumstances might require. On the other hand, the Mandatory was to observe a number of obligations, and the Council of the League was to supervise the administration and see to it that these obligations were fulfilled.

The terms of this Mandate, as well as the provisions of Article 22 of the Covenant and the principles embodied therein, show that the creation of this new international institution did not involve any cession of territory or transfer of sovereignty to the Union of South Africa. The Union Government was to exercise an international function of administration on behalf of the League, with the object of promoting the well-being and development of the inhabitants.

It is now contended on behalf of the Union Government that this Mandate has lapsed, because the League has ceased to exist. This contention is based on a misconception of the legal situation created by Article 22 of the Covenant and by the Mandate itself. The League was not, as alleged by that Government, a "mandator" in the sense in which this term is used in the national law of certain States. It had only assumed an international function of supervision and control. The "Mandate" had only the name in common with the several notions of mandate in national law. The object of the Mandate regulated by international rules far exceeded that of contractual relations regulated by national law. The Mandate was created, in the interest of the inhabitants of the territory, and of humanity in general, as an international institution with an international object—a sacred trust of civilization. . . .

*   *   *

The authority which the Union Government exercises over the Territory is based on the Mandate. If the Mandate lapsed, as the Union Government contends, the latter's authority would equally have lapsed. To retain the rights derived from the Mandate and to deny the obligations thereunder could not be justified.

*   *   *

The first-mentioned group of obligations are defined in Article 22 of the Covenant and in Articles 2 to 5 of the Mandate. The Union undertook the general obligation to promote to the utmost the material and moral well-being and the social progress of the inhabitants. It assumed particular obligations relating to slave trade, forced labour, traffic in arms and ammunition, intoxicating spirits and beverages, military training and establishments, as well as obligations relating to freedom of conscience and free exercise of worship, including special obligations with regard to missionaries.

These obligations represent the very essence of the sacred trust of civilization. Their *raison d'etre* and original object remain. Since their fulfilment did not depend on the existence of the League of Nations, they could not be brought to an end merely because this supervisory organ ceased to exist. Nor could the right of the population to have the Territory administered in accordance with these rules depend thereon.

This view is confirmed by Article 80, paragraph 1, of the Charter, which maintains the rights of States and peoples and the terms of existing international instruments until the territories in question are placed under the Trusteeship System. It is true that this provision only says that nothing in Chapter XII shall be construed to alter the rights of States or peoples or the terms of existing international instruments. But—as far as mandated territories are concerned, to which paragraph 2 of this article refers—this provision presupposes that the rights of States and peoples shall not lapse automatically on the dissolution of the League of Nations. It obviously was the intention to safeguard the rights of States and peoples under all circumstances and in all respects, until each territory should be placed under the Trusteeship System.

*   *   *

A similar view has on various occasions been expressed by the Union of South Africa. In declarations made to the League of Nations, as well as to the United Nations, the Union Government has acknowledged that its obligations under the Mandate continued after the disappearance of the League. . . .

*   *   *

These declarations constitute recognition by the Union Government of the continuance of its obligations under the Mandate and not a mere indication of the future conduct of that Government. Interpretations placed upon legal instruments by the parties to them, though not conclusive as to their meaning, have considerable probative value when they contain recognition by a party of its own obligations under an instrument. In this case the declarations of the Union of South Africa support the conclusions already reached by the Court.

The Court will now consider the above-mentioned second group of obligations. These obligations related to the machinery for implementation and were closely linked to the supervisory functions of the League of Nations—particularly the obligation of the Union of South Africa to submit to the supervision and control of the Council of the League and the obligation to render to it annual reports in accordance with Article 22 of the Covenant and Article 6 of the Mandate. Since the Council disappeared by the dissolution of the League, the question arises whether these supervisory functions are to be exercised by the new international organization created by the Charter, and whether the Union of South Africa is under an obligation to submit to a supervision by this new organ and to render annual reports to it.

Some doubts might arise from the fact that the supervisory functions of the League with regard to mandated territories not placed under the new Trusteeship System were neither expressly transferred to the United Nations nor expressly assumed by that organization. Nevertheless, there seem to be decisive reasons for an affirmative answer to the above-mentioned question.

The obligation incumbent upon a mandatory State to accept international supervision and to submit reports is an important part of the Mandates System. When the authors of the Covenant created this system, they considered that the effective performance of the sacred trust of civilization by the mandatory Powers required that the administration of mandated territories should be subject to international supervision. The authors of the Charter had in mind the same necessity when they organized an International Trusteeship System. The necessity for supervision continues to exist despite the disappearance of the supervisory organ under the Mandates System. It cannot be admitted that the obligation to submit to supervision has disappeared merely because the supervisory organ has ceased to exist, when the United Nations has another international organ performing similar, though not identical, supervisory functions.

*   *   *

The Assembly of the League of Nations, in its Resolution of April 18th, 1946, gave expression to a corresponding view. It recognized, as mentioned above, that the League's functions with regard to the mandated territories would come to an end, but noted that Chapters XI, XII and XIII of the Charter of the United Nations embody principles corresponding to those declared in Article 22 of the Covenant. It further took note of the intentions of the mandatory States to continue to administer the territories in accordance with the obligations contained in the Mandates until other arrangements should be agreed upon between the United Nations and the mandatory Powers. This resolution presupposes that the supervisory functions exercised by the League would be taken over by the United Nations.

The competence of the General Assembly of the United Nations to exercise such supervision and to receive and examine reports is derived from the provisions of Article 10 of the Charter, which authorizes the General Assembly to discuss any questions or any matters within the scope of the Charter and to make recommendations on these questions or matters to the Members of the United Nations. . . .

For the above reasons, the Court has arrived at the conclusion that the General Assembly of the United Nations is legally qualified to exercise the supervisory functions previously exercised by the League of Nations with regard to the administration of the Territory, and that the Union of South Africa is under an obligation to submit to supervision and control of the General Assembly and to render annual reports to it.

The right of petition was not mentioned by Article 22 of the Covenant or by the provisions of the Mandate. But on January 31st, 1923, the Council of the League of Nations adopted certain rules relating to this matter. Petitions to the League from communities or sections of the populations of mandated territories were to be transmitted by the mandatory Governments, which were to attach to these petitions such comments as they might consider desirable. . . .

The Court is of opinion that this right, which the inhabitants of South-West Africa had thus acquired, is maintained by Article 80, paragraph 1, of the Charter, as this clause has been interpreted above. . . .

It follows from what is said above that South-West Africa is still to be considered as a territory held under the mandate of December 17th, 1920. The degree of supervision to be exercised by the General Assembly should not therefore exceed that which applied under the Mandates System, and should conform as far as possible to the procedure followed in this respect by the Council of the League of Nations. These observations are particularly applicable to annual reports and petitions.

*   *   *

QUESTION (b): *"Are the provisions of Chapter XII of the Charter applicable and, if so, in what manner, to the Territory of South-West Africa?"*

Territories held under Mandate were not by the Charter automatically placed under the new International Trusteeship System. This system should, according to Articles 75 and 77, apply to territories which are placed thereunder by means of Trusteeship Agreements. South-West Africa, being a territory held under Mandate (Article 77 *a*), may be placed under the Trusteeship System in accordance with the provisions of Chapter XII. . . .

. . . It appears from a number of documents submitted to the Court in accordance with the General Assembly's Resolution of December 6th, 1949, as well as from the written and the oral observations of several Governments, that the General Assembly, in asking about the manner of application of Chapter XII, was referring to the question whether the Charter imposes upon the Union of South Africa an obligation to place the Territory under the Trusteeship System by means of a Trusteeship Agreement.

Articles 75 and 77 show, in the opinion of the Court, that this question must be answered in the negative. The language used in both articles is permissive ("as may be placed thereunder"). Both refer to subsequent agreements by which the territories in question may be placed under the Trusteeship System. An "agreement" implies consent of the parties concerned, including the mandatory Power in the case of territories held under Mandate (Article 79). The parties must be free to accept or reject the terms of a contemplated agreement. No party can impose its terms on the other party. Article 77, paragraph 2, moreover, presupposes agreement not only with regard to its particular terms, but also as to which territories will be brought under the Trusteeship System.

*　　　*　　　*

For these reasons, the Court considers that the Charter does not impose on the Union an obligation to place South-West Africa under the Trusteeship System.

QUESTION (c): *"Has the Union of South Africa the competence to modify the international status of the Territory of South-West Africa, or, in the event of a negative reply, where does competence rest to determine and modify the international status of the Territory?"*

The international status of the Territory results from the international rules regulating the rights, powers and obligations relating to the administration of the Territory and the supervision of that administration, as embodied in Article 22 of the Covenant and in the Mandate. It is clear that the Union has no competence to modify unilaterally the international status of the Territory or any of these international rules. This is shown by Article 7 of the Mandate, which expressly provides that the consent of the Council of the League of Nations is required for any modification of the terms of the Mandate.

The Court is further requested to say where competence to determine and modify the international status of the Territory rests.

*   *   *

Article 26 of the Covenant laid down the procedure for amending provisions of the Covenant, including Article 22. On the other hand, Article 7 of the Mandate stipulates that the consent of the Council of the League was required for any modification of the terms of that Mandate. The rules thus laid down have become inapplicable following the dissolution of the League of Nations. But one cannot conclude therefrom that no proper procedure exists for modifying the international status of South-West Africa.

Article 7 of the Mandate, in requiring the consent of the Council of the League of Nations for any modification of its terms, brought into operation for this purpose the same organ which was invested with powers of supervision in respect of the administration of the Mandates. In accordance with the reply given above to Question (a), those powers of supervision now belong to the General Assembly of the United Nations. On the other hand, Articles 79 and 85 of the Charter require that a Trusteeship Agreement be concluded by the mandatory Power and approved by the General Assembly before the International Trusteeship System may be substituted for the Mandates System. These articles also give the General Assembly authority to approve alterations or amendments of Trusteeship Agreements. By analogy, it can be inferred that the same procedure is applicable to any modification of the international status of a territory under Mandate which would not have for its purpose the placing of the territory under the Trusteeship System. This conclusion is strengthened by the action taken by the General Assembly and the attitude adopted by the Union of South Africa which is at present the only existing mandatory Power.

On January 22nd, 1946, before the Fourth Committee of the General Assembly, the representative of the Union of South Africa explained the special relationship between the Union and the Territory under its Mandate. There would—he said—be no attempt to draw up an agreement until the freely expressed will of both the European and native populations had been ascertained. He continued: "When that had been done, the decision of the Union would be submitted to the General Assembly for judgment."

On April 9th, 1946, before the Assembly of the League of Nations, the Union representative declared that "it is the intention of the Union

Government, at the forthcoming session of the United Nations General Assembly in New York, to formulate its case for according South-West Africa a status under which it would be internationally recognized as an integral part of the Union."

In accordance with these declarations, the Union Government, by letter of August 12th, 1946, from its Legation in Washington, requested that the question of the desirability of the territorial integration in, and the annexation to, the Union of South Africa of the mandated Territory of South-West Africa, be included in the Agenda of the General Assembly. In a subsequent letter of October 9th, 1946, it was requested that the text of the item to be included in the Agenda be amended as follows: "Statement by the Government of the Union of South Africa on the outcome of their consultations with the peoples of South-West Africa as to the future status of the mandated Territory, and implementation to be given to the wishes thus expressed."

On November 4th, 1946, before the Fourth Committee, the Prime Minister of the Union of South Africa stated that the Union clearly understood "that its international responsibility precluded it from taking advantage of the war situation by effecting a change in the status of South-West Africa without proper consultation either of all the peoples of the Territory itself, or with the competent international organs."

By thus submitting the question of the future international status of the Territory to the "judgment" of the General Assembly as the "competent international organ," the Union Government recognized the competence of the General Assembly in the matter.

The General Assembly, on the other hand, affirmed its competence by Resolution 65 (I) of December 14th, 1946. It noted with satisfaction that the step taken by the Union showed the recognition of the interest and concern of the United Nations in the matter. It expressed the desire "that agreement between the United Nations and the Union of South Africa may hereafter be reached regarding the future status of the Mandated Territory of South-West Africa," and concluded: "The General Assembly, therefore, is unable to accede to the incorporation of the Territory of South-West Africa in the Union of South Africa."

Following the adoption of this resolution, the Union Government decided not to proceed with the incorporation of the Territory, but to maintain the *status quo*. . . .

*   *   *

For these reasons,

The Court is of opinion,

On the General Question:

unanimously,

that South-West Africa is a territory under the international Mandate assumed by the Union of South Africa on December 17th, 1920;

On Question (a):

by twelve votes to two,

that the Union of South Africa continues to have the international obligations stated in Article 22 of the Covenant of the League of Nations and in the Mandate for South-West Africa as well as the obligation to transmit petitions from the inhabitants of that Territory, the supervisory functions to be exercised by the United Nations, to which the annual reports and the petitions are to be submitted, . . .

On Question (b):

unanimously,

that the provisions of Chapter XII of the Charter are applicable to the Territory of South-West Africa in the sense that they provide a means by which the Territory may be brought under the Trusteeship System;

and by eight votes to six,

that the provisions of Chapter XII of the Charter do not impose on the Union of South Africa a legal obligation to place the Territory under the Trusteeship System;

On Question (c):

unanimously,

that the Union of South Africa acting alone has not the competence to modify the international status of the Territory of South-West Africa, and that the competence to determine and modify the international status of the Territory rests with the Union of South Africa acting with the consent of the United Nations.

* * *

Neutralization of Territory

The projection into space of manned missiles by states of this world—missiles now capable of circling the earth and ultimately destined to land on the moon, planets, or beyond—will raise legal questions of ownership as surely as the discovery of new continents.

Because of the urgent need of a whole community of states to exchange their products and people, to trade and thrive with all their potential, international law prohibits the appropriation of the high seas or the skies above them by any one state. Practice already demonstrates the same law-in-the-making about sovereignty over space. Meanwhile, some territorial claims touching vital political interests have not, and probably will not, come up for adjudication, while other claims have been suspended. Antarctica is an excellent case in point of the suspension of claims while states dealt with the urgent problem of limiting the growth of armaments.

Several conflicting international claims over the ownership of territory in Antarctica have been advanced in the 20th century. Some states have invoked discovery dating back as far as 1820 (U.S.S.R.) and 1840 (France); some have relied on a partial exercise of sovereign administration, such as establishment of a weather station; and others have justified their possession on an extension of the sector principle from their own mainland or from bases of exploration along the fringe of the Antarctic continent. In 1955, the United Kingdom filed applications with the International Court of Justice against Argentina and Chile, alleging encroachment on territory claimed to be under British sovereignty. Since neither of the Latin-American states had accepted the jurisdiction of the Court, the cases were withdrawn.

In 1959, 12 interested states concluded the extraordinary *Antarctic Treaty*, which follows. Underlying the agreement was the dread of any further expansion of military preparation to remote areas of the earth by states already capable of destroying most of the physical and moral achievements of mankind. Legally, the treaty neither confirmed nor denied claims, but it gave rise to a unique international cooperative arrangement by which states both renounced Antarctica as a military base and provided for actual inspections, as shown by the *Report of United States Observers of Antarctic Stations*, which also follows.

ANTARCTIC TREATY
Signed at Washington, 1 December 1959*
41 Department of State Bulletin

The Governments of Argentina, Australia, Belgium, Chile, the French Republic, Japan, New Zealand, Norway, the Union of South Africa, the Union of Soviet Socialist Republics, the United Kingdom of Great Britain and Northern Ireland, and the United States of America,

Recognizing that it is in the interest of all mankind that Antarctica shall continue forever to be used exclusively for peaceful purposes and shall not become the scene or object of international discord;

Acknowledging the substantial contributions to scientific knowledge resulting from international cooperation in scientific investigation in Antarctica;

Convinced that the establishment of a firm foundation for the continuation and development of such cooperation on the basis of freedom of scientific investigation in Antarctica as applied during the International Geophysical Year accords with the interests of science and the progress of all mankind;

Convinced also that a treaty ensuring the use of Antarctica for peaceful purposes only and the continuance of international harmony in Antarctica will further the purposes and principles embodied in the Charter of the United Nations:

Have agreed as follows:

Article I

1. Antarctica shall be used for peaceful purposes only. There shall be prohibited, *inter alia*, any measures of a military nature, such as the establishment of military bases and fortifications, the carrying out of military maneuvers, as well as the testing of any type of weapons.

2. The present treaty shall not prevent the use of military personnel or equipment for scientific research or for any other peaceful purpose.

Article II

Freedom of scientific investigation in Antarctica and cooperation toward that end, as applied during the International Geophysical Year, shall continue, subject to the provisions of the present treaty.

Article III

1. In order to promote international cooperation in scientific investigation in Antarctica, as provided for in Article II of the present treaty, the

---

* In force 23 June, 1961.

Contracting Parties agree that, to the greatest extent feasible and practicable:

(a) information regarding plans for scientific programs in Antarctica shall be exchanged to permit maximum economy and efficiency of operations;

(b) scientific personnel shall be exchanged in Antarctica between expeditions and stations;

(c) scientific observations and results from Antarctica shall be exchanged and made freely available.

2. In implementing this article, every encouragement shall be given to the establishment of cooperative working relations with those Specialized Agencies of the United Nations and other international organizations having a scientific or technical interest in Antarctica.

Article IV

1. Nothing contained in the present treaty shall be interpreted as:

(a) a renunciation by any Contracting Party of previously asserted rights of or claims to territorial sovereignty in Antarctica;

(b) a renunciation or diminution by any Contracting Party of any basis of claim to territorial sovereignty in Antarctica which it may have whether as a result of its activities or those of its nationals in Antarctica or otherwise;

(c) prejudicing the position of any Contracting Party as regards its recognition or non-recognition of any other State's right of or claim or basis of claim to territorial sovereignty in Antarctica.

2. No acts or activities taking place while the present treaty is in force shall constitute a basis for asserting, supporting or denying a claim to territorial sovereignty in Antarctica or create any rights of sovereignty in Antarctica. No new claim, or enlargement of an existing claim, to territorial sovereignty in Antarctica shall be asserted while the present treaty is in force.

Article V

1. Any nuclear explosions in Antarctica and the disposal there of radioactive waste material shall be prohibited.

2. In the event of the conclusion of international agreements concerning the use of nuclear energy, including nuclear explosions and the disposal of radioactive waste material, to which all of the Contracting Parties whose representatives are entitled to participate in the meetings provided for under Article IX are parties, the rules established under such agreements shall apply in Antarctica.

*   *   *

Article VII

1. In order to promote the objectives and ensure the observance of the provisions of the present treaty, each Contracting Party whose repre-

sentatives are entitled to participate in the meetings referred to in Article IX of the treaty shall have the right to designate observers to carry out any inspection provided for by the present article. Observers shall be nationals of the Contracting Parties which designate them. The names of observers shall be communicated to every other Contracting Party having the right to designate observers, and like notice shall be given of the termination of their appointment.

2. Each observer designated in accordance with the provisions of paragraph 1 of this article shall have complete freedom of access at any time to any or all areas of Antarctica.

3. All areas of Antarctica, including all stations, installations and equipment within those areas, and all ships and aircraft at points of discharging or embarking cargoes or personnel in Antarctica, shall be open at all times to inspection by any observers designated in accordance with paragraph 1 of this article.

4. Aerial observation may be carried out at any time over any or all areas of Antarctica by any of the Contracting Parties having the right to designate observers.

5. Each Contracting Party shall, at the time when the present treaty enters into force for it, inform the other Contracting Parties, and thereafter shall give them notice in advance, of

(a) all expeditions to and within Antarctica, on the part of its ships or nationals, and all expeditions to Antarctica organized in or proceeding from its territory;

(b) all stations in Antarctica occupied by its nationals; and

(c) any military personnel or equipment intended to be introduced by it into Antarctica subject to the conditions prescribed in paragraph 2 or Article I of the present treaty.

*   *   *

Article XI

1. If any dispute arises between two or more of the Contracting Parties concerning the interpretation or application of the present treaty, those Contracting Parties shall consult among themselves with a view to having the dispute resolved by negotiation, inquiry, mediation, conciliation, arbitration, judicial settlement or other peaceful means of their own choice.

2. Any dispute of this character not so resolved shall, with the consent, in each case, of all parties to the dispute, be referred to the International Court of Justice for settlement; but failure to reach agreement on reference to the International Court shall not absolve parties to the dispute from the responsibility of continuing to seek to resolve it by any of the various peaceful means referred to in paragraph 1 of this article.

*   *   *

REPORT OF UNITED STATES OBSERVERS ON INSPECTION OF ANTARCTIC STATIONS
1963–64 Austral Summer Season
3 International Legal Materials 65

Pursuant to the provisions of Article VII of the Antarctic Treaty, the stations tabulated below were inspected by designated United States Observers. . . . [Decepcion, Esperanza (Argentina); Gabriel Gonzolez Videla, Pedro Aguirre Cerda (Chile); Dumont d'Urville (overflight only) (France); Scott (New Zealand); Base B and Base F (United Kingdom); Mirnyy and Vostok (Union of Soviet Socialist Republics.]

Attitudes of host Government personnel to the inspections were frank, helpful, courteous and in keeping with the already existing cordiality of international relations and cooperation in the Antarctic area.

Access was freely accorded to all buildings and rooms; and there were no prohibitions on examining equipment.

Observations revealed a variety of scientific and other peaceful activities; no evidence of measures of a military nature was found.

No evidence was discovered which would indicate utilization of Antarctica for nuclear explosion or the disposal there of radioactive waste material.

The scientific work programs, equipment and arms observed were found to be in general agreement with the advance information provided by Governments.

In general, personnel in Antarctica were found to be adhering to sound practices regarding preservation and conservation of living resources in this area. The variations in such practices were extensive, however.

The atmosphere of cooperation which has characterized the relationship of all parties to the Antarctic Treaty in respect to matters affecting the Antarctic Continent continued to be evident during the conduct of these inspections.

*   *   *

Mirnyy

This Soviet station was observed to be engaged in scientific activities including meteorology, upper air observations, cosmic ray research, geomagnetism, ionospheric and aurora observations, earth current research and seismology. It appeared to be serving as a principal scientific and logistical station and communication center for Soviet activities in Antarctica.

The station and surrounding areas were observed from the air. All buildings and areas of activity except for a few living quarters were inspected including the geomagnetic pavilion, cosmic ray pavilion, ionosphere pavilion, seismology station, radio theodolite station and the weather balloons launching facility.

Scientific work programs and equipment observed were found to be in general agreement with the advance information provided by the Soviet Government in accordance with Article VII, paragraph 5 of the Treaty. All equipment examined appeared to be of a standard type and typical of that used for peaceful research of the type described above.

There were no arms seen at this station.

No biological program appeared to be in progress and no disturbance of wildlife was observed.

Vostok

This Soviet station was observed to be serving as an Antarctic research base. Its scientific activities were found to include meteorology, upper air observations, cosmic ray research, geomagnetism, ionospheric research, and geodetic surveying.

*   *   *

Scientific work programs and equipment observed were found to be in general agreement with advance information provided by the Soviet Government in accordance with Article VII, paragraph 5 of the Treaty. All equipment examined appeared to be of a standard type and typical of that used for peaceful research of the types described above.

There were no arms seen at this station.

*   *   *

FOR FURTHER STUDY

GEORGE THULLEN. *Problems of the Trusteeship System.* Geneva: Librairie E. Droz, 1964.

R. Y. JENNINGS. *The Acquisition of Territory in International Law.* Dobbs Ferry, N.Y.: Oceana Publications, 1963.

NORMAN L. HILL. *Claims to Territory in International Law and Relations.* New York: Oxford University Press, 1945.

A. S. KELLER, O. J. LISSITZYN, and F. J. MANN. *Creation of Rights of Sovereignty Through Symbolic Acts, 1400–1800.* New York: Columbia University Press, 1938.

V

Jurisdiction: The Seas, Vessels, Space, and Carriers

Who has the right to make law for a community? At what place and to whom does the law extend? On what authority does a court interpret the law and apply it to cases before it? All such questions pertain to "the saying of the law," or jurisdiction.

Jurisdiction may depend on *where* an act or event transpires or *who* has been involved in the act or event. The territorial principle has generally dominated the Anglo-American system of law, while the personal principle has a stronger hold on the European systems of law. But all states utilize both principles in their exercise of jurisdiction.

International law places very few limits on the right of a state to assert its jurisdiction in areas under its sovereignty; on the contrary, as the Permanent Court of International Justice warned,

. . . the first and foremost restriction placed upon a State is that—failing the existence of a permissive rule to the contrary—it may not exercise its power in any form in the territory of another State. In this sense jurisdiction is certainly territorial; it cannot be exercised by a State outside its territory except by virtue of a permissive rule derived from international custom or convention.[1]

Yet, where does a state's territory begin and end? For "territory" does not merely include (*a*) the land under the state's sovereignty, it also comprehends (*b*) the territorial or marginal seas adjacent to its land, (*c*) the extension of that land known as the continental shelf beyond the territorial seas under the high seas, and (*d*) the airspace above both the land and the territorial seas of the state.

---

[1] *The Lotus Case*, P.C.I.J., Series A, No. 10 (1927), p. 19.

The Seas

The high seas begin at the boundary of the state's territorial seas. However, as yet no universal agreement exists on the limits of the territorial waters over which a state exercises its jurisdiction, although most claims range from 3 to 12 miles seaward from the low-tide mark of the national shorelines. A difficult problem in defining territorial waters has been the ragged shorelines of such states as Norway, where countless bays, rocks, reefs, islets, and other indentures of the coast make impossible the drawing of a single line parallel to the shore. In the 1951 *Fisheries* case (*United Kingdom* v. *Norway*), Great Britain had objected to Norway's claim that large areas of the sea abutting the Norwegian coast were inland waters, thus eliminating the freedom of British fishing rights in those areas. The United Kingdom particularly denied Norwegian enclosure lines across bays and fjords beyond a maximum length of 10 miles. The International Court of Justice rejected the British contention, holding that although the 10-mile rule had been accepted by certain states both in their national law and in their treaties and conventions, and although certain arbitral decisions had applied it to the arbitrating states, other states had adopted a different limit. Consequently, the 10-mile rule had not acquired the authority of a general rule of international law.[2] In effect, moreover, the Court turned away from any mathematical limit of baselines demarcating the territorial seas, but rather looked to the close dependence on and relationship of the territorial seas to the land domain, as well as their economic exploitation by long usage.

Nevertheless, many questions about the law of the high seas, the territorial waters of states, and the newer problems of fisheries and exploitation of the continental shelf remained unsatisfactory. Therefore, in 1958, pursuant to a resolution of the United Nations General Assembly, more than 700 delegates from 86 nations gathered in Geneva to fashion 4 major conventions. These conventions, now in force for many, but not all, states, represent a significant framework of international law, although some issues like the width of the territorial sea have not been resolved, and other issues like "historic bays" are open to diplomatic and judicial interpretation.

Outside the territorial waters, the vast high seas by international law are open to free navigation, fishing, laying of cables and pipelines, and overflight by all states. The United States Supreme Court in 1826 epitomized the customary international law of the high seas when it said:

---

[2] 1951 I.C.J. Reports 116.

Upon the ocean, then, in time of peace, all possess an entire equality. It is the common highway of all, appropriated to the use of all; and no one can vindicate to himself a superior or exclusive prerogative there.[3]

On the high seas, vessels registered with a state and flying the flag of that state may proceed freely without interference or arrest from any other state. Specific treaties, of course, can be made between states to permit the reciprocal stopping and searching of each other's vessels on the high seas for special causes, such as a suspicion of whaling out of season or the cutting of submarine cables. But such agreements are exceptional, and any prosecution of individuals aboard a vessel for such alleged offenses has generally been referred to the flag state. In time of peace, a public vessel may also apprehend a ship on the high seas on suspicion of piracy, violence, detention, and robbery for personal motives. But all such approaches indicated above must be wary. If a demand for stop and search on the high seas reveals innocence, the arresting state may become seriously liable to claims from the state whose flag the vessel flies.

During a war, the belligerent states have customarily had the right to visit and search merchant vessels on the high seas on suspicion of assistance to the enemy either through transport of contraband goods or by running through an actual blockade. If evidence of such conduct existed, the vessel and/or its cargo could be brought by the belligerent state before its courts and claimed as a prize of war after legal condemnation. Some of these rules on naval warfare, although still legitimate international practice, have an archaic ring under the principles of the United Nations Charter, and they must be understood as in transition.

Such a transition is shown by the uncertain legal practice of the United States in 1962. On October 22, the President announced the intention of the United States to "quarantine" Cuba and turn back vessels carrying offensive military weapons. The Executive Proclamation, signed at 7:06 P.M., October 23, immediately followed a resolution of the Organization of American States recommending that member states take all measures necessary to prevent Cuba from receiving military material from Sino-Soviet powers. These actions were immediately reported to the United Nations Security Council. No legal test really occurred. United States naval units actually boarded only one ship (Lebanese) chartered by the Soviet Union, one Soviet tanker was intercepted and visually checked, and other vessels altered their routes, but no forcible measures were employed. Political understandings between the main antagonists—the United States and the Soviet Union—eased the tension and ended the quarantine on November 20.

According to some statesmen and scholars, the measures and procedure of the Cuban quarantine were justified by customary international law, with its inherent right of individual or collective self-defense; by Article

---

[3] *The Mariana Flora* case, 11 Wheaton 1.

51 of the United Nations Charter, which provides for self-defense; and by the right of collective action for hemispheric security under the Organization of American States and the Rio Treaty of 1947. Other opinions differ. In any event, the laws of war and the use of force on the high seas are open to great political questions and subject to change as the legality of force in international relations is increasingly challenged.

All states, including landlocked states, have the right to sail on the high seas both public and private vessels under their registry. A state can assert jurisdiction over all vessels flying its flag on the high seas; it can apply its laws to *all* persons aboard, thus ensuring the public order of the ship. Moreover, even when in the territorial waters of another State, conduct aboard a ship is usually held to be regulated by the flag of the vessel. Only when the disorder aboard a foreign ship becomes so grave that it plainly imperils the peace and security of the shore or the port of the host state will its authorities intervene. As noted in the often-cited *Wildenhus* case, when a Belgian crew member killed another Belgian crew member in an American port:

> And so by comity it came to be generally understood among civilized nations that all matters of discipline and all things done on board which affected only the vessel or those belonging to her, and did not involve the peace or dignity of the country, or the tranquillity of the port, should be left by the local government to be dealt with by the authorities of the nation to which the vessel belonged as the laws of that nation or the interests of its commerce should require . . . but all must concede that felonious homicide is a subject for the local jurisdiction; and that if the proper authorities are proceeding with the case in a regular way, the consul has no right to interfere to prevent it.[4]

Under international law, the merchant ships of a state generally enjoy a right of "innocent passage" through the territorial waters or international canals of a friendly state without actually notifying the authorities or visiting the ports. Of course, for any offenses against the public order of the state, such as illegal pollution or violation of import-export regulations, the vessel would be subject to the jurisdiction of the state while traversing territorial waters. An important question of jurisdiction over vessels and their seamen has arisen in recent years as a result of the use of "flags of convenience." That is, American, British, or other owners register vessels with such states as Panama, Liberia, Honduras, and others in order to avoid high taxes, high wages to seamen, insurance requirements, or other stringent legislation for vessels and shipping that may be in effect in the owner's state.

In addition to the prescriptions about the rights of states and vessels on the high seas, the Geneva Convention on the High Seas in 1958 had called for a "genuine link" between a state and a vessel registered with its

---

[4] 120 U.S. 1 (1887).

nationality. Yet, what action can a state take against a vessel whose link of ownership, purpose, and nationality may be tenuous?

In the first two documents that follow, the *Convention on the Territorial Sea and the Contiguous Zone* and the *Convention on the High Seas* —two of the four major conventions signed at Geneva in 1958—some of the articles illustrate central principles of international law with respect to the seas.

The third document that follows, the 1965 case of *United States* v. *California*, shows the vigorous dispute between the federal government and the state of California about the definition of "inland waters." This was of great importance in establishing the extent out to sea that California, rather than the United States, could exploit the submerged lands for oil and other natural resources. Following a 1947 decree favoring the United States title to the seabed beyond the "inland waters" of California, a Special Master was appointed by the Court to define more clearly the inland waters. His report was filed in 1952, but, meanwhile, Congress had, by the Submerged Lands Act, given title to ordinary low water along that portion of the coast in direct contact with the open sea "*and the line marking* the seaward limit of inland water." However, no definition was given to "inland waters." The Supreme Court, in *United States* v. *California*, addressed itself to this problem.

Finally, the case of *McCulloch* v. *Sociedad Nacional de Marineros de Honduras*, the fourth document that follows, went to the Supreme Court for a final determination of the jurisdictional reach of the United States National Labor Relations Act to a vessel indirectly, but wholly, owned by an American corporation allegedly sailing under a foreign "flag of convenience."

Territorial Seas

CONVENTION ON THE TERRITORIAL SEA AND THE CONTIGUOUS ZONE,
Signed at Geneva 29 April 1958*
U.N. Document A/Conf.13/L.52

Article 1

1. The sovereignty of a state extends beyond its land territory and its internal waters to a belt of sea adjacent to its coast, described as the territorial sea.

---

* In force 10 September, 1964.

2. This sovereignty is exercised subject to the provisions of these articles and to other rules of international law.

Article 2

The sovereignty of a coastal state extends to the airspace over the territorial sea as well as to its bed and subsoil.

Article 3

Except where otherwise provided in these articles, the normal baseline for measuring the breadth of the territorial sea is the low-water line along the coast as marked on large-scale charts officially recognized by the coastal state.

*　　　*　　　*

Article 7

1. This article relates only to bays the coasts of which belong to a single state.

2. For the purposes of these articles, a bay is a well-marked indentation whose penetration is in such proportion to the width of its mouth as to contain landlocked waters and constitute more than a mere curvature of the coast. An indentation shall not, however, be regarded as a bay unless its area is as large as, or larger than, that of the semi-circle whose diameter is a line drawn across the mouth of that indentation.

*　　　*　　　*

4. If the distance between the low-water marks of the natural entrance points of a bay does not exceed twenty-four miles, a closing line may be drawn between these two low-water marks, and the waters enclosed thereby shall be considered as internal waters.

5. Where the distance between the low-water marks of the natural entrance points of a bay exceeds twenty-four miles, a straight baseline of twenty-four miles shall be drawn within the bay in such a manner as to enclose the maximum area of water that is possible with a line of that length.

6. The foregoing provisions shall not apply to so-called "historic" bays, or in any case where the straight baseline system provided for in Article 4 is applied.

*　　　*　　　*

Article 12

1. Where the coasts of two states are opposite or adjacent to each other, neither of the two states is entitled, failing agreement between them to the contrary, to extend its territorial sea beyond the median line every point of which is equidistant from the nearest points on the base-

lines from which the breadth of the territorial seas of each of the two states is measured. The provisions of this paragraph shall not apply, however, where it is necessary by reason of historic title or other special circumstances to delimit the territorial seas of the two states in a way which is at variance with this provision.

*   *   *

Article 14

1. Subject to the provisions of these articles, ships of all states, whether coastal or not, shall enjoy the right of innocent passage through the territorial sea.

2. Passage means navigation through the territorial sea for the purpose either of traversing that sea without entering internal waters, or of proceeding to internal waters, or of making for the high seas from internal waters.

3. Passage includes stopping and anchoring, but only insofar as the same are incidental to ordinary navigation or are rendered necessary by *force majeure* or by distress.

4. Passage is innocent so long as it is not prejudicial to the peace, good order or security of the coastal state. Such passage shall take place in conformity with these articles and with other rules of international law.

5. Passage of foreign fishing vessels shall not be considered innocent if they do not observe such laws and regulations as the coastal state may make and publish in order to prevent these vessels from fishing in the territorial sea.

6. Submarines are required to navigate on the surface and to show their flag.

Article 15

1. The coastal state must not hamper innocent passage through the territorial sea.

2. The coastal state is required to give appropriate publicity to any dangers to navigation, of which it has knowledge, within its territorial sea.

Article 16

1. The coastal state may take the necessary steps in its territorial sea to prevent passage which is not innocent.

*   *   *

4. There shall be no suspension of the innocent passage of foreign ships through straits which are used for international navigation between one part of the high seas and another part of the high seas or the territorial sea of a foreign state.

Article 17

Foreign ships exercising the right of innocent passage shall comply with the laws and regulations enacted by the coastal state in conformity with these articles and other rules of international law and, in particular, with such laws and regulations relating to transport and navigation.

*   *   *

Article 19

1. The criminal jurisdiction of the coastal state should not be exercised on board a foreign ship passing through the territorial sea to arrest any person or to conduct any investigation in connexion with any crime committed on board the ship during its passage, save only in the following cases:

(a) If the consequences of the crime extend to the coastal state; or

(b) If the crime is of a kind to disturb the peace of the country or the good order of the territorial sea; or

(c) If the assistance of the local authorities has been requested by the captain of the ship or by the consul of the country whose flag the ship flies; or

(d) If it is necessary for the suppression of illicit traffic in narcotic drugs.

*   *   *

3. In the cases provided for in paragraphs 1 and 2 of this article, the coastal state shall, if the captain so requests, advise the consular authority of the flag state before taking any steps, and shall facilitate contact between such authority and the ship's crew. In cases of emergency this notification may be communicated while the measures are being taken.

*   *   *

5. The coastal state may not take any steps on board a foreign ship passing through the territorial sea for the purpose of exercising civil jurisdiction in relation to a person on board the ship.

Article 20

1. The coastal state should not stop or divert a foreign ship passing through the territorial sea for the purpose of exercising civil jurisdiction in relation to a person on board the ship.

2. The coastal state may not levy execution against or arrest the ship for the purpose of any civil proceedings, save only in respect of obligations or liabilities assumed or incurred by the ship itself in the course or for the purpose of its voyage through the waters of the coastal state.

3. The provisions of the previous paragraphs are without prejudice to the right of the coastal state, in accordance with its laws, to levy execu-

tion against or to arrest, for the purpose of any civil proceedings, a foreign ship lying in the territorial sea, or passing through the territorial sea after leaving internal waters.

*   *   *

Article 23

If any warship does not comply with the regulations of the coastal state concerning passage through the territorial sea and disregards any request for compliance which is made to it, the coastal state may require the warship to leave the territorial sea.

Article 24

1. In a zone of the high seas contiguous to its territorial sea, the coastal state may exercise the control necessary to:

(a) Prevent infringement of its customs, fiscal, immigration or sanitary regulations within its territory or territorial sea;

(b) Punish infringement of the above regulations committed within its territory or territorial sea.

2. The contiguous zone may not extend beyond twelve miles from the baseline from which the breadth of the territorial sea is measured.

*   *   *

The High Seas and Vessels

CONVENTION ON THE HIGH SEAS
Signed at Geneva 29 April 1958*
U.N. Document A/Conf. 13/L.53

The States Parties to this Convention

Desiring to codify the rules of international law relating to the high seas,

Recognizing that the United Nations Conference on the Law of the Sea, held at Geneva from 24 February to 27 April 1958, adopted the following provisions as generally declaratory of established principles of international law,

Have agreed as follows:

---

* In force 30 September, 1962.

Article 1

The term "high seas" means all parts of the sea that are not included in the territorial sea or in the internal waters of a state.

Article 2

The high seas being open to all nations, no state may validly purport to subject any part of them to its sovereignty. Freedom of the high seas is exercised under the conditions laid down by these articles and by the other rules of international law. It comprises, *inter alia*, both for coastal and non-coastal states:

(1) Freedom of navigation;
(2) Freedom of fishing;
(3) Freedom to lay submarine cables and pipelines;
(4) Freedom to fly over the high seas.

These freedoms, and others which are recognized by the general principles of international law, shall be exercised by all states with reasonable regard to the interests of other states in their exercise of the freedom of the high seas.

*   *   *

Article 4

Every state, whether coastal or not, has the right to sail ships under its flag on the high seas.

Article 5

1. Each state shall fix the conditions for the grant of its nationality to ships, for the registration of ships in its territory, and for the right to fly its flag. Ships have the nationality of the state whose flag they are entitled to fly. There must exist a genuine link between the state and the ship; in particular, the state must effectively exercise its jurisdiction and control in administrative, technical and social matters over ships flying its flag.

*   *   *

Article 6

1. Ships shall sail under the flag of one state only and, save in exceptional cases expressly provided for in international treaties or in these articles, shall be subject to its exclusive jurisdiction on the high seas. A ship may not change its flag during a voyage or while in a port of call, save in the case of a real transfer of ownership or change in registry.

*   *   *

Article 8

1. Warships on the high seas have complete immunity from the jurisdiction of any state other than the flag state.

* * *

Article 9

Ships owned or operated by a state and used only on government non-commercial service shall, on the high seas, have complete immunity from the jurisdiction of any state other than the flag state.

* * *

Article 11

1. In the event of a collision or of any other incident of navigation concerning a ship on the high seas, involving the penal or disciplinary responsibility of the master or of any other person in the service of the ship, no penal or disciplinary proceedings may be instituted against such persons except before the judicial or administrative authorities either of the flag state or of the state of which such person is a national.

* * *

3. No arrest or detention of the ship, even as a measure of investigation, shall be ordered by any authorities other than those of the flag state.

* * *

Article 13

Every state shall adopt effective measures to prevent and punish the transport of slaves in ships authorized to fly its flag, and to prevent the unlawful use of its flag for that purpose. Any slave taking refuge on board any ship, whatever its flag, shall *ipso facto* be free.

Article 14

All states shall co-operate to the fullest possible extent in the repression of piracy on the high seas or in any other place outside the jurisdiction of any state.

Article 15

Piracy consists of any of the following acts:

(1) Any illegal acts of violence, detention or any act of depredation, committed for private ends by the crew or the passengers of a private ship or a private aircraft, and directed:

(a) On the high seas, against another ship or aircraft, or against persons or property on board such ship or aircraft;

(b) Against a ship, aircraft, persons or property in a place outside the jurisdiction of any state;

(2) Any act of voluntary participation in the operation of a ship or of an aircraft with knowledge of facts making it a pirate ship or aircraft;

*   *   *

Article 17

A ship or aircraft is considered a pirate ship or aircraft if it is intended by the persons in dominant control to be used for the purpose of committing one of the acts referred to in Article 15. The same applies if the ship or aircraft has been used to commit any such act, so long as it remains under the control of the persons guilty of that act.

Article 18

A ship or aircraft may retain its nationality although it has become a pirate ship or aircraft. The retention or loss of nationality is determined by the law of the state from which such nationality was derived.

Article 19

On the high seas, or in any other place outside the jurisdiction of any state, every state may seize a pirate ship or aircraft, or a ship taken by piracy and under the control of pirates, and arrest the persons and seize the property on board. The courts of the state which carried out the seizure may decide upon the penalties to be imposed, and may also determine the action to be taken with regard to the ships, aircraft or property, subject to the rights of third parties acting in good faith.

*   *   *

Article 22

1. Except where acts of interference derive from powers conferred by treaty, a warship which encounters a foreign merchant ship on the high seas is not justified in boarding her unless there is reasonable ground for suspecting:

(a) That the ship is engaged in piracy; or

(b) That the ship is engaged in the slave trade; or

(c) That, though flying a foreign flag or refusing to show its flag, the ship is, in reality, of the same nationality as the warship.

*   *   *

3. If the suspicions prove to be unfounded, and provided that the ship boarded has not committed any act justifying them, it shall be compensated for any loss or damage that may have been sustained.

Article 23

1. The hot pursuit of a foreign ship may be undertaken when the competent authorities of the coastal state have good reason to believe that the ship has violated the laws and regulations of that state. Such pursuit must be commenced when the foreign ship or one of its boats is within the internal waters or the territorial sea or the contiguous zone of the

pursuing state, and may only be continued outside the territorial sea or the contiguous zone if the pursuit has not been interrupted. . . .

2. The right of hot pursuit ceases as soon as the ship pursued enters the territorial sea of its own country or of a third state.

*   *   *

UNITED STATES v. CALIFORNIA
United States Supreme Court, 1965
381 U.S. 139

Mr. Justice Harlan delivered the opinion of the Court.

The United States contends that we must ignore the Convention of the Territorial Sea and the Contiguous Zone in performing our duty of giving content to "inland waters" as used in the Submerged Lands Act, and must restrict ourselves to determining what our decision would have been had the question been presented to us for decision on May 22, 1953, the passage date of the Act. At that time there was no international accord on any definition of inland waters, and the best evidence (although strenuously contested by California) of the position of the United States was the letters of the State Department which the Special Master refused to treat as conclusive.

We do not think that the Submerged Lands Act has so restricted us. Congress, in passing the Act, left the responsibility for defining inland waters to this Court. We think that it did not tie our hands at the same time. Had Congress wished us simply to rubber-stamp the statements of the State Department as to its policy in 1953, it could readily have done so itself. It is our opinion that we best fill our responsibility of giving content to the words which Congress employed by adopting the best and most workable definitions available. The Convention of the Territorial Sea and the Contiguous Zone, approved by the Senate and ratified by the President, provides such definitions. We adopt them for purposes of the Submerged Lands Act. This establishes a single coastline for both the administration of the Submerged Lands Act and the conduct of our future international relations (barring an unexpected change in the rules established by the Convention). Furthermore the comprehensiveness of the Convention provides answers to many of the lesser problems related to coastlines which, absent the Convention, would be most troublesome.

California argues, alternatively to its claim that "inland waters" embrace all ocean areas lying within a State's historic seaward boundaries, that if Congress intended "inland waters" to be judicially defined in accordance with international usage, such definition should possess an ambulatory quality so as to encompass future changes in international law or practice. Thus, if 10 years from now the definitions of the Convention were amended, California would say that the extent of the Submerged Lands Act grant would automatically shift, at least if the effect of such amendment were to enlarge the extent of submerged lands available to the States. We reject this open-ended view of the Act for several reasons. Before today's decision no one could say with assurance where lay the line of inland waters as contemplated by the Act; hence there could have been no tenable reliance on any particular line. After today that situation will have changed. Expectations will be established and reliance placed on the line we define. Allowing future shifts of international understanding respecting inland waters to alter the extent of the Submerged Lands Act grant would substantially undercut the definiteness of expectation which should attend it. Moreover, such a view might unduly inhibit the United States in the conduct of its foreign relations by making its ownership of submerged lands *vis-à-vis* the States continually depended upon the position it takes with foreign nations. "Freezing" the meaning of "inland waters" in terms of the Convention definition largely avoids this, as well as serving to fulfill the requirements of definiteness and stability which should attend any congressional grant of property rights belonging to the United States.

Once it is decided that the definitions of the Convention on the Contiguous Zone apply, many of the subsidiary issues before us fall into place.

1. *Straight Base Lines.*—California argues that because the Convention permits a nation to use the straight base line method for determining its seaward boundaries if its "coast line is deeply indented and cut into, or if there is a fringe of islands along the coast in its immediate vicinity," California is therefore free to use such boundary lines across the openings of its bays and around its islands. We agree with the United States that the Convention recognizes the validity of straight base lines used by other countries, Norway for instance, and would *permit* the United States to use such base lines if it chose, but that California may not use such base lines to extend our international boundaries beyond their traditional international limits against the expressed opposition of the United States. The national responsibility for conducting our international relations obviously must be accommodated with the legitimate interests of the States in the territory over which they are sovereign. Thus a contraction of a State's recognized territory imposed by the Federal Government in the name of foreign policy would be highly questionable. But an extension of state sovereignty to an international area by claiming it as inland water would necessarily also extend national sovereignty, and unless the Federal Government's responsibility for questions of external sovereignty is hollow, it must have the power to prevent States from so enlarging them-

selves. We conclude that the choice under the Convention to use the straight baseline method for determining inland waters claimed against other nations is one that rests with the Federal Government, and not with the individual States. . . .

2. *Twenty-four Mile Closing Rule.*—The Convention recognizes, and it is the present United States position, that a 24-mile closing rule together with the semicircle test should be used for classifying bays in the United States. Applying these tests to the segments of California's coast here in dispute, it appears that Monterey Bay is inland water and that none of the other coastal segments in dispute fulfill these aspects of the Convention test. We so hold.

*   *   *

3. *Historic Inland Waters.*—By the terms of the Convention the 24-mile closing rule does not apply to so-called "historic" bays. Essentially these are bays over which a coastal nation has traditionally asserted and maintained dominion with the acquiescence of foreign nations. California claims that virtually all the waters here in dispute are historic inland waters as the term is internationally understood. It relies primarily on an interpretation of its State Constitution to the effect that the State boundaries run three miles outside the islands and bays, plus several court decisions which so interpret it as applied to Monterey, Santa Monica, and San Pedro Bays. The United States counters that, as with straight base lines, California can maintain no claim to historic inland waters unless the claim is endorsed by the United States. The Special Master found it unnecessary to decide that question because, on the evidence before him, he concluded that California had not traditionally exercised dominion over any of the claimed waters.

Since the 24-mile rule includes Monterey Bay, we do not consider it here. As to Santa Monica Bay, San Pedro Bay, and the other water areas in dispute, we agree with the Special Master that they are not historic inland waters of the United States.

*   *   *

The Chief Justice and Mr. Justice Clark took no part in the consideration or decision of this case.

Mr. Justice Black, with whom Mr. Justice Douglas joined, dissented.

*   *   *

In light of this legislative history, of which I have set forth only a small part, I think that under the Submerged Lands Act California is entitled to all the submerged lands within its historic boundaries, and that it should be given an opportunity to try to prove in hearings before a Master where those historic boundaries were. The Court says that Congress left it up to this Court to expound the legal principles which shall determine California's claims, without any reference to the Submerged Lands Act's stated purpose to restore the mineral rights of the States in submerged lands within their historic boundaries. I think the Court is completely misreading the intentions of the authors and supporters of the Act. If there is anything clear in the legislative history, it is that Congress was not satisfied with the way in which this Court had decided the *California* case and did not approve of the considerations of external sovereignty used there in determining a domestic dispute over title. It seems to me the height of irony to hold that an Act passed expressly to escape the effect of this Court's opinion in this field is now construed as leaving us free to announce principles directly antithetic to the basic purpose of Congress of deciding that question for itself once and for all. True, the Congress left to the courts the exercise of their historic function to decide the factual question of where a State's historic boundaries, based on those approved when it was admitted to the Union, lie. But I think the Court errs in arguing repeatedly that by leaving it to the courts to decide the issues of fact in particular cases, Congress meant to leave it to this Court to determine the legal principles governing California's claim, and in particular to do so by adopting a formula of its own devising based on one used by the State Department in its handling of foreign affairs.

*   *   *

McCULLOCH v. SOCIEDAD NACIONAL DE MARINEROS DE HONDURAS
United States Supreme Court, 1963
372 U.S. 10

Mr. Justice Clark delivered the opinion of the Court.

*   *   *

I

The National Maritime Union of America, AFL–CIO, filed a petition in 1959 with the National Labor Relations Board seeking certification under Sec. 9 (c) of the Act, 29 U.S.C. Sec. 159 (c), as the representative of the unlicensed seamen employed upon certain Honduran flag vessels owned by Empresa Hondurena de Vapores, S.A., a Honduran corporation. The petition was filed against United Fruit Company, a New Jersey corporation which was alleged to be the owner of the majority of Empresa's stock. Empresa intervened and on hearing it was shown that United Fruit owns all of its stock and elects its directors, though no officer or director of Empresa is an officer or director of United Fruit and all are residents of Honduras. In turn the proof was that United Fruit is owned by citizens of the United States, and maintains its principal office at Boston. Its business was shown to be the cultivation, gathering, transporting and sale of bananas, sugar, cacao and other tropical produce raised in Central and South American countries and sold in the United States.

United Fruit maintains a fleet of cargo vessels which it utilizes in this trade. A portion of the fleet consists of 13 Honduran-registered vessels operated by Empresa and time chartered to United Fruit, which vessels were included in National Maritime Union's representation proceeding. The crews on these vessels, including the officers, are recruited by Empresa in Honduras. They are Honduran citizens (save one Jamaican) and claim that country as their residence and home port. The crew is required to sign Honduran shipping articles, and their wages, terms and condition of employment, discipline, etc., are controlled by a bargaining agreement between Empresa and a Honduran union, Sociedad Nacional de Marineros de Honduras. Under the Honduran Labor Code only a union whose "juridic personality" is recognized by Honduras and which is composed of at least 90% of Honduran citizens can represent the seamen on Honduran-registered ships. The N.M.U. fulfills neither requirement. Further, under Honduran law recognition of Sociedad as the bargaining agent compels Empresa to deal exclusively with it on all matters covered by the contract. The current agreement in addition to recognition of Sociedad provides for a union shop, with a no-strike-or-lockout provision, and sets up wage scales, special allowances, maintenance and cure provisions, hours of work, vacation time, holidays, overtime, accident prevention, and other details of employment as well.

United Fruit, however, determines the ports of call of the vessels, their cargoes and sailings, integrating the same into its fleet organization. While the voyages are for the most part between Central and South American ports and those of the United States, the vessels each call at regular intervals at Honduran ports for the purpose of taking on and discharging cargo and, where necessary, renewing the ship's articles.

II

The Board concluded from these facts that United Fruit operated a single, integrated maritime operation within which were the Empresa vessels, reasoning that United Fruit was a joint employer with Empresa of the seamen covered by N.M.U.'s petition. Citing its own *West India Fruit & Steamship Co.* opinion, 130 NLRB 343 (1961), it concluded that the maritime operations involved substantial United States contacts, outweighing the numerous foreign contacts present. The Board held that Empresa was engaged in "commerce" within the meaning of Sec. 2 (6) of the Act and that the maritime operations "affected commerce" within

Sec. 2 (7), meeting the jurisdictional requirement of Sec. 9 (c) (1). It therefore ordered an election to be held among the seamen signed on Empresa's vessels to determine whether they wished N.M.U., Sindicato Maritime Nacional de Honduras, or no union to represent them.

As we have indicated, both Empresa and Sociedad brought suits in Federal District Courts to prevent the election, Empresa proceeding in New York against the Regional Director—Nos. 91 and 93—and Sociedad in the District of Columbia against the members of the Board—No. 107. In Nos. 91 and 93 the jurisdiction of the District Court was challenged on two grounds . . . Sociedad is not a party in Nos. 91 and 93, although the impact of the Board order—the same order challenged in No. 107—is felt by it. That order has the effect of cancelling Sociedad's bargaining agreement with Empresa's seamen, since Sociedad is not on the ballot called for by the Board. No. 107, therefore, presents the question in better perspective, and we have chosen it as the vehicle for our adjudication on the merits. This obviates our passing on the jurisdictional questions raised in Nos. 91 and 93, since the disposition of those cases is controlled by our decision in No. 107.

We are not of course precluded from reexamining the jurisdiction of the District Court in Sociedad's action, merely because no challenge was made by the parties. *Mitchell* v. *Maurer* 293 U.S. 237, 244 (1934). Having examined the question whether the District Court had jurisdiction at the instance of Sociedad to enjoin the Board's order, we hold that the action falls within the limited exception fashioned in *Leedom* v. *Kyne*, 358 U.S. 184 (1958). In that case judicial intervention was permitted since the Board's order was "in excess of its delegated powers and contrary to a specific prohibition in the Act." *Id* at 188. While here the Board has violated no specific prohibition in the Act, the overriding consideration is that the Board's assertion of power to determine the representation of foreign seamen aboard vessels under foreign flags has aroused vigorous protests from foreign governments and created international problems for our Government. Important interests of the immediate parties are of course at stake. But the presence of public questions particularly high in the scale of our national interest because of their international complexion is a uniquely compelling justification for prompt judicial resolution of the controversy over the Board's power. . . .

III

Since the parties all agree that the Congress has constitutional power to apply the National Labor Relations Act to the crews working foreign flag ships, at least while they are in American waters, the *Exchange*, 11 U.S. (7 Cranch) 116, 143, (1812), *Wildenhus's Case*, 120 U.S. 1, 11, (1887); *Benz* v. *Compania Naviera Hidalgo* 353 U.S. 138, 142 (1957), we go directly to the question whether Congress exercised that power. Our decision on this point being dispositive of the case, we do not reach the other questions raised by the parties and the *amici curiae.*

The question of application of the laws of the United States to foreign flagships and the crews has arisen often and in various contexts. As to the application of the National Labor Relations Act and its amendments, the Board has evolved a test relying on the relative weight of a ship's foreign as compared with its American contacts. That test led the Board to conclude here, as in *West India Fruit & Steamship Co., supra,* that the foreign flagship's activities affected "commerce" and brought them within the coverage of the Act. Where the balancing of the vessel's contacts has resulted in a contrary finding the Board has concluded that the Act does not apply.

Six years ago this Court considered the question of the application of the Taft-Hartley amendments to the Act in a suit for damages "resulting from the picketing of a foreign ship operated entirely by foreign seamen under foreign articles while the vessel (was) temporarily in an American port." *Benz* v. *Compania Naviera Hidalgo, supra* at 139. We held that the Act did not apply, searching the language and the legislative history and concluding that the latter "inescapably describes the boundaries of the Act as including only the workingmen of our own country and its possessions. . . ." Subsequently in *Marine Cooks & Stewards* v. *Panama S. S. Co.* 362 U.S. 365 (1960) we held that the Norris-LaGuardia Act, 29 U.S.C., §101, deprived a Federal District Court of jurisdiction to enjoin picketing of a foreign flagship, specifically limiting the holding to the jurisdiction of the court "to issue the injunction it did under the circumstances shown. . . ." That case cannot be regarded as limiting the earlier *Benz* holding, however, since no question as to "whether the picketing . . . was tortious under state or federal law" was either presented or decided. . . . Indeed, the Court specifically noted that the application of the Norris-LaGuardia Act "to curtail and regulate the jurisdiction of the courts" differs from the application of the Taft-Hartley Act "to regulate the conduct of people engaged in labor disputes. . . ."

It is contended that this case is nonetheless distinguishable from *Benz* in two respects. First, here there is a fleet of vessels not temporarily in United States waters but operating in a regular course of trade between foreign ports and those of the United States; and, second, the foreign owner of the ships is in turn owned by an American corporation. We note that both of these points rely on additional American contacts and therefore necessarily presume the validity of the "balancing of contacts" theory of the Board. But to follow such a suggested procedure to the ultimate might require that the Board inquire into the internal discipline and order of all foreign vessels calling at American ports. Such activity would raise considerable disturbance not only in the field of maritime law but in our international relations as well. In addition enforcement of

Board orders would project the courts into application of the sanctions of the Act to foreign flagships on a purely *ad hoc* weighing of contracts basis. This would inevitably lead to embarrassment in foreign affairs and be entirely infeasible in actual practice. The question, therefore, appears to us more basic; namely, whether the Act as written was intended to have any application to foreign registered vessels employing alien seamen.

Petitioners say that the language of the Act may be read literally as including foreign flag vessels within its coverage. But, as in *Benz*, they have been unable to point to any specific language in the Act itself or in its extensive legislative history that reflects such a congressional intent. Indeed, the opposite is true as we found in *Benz*, where we pointed to the language of Chairman Hartley characterizing the Act as a "bill of rights both for American working men and for their employers." 353 U.S., at 144. We continue to believe that if the sponsors of the original Act or of its amendments conceived of the application now sought by the Board they failed to translate such thoughts into describing the boundaries of the Act as including foreign flag vessels manned by alien crews. Therefore, we find no basis for a construction which would exert United States jurisdiction over and apply its laws to the internal management and affairs of the vessels here flying the Honduran flag, contrary to the recognition long afforded them not only by our State Department but also by the Congress. In addition, our attention is called to the well-established rule of international law that the law of the flag state ordinarily governs the internal affairs of a ship. See *Wildenhus's Case, supra* at 12; Colombos *The International Law of the Sea* (3d rev., ed. 1954) 222–223. The possibility of international discord cannot therefore be gainsaid. Especially is this true on account of the concurrent application of the Act and the Honduran Labor Code that would result with our approval of jurisdiction. Sociedad, currently the exclusive bargaining agent of Empresa under Honduran law, would have a head-on collision with N.M.U. should it become the exclusive bargaining agent under the Act. This would be aggravated by the fact that under Honduran law N.M.U. is prohibited from representing the seamen on Honduran flagships even in the absence of a recognized bargaining agent. Thus even though Sociedad withdrew from such an intra-mural labor fight—a highly unlikely circumstance—questions of such international import would remain as to invite retaliatory action from other nations as well as Honduras.

The presence of such highly charged international circumstances brings to mind the admonition of Mr. Chief Justice Marshall in *The Charming Betsy*, 6 U.S. (2 Cranch) 64, 118 (1804) that "an act of Congress ought never to be construed to violate the law of nations if any other possible construction remains. . . ." We therefore conclude, as we did in *Benz*, that for us to sanction the exercise of local sovereignty under such conditions in this "delicate field of international relations there must

be present the affirmative intention of the Congress clearly expressed."
353 U.S., at 147. Since neither we nor the parties are able to find any such
clear expression we hold that the Board was without jurisdiction to order
the election. This is not to imply, however, "any impairment of our own
sovereignty, or limitation of the power of Congress" in this field. *Laurit-
zen* v. *Larsen* 345 E.U. 571, 578 (1953). In fact, just as we directed the
parties in *Benz* to the Congress, which "alone has the facilities necessary
to make fairly such an important policy decision," 353 U.S., at 147, we
conclude here that the arguments should be directed to the Congress
rather than to us. . . .

   The judgment of the District Court (enjoining the National Labor
Relations Board from ordering an election by the National Maritime
Union) is therefore affirmed in No. 107. The judgment of the Court of
Appeals in Nos. 91 and 93 is vacated and the cases are remanded to that
court, with instructions that it remand to the District Court for dismissal
of the complaint in light of our decision in No. 107.

   Justice Goldberg took no part in the consideration or decisions of these
cases.

Fisheries

On 28 September 1945, the President of the United States issued two proclamations, one on fisheries and the other on the continental shelf. The first called attention to the inadequacy of arrangements for the protection and perpetuation of the fisheries in high seas contiguous to the American shores. The proclamation stressed the need to establish conservation zones in which fisheries used by nationals of the United States and other nationals could be regulated by international agreement, although the character of the high seas in these zones would remain as free and unimpeded highways of navigation under international law.

Neither the Geneva Conference on the Law of the Sea in 1958 nor a subsequent conference in 1960 had succeeded in establishing an international agreement on the maritime boundaries of states; proposals to retain the limit of territorial waters at 3 miles and proposals to extend the limit to 12 miles from the low-water mark of a state's coast were both defeated. At the 1960 conference, the United States, the United Kingdom, and Canada made a compromise proposal to extend the maritime boundary to six miles, but to allow the coastal state an additional six miles for jurisdiction over fishing and exploitation of the resources of the sea. The compromise failed by one vote to achieve a two-thirds majority.

The *Convention on Fishing and Conservation of the Living Resources on the High Seas*, the first document following, indicates the general agreement of states that a coastal state has a special interest in fisheries on the high seas contiguous to its maritime boundaries, and recommends international agreements and cooperation to conserve resources in areas where the nationals of two or more states fish. It also provides for "compulsory jurisdiction" with respect to certain disputes arising out of the convention, but has left unsettled many existing claims to fisheries and has relied for conservation on agreements by states, such as the treaty between Japan and the United States. That treaty, which may terminate in 1973, limits Japan to the Western Pacific for salmon, halibut, and herring.

Since the Geneva conferences on the Law of the Sea, several states have made new international agreements on fisheries zones and a few have issued unilateral declarations extending their jurisdiction over fisheries beyond the territorial seas. The second document that follows, the *Proposed U.S. 12-Mile Fishery Zone* letter from the Department of State, indicates United States policy.

CONVENTION ON FISHING AND CONSERVATION OF THE LIVING RESOURCES OF THE HIGH SEAS
Signed at Geneva 29 April 1958*
U.N. Document A/Conf.13/L.54

* * *

Article 1

1. All states have the right for their nationals to engage in fishing on the high seas, subject (a) to their treaty obligations, (b) to the interests and rights of coastal states as provided for in this Convention, and (c) to the provisions contained in the following articles concerning conservation of the living resources of the high seas.

2. All states have the duty to adopt, or to co-operate with other states in adopting, such measures for their respective nationals as may be necessary for the conservation of the living resources of the high seas.

* * *

Article 3

A state whose nationals are engaged in fishing any stock or stocks of fish or other living marine resources in any area of the high seas where the nationals of other states are not thus engaged shall adopt, for its own nationals, measures in that area when necessary for the purpose of the conservation of the living resources affected.

Article 4

1. If the nationals of two or more states are engaged in fishing the same stock or stocks of fish or other living marine resources in any area or areas of the high seas, these states shall, at the request of any of them, enter into negotiations with a view to prescribing by agreement for their nationals the necessary measures for the conservation of the living resources affected.

2. If the states concerned do not reach agreement within twelve months, any of the parties may initiate the procedure contemplated by Article 9.

* * *

Article 6

1. A coastal state has a special interest in the maintenance of the productivity of the living resources in any area of the high seas adjacent to its territorial sea.

---

* In force 20 March 1966.

*   *   *

3. A state whose nationals are engaged in fishing in any area of the high seas adjacent to the territorial sea of a coastal state shall, at the request of that coastal state, enter into negotiations with a view to prescribing by agreement the measures necessary for the conservation of the living resources of the high seas in that area.

*   *   *

Article 7

1. Having regard to the provisions of paragraph 1 of Article 6, any coastal state may, with a view to the maintenance of the productivity of the living resources of the sea, adopt unilateral measures of conservation appropriate to any stock of fish or other marine resources in any area of the high seas adjacent to its territorial sea, provided that negotiations to that effect with the other states concerned have not led to an agreement within six months.

*   *   *

Article 8

1. Any state which, even if its nationals are not engaged in fishing in an area of the high seas not adjacent to its coast, has a special interest in the conservation of the living resources of the high seas in that area, may request the state or states whose nationals are engaged in fishing there to take the necessary measures of conservation under Articles 3 and 4 respectively, at the same time mentioning the scientific reasons which in its opinion make such measures necessary, and indicating its special interest.

2. If no agreement is reached within twelve months, such state may initiate the procedure contemplated by Article 9.

*   *   *

Article 9

1. Any dispute which may arise between states under Articles 4, 5, 6, 7, and 8, shall, at the request of any of the parties, be submitted for settlement to a special commission of five members, unless the parties agree to seek a solution by another method of peaceful settlement, as provided for in Article 33 of the Charter of the United Nations.

*   *   *

7. Decisions of the commission shall be by majority vote.

*   *   *

Article 11

The decisions of the special commission shall be binding on the states concerned. . . .

PROPOSED U.S. 12-MILE FISHERY ZONE
United States Senate Report, 89th Congress, 2nd Session
15 June 1966

DEPARTMENT OF STATE
Washington, May 18, 1966

HON. WARREN G. MAGNUSON,
Chairman, Committee on Commerce,
U.S. SENATE

DEAR MR. CHAIRMAN: Your letter of June 30, 1965, enclosed copies of S. 2218, introduced by Senator Bartlett, and S. 2225, introduced by Senator Magnuson, on which the Department of State's comments were requested.

The purpose of the proposed legislation is to establish for the United States a 12-mile exclusive fisheries zone measured from the baseline from which the breadth of the territorial sea is measured but subject to the continuation of such traditional fishing by foreign states and their nationals as may be recognized by the U.S. Government.

Although the Geneva Conference of 1958 adopted four conventions on the law of the sea, it was recognized that the conventions left unresolved the twin questions of the width of the territorial sea and the extent to which a coastal state could claim exclusive fishing rights in the high seas off its coast. The Conference adopted a resolution suggesting that the United Nations call a second conference to deal with these unresolved problems, which the United Nations did. At the second conference, which was held in 1960, the United States and Canada put forward a compromise proposal for a 6-mile territorial sea, plus a 6-mile exclusive fisheries zone (12 miles of exclusive fisheries jurisdiction in all) subject to the continuation for 10 years of traditional fishing by other states in the outer 6 miles. This compromise proposal failed by one vote to obtain the two-thirds vote necessary for adoption.

Since the 1960 Law of the Sea Conference there has been a trend toward the establishment of a 12-mile fisheries rule in international practice. Many states acting individually or in concert with other states have extended or are in the process of extending their fisheries limits to 12 miles. Such actions have no doubt been accelerated by the support for the proposals made at the Geneva Law of the Sea Conferences in 1958 and 1960, of a fisheries zone totaling 12 miles as part of a package designed to achieve international agreement on the territorial sea.

In view of the recent developments in international practice, action by the United States at this time to establish an exclusive fisheries zone extending 9 miles beyond the territorial sea would not be contrary to international law. It should be emphasized that such action would not extend the territorial sea beyond our traditional 3-mile limit and would not affect such traditional freedoms of the sea as freedom of navigation or of overflight. With one or two possible exceptions, it is not likely that such action would be unfavorably received by other governments in view of the provision for recognition of traditional fishing, which the Department regards as a desirable provision.

In the above circumstances, the Department has no objection from the standpoint of U.S. foreign relations to establishing a 12-mile exclusive fisheries zone subject to the continuation of such traditional fishing by foreign states as may be recognized by the U.S. Government.*

Whether the establishment at this time of a 12-mile exclusive fisheries zone would serve the longer term economic interests of the United States and the U.S. fishing industry is, of course, a separate question which is discussed in a report prepared by the Department of the Interior. Inasmuch as U.S. establishment of a 12-mile exclusive fisheries zone would tend to support the trend already referred to, the passage of the proposed legislation would make it more difficult, from the standpoint of international law, to extend the zone beyond 12 miles in the future.

Time has not permitted the Department to obtain the advice of the Bureau of the Budget with respect to this report.

Douglas MacArthur II
Assistant Secretary for Congressional Relations
(For the Secretary of State)

---

* Public Law 89–658 based upon House of Representatives' Bill 9531 and above cited Senate bills was signed by the President on 14 October 1966.

Continental Shelf

The second executive proclamation of the President on 28 September 1945 dealt with control over the continental shelf of the United States, and it was followed by an act of Congress in 1953, affirming jurisdiction over the subsoil and seabed of the shelf beneath the high seas but contiguous to American coasts. Nothing in the act affected international law with respect to navigation and fishing in the high seas above the continental shelf. Many states followed the United States action, but claims to the shelf, with its potential of pearls and petroleum and other resources, were broad and vague, since no much depended on the technology of exploitation.

How far out can a state exercise jurisdiction over its continental shelf? In the 1958 *Convention of the Continental Shelf*, extracts of which follow, the depth of 200 meters was agreed on, but beyond that a state could go virtually to the limits of technical exploitation. The seas and the seabeds contain vast resources only beginning to be realized. The scientific farming of the oceans could obtain large protein foodstuffs for the rapidly growing population of the world. Untapped petroleum pools and other valuable minerals, such as manganese, undoubtedly lie on or in the seabed, waiting to be exploited. Without planning or mutual agreement, the states of the world may undertake a race for occupation of the seabed, staking out claims more fictitious and troublesome than those in the division of Africa in the 19th century. The legal issue of title to almost three quarters of the earth's surface must be faced again, as it was in the early history of the law of nations, only in a new technological complex. International law will be required to control, conserve, and exploit resources for the benefit of mankind as the competence of states to discover and produce wealth from the sea and seabeds steadily increases.

CONVENTION ON THE CONTINENTAL SHELF
Signed at Geneva 29 April 1958*
U.N. Document A/Conf.13/L.55

*   *   *

Article 1

For the purpose of these articles, the term "continental shelf" is used as referring (a) to the seabed and subsoil of the submarine areas adjacent to the coast but outside the area of the territorial sea, to a depth of 200 metres or, beyond that limit, to where the depth of the superjacent waters admits of the exploitation of the natural resources of the said areas; (b) to the seabed and subsoil of similar submarine areas adjacent to the coasts of islands.

Article 2

1. The coastal state exercises over the continental shelf sovereign rights for the purpose of exploring it and exploiting its natural resources.

2. The rights referred to in paragraph 1 of this article are exclusive in the sense that if the coastal state does not explore the continental shelf or exploit its natural resources, no one may undertake these activities, or make a claim to the continental shelf, without the express consent of the coastal state.

3. The rights of the coastal state over the continental shelf do not depend on occupation, effective or notional, or on any express proclamation.

4. The natural resources referred to in these articles consist of the mineral and other non-living resources of the seabed and subsoil together with living organisms belonging to sedentary species, that is to say, organisms which, at the harvestable stage, either are immobile on or under the seabed or are unable to move except in constant physical contact with the seabed or the subsoil.

Article 3

The rights of the coastal state over the continental shelf do not affect the legal status of the superjacent waters as high seas, or that of the airspace above those waters.

*   *   *

----
* In force 10 June 1964.

Air and Outer Space

A state's airspace over its land and marginal seas is completely and exclusively within the jurisdiction of that state. Landings for traffic purposes are permitted to the carriers of other states only by international agreement, although a general right of overflying or landing for nontraffic purposes has been granted to the scheduled aircraft of foreign states through the multilateral Air Services Transit Agreement, now widely in force.

The 1944 Chicago Civil Aviation Conference, which led to a comprehensive convention on civil aviation and to establishment of the International Civil Aviation Organization, produced the Air Services Transit Agreement. The conference also drew up an Air Transport Agreement to give contracting states the reciprocal right, in any of the other territories, to put down or pick up their national passengers, cargo, and mail originating from or proceeding to their own state, or even traffic coming from or going to a third state. But the agreement has little force today. International air transport depends on numerous other bilateral or multilateral arrangements with specific regulations.

There is no customary "innocent passage" of airspace comparable to foreign merchant ship passage through the territorial seas of a state; nevertheless, comity between friendly nations can allow an emergency incursion of airspace due to bad weather and navigational difficulties. However, many incidents of alleged violations of airspace have arisen, with grave retaliatory action. Two examples are Yugoslavia's destruction of an unarmed American transport in 1946, and the Bulgarian destruction of an Israeli plane in 1955, both involving a great loss of life. Diplomatic protests have attempted to fix liability and have sometimes obtained compensation, but no case has been adjudicated.

Many other legal problems arise in the airspace. Each airplane must be registered with one nationality, but this does not answer the problem of ownership and the "genuine link" of nationality suggested for vessels in the Geneva Convention on the High Seas. Moreover, which law governs collisions of different national aircraft above the high seas? Which governs a crime committed by a Frenchman aboard a Canadian carrier over the United States en route to Mexico? A *Convention on Aerial Collisions* and a *Convention on Offenses and Certain Other Acts Committed on Board Aircraft* have been drafted and are beginning to give guidance to new rules of law for airspace that will eventually be applied by the national courts of the participating states. Meanwhile, how far up is airspace?

Outer Space

International law presently recognizes two zones—airspace and outer space—but no measurement of them has gained legal acceptance. Until the Soviet Union launched an artificial satellite into space in October, 1957, there was little relevant debate about how far up the airspace and jurisdiction of a state extended. The immediate effect of the Russian satellite was to put outer space beyond the jurisdiction of any single state, for the satellite necessarily circled somewhere above the airspace of many states that had neither the will nor the capacity to arrest its flight. The United Nations in 1958 established an *ad hoc* committee and in 1959 a permanent Committee on the Peaceful Uses of Outer Space. This led to the epoch-making Resolution 1721 (XVI), unanimously adopted by the General Assembly on 20 December 1961, which

> Commends to States for their guidance in the exploration and use of outer space the following principles:
> (a) International law, including the Charter of the United Nations, applies to outer space and celestial bodies;
> (b) Outer space and celestial bodies are free for exploration and use by all States in conformity with international law, and are not subject to national appropriation.

The resolution also called on states that launch objects into orbit or beyond to promptly furnish information to the Committee on the Peaceful Uses of Outer Space, through the Secretary General, for the registration of launchings. Although the resolution "commends" the principles to member states, the United States has taken the position that these principles are presently the law, especially as demonstrated by the unanimous action of the General Assembly.[5]

Although only the Soviet Union and the United States have launched a number of earth-orbiting satellites as well as moon, sun, and planet probes, other states will certainly be launching objects and agents into outer space in the future. All the legal problems of the nationality of carriers, the liability for collisions, and jurisdiction for offenses, as well as questions of title and exploitation of resources are bound to arise.

In the documents that follow: (*a*) the *Convention on Offenses and Certain Other Acts Committed on Board Aircraft*, signed by 16 states in Tokyo in September 1963 proposes a determination of jurisdiction over events on board airspace carriers; (*b*) the *Survey of Space Law* recites some of the background to definitions of airspace and emergence of the concept of outer space; and (*c*) the *Declaration of Legal Principle Governing the Activities of States in the Exploration of Outer Space*, adopted unanimously by the General Assembly on 24 December 1963, reiterates

---

[5] See Statement of the United States Secretary of State before the Senate Foreign Relations Committee, 6 August 1962 in 47 *Department of State Bulletin* 318 (1962).

the principles of the 1961 Resolution on Outer Space, and further recommends new legal principles for the conduct of states with respect to outer space, carriers, and astronauts.

CONVENTION ON OFFENSES AND CERTAIN OTHER ACTS COMMITTED ON BOARD AIRCRAFT, TOKYO, 1963*
2 International Legal Materials 1042

Article 1

1. This Convention shall apply in respect of:

(a) offenses against penal law;

(b) acts which, whether or not they are offenses, may or do jeopardize the safety of the aircraft or of persons or property therein or which jeopardize good order and discipline on board.

2. Except as provided in Chapter III, this Convention shall apply in respect of offenses committed or acts done by a person on board any aircraft registered in a Contracting State, while that aircraft is in flight or on the surface of the high seas or of any other area outside the territory of any State.

*   *   *

Article 3

1. The State of registration of the aircraft is competent to exercise jurisdiction over offenses and acts committed on board.

2. Each Contracting State shall take such measures as may be necessary to establish its jurisdiction as the State of registration over offenses committed on board aircraft registered in such State.

3. This Convention does not exclude any criminal jurisdiction exercised in accordance with national law.

Article 4

A Contracting State which is not the State of registration may not interfere with an aircraft in flight in order to exercise its criminal jurisdiction over an offense committed on board except in the following cases:

(a) the offense has effect on the territory of such State;

(b) the offense has been committed by or against a national or permanent resident of such State;

(c) the offense is against the security of such State;

(d) the offense consists of a breach of any rules or regulations relating to the flight or manoeuvre of aircraft in force in such State;

---

* Not in force as of October 1966. Three states out of twelve required had ratified.

(e) the exercise of jurisdiction is necessary to ensure the observance of any obligation of such State under a multilateral international agreement.

Article 5

1. The provisions of this Chapter shall not apply to offenses and acts committed or about to be committed by a person on board an aircraft in flight in the airspace of the State of registration or over the high seas or any other area outside the territory of any State unless the last point of take-off or the next point of intended landing is situated in a State other than that of registration, or the aircraft subsequently flies in the airspace of a State other than that of registration with such person still on board.

*   *   *

Article 6

1. The aircraft commander may, when he has reasonable grounds to believe that a person has committed, or is about to commit, on board the aircraft, an offense or act contemplated in Article 1, paragraph 1, impose upon such person reasonable measures including restraint which are necessary:

(a) to protect the safety of the aircraft, or of persons or property therein; or

(b) to maintain good order and discipline on board; or

(c) to enable him to deliver such person to competent authorities or to disembark him in accordance with the provisions of this.

*   *   *

Article 7

1. Measures of restraint imposed upon a person in accordance with Article 6 shall not be continued beyond any point at which the aircraft lands unless:

(a) such point is in the territory of a non-Contracting State and its authorities refuse to permit disembarkation of that person or those measures have been imposed in accordance with Article 6, paragraph 1(c) in order to enable his delivery to competent authorities;

(b) the aircraft makes a forced landing and the aircraft commander is unable to deliver that person to competent authorities; or

(c) that person agrees to onward carriage under restraint.

*   *   *

Article 9

1. The aircraft commander may deliver to the competent authorities of any Contracting State in the territory of which the aircraft lands any person who he has reasonable grounds to believe has committed on board

the aircraft an act which, in his opinion, is a serious offense according to the penal law of the State of registration of the aircraft.

*　　　*　　　*

Article 11

1. When a person on board has unlawfully committed by force or threat thereof an act of interference, seizure, or other wrongful exercise of control of an aircraft in flight or when such an act is about to be committed, Contracting States shall take all appropriate measures to restore control of the aircraft to its lawful commander or to preserve his control of the aircraft.

*　　　*　　　*

Article 13

1. Any Contracting State shall take delivery of any person whom the aircraft commander delivers pursuant to Article 9, paragraph 1.

2. Upon being satisfied that the circumstances so warrant, any Contracting State shall take custody or other measures to ensure the presence of any person suspected of an act contemplated in Article 11, paragraph 1, and of any person of whom it has taken delivery. The custody and other measures shall be as provided in the law of that State but may only be continued for such time as is reasonably necessary to enable any criminal or extradition proceedings to be instituted.

*　　　*　　　*

5. When a State, pursuant to this Article, has taken a person into custody, it shall immediately notify the State of registration of the aircraft and the State of nationality of the detained person and, if it considers it advisable, any other interested State of the fact that such person is in custody and of the circumstances which warrant his detention. The State which makes the preliminary enquiry contemplated in paragraph 4 of this Article shall promptly report its findings to the said States and shall indicate whether it intends to exercise jurisdiction.

*　　　*　　　*

Article 16

1. Offenses committed on aircraft registered in a Contracting State shall be treated, for the purpose of extradition, as if they had been committed not only in the place in which they have occurred but also in the territory of the State of registration of the aircraft.

2. Without prejudice to the provisions of the preceding paragraph, nothing in this Convention shall be deemed to create an obligation to grant extradition.

*　　　*　　　*

SURVEY OF SPACE LAW
Select Committee on Astronautics and Space Exploration
U.S. 85th Congress, 2d Session, 1958

*   *   *

Existing international flight agreements refer to sovereignty only in the airspace over national territory, and hence do not apply, in their terms, to outer space. Today, the only generally accepted agreement of this kind is the Chicago Convention. (Convention on International Civil Aviation, 61 Stat. 1180 [1944]) Although the United States and most other advanced Western countries are parties to this Convention, the Soviet Union and Communist China are not.

Article 1 of the Chicago Convention provides that—every state has complete and exclusive jurisdiction over the airspace above its territory.

But the Convention contains no definition of the term "airspace" or of any equivalent term such as "air" or "atmosphere."

In later annexes to the Chicago Convention, the related term "aircraft" is defined in language adopted from the Paris Convention of 1919 (International Convention for the Regulation of Air Navigation, 11 League of Nations Treaty Series 173) as—

any machine which can derive support in the atmosphere from the reactions of the air.

This definition is not literally applicable to satellites or other spacecraft. Furthermore, the Chicago Convention was never intended to regulate anything but conventional civil aviation, and its definition of "aircraft" cannot reasonably be stretched to fit new and then unforeseen devices and situations.

John Cobb Cooper has argued convincingly that the term "aircraft" as used in the Chicago Convention is limited to the atmosphere (i.e., the region of aerodynamic flight). Most of the other leading commentators on space law have taken the same view.

Like the Chicago Convention, the pertinent domestic legislation of many countries, including the United States and the Soviet Union, is limited to "airspace" and "aircraft."

In both the Air Commerce Act of 1926 and the civil Aeronautics Act of 1938, the United States asserted its sovereignty in the "air space" above its lands and waters. But the term "airspace" is not defined in either act.

It is true that the term "aircraft" is defined in the Air Commerce Act as—

any contrivance now known or hereafter invented, used or designed for navigation or flight in the air.

This appears somewhat broader than the definition contained in the annexes to the Chicago convention. Although it has been seriously argued that spacecraft are accordingly "aircraft" under American domestic law *and therefore under international law as well*, this argument seems rather farfetched when applied to satellites and long-range missiles which merely pass through the atmosphere on their way to or from outer space.

*   *   *

At present, the United States is not taking any steps to broaden its flight jurisdiction even for domestic purposes. The assertion of air sovereignty and the previously quoted definition of "aircraft" contained in the earlier acts of Congress remain unchanged by the Federal Aviation Act of 1958.

In the Soviet Union, also, the principle of air sovereignty is set forth in domestic law. Article 1 of the Air Code of the U.S.S.R. (1932) asserts complete and exclusive sovereignty in the airspace (*vozdushnoye prostrantsvo*) above the Soviet Union. Although the term "airspace" is not defined in the code or elsewhere in the Soviet law, it appears that the Soviet Union, like the United States, has never recognized any upper limit to its sovereignty.

Some Soviet legal writers have asserted that air sovereignty is a principle of international as well as domestic law. On the other hand, Soviet legal articles published since the launching of Sputnik I have taken a different position. Thus, one writer has likened a satellite in outer space to a ship on the high seas. A more recent and scholarly Soviet legal article states that there is no legal regime for outer space.

No nation has yet objected to the orbiting of artificial satellites above its territory. It should be clear from the previous discussion that, in the opinion of the leading commentators on space law, no nation would have a legal right to raise such an objection. Satellite flights are not considered a violation of international law because satellites are not "aircraft" within the meaning of the Chicago Convention (particularly article 8, which concerns pilotless aircraft).

In any event, as was stated above, the Soviet Union is not a party to the Chicago Convention, and is therefore not obliged by it to recognize the sovereignty of other nations, even in the airspace above their territories, let alone the space at higher altitudes.

In addition, the space above the high seas, which cover most of the globe, and the space above unclaimed land areas, are free, according to general international law.

The foregoing considerations indicate that consent to satellite flights is unnecessary.

*   *   *

In private Anglo-American law, the counterpart of air sovereignty is the maxim *cuius est solum, eius est usque ad coelum* (he who owns the land owns it up to the sky). Some writers have argued from this maxim that national sovereignty extends without limit into outer space.

*   *   *

The Supreme Court of the United States has rejected the maxim as a doctrine of air law in the following language:

It is ancient doctrine that, at common law, ownership of the land extended to the periphery of the universe—*cuius est solum eius est usque ad coelum*. But that doctrine has no place in the modern world.

*   *   *

According to the maxim, a landowner's property rights extend to an indefinite distance both upward (*ad coelum*) and downward (*ad inferos*, as was often added). The application of this principle to the sovereign rights of nations has led some writers to postulate a zone of sovereignty stretching into space from the center of the earth through the land boundaries of each nation and the limits of its territorial seas. As Hanover pointed out and Jenks has since expressed more vividly, this conception will not fit the facts of astronomy. With the movement of the earth and other astronomical bodies, the content of a nation's zone of sovereignty would be constantly changing. Any given point in space, such as a part of the moon, would, therefore, be passing constantly from the sovereignty of one nation to that of another. A spaceship could not go from New York City to the moon, for example, without crossing the zones of sovereignty, and presumably getting the consent, of many nations. Static conceptions of sovereignty are not likely to yield acceptable results in outer space.

*   *   *

DECLARATION OF LEGAL PRINCIPLES GOVERNING ACTIVITIES IN OUTER SPACE,* 24 December 1963 U.N. Document A/Res/1962 (XVIII)

The General Assembly,

Inspired by the great prospects opening up before mankind as a result of man's entry into outer space,

---

* A treaty embodying the principles of this declaration was finally negotiated in the U.N. Outer Space Committee in December 1966 and commended by the General Assembly to all states for signature and ratification.

Recognizing the common interest of all mankind in the progress of the exploration and use of outer space for peaceful purposes,

Believing that the exploration and use of outer space should be carried on for the betterment of mankind and for the benefit of States irrespective of their degree of economic or scientific development,

Desiring to contribute to broad international co-operation in the scientific as well as in the legal aspects of exploration and use of outer space for peaceful purposes,

Believing that such co-operation will contribute to the development of mutual understanding and to the strengthening of friendly relations between nations and peoples,

Recalling its resolution 110 (II) of 3 November 1947, which condemned propaganda designed or likely to provoke or encourage any threat to the peace, breach of the peace, or act of aggression, and considering that the aforementioned resolution is applicable to outer space,

Taking into consideration its resolutions 1721 (XVI) of 20 December 1961 and 1802 (XVII) of 14 December 1962, adopted unanimously by the States Members of the United Nations,

Solemnly declares that in the exploration and use of outer space States should be guided by the following principles:

1. The exploration and use of outer space shall be carried on for the benefit and in the interests of all mankind.

2. Outer space and celestial bodies are free for exploration and use by all States on a basis of equality and in accordance with international law.

3. Outer space and celestial bodies are not subject to national appropriation by claim of sovereignty, by means of use or occupation, or by any other means.

4. The activities of States in the exploration and use of outer space shall be carried on in accordance with international law, including the Charter of the United Nations, in the interest of maintaining international peace and security and promoting international co-operation and understanding.

5. States bear international responsibility for national activities in outer space, whether carried on by governmental agencies or by non-governmental entities, and for assuring that national activities are carried on in conformity with the principles set forth in the present Declaration. The activities of non-governmental entities in outer space shall require authorization and continuing supervision by the State concerned. When activities are carried on in outer space by an international organization, responsibility for compliance with the principles set forth in this Declaration shall be borne by the international organization and by the States participating in it.

6. In the exploration and use of outer space, States shall be guided by the principle of co-operation and mutual assistance and shall conduct all their activities in outer space with due regard for the corresponding

interests of other States. If a State has reason to believe that an outer space activity or experiment planned by it or its nationals would cause potentially harmful interference with activities of other States in the peaceful exploration and use of outer space, it shall undertake appropriate international consultations before proceeding with any such activity or experiment. A State which has reason to believe that an outer space activity or experiment planned by another State would cause potentially harmful interference with activities in the peaceful exploration and use of outer space may request consultation concerning the activity or experiment.

7. The State on whose registry an object launched into outer space is carried shall retain jurisdiction and control over such object, and any personnel thereon, while in outer space. Ownership of objects launched into outer space, and of their component parts, is not affected by their passage through outer space or by their return to the earth. Such objects or component parts found beyond the limits of the State of registry shall be returned to that State, which shall furnish identifying data upon request prior to return.

8. Each State which launches or procures the launching of an object into outer space, and each State from whose territory or facility an object is launched, is internationally liable for damage to a foreign State or to its natural or judicial persons by such object or its component parts on the earth, in air space, or in outer space.

9. States shall regard astronauts as envoys of mankind in outer space, and shall render to them all possible assistance in the event of accident, distress, or emergency landing on the territory of a foreign State or on the high seas. Astronauts who make such a landing shall be safely and promptly returned to the State of registry of their space vehicle.

FOR FURTHER STUDY

Douglas M. Johnston. *The International Law of Fisheries*. New Haven, Conn.: Yale University Press, 1965.

C. W. Jenks. *Space Law*. New York: Frederick A. Praeger, Inc., 1965.

U.S. Senate Committee on Commerce. *Air Laws and Treaties of the World*. Washington, D.C.: U.S. Government Printing Office, 1965.

Maxwell Cohen (ed.). *Law and Politics in Space*. Montreal: McGill University Press, 1964.

Boleslaw Adam Boczek. *Flags of Convenience: An International Legal Study*. Cambridge, Mass.: Harvard University Press, 1962.

T. Kocher Thommen. *Legal Status of Government and Merchant Ships in International Law*. The Hague: Martinus Nijhoff, 1962.

A. P. Higgens and C. J. Colombos. *The International Law of the Sea*. London: Longmans Green, 1943 (4th ed. by C. J. Colombos, 1959).

VI

Nationality: Jurisdiction over Persons

PEOPLE are physical persons, of stature, weight, and pulse; they are moral persons, of reason, faith, and discrimination; but they are also persons who have a legal status, who possess a legal identity, with rights and obligations that may be adjudicated under a system of law. One of the most important legal identifications attached to a person in the modern world is his nationality.

Nationality is the legal status of a natural person who owes an enduring, rather than a temporary, allegiance to a state.

The Fourteenth Amendment of the United States Constitution provides that "all persons born or naturalized in the United States and subject to the jurisdiction thereof are citizens of the United States and of the State wherein they reside." The nationality law also permits children of American citizens born abroad to retain or opt for United States citizenship. The Japanese nationality law of 1950, on the other hand, emphasized parentage in prescribing that a child shall, in any of the following cases, be a Japanese national:

(1) When, at the time of its birth, the father is a Japanese national;
(2) When the father who died prior to the birth of the child was a Japanese national at the time of his death;
(3) When the mother . . .[1]

and so forth. The contemporary practice in the nationality laws of most states is a combination of both *jus soli*, right by soil or place of birth, and *jus sanguinis*, right by blood or descent.

---

[1] Law No. 157 of 1950, *Works of the Second Session of the Asian–African Legal Consultative Committee*, held at Cairo, October 1958, p. 267. The Secretariat of the Committee is located in New Delhi.

A distinction ought to be drawn between "national" and "citizen," although the words often may be used interchangeably. Citizenship refers to political and civil rights that a state may grant to its nationals. Citizenship, therefore, is regulated by municipal law only. A person may be a national of a state but not possess the rights of citizenship. For instance, under the Philippine Independence Act of 1934, Philippine citizens were not citizens of the United States, although they owed allegiance to it. The U.S. Immigration and Nationality Act of 1952 plainly defines an American "national" as *either* a citizen *or* "a person, who though not a citizen of the United States, owes permanent allegiance to the United States."

In brief, "Every citizen is a national, but not every national is necessarily a citizen of the State concerned; whether this is the case depends upon municipal law; the question is not relevant for international law."[2]

Nationality also refers to the legal status of vessels, carriers, and fictitious persons, such as business corporations. Although such entities cannot demonstrate allegiance in the same sense as natural persons, they also fall under the jurisdiction of their states, not only within the territories of their states, but also on the high seas and, under certain conditions, while situated or active in other states. Aliens, who are nationals of another state, also owe loyalty to the state where they reside and are subject to the national laws. As expressed by the United States Supreme Court in 1872:

> The alien, whilst domiciled in the country, owes a local and temporary allegiance, which continues during the period of his residence. This obligation of temporary allegiance by an alien resident in a friendly country is everywhere recognized by publicists and statesmen. . . . It is well known that, by the public law, an alien or a stranger born, for so long a time as he continues within the dominions of a foreign government, owes obedience to the laws of that government, and may be punished for treason or other crimes as a native born subject might be. . . .[3]

An English court tried and convicted United States-born Lord Haw-Haw of treason for his broadcasts of enemy propaganda for Germany. England asserted jurisdiction because he had obtained a British passport, although fraudulently, and thus continued to owe allegiance to Great Britain.[4] Aliens can also be employed as officials of a foreign state, or as members of a crew aboard a foreign ship or aircraft, with the possibility of a temporary allegiance to that state and subjection to its laws beyond its territory.

States do not zealously seek to enforce their laws on their nationals abroad, for neither circumstances nor policy warrant such measures.

---

[2] Paul Weiss, *Nationality and Statelessness in International Law* (London: Stevens and Sons, 1956), p. 6.

[3] *Carlisle* v. *United States*, 83 U.S. (16 Wall) 147.

[4] *Joyce* v. *Director of Public Prosecutions*, British House of Lords (1946), Appeals Case, 347.

Nevertheless, the state can prosecute its nationals within its own jurisdiction for offenses that were punishable in both the resident state and the national's state, or for specific kinds of offenses or offenses against co-nationals abroad. One celebrated case involved two fines of $30,000 each imposed on Harry M. Blackmer and his property, situated in the United States, as a punishment for contempt of court. A resident of France but a citizen of the United States, Mr. Blackmer had failed to respond to subpoenas served on him in France, which required him to appear as a witness for the United States in a criminal trial before the Supreme Court of the District of Columbia. Hearing the case on an appeal that the governing statute of Congress was unconstitutional, the Supreme Court of the United States said:

> He continued to owe allegiance to the United States. By virtue of the obligations of citizenship, the United States retained its authority over him, and he was bound by its laws made applicable to him in a foreign country. . . . With respect to such an exercise of authority, there is no question of international law, but solely of the purport of the municipal law which establishes the duties of the citizen in relation to his own government.[5]

Beyond such a general duty, however, doubt may exist as to whether a particular statute was intended to apply to nationals abroad, as in the *Bulova Watch* case. Steele, an American national, committed his acts in Mexico City. The Supreme Court held:

> This Court has often stated that the legislation of Congress will not extend beyond the boundaries of the United States unless a contrary legislative intent appears. . . . His operations and their effects were not confined within the territorial limits of a foreign nation. He bought component parts of his wares in the United States, and spurious "Bulovas" filtered through the Mexican border into this country. . . . We do not deem material that petitioner affixed the mark "Bulova" in Mexico City rather than here, or that his purchases in the United States when viewed in isolation do not violate any of our laws . . . we do not think that petitioner by so simple a device can evade the thrust of the laws of the United States in a privileged sanctuary beyond our borders. . . . Where, as here, there can be no interference, with the sovereignty of another nation, the District Court in exercising its equity powers may command persons properly before it to cease or perform acts outside its territorial jurisdiction.[6]

States have frequently stretched the meaning of territorial jurisdiction to cover acts performed, strictly speaking, outside the boundaries of sovereignty. For example, an individual who plans and intends certain crimes in one state, but actually carries them out in another, might under certain statutes be arrested and tried for the crime by the first state if he returns to its territory. Or an individual who shoots across a frontier and kills a man in another state might, if he falls into the hands of the authorities of that state, be tried by its courts. Similarly, such acts as

---

[5] *Harry M. Blackmer* v. *United States of America*, 284 U.S. 421 (1932).

[6] *Steele* v. *Bulova Watch Company*, 344 U.S. 280 (1952).

counterfeiting money, mail fraud, or illegal trade combinations that affect the state's market may be construed as an injury to a state, punishable if the agent enters, is delivered to, or has assets in the state's territory, even though the acts took place entirely in other states. The outreach of a state's jurisdiction to its own nationals beyond its territory poses far fewer problems than its outreach to aliens. Nevertheless, a United States Court of Appeals has said, ". . . it is settled law . . . that any state may impose liabilities, even upon persons not within its allegiance, for conduct outside its borders which the state reprehends; and these liabilities other states will ordinarily recognize."[7]

However, an extreme illustration of the outreach of jurisdiction by a state occurred when Turkey asserted criminal jurisdiction over a French officer of a French ship that had collided with a Turkish vessel on the high seas and had caused the deaths of eight Turkish sailors and passengers. In 1927, in the *Lotus* case the Permanent Court of International Justice found that no rule of international law prevented such a claim by a state to jurisdiction. But the dissenting opinion of six judges then, the subsequent reaction of several governments, and the provisions of Article II of the Geneva Convention on the High Seas in 1958 seem to indicate that such an assertion of criminal jurisdiction goes far beyond what most states will tolerate today.

States, of course, cannot exercise their jurisdiction over persons within the territory of another state. In civil law, however, states generally assist each other in the administration of justice by allowing their courts on the request of another state to compel testimony of persons within their jurisdiction in the form of a "letter rogatory." Such depositions are sent to the foreign court at which an action is in progress. Furthermore, where diverse citizenship or locality or foreign law is involved in arriving at a decision, by custom several national courts make use of the laws and judgments of foreign states in their application of law (private international law) to cases before them involving title to property, family relations, inheritance, contracts, and so forth.

In criminal law, both nationals and aliens may be returned to a state's domain by its agreement with other states on the extradition of alleged criminals. Treaties of extradition usually specify the offenses for which extradition will be effected. They generally include well-recognized crimes, such as murder, forgery, and robbery, that would be punishable in both contracting states. A state that receives an extradited person from another state under a treaty is under an international obligation to try that individual for the offense actually specified in the request for extradition.

States are notoriously reluctant to surrender their own nationals to the jurisdiction of another state under the procedure of extradition. In some states, nationals may be tried for crimes committed within the territory

---

[7] *United States* v. *Aluminum Company of America*, 148 F. 2d 416 (1945).

and against the laws of another state, but the United States and Great Britain, bound by the common law, generally require trial at the place of the crime. Political offenses are regularly excepted from extradition treaties, but what is a "political" offense? Where does one draw the line between an act in pursuance of political or governmental ends and plain crimes?

In the *International Judicial Procedure* amendment to the United States Code by Public Law 88–619 (1964), the first document that follows, the assistance rendered to foreign tribunals by law is indicated, as is the power of American courts to reach nationals or residents of the United States in a foreign country. In the *Jimenez v. Aristigueta* case, which also follows, part of the legal procedure used by Jiminez to resist extradition by Venezuela from the United States is shown, as is the role of the American court in determining grounds for extradition in accordance with the United States–Venezuela treaty.

International Subpoena Power and Extradition

INTERNATIONAL JUDICIAL PROCEDURE
Public Law 88–619, 88th Congress, H.R. 9435
3 October 1964

*   *   *

#1782. *Assistance to foreign and international tribunals and to litigants before such tribunals*

(a) The district court of the district in which a person resides or is found may order him to give his testimony or statement or to produce a document or other thing for use in a proceeding in a foreign or international tribunal. The order may be made pursuant to a letter rogatory issued, or request made, by a foreign or international tribunal or upon the application of any interested person and may direct that the testimony or statement be given, or the document or other thing be produced, before a person appointed by the court. . . .

#1783. *Subpoena of person in foreign country*

(a) A court of the United States may order the issuance of a subpoena requiring the appearance as a witness before it, or before a person or body designated by it, of a national or resident of the United States who is in a foreign country, or requiring the production of a specified document or other thing by him, if the court finds that particular testimony or the production of the document or other thing by him is necessary in the interest of justice, and, in other than a criminal action or proceeding, if the court finds, in addition, that it is not possible to obtain his testimony in admissible form without his personal appearance or to obtain the production of the document or other thing in any other manner. . . .

(b) . . . The person serving the subpoena shall tender to the person to whom the subpoena is addressed his estimated necessary travel and attendance expenses, the amount of which shall be determined by the court and stated in the order directing the issuance of the subpoena. . . .

* * *

#1784. *Contempt*

(a) The court of the United States which has issued a subpoena served in a foreign country may order the person who failed to appear or who has failed to produce a document or other thing as directed therein to show cause before it at a designated time why he should not be punished for contempt.

(b) The court, in the order to show cause, may direct that any of the person's property within the United States be levied upon or seized, in the manner provided by law or court rules governing levy or seizure under execution, and held to satisfy any judgment that may be rendered against him pursuant to subjection (d) of this section if adequate security, in such amount as the court may direct in the order, be given for any damage that he might suffer should he not be found in contempt. Security under this subsection may not be required of the United States. . . .

* * *

(d) On the return day of the order to show cause or any later day to which the hearing may be continued, proof shall be taken. If the person is found in contempt, the court, notwithstanding any limitation upon its power generally to punish for contempt, may fine him not more than $100,000 and direct that the fine and costs of the proceedings be satisfied by a sale of the property levied upon or seized, conducted upon the notice required and in the manner provided for sales upon execution.

JIMENEZ V. ARISTIGUETA
United States Court of Appeals, 1962
311 F. 2d 547

Estes, District Judge

This is an appeal from the judgment of the United States District Court for the Southern District of Florida, Judge Wm. A. McRae, Jr., dated August 23, 1961, dismissing the original and amended petitions for habeas corpus filed by appellant, Marcos Perez Jimenez, and discharging the original and amended orders to show cause issued on the petitions for habeas corpus. The petitions for habeas corpus incorporate by reference the entire file in an international extradition proceeding under 18 U.S.C. § 3184 ct seq. filed in the United States District Court for the Southern District of Florida, Miami Division, on August 24, 1959, by Manuel Aristigueta, Consul General of the Republic of Venezuela, on behalf of appellee, the Republic of Venezuela (Venezuela), in which the return to Venezuela of appellant, a former president of Venezuela, now in Miami, Florida, is sought under the Treaty of Extradition between the United States and Venezuela (43 Stat. 1698).

The extradition proceeding was initially heard by Judge William C. Mathes, of the United States District Court for the Southern District of California, sitting in Miami by designation. On March 8, 1960, Judge Mathes permitted the filing of Venezuela's Second Amended Complaint; issued a new warrant for the arrest of appellant returnable "before me," and "with the consent of both plaintiff and defendant" continued appellant's release on bond previously posted. Thereafter the extradition case proceeded before Judge Mathes until Venezuela closed its evidence, all of which was documentary. Appellant's motion to dismiss was denied by Judge Mathes "without prejudice to a renewal of it at the close of the evidence."

In accordance with an order of the Judicial Council of the Fifth Circuit of October 7, 1960, for assignment "to some other judge" of any "unfinished business" of Judge Mathes, Chief Judge Whitehurst ordered the extradition case assigned to himself on March 6, 1961, and proceeded with hearings therein.

* * *

Venezuela's Second Amended Complaint, upon which the extradition proceeding and orders under attack were based, charged appellant, chief executive of Venezuela (first as a member of a three-man junta, then as provisional President, and later as President), having legal responsibility for the administration of the funds and contracting authority of Venezuela, with two distinct groups of crimes committed in Venezuela during the years 1948–1958, the first group composed of four charges of murder and participation in murder as an accessory before the fact, the second group comprised financial crimes for his own private personal gain. . . .

* * *

Appellant first urges that Judge Whitehurst did not have jurisdiction to conduct the extradition proceeding because the warrant of arrest was made returnable before Judge Mathes—not Judge Whitehurst, contending that the statute (18 U.S.C. § 3184) and the Treaty (Article XII) authorize only that particular justice, judge or commissioner who issues the warrant of arrest or who is "designated in the warrant of arrest" to hear and consider the evidence of criminality. . . .

*   *   *

Appellant's second point urges that Judge McRae erred in restricting his review of the extradition proceedings on habeas corpus to the following: "(1) whether the magistrate has jurisdiction, (2) whether the offense charged is within the Treaty, and (3) whether there was any evidence warranting the finding that there was reasonable ground to believe the accused guilty"; and in not determining that appellant was denied due process of law in that (1) Judge Whitehurst had not heard, examined, considered, and read all of the evidence of criminality as required by Article XII of the Treaty and 18 U.S.C. § 3184, (2) Judge Whitehurst did not examine and consider separately the evidence presented to determine whether in each case there existed probable cause that a crime enumerated within the Treaty had been committed by appellant as charged, and (3) Judge Whitehurst refused appellant's request to take the deposition of Dupouy.

All of Venezuela's evidence of criminality was documentary and was presented before Judge Mathes. . . . All of appellant's evidence (including testimony of witnesses) was presented before Judge Whitehurst. Both sides had, at the request of Judges Mathes and Whitehurst, submitted fact memoranda or analyses of the evidence. On June 16, 1961 Judge Whitehurst announced at the conclusion of extended hearings and arguments before him that probable cause had not been established with respect to the murders, but that probable cause had been established with respect to the financial crimes charged.

*   *   *

In support of his contention that he was denied due process of law in Judge Whitehurst's refusal of his request to take the deposition of Napoleon Dupouy appellant points to 18 U.S.C. § 3191 which provides that "witnesses" whose evidence is material to his defense may be subpoenaed on behalf of persons unable to pay the fees of "such witnesses." Section 3191 relates to the subpoenaing of *witnesses* and *not* to *depositions*.

*   *   *

. . . The accused is not entitled to introduce evidence which merely goes to his defense but he may offer limited evidence to explain elements in the case against him, since the extradition proceeding is not a trial of the guilt or innocence but of the character of a preliminary examination held before a committing magistrate to determine whether the accused shall be held for trial in another tribunal.

*   *   *

There is no merit to appellant's contention that he was denied due process of law in the extradition proceeding.

* * *

Appellant contends that the acts with which he is charged are "acts done in the exercise of or in color of his sovereign authority and by virtue of the law of nations as stated in *Underhill* v. *Hernandez*, 168 U.S. 250 . . . was entitled to be discharged from custody inasmuch as the judicial authorities cannot review the acts done by a sovereign in his own territory to determine illegality."

Seizing upon Venezuela's characterization of appellant as a "dictator" he argues that as a "dictator" he himself would be the sovereign—the government of Venezuela—and that all his acts constituting the financial crimes with which he is charged and as to which probable cause of guilt has been found are acts of state or sovereign acts, the legality of which the Act of State Doctrine precludes an extradition judge or magistrate from adjudicating.

* * *

Even though characterized as a dictator, appellant was not himself the sovereign—government—of Venezuela within the Act of State Doctrine. He was chief executive, a public officer, of the sovereign nation of Venezuela. It is only when officials having sovereign authority act in an official capacity that the Act of State Doctrine applies. . . .

Appellant's acts constituting the financial crimes of embezzlement or malversation, fraud or breach of trust, and receiving money or valuable securities knowing them to have been unlawfully obtained as to which probable cause of guilt had been shown were not acts of Venezuela sovereignty. Judge Whitehurst found that each of these acts was "for the private financial benefit" of the appellant. They constituted common crimes committed in pursuance of it. They are as far from being an act of state as rape which appellant concedes would not be an "Act of State."

* * *

The very reason for this extradition case is that the United States has agreed with Venezuela for the extradition of persons charged with crimes enumerated in the Treaty. This Treaty deals expressly in paragraph 14 of Article II with embezzlement or criminal malversation by public officers. Appellant notes that a public officer is one who exercises "in part sovereign power." The two governments intended the tribunals to act when the accused is a public officer charged with crimes enumerated in the Treaty. The acts constituting crimes charged for which the extradition of appellant is sought are not "acts of Venezuela" as in Hernandez, and the Act of State doctrine is no bar to this extradition proceeding or justification for the discharge from custody of appellant.

*   *   *

Since appellant had no connection with the murders charged in the complaint, those acts could not be political acts or crimes attributable to appellant and whether or not the homicides were political crimes by those who committed them can have no bearing on the appellant.

The murders are no longer in the case.

Judge Whitehurst's decision that the financial crimes were not political was based upon the evidence and is not reviewable here.

*   *   *

There is no evidence that the financial crimes charged were committed in the course of and incidentally to a revolutionary uprising or other violent political disturbance.

Venezuela seeks the surrender of appellant by the executive officers of the United States (who must ultimately determine whether fugitives shall be surrendered) for trial of appellant on the financial crimes only. The claim of extradition for appellant within the meaning of the Treaty, is not based on any crime or offense of a political character or on acts connected with such crimes or offenses. Judge McRae did not err in failing to remand the extradition proceedings for further findings.

*   *   *

The record shows that appellant, in November, 1948, was a young lieutenant colonel in the Venezuelan army, of very modest means. By a coup d'etat, appellant and two other lieutenant colonels established a three-man military junta, which was to rule in accordance with the Constitution and laws of Venezuela. As a member of the Junta, the appellant was required by law to file a statement of his assets upon taking office. His sworn statement, filed on March 14, 1949, showed that he and his wife then possessed total net assets equivalent to $31,343.28.

In the succeeding nine years the record discloses that appellant was enriched by more than $13,000,000 in excess of his opening net worth and his legitimate compensation. All during this period the laws of Venezuela prohibited anyone in appellant's position from engaging in commercial transactions with the nation, directly or indirectly. Evidence of appellant's financial dealings was found in a suitcase which he left behind when he hastily fled Venezuela, on January 23, 1958. The suitcase bore the initials of appellant's wife, "F.P.J.," and contained securities, title deeds, banking documents, personal memoranda, currency, and a major general's uniform. That the suitcase and its contents belonged to appellant is clear from a radiogram sent by appellant's wife from the Dominican Republic, appellant's first stop in his flight from Venezuela, and from a letter he wrote on October 24, 1958 from Miami, Florida.

The record reflects that Dr. Napoleon Dupouy was an intimate and close associate of appellant; that he exerted a strong influence in connection with government contracts; that he reported regularly to appellant and received commissions on government contracts which were shared with appellant. Papers and memoranda in the handwriting of Dupouy and appellant, found in appellant's suitcase, evidence the fact that appellant received commissions or "kickbacks" in the ten specific instances alleged in the second amended complaint.

Dupouy was nominal president of a construction company, Empress Champenon Bernard de Venezuela, S.A., a subsidiary of the French firm Champenon Bernard. On September 12, 1950, Champenon Bernard entered into a contract with the Venezuelan government for the construction of three viaducts on the Caracas–LaGuaira expressway. Dupouy received as his commission 250,000 bolivares, which the written memoranda reflect that he shared equally with appellant.

On March 18, 1949, the appellant, as Minister of Defense, contracted with the Swedish armaments manufacture Aktiebolaget Bofors for cannon, guns, parts and ammunition for the amount of $2,358,060. Evidence from appellant's suitcase reflects that he received $58,951.50, which is precisely 2½ percent of the Bofors contracts.

Appellant, as Minister of Defense, on July 24, 1951 contracted with the British firm Vickers-Armstrong (Shipbuilders), Ltd., for the construction of a destroyer, "Aragua," for the amount of £2,637,000. A memorandum by Dupouy evidences the fact that appellant received $168,979.

In connection with a contract for a ground-to-air communications system for 47 airports in Venezuela with International Standard Electric Company of New York, at a cost of $2,948,754, the evidence shows that appellant received $60,000 through checks from one Virgil G. Applewhite, who was vice-president of a Caracas firm which did preliminary work on the communications contract.

A handwritten memorandum prepared by Dupouy, found in appellant's suitcase, indicated that appellant received $785,000 on the purchase of six destroyers from the Italian firm of Ansaldo, S.A.; $190,272 on a contract for the purchase of three Viscount aircraft, spare parts and spare engines; $258,744 on the purchase of 40 tanks with spare parts and ammunition from two French concerns; and $170,175 on the purchases of boats by the government of Venezuela.

* * *

The record shows that appellant, through a close associate, Fortunato Herrera, and a corporation called Polinversiones, received a portion of the compensation paid by the Venezuelan Government for two tracts of land expropriated by decrees promulgated by appellant. One of the transactions involved the property of a Mrs. Carmen Rafaela Agreda de Jiminez which the government was taking over pursuant to a decree issued by appellant on August 15, 1952.

*   *   *

The official government appraisal of the property was B's 13,320,210.50. The government paid Mrs. de Jiminez with interest-bearing obligations, and Mrs. de Jiminez turned over the amount in excess of B's 10,000,000 to Herrera.

In the acquisition of land for highway construction Herrera acquired for Polinversiones an option from Industrial del Carton for the purchase of 40,304 square meters of land at B's 30 per square meter. The land was subsequently appraised by the government at B's 120 per square meter. Thus Polinversiones received a profit of B's 3,627,360 in less than a year on an investment of B's 1,209,130. It is clear from the evidence that appellant shared with Herrera in the profits of Polinversiones.

*   *   *

The evidence of appellant's enrichment, with no proof of any lawful source of the funds, when considered with the evidence of appellant's transactions . . . is sufficient to warrant the finding that there was reasonable ground to believe the accused guilty of the financial crimes charged.

The crimes charged to appellant as to which probable cause has been found are offenses extraditable by Article II of the Treaty of Extradition. The record is clear that these charges are, if proved, crimes in the demanding nation, that question having been determined by the highest court of Venezuela. It is significant in this regard that the charges come here as a result of proceedings before the Supreme Court of Justice of Venezuela.

The crimes as to which probable cause has been shown are within Article II, paragraph 14, of the Treaty—"embezzlement or criminal malversation."

The crimes as to which probable cause has been shown are within Article II, paragraph 20, of the Treaty—"fraud or breach of trust. . . ."

Appellant contends that the extradition magistrate was without jurisdiction by virtue of Article XII of the Treaty because appellee failed to lay before the extradition magistrate legal evidence of the appellant's guilt within the two months prescribed by the treaty.

*   *   *

The Second Amended Complaint was filed on March 8, 1960, and a new warrant of arrest was issued and executed the same day. Almost all of the evidence of appellee was on file by April 9, 1960, well within the two-month period. In *Voloshin* v. *Ridenour*, 299 F. 134, 137–38 (5 Cir. 1924), it was held by this court that the period prescribed by a treaty is measured from the date on which the defendant is arrested on the basis of the complaint on which the hearing is held. It is therefore evident that the two-month limitation period of Article XII was not exceeded on either of the two warrants.

The record contains no reversible error and the judgment of the District Court dismissing the appellant's petition for habeas corpus and discharging the orders to show cause issued thereon is hereby Affirmed. The mandate of the Court will issue forthwith.

Dual Nationality and Effective Bond

Because each state can make its own nationality laws, it frequently happens that a person may have a claim to being a national of two states. For example, a person born in the United States and subject to the jurisdiction thereof would be an American national, but if his parents were Japanese he would also have a right to Japanese nationality. To give another illustration, if an American woman were to marry an alien she would not lose her United States nationality, but she might additionally acquire her husband's nationality under the laws of his state.

Again, the municipal laws of each state must be studied to see what steps such an individual might have to take in order to maintain a continuing claim to the nationality of a state, or to determine what acts he might have to perform to denationalize himself from one of the two states. Generalizations in this field would be useless and largely irrelevant to international law. But when a state exercises its right of diplomatic protection for one of its nationals under international law, certain problems may arise if the individual has a dual legal status.

Customarily, under international law states have been barred from extending their diplomatic protection to one of their nationals against another state that also claims the same individual as its national. For example, an individual with American and Japanese nationality could not rely on the diplomatic protection of the United States against Japan. Too often, dual nationality is thought of as an advantage, allowing a certain flexibility in residence, in obligations to national law, and so forth; but it could prove a genuine liability, for a dual national may owe allegiance to two states and may be subject to the laws of both states with regard to military service, taxes, and other obligations placed on nationals. States have been concerned about the problem of dual nationality. The *European Convention on Reduction of Cases of Multiple Nationality and Military Obligations in Cases of Multiple Nationality*, signed at Strasbourg in 1963, was one of several earnest efforts to bring state practices in allowing a choice of nationality into harmony with its consequent military obligations.

Although each state may make its own nationality laws, its "right" to do so may come into conflict with its obligations to other states of the community under international law. A respected statement on this point was rendered by the Permanent Court of International Justice in 1923 in an advisory opinion to the Council of the League of Nations. In Tunis and Morocco, France had promulgated nationality decrees that conferred French nationality, with liability for military service, on persons born in

Tunis or Morocco who also had at least one parent born there. Great Britain protested the enforcement of these decrees against British subjects, denying the exclusive jurisdiction of France over these protected states in the light of their previous treaties with Great Britain, while France rejoined that the issue was solely a matter of domestic jurisdiction and not justiciable under international law. The Court said:

. . . it is enough to observe that it may well happen that, in a matter which, like that of nationality, is not, in principle, regulated by international law, the right of a State to use its discretion is nevertheless restricted by obligations which it may have undertaken towards other States. In such a case, jurisdiction which, in principle belongs solely to the State, is limited by rules of international law.[8]

However, the degree to which international law limits municipal laws on nationality has thus far been very slight, and even then open to profound argument. As Lord McNair wrote, with brevity and cogency, "Nationality stands on the frontier which is common to international law and municipal law . . . little authority exists as to the extent to which international law can control, and in extreme cases, refuse to recognize municipal regulations on the matter."[9]

One international legal problem, distinctly related to the effective identification of nationality, may occur when there is a mixed nationality or doubts about the "national character" of corporations. Nationality for legal purposes applies to corporations as well as to individuals. With a modern international economy, corporations today can have their headquarters in one state while transacting most of their business in others; they can be incorporated in one state, but a majority of their shareholders may be individuals of another nationality. Therefore, questions can arise about the "enemy character" of a corporation chartered by a neutral state to stockholders who are nationals of a belligerent. As with individuals, moreover, the diplomatic protection of a corporation by a state against another state will hinge on a determination of nationality, at the time of both the alleged injury and prosecution of the claim.

A new departure in international judgments on nationality has been the majority opinion in the Nottebohm case, which held that one state did not have to recognize the nationality granted to an individual by another state when there was an absence of any bond of attachment or durable link between the individual and that state; consequently, the state that granted nationality to the individual in such circumstances could not under international law claim the right of diplomatic protection for him against a state that contested the validity of the naturalization.

In *Perkins* v. *Elg*, the first case that follows, the acquisition of dual

---

[8] P.C.I.J. Series B, No. 4.

[9] *International Law Opinions* (Cambridge: Cambridge University Press, 1956), Vol. II, p. 3.

nationality under United States law is illustrated; in *Kawakita* v. *United States*, the second case that follows, a further definition of dual citizenship and the responsibilities of dual allegiance are forcefully indicated; in the *Nottebohm Case*, the third case that follows, the majority and dissenting opinions reflect a strong divergence of view on the requirements for obtaining nationality and the allowable exercise of diplomatic protection by states on behalf of their nationals.

Dual Nationality

PERKINS v. ELG
United States Supreme Court, 1938
307 U.S. 525

Mr. Chief Justice Hughes delivered the opinion of the Court.

The question is whether the plaintiff, Marie Elizabeth Elg, who was born in the United States of Swedish parents then naturalized here, has lost her citizenship and is subject to deportation because of her removal during minority to Sweden, it appearing that her parents resumed their citizenship in that country but that she returned here on attaining majority with intention to remain and to maintain her citizenship in the United States.

Miss Elg was born in Brooklyn, New York, on October 2, 1907. Her parents, who were natives of Sweden, emigrated to the United States sometime prior to 1906 and her father was naturalized here in that year. In 1911, her mother took her to Sweden where she continued to reside until September 7, 1929. Her father went to Sweden in 1922 and has not since returned to the United States. In November, 1934, he made a statement before an American consul in Sweden that he had voluntarily expatriated himself for the reason that he did not desire to retain the status of an American citizen and wished to preserve his allegiance to Sweden.

In 1928, shortly before Miss Elg became twenty-one years of age, she inquired of an American consul in Sweden about returning to the United States and was informed that if she returned after attaining majority she should seek an American passport. In 1929, within eight months after attaining majority, she obtained an American passport which was issued on the instructions of the Secretary of State. She then returned to the United States, was admitted as a citizen and has resided in this country ever since.

In April, 1935, Miss Elg was notified by the Department of Labor that she was an alien illegally in the United States and was threatened with deportation. Proceedings to effect her deportation have been postponed from time to time. In July, 1936, she applied for an American passport but it was refused by the Secretary of State upon the sole ground that he was without authority to issue it because she was not a citizen of the United States.

Thereupon she began this suit against the Secretary of Labor, the Acting Commissioner of Immigration and Naturalization, and the Secretary of State to obtain (1) a declaratory judgment that she is a citizen of the United States and entitled to all the rights and privileges of citizenship, and (2) an injunction against the Secretary of Labor and the Commissioner of Immigration restraining them from prosecuting proceedings for her deportation, and (3) an injunction against the Secretary of State from refusing to issue to her a passport upon the ground that she is not a citizen.

The defendants moved to dismiss the complaint, asserting that plaintiff was not a citizen of the United States by virtue of the Naturalization Convention and Protocol of 1869 (proclaimed in 1872) between the United States and Sweden (17 Stat. 809) and the Swedish Nationality Law, and paragraph 2 of the Act of Congress of March 2, 1907, 8 U.S.C. 17. The District Court overruled the motion as to the Secretary of Labor and the Commissioner of Immigration and entered a decree declaring that the plaintiff is a native citizen of the United States but directing that the complaint be dismissed as to the Secretary of State because of his official discretion in the issue of passports. On cross appeals, the Court of Appeals affirmed the decree. 69 App. D.C. 175; 99 F. 2d. 408. Certiorari was granted, December 5, 1938.

First. On her birth in New York, the plaintiff became a citizen of the United States. Civil Rights Act of 1866, 14 Stat. 27; Fourteenth Amendment, paragraph 1; *United States* v. *Wong Kim Ark*, 169 U.S. 649. In a comprehensive review of the principles and authorities governing the decision in that case—that a child born here of alien parentage becomes a citizen of the United States—the Court adverted to the "inherent right of every independent nation to determine for itself, and according to its own constitution and laws, what classes of persons shall be entitled to its citizenship." *United States* v. *Wong Kim Ark*. As municipal law determines how citizenship may be acquired, it follows that persons may have a dual nationality. And the mere fact that the plaintiff may have acquired Swedish citizenship by virtue of the operation of Swedish law, on the resumption of that citizenship by her parents, does not compel the conclusion that she has lost her own citizenship acquired under our law. As at birth she became a citizen of the United States, that citizenship must be deemed to continue unless she has been deprived of it through the operation of a treaty of congressional enactment or by her voluntary action in conformity with applicable legal principles.

Second. It has long been a recognized principle in this country that if a child born here is taken during minority to the country of his parents' origin, where his parents resume their former allegiance, he does not thereby lose his citizenship in the United States provided that on attaining majority he elects to retain that citizenship and to return to the United States to assume its duties.

*   *   *

Petitioners stress the American doctrine relating to expatriation. By the Act of July 27, 1868, Congress declared that "the right of expatriation is a natural and inherent right of all people." Expatriation is the voluntary renunciation or abandonment of nationality and allegiance. It has no application to the removal from this country of a native citizen during minority. In such a case the voluntary action which is of the essence of the right of expatriation is lacking. That right is fittingly recognized where a child born here, who may be, or may become, subject to a dual nationality, elects on attaining majority citizenship in the country to which he has been removed. But there is no basis for invoking the doctrine of expatriation where a native citizen who is removed to his parents' country of origin during minority returns here on his majority and elects to remain and to maintain his American citizenship. Instead of being inconsistent with the right of expatriation, the principle which permits that election conserves and applies it.

The question then is whether this well recognized right of election has been destroyed by treaty or statute.

Third. Petitioners invoke our treaty with Sweden of 1869 . . . Article I of the treaty provided:

"Citizens of the United States of America who have resided in Sweden or Norway for a continuous period of at least five years, and during such residence have become and are lawfully recognized as citizens of Sweden or Norway, shall be held by the government of the United States to be Swedish or Norwegian citizens, and shall be treated as such.

"Reciprocally, citizens of Sweden or Norway who have resided in the United States of America for a continuous period of at least five years, and during such residence have become naturalized citizens of the United States, shall be held by the government of Sweden and Norway to be American citizens, and shall be treated as such.

"The declaration of an intention to become a citizen of one or the other country has not for either party the effect of citizenship legally acquired."

We think that this provision in its direct application clearly implies a voluntary residence and it would thus apply in the instant case to the father of respondent. There is no specific mention of minor children who have obtained citizenship by birth in the country which their parents have left. And if it be assumed that a child born in the United States would be deemed to acquire the Swedish citizenship of his parents through their return to Sweden and resumption of citizenship there, still nothing is said in the treaty which in such a case would destroy the right of election which appropriately belongs to the child on attaining majority. . . .

* * *

Fourth. We think that petitioners' contention under paragraph 2 of the Act of March 2, 1907, is equally untenable. That statutory provision is as follows:

"That any American citizen shall be deemed to have expatriated himself when he has been naturalized in any foreign state in conformity with its laws, or when he has taken an oath of allegiance to any foreign state.

"When any naturalized citizen shall have resided for two years in the foreign state from which he came, or for five years in any other foreign state it shall be presumed that he has ceased to be an American citizen, and the place of his general abode shall be deemed his place of residence during said years: *Provided, however,* That such presumption may be overcome on the presentation of satisfactory evidence to a diplomatic or consular officer of the United States, under such rules and regulations as the Department of State may prescribe: *And provided also,* That no American citizen shall be allowed to expatriate himself when this country is at war."

Petitioners contend that respondent's acquisition of derivative Swedish citizenship makes her a person who has been "naturalized under Swedish law," and that therefore "she has lost her American citizenship" through the operation of this statute. We are unable to accept that view. We think that the statute was aimed at a voluntary expatriation and we find no evidence in its terms that it was intended to destroy the right of a native citizen, removed from this country during minority, to elect to retain the citizenship acquired by birth and to return here for that purpose. . . .

It should also be noted that the Act of 1907 in paragraphs 5 and 6 has specific reference to children born without the United States of alien parents but says nothing as to the loss of citizenship by minor children born in the United States.

That in the latter case the child was not deemed to have lost his American citizenship by virtue of the terms of the statute but might still with reasonable promptness on attaining majority manifest his election is shown by the views expressed in the instructions issued under date of November 24, 1923, by the Department of State to the American Diplomatic and Consular Officers. . . .

"The term 'dual nationality' needs exact appreciation. It refers to the fact that two States make equal claim to the allegiance of an individual at the same time. Thus, one State may claim his allegiance because of his birth within its territory, and the other because at the time of his birth in foreign territory his parents were its nationals. The laws of the United States purport to clothe persons with American citizenship by virtue of both principles."

And after referring to the Fourteenth Amendment and the Act of February 2, 1855, R.S. 1993, the instructions continued:

"It thus becomes important to note how far these differing claims of American nationality are fairly operative with respect to persons living abroad, whether they were born abroad or were born in the United States of alien parents and taken during minority to reside in the territory of States to which the parents owed allegiance. It is logical that, while the child remains or resides in territory of the foreign State claiming him as a national, the United States should respect its claim to allegiance. The important point to observe is that the doctrine of dual allegiance ceases, in American contemplation, to be fully applicable after the child has reached adult years. Thereafter two States may in fact claim him as a national. Those claims are now, however, regarded as of equal merit, because one of the States may then justly assert that his relationship to itself as a national is, by reason of circumstances that have arisen, inconsistent with, and reasonably superior to, any claim of allegiance asserted by any other State. Ordinarily the State in which the individual retains his residence after attaining his majority has the superior claim. The statutory law of the United States affords some guidance but not all that could be desired, because it fails to announce the circumstances when the child who resides abroad within the territory of a State reasonably claiming his allegiance forfeits completely the right to perfect his inchoate right to retain American citizenship. The department must, therefore, be reluctant to declare that particular conduct on the part of a person after reaching adult years in foreign territory produces a forfeiture or something equivalent to expatriation.

*   *   *

"The child born of foreign parents in the United States who spends his minority in the foreign country of his parents' nationality is not expressly required by any statute of the United States to make the same election as he approaches or attains his majority. It is, nevertheless, believed that his retention of a right to demand the protection of the United States should, despite the absence of statute, be dependent upon his convincing the department within a reasonable period after the attaining of his majority of an election to return to the United States, there to assume the duties of citizenship. In the absence of a definite statutory requirement, it is impossible to prescribe a limited period within which such election should be made. On the other hand, it may be asserted negatively that one who has long manifested no indication of a will to make such an election should not receive the protection of the United States save under the express approval of the department."

. . . Having regard to the plain purpose of paragraph 2 of the Act of 1907, to deal with voluntary expatriation, we are of the opinion that its provisions do not affect the right of election, which would otherwise exist, by reason of a wholly involuntary and merely derivative naturalization in another country during minority. And, on the facts of the instant case, this view apparently obtained when in July, 1929, on the instructions of the Secretary of State, the Department issued the passport to respondent as a citizen of the United States.

But although respondent promptly made her election and took up her residence in this country accordingly, and had continued to reside here, she was notified in April, 1935, that she was an alien and was threatened with deportation.

*   *   *

We conclude that respondent has not lost her citizenship in the United States and is entitled to all the rights and privileges of that citizenship.

* * *

Dual Allegiance

KAWAKITA v. UNITED STATES
United States Supreme Court, 1952
343 U.S. 717

Mr. Justice Douglas delivered the opinion of the Court.

First. The important question that lies at the threshold of the case relates to expatriation. Petitioner was born in this country in 1921 of Japanese parents who were citizens of Japan. He was thus a citizen of the United States by birth (Amendment XIV, section 1) and, by reason of Japanese law, a national of Japan. See *Hirabayashi* v. *United States,* [1943] 320 U.S. 81, 97.

In 1939 shortly before petitioner turned 18 years of age he went to Japan with his father to visit his grandfather. He traveled on a United States passport; and to obtain it he took the customary oath of allegiance. In 1940 he registered with an American consul in Japan as an American citizen. Petitioner remained in Japan, his father returning to this country. In March, 1941, he entered Meiji University and took a commercial course and military training. In April, 1941, he renewed his United States passport, once more taking the oath of allegiance to the United States. During this period he was registered as an alien with the Japanese police. When war was declared, petitioner was still a student at Meiji University. He became of age in 1942 and completed his schooling in 1943, at which time it was impossible for him to return to the United States. In 1943 he registered in the Koseki, a family census register. Petitioner did not join the Japanese Army nor serve as a soldier. Rather, he obtained employment as an interpreter with the Oeyama Nickel Industry Co., Ltd., where he worked until Japan's surrender. He was hired to interpret communications between the Japanese and the prisoners of war who were assigned to work at the mine and in the factory of this company. The treasonable acts for which he was convicted involved his conduct toward American prisoners of war.

In December, 1945, petitioner went to the United States consul at Yokohama and applied for registration as an American citizen. He stated under oath that he was a United States citizen and had not done various acts amounting to expatriation. He was issued a passport and returned to the United States in 1946. Shortly thereafter he was recognized by a former American prisoner of war, whereupon he was arrested, and indicted, and tried for treason.

*　　*　　*

The (trial) court charged that if the jury found that petitioner had lost his American citizenship prior to or during the period specified in the indictment, they must acquit him even if he did commit the overt acts charged in the indictment, since his duty of allegiance would have ceased with the termination of his American citizenship. The court further charged that if the jury should find beyond a reasonable doubt that during the period in question petitioner was an American citizen, he owed the United States the same duty of allegiance as any other citizen. The court also charged that even though the jury found that petitioner was an American citizen during the period in question, they must acquit him if at the time of the overt acts petitioner honestly believed he was no longer a citizen of the United States, for then he could not have committed the overt acts with treasonable intent. The special verdicts of the jury contain, with respect to each overt act as to which petitioner was found guilty, an affirmative answer to an interrogatory that he was at that time "an American citizen owing allegiance to the United States, as charged in the indictment."

Petitioner asks us to hold as a matter of law that he had expatriated himself by his acts and conduct beginning in 1943. He places special emphasis on the entry of his name in the Koseki. Prior to that time he had been registered by the police as an alien. There is evidence that after that time he was considered by Japanese authorities as a Japanese and that he took action which might give rise to the inference that he had elected the Japanese nationality: he took a copy of the Koseki to the police station and had his name removed as an alien; he changed his registration at the University from American to Japanese and his address from California to Japan; he used the Koseki entry to get a job at the Oeyama camp; he went to China on a Japanese passport (see *United States* v. *Husband*, 6 F. 2d 957, 958); he accepted labor draft papers from the Japanese government; he faced the east each morning and paid his respects to the Emperor.

The difficulty with petitioner's position is that the implications from the acts, which he admittedly performed, are ambiguous. He had a dual nationality, a status long recognized in the law. *Perkins* v. *Elg*, 307 U.S. 325, 344–349. The concept of dual citizenship recognizes that a person may have and exercise rights of nationality in two countries and be subject to the responsibilities of both. The mere fact that he asserts the rights of one citizenship does not without more mean that he renounces the other. . . .

* * *

As we have said, dual citizenship presupposes rights of citizenship in each country. It could not exist if the assertion of rights or the assumption of liabilities of one were deemed inconsistent with the maintenance of the other. For example, when one has a dual citizenship, it is not necessarily inconsistent with his citizenship in one nation to use a passport proclaiming his citizenship in the other. See 3 Hackworth, p. 353. Hence the use by petitioner of a Japanese passport on his trip to China, his use of the Koseki entry to obtain work at the Oeyama camp, the bowing to the Emperor, and his acceptance of labor draft papers from the Japanese government might reasonably mean no more than acceptance of some of the incidents of Japanese citizenship made possible by his dual citizenship.

* * *

On December 31, 1945, he applied for registration as an American citizen, and in that connection he made an affidavit in which he stated that he had been "temporarily residing" in Japan since August 10, 1939; that he came to Japan to study Japanese; that he possessed dual nationality from birth but that his name was not entered in the census register until March 8, 1943; and that he had "never been naturalized, taken an oath of allegiance, or voted as a foreign citizen or subject, or in any way held myself out as such."

* * *

If petitioner were to be believed in December, 1945, he never once renounced his American citizenship. If what petitioner now says were his thoughts, attitudes, and motives in 1943 and 1944 and in part of 1945, he did intend to renounce his American citizenship. . . . The charge was that the jury must be satisfied beyond a reasonable doubt that during the period specified in the indictment, petitioner was an American citizen. We cannot say there was insufficient evidence for that finding.

Petitioner concedes he did not enter the armed services of Japan within the meaning of section 401 (c) of the Act but claims that during his tour of duty at the Oeyama camp he was "serving in" the Japanese armed services within the statutory meaning of those words. In this connection he also argues that his work in the Oeyama camp was the performance of the duties of an "office, post, or employment under the government" of Japan "for which only nationals of such state are eligible" within the meaning of section 401 (d) of the Act.

The Oeyama Nickel Industry Co., Ltd., was a private company, organized for profit. It was engaged in producing metals used for war under contracts with the Japanese government. In 1944 it was designated by the Japanese government as a munitions corporation and under Japanese law civilian employees were not allowed to change or quit their employment without the consent of the government. The company's mine and factory were manned in part by prisoners of war. They lived in a camp controlled by the Japanese army. Though petitioner took orders from the military, he was not a soldier in the armed services; he wore insignia on his uniform distinguishing him as nonmilitary personnel; he had no duties to perform in relation to the prisoners, except those of an interpreter. . . .

*   *   *

Second. Petitioner contends that a person who has a dual nationality can be guilty of treason only to the country where he resides, not to the other country which claims him as a national. More specifically, he maintains that while petitioner resided in Japan he owed his paramount allegiance to that country and was indeed, in the eyes of our law, an alien enemy.

The argument in its broadest reach is that treason against the United States cannot be committed abroad or in enemy territory, at least by an American with a dual nationality residing in the other country which claims him as a national. The definition of treason, however, contained in the Constitution contains no territorial limitation. "Treason against the United States, shall consist only in levying War against them, or in adhering to their Enemies, giving them Aid and Comfort . . ." Art. III, section 3. A substitute proposal containing some territorial limitations was rejected by the Constitutional Convention. . . . We must therefore reject the suggestion that an American citizen living beyond the territorial limits of the United States may not commit treason against them. . . .

One who has a dual nationality will be subject to claims from both nations, claims which at times may be competing or conflicting. The nature of those claims has recently been stated as follows:

"A person with dual nationality may be subjected to taxes by both states of which he is a national. He is not entitled to protection by one of the two states of which he is a national while in the territorial jurisdiction of the other. Either state not at war with the other may insist on military service when the person is present within its territory. In time of war if he supports neither belligerent, both may be aggrieved. If he supports one belligerent, the other may be aggrieved. One state may be suspicious of his loyalty to it and subject him to the disabilities of an enemy alien, including sequestration of his property, while the other holds his conduct treasonable." Orfield, The Legal Effects of Dual Nationality, 17 Geo. Wash. L. Rev. 427, 429.

Dual nationality, however, is the unavoidable consequence of the conflicting laws of different countries. . . . But American citizenship, until lost, carries obligations of allegiance as well as privileges and benefits. For one who has a dual status the obligations of American citizenship may at times be difficult to discharge. An American who has a dual nationality may find himself in a foreign country when it wages war on us. . . . He may be coerced by his employer or supervisor or by the force of circumstances to do things which he has no desire or heart to do. That was one of petitioner's defenses in this case. Such acts—if done voluntarily and willfully—might be treasonable. But if done under the compulsion of the job or the law or some other influence, those acts would not rise to the gravity of that offense. The trial judge recognized the distinction in his charge when he instructed the jury to acquit petitioner if he did not do the acts willingly or voluntarily "but so acted only because performance of the duties of his employment required him to do so or because of other coercion or compulsion." In short, petitioner was held accountable by the jury only for performing acts of hostility toward this country which he was not required by Japan to perform.

* * *

The jury found petitioner guilty of eight overt acts. . . .

Each of these related to his treatment of American prisoners of war at the Oeyama camp. . . .

* * *

Overt act (k) as alleged in the indictment and developed at the trial was that in the spring or summer of 1945 petitioner participated in the inhuman punishment of one Shaffer, an American prisoner of war. Shaffer was forced to kneel on bamboo sticks on a platform with a bamboo stick inside the joints of his knees, and to keep his arms above his head holding a bucket of water and later a log. When Shaffer became tired and bent his elbows, petitioner would strike him. When Shaffer leaned over and spilled some water, petitioner would take the bucket, throw the water on Shaffer, and have the bucket refilled. Then Shaffer was required to hold up a log. It fell on him, causing a gash. After the wound was treated, petitioner placed bamboo sticks on the ground and once more made Shaffer kneel on them and go through the same performance.

As we have said, petitioner was not required by his employment to inflict punishment on the prisoners. His duties regarding the prisoners related solely to the role of interpreter. His acts of cruelty toward the prisoners were over and beyond the call of duty of his job, or so the jury might have found. We cannot say as a matter of law that petitioner did these acts under compulsion. He seeks, however, to find protection under Japanese municipal law. It is difficult to see how that argument helps petitioner. The source of the law of treason is the Constitution. If an American citizen is a traitor by the constitutional definition, he gains no immunity because the same acts may have been unlawful under the law of the country where the acts were performed. Treason is a separate offense; treason can be committed by one who scrupulously observes the laws of other nations; and his acts may be nonetheless treasonable though the same conduct amounts to a different crime. . . .

* * *

Petitioner contends that the overt acts were not sufficiently proved by two witnesses. Each witness who testified to an overt act was, however, an eye-witness of the commission of that act. They were present and saw or heard that to which they testified. . . .

Fourth. Petitioner challenges the sufficiency of the evidence to show the second element in the crime of treason—adhering to the enemy. The two-witness requirement does not extend to this element. *Cramer* v. *United States,* p. 31. Intent to betray must be inferred from conduct. It may be inferred from the overt acts themselves (*Cramer* v. *United States, supra,* p. 31), from the defendant's own statements of his attitudes toward the war effort (*Haupt* v. *United States,* p. 642), and from his own professions of loyalty to Japan.

Evidence of what petitioner said during this period concerning the war effort and his professions of loyalty, if believed by the jury, leaves little doubt of his traitorous intent. "It look like MacArthur took a run-out powder on you boys"; "The Japanese were a little superior to your American soldiers"; "You Americans don't have no chance. We will win the war." "Well, you guys needn't be interested in when the war will be over because you won't go back; you will stay here and work. I will go back to the States because I am an American citizen"; "We will kill all you prisoners right here anyway, whether you win the war or lose it. You will never get to go back to the States"; "I will be glad when all of the Americans is dead, and then I can go home and live happy." These are some of the statements petitioner made aligning himself with the Japanese cause. . . .

*   *   *

If the versions of petitioner's words and conduct at the Oeyama camp, testified to by the various witnesses, were believed, the traitorous intent would be shown by overwhelming evidence. Petitioner indeed conceded at the trial that he felt no loyalty to the United States at this time and had thrown his lot in with Japan. Yet at the end of the war he had taken the oath of allegiance to the United States, claiming he had been a United States citizen all along. The issue of intent to betray, like the citizenship issue, was plainly one for the jury to decide. We would have to reject all the evidence adverse to petitioner and accept as the truth his protestations when the shadow of the hangman's noose was on him in order to save him from the finding that he did have the intent to betray. That finding of the jury was based on its conclusion that what he did was done willingly and voluntarily and not because the duty of his office or any coercion compelled him to do it. The finding that he had an uncoerced and voluntary purpose was amply supported by the evidence. . . .

. . . The trial judge imposed the death sentence. The argument is that that sentence was so severe as to be arbitrary. It was, however, within the statutory limits. Whether a sentence may be so severe and the offense so trivial that an appellate court should set it aside is a question we need not reach. The flagrant and persistent acts of petitioner gave the trial judge such a leeway in reaching a decision on the sentence that we would not be warranted in interfering. . . .*

*   *   *

Effective Bond of Nationality

NOTTEBOHM CASE (LIECHTENSTEIN v. GUATEMALA)
International Court of Justice, 1955
1955 I.C.J. Reports 4

*   *   *

Nottebohm was born at Hamburg on September 16th, 1881. He was German by birth, and still possessed German nationality when, in October 1939, he applied for naturalization in Liechtenstein.

In 1905 he went to Guatemala. He took up residence there and made that country the headquarters of his business activities, which increased and prospered; these activities developed in the field of commerce, banking and plantations. Having been an employee in the firm of Nottebohm Hermanos, which had been founded by his brothers Juan and Arturo, he became their partner in 1912 and later, in 1937, he was made head of the firm. After 1905 he sometimes went to Germany on business and to other countries for holidays. He continued to have business connections in Germany. He paid a few visits to a brother who had lived in Liechtenstein since 1931. Some of his other brothers, relatives and friends were in Germany, others in Guatemala. He himself continued to have his fixed abode in Guatemala until 1943, that is to say, until the occurrence of the events which constitute the basis of the present dispute.

In 1939, after having provided for the safeguarding of his interests in Guatemala by a power of attorney given to the firm of Nottebohm Hermanos on March 22nd, he left that country at a date fixed by Counsel for Liechtenstein as at approximately the end of March or the beginning of April, when he seems to have gone to Hamburg, and later to have paid a few brief visits to Vaduz where he was at the beginning of October 1939. It was then, on October 9th, a little more than a month after the

---

* President Eisenhower later commuted this sentence to life imprisonment. In 1963, one of the last acts of President Kennedy was the pardon of Kawakita, on condition that he depart from and never return to the United States.

opening of the second World War marked by Germany's attack on Poland, that his attorney, Dr. Marxer, submitted an application for naturalization on behalf of Nottebohm.

*   *   *

A certificate of nationality has also been produced, signed on behalf of the Government of the Principality and dated October 20th, 1939, to the effect that Nottebohm was naturalized by Supreme Resolution of the Reigning Prince dated October 13th, 1939.

Having obtained a Liechtenstein passport, Nottebohm had it visaed by the Consul General of Guatemala in Zurich on December 1st, 1939, and returned to Guatemala at the beginning of 1940, where he resumed his former business activities and in particular the management of the firm of Nottebohm Hermanos.

Relying on the nationality thus conferred on Nottebohm, Liechtenstein considers itself entitled to seize the Court of its claim on his behalf, and its Final Conclusions contain two submissions in this connection. Liechtenstein requests the Court to find and declare, first, "that the naturalization of Mr. Frederic Nottebohm in Liechtenstein on October 13th, 1939, was not contrary to international law," and, secondly, "that Liechtenstein's claim on behalf of Mr. Nottebohm as a national of Liechtenstein is admissible before the Court."

The Final Conclusions of Guatemala, on the other hand, request the Court "to declare that the claim of the Principality of Liechtenstein is inadmissible," and set forth a number of grounds relating to the nationality of Liechtenstein granted to Nottebohm by naturalization.

Thus, the real issue before the Court is the admissibility of the claim of Liechtenstein in respect of Nottebohm. . . .

*   *   *

In order to establish that the Application must be held to be admissible, Liechtenstein has argued that Guatemala formerly recognized the naturalization which it now challenges and cannot therefore be heard to put forward a contention which is inconsistent with its former attitude.

Various documents, facts and actions have been relied upon in this connection.

Reliance has been placed on the fact that, on December 1st, 1939, the Consul General of Guatemala in Zurich entered a visa in the Liechtenstein passport of Mr. Nottebohm for his return to Guatemala; that on January 29th, 1940, Nottebohm informed the Ministry of External Affairs in Guatemala that he had adopted the nationality of Liechtenstein and therefore requested that the entry relating to him in the Register of Aliens should be altered accordingly, a request which was granted on January 31st; that on February 9th, 1940, a similar amendment was made to his identity document, and lastly, that a certificate to the same effect was issued to him by the Civil Registry of Guatemala on July 1st, 1940.

The acts of the Guatemalan authorities just referred to proceeded on the basis of the statements made to them by the person concerned. The one led to the other. The only purpose of the first, as appears from Article 9 of the Guatemalan law relating to passports, was to make possible or facilitate entry into Guatemala, and nothing more. According to the Aliens Act of January 25th, 1936, Article 49, entry in the Register "constitutes a legal presumption that the alien possesses the nationality there attributed to him, but evidence to the contrary is admissible." All of these acts have reference to the control of aliens in Guatemala and not to the exercise of diplomatic protection. When Nottebohm thus presented himself before the Guatemalan authorities, the latter had before them a private individual: there did not thus come into being any relationship between governments. There was nothing in all this to show that Guatemala then recognized that the naturalization conferred upon Nottebohm gave Liechtenstein any title to the exercise of protection.

*   *   *

Since no proof has been adduced that Guatemala has recognized the title to the exercise of protection relied upon by Liechtenstein as being derived from the naturalization which it granted to Nottebohm, the Court must consider whether such an act of granting nationality by Liechtenstein directly entails an obligation on the part of Guatemala to recognize its effect, namely, Liechtenstein's right to exercise its protection. In other words, it must be determined whether that unilateral act by Liechtenstein is one which can be relied upon against Guatemala in regard to the exercise of protection. The Court will deal with this question without considering that of the validity of Nottebohm's naturalization according to the law of Liechtenstein.

It is for Liechtenstein, as it is for every sovereign State, to settle by its own legislation the rules relating to the acquisition of its nationality, and to confer that nationality by naturalization granted by its own organs in accordance with that legislation. It is not necessary to determine whether international law imposes any limitations on its freedom of decision in this domain. Furthermore, nationality has its most immediate, its most far-reaching and, for most people, its only effects within the legal system of the State conferring it. Nationality serves above all to determine that the person upon whom it is conferred enjoys the rights and is bound by the obligations which the law of the State in question grants to or imposes on its nationals. This is implied in the wider concept that nationality is within the domestic jurisdiction of the State.

But the issue which the Court must decide is not one which pertains to the legal system of Liechtenstein. It does not depend on the law or on the decision of Liechtenstein whether that State is entitled to exercise its protection, in the case under consideration. To exercise protection, to apply to the Court, is to place oneself on the plane of international law. It is international law which determines whether a State is entitled to exercise protection and to seise the Court.

The naturalization of Nottebohm was an act performed by Liechtenstein in the exercise of its domestic jurisdiction. The question to be decided is whether that act has the international effect here under consideration.

International practice provides many examples of acts performed by States in the exercise of their domestic jurisdiction which do not necessarily or automatically have international effect, which are not necessarily and automatically binding on other States or which are binding on them only subject to certain conditions: this is the case, for instance, of a judgment given by the competent court of a State which it is sought to invoke in another State.

In the present case it is necessary to determine whether the naturalization conferred on Nottebohm can be successfully invoked against Guatemala, whether, as has already been stated, it can be relied upon as against that State, so that Liechtenstein is thereby entitled to exercise its protection in favour of Nottebohm against Guatemala.

*   *   *

The practice of certain States which refrain from exercising protection in favour of a naturalized person when the latter has in fact, by his prolonged absence, severed his links with what is no longer for him anything but his nominal country, manifests the view of these States that, in order to be capable of being invoked against another State, nationality must correspond with the factual situation. A similar view is manifested in the relevant provisions of the bilateral nationality treaties concluded between the United States of America and other States since 1868, such as those sometimes referred to as the Bancroft Treaties, and in the Pan-American Convention, signed at Rio de Janeiro on August 13th, 1906, on the status of naturalized citizens who resume residence in their country of origin.

The character thus recognized on the international level as pertaining to nationality is in no way inconsistent with the fact that international law leaves it to each State to lay down the rules governing the grant of its own nationality. The reason for this is that the diversity of demographic conditions has thus far made it impossible for any general agreement to be reached on the rules relating to nationality, although the latter by its very nature affects international relations. It has been considered that the best way of making such rules accord with the varying demographic conditions in different countries is to leave the fixing of such rules to the competence of each State. On the other hand, a State cannot claim that the rules it has thus laid down are entitled to recognition by another State unless it has acted in conformity with this general aim of making the legal bond of nationality accord with the individual's genuine connection with the State which assumes the defence of its citizens by means of protection as against other states.

* * *

According to the practice of States, to arbitral and judicial decisions and to the opinions of writers, nationality is a legal bond having as its basis a social fact of attachment, a genuine connection of existence, interests and sentiments, together with the existence of reciprocal rights and duties. It may be said to constitute the juridical expression of the fact that the individual upon whom it is conferred, either directly by the law or as the result of an act of the authorities, is in fact more closely connected with the population of the State conferring nationality than with that of any other State. Conferred by a State, it only entitles that State to exercise protection vis-à-vis another State, if it constitutes a translation into juridical terms of the individual's connection with the State which has made him its national.

* * *

The essential facts are as follows:

At the date when he applied for naturalization Nottebohm had been a German national from the time of his birth. He had always retained his connections with members of his family who had remained in Germany and he had always had business connections with that country. His country had been at war for more than a month, and there is nothing to indicate that the application for naturalization then made by Nottebohm was motivated by any desire to dissociate himself from the Government of his country.

He had been settled in Guatemala for 34 years. He had carried on his activities there. It was the main seat of his interests. He returned there shortly after his naturalization, and it remained the centre of his interests and of his business activities. He stayed there until his removal as a result of war measures in 1943. He subsequently attempted to return there, and he now complains of Guatemala's refusal to admit him. There, too, were several members of his family who sought to safeguard his interests.

In contrast, his actual connections with Liechtenstein were extremely tenuous. No settled abode, no prolonged residence in that country at the time of his application for naturalization: the application indicates that he was paying a visit there and confirms the transient character of this visit by its request that the naturalization proceedings should be initiated and concluded without delay. No intention of settling there was shown at that time or realized in the ensuing weeks, months or years—on the contrary, he returned to Guatemala very shortly after his naturalization and showed every intention of remaining there. If Nottebohm went to Liechtenstein in 1946, this was because of the refusal of Guatemala to admit him. No indication is given of the grounds warranting the waiver of the condition of residence, required by the 1934 Nationality Law, which waiver was implicitly granted to him. There is no allegation of any economic interests or of any activities exercised or to be exercised in Liechtenstein, and no manifestation of any intention whatsoever to transfer all or some of his interests and his business activities to Liechtenstein. It is unnecessary in this connection to attribute much importance to the promise to pay the taxes levied at the time of his naturalization. The only links to be discovered between the Principality and Nottebohm are the short sojourns already referred to and the presence in Vaduz of one of his brothers: but his brother's presence is referred to in his application for naturalization only as a reference to his good conduct. Furthermore, other members of his family have asserted Nottebohm's desire to spend his old age in Guatemala.

These facts clearly establish, on the one hand, the absence of any bond of attachment between Nottebohm and Liechtenstein and, on the other hand, the existence of a long-standing and close connection between him and Guatemala, a link which his naturalization in no way weakened. That naturalization was not based on any real prior connection with Liechtenstein, nor did it in any way alter the manner of life of the person upon whom it was conferred in exceptional circumstances of speed and accommodation. In both respects, it was lacking in the genuineness requisite to an act of such importance, if it is to be entitled to be respected by a State in the position of Guatemala. It was granted without regard to the concept of nationality adopted in international relations.

Naturalization was asked for not so much for the purpose of obtaining a legal recognition of Nottebohm's membership in fact in the population of Liechtenstein, as it was to enable him to substitute for his status as a national of a belligerent State that of a national of a neutral State, with the sole aim of thus coming within the protection of Liechtenstein but not of becoming wedded to its traditions, its interest, its way of life or of assuming the obligations—other than fiscal obligations—and exercising the rights pertaining to the status thus acquired.

Guatemala is under no obligation to recognize a nationality granted in such circumstances. Liechtenstein consequently is not entitled to extend its protection to Nottebohm vis-à-vis Guatemala and its claim must, for this reason, be held to be inadmissible.

*   *   *

For these reasons,

The Court,

by eleven votes to three,
holds that the claim submitted by the Government of the Principality of Liechtenstein is inadmissible.

Dissenting Opinion of Judge Read

I am unable to concur in the Judgment of the Court, which holds that the claim submitted by the Principality of Liechtenstein is inadmissible. . . .

*   *   *

In 1944 a series of fifty-seven legal proceedings was commenced against Mr. Nottebohm, designed to expropriate, without compensation to him, all of his properties, whether movable or immovable. The proceedings involved more than one hundred and seventy-one appeals of various kinds. Counsel for Guatemala has demonstrated, in a fair and competent manner, the existence of a network of litigation, which could not be dealt with effectively in the absence of the principally interested party. Further, all of the cases involved, as a central and vital issue, the charge against Mr. Nottebohm of treasonable conduct.

It is common ground that Mr. Nottebohm was not permitted to return to Guatemala. He was thus prevented from assuming the personal direction of the complex network of litigation. He was allowed no opportunity to give evidence of the charges made against him, or to confront his accusers in open court. In such circumstances I am bound to proceed on the assumption that Liechtenstein might be entitled to a finding of denial of justice, if the case should be considered on the merits.

*   *   *

The issue for decision is: *whether, in the circumstances of this case and vis-à-vis Guatemala, Liechtenstein is entitled, under the rules of international law, to afford diplomatic protection to Mr. Nottebohm.*

*   *   *

. . . The Judgment of the Court is based upon the ground that the naturalization of Mr. Nottebohm was not a genuine transaction. It is pointed out that it did not lead to any alteration in his manner of life; and that it was acquired, not for the purpose of obtaining legal recognition of his membership in fact of the population of Liechtenstein, but for the purpose of obtaining neutral status and the diplomatic protection of a neutral state.

*   *   *

To begin with, I do not question the desirability of establishing some limitation on the wide discretionary power possessed by sovereign states: the right, under international law, to determine, under their own laws, who are their own nationals and to protect such nationals.

Nevertheless, I am bound, by Article 38 of the Statute, to apply international law as it is—positive law—and not international law as it might be if a Codification Conference succeeded in establishing new rules limiting the conferring of nationality by sovereign states. It is, therefore, necessary to consider whether there are any rules of positive international law requiring a substantial relationship between the individual and the state, in order that a valid grant of nationality may give rise to a right of diplomatic protection.

Both Parties rely on Article I of The Hague Draft Convention of 1930 as an accurate statement of the recognized rules of international law. Commenting on it, the Government of Guatemala stated in the Counter-Memorial (p. 7) that "there can be no doubt that its Article I represented the existing state of international law." It reads as follows:

> "It is for each State to determine under its own law who are its nationals. This law shall be recognized by other States in so far as it is consistent with international conventions, international custom, and the principles of law generally recognized with regard to nationality."

Applying this rule to the case, it would result that Liechtenstein had the right to determine under its own law that Mr. Nottebohm was its own national, and that Guatemala must recognize the Liechtenstein law, in this regard *in so far as it is consistent with international conventions, international custom, and the principles of law generally recognized with regard to nationality. . . .*

*   *   *

I have mentioned that no "international conventions" are involved and that no "international custom has been proved." It has been conceded by Guatemala that "there is no system of customary rules," but the link theory is supported by the view that certain international conventions suggest the existence of a trend. . . .

The first international convention is Article 3 (2) of the Statute, which deals with the problem of double nationality. It has nothing to do with diplomatic protection and is not in any sense relevant to the problem under consideration. It is true that it accepts as a test in the case of double nationality the place in which the person "ordinarily exercises civil and political rights." Even if this test can be dragged from an entirely different setting and applied to the present case, it does not contribute much to the solution. Mr. Nottebohm has, in the course of the last fifty years, been linked with four states. He was a German national during thirty-four years, but exercised neither civil nor political rights in that country. He was ordinarily resident in Guatemala for nearly forty years, but exercised no political rights at any time in that country and has been prevented from exercising important civil rights for twelve years. He was a prisoner in the United States of America for more than two years, where he exercised neither civil nor political rights. Since his release, he has been accorded full civil rights in the United States and has exercised them freely, but he has had no political rights in that country. He has had full civil rights in Liechtenstein for nearly sixteen years, and has exercised full political rights for nine. Article 3 (2) certainly does not weaken the Liechtenstein position.

* * *

There have been many instances of double nationality in which international tribunals have been compelled to decide between conflicting claims. In such cases, it has been necessary to choose; and the choice has been determined by the relative strength of the association between the individual concerned and his national state. There have been many instances in which a state has refused to recognize that the naturalization of one of its own citizens has given rise to the right of diplomatic protection, or in which it has refused to treat naturalization as exempting him from the obligations incident to his original citizenship, such as military service.

But the problems presented by conflicting claims to nationality and by double nationality do not arise in this case. There can be no doubt that Mr. Nottebohm lost his German nationality of origin upon his naturalization in Liechtenstein in October 1939. I do not think that it is permissible to transfer criteria designed for cases of double nationality to an essentially different type of relationship.

* * *

There are other difficulties presented by the link theory. In the case of Mr. Nottebohm, it relies upon a finding of fact that there is nothing to indicate that his application for naturalization abroad was motivated by any desire to break his ties with the Government of Germany. . . .

In the first place, I do not think that international law, apart from abuse of right and fraud, permits the consideration of the motives which led to naturalization as determining its effects.

In the second place, the finding depends upon the examination of issues which are part of the merits and which cannot be decided when dealing with the plea in bar.

In the third place, the breaking of ties with the country of origin is not essential to valid and opposable naturalization. International law recognizes double nationality and the present trend in state practice is towards double nationality, which necessarily involves maintenance of the ties with the country of origin. It is noteworthy that in the United Kingdom the policy of recognizing the automatic loss of British nationality on naturalization abroad, which had been adopted in 1870, was abandoned in 1948. Under the new British legislation, on naturalization abroad, a British citizen normally maintains his ties with his country of origin.

In the fourth place, I am unable to agree that there is nothing to indicate that Mr. Nottebohm's naturalization was motivated by a desire to break his ties with Germany. There are three facts which prove that he was determined to break his ties with Germany. The first is the fact of his application for naturalization, the second is the taking of his oath of allegiance to Liechtenstein, and the third is his obtaining a certificate of naturalization and a Liechtenstein passport.

*   *   *

It is also suggested that the naturalization of Mr. Nottebohm was lacking in genuineness, and did not give rise to a right of protection, because of his subsequent conduct: that he did not abandon his residence and his business activities in Guatemala, establish a business in Liechtenstein, and take up permanent residence. Along the same lines, it is suggested that he did not incorporate himself in the body politic which constitutes the Liechtenstein state.

*   *   *

. . . To my mind the state is a concept broad enough to include not merely the territory and its inhabitants but also those of its citizens who are resident abroad but linked to it by allegiance. Most states regard non-resident citizens as a part of the body politic. In the case of many countries such as China, France, the United Kingdom and the Netherlands, the non-resident citizens form an important part of the body politic and are numbered in their hundreds of thousands or millions. Many of these non-resident citizens have never been within the confines of the home state. I can see no reason why the pattern of the body politic of Liechtenstein should or must be different from that of other states.

*   *   *

Further, I have difficulty in accepting two closely related findings of fact. The first is that the naturalization did not alter the manner of life of Mr. Nottebohm. In my opinion, a naturalization which led ultimately to his permanent residence in the country of his allegiance altered the manner of life of a merchant who had hitherto been residing in and conducting his business activities in Guatemala.

The second finding is that the naturalization was conferred in exceptional circumstances of speed and accommodation. There are many countries, beside Liechtenstein, in which expedition and good will are regarded as administrative virtues. I do not think that these qualities impair the effectiveness or genuineness of their administrative acts.

*   *   *

Nationality and diplomatic protection are closely interrelated. The general rule of international law is that nationality gives rise to a right of diplomatic protection.

*   *   *

As a result of the naturalization in October 1939, the whole network of legal relationships between Guatemala and Germany as regards Mr. Nottebohm came to an end.

Mr. Nottebohm returned to Guatemala in January 1940, having brought about a fundamental change in his legal relationships in that country. He no longer had the status of a permanently settled alien of German nationality. He was entering with a Liechtenstein passport and with Liechtenstein protection.

The first step taken by him was the obtaining of a visa from the Guatemalan Consul before departure. On arrival in Guatemala he immediately brought his new national status to the attention of the Guatemalan Government on the highest level. His registration under the Alien's Act as a German national was cancelled and he was registered as a Liechtenstein national. From the end of January 1940 he was treated as such in Guatemala.

. . . From that time on Guatemala had the right to deport Mr. Nottebohm to Liechtenstein, and Liechtenstein was under the correlative obligation to receive him on deportation. Liechtenstein was entitled as of right to furnish diplomatic protection to Mr. Nottebohm in Guatemala and when that right was exercised in October 1943, it was not questioned by Guatemala.

*   *   *

. . . It has been complained that the purpose of the naturalization was to avoid the operation of war-time measures in the event that Guatemala ultimately became involved in war with Germany. . . . Even if his main purpose had been to protect his property and business in the event of Guatemalan belligerency, I do not think that it affected the validity or opposability of the naturalization. There was no rule of international law and no rule in the laws of Guatemala at the time forbidding such a course of action. Mr. Nottebohm did not conceal the naturalization and informed the Government of Guatemala on the highest level on his return to the country.

I do not think that I am justified in taking Mr. Nottebohm's motives into consideration—in the absence of fraud or injury to Guatemala—but even if this particular motive is considered, it cannot be regarded as preventing the existence of the right of diplomatic protection.

*   *   *

Statelessness

A man without a country is generally pathetic. Apart from the psychological-sentimental damage that may affect an individual deprived of nationality for one reason or another, his legal status alone portends trouble. An alien—that is, the national of a foreign state—never has all the legal rights of the citizens or nationals of the state where he resides. But he may have a considerable number of them, such as the right to use the courts, the right to inherit property, the right to conduct business, and so forth. These rights (*a*) can be granted directly by the municipal laws, (*b*) can stem from international agreements in force between the state of his residence and the state of his nationality, and (*c*) may be due to him under general principles of international law. In any case, when one of his rights under international law is offended or ignored, he may appeal to the protection of his state.

A stateless person has far fewer legal grounds to stand upon. There may be situations, of course, in which an individual prefers statelessness to his original nationality. In the much-cited case of *Stoeck* v. *Public Trustee*, Stoeck claimed he was *not* a German national, whose property would then be subject to a charge by virtue of a Treaty of Peace Order in England. The Court agreed. Stoeck had obtained a discharge from Prussian nationality in 1896.

The evidence satisfies me that the plaintiff has lost his German nationality. It is not suggested that he has acquired any other. If then such a condition is possible in law the person is of no nationality; he is a stateless person. Is such a condition possible in law? So far as international law is concerned, opinions appear to differ. . . .
Whether a person is a national of a country must be determined by the municipal law of that country. . . . How could the municipal law of England determine that a person *is* a national of Germany. . . . In truth, there is not and cannot be such an individual as a German national according to English law. . . .[10]

Statelessness could be the fate of a woman who on marriage to a foreigner loses her nationality and does not acquire her husband's nationality; a person whose place of birth or parentage cannot be established; or an individual who by his own action has disclaimed his nationality or through the laws of his state has been deprived of it without acquiring another. Such persons would be under a grievous legal disadvantage, ultimately lacking the identification and protection that states generally afford their nationals.

[10] Great Britain, 2 Chancery 67 (1921).

Expatriation

Courts will be wary in accepting disclaimers of nationality or expatriation by an individual. Much will depend on its intention and good faith. An act of expatriation during wartime, for example, can be tantamount to treason. Generally speaking, however, the acquisition of a new nationality will be matched by a willingness of a former state to allow the individual to release himself from his former nationality *if he so desires*. Expatriation permits may be required by municipal law, and services still owed to the state may have to be discharged before the first nationality is fully divested, but the international practice of states to allow expatriation is widely accepted.

The right of the individual to expatriate himself also forms an essential element in determining a change of his nationality beyond his immediate control. Suppose after war and by peace treaty the state of an individual legally disappears. Sovereignty is transferred to a new state. Momentarily, the individual becomes stateless, although it is usual, though not compulsory, for the new state to grant its nationality to the nationals of the extinguished state. Continued residence in the new state or other acts of acquiescence, of course, will be evidence of the individual's acceptance of his new nationality. But the person who immediately emigrates or who resides abroad and never accepts the new sovereign may continue to be stateless.

In 1948, the right of nationality was proclaimed in the Universal Declaration of Human Rights. Both the League of Nations and the United Nations through their agencies have sought legal protection for persons of uncertain nationality. Since 1954, multilateral conventions on the Status of Refugees, the Status of Stateless Persons, and the Reduction of Statelessness have begun to come into force. Such positive agreements have partly redefined international law, easing some of the past legal difficulties of individuals, but their application is still limited.

The case that follows, *United States ex rel. Schwarzkopf* v. *Uhl*, illustrates the problems of expatriation by virtue of the extinction of a state, transfer of nationality, and statelessness.

UNITED STATES ex rel. SCHWARZKOPF v. UHL
U.S. Circuit Court of Appeals, 1943
137 F. 2d. 898

Swan, Circuit Judge

*　　*　　*

. . . The relator is a Jew born in 1886 in the city of Prague, Bohemia, which was then within the Austro-Hungarian Empire. In 1919 Prague became part of Czechoslovakia and the relator became a citizen of that country. In 1925 he became a citizen of the German Republic by naturalization, being then in business in Berlin. In 1927 he removed from Germany to the Austrian Tyrol and in 1933 became a naturalized citizen of Austria, his former German citizenship being thereby automatically terminated. In October 1936 he arrived in the United States for permanent residence as a quota immigrant under the Czechoslovakian quota. When Hitler's forces invaded Austria in March 1938, the relator was resident in the United States and on June 17, 1938, he declared his intention to become a United States citizen. He applied for naturalization on September 26, 1941. This application was pending when he was taken into custody as an alien enemy on December 9, 1941.

The legal question for decision is whether the conceded facts bring the appellant within the class of aliens whose restraint is authorized under the statute, 50 U.S.C.A. paragraph 21, and the presidential proclamation pursuant to which he is held. That statute provides that: "Whenever . . . any invasion or predatory incursion is . . . threatened against the territory of the United States by any foreign nation or government, and the President makes public proclamation of the event, all natives, citizens, denizens, or subjects of the hostile nation or government, being of the age of fourteen years and upward, who shall be within the United States and not actually naturalized, shall be liable to be apprehended, restrained, secured, and reapprehended, restrained, secured, and removed as alien enemies." The President is authorized to direct "the manner and degree" of their restraint "and in what cases," and "to establish any other regulations which are found necessary in the premises and for the public safety." On December 8, 1941, the President issued Proclamation No. 2526, published in 6 Fed. Reg. 6323, by which he proclaimed that "an invasion or predatory incursion is threatened upon the territory of the United States by Germany," and directed the attorney general to cause the apprehension of such alien enemies as in his judgment are subject to apprehension under regulations incorporated in the presidential proclamation.

With the attorney general's finding that restraint of the appellant is required as a measure of public safety the courts have no concern . . . the relator's writ of habeas corpus can raise only the question whether he is an alien enemy within the statutory definition, that is, whether he is a "native, citizen, denizen or subject" of Germany.

The United States attorney relies solely on the word "citizen." He argues that the relator was an Austrian citizen on March 13, 1938, the date of the annexation of Austria by Germany, and became a German citizen by virtue of the German decree of July 3, 1938, which granted German citizenship to all Austrian citizens; that the United States has recognized the de facto sovereignty of Germany over the territory formerly Austria, and our courts must recognize and give effect to the German decree of July 3rd. It is further contended that our courts must disregard the German "Executive Order" of November 25, 1941 which purports to deprive Jews residing abroad of German citizenship and to subject their property to confiscation.

It is not claimed that the United States has accorded de jure recognition to Germany's annexation of Austrian territory. Clearly no such claim could be successfully asserted in view of the public declaration by the Secretary of State that "This Government has never taken the position that Austria was legally absorbed into the German Reich." The claim that de facto recognition has been given is rested chiefly upon two notes which the Secretary of State delivered to the German foreign minister on April 6, 1938. One of the notes recited that on March 17, 1938 the Austrian minister had informed the Department of State that Austria had ceased to exist as an independent state, the Austrian ministry to this country has been abolished and its affairs had been taken over by the Embassy of Germany. It was then stated that "The Government of the United States finds itself under the necessity as a practical measure of closing its Legation at Vienna and of establishing a Consulate General," and "provisional consular status" was requested for certain persons. The other note referred to Austrian indebtedness to the United States and said: "This Government will expect that these obligations will continue to be fully recognized and that service will be continued by the German authorities which have succeeded in control of the means and machinery of payment in Austria. . . ." The respondent's brief also directs attention to Executive Proclamation No. 2283 of April 28, 1938, which increased the German immigration quota to include the quota formerly allocated to Austria; to a letter of instructions dated February 19, 1939, in which the Commissioner of Immigration and Naturalization stated that former Austrian citizens, "who automatically became German citizens by the turn of events on March 13, 1938" should renounce "The German Reich" in petitioning for naturalization; and to Local Board Release No. 112 of March 16, 1942, in which the National Director of the Selective Service System listed among enemy countries, "Germany including Austria."

. . . Even if de facto recognition be assumed it does not follow that it affects the nationality of those under the domination of the de facto power (1 Hackworth, Digest of International Law, 377–383) or that the relator thereby becomes a citizen of Germany within the meaning of a statute of the United States. Indeed, in our view, the dispute as to recognition or non-recognition by the United States of the conquest of Austria raises a wholly irrelevant issue.

The issue for decision is whether the relator is a "citizen" of Germany within the meaning of the Alien Enemy Act. The obvious purpose of that Act was to include within its ambit all aliens who by reason of ties of nativity or allegiance might be likely to favor "the hostile nation or government" and might therefore commit acts dangerous to our public safety if allowed to remain at large. Congress selected the words "natives, citizens, denizens, or subjects" as an all inclusive description. In determining who are "citizens" of a foreign nation our courts must consider not only the municipal law of the foreign nation but also the accepted rules and practices under international law. If the relator's citizenship be tested by the municipal law of Germany—disregarding for the moment the cancellation of his German citizenship by the November 1941 "Executive Order"—the claim that he is a citizen of Germany must be based upon the conquest and annexation of Austria and the decree of July 3, 1938 granting German citizenship to all citizens of Austria. But under generally accepted principles of international law Germany could impose citizenship by annexation (collective naturalization) only on those who were inhabitants of Austria in 1938. This question is discussed in Oppenheim, International Law, 5th Ed., I, sec. 240. He states that it is the American view that only the "inhabitants" who "remain" in the territory, or by treaty are permitted to elect the new nationality, are to be deemed nationals of the annexing state . . . commentators maintain that when territory is transferred to a new sovereign by conquest or cession the inhabitants of the territory become nationals of the new government only by their own consent, express or implicit. This generally accepted principle of international law has been recognized in the decisions of the Supreme Court. If the inhabitants remain within the territory their allegiance is transferred to the new sovereign. . . . If they have voluntarily departed before the annexation and have never elected to accept the sovereignty of the new government, their allegiance is not so transferred. . . .

The respondent concedes the principle that an inhabitant of conquered or ceded territory can elect whether to retain his old nationality or accept the nationality of the new sovereign, but denies its applicability because there is no Austrian government in exile, as there is in the case of certain countries invaded by Germany, for example, Norway and Holland. . . . On the general principles of justice we think that civilized nations should not recognize the asserted distinction. If the invaded country has ceased to exist as an independent state there would seem to be all the more reason for allowing its former nationals, who have fled from the invader and established a residence abroad, the right of voluntarily electing a new nationality and remaining "stateless" until they can acquire it. In our view an invader cannot under international law impose its nationality upon non-residents of the subjugated country without their consent, express or tacit.

*   *   *

Moreover, if we were to deny the relator the right of election and were to look solely to German law to determine his status, he would not be a German citizen. If it be assumed that he acquired German citizenship by the annexation of Austria and the decree of July 3rd, such citizenship was lost under German law in November 1941. There is no public policy of this country to preclude an American court from recognizing the power of Germany to disclaim Schwarzkopf as a German citizen. . . . The statute does not authorize the apprehension and detention of all persons whose presence here may be found by the President to be dangerous to public safety. Unfortunately, even citizens of the United States or aliens owing allegiance to some friendly nation, may disregard their duty and commit acts favoring the enemy. But they cannot for that reason be held in custody under the statute in question. No more can the appellant. Upon the conceded facts he is not a German citizen and that is the only ground upon which the respondent justifies detention of him. The writ must be sustained and the appellant discharged from custody. It is so ordered.

Denationalization

In the early 1920's, for political reasons the Soviet Union denationalized somewhere up to 2 million Russian nationals, mostly resident abroad; in 1941, the National Socialist government of Germany denationalized all German Jews residing abroad. Other states have also penalized their minorities. Unfortunate and disturbing as these acts may be, nothing in international law forbids the right of states to withdraw their nationality from individuals; nothing forbids even a mass denationalization.

Deprivation of a man's nationality has long been employed as a penalty by states. Individuals have been denationalized for entering the civil or military service of another state, or for living permanently abroad, or for committing a crime. In the case of dual nationality, the loss of one nationality does not affect the other, and it leaves the individual with the diplomatic protection of one state when abroad, as well as with other rights conferred on nationals and/or citizens by the municipal laws. But in other cases, the hardship on a person is evident. It creates statelessness. While the state might not order deportation of such a resident individual, a person who loses his nationality while living abroad could be deprived of the right of residence itself. Suppose a Russian resident in Australia is denationalized by the Soviet government. He may also become unwelcome to Australia so that the government orders him out of the state. No other state will receive him. The U.S.S.R. states that he is not a Russian national. What then?

Denationalization in the modern world has become so dreadful that in 1958 the Supreme Court of the United States in *Trop* v. *Dulles*, by a five-to-four vote, found unconstitutional a statute of Congress providing for loss of United States citizenship in the event of conviction for wartime desertion. In that case the Court said:

Section 401 (g) is a penal law, and we must face the question whether the Constitution permits the Congress to take away citizenship as a punishment for crime. If it is assumed that the power of Congress extends to divestment of citizenship, the problem still remains as to this statute whether denationalization is a cruel and unusual punishment within the meaning of the Eighth Amendment. . . .

We believe, as did Chief Judge Clark in the court below, that use of denationalization as a punishment is barred by the Eighth Amendment. There may be involved no physical mistreatment, no primitive torture. There is instead the total destruction of the individual's status in organized society. It is a form of punishment more primitive than torture, for it destroys for the individual the political existence that was centuries in the development. The

242

punishment strips the citizen of his status in the national and international political community. . . .[11]

The *Kennedy* v. *Mendoza-Martinez* and *Rusk* v. *Cort* cases, which follow, continue the development of American constitutional law on the subject of denationalization. In *Perez* v. *Brownell*,[12] the Court by a close vote had upheld congressional power to impose loss of nationality for voting in a political election or participating in an election or plebiscite to determine sovereignty over foreign territory, while in *Trop* v. *Dulles*, on the other hand, a scant four-member opinion in the Court denied congressional power to denationalize for wartime desertion. Both Mendoza-Martinez and Cort deliberately evaded American military service. Did Congress have the constitutional power in such circumstances to deprive them of United States nationality?

KENNEDY v. MENDOZA-MARTINEZ
RUSK v. CORT
United States Supreme Court, 1963
372 U.S. 44

Mr. Justice Goldberg delivered the opinion of the Court.

The facts of both cases are not in dispute. Mendoza-Martinez, the appellee in No. 2, was born in this country in 1922 and therefore acquired American citizenship by birth. By reason of his parentage, he also, under Mexican law, gained Mexican citizenship, thereby possessing dual nationality. In 1942 he departed from this country and went to Mexico solely, as he admits, for the purpose of evading military service in our armed forces. He concedes that he remained there for that sole purpose until November 1946, when he voluntarily returned to this country. In 1947, in the United States District Court for the Southern District of California, he pleaded guilty to and was convicted of evasion of his service obligations in violation of Section 11 of the Selective Training and Service Act of 1940. He served the imposed sentence of a year and a day. For all that appears in the record, he was, upon his release, allowed to reside undisturbed in this country until 1953, when, after a lapse of five years, he was served with a warrant of arrest in deportation proceedings. This was premised on the assertion that, by remaining outside the United States to avoid military service after September 27, 1944, when Section 401 (j) took effect, he had lost his American citizenship. Following hearing, the Attorney

[11] 356 U.S. 86 (1958).
[12] 356 U.S. 44 (1958).

General's special inquiry officer sustained the warrant and ordered that Mendoza-Martinez be deported as an alien. He appealed to the Board of Immigration Appeals of the Department of Justice, which dismissed his appeal.

Thereafter, Mendoza-Martinez brought a declaratory judgment action in Federal District Court in the Southern District of California, seeking a declaration of his status as a citizen, of the unconstitutionality of Section 401 (j), and of the voidness of all orders of deportation directed against him. A single-judge District Court in an unreported decision entered judgment against Mendoza-Martinez in 1955, holding that by virtue of Section 401 (j), which the court held to be constitutional, he had lost his nationality by remaining outside the jurisdiction of the United States after September 27, 1944. The Court of Appeals for the Ninth Circuit affirmed the judgment, 238 F. 2d 239. This Court, in 1958, *Mendoza-Martinez* v. *Mackey* 356 U.S. 258, granted certiorari, vacated the judgment, and remanded the cause to the District Court for reconsideration in light of its decision a week earlier in *Trop* v. *Dulles,* 356 U.S. 86.

On September 24, 1958, the District Court announced its new decision, also unreported, that in light of *Trop* Section 401 (j) is unconstitutional because not based on any "rational nexus . . . between the content of a specific power in Congress and the action of Congress in carrying that power into execution." On direct appeal under 28 U.S.C. Section 1252, this Court noted probable jurisdiction, 359 U.S. 933, and then of its own motion remanded the cause, this time with permission to the parties to amend the pleadings to put in issue the question of whether the facts as determined on the draft-evasion conviction in 1947 collaterally estopped the Attorney General from now claiming that Mendoza-Martinez had lost his American citizenship while in Mexico. *Mackey* v. *Mendoza-Martinez,* 362 U.S. 384.

The District Court on remand held that the Government was not collaterally estopped because the 1947 criminal proceedings entailed no determination of Mendoza-Martinez' citizenship. The court, however, reaffirmed its previous holding that Section 401 (j) is unconstitutional, adding as a further basis of invalidity that Section 401 (j) is "essentially penal in character and deprives the plaintiff of procedural due process. . . . The requirements of procedural due process are not satisfied by the administrative hearing of the Immigration Service nor in this present proceedings." The Attorney General's current appeal is from this decision. . . .

Cort, the appellee in No. 3, is also a native-born American, born in Boston in 1927. Unlike Mendoza-Martinez, he has no dual nationality. His wife and two young children are likewise American citizens by birth. Following receipt of his M.D. degree from Yale University School of Medicine in 1951, he went to England for the purpose of undertaking a position as a Research Fellow at Cambridge University. He had earlier registered in timely and proper fashion for the draft and shortly before his departure supplemented his regular Selective Service registration by registering under the newly enacted Doctors' Draft Act. In late 1951 he received a series of letters from the American Embassy in London instructing him to deliver his passport to it to be made "valid only for return to the United States." He did not respond to these demands because, he now says in an affidavit filed in the trial court in this proceeding, "I believed that they were unlawful and I did not wish to subject myself to this and similar forms of political persecution then prevalent in the United States . . . I was engaged in important research and teaching work in physiology and I desired to continue earning a livelihood for my family." Cort had been a member of the Communist Party while he was a medical student at Yale from 1946 to 1951, except for the academic year 1948–1949 when he was in England. In late 1952, while still in England at Cambridge, he accepted a teaching position for the following academic year at Harvard University Medical School. When, however, the school discovered through further correspondence that he had not yet fulfilled his military obligations, it advised him that it did not regard his teaching position as essential enough to support his deferment from military service in order to enter upon it. Thereafter, his local draft board in Brookline, Massachusetts, notified him in February 1953 that his request for deferment was denied and that he should report within 30 days for a physical examination either in Brookline or in Frankfurt, Germany. On June 4 and on July 3 the draft board again sent Cort notices to report for a physical examination, the first notice for examination on July 1 in Brookline, and the second for examination within 30 days in Frankfurt. He did not appear at either place, and the board on August 13 ordered him to report for induction on September 14, 1953. He did not report and consequently he was indicted in December 1954 for violation of Section 12 (a) of the Selective Service Act of 1948 by reason of his failure to report for induction. This indictment is still outstanding. His complaint in this action states that he did not report for induction because he believed "that the induction order was not issued in good faith to secure his military services, that his past political associations and present physical disabilities made him ineligible for such service, and that he was being ordered to report back to the United States to be served with a Congressional Committee subpoena or indicted under the Smith Act. . . ." Meanwhile, the British Home Office had refused to renew his residence permit, and in mid-1954 he and his family moved to Prague, Czechoslovakia, where he took a position as Senior Scientific Worker at the Cardiovascular Institute. He has lived there since.

In April 1959, his previous United States passport having long since expired, Cort applied at the American Embassy in Prague for a new one. His complaint in this action states that he wanted the passport "in order to return to the United States with his wife and children so that he might fulfill his obligations under the Selective Service laws and his wife might secure medical treatment for multiple sclerosis." Mrs. Cort received a passport and came to this country temporarily in late 1959, both for purposes of medical treatment and to facilitate arrangements for her husband's return. Cort's application, however, was denied on the ground that he had, by his failure to report for induction on September 14, 1953, as ordered, remained outside the country to avoid military service and thereby automatically forfeited his American citizenship by virtue of Section 349 (a) (10) of the Immigration and Nationality Act of 1952, which had superseded Section 401 (j). The State Department's Passport Board of Review affirmed the finding of expatriation, and the Department's legal adviser affirmed the decision. Cort, through counsel, thereupon brought this suit in the District Court for the District of Columbia for a declaratory judgment that he is a citizen of the United States, for an injunction against enforcement of Section 349 (a) (10) because of its unconstitutionality, and for an order directing revocation of the certificate of loss of nationality and issuance of a United States passport to him. Pursuant to Cort's demand, a three-judge court was convened. The court held that he had remained outside the United States to evade military service, but that Section 349 (a) (10) is unconstitutional because "We perceive no substantial difference between the constitutional issue in the Trop case and the one facing us." It therefore concluded that Cort is a citizen of this country and enjoined the Secretary of State from withholding a passport from Cort on the ground that he is not a citizen and from otherwise interfering with his rights of citizenship. *Cort* v. *Herter*, 187 F. Suppl. 683.

*				*				*

We deal with the contending constitutional arguments in the context of certain basic and sometimes conflicting principles. Citizenship is a most precious right. It is expressly guaranteed by the Fourteenth Amendment to the Constitution, which speaks in the most positive terms. The Constitution is silent about the permissibility of involuntary forfeiture of citizenship rights. While it confirms citizenship rights, plainly there are imperative obligations of citizenship, performance of which Congress in the exercise of its powers may constitutionally exact. One of the most important of these is to serve the country in time of war and national emergency. The powers of Congress to require military service for the common defense are broad and far-reaching, for while the Constitution protects against invasions of individual rights, it is not a suicide pact. Similarly, Congress has broad power under the Necessary and Proper Clause to enact legislation for the regulation of foreign affairs. Latitude in this area is necessary to ensure effectuation of this indispensable function of government.

. . . The Government argues that Sections 401 (j) and 349 (a) (10) are valid as an exercise of Congress' power over foreign affairs, of its war power, and of the inherent sovereignty of the Government. Appellees urge the provisions' invalidity as not within any of the powers asserted, and as imposing a cruel and unusual punishment.

We recognize at the outset that we are confronted here with an issue of the utmost import. Deprivation of citizenship . . . has grave practical consequences. An expatriate who, like Cort, had no other nationality becomes a stateless person—a person who not only has no rights as an American citizen, but no membership in any national entity whatsoever. "Such individuals as do not possess any nationality enjoy, in general, no protection whatever, and if they are aggrieved by a State they have no means of redress, since there is no State which is competent to take their case in hand. As far as the Law of Nations is concerned, there is, apart from restraints of morality or obligations expressly laid down by treaty . . . no restriction whatever to cause a State to abstain from maltreating to any extent such stateless individuals." 1 Oppenheim, International Law (8th ed., Lauterpacht, 1955), Section 291, at 640. . . . The stateless person may end up shunted from nation to nation, there being no one obligated or willing to receive him, or, as in Cort's case, may receive the dubious sanctuary of a Communist regime lacking the essential liberties precious to American citizenship.

*   *   *

In *Perez*, Section 401 (e), which imposes loss of nationality for "voting in a political election or plebiscite to determine the sovereignty over foreign territory," was upheld by a closely divided Court as a constitutional exercise of Congress' power to regulate foreign affairs. The Court reasoned that since withdrawal of citizenship of Americans who vote in foreign elections is reasonably calculated to effect the avoidance of embarrassment in the conduct of foreign relations, such withdrawal is within the power of Congress, acting under the Necessary and Proper Clause. Since the Court sustained the application of Section 401 (e) to denationalize Perez, it did not have to deal with Section 401 (j), upon which the Government had also relied, and it expressly declined to rule on the constitutionality of that section, 356 U.S., at 62. There were three opinions written in dissent. . . .

In *Trop*, Section 401 (g), forfeiting the citizenship of any American who is guilty of "deserting the military or naval forces of the United States in time of war, provided he is convicted thereof by court martial and as the result of such conviction is dismissed or dishonorably discharged . . . ," was declared unconstitutional. There was no opinion of the Court. THE CHIEF JUSTICE wrote an opinion for four members of the Court, concluding that Section 401 (g) was invalid for the same reason that he had urged as to Section 401 (e) in his dissent in *Perez*, and that it was also invalid as a cruel and unusual punishment imposed in violation of the Eighth Amendment. Justice BRENNAN conceded that it is "paradoxical to justify as constitutional the expatriation of the citizen who has committed no crime by voting in a Mexican political election, yet find unconstitutional a statute which provides for the expatriation of a soldier guilty of the very serious crime of desertion in time of war," 356 U.S., at 105. Notwithstanding, he concurred because "the requisite rational relation between this statute and the war power does not appear . . . ," *id.*, at 114. Justice Frankfurter, joined by three other Justices, dissented on the ground that Section 401 (g) did not impose punishment at all, let alone cruel and unusual punishment, and was within the war powers of Congress.

The present cases present for decision the constitutionality of a section not passed upon in either *Perez* or *Trop*—Section 401 (j), added in 1944, and its successor and present counterpart, Section 349 (a) (10) of the Immigration and Nationality Act of 1952. We have come to the conclusion that there is a basic question in the present cases, the answer to which obviates a choice here between the powers of Congress and the constitutional guarantee of citizenship. That issue is whether the statutes here, which automatically—without prior court or administrative proceedings —forfeit citizenship, are essentially penal in character, and consequently have deprived the appelles of their citizenship without due process of law and without according them the rights guaranteed by the Fifth and Sixth Amendments, including notice, confrontation, compulsory process for obtaining witnesses, trial by jury, and assistance of counsel. This issue was not relevant in *Trop* because, in contrast to Sections 401 (j) and 349 (a) (10), Section 401 (g) required conviction by court-martial for desertion before forfeiture of citizenship could be inflicted. In *Perez* the contention that Section 401 (e) was penal in character was impliedly rejected by the Court's holding, based on legislative history totally different from that underlying Sections 401 (j) and 349 (a) (10), that voting in a political election in a foreign state "is regulable by Congress under its power to deal with foreign affairs.". . .

It is fundamental that the great powers of Congress to conduct war and to regulate the Nation's foreign relations are subject to the constitutional requirements of due process. The imperative necessity for safeguarding these rights to procedural due process under the gravest of emergencies has existed throughout our constitutional history, for it is then, under the pressing exigencies of crisis, that there is the greatest temptation to dispense with fundamental constitutional guarantees which, it is feared, will inhibit governmental action. . . .

We hold Sections 401 (j) and 349 (a) (10) invalid because in them Congress has plainly employed the sanction of deprivation of nationality as a punishment—for the offense of leaving or remaining outside the country to evade military service—without affording the procedural safeguards guaranteed by the Fifth and Sixth Amendments. . . .

As the Government concedes, Sections 401 (j) and 349 (a) (10) automatically strip an American of his citizenship, with concomitant deprivation "of all that makes life worth living." *Ng Gung Ho* v. *White*, 259 U.S. 276, 284–285, whenever a citizen departs from or remains outside the jurisdiction of this country for the purpose of evading his military obligations. Conviction for draft evasion, as Cort's case illustrates, is not prerequisite to the operation of this sanction. Independently of prosecution, forfeiture of citizenship attaches when the statutory set of facts develops. . . . This being so, the Fifth and Sixth Amendments mandate that this punishment cannot be imposed without a prior criminal trial and all its incidents, including indictment, notice, confrontation, jury trial, assistance of counsel, and compulsory process for obtaining witnesses. If the sanction these sections impose is punishment, and it plainly is, the procedural safeguards required as incidents of a criminal prosecution are lacking. We need go no further.

The punitive nature of the sanction here is evident under the tests traditionally applied to determine whether an Act of Congress is penal or regulatory in character, even though in other cases this problem has been extremely difficult and elusive of solution. Whether the sanction involves an affirmative disability or restraint, whether it has historically been regarded as a punishment, whether it comes into play only on a finding of *scienter*, whether its operation will promote the traditional aims of punishment—retribution and deterrence, whether the behavior to which it applies is already a crime, whether an alternative purpose to which it may rationally be connected is assignable for it, and whether it appears excessive in relation to the alternative purpose assigned are all relevant to the inquiry, and may often point in differing directions. Absent conclusive evidence of congressional intent as to the penal nature of the statute, these factors must be considered in relation to the statute on its face. Here, although we are convinced that application of these criteria to the face of the statutes supports the conclusion that they are punitive, a detailed examination along such lines is unnecessary, because the objective manifestations of congressional purpose indicate conclusively that the provisions in question can only be interpreted as punitive.

*   *   *

It is argued that our holding today will have the unfortunate result of immunizing the draft evader who has left the United States from having to suffer any sanction against his conduct, since he must return to this country before he can be apprehended and tried for his crime. The compelling answer to this is that the Bill of Rights which we guard so jealously and the procedures it guarantees are not to be abrogated merely because a guilty man may escape prosecution or for any other expedient reason. Moreover, the truth is that even without being expatriated, the evader living abroad is not in a position to assert the vast majority of his component rights as an American citizen. If he wishes to assert those rights in any real sense he must return to this country, and by doing that he will subject himself to prosecution. In fact, while he is outside the country evading prosecution, the United States may, by proper refusal to exercise its largely discretionary power to afford him diplomatic protection, decline to invoke its sovereign power on his behalf. Since the substantial benefits of American citizenship only come into play upon return to face prosecution, the draft evader who wishes to exercise his citizenship rights will inevitably come home and pay his debt, which within constitutional limits Congress has the power to define. This is what Mendoza-Martinez did, what Cort says he is willing to do, and what others have done. Thus our holding today does not frustrate the effective handling of the problem of draft evaders who leave the United States.

We conclude, for the reasons stated, that Sections 401 (j) and 349 (a) (10) are punitive and as such cannot constitutionally stand, lacking as they do the procedural safeguards which the Constitution commands. We recognize that draft evasion, particularly in time of war, is a heinous offense, and should and can be properly punished. Dating back to Magna Carta, however, it has been an abiding principle governing the lives of civilized men that "no freeman shall be taken or imprisoned or disseised or outlawed or exiled . . . without the judgment of his peers or by the law of the land. . . ." What we hold is only that, in keeping with this cherished tradition, punishment cannot be imposed "without due process of law." Any lesser holding would ignore the constitutional mandate upon which our essential liberties depend. Therefore the judgments of the District Courts in these cases are

Affirmed.

*   *   *

Mr. Justice Douglas and Mr. Justice Black, while joining the opinion of the Court, adhere to the views expressed in the dissent of Mr. Justice Douglas, in which Mr. Justice Black joined, in *Perez* v. *Brownell,* that Congress has no right to deprive a person of the citizenship granted the native-born by Sec., cl. 1, of the Fourteenth Amendment.

*   *   *

Mr. Justice Brennan, concurring.

*   *   *

It is apparent, then, that today's cases are governed by *Trop* no matter which of the two controlling opinions is consulted. Expatriation is here employed as "punishment," cruel and unusual here if it was there. Nor has expatriation as employed in these cases any more rational or necessary a connection with a war power than it had in *Trop.*

Mr. Justice Stewart with whom Mr. Justice White joins dissenting.

The Court's opinion is lengthy, but its thesis is simple: (1) The withdrawal of citizenship which these statutes provide is "punishment." (2) Punishment cannot constitutionally be imposed except after a criminal trial and conviction. (3) The statutes are therefore unconstitutional. As with all syllogisms, the conclusion is inescapable if the premises are correct. But I cannot agree with the Court's major premise—that the divestiture of citizenship which these statutes prescribe is punishment in the constitutional sense of that term.

Despite the broad sweep of some of the language of its opinion, the Court as I understand it does not hold that involuntary deprivation of citizenship is inherently and always a penal sanction. In support of this position, the Court devotes many pages of its opinion to a discussion of a quite different law, enacted in 1865, amended in 1912, and repealed in 1940. . . .

* * *

. . . Unlike the 1865 law, the legislation at issue in the cases before us is *not* "in terms punitive." And there is nothing in the history of *this* legislation which persuades me that these statutes, though not in terms penal, nonetheless embody a purpose of the Congresses which enacted them to impose criminal punishment without the safeguards of the criminal trial.

Unlike the two sections of the Nationality Act of 1940 which were in issue in *Perez* v. *Brownell* and *Trop* v. *Dulles*, Sec. 401 (j) did not have its genesis in the Cabinet Committee's draft code which President Roosevelt submitted to Congress in 1938. Indeed, Sec. 401 (j) was the product of a totally different environment—the experience of a nation engaged in a global war.

* * *

The question of whether or not a statute is punitive ultimately depends upon whether the disability it imposes is for the purpose of vengeance or deterrence, or whether the disability is but an incident to some broader regulatory objective. . . .

. . . I can find no clear proof that the prime purpose of this legislation was punitive. To be sure, there is evidence that the deterrent effect of the legislation was considered. Moreover, the attitude of some members of Congress toward those whom the legislation was intended to reach was obviously far from neutral. But the fact that the word "penalty" was used by an individual Senator in the congressional debates is hardly controlling. . . .

It seems clear to me that these putative indicia of punitive intent are far overbalanced by the fact that this legislation dealt with a basic problem of wartime morale reaching far beyond concern for any individual affected. . . .

* * *

. . . it is unnecessary to pursue further an inquiry as to whether the power to regulate foreign affairs could justify denationalization for the conduct in question. For I think it apparent that Congress in enacting the statute was drawing upon another power, broad and far reaching.

A basic purpose of the Constitution was to "provide for the common defense." . . .

It seems to me evident that Congress was drawing upon this power when it enacted the legislation before us. . . .

* * *

This Court has never held that Congress' power to expatriate may be used unsparingly in every area in which it has general power to act. Our previous decisions upholding involuntary denationalization all involved conduct inconsistent with undiluted allegiance to this country. But I think the legislation at issue in these cases comes so clearly within the compass of those decisions as to make unnecessary in this case an inquiry as to what the ultimate limitation upon the expatriation power may be.

The conduct to which this legislation applies, involving not only the attribute of flight or absence from this country in time of war or national emergency, but flight or absence for the express purpose of evading the duty of helping to defend this country, amounts to an unequivocal and conspicuous manifestation of nonallegiance, whether considered objectively or subjectively. . . . It is hardly an improvident exercise of constitutional power for Congress to disown those who have disowned this Nation in time of ultimate need.

. . . Sec. 349 (a) (10) declares:

"For the purposes of this paragraph failure to comply with any provision of any compulsory service laws of the United States shall raise the presumption that the departure from or absence from the United States was for the purpose of evading or avoiding training and service in the military, air, or naval forces of the United States."

I think the evidentiary presumption which the statute creates is clearly invalid, and that it fatally infected the administrative determination that Joseph Henry Cort had lost his citizenship.

* * *

The presumption created by Sec. 349 (a) (10) is wholly at odds with the decisions of the Court which hold that in cases such as this a heavy burden is upon the Government to prove an act of expatriation by clear, convincing, and unequivocal evidence. . . .

*　　*　　*

It is clear from the record in this case that Cort's sole purpose in leaving the United States in 1951 was to accept a position as a Research Fellow at the University of Cambridge, England. The record also makes clear that in 1946 Cort was called up under the Selective Service law, physically examined, and classified as 4F because of physical disability. The record further shows that Cort voluntarily registered under the Doctors Draft Act, making special arrangements with his draft board to do so in advance of the effective date for registration under the statute, a few days before he left for Europe. Cort filed an affidavit in which he swore that it was his belief, in the light of his physical disability, that the induction order which he received in England was not issued in good faith to secure his military service, but that its purpose instead was to force him to return to the United States to be investigated by the House Committee on Un-American Activities or prosecuted under the Smith Act. He has made repeated efforts to arrange with Selective Service officials for the fulfillment, albeit belatedly, of his military obligations, if any, and. . . . I mention this evidence as disclosed by the present record only to indicate why I think a new administrative hearing freed from the weight of the statutory presumption is in order, not to imply any pre-judgment of what I think the ultimate administrative decision should be.

In No. 3, *Rusk* v. *Cort*, I would vacate the judgment of the District Court and remand the case with instructions to declare null and void the certificate of loss of nationality issued to Cort by the Secretary of State, so that upon Cort's renewed application for a passport, an administrative hearing could be had, free of the evidentiary presumption of Sec. 349 (a) (10). In the event that such administrative proceedings should result in a finding that Cort had lost his United States citizenship, he would be entitled to a *de novo* judicial hearing in which the Government would have the burden of proving an act of expatriation by clear, convincing, and unequivocal evidence. . . .

In No. 2, *Kennedy* v. *Mendoza-Martinez*, I would reverse the judgment of the District Court.

Mr. Justice Harlan, whom Mr. Justice Clark joins dissenting.

I agree with and join in Parts I, II, III, and IV of my Brother Stewart's opinion, leading to the conclusion that Sec. 401 (j) of the Nationality Act of 1940, applicable in No. 2 (Mendoza), is constitutional. I also agree with his conclusion that, for the same reasons, the substantive provisions of Sec. 349 (a) (10) of the 1952 Act, applicable in No. 3 (Cort), are constitutional. I disagree, however, with his view that the evidentiary presumption contained in Sec. 349 (a) (10) is unconstitutional. . . .

*　　*　　*

VII

Human Rights and International Crimes

THE problem of jurisdiction over individuals in international law can be brought into sharp focus by a study of international human rights and international crimes. This subject owes its history to the determined efforts of statesmen, lawyers, and political-legal philosophers to give universal justice to the individual by ending the fiction of the sovereign state as (*a*) sole judge of all matters within its territorial jurisdiction and (*b*) the only "person" for whom rights are created by international law.

For more than half a century, by political rhetoric, social philosophy, and modern law the governments of the world have taken increasing responsibility for individual welfare. Much of this mood first crept into the conditions for maintaining international peace after World War I. The Treaty of Versailles and the Covenant of the League of Nations contained many auspicious phrases that called for elimination of privation, prevention of disease, improvement of working conditions, curtailment of traffic in women, protection of minorities, and just treatment of native inhabitants in dependent territories. Thus, a new plea for considering individuals as members of a world community with their own legal rights began to be heard beside the traditional assertions of the rights of states under international law.

The joint United States–Great Britain proposal in the 1941 Atlantic Charter "to bring about the fullest collaboration between all nations in the economic field with the object of securing for all, improved labor standards, economic advancement, and social security" was followed by the Declaration of United Nations in 1942, which stated "complete victory over their enemies is necessary to preserve human rights and justice in

254

their own lands as well as other lands." The way was thereby prepared for the 1945 United Nations Charter. One of the major purposes of the organization, as stated in Article I, is "to achieve international cooperation . . . in promoting and encouraging respect for human rights and for fundamental freedoms for all without distinction as to race, sex, language, or religion. . . ." Five other articles in the Charter also called on the United Nations to study, encourage, and promote human rights, as well as to establish a commission for that purpose.[1]

After two years of study and drafting by the new U.N. Commision on Human Rights, a Universal Declaration of Human Rights was approved on 10 December 1948 without a dissenting vote. The declaration was a bold and comprehensive statement of the rights due to individuals, such as freedom of speech and religion, a free choice of nationality, an asylum from persecution, a choice of employment, and an opportunity for education—all without distinction of race, religion, sex, color, national origin, and so forth.

The Universal Declaration of Human Rights is not a convention and lacks the binding force of a treaty obligation. Nevertheless, its standards have become a guiding star to international jurisprudence, and the high tone of its exhortation continues to influence national policies and their legal application. However, the ultimate difficulty of maintaining international human rights lies in the prosecution and enforcement of those rights against states. At issue is the doctrine that individuals derive such rights as they may have under international law only *through* states. Advocates of international human rights argue that the individual must derive his rights directly from international law, that is, by an international convention making the states, not only liable to one another for a breach of obligation with respect to human rights, but also liable to the individual himself, even if a national of the state.

To achieve this radical change of legal relationships between states and individuals in the field of human rights, three steps must be mounted: first, a declaration of common standards of human rights on which states can generally agree, such as "no one shall be held in slavery," "no one shall be subjected to arbitrary arrest," or "everyone has the right to leave any country"; second, signing and ratification of a treaty in which the states undertake to provide specific human rights through their municipal laws; third, establishment of some international judicial machinery by which *both* the rights of states against one another and the rights of individuals against states under the treaty can be maintained.

Several treaties of the past, beginning with the Treaty of Augsburg in 1555, guaranteed religious freedom to individuals or special civil rights for minority groups. The obligation for enforcement always rested on the state through its own municipal laws. After World War I, several "minor-

---

[1] United Nations Charter, Article I, Section 3. See also Articles 13, 55, 62, 68, and 76.

ities treaties" were signed. In these, the Allied and Associated Powers imposed obligations on new or enlarged states, like Poland or Czechoslovakia, for the protection of racial, religious, or linguistic groups within their borders, with the Council of the League as the supervising body. Any breach of obligation was considered a matter between the state and the League of Nations. However, only in the Geneva Convention on Upper Silesia in 1922 was an individual—probably for the first time in modern history—enabled to petition an international organ regarding acts of his own government that affected his political and civil rights.

After World War II, many states of the world indicated either their willingness or their legal obligation to promote and encourage a respect for human rights through the United Nations Charter in 1945, the constitutions of the United Nations specialized agencies, the Paris peace treaties of 1947 with Bulgaria, Hungary, Italy, Roumania, and Finland, and, most notably, through the Universal Declaration of Human Rights in 1948.

Many conventions dealing with stateless persons, refugees, forced labor, slavery, organized labor, women, minority groups, education, children, freedom of information, and others have been drafted, signed, and submitted for state ratification under the auspices of the United Nations and the specialized agencies.[2] Some were in force in 1967, and some had not yet received the necessary number of ratifications to put them into force, but all represented a substantial thrust forward to realize worldwide principles of protection for human rights.

But the nub of the problem of all human rights conventions still lies in the states' acceptance of review and possible prosecution of alleged violations within their territorial jurisdiction. Methods to implement human rights conventions now range all the way from a committee to mediate between states when a breach of international obligation has been charged, to an immediate and direct appeal by individuals to an international tribunal where the state would be a defendant.

In December 1966 the U.N. General Assembly unanimously adopted the International Covenant on Civil and Political Rights and the International Covenant on Economic, Social, and Cultural Rights. Both conventions are far-reaching in their expectations that states will recognize the equality of all persons before the law, grant freedom of opinion, provide opportunities for work and leisure, and protect the family. An optional protocol, moreover, to which states may agree would allow the Human Rights Committee, established by the covenants, to receive and consider communications from individuals alleging a violation of human rights and require an impugned state to explain or clarify the allegation within six months.

---

[2] See, for example, the conventions on Abolition of Forced Labor, 1957; Against Discrimination in Education, 1960; Reduction of Statelessness, 1961; Consent to Marriage, Minimum Age of Marriage, and Registration of Marriages, 1962; Elimination of All Forms of Racial Discrimination, 1965.

Contrasted with the lack of universal agreement on enforcement procedures, the achievement of the European Convention on Human Rights seems formidable. In 1950, 15 foreign ministers of European states signed the text of a European Convention for the Protection of Human Rights and Fundamental Freedoms, and the convention entered into force in 1953. But the key question of international supervision of the rights and freedoms guaranteed in the convention by states to individuals under their jurisdiction had to be approached gingerly. Therefore, each contracting state was given the option to accept or reject (*a*) the provisions that allowed a European Commission of Human Rights to investigate and report on violations *upon the petition of individuals or nongovernmental agencies;* and (*b*) the provisions for submitting to the jurisdiction of a European Court of Human Rights.

The right of individuals to make applications to the Commission came into force in 1955, and by 1966, 11 of the 15 member states of the Council of Europe recognized the competence of the Commission in this respect. Between 1955 and 1963, the Commission was flooded with 2,095 individual applications, of which 1,515 were rejected directly by decision of the Commission, 45 were rejected after communication with the respondent government, and 64 were stricken from the list. Of the balance 27 were ultimately found to be admissible complaints for which remedies might be obtained either (*a*) through friendly adjustment with the state concerned or (*b*) by action of the Committee of Ministers of the Council of Europe or (*c*) by recourse to the European Court of Human Rights.

The European Court of Human Rights, whose jurisdiction was described in Section I, came into legal existence in 1958, and by 1966, 11 states had accepted its jurisdiction. Through a protocol to the Convention on Human Rights, in 1963, it may eventually become competent to give advisory opinions in certain circumstances.

On 13 April 1960, the Court accepted its first case, *Gerard Lawless* v. *the Government of Ireland.* A partial text of the decision follows. The case was a landmark of international jurisprudence, not for its substance but for the litigation between an individual and a state. The Court also heard the *"De Becker"* case in 1961 and 1962. Part of the proceedings follow; as the text indicates, they were halted due to a change in Belgian law. Up to 1966, the Court had decided only one case, but the scant record does not reveal the whole impact that the very existence of the European Convention on Human Rights, the Commission, and the Court are having on national laws and the judgment of national courts. From the point of view of international law, an international organ—the Human Rights Commission—still stands before the Court, not the individual himself; but practically, the European Convention on Human Rights can afford a rare protection for an individual against a state before an international tribunal. While the step is extremely modest and particular to the European Community, it marks one of those bold departures in international legal theory that bear watching.

International Protection

LAWLESS CASE (Merits)
European Court of Human Rights, 1961
56 A.J.I.L. 187

*   *   *

1. The present case was referred to the Court on 13th April 1960 by the European Commission of Human Rights (hereinafter called "the Commission") (by a request) dated 12th April 1960. Attached to the request was the Report drawn up by the Commission in accordance with Article 31 of the Convention. The case relates to the Application submitted to the Commission under Article 25 of the Convention by G. R. Lawless, a national of the Republic of Ireland, against the Government of that State.

*   *   *

Whereas it has been established that G. R. Lawless was arrested by the Irish authorities on 11th July 1957 under Sections 21 and 30 of the Offences against the State Act (1939) No. 13; that on 13th July 1957, before the expiry for the order for arrest made under Act No. 13 of 1939, G. R. Lawless was handed a copy of a Detention Order made on 12th July 1957 by the Minister of Justice under Section 4 of the Offences against the State (Amendment) Act 1940; and that he was subsequently detained, first in the military prison in the Curragh and then in the Curragh Internment Camp, until his release on 11th December 1957 without having been brought before a judge during that period;

Whereas the Court is not called upon to decide on the arrest of G. R. Lawless on 11th July 1957, but only, in the light of the submissions put forward both by the Commission and by the Irish Government, whether or not the detention of G. R. Lawless from 13th July to 11th December 1957 under Section 4 of the Offences against the State (Amendment) Act, 1940, complied with the stipulations of the Convention.

Whereas, in this connection the Irish Government has put in against the Application of G. R. Lawless a plea in bar as to the merits derived from Article 17 of the Convention; whereas this plea in bar should be examined first;

. . . *Whereas* Article 17 of the Convention provides as follows:

"Nothing in this Convention may be interpreted as implying for any State, group or person any right to engage in any activity or perform any act aimed at the destruction of any of the rights and freedoms set forth herein or at their limitation to a greater extent than is provided for in the Convention";

Whereas the Irish Government submitted to the Commission and reaffirmed before the Court (i) that G. R. Lawless, at the time of his arrest in July 1957, was engaged in IRA activities; (ii) that the Commission, in paragraph 138 of its Report, had already observed that his conduct was "such as to draw upon the Applicant the gravest suspicion that, whether or not he was any longer a member, he was still concerned with the activities of the IRA at the time of his arrest in July 1957"; (iii) that the IRA was banned on account of its activity aimed at the destruction of the rights and freedoms set forth in the Convention; that, in July 1957, G. R. Lawless was thus concerned in activities falling within the terms of Article 17 of the Convention; that he therefore no longer had a right to rely on Article 5, 6, 7 or any other Article of the Convention; . . .

* * *

. . . whereas this provision, which is negative in scope, cannot be construed *a contrario* as depriving a physical person of the fundamental individual rights guaranteed by Articles 5 and 6 of the Convention; whereas, in the present instance G. R. Lawless has not relied on the Convention in order to justify or perform acts contrary to the rights and freedoms recognized therein but has complained of having been deprived of the guarantees granted in Articles 5 and 6 of the Convention; whereas, accordingly, the Court cannot, on this ground, accept the submissions of the Irish Government.

As to whether the detention of G. R. Lawless without trial from 13th July to 11th December 1957 under Section 4 of the Offences against the State (Amendment) Act 1940, conflicted with the Irish Government's obligations under Articles 5 and 6 of the Convention.

Whereas Article 5 of the Convention reads as follows:

"(1) Everyone has the right to liberty and security of person.
No one shall be deprived of his liberty save in the following cases and in accordance with a procedure prescribed by law:
(a) the lawful detention of a person after conviction by a competent court;
(b) the lawful arrest or detention of a person for non-compliance with the lawful order of a court or in order to secure the fulfilment of any obligation prescribed by law;
(c) the lawful arrest or detention of a person effected for the purpose of bringing him before the competent legal authority on reasonable suspicion of having committed an offence or when it is reasonably considered necessary to prevent his committing an offence or fleeing after having done so;
(d) the detention of a minor by lawful order for the purpose of educational supervision or his lawful detention for the purpose of bringing him before the competent legal authority;
(e) the lawful detention of persons for the prevention of the spreading of infectious diseases; of persons of unsound mind; alcoholics or drug addicts or vagrants;

(f) the lawful arrest or detention of a person to prevent his effecting an unauthorised entry into the country or of a person against whom action is being taken with a view to deportation or extradition.

(2) Everyone who is arrested shall be informed promptly, in a language which he understands, of the reasons for his arrest and of any charge against him.

(3) Everyone arrested or detained in accordance with the provisions of paragraph 1(c) of this Article shall be brought promptly before a judge or other officer authorised by law to exercise judicial power and shall be entitled to trial within a reasonable time or to release pending trial. Release may be conditioned by guarantees to appear for trial.

(4) Everyone who is deprived of his liberty by arrest or detention shall be entitled to take proceedings by which the lawfulness of his detention shall be decided speedily by a court and his release ordered if the detention is not lawful.

(5) Everyone who has been the victim of arrest or detention in contravention of the provisions of this Article shall have an enforceable right to compensation."

*   *   *

Whereas it has been shown that the detention of G. R. Lawless from 13th July to 11th December 1957 was not "effected for the purpose of bringing him before the competent legal authority" and that during his detention he was not in fact brought before a judge for trial "within a reasonable time"; whereas it follows that his detention under Section 4 of the Irish 1940 Act was contrary to the provisions of Article 5, paras. 1(c) and 3 of the Convention; whereas it will therefore be necessary to examine whether, in the particular circumstances of the case, the detention was justified on other legal grounds;

*   *   *

Whereas the Commission referred before the Court to the renewed allegation of G. R. Lawless that his detention constituted a violation of Article 7 of the Convention; whereas the said Article reads as follows:

"(1) No one shall be held guilty of any criminal offence on account of any act or omission which did not constitute a criminal offence under national or international law at the time when it was committed. Nor shall a heavier penalty be imposed than the one that was applicable at the time the criminal offence was committed.

(2) This Article shall not prejudice the trial and punishment of any person for any act or omission which, at the time when it was committed, was criminal according to the general principles of law recognised by civilised nations."

*   *   *

Whereas the proceedings show that the Irish Government detained G. R. Lawless under the Offences against the State (Amendment) Act, 1940, for the sole purpose of restraining him from engaging in activities prejudicial to the preservation of public peace and order or the security of the

State; whereas his detention, being a preventive measure, cannot be deemed to be due to his having been held guilty of a criminal offence within the meaning of Article 7 of the Convention; whereas it follows that Article 7 has no bearing on the case . . .

*   *   *

Whereas Article 15 reads as follows:

"(1) In time of war or other public emergency threatening the life of the nation any High Contracting Party may take measures derogating from its obligations under this Convention to the extent strictly required by the exigencies of the situation, provided that such measures are not inconsistent with its other obligations under international law.

(2) No derogation from Article 2, except in respect of deaths resulting from lawful acts of war, or from Articles 3, 4 (paragraph 1) and 7 shall be made under this provision.

(3) Any High Contracting Party availing itself of this right of derogation shall keep the Secretary-General of the Council of Europe fully informed of the measures which it has taken and the reasons therefor. It shall also inform the Secretary-General of the Council of Europe when such measures have ceased to operate and the provisions of the Convention are again being fully executed."

Whereas it follows from these provisions that, without being released from all its undertakings assumed in the Convention, the Government of any High Contracting Party has the right, in case of war or public emergency threatening the life of the nation, to take measures derogating from its obligations under the Convention other than those named in Article 15, paragraph 2, provided that such measures are strictly limited to what is required by the exigencies of the situation and also that they do not conflict with other obligations under international law; . . .

*   *   *

Whereas, in the general context of Article 15 of the Convention, the natural and customary meaning of the words "other public emergency threatening the life of the nation" is sufficiently clear; whereas they refer to an exceptional situation of crisis or emergency which affects the whole population and constitutes a threat to the organised life of the community of which the State is composed; whereas, having thus established the natural and customary meaning of this conception, the Court must determine whether the facts and circumstances which led the Irish Government to make their Proclamation of 5th July 1957 come within this conception; whereas the Court, after an examination, find this to be the case; . . .

Whereas, despite the gravity of the situation, the Government had succeeded, by using means available under ordinary legislation, in keeping public institutions functioning more or less normally, but whereas the homicidal ambush on the night of 3rd to 4th July 1957 in the territory of

Northern Ireland near the border had brought to light, just before 12th July—a date, which, for historical reasons is particularly critical for the preservation of public peace and order—the imminent danger to the nation caused by the continuance of unlawful activities in Northern Ireland by the IRA and various associated groups, operating from the territory of the Republic of Ireland.

Whereas, in conclusion, the Irish Government were justified in declaring that there was a public emergency in the Republic of Ireland threatening the life of the nation and were hence entitled, applying the provisions of Article 15, paragraph 1, of the Convention for the purposes for which those provisions were made, to take measures derogating from their obligations under the Convention;

*   *   *

Whereas Article 15, paragraph 1, provides that a High Contracting Party may derogate from its obligations under the Convention only "to the extent strictly required by the exigencies of the situation"; whereas it is therefore necessary, in the present case, to examine whether the bringing into force of Part II of the 1940 Act was a measure strictly required by the emergency existing in 1957;

*   *   *

Whereas, however, considering, in the judgment of the Court, that in 1957 the application of the ordinary law had proved unable to check the growing danger which threatened the Republic of Ireland; whereas the ordinary criminal courts, or even the special criminal courts or military courts, could not suffice to restore peace and order; whereas, in particular, the amassing of the necessary evidence to convict persons involved in activities of the IRA and its splinter groups was meeting with great difficulties caused by the military, secret and terrorist character of those groups and the fear they created among the population; whereas the fact that these groups operated mainly in Northern Ireland, their activities in the Republic of Ireland being virtually limited to the preparation of armed raids across the border was an additional impediment to the gathering of sufficient evidence; whereas the sealing of the border would have had extremely serious repercussions on the population as a whole, beyond the extent required by the exigencies of the emergency;

*   *   *

Whereas, therefore, it follows from the foregoing that the detention without trial provided for by the 1940 Act, subject to the above-mentioned safeguards, appears to be a measure strictly required by the exigencies of the situation within the meaning of Article 15 of the Convention;

*   *   *

Whereas the Court is called upon in the first instance, to examine whether, in pursuance of paragraph 3 of Article 15 of the Convention, the Secretary-General of the Council of Europe was duly informed both of the measures taken and of the reasons therefor; . . .

Whereas the Court accordingly finds that, in the present case, the Irish Government fulfilled their obligations as Party to the Convention under Article 15, paragraph 3, of the Convention;

For these reasons,

The Court

Unanimously

(i) *Dismisses* the plea in bar derived by the Irish Government from Article 17 of the Convention;

(ii) *States* that Articles 5 and 6 of the Convention provided no legal foundation for the detention without trial of G. R. Lawless from 13th July to 11th December 1957, by virtue of Article 4 of the Offences against the State (Amendment) Act, 1940;

(iii) *States* that there was no breach of Article 7 of the Convention;

(iv) *States* that the detention of G. R. Lawless from 13th July to 11th December 1957 was founded on the right of derogation duly exercised by the Irish Government in pursuance of Article 15 of the Convention in July 1957;

(v) *States* that the communication addressed by the Irish Government to the Secretary-General of the Council of Europe on 20th July 1957 constituted sufficient notification within the meaning of Article 15, paragraph 3, of the Convention.

Decides, accordingly, that in the present case the facts found do not disclose a breach by the Irish Government of their obligations under the European Convention for the Protection of Human Rights and Fundamental Freedoms;

Decides, therefore, that the question of entitlement by G. R. Lawless to compensation in respect of such a breach does not arise.

* * *

"DE BECKER" CASE
European Court of Human Rights, 1962
Series B, Registry of the Court, 1962

Memorial Submitted by the European Commission of Human Rights:

*   *   *

The case as submitted to the Commission was mainly concerned with questions of law. There was virtually no controversy between the Applicant and the Respondent Government as to the actual facts of the case. . . .

Mr. Raymond De Becker, a Belgian journalist and writer, is at present resident in Paris. On 24 July 1946 the Brussels *Conseil de Guerre* sentenced him to death on the ground that, between 13 June 1940 and 5 October 1943, he had collaborated with the German authorities in Belgium in various ways and capacities, principally in his position as editor of the Belgian daily newspaper "Le Soir". . . .

This judgment carried with it, *inter alia*, forfeiture by Mr. De Becker of the rights set out in Article 123 *sexies* of the Belgian Penal Code.

On appeal by Mr. De Becker, the Brussels Military Court, while confirming the facts and the Applicant's criminal intent, took into account certain entenuating circumstances, namely the Applicant's opposition to the "annexionist and separatist" intentions of the German authorities, which had led to his arrest in 1943 and to his deportation to Germany for a period of two years; and, in consequence, in its judgment of 14 June 1947, the Court had commuted the death-penalty to one of life imprisonment and confirmed the sentence in all other respects, including the forfeiture of the rights enumerated in Article 123 *sexies*.

This Article . . . then provided:

Any person convicted of an offense or attempted offense under Title I, Vol. 2, Chapter II of the Penal Code or Articles 17 and 18 of the Military Penal Code, committed in time of war, shall, *ipso facto*, be deprived for life of the following rights:

(a) the rights set out in Article 31 of the Penal Code, including the right to vote and the right to be elected;

(b) the right to appear on any roll of barristers, honorary counsel or probationary barristers;

(c) the right to take part, in any capacity whatsoever, in instruction provided by a public or private establishment;

(d) the right to receive remuneration from the State as a minister of religion;

(e) the right to have a proprietary interest in, or to take part in any capacity whatsoever in the administration, editing, printing or distribution of a newspaper or any other publication;

(f) the right to take part in organising or managing any cultural, philanthropic or sporting activity or any public entertainment;

(g) the right to have a proprietary interest in, or to be associated with, the administration or in any way with the activity of any undertaking concerned with theatrical production, films or broadcasting;

(h) the right to carry out the duties of director or manager or authorised representative of a private company . . .

(i) the right to be associated in any way with the administration, management or direction of a professional association or a non-profit-making association;

(j) the right to be a leader of a political association.

Article 123 *sexies* has since been modified by the laws of 14 June 1948 and 29 February 1952, but only in respect of the class of conviction to which it applied. . . . In its present form it applies only to "a criminal offense entailing a sentence of more than five years' imprisonment" wherefor it follows that the terms of this Article remain in force in the case of the Applicant.

In 1950, by an act of clemency, the sentence imposed on Mr. De Becker was reduced to seventeen years.

On 22 February 1951 Mr. De Becker was released conditionally upon his signing an "undertaking" that he would take up residence in France within one month from the date of his release; he also promised that he would not engage in politics. After spending some time in Switzerland, the Applicant took up residence in Paris.

Subsequently, Mr. De Becker asked on several occasions, but in vain, for the removal of the ban which forbade him to reside in Belgium and to practice his profession. He did, however, succeed in establishing *legal* domicile in that country. . . .

*   *   *

In view of the gravity of the crimes to which Article 123 *sexies* is applicable and the nature of modern warfare, the Commission "readily conceded the need for strong sanctions and effective preventive measures to protect the community against crimes of the kind committed by the Applicant." It considered, however, that Article 10 (2) of the Convention "does not permit the infliction of incapacities in regard to freedom of expression . . . except where the very nature of the offense obviously necessitates such incapacities."

The Commission further considered that "to impose on persons convicted of treason in time of war a total incapacity for life to publish their *political* opinions may be justifiable" under Article 10, paragraph 2. "But Article 123 *sexies* goes beyond the imposition of incapacities in regard to the publication of political opinions and includes incapacities which have no direct relation to the offense committed." The Commission nevertheless believed "that the imposition of the incapacities contained in paragraphs (e), (f) and (g) of that Article may be justifiable in time of war

and for such period as may be necessary after the conclusion of a war."
However, "a law which inflexibly takes away for life, without reference
to the evolution of public morale and public order, all freedom of publication in regard to non-political as well as political writings, appears to
the Commission to go beyond what is justifiable under paragraph 2 of
Article 10."

*   *   *

As it stated in its request of 28 April 1960 (page 91), the Commission,
in deciding to refer the matter to the Court, did not disregard the
existence of several proposals and bills designed to vary or restrict the
application of Article 123 *sexies* of the Belgian Penal Code. In particular,
it took note of the Government's Bill of 23 February 1960, added to the
file on 25 March.

*   *   *

Since 28 April 1960 the Commission has not received any information
modifying to any extent the situation described in the preceding paragraph. It did, of course, learn that on 7 April 1960 the Belgian Chamber of
Representatives passed the Government's Bill of 23 February. This Bill
has not however yet been passed by the Senate. In addition, it has brought
forth a whole series of draft amendments. According to the Belgian
constitution, the new legislation will not enter into force until both
Chambers of the Parliament have agreed on a uniform text.

*   *   *

Public Hearing by the Chamber of the Court

Mr. VAN RYN (Representative of the Belgium Government):
    As the Principal Delegate of the Commission has very rightly pointed
out, the proceedings in this case before the Court have been decisively
influenced by two new essential facts:
    —the first, as you know, is that of the entry into force of the Belgian
Law of 30th June 1961, amending and supplementing Article 123 *sexies* of
the Belgian Penal Code;
    —the second and more recent fact is that of the memorandum ad-
dressed to the Commission by Mr. De Becker, on 5th October 1961, the
contents of which were unknown to us at the time of the last hearing and
in which the Applicant stated that the Law of 30th June 1961 accorded
him once more freedom of expression, at least in what he considers to be
the most essential sphere, namely the non-political sphere. Mr. De Becker
added that he accordingly thought that he could and must withdraw his
application.

*   *   *

The Belgian Government takes the view that the solution consisting of now putting an end to these proceedings and, consequently, striking the case off the list is both logical and reasonable and, indeed, necessary if it is borne in mind that—as ruled by this Court in its judgment on the Lawless Case—"the whole of the proceedings in the Court, as laid down by the Convention and the Rules of Court, are upon issues which concern the Applicant."

In this connection the Belgian Government wishes to emphasize the very proper conception of the role of the Commission as expressed in particularly appropriate terms in the last conclusions of the Commission submitted to you, in which it is stated—and I quote: "whereas, however, the Commission does not conceive that the function entrusted to it under Article 19 'to ensure the observance of the engagements undertaken by the High Contracting Parties in the present Convention requires it in every case to seek from the Court a ruling as to whether or not there has been a violation of the Convention.' '

"Whereas, on the contrary, the Commission, when it brings a case before the Court, does not attempt to bring an accusation, but rather to watch over the maintenance of restoration of European public order."

* * *

The Belgian Government has always believed that the severity of these penalties imposed after the war in pursuance of Article 123 *sexies* should inevitably be attenuated after a time when feelings had calmed down. The Belgian Government has considered and still considers today that this is a question of a political gesture, the extent and timeliness of which is a matter solely for the discretion of the national authorities and primarily the Belgian Parliament, who are sole judges of the time at which this gesture can be made and of the extent to which it may be made.

This gesture of moderation, as you know from the explanation which I previously had the honour to give to the Court, was in course of preparation in Belgium for several years and, indeed, before Mr. De Becker lodged his application. The proposals which had been made to this end had met with a very hostile reception from a large section of the public in Belgium. The opinion expressed by the Commission in the De Becker case has, without any doubt, served to expedite the fulfillment of this gesture. And as, very rightly, pointed out by the Commission in its submissions, its opinion was taken into account during the preparatory work on the Law of 30 June 1961. Account was taken of it, Gentlemen, but I venture to warn the Court against a mistaken view, namely that alleging that the Law of 30 June 1961 was passed only because Belgium recognized that it was guilty of a violation of the Convention, a violation allegedly due to the existence in the Belgian Penal Code of an Article 123 *sexies* conflicting with the provisions of the Convention.

* * *

International Punishment

Is there a need for an international criminal court that can try offenses that take place outside the territory of any state? Is a court needed for crimes that transcend the borders of all states, for acts so universally acknowledged to be crimes, regardless of where committed, that an international tribunal would be competent to assert jurisdiction over the wrongdoers wherever they were seized?

These are questions that intrigue speculation on the future development of international law. Piracy, for example, has long been recognized under the law of nations as a crime against the human race. Both the seizure and punishment of pirates, regardless of nationality, have been undertaken by individual states. Moreover, nothing precludes a state from conferring jurisdiction over its nationals on another state when such nationals are taken on the high seas for committing international offenses outlawed by treaty, such as slave trading, cable cutting, or whale killing. But thus far states have shown little willingness to allow their nationals to fall under the nonterritorial jurisdiction of another state when criminal penalties are involved.

Of course, states have punished their own nationals and aliens brought under their jurisdiction for violations of the international laws of war, usually by military tribunals and generally on the assumption that such international law has been incorporated into the municipal law of the state. But prior to 1945, no *international* military tribunal had ever been created.

Napoleon had been called an enemy and disruptor of the world "who has exposed himself to public prosecution" by the Allies in 1815, but after capture he was exiled without trial. The Treaty of Versailles in 1919 had provided for the trial of William II of Germany "for a supreme offense against international morality and the sanctity of treaties . . . vindicating . . . the validity of international law," but he fled to the Netherlands, which refused to surrender him to the Allied Powers. After World War I, Germany recognized the right of the Allies to try persons accused of war crimes, but in the end only 12 trials were held, all before German courts.

In 1943, the leaders of the Allied Powers resolved that all Germans responsible for atrocities, massacres, or executions would be punished in the countries where they had committed their excesses, but those major criminals whose offenses had no particular geographical location would be punished under a joint decision of the Allies. Therefore, in 1945 they established an International Military Tribunal, composed of members from the United States, the Union of Soviet Socialist Republics, the United Kingdom, and France, to try those German leaders accused of crimes against peace, war crimes, and crimes against humanity. The Nuremberg trial of 22 Germans began 14 November, 1945. For the first time in history, an international tribunal heard an indictment against the political and military leaders of a state for war crimes as well as crimes against peace and crimes against humanity that were untested legal concepts. Judgment was delivered on 1 October, 1946. There were 19 convictions—12 with death sentences—and 3 acquittals. Later, the International Military Tribunal for the Far East in Tokyo gave a judgment on 12 November 1947, against 25 war criminals, all of whom were found guilty. Seven received the death sentence.[3]

To the present day, arguments continue on whether the Nuremberg Tribunal, as constituted, had jurisdiction over the alleged offenses against international law, and whether such crimes, internationally acknowledged today, were crimes for individuals at the time of their commission. Nevertheless, the General Assembly late in 1946 unanimously adopted a resolution affirming the principles of international law recognized by the Charter of the Nuremberg Tribunal and the judgment of that tribunal. The United Nations International Law Commission, proceeding on the recommendation of the General Assembly, in 1950 formulated a draft Code on Offenses against the Peace and Security of Mankind. The draft specifically refers to the fact that individuals can be found guilty of crimes against the peace and security of mankind under international law, but the document has not yet been signed and ratified by the states of the world.

Contemporary with this ideological thrust to place direct responsibility on individuals for violations of international law was the Genocide Convention adopted by the United Nations General Assembly in 1948. It entered into force early in 1951, and has been ratified by more than half the states of the world, subject to a number of confusing reservations. Essentially, genocide, consisting of acts to destroy religious, ethnic, or racial groups by calculated bodily or mental harm, is declared an international crime both in peace and war. The trial of individuals for such acts "shall" take place either before a competent national tribunal or an international criminal court to be given jurisdiction by the parties to the convention, with the necessary rights of extradition.

Lines are beginning to be drawn in the definition of crimes to be judged under international law. There is a plain warning that individuals can no longer hide behind the legal fiction of the state to exonerate atrocious deeds, and that individuals, regardless of their official cloak, may be held responsible for acts that outrage the law of nations. The United Nations has begun to draft a statute for a permanent international court

---

[3] In addition to the international tribunals, American, British, French, and other military tribunals held trials, convicted, and sentenced Germans, Italians, and Japanese accused of war crimes.

for such offenses, but candor again compels the observation that thus far states have shown little enthusiasm for establishing a court for war crimes, crimes against peace and humanity, or any other crimes, which through diversity of nationality or locus of the act might be tried more fairly and satisfactorily before an international tribunal. The Nuremberg opinion and judgment on *Nazi Conspiracy and Aggression*, which follows, raises many questions of substance and procedure in international law.

NAZI CONSPIRACY AND AGGRESSION
Opinion and Judgment, 1946
International Military Tribunal, Nuremberg, 1947

*   *   *

The jurisdiction of the Tribunal is defined in the Agreement and Charter, and the crimes coming within the jurisdiction of the Tribunal, for which there shall be individual responsibility, are set out in Article 6. The law of the Charter is decisive, and binding upon the Tribunal.

The making of the Charter was the exercise of the sovereign legislative power by the countries to which the German Reich unconditionally surrendered; and the undoubted right of these countries to legislate for the occupied territories has been recognized by the civilized world. The Charter is not an arbitrary exercise of power on the part of the victorious nations, but in the view of the Tribunal, as will be shown, it is the expression of international law existing at the time of its creation; and to that extent is itself a contribution to international law.

*   *   *

The Charter makes the planning or waging of a war of aggression or a war in violation of international treaties a crime; and it is therefore not strictly necessary to consider whether and to what extent aggressive war was a crime before the execution of the London Agreement. But in view of the great importance of the questions of law involved, the Tribunal has heard full argument from the prosecution and the defense, and will express its view on the matter.

It was urged on behalf of the defendants that a fundamental principle of all law—international and domestic—is that there can be no punishment of crime without a pre-existing law. "*Nullum crimen sine lege, nulla poena sine lege.*" It was submitted that *ex post facto* punishment is abhorrent to the law of all civilized nations, that no sovereign power had made aggressive war a crime at the time the alleged criminal acts were committed, that no statute had defined aggressive war, that no penalty had been fixed for its commission, and no court had been created to try and punish offenders.

In the first place, it is to be observed that the maxim *nullum crimen sine lege* is not a limitation of sovereignty, but is in general a principle of justice. To assert that it is unjust to punish those who in defiance of treaties and assurances have attacked neighboring states without warning is obviously untrue, for in such circumstances the attacker must know that he is doing wrong, and so far from it being unjust to punish him, it would be unjust if his wrong were allowed to go unpunished. Occupying the positions they did in the government of Germany, the defendants, or at least some of them must have known of the treaties signed by Germany, outlawing recourse to war for the settlement of international disputes; they must have known that they were acting in defiance of all international law when in complete deliberation they carried out their designs of invasion and aggression. On this view of the case alone, it would appear that the maxim has no application to the present facts.

This view is strongly reinforced by a consideration of the state of international law in 1939, so far as aggressive war is concerned. The General Treaty for the Renunciation of War of August 27, 1928, more generally known as the Pact of Paris or the Kellogg-Briand Pact, was binding on 63 nations, including Germany, Italy, and Japan at the outbreak of war in 1939. . . .

The first two articles are as follows:

"ARTICLE I. The High Contracting Parties solemnly declare in the names of their respective peoples that they condemn recourse to war for the solution of international controversies and renounce it as an instrument of national policy in their relations to one another.

"ARTICLE II. The High Contracting Parties agree that the settlement or solution of all disputes or conflicts of whatever nature or of whatever origin they may be, which may arise among them, shall never be sought except by pacific means."

The question is, what was the legal effect of this pact? The nations who signed the pact or adhered to it unconditionally condemned recourse to war for the future as an instrument of policy, and expressly renounced it. After the signing of the pact, any nation resorting to war as an instrument of national policy breaks the pact. In the opinion of the Tribunal, the solemn renunciation of war as an instrument of national policy necessarily involves the proposition that such a war is illegal in international law; and that those who plan and wage such a war, with its inevitable and terrible consequences, are committing a crime in so doing. . . .

But it is argued that the pact does not expressly enact that such wars are crimes, or set up courts to try those who make such wars. To that extent the same is true with regard to the laws of war contained in the Hague Convention. The Hague Convention of 1907 prohibited resort to certain methods of waging war. These included the inhumane treatment of prisoners, the employment of poisoned weapons, the improper use of flags or truce, and similar matters. Many of these prohibitions had been enforced long before the date of the Convention; but since 1907 they have certainly been crimes, punishable as offenses against the laws of war; yet the Hague Convention nowhere designates such practices as criminal, nor is any sentence prescribed, nor any mention made of a court to try and punish offenders. For many years past, however, military tribunals have tried and punished individuals guilty of violating the rules of land warfare laid down by this Convention. In the opinion of the Tribunal, those who wage aggressive war are doing that which is equally illegal, and of much greater moment than a breach of one of the rules of the Hague Convention. In interpreting the words of the pact, it must be remembered that international law is not the product of an international legislature, and that such international agreements as the Pact of Paris have to deal with general principles of law, and not with administrative matters of procedure. The law of war is to be found not only in treaties, but in the customs and practices of states which gradually obtained universal recognition, and from the general principles of justice applied by jurists and practiced by military courts. This law is not static, but by continual adaptation follows the needs of a changing world. Indeed, in many cases treaties do no more than express and define for more accurate reference the principles of law already existing.

The view which the Tribunal takes of the true interpretation of the pact is supported by the international history which preceded it. In the year 1923 the draft of a Treaty of Mutual Assistance was sponsored by the League of Nations. In Article I the treaty declared "that aggressive war is an international crime," and that the parties would "undertake that no one of them will be guilty of its commission." The draft treaty was submitted to twenty-nine states, about half of whom were in favor of accepting the text. . . .

*   *   *

At the meeting of the Assembly of the League of Nations on the 24th September 1927, all the delegations then present (including the German, the Italian, and the Japanese), unanimously adopted a declaration concerning wars of aggression. The preamble to the declaration stated:

"The Assembly: Recognizing the solidarity which unites the community of nations;

"Being inspired by a firm desire for the maintenance of general peace;

"Being convinced that a war of aggression can never serve as a means of settling international disputes, and is in consequence an international crime. . . ."

The unanimous resolution of the 18th February 1928, of 21 American republics at the sixth (Havana) Pan-American Conference, declared that "war of aggression constitutes an international crime against the human species."

All these expressions of opinion, and others that could be cited, so solemnly made, reinforce the construction which the Tribunal placed upon the Pact of Paris, that resort to a war of aggression is not merely illegal, but is criminal. The prohibition of aggressive war demanded by the conscience of the world, finds its expression in the series of Pacts and Treaties to which the Tribunal has just referred.

*   *   *

In the previous recital of the facts relating to aggressive war, it is clear that planning and preparation had been carried out in the most systematic way at every stage of the history.

Planning and preparation are essential to the making of war. In the opinion of the Tribunal aggressive war is a crime under international law. . . .

*   *   *

. . . That Germany was rapidly moving to complete dictatorship from the moment that the Nazis seized power, and progressively in the direction of war, has been overwhelmingly shown in the ordered sequence of aggressive acts and wars already set out in this judgment.

In the opinion of the Tribunal, the evidence establishes the common planning to prepare and wage war by certain of the defendants. . . .

The argument that such common planning cannot exist where there is complete dictatorship is unsound. A plan in the execution of which a number of persons participate is still a plan, even though conceived by only one of them; and those who execute the plan do not avoid responsibility by showing that they acted under the direction of the man who conceived it. Hitler could not make aggressive war by himself. He had to have the cooperation of statesmen, military leaders, diplomats, and businessmen. When they, with knowledge of his aims, gave him their cooperation, they made themselves parties to the plan he had initiated. They are not to be deemed innocent because Hitler made use of them, if they knew what they were doing. That they were assigned to their tasks by a dictator does not absolve them from responsibility for their acts. The relation of leader and follower does not preclude responsibility here any more than it does in the comparable tyranny of organized domestic crime.

*   *   *

The evidence relating to war crimes has been overwhelming, in its volume and its detail. It is impossible for this judgment adequately to review it, or to record the mass of documentary and oral evidence that has been presented. The truth remains that war crimes were committed on a vast scale, never before seen in the history of war. They were perpetrated in all the countries occupied by Germany, and on the high seas, and were attended by every conceivable circumstance of cruelty and horror. There can be no doubt that the majority of them arose from the Nazi conception of "total war," with which the aggressive wars were waged. For in this conception of "total war" the moral ideas underlying the conventions which seek to make war more humane are no longer regarded as having force or validity. Everything is made subordinate to the overmastering dictates of war. Rules, regulations, assurances, and treaties, all alike, are of no moment; and so, freed from the restraining influence of international law, the aggressive war is conducted by the Nazi leaders in the most barbaric way. . . .

*   *   *

. . . Prisoners of war were ill-treated and tortured and murdered, not only in defiance of the well-established rules of international law, but in complete disregard of the elementary dictates of humanity. Civilian populations in occupied territories suffered the same fate. Whole populations were deported to Germany for the purposes of slave labor upon defense works, armament production and similar tasks connected with the war effort. Hostages were taken in very large numbers from the civilian populations in all the occupied countries, and were shot as suited the German purposes. Public and private property was systematically plundered and pillaged in order to enlarge the resources of Germany at the expense of the rest of Europe. Cities and towns and villages were wantonly destroyed without military justification or necessity.

*   *   *

The Tribunal is of course bound by the Charter, in the definition which it gives both of war crimes and crimes against humanity. With respect to war crimes, however, as has already been pointed out, the crimes defined by Article 6, section (b), of the Charter were already recognized as war crimes under international law. They were covered by Articles 46, 50, 52, and 56 of the Hague Convention of 1907, and Articles 2, 3, 4, 46, and 51 of the Geneva Convention of 1929. That violation of these provisions constituted crimes for which the guilty individuals were punishable is too well settled to admit of argument.

But it is argued that the Hague Convention does not apply in this case, because of the "general participation" clause in Article 2 of the Hague Convention of 1907. That clause provided:

"The provisions contained in the regulations (rules of land warfare) referred to in Article 1 as well as in the present convention do not apply except between contracting powers, and then only if all the belligerents are parties to the convention."

Several of the belligerents in the recent war were not parties to this convention.

In the opinion of the Tribunal it is not necessary to decide this question. The rules of land warfare expressed in the convention undoubtedly represented an advance over existing international law at the time of their adoption. But the convention expressly stated that it was an attempt "to revise the general laws and customs of war," which it thus recognized to be then existing, but by 1939 these rules laid down in the convention were recognized by all civilized nations, and were regarded as being declaratory of the laws and customs of war which are referred to in Article 6 (b) of the Charter.

*   *   *

With regard to crimes against humanity, there is no doubt whatever that political opponents were murdered in Germany before the war, and that many of them were kept in concentration camps in circumstances of great horror and cruelty. The policy of terror was certainly carried out on a vast scale, and in many cases was organized and systematic. The policy of persecution, repression, and murder of civilians in Germany before the war of 1939, who were likely to be hostile to the Government, was most ruthlessly carried out. The persecution of Jews during the same period is established beyond all doubt. To constitute crimes against humanity, the acts relied on before the outbreak of war must have been in execution of, or in connection with, any crime within the jurisdiction of the Tribunal. The Tribunal is of the opinion that revolting and horrible as many of these crimes were, it has not been satisfactorily proved that they were done in execution of, or in connection with, any such crime. The Tribunal therefore cannot make a general declaration that the acts before 1939 were crimes against humanity within the meaning of the Charter, but from the beginning of the war in 1939 war crimes were committed on a vast scale, which were also crimes against humanity; and insofar as the inhumane acts charged in the indictment, and committed after the beginning of the war, did not constitute war crimes, they were all committed in execution of, or in connection with, the aggressive war, and therefore constituted crimes against humanity.

*   *   *

Article 20 of the Charter provides that the judgment of the Tribunal as to the guilt or innocence of any defendant shall give the reasons on which it is based.

The Tribunal will now state those reasons in declaring its judgment on such guilt or innocence.

Goering is indicted on all four counts. . . .

National Punishment for Universal Crimes

If states have been so negligent as to define international crimes without providing international agencies for the arrest, trial, and punishment of criminals, may individual states prosecute the wrongdoers? May states assume that such internationally proscribed evils repel all sense of justice in the world, and, therefore, (*a*) whatever the nationality of the wrongdoer and (*b*) wherever the act was committed the state can assert its authority over the individual on the basis of universal jurisdiction?

In 1961, the state of Israel took into its own hands the prosecution of Adolph Eichmann, an individual who as a German national during the Nazi regime in Germany and during World War II allegedly performed acts constituting a crime against the Jewish people, a crime against humanity, and a war crime.

One disturbing element of this singular case arose from Eichmann's deliberate abduction from Argentina, where he was a resident, to Israel. While this could be a violation of international law in itself, if the act were sanctioned by Israel, under the law of nations it created a wrong only against Argentina. Another peculiar circumstance of the case was the German failure to extend diplomatic protection to one of its nationals, although admittedly Eichmann's status was not clear.

Moreover, Eichmann's alleged crimes were committed before Israel became a state, outside Israel, and not against Israeli nationals. Finally, Article 6 of the Genocide Convention, on which much reliance was placed to underline the international nature of the crimes, specifically requires that persons charged with genocide,

. . . shall be tried by a competent tribunal of the State in the territory of which the act was committed, or by such international penal tribunal as may have jurisdiction with respect to those Contracting Parties which shall have accepted its jurisdiction.

To this, the Israeli court answered that Article 6 pertained to *future* crimes, that it was a "conventional" arrangement that did not supersede or negate the principles of customary international law, which would allow a state to punish any individual for a crime against humanity even if committed outside its territory.

All these points of doubt or contention at least illustrate the difficult issues of jurisdiction that would have to be ironed out through any future international convention on war crimes or crimes against humanity. Whatever position states may take henceforth, it seems reasonable to say that in the *Eichmann* case several problems were circumvented through rather extraordinary circumstances.

If an international criminal court is not available to the world community, national law can still be rather effective in meting out justice once an alleged criminal is brought within the territorial jurisdiction of the state. But this will require a rehabilitation of extradition procedures, *first*, by treaty definition of crimes against peace and humanity as extraditable offenses and, *second*, by a willingness of national judges to recognize that offenses extending to mass murder, pillage, torture, and so forth cannot be screened from extradition as "political" acts.

A case in point is the United States refusal to surrender Andrija Artukovic to Yugoslavia in 1959. Artukovic had been a former minister and president of the State Council of Croatia. Yugoslavia alleged that he was responsible for the brutal deaths of thousands of victims during World War II. The State Department delicately cloaked its position on whether it judged his acts to be "political" and, therefore, of a nonextraditable character, leaving this thorny matter to the courts. Yet, in a note to the United States Supreme Court in this case, the department chose the exact words of the Genocide Convention: the offense of murder, even though committed solely or predominantly "with the intent to destroy, in whole or in part, a national, ethnical, racial or religious group," is nonetheless murder, and not a political offense. Nevertheless, Artukovic was not extradited from the United States.

If states continue to pontificate about the universality of war crimes or crimes against humanity while refraining from delegating jurisdiction to an international agency, they will have to recognize that the surrender of alleged criminals to other states must be facilitated. If they are not willing to entertain the notion of the nonpolitical character of war crimes and crimes against humanity in their extradition proceedings, then all the pious platitudes about universal crimes may come to naught as the old doctrines of jurisdiction are reiterated.

The *Eichmann* case, which follows, raises important issues about the prosecution of international crimes by a national court whose jurisdiction is based upon national law.

ATTORNEY GENERAL v. EICHMANN
Jerusalem District Court of Israel, 1961
56 A.J.I.L. 805

The law which confers on us jurisdiction to try the accused in this case is the Nazis and Nazi Collaborators (Punishment) Law 5710–1950 . . . Section 1(a) of the law provides:

"A person who has committed one of the following offenses—
(1) did, during the period of the Nazi regime, in a hostile country, an act constituting a crime against the Jewish people;
(2) did, during the period of the Nazi regime, in a hostile country, an act constituting a crime against humanity;
(3) did, during the period of the Second World War, in a hostile country, an act constituting a war crime; is liable to the death penalty."

The three above-mentioned classes of crimes—crime against the Jewish people, crime against humanity, war crime—are defined in Section 1(b).

*   *   *

(The Defense contends)
(a) That the Israel Law, by inflicting punishment for acts done outside the boundaries of the State and before its establishment, against persons who were not Israel citizens, and by a person who acted in the course of duty on behalf of a foreign country ("Act of State") conflicts with international law and exceeds the powers of the Israel legislator;
(b) That the prosecution of the accused in Israel upon his abduction from a foreign country conflicts with international law and exceeds the jurisdiction of the Court.

*   *   *

Our jurisdiction to try this case is based on the Nazis and Nazi Collaborators (Punishment) Law, *a statutory law the provisions of which are unequivocal.* The Court has to give effect to the law of the Knesset, and we cannot entertain the contention that this law conflicts with the principles of international law. For this reason alone Counsel's first contention must be rejected.

But we have also perused the sources of international law, including the numerous authorities mentioned by learned Counsel in his comprehensive written brief upon which he based his oral pleadings, and by the learned *Attorney-General* in his comprehensive oral pleadings, and failed to find any foundation for the contention that Israel law is in conflict with the principles of international law. On the contrary, we have reached the conclusion that the law in question conforms to the best traditions of the law of nations.

The power of the State of Israel to enact the law in question or Israel's "right to punish" is based, with respect to the offences in question, from the point of view of international law, on a dual foundation: The universal character of the crimes in question and their specific character as being designed to exterminate the Jewish people. In what follows we shall deal with each of these two aspects separately.

The abhorrent crimes defined in this law are crimes not under Israel law alone. These crimes which afflicted the whole of mankind and shocked the conscience of nations are grave offences against the law of nations itself ("delicta juris gentium"). Therefore, so far from international law negating or limiting the jurisdiction of countries with respect to such crimes, in the absence of an International Court the international law is in need of the judicial and legislative authorities of every country, to give effect to its penal injunctions and to bring criminals to trial. The authority and jurisdiction to try crimes under international law are *universal*.

* * *

Instances of the extensive use made by the Allied Military Tribunals of the principle of universality of jurisdiction of war crimes of all classes (including "crimes against humanity") will be found in Vols. 1–15 of the Law Reports of Trials of War Criminals.

We have said that the crimes dealt with in this case are not crimes under Israel law alone, but are in essence offences against the law of nations. Indeed, the crimes in question are not a figment of the imagination of the legislator who enacted the law for the punishment of Nazis and Nazi collaborators, but have been stated and defined in that law according to a precise pattern of international laws and conventions which define crimes under the law of nations. The "crime against the Jewish people" is defined on the pattern of the genocide crime defined in the "Convention for the prevention and punishment of genocide" which was adopted by the United Nations Assembly on 9.12.48. The "crime against humanity" and the "war crime" are defined on the pattern of crimes of identical designations defined in the Charter of the International Military Tribunal (which is the Statute of the Nuremberg Court) annexed to the Four-Power Agreement of 8.8.45 on the subject of the trial of the principal war criminals (the London Agreement), and also in Law No. 10 of the Control Council of Germany of 20.12.45. . . .

* * *

It is hardly necessary to add that the "crime against the Jewish people," which constitutes the crime of "genocide" is nothing but the gravest type of "crime against humanity" (and all the more so because both under Israel law and under the convention a special intention is requisite for its commission, an intention that is not required for the commission of a "crime against humanity"). Therefore, all that has been said in the Nuremberg principles on the "crime against humanity" applies *a fortiori* to the "crime against the Jewish people.". . .

*   *   *

We have already dealt with the 'principle of legality' that postulates *"Nullum crimen sine lege, nulla poena sine lege,"* and what has been stated above with respect to the municipal law is also applicable to international law. In the Judgment against the "Major War Criminals" it is stated (p. 219):

"In the first place, it is to be observed that the maxim *nullum crimen sine lege* is not a limitation of sovereignty, but it is in general a principle of justice."

That is to say, the penal jurisdiction of a State with respect to crimes committed by 'foreign offenders' insofar as it does not conflict on other grounds with the principles of international law, is not limited by the prohibition of retroactive effect.

It is indeed difficult to find a more convincing instance of a just retroactive legislation than the legislation providing for the punishment of war criminals and criminals against humanity and against the Jewish people, and all the reasons justifying the Nuremberg judgments justify *eo ipse* the retroactive legislation of the Israel legislator. . . .

*   *   *

Learned Counsel seeks to negate the jurisdiction of the State by contending that the crimes attributed to the accused in counts 1–12 had been committed, according to the Charge Sheet itself, in the course of duty, and constitute "acts of State," acts for which, according to his contention, only the German State is responsible. . . . Learned Counsel bases himself on the rule "par in parem non habet imperium," that is to say—a sovereign State does not dominate, and does not sit in judgment against, another sovereign State, and deduces therefrom that a State may not try a person for a criminal act that constitutes an "act of State" of another State, without the consent of such other State to that person's trial. In the view of Kelsen only the State in whose behalf the "organ" (ruler or official) had acted is responsible for the violation, through such act, of international law, (for) which the perpetrator himself is not responsible (with the two exceptions of espionage and war treason).

The theory of "Act of State" was repudiated by the International Military Tribunal at Nuremberg, when it said (pp. 222–223):

*   *   *

". . . The principle of international law which, under certain circumstances, protects the representatives of a state, cannot be applied to acts which are condemned as criminal by international law. The authors of these acts cannot shelter themselves behind their official position in order to be freed from punishment in appropriate proceedings. Article 7 of the Charter expressly declares:

'The official position of defendants, whether as heads of States, or responsible officials in Government departments, shall not be considered as freeing them from responsibility, or mitigating punishment.' . . .

On the other hand the very essence of the Charter is that individuals have international duties which transcend the national obligations of obedience imposed by the individual state. He who violates the laws of war cannot obtain immunity while acting in pursuance of the authority of the state if the state in authorising action moves outside its competence under international law."

* * *

We have discussed at length the international character of the crimes in question because this offers the broadest possible, though not the only, basis for Israel's jurisdiction according to the law of nations. No less important from the point of view of international law is the special connection the State of Israel has with such crimes, seeing that the people of Israel (Am Israel)—the Jewish people (Ha'am Ha'yehudi—to use the term in the Israel legislation)—constituted the target and the victim of most of the crimes in question. The State of Israel's "right to punish" the accused derives, in our view, from two cumulative sources: a universal source (pertaining to the whole of mankind) which vests the right to prosecute and punish crimes of this order in every State within the family of nations; and a specific or national source which gives the victim nation the right to try any who assault their existence.

* * *

The second contention of Learned Counsel was that the trial in Israel of the accused following upon his capture in a foreign land is in conflict with international law, and takes away the jurisdiction of the Court. . . .

* * *

It is an established rule of law that a person standing trial for an offence against the laws of the land may not oppose his being tried by reason of the illegality of his arrest or of the means whereby he was brought to the area of jurisdiction of the country. The courts in England, the United States and Israel have ruled continuously that the circumstances of the arrest and the mode of bringing of the accused into the area of the State have no relevance to his trial, and they consistently refused in all cases to enter into the examination of these circumstances. . . .

* * *

Indeed there can be no escaping the conclusion that the violation of international law through the mode of the bringing of the accused into the territory of the country pertains to the international level, namely the relations between the two countries concerned only, and must find its solution at such level. The violation of the international law of this order constitutes an international tort to which the usual rules of current international law apply. . . .

* * *

. . . If the violation of Argentina's sovereignty is excluded from consideration, then the abduction of the accused is no different from any unlawful abduction, whether it constituted a contravention of Argentine law or Israeli law or both. Thus after the enactment of the Federal Kidnaping Act the United States Supreme Court ruled unanimously in *Frisbie* v. *Collins* (1952) 342 U.S. 512 (96 L.Ed. 541), (p. 545):

This Court has never departed from the rule announced in *Ker* v. *Illinois*, 119 U.S. 436, 444, that the power of a court to try a person for crime is not impaired by the fact that he had been brought within the court's jurisdiction by reason of a "forcible abduction." No persuasive reasons are now presented to justify overruling this line of cases. They rest on the sound basis that due process of law is satisfied when one present in court is convicted of crime after having been fairly apprized of the charges against him and after a fair trial in accordance with constitutional procedural safeguards. There is nothing in the Constitution that requires a court to permit a guilty person rightfully convicted to escape justice because he was brought to trial against his will.

* * *

It is hardly necessary to state, with reference to the above, that the accused is not at all a "political" criminal; the reverse is the case: The crimes which are attributed to the accused have been condemned by all nations as "abhorrent crimes" whose perpetrators do not deserve any asylum, "political" or other. . . . There is considerable foundation for the view that the grant by any country of asylum to a person accused of a major crime of this type and the prevention of his prosecution constitute an abuse of the sovereignty of the country contrary to its obligation under international law. . . .

* * *

To sum up, the contention of the accused against the jurisdiction of the Court by reason of his abduction from Argentina is in essence nothing but a plea for immunity by a fugitive offender on the strength of the refuge given him by a sovereign State. That contention does not avail the accused for two reasons: (a) According to the established rule of law there is no immunity for a fugitive offender save in the one and only case where he has been extradited by the country of asylum to the country applying for extradition by reason of a specific offence, which is not the offence tried in his case. The accused was not surrendered to Israel by

Argentina and the State of Israel is not bound by any agreement with Argentina to try the accused for any other specific offence, or not to try him for the offence with which the Court is concerned in this case. (b) The rights of asylum and immunity belong to the country of asylum and not to the offender, and the accused cannot compel a foreign sovereign country to give him protection against its will. The accused was a wanted war criminal when he escaped to Argentina by concealing his true identity. It was only after he was captured and brought to Israel that his identity has been revealed, and after negotiations between the two Governments, the Government of Argentina waived its demand for his return and declared that it viewed the incident as settled. The Government of Argentina thereby refused definitely to give the accused any sort of protection. The accused has been brought to trial before a Court of a State which accuses him of grave offences against its laws. The accused has no immunity against this trial, and must stand his trial in accordance with the Charge Sheet.

* * *

This Court sentences Adolf Eichmann to death for his guilt in performing crimes against the Jewish people and against humanity, and war crimes.*

FOR FURTHER STUDY

PETER PAPADATOS. *The Eichmann Trial.* New York: Frederick A. Praeger, Inc., 1964.

ROBERT K. WOETZEL. *The Nuremberg Trials in International Law.* Rev. ed. New York: Frederick A. Praeger, Inc., 1962.

PIETER N. DROST. *The Crimes of State.* Vol. I, *Humanicide;* Vol. II, *Genocide.* Leiden: A. W. Sijthoff, 1959.

MOSES MOSKOWIVITZ. *Human Rights and World Order.* New York: Oceana Publications, 1958.

J. A. APPLEMAN. *Military Tribunals and International Crimes.* Indianapolis: Bobbs-Merrill Co., Inc., 1954.

---

* Appeal from the principle of guilt and the sentence was denied by the Supreme Court of Israel, which held seven sessions. Petition for clemency was denied by the head of state, and Eichmann was hanged on 31 May 1962.

VIII

Immunities from Jurisdiction

THE complete jurisdiction of states over their territory, including persons, things, and acts therein, has only a few exceptions, but these date back to the very beginnings of the modern international legal system. One of the most frequently cited cases in international law is *The Schooner Exchange* v. *M'Faddon*. The opinion was delivered by United States Supreme Court Chief Justice Marshall in 1812.

This full and absolute territorial jurisdiction being alike the attribute of every sovereign . . . would not seem to contemplate foreign sovereigns nor their rights as its objects. One sovereign being in no respect amenable to another, and being bound by obligations of the highest character not to degrade the dignity of his nation, by placing himself or its sovereign rights within the jurisdiction of another, can be supposed to enter a foreign territory only under an express license, or in the confidence that the immunities belonging to his independent sovereign station, though not expressly stipulated, are reserved by implication, and will be extended to him.[1]

Marshall then went on to detail the exemption of the person of the sovereign from any arrest or detention within a foreign territory, the immunity from local jurisdiction also accorded to foreign ministers, the waiver of jurisdiction by a state over foreign troops once it had granted them the right of passage through its territory, and the immunity from process, suit, or seizure that was due a sovereign's public armed ships that peacefully entered the ports of a friendly state.

The fundamental doctrine of a sovereign's immunity[2] from local jurisdiction still forms an important part of international law. However, the (*a*) devolution of sovereignty from a personal king to an abstract "people"; (*b*) large increase of diplomatic, consular, and financial, trading, and

---

[1] 7 Cranch 116.

[2] The use of this term should not be confused with the unwillingness of a sovereign to allow itself to be sued *in its own courts*, except by its own consent through permissive legislation. This is a matter of municipal law, touching international law only indirectly.

technical intercourse between nations; (*c*) socialization of national economics, with state capitalism and state controls; and (*d*) emergence of international organizations with their own legal personalities have all had important effects on the development and interpretation of the doctrine of sovereign immunity.

Diplomatic Immunities

The most ancient form of immunity from local jurisdiction conceded by states was to the persons of sovereigns and their representatives or diplomatic agents. European states began to exchange resident ambassadors in the 15th century. In 1710, the attorney general of England said:

The person of an ambassador has ever been held sacred and inviolable by the law of nations. The goods of an ambassador are not liable to distress, a fortiori, nor his person. . . . The same fiction of law that makes him represent the person of his master, makes him extraparochial and quasi, in the dominions of his master. The ill treatment of an ambassador is a thing of dangerous consequence, for it may involve the nation in a war, and it would be very inconvenient that this should be in the power of any private person whatsoever.[3]

With few exceptions, a diplomatic agent is immune from *all criminal, civil, and administrative processes* in the state to which he is accredited. Not only are the diplomatic agent and his effects free of any harassment from local jurisdiction, but so is his family. To a more limited extent, other members of the diplomatic mission, including staff and servants, enjoy similar legal immunities always providing they are not nationals of the receiving state. Embassies may once have been regarded as "extraterritorial," literally outside the territorial jurisdiction of the host state, as enclaves immune from all local control, but this is not modern legal practice. For example, under international law a state cannot use its diplomatic missions in the host state to detain people against their wills, to give asylum to felons, or to disturb and endanger the local community.

The ambassador, moreover, was once regarded as the *alter ego* of his sovereign and entitled to all rights, privileges, and immunities for himself, his staff, and his household as if he were the sovereign himself. However, the modern trend is to examine the functional necessity of sovereign immunities—that is, to exempt the agents or property of the sovereign

---

[3] *Case of Andrew Artemonowitz Mattueof*, Queen's Bench, 8 Queen Anne (1710). Partial text in James Brown Scott, *Cases in International Law* (St. Paul, Minn.: West Publishing Co., 1922), p. 286.

from local jurisdiction only to the extent required by the official and orderly conduct of international relations between states.

The premises of a diplomatic mission, its archives, the diplomatic pouch, and the personal residence of a diplomatic agent are considered inviolable, and neither the premises nor residence can be entered without the consent of the head of the mission. States are ultracautious in approaching the premises of a diplomatic mission, even though allegations of espionage within embassies have been abundant. Host states have occasionally surrounded diplomatic premises or guarded entries and exits, either to protect the premises from local disorder or to arrest persons harbored therein. For example, the Colombian Embassy in Peru granted political asylum to Víctor Raúl Haya de la Torre, leading to the case documented in Section I; the United States Embassy granted prolonged asylum to Cardinal Mindszenty in Hungary. The embassies of the Soviet Union in Peking and the United States in Moscow have heard insults, seen demonstrations outside their windows, and had their walls defaced. But the actual violation of diplomatic premises has been rare.

Too often it is assumed that diplomats, being beyond the immediate reach of the local law, may take advantage of a community that has no apparent redress against their activities. Some abuses have occurred, but diplomats represent states; their conduct is public conduct, and they must be extraordinarily circumspect about their reputations both at home and abroad. Even while representing his state, a diplomatic agent in a foreign state may not enjoy complete immunity from civil and administrative jurisdiction. Case law has been far from clear on the general principle of granting diplomatic agents immunity from actions that relate to professional or commercial activities outside their diplomatic functions. Practice has varied from state to state and within the courts of a single state. Some judges have followed an absolute view of immunity, while others have denied immunity in cases relating to: (*a*) private immovable property; (*b*) inheritances, when the diplomatic agent is an executor, administrator, heir, or legatee as a private person; (*c*) where personal gain is involved through commercial transactions.

Moreover, immunity from jurisdiction does not mean immunity from liability. First, for a person in his mission an ambassador could waive immunity from local jurisdiction and thereby allow prosecution, or in the case of the ambassador himself his state might waive immunity. Second, a diplomatic agent may lose his diplomatic status, and if he remains in or returns to the state to which he was accredited he will be subject to the state's jurisdiction for a previous act of a private or unofficial character. Finally, although the criminal prosecution of a diplomatic agent may be impossible in the host state, he does not necessarily escape justice on his return home; as a national of the state and having been especially subject to its jurisdiction as a diplomat, he might be tried for criminal acts committed abroad.

Until 1961, there existed a very large body of customary international law on diplomatic intercourse and immunities, but there was rather little in the way of positive conventions. The Congress of Vienna in 1815 and the Conference of Aix-la-Chappelle in 1818 led to regulations that classified diplomatic ranks and dealt with problems of precedence, which previously had greatly troubled states in their international negotiations. The eight leading European powers signed the regulations made at Vienna, and virtually all states have since accepted the rules. During the Sixth International Conference of American States at Havana in 1928, a limited convention on the rights, duties, and privileges of diplomatic officers was approved. But only the United Nations call to a conference of 81 states in Vienna in the spring of 1961 led to the adoption of a comprehensive Convention on Diplomatic Relations.[4] By 1964, the convention was in force, and by 1967 more than 50 states had ratified it—a remarkable codification of many long-established usages of international law in the light of modern practice.

In the documents that follow, (a) *Carrera* v. *Carrera* illustrates the scope of diplomatic immunity from local jurisdiction, (b) articles from the *Convention on Diplomatic Relations* point up a positive agreement on diplomatic immunities, and (c) the *Statement on the Vienna Convention on Diplomatic Relations* by the Legal Adviser of the U.S. State Department indicates the effect of the convention on customary international law.

CARRERA v. CARRERA
United States Court of Appeals, 1949
174 F. 2d 496

Wilbert K. Miller, Circuit Judge

* * *

Rosa H. Carrera sued her husband, Amable H. Carrera, in the United States District Court for the District of Columbia for separate maintenance for herself, and for the custody of and support for their fifteen-year-old son. The Carreras are nationals of Ecuador, permanently resident in the United States. When the action was instituted, both were domestic servants in the Czechoslovakian Embassy.

Amable moved to quash the return showing service of process upon him and also moved to dismiss the complaint, claiming diplomatic immu-

---

[4] U.S. Department of State Publication 7289, *United Nations Conference on Diplomatic Intercourse and Immunities* (Vienna, Austria, March 2–April 14, 1961), Washington, D.C., 1962, which contains text of the convention and other documentary material.

nity from the action. Such immunity was requested for him by the Czechoslovakian Ambassador in a communication to the Secretary of State. A copy of the Ambassador's note was transmitted to the district judge by the legal adviser to the Secretary of State with the following letter.

"There is enclosed for the information of the District Court of the United States for the District of Columbia a copy of a note received by the Department of State from the Czechoslovak Ambassador in which diplomatic immunity is requested on behalf of Amable Hidalgo Carrera, an Ecuadoran national, employed by the Czechoslovak Ambassador as a butler and chauffeur.

"The name of Mr. Carrera has been previously registered in the Department of State in accordance with Section 254 of Title 22 of the United States Code and has been included in the 'List of Employees in the Embassies and Legations in Washington not Printed in the Diplomatic List,' commonly known as the 'White List,' which has been transmitted by the Secretary of State to the Marshal of the District of Columbia.

"It would be appreciated if the Court would take into consideration the request of the Czechoslovak Ambassador and take such action as the Court deems to be appropriate in the circumstances."

The District Court dismissed the complaint on the ground that Amable was diplomatically immune from the action. Rosa appeals.

Her first ground for reversal is that the right of the appellee to diplomatic immunity was not properly presented to the District Court. We find, however, that the process by which the claim of immunity made by the Czechoslovakian Ambassador to the State Department was communicated to the court is that which was approved by the Supreme Court in *In re Baiz*, 1890, 135 U.S. 403, 421, 10 S.Ct. 854, 34 L.Ed. 222. It is enough that an ambassador has requested immunity, that the State Department has recognized that the person for whom it was requested is entitled to it, and that the Department's recognition has been communicated to the court. "The courts are disposed to accept as conclusive of the fact of the diplomatic status of an individual claiming an exemption, the views thereon of the political department of their government."

The next contention of the appellant is that the inclusion of Amable's name on the so-called "White List" was not sufficient to bring him within the second clause of section 254 which would extend to him the protection of sections 252 and 253. In support of this proposition the appellant cites *Trost* v. *Tompkins*, D.C. Mun. App. 1945, 44 A.2d 226. But in the Trost case the court held no more than that, certification of the Secretary of State being absent, a court otherwise having jurisdiction should determine whether the person claiming immunity was properly placed on the "White List." But here, the Secretary having certified Carrera's name as included in the list, judicial inquiry into the propriety of its listing was not appropriate.

It is further suggested by the appellant that this action is not within the purview of section 252 since it is not one in which the defendant's goods or chattels were distrained, seized or attached. The rule of immunity is not confined to those actions which have as a direct objective the distraint, seizure or attachment of goods or chattels. "It has long been a settled rule of law that foreign diplomatic representatives are exempt from all local processes in the country to which they are accredited. 1 Kent's Commentaries 15, 38. The same immunity is not only given to an ambassador himself, but to his subordinates, family and servants as well." 27 Harv. L. Rev. 489 (1914). . . .

The appellant also invokes the first portion of section 254, which is:

"Sections 252 and 253 of this title shall not apply to any case where the person against whom the process is issued is a citizen or inhabitant of the United States, in the service of an ambassador or a public minister, and the process is founded upon a debt contracted before he entered upon such service; . . ."

The suggestion is that Amable is an inhabitant of the United States in the service of an ambassador and that the process against him in this case was founded upon a debt contracted before he entered upon such service, in that the child for whom support was sought was born before he began to serve the Ambassador. A parent's moral or legal obligation to support his infant child is not usually considered as a debt within the ordinary significance of the word. We are here concerned with the word "debt" as it is used in section 254; and we do not regard Amable's moral or legal obligation to support his child, which this action sought to enforce, as a "debt contracted before he entered upon" the Ambassador's service.

The final contention of the appellant is that the rule of diplomatic immunity does not apply in the field of domestic relations, in support of which she cites State of Ohio ex rel. *Popovici* v. *Agler*, 1930, 280 U.S. 379, 50 S.Ct. 154, 74 L.Ed. 489. But the question of diplomatic immunity was not raised in that case, as Popovici was a vice consul of Rumania, and it is universally recognized as a principle of international law that, in the absence of express agreement therefor, immunity does not extend to consuls, who are merely commercial representatives of foreign states. 16 Am Jur. 964. Cf. The Sao Vicente, 1922, 260 U.S. 151, 155, 42 S.Ct. 15, 67 L.Ed. 179.

We have no doubt that the case was properly decided by the District Court.

Affirmed.

CONVENTION ON DIPLOMATIC RELATIONS
Signed at Vienna, 1961*
United Nations Document A/Conf. 20/13, 16 April 1961

The *States Parties to the present Convention*, . . .
Have agreed as follows:

*   *   *

Article 22

1. The premises of the mission shall be inviolable. The agents of the receiving state may not enter them, except with the consent of the head of the mission.

2. The receiving state is under a special duty to take all appropriate steps to protect the premises of the mission against any intrusion or damage and to prevent any disturbance of the peace of the mission or impairment of its dignity.

3. The premises of the mission, their furnishings and other property thereon and the means of transport of the mission shall be immune from search, requisition, attachment or execution.

Article 23

1. The sending state and the head of the mission shall be exempt from all national, regional or municipal dues and taxes in respect of the premises of the mission, whether owned or leased, other than such as represent payment for specific services rendered.

*   *   *

Article 24

The archives and documents of the mission shall be inviolable at any time and wherever they may be.

*   *   *

Article 27

1. The receiving state shall permit and protect free communication on the part of the mission for all official purposes. In communicating with the government and the other missions and consulates of the sending state, wherever situated, the mission may employ all appropriate means, including diplomatic couriers and messages in code or cipher. However, the mission may install and use a wireless transmitter only with the consent of the receiving state.

---

* In force 24 April 1964.

2. The official correspondence of the mission shall be inviolable. Official correspondence means all correspondence relating to the mission and its functions.

3. The diplomatic bag shall not be opened or detained.

*   *   *

Article 29

The person of a diplomatic agent shall be inviolable. He shall not be liable to any form of arrest or detention. The receiving state shall treat him with due respect and shall take all appropriate steps to prevent any attack on his person, freedom or dignity.

Article 30

1. The private residence of a diplomatic agent shall enjoy the same inviolability and protection as the premises of the mission.

*   *   *

Article 31

1. A diplomatic agent shall enjoy immunity from the criminal jurisdiction of the receiving state. He shall also enjoy immunity from its civil and administrative jurisdiction, except in the case of:
   (a) a real action relating to private immovable property situated in the territory of the receiving state, unless he holds it on behalf of the sending state for the purposes of the mission;
   (b) an action relating to succession in which the diplomatic agent is involved as executor, administrator, heir or legatee as a private person and not on behalf of the sending state;
   (c) an action relating to any professional or commercial activity exercised by the diplomatic agent in the receiving state outside his official functions.

2. A diplomatic agent is not obliged to give evidence as a witness.

*   *   *

4. The immunity of a diplomatic agent from the jurisdiction of the receiving state does not exempt him from the jurisdiction of the sending state.

Article 32

1. The immunity from jurisdiction of diplomatic agents and of persons enjoying immunity under Article 37 may be waived by the sending state.

*   *   *

Article 34

A diplomatic agent shall be exempt from all dues and taxes, personal or

real, national, regional or municipal, except:
- (a) indirect taxes of a kind which are normally incorporated in the price of goods or services;
- (b) dues and taxes on private immovable property situated in the territory of the receiving state . . . ;
- (c) estate, succession or inheritance duties levied by the receiving state, . . . ;
- (d) dues and taxes on private income having its source in the receiving state and capital taxes on investments made in commercial undertakings in the receiving state;
- (e) charges levied for specific services rendered;
- (f) registration, court or record fees, mortgage dues and stamp duty, with respect to immovable property, . . .

* * *

Article 36

1. The receiving state shall, in accordance with such laws and regulations as it may adopt, permit entry of and grant exemption from all customs duties, taxes, and related charges other than charges for storage, cartage and similar services, on:
- (a) articles for the official use of the mission;
- (b) articles for the personal use of a diplomatic agent or members of his family forming part of his household, including articles intended for his establishment.

* * *

Article 37

1. The members of the family of a diplomatic agent forming part of his household shall, if they are not nationals of the receiving state, enjoy the privileges and immunities specified in Articles 29 to 36.

* * *

Article 40

1. If a diplomatic agent passes through or is in the territory of a third state, which has granted him a passport visa if such visa was necessary, while proceeding to take up or to return to his post, or when returing to his own country, the third state shall accord him inviolability and such other immunities as may be required to ensure his transit or return. . . .

* * *

Article 41

1. Without prejudice to their privileges and immunities, it is the duty of all persons enjoying such privileges and immunities to respect the laws

and regulations of the receiving state. They also have a duty not to interfere in the internal affairs of that state.

* * *

Article 44

The receiving state must, even in case of armed conflict, grant facilities in order to enable persons enjoying privileges and immunities, other than nationals of the receiving state, and members of the families of such persons irrespective of their nationality, to leave at the earliest possible moment. It must, in particular, in case of need, place at their disposal the necessary means of transport for themselves and their property.

Article 45

If diplomatic relations are broken off between two states, or if a mission is permanently or temporarily recalled:
   (a) the receiving state must, even in case of armed conflict, respect and protect the premises of the mission, together with its property and archives;
   (b) the sending state may entrust the custody of the premises of the mission, together with its property and archives to a third state acceptable to the receiving state;
   (c) the sending state may entrust the protection of its interests and those of its nationals to a third state acceptable to the receiving state.

* * *

STATEMENT ON THE VIENNA CONVENTION ON DIPLOMATIC RELATIONS
Legal Adviser, U.S. Department of State
Hearing, Subcommittee of Senate Committee on Foreign Relations
89th Congress, 1st Session, 6 July 1965

* * *

First I should like to emphasize that this convention is for the most part a codification of principles heretofore observed by governments in their practice. For instance, the division of chiefs of mission into three classes—ambassadors, ministers, and chargé d'affaires—and the provision that they shall rank in each class in order of seniority as determined by their arrival in the receiving state, is essentially a restatement of the

Vienna regulation which was adopted in 1815, at the end of the Napo-
leonic wars.

Similarly, the provisions regarding the inviolability of the premises of
the mission, its archives, and its communications, and the immunity of the
chief of mission and other diplomatic officers and their families from
arrest and prosecution reflect practice which developed long before 1815,
in fact go very far back in history.

In some areas where practice has not been uniform or has not been
considered appropriate in the light of modern conditions, the convention
establishes new rules. One such change provides that while members of
the administrative and technical staff of the mission shall continue to have
the same complete immunity from criminal jurisdiction which diplomatic
agents presently enjoy, they shall have immunity from civil jurisdiction
only with respect to their official acts. Another new rule is that a diplomatic agent and his family will have no immunity from jurisdiction with
respect to certain nonofficial matters such as private professional or commercial activities.

The convention does not increase the number of persons in the United
States who will be entitled to diplomatic privileges and immunities except
in one limited respect; it provides that families of members of the administrative and technical staff of a diplomatic mission will have immunity
from criminal jurisdiction.

*   *   *

I would like to say a word now about the optional protocol concerning
the compulsory settlement of disputes which provides that disputes arising
out of the interpretation or application of the convention shall lie within
the compulsory jurisdiction of the International Court of Justice, and may
be brought before the Court by any party to the dispute, unless the
parties have agreed that before resorting to the Court they will first resort
to an arbitral tribunal or will adopt a conciliation procedure. The protocol is in keeping with the U.S. position in favor of the use of the Court for
the resolution of legal disputes. Adoption of the protocol is desirable as a
means of securing uniformity in the interpretation of the provisions of the
convention.

*   *   *

. . . one of the principal differences between this convention and
existing international law lies in the following new disposition which the
convention makes in the area of immunities.

The convention divides the personnel of a diplomatic mission into three
groups.

First, by the diplomatic agents who are the head of mission and other
professional diplomatic officers; second, the class of administrative and
technical personnel; and finally, the service staff.

Under the convention the rules of immunity will be different for those three groups. The first class of diplomatic agents will have virtually complete immunity from both civil and criminal jurisdiction. There is a little difference here regarding diplomatic agents under the convention. Under international law today, diplomatic agents have complete immunity without exceptions.

However, under the Vienna Convention there will be some exceptions. . . . If there is a civil action, a judicial proceeding, relating to real estate in the territory of the receiving state, and if a diplomatic agent is a party thereto he is subject to jurisdiction unless he happens to hold the property on behalf of his government. But if he holds it for himself and in his own name, then he would be subject to suit.

The same would be true . . . if the diplomatic agent were involved in some probate proceedings as executor, administrator, heir or legatee in a private capacity.

And finally, if the diplomatic agent engages in any professional or commercial activity outside of his official duties as a diplomatic agent when he would be subject to the jurisdiction of the receiving state with respect to those nonofficial acts of a professional or commercial character.

*   *   *

The next category is the administrative and technical staff. Under the convention they will have a degree of immunity which is less than what diplomatic agents have. They will have full immunity from criminal jurisdiction but they will have immunity from civil jurisdiction only with respect to official acts. So this is somewhat narrower. . . .

Today those persons have full immunity. Then the service staff have an even narrower degree of immunity. Their immunity is limited to immunity from income tax, from social security tax, and from process with respect to official acts. With respect to nonofficial matters they are subject not only to civil jurisdiction but even to criminal prosecution as well.

Today a chauffeur or another member of the service staff of an embassy would have full immunity unless, of course, in this country he were an American citizen or permanent resident of the United States . . . in those respects, the Vienna Convention will cut down the degree of immunity which is provided for in international law as it is currently being applied.

*   *   *

. . . In the past there has been some unclarity and at times some difference of view about the applicability of exemption from taxes and in certain tax situations.

Article 34 undertakes to settle this by providing that a diplomatic agent, a member of the first group, diplomatic officers, shall be exempt from all dues and taxes, personal or real, national, regional or municipal, except, among others, for the following:

Indirect taxes of a kind which are normally incorporated in the price of goods and services.

Second, dues and taxes on private immovable property, land situated in the territory of the receiving state, unless the diplomatic agent holds it for the use of the mission.

Third, estate, succession or inheritance duties levied by the receiving state subject to the provisions of paragraph 4 in article 39, which provides if a diplomatic agent dies while in service in the receiving state then his property, movable property, may be taken from the country and is exempt from estate tax.

Fourth, dues and taxes on private income having its source in the receiving state and capital taxes on investments made in commercial undertakings.

*   *   *

There is one new article in the convention which hopefully will have a good deal of helpful influence. This is a new provision in article 41 which states:

Without prejudice to their privileges and immunities, it is the duty of all persons enjoying such privileges and immunities to respect the laws and regulations of the receiving state. They also have a duty not to interfere in the internal affairs of that state.

What this does is to say that although a diplomat may not be subject to prosecution or subject to civil action with respect to his activities while in the receiving state, nevertheless, his enjoyment of immunity is not a license to disregard the laws of the receiving state . . . and ultimately, if the situation becomes serious enough, we would have to in certain cases perhaps require the departure of members of diplomatic missions as we [now] have a right to require and will have that right under the convention. . . .

*   *   *

It does make new international law in the field of immunities and in setting up the groups and narrowing the relation of each. It makes some new international law in regard to the matter of taxation in certain instances as with regard to the estate taxes on diplomatic agents dying in the service, and it makes a little new international law, I suppose, in article 41 which sets forth flatfootedly the obligation of members of diplomatic missions to abide by the laws and regulations of the receiving state. . . .

*   *   *

Consular Immunities

From the earliest times of the modern state system, consuls have not been entitled to the same considerations as diplomatic agents under international law. A well-known statement of the consul's status appears in the famous *Barbuit's Case*, decided in 1737. Barbuit held a commission from the King of Prussia to be his agent of commerce in Great Britain, and he therefore claimed the privilege of a foreign minister to be free from arrest by the local authorities. The English judge denied this.

. . . what creates my difficulty is, that I do not think that he is intrusted to transact affairs between the two crowns: the commission is to assist his Prussian Majesty's subjects here in their commerce. . . . Now this gives him no authority to intermeddle with the affairs of the King; which makes his employment to be in the nature of a consul.[5]

Diplomatic duties may sometimes be imposed on consuls, but a consul will obtain diplomatic privileges only through a special agreement with a host state. Normally, a consul's duties are of a limited nature, dealing with his state's commercial interests, shipping, immigration, and the legal problems of its nationals. Consuls may be appointed only with the consent of the host state, and to perform consular duties they usually obtain an exequatur or certificate, which may be revoked at any time.

Although the premises of consulates do not have the customary inviolability attached to embassies or legations, the host state generally recognizes their special character and by consular conventions may provide for their immunities. Moreover, in nearly all courts consuls will be held immune from local jurisdiction for acts performed in their official capacity and, in some courts, for private acts. Occasionally, states have directly punished consuls for serious offenses not consonant with their duties. Therefore, consuls can claim rather few immunities under the general principles of international law, but the existence of many bilateral conventions and the municipal regulations of states themselves have conferred on them a substantial freedom from local jurisdiction.

The first multilateral convention on the legal status of consuls was the regional Havana Convention on Consular Agents in 1928, but in 1963, following the success of the Conference on Diplomatic Intercourse and Immunities in 1961, 92 states met again in Vienna to conclude the Convention on Consular Relations.[6]

---

[5] High Court of Chancery, 1737, text taken from Scott, *op. cit.*, p. 311.

[6] United Nations Document A/Conf. 25/12, 25 April 1963. By mid-1966, 20 states had ratified the convention; thus, only two more ratifications were required to put it in force.

In the following cases (*a*) *Waltier* v. *Thompson* shows the immunity of a consul for his official acts, (*b*) articles from the *Vienna Convention on Consular Relations* point up a positive agreement on consular immunities, and (*c*) *Republic of Finland* v. *Town of Pelham* clarifies the legal status of a foreign consul's residence in the United States.

WALTIER v. THOMSON
United States District Court, 1960
189 F. Supp. 319

Bicks, District Judge

Plaintiff is a physician and surgeon. At all times here material, the defendant Thomson was officer in charge of the Canadian Government Immigration Service at the Canadian Consulate General in the City of New York. Mr. Thomson was certified to the Department of State as an officer of Canada whose "official activities . . . include the interviewing of residents of the United States of America who might wish to immigrate to Canada. . . ."

Plaintiff's complaint, as amended, alleges that the individual defendant herein made false statements which induced plaintiff to immigrate to Edmonton, Alberta, Canada. Among the offending statements alleged are the following:

"You're a surgeon—don't worry about anything. There's an exam you must take to be licensed, which is just a matter of form. Alberta is my favorite place —they have just discovered gas, oil, titanium and gold. You will be a success there, and it's the one place in Canada for you. I wish my stocks and bonds were as safe as your chances of success in Alberta.

"The exam is your only requirement. I anticipate that in your second year you will be making $30,000. Once you get to Edmonton and you're a surgeon, which will take you only thirty days after you arrive, you'll have much happier birthdays."

A. D. P. Heeney, Ambassador of Canada to the United States appears as *amicus curiae* for the defendant Thomson and has submitted the suggestion of Her Majesty in Right of Canada, Queen Elizabeth II, that Canada "is not subject to suit . . . without Her consent whether the suit be brought directly against Her or Her Government or by way of suit against an officer of Her Majesty's Government acting in course of his official duties and in Her Majesty's behalf in the City of New York."

Plaintiff consenting, the United States Attorney has informed the Court of the Department of State's response to a note, dated March 17, 1960, from the Charge d'Affaires of Canada to the Secretary of State concerning the complaint herein. The Charge's note requested the assistance of the Secretary of State in bringing to the Court's attention that the defendant Thomson enjoys sovereign immunity. The Department's reply, as communicated to this Court, is:

> "It is a matter of record in the Department of State that Mr. Hubert W. P. Thomson is 'Settlement Officer—Department of Citizenship and Immigration' of the Canadian Government on duty at the Canadian Consulate General in New York City, that he held that position on and continuously subsequent to March 6, 1957, and that Mr. Thomson's official duties include interviewing and advising prospective immigrants to Canada."

The statements which form the matrix of plaintiff's claim, as reflected in the amended complaint, are all comments made by Mr. Thomson to plaintiff with respect to what plaintiff might anticipate upon arrival in Edmonton. The complaint specifically alleges that Mr. Thomson, at all times material herein, was an officer of the Canadian Government. We address ourselves solely to the application of sovereign immunity to the facts of this case.

A consular official is immune from suit when the acts complained of were performed in the course of his official duties. . . . Thus, if the statements allegedly made to Waltier by Thomson were uttered in pursuance of Thomson's official functions as a consular officer, then the suggestion of the Ambassador of Canada should be adopted and the defendant held immune.

*   *   *

Here, the parties, the Ambassador of Canada to the United States, and the Department of State are in accord that Mr. Thomson was sent to New York to interview and advise prospective immigrants to Canada. Since the complaint itself alleges that the statements were "designed to induce the plaintiff to leave the United States," it appears beyond peradventure that Mr. Thomson was acting in the course of his official duties.

Accordingly, the complaint and amended complaint must be dismissed. So ordered.

VIENNA CONVENTION ON CONSULAR RELATIONS
Signed at Vienna, 1963*
United Nations Document A/Conf. 25/12, 23 April 1963

The States Parties to the present Convention, . . .
Have agreed as follows:

*　　　*　　　*

Article 31
Inviolability of the Consular Premises

1. Consular premises shall be inviolable to the extent provided in this Article.

2. The authorities of the receiving State shall not enter that part of the consular premises which is used exclusively for the purpose of the work of the consular post except with the consent of the head of the consular post or of his designee or of the head of the diplomatic mission of the sending State. The consent of the head of the consular post may, however, be assumed in case of fire or other disaster requiring prompt protective action.

3. Subject to the provisions of paragraph 2 of this Article, the receiving State is under a special duty to take all appropriate steps to protect the consular premises against any intrusion or damage and to prevent any disturbance of the peace of the consular post or impairment of its dignity.

4. The consular premises, their furnishings, the property of the consular post and its means of transport shall be immune from any form of requisition for purposes of national defense or public utility. If expropriation is necessary for such purposes, all possible steps shall be taken to avoid impeding the performance of consular functions, and prompt, adequate and effective compensation shall be paid to the sending State.

Article 32
Exemption from Taxation of Consular Premises

1. Consular premises and the residence of the career head of consular post of which the sending State or any person acting on its behalf is the owner or lessee shall be exempt from all national, regional or municipal dues and taxes whatsoever, other than such as represent payment for specific services rendered.

*　　　*　　　*

---

* Twenty-two state ratifications required to put the convention in force. Twenty states had deposited ratifications with the U.N. as of October, 1966.

Article 33
Inviolability of the Consular Archives and Documents

The consular archives and documents shall be inviolable at all times and wherever they may be.

*   *   *

Article 40
Protection of Consular Officers

The receiving State shall treat consular officers with due respect and shall take all appropriate steps to prevent any attack on their person, freedom or dignity.

Article 41
Personal Inviolability of Consular Officers

1. Consular officers shall not be liable to arrest or detention pending trial, except in the case of a grave crime and pursuant to a decision by the competent judicial authority.

2. Except in the case specified in paragraph 1 of this Article, consular officers shall not be committed to prison or liable to any other form of restriction on their personal freedom save in execution of a judicial decision of final effect.

3. If criminal proceedings are instituted against a consular officer, he must appear before the competent authorities. Nevertheless, the proceedings shall be conducted with the respect due him by reason of his official position and, except in the case specified in paragraph 1 of this Article, it has become necessary to detain a consular officer, the proceedings against him shall be instituted with the minimum of delay.

*   *   *

Article 43
Immunity from Jurisdiction

1. Consular officers and consular employees shall not be amenable to the jurisdiction of the judicial or administrative authorities of the receiving State in respect to acts performed in the exercise of consular functions.

2. The provisions of paragraph 1 of this Article shall not, however, apply in respect of a civil action either:
   (a) arising out of a contract concluded by a consular officer or a consular employee in which he did not contract expressly or impliedly as an agent of the sending State; or
   (b) by a third party for damage arising from an accident in the receiving State caused by a vehicle, vessel or aircraft.

Article 44
Liability to Give Evidence

1. Members of a consular post may be called upon to attend as witnesses in the course of judicial or administrative proceedings. A Consular employee or a member of the service staff shall not, except in the cases mentioned in paragraph 3 of this Article, decline to give evidence. If a consular officer should decline to do so, no coercive measure or penalty may be applied to him.

2. The authority requiring the evidence of a consular officer shall avoid interference with the performance of his functions. It may, when possible, take such evidence at his residence or at the consular post or accept a statement from him in writing.

3. Members of a consular post are under no obligation to give evidence concerning matters connected with the exercise of their functions or to produce official correspondence and documents relating thereto. They are also entitled to decline to give evidence as expert witnesses with regard to the law of the sending State.

Article 45
Waiver of Privileges and Immunities

1. The sending State may waive, with regard to a member of the consular post, any of the privileges and immunities provided for in Articles 41, 43 and 44. . . .

*   *   *

Article 49
Exemption from Taxation

1. Consular officers and consular employees and members of their families forming part of their households shall be exempt from all dues and taxes, personal or real, national, regional, or municipal, except:
   (a) indirect taxes of a kind which are normally incorporated in the price of goods or services.
   (b) dues or taxes on private immovable property situated in the territory of the receiving State, subject to the provisions of Article 32,
   (c) estate, succession or inheritance duties, and duties on transfers, levied by the receiving State, subject to the provisions of paragraph (b) of Article 51,
   (d) dues and taxes on private income, including capital gains, having its source in the receiving State and capital taxes relating to investments made in commercial or financial undertakings in the receiving State,
   (e) charges levied for specific services rendered;

(f) registration, court or record fees, mortgage dues and stamp duties, subject to the porvisions of Article 32.

2. Members of the service staff shall be exempt from dues and taxes on the wages which they receive for their services.

3. Members of the consular post who employ persons whose wages or salaries are not exempt from income tax in the receiving State shall observe the obligations which the laws and regulations of that State impose upon employers concerning the levying of income tax.

Article 50
Exemption from Customs Duties and Inspection

1. The receiving State shall, in accordance with such laws and regulations as it may adopt, permit entry of and grant exemption from all customs duties, taxes, and related charges other than charges for storage, cartage and similar services, on:
   (a) articles for the official use of the consular post;
   (b) articles for the personal use of a consular officer or members of his family forming part of his household, including articles intended for his establishment. . . .

*   *   *

Article 57
Special Provisions Concerning Private Gainful Occupation

1. Career consular officers shall not carry on for personal profit any professional or commercial activity in the receiving State.

2. Privileges and immunities provided in this Chapter shall not be accorded:
   (a) to consular employees or to members of the service staff who carry on any private gainful occupation in the receiving State;
   (b) to members of the family. . . .

*   *   *

Article 71
Nationals or Permanent Residents of the Receiving State

1. Except insofar as additional facilities, privileges and immunities may be granted by the receiving State, consular officers who are nationals of or permanently resident in the receiving State shall enjoy only immunity from jurisdiction and personal inviolability in respect of official acts performed in the exercise of their functions. . . .

2. Other members of the consular post who are nationals of or permanently resident in the receiving State and members of their families as well as members of the families of consular officers referred to in paragraph 1 of this Article, shall enjoy facilities, privileges and immunities only in so far as these are granted to them by the receiving state.

*   *   *

REPUBLIC OF FINLAND v. TOWN OF PELHAM
New York Supreme Court, 1966
35 Law Week 2021

Christ, Justice

*   *   *

We meet squarely the argument that the residence use by the Consul destroys the exemption because this is not a governmental purpose; and that, no matter what governmental use is made of the property, there can be no exclusive governmental purpose, because of the residence use. Finland considers this residence use a governmental purpose, for it has expended its public money to purchase the property, presumably to make the position of Consul General more attractive, to give it greater dignity and rank and perhaps to provide some security.

We have in this country recognized that providing a residence for certain officials is a government purpose. The White House in Washington for the President, the Executive Mansion in Albany for the Governor, Gracie Mansion in New York for the Mayor and a suite in the Waldorf Towers for the Ambassador to the United Nations are examples of expenditures of public funds for the private living accommodations of public officials. This practice is common in the area of foreign, diplomatic and consular relations. We believe that the residence purpose is a government use by the Finnish Government and that the treaty standard of exclusive governmental purposes is met.

*   *   *

The Supreme Court of the United States has warned "that rules of international law should not be left to divergent and perhaps parochial state interpretations," emphasizing in its opinion the serious consequences and dangers of permitting interpretive conflicts to arise (*Banco Nacional de Cuba* v. *Sabbatino*, 376 U.S. 398, 32 LW 4229).

*   *   *

. . . We agree that the State or its civil divisions, including local municipalities, cannot frustrate the tax-exemption provision of the treaty between the United States and Finland.

*   *   *

Sovereign Immunities

A foreign state or a head of state cannot be made a party to legal proceedings in another state against its will; the general rule is that it cannot be enjoined from its actions or sued for recovery of damages in the local courts. This immunity from process extends to property, including vessels, bank deposits, and other assets within the territorial jurisdiction of the host state. Exceptions tend to be in questions of land title or in litigation where the foreign state has a partial interest, such as in a corporation, bond issue, or trust fund.

In the 20th century, the central problem of local immunity from legal process against a sovereign's property has been the ever-increasing scope of state activities in national and international economic activities. Socialist and quasi-socialist governments have created state-owned agencies or corporations for international trade, shipping, communications, and finance, or they have licensed and chartered such activities under state authority. Even in so-called private enterprise countries, complex corporate and fiscal arrangements mix state capital with private management and money. Therefore, the right of a sovereign to legal immunity in his capacity as an entrepreneur has been increasingly questioned.

Nevertheless, as late as 1926 the Supreme Court of the United States held:

> The single question presented for decision by us is whether a ship owned and possessed by a foreign government, and operated by it in the carriage of merchandise for hire, is immune from arrest under process based on a libel in rem by a private suitor in a federal district court exercising admiralty jurisdiction. . . . We think the principles (of *The Schooner Exchange* v. *M'Faddon*) are applicable alike to all ships held and used by a government for a public purpose, and that when, for the purpose of advancing the trade of its people or providing revenue for its treasury, a government acquires, mans, and operates ships in the carrying trade, they are public ships in the same sense that war ships are.[7]

In 1945, however, the Court would not admit the suggested immunity from suit filed by the Mexican government in a collision case that involved a vessel to which the state of Mexico held title, but which was operated completely by a private Mexican company under contract.[8] To illustrate further, Belgium and Italy have in the past followed a policy of granting immunities only in cases clearly involving sovereign or public acts by a state, while at the other extreme the United Kingdom and the

---

[7] *Berizzi Bros. Co.* v. *S.S. Pesaro*, 271 U.S. 562 [1926].
[8] *Republic of Mexico* v. *Hoffmann* (*The Baja California*), 324 U.S. 30 [1945].

United States have tended to follow a generous policy in granting immunities when the interests of a foreign state were touched, connected, or related. The courts of other states have followed lines of reasoning somewhere between these positions.

The United States attitude toward sovereign immunity has in recent years undergone a change from its rather generous exemption from local jurisdiction of sovereign acts of a commercial character. In 1952, Acting Legal Adviser of the Department of State Jack B. Tate indicated by letter to the Justice Department that in the future the department policy would be to follow the *"restrictive theory"* of sovereign immunity in considering requests from foreign governments due to the widespread and increasing practice of engagement in commercial activities on the part of governments. This shift in policy, however, cannot and does not control American courts, although they are bound to be attentive to the prerogatives of the Executive Branch in conducting United States foreign relations.

In any event, immunity of the sovereign and his property from local suit is a long-standing legal practice followed by one sovereign with respect to another in the interests of friendly, peaceful international relations. But it is not a definitive and wholesale right, particularly where the question arises whether the state is involved in its sovereign capacity (*jure imperii*) or in its managerial-commercial role (*jure gestionis*).

States may waive their immunities from local jurisdiction, either by express consent to an action before the court, such as a voluntary appearance, or by implied consent, such as a previous agreement with a party to arbitrate an issue. Moreover, if a foreign state initiates suit in the courts of another state, it cannot claim sovereign immunity when the local defendant appeals the same case. Or if a foreign state claims restitution or damages against a defendant, it usually cannot claim sovereign immunity when the defendant initiates a *counterclaim* or a *setoff* on the same matter in dispute or transaction. A more thorny problem, however, is whether courts will allow a counterclaim against a sovereign who pleads immunity, when the counterclaim is not limtied to the same transaction.

In the cases that follow, *Chemical Natural Resources* v. *Republic of Venezuela* largely illustrates the problem of sovereign immunity from local jurisdiction; *Victory Transport* brings out distinctions between *jure imperii* and *jure gestionis;* while *National City Bank* v. *Republic of China* is important for its denial of sovereign immunity where a counterclaim was not based on the subject matter of the original suit.

CHEMICAL NATURAL RESOURCES v. REPUBLIC OF VENEZUELA
Supreme Court of Pennsylvania, 1966
215 Atlantic Reporter, 2d Series, 864

Bell, Chief Justice

*   *   *

Chemical Natural Resources, Inc., and Venezuelan Sulphur Corporation, C.A. sued Venezuela in an action of assumpsit commenced by a writ of foreign attachment which in this case is an action quasi in rem. Chemical is a Delaware Corporation of which not less than 50 percent of its stock is beneficially owned by United States citizens. Sulphur is a corporation organized under the laws of Venezuela and is a wholly owned subsidiary of Chemical.

On October 21, 1963, the plaintiffs (Chemical and Sulphur) commenced their action of assumpsit against Venezuela by filing a (praecipe for a) writ of foreign attachment (together with a complaint) under which writ the sheriff was directed to attach and seize the S.S. CUIDAD DE VALENCIA, allegedly the property of defendant Venezuela, which was then in the Port of Philadelphia and in the custody of Stockyard Shipping and Terminal Corp. The complaint demanded damages in the sum of $116,807,258.28.

On October 22, 1963, the day after the writ was issued, the sheriff attached and seized the Steamship and took it into his possession. He also served copies of plaintiffs' complaint on the ship's Master and on Stockyard as garnishee. However, two days later, on October 24, 1963, *the attachment was dissolved without prejudice* upon the order of plaintiffs' attorney.

Plaintiffs' pertinent allegations in its amended complaint may be thus summarized:

In April of 1952 the plaintiffs, acting through Sulphur, purchased all mineral rights and interest or denouncements located in the Municipality of El Pilar, State of Sucre, Venezuela. Solely by reason of plaintiffs' exploitation reservoirs of mineral-laden geothermal steam were discovered in El Pilar. Subsequently, plaintiffs through Sulphur entered into several contracts with a department of the Venezuelan Government under which, inter alia, plaintiffs agreed to erect facilities for converting the steam into electrical power and defendant agreed to purchase the resulting power. Plaintiffs expended large sums of money in order to carry out their part of the contract. Thereafter, Venezuela unilaterally and without any justifiable cause cancelled the contract and confiscated plaintiffs' property and property rights with a resulting loss to plaintiffs of over $116,000,000. Plaintiffs further averred that Venezuela operates its merchant vessels, including the ship which was seized, through a nationalized company wholly owned by Venezuela, and thus was engaged in a commercial and private or proprietary capacity as distinguished from a Governmental or public capacity. Plaintiffs further averred that they could not obtain justice in any Venezuelan Court.

Venezuela has never entered a general appearance in this action, but improperly entered a special appearance for the purpose of challenging the jurisdiction of the Court of Common Pleas. However, Venezuela, more importantly and properly, challenged the jurisdiction of the Court by filing preliminary objections to plaintiffs' complaint and writ of foreign attachment. On December 5, 1963, Venezuela averred in its preliminary objections (a) that plaintiffs did not have a cause of action, and (b) that the Courts of Venezuela are available to the plaintiffs to assert any claim they may have, and (c) that the vessel allegedly operated by the nationalized Company is not, in fact, the property of Venezuela, and (d) that under the principle or doctrine of Sovereign Immunity the Court below could not obtain jurisdiction through an action quasi in rem. Plaintiffs filed an answer which denied virtually all of Venezuela's material averments of fact and conclusions of law.

*　　　　*　　　　*

The Court below undoubtedly acquired jurisdiction by service of the writ of foreign attachment upon the Captain of the vessel, and its jurisdiction was not subsequently divested or lost as a result of plaintiffs' voluntary dissolution of the (foreign) attachment without prejudice. . . .

*　　　　*　　　　*

. . . the question is not whether the Court had jurisdiction—which it had—but *whether the jurisdiction which the Court had acquired should be relinquished* for diplomatic reasons in order to promote our foreign relations or to prevent a possible war. . . .

*　　　　*　　　　*

It is a long and well established general rule that *foreign Sovereigns, which are duly recognized by appropriate action by the State Department*, and their property *are not amenable* without their waiver or consent, *to suit* in the Courts of this Country. This widely accepted National and International diplomatic policy has been established among many civilized non-communist Nations on the principle of comity and for the preservation of International friendships and Peace. In order to preserve this policy of Sovereign Immunity from conflict, confusion and erosion, and to prevent a breach of friendly relations or a severance of diplomatic relations or a possible war with a foreign nation, the *Supreme Court of the*

United States has held that in the realm of Foreign Relations or Foreign Affairs, *a determination of Sovereign Immunity by the Executive branch of our Government,* namely, the State Department, when conveyed to a Court through proper channels or officials, is—in the absence of waiver or consent—*binding and conclusive* upon all our Courts. If and when the State Department concludes that a foreign Nation is entitled to Sovereign immunity that determination, we repeat, is conclusive no matter how unwise or, in a particular case how unfair or unjust the Department's determination appears to be (a) to injured American citizens and (b) to vast numbers of the American people and (c) to our Courts. . . .

Ex Parte Peru, 318 U.S. 578, 63 S.Ct. 793, *supra,* is factually similar and legally controlling. That case involved the libeling of the ship UCAYALI belonging to the Republic of Peru to enforce a claim by a Cuban corporation arising out of the alleged breach (by a corporation acting for the Peruvian Government) of a charter party involving that ship. The case was commenced by *a writ of prohibition* filed in the Supreme Court of the United States after a lower Federal Court had refused to dismiss the libel, even after a Suggestion of Foreign Sovereign Immunity had been filed on behalf of the State Department. The Government of Peru asked for a dismissal of the action on the basis of a Suggestion of Immunity— filed (as in the case at bar) by the United States Attorney at the behest of the Attorney General, acting upon the request of the State Department which, in turn, was based upon a letter from the State Department's legal adviser—which therein had "recognized" Peru's claim to Sovereign Immunity. The Supreme Court held (a) that the doctrine of Sovereign Immunity applied; (b) that Peru had not waived such immunity. (c) that upon submission of the State Department's certification that it recognized Peru's right to Sovereign Immunity *"it became the court's duty,* in conformity *to established principles, to release the vessel and to proceed no further in the cause."* . . . The Court pertinently said . . .

*   *   *

"This case presents no question of the jurisdiction of the district court over the person of a defendant. Such jurisdiction must be acquired either by the service of process or by the defendant's appearance or participation in the litigation. Here the district court acquired jurisdiction in rem by the seizure and control of the vessel, and the libelant's claim against the vessel constituted a case or controversy which the court had authority to decide. . . . Therefore the question which we must decide is not whether there was jurisdiction in the district court, acquired by the appearance of petitioner, but whether the jurisdiction which the court had already acquired by seizure of the vessel should have been relinquished in conformity to an overriding principle of substantive law.

"That principle is that courts may not so exercise their jurisdiction, by the seizure and detention of the property of a friendly sovereign, as to embarrass the executive arm of the government in conducting foreign relations. 'In such cases the judicial department of this government follows the action of the political branch, and will not embarrass the latter by assuming an antagonistic jurisdiction.' *United States* v. *Lee*, 106 U.S. 196, 209, 1 S.Ct. 240, 251, 27 L.Ed. 171. More specifically the judicial seizure of the vessel of a friendly foreign state is so serious a challenge to its dignity, and may so affect our friendly relations with it, that courts are required to accept and follow the executive determination that the vessel is immune. When such a seizure occurs the friendly foreign sovereign may present its claim of immunity by appearance in the suit and by way of defense to the libel. . . . But it may also present its claim to the Department of State, the political arm of the Government charged with the conduct of our foreign affairs. Upon recognition and allowance of the claim by the State Department and certification of its action presented to the court by the Attorney General, it is the court's duty to surrender the vessel and remit the libellant to the relief obtainable through diplomatic negotiations. . . . This practice is founded upon the policy, recognized both by the Department of State and the courts, that our national interest will be better served in such cases if the wrongs to suitors, involving our relations with a friendly foreign power, are righted through diplomatic negotiations rather than by the compulsions of judicial proceedings.

"We cannot say that the Republic of Peru has waived its immunity. It has consistently declared its reliance on the immunity, both before the Department and in the district court. Neither method of asserting the immunity is incompatible with the other. . . ."

*   *   *

F. W. Stone Engineering Co. v. *Petroleos Mexicanos,* 352 Pa. 12, 42 A.2d 57, *supra* is likewise pertinent and controlling. That case was very similar to the case at bar. Plaintiff sued defendant which was an instrumentality of the Mexican Government and wholly owned and controlled by that Government, in a foreign attachment proceedings and attached funds of the defendant which had been deposited and were in the possession of the Butler County National Bank & Trust Company. Defendant moved to dissolve the attachment and based its motion upon a communication from the Secretary of State to the Attorney General of the United States which recognized defendant as an instrumentality of Mexico. . . . Although the defendant was admittedly an instrumentality of Mexico and was engaged in a commercial enterprise for profit, this Court affirmed the Order of the lower Court which dissolved the attachment and said . . .

"*When the Department of State makes known its determination* with respect to political matters growing out of or incidental to our Government's relations with a friendly foreign state, *it is the duty of the courts to abide by the status so indicated or created* and to refrain from making independent inquiries into the merit of the State Department's determination or from taking any steps that might prove embarrassing to the Government in the handling of its foreign relations. . . .

*   *   *

Chemical and Sulphur . . . first contend that the *Schooner Exchange, Ex Parte Peru* and the *Stone* cases are restricted and limited in their effect and do not apply to the case at bar because (1) procedurally those cases arose out of a seizure (by libel or writ of foreign attachment) of property of a foreign Government or of its instrumentality and that through appellees' voluntary dissolution of the attachment without prejudice, this is no longer a "seizure" case and (2) consequently friendly foreign relations cannot be jeopardized by this suit. Appellees further contend that in spite of the release by them of the property seized, jurisdiction over the person of the defendant was obtained and still remains by way of the writ of foreign attachment, as well as by actual service of the writ and the complaint on the captain of Venezuela's ship. Appellees' attempted distinction of the Supreme Court cases previously cited in this opinion, and their aforesaid contentions are devoid of merit.

The principle or doctrine of absolute Sovereign Immunity has been attacked for many years by legal writers, by text authorities and by numerous Judges. The absolute doctrine is recognized by only a few countries in the world. These authorities assert and appellees contend that even when Sovereign Immunity has been recognized and suggested by the State Department, the acceptance or rejection thereof is nevertheless a matter for the Courts—whether the action be in rem, or quasi in rem or in personam—and the Courts in their sole discretion may accept or reject the plea of Sovereign Immunity. They further assert that this principle of absolute Sovereign Immunity should be restricted and should apply only to situations and activities in which the foreign Country is acting or is involved in its national or governmental or public capacity and not in a proprietary or a commercial or private or non-governmental activity or capacity. However, where the State Department has (through appropriate channels) recognized the Sovereign Immunity of the foreign Country which is involved, and that Country has not waived its immunity or consented to the suit, the Supreme Court of the United States has never recognized this proposed *restricted* doctrine.

*   *   *

In *Rich* v. *Naviera Vacuba, S.A.*, 295 F. 2d 24, 25–26 (C.C.A. 4, 1961), a Cuban ship had been libeled by an American corporation. In spite of Cuba's hostile attitude and belligerent actions toward our Country, and the fact that the ship was engaged in a commercial enterprise, a Suggestion of Immunity was filed by the United States Attorney General at the request of our State Department. The Circuit Court (for the 4th District) sustained the Suggestion of Immunity and dismissed the libel. The Court rejected all the arguments therein made, which were repeated by appellees in this case, and said . . .

"The vessel Bahia de Nipe sailed on August 8, 1961, from Cuba with a cargo of 5,000 bags of sugar destined for a Russian port. . . .
"The libellants argue that before sovereign immunity may be granted they should be heard by the court on whether the foreign government is in fact the

owner and possessor of the property in question and, as to the ship, whether she was operated by that government not commercially but in a public capacity.

"Despite these contentions, *we conclude that* the certificate and *grant of immunity issued by the Department of State should be* accepted by the court without further inquiry. . . ."

Two individual claimants in the *Rich* case on September 9, 1961, petitioned the Supreme Court of the United States for a stay on the ground that ". . . the suggestion of immunity had been issued in violation of the State Department's policy as set forth in the Tate letter." In response and in opposition to that application, the Solicitor General filed a Memorandum for the United States and said:

" 'Similarly, the applicants' reliance on the so-called 'Tate letter'—dealing with the State Department's policy towards foreign government-owned vessels operated in commercial or mercantile pursuits—is misplaced. That letter does set forth the considerations which the Department will take into account in determining whether or not to recognize a claim of immunity by a foreign sovereign. *But it is wholly and solely a guide to the State Department's own policy, not the declaration of a rule of law or even of an unalterable policy position;* and, in addition, it sets forth only some of the governing considerations and does not purport to be all-inclusive or exclusive. Here, the State Department has, in fact, recognized Cuba's claim to immunity, after taking into account all pertinent factors . . .' . . ."

On September 11, 1961, Chief Justice Warren denied the application for a stay. . . .

It is our conclusion, therefore, (1) that Sovereign Immunity of foreign Governments is a matter for determination in the first instance by the Executive Branch of the Government, namely, the State Department; and (2) if and when that Department's determination has been made and has been appropriately presented to the Courts, the Department's determination is binding and conclusive upon the Courts.

*   *   *

. . . A writ of prohibition is issued, directed to the Judges of the lower Court dissolving plaintiffs' attachment and dismissing plaintiffs' complaint.

Justice JONES files a concurring opinion.

Justice ROBERTS files a concurring and dissenting opinion.

Justices MUSMANNO and COHEN file dissenting opinions.

*   *   *

Dissenting Opinion of Justice Musmanno

Involved in this case is an expropriation of the property of American citizens by the Venezuelan government not only without fair compensation as required by International Law but with an accompanying arrogant refusal to even enter into any settlement negotiations. Moreover, the role of our State Department is most puzzling and inconsistent with its own expressed policy.

The plaintiff began its lawsuit after the State Department tried unsuccessfully to bring the Venezuelan Government to a conference discussion. After the action was filed, the State Department scheduled a hearing and received briefs to determine whether—*as a matter of law,* not policy—the Venezuelan Government was immune from suit under the Sovereign Immunity doctrine. The legal advisor of the Secretary of State decided as a *legal* matter that the Sovereign Immunity doctrine should be invoked and filed such a plea in behalf of the Venezuelan government. In so doing the State Department obviously invaded the jurisdiction of the Courts and for that reason alone the judiciary must approach the problem as if the State Department had not intervened at all.

*   *   *

Of course, it is obvious and indisputable that where the nation's security is involved, the Courts will support the foreign policy of the nation, as it is officially made known by the President of the United States. But that is not this case. It is not even close. We have here outrightly a commercial transaction. We have here the case of American businessmen, under the most absolute assurance of safeguarding by Venezuela, going into Venezuela, investing huge sums of money to develop Venezuela's resources with the official sanction and urging of the Venezuelan government, and then that same government confiscating, without compensation, the property of these American businessmen, property amounting, as already stated, to over a hundred million dollars.

*   *   *

The Majority Opinion in this case is built on an erroneous concept of the law, namely, that once the State Department whispers sovereign immunity the Courts must close their doors to everyone who may come within the breeze of the zephyric suggestion. Fortunately, for the majesty of the law, the dignity of the courts, and the fair-minded administration of justice in America, that is not the case. In fact, that is not even the view of the State Department.

The State Department intervened in this litigation on the basis of a question of law, not policy. In a letter to the President of the plaintiff corporation, Chemical Natural Resources, Inc., the State Department said: "The decision of the Department of State in this matter was made in the light of *legal issues.*" (Emphasis supplied.)

Thus, it must be obvious that we are not here considering any question of United States foreign policy. We are adjudicating legal issues and I certainly should not have to emphasize that legal issues are resolved by the judicial branch of our government, not the executive branch. . . .

*   *   *

Instead of accepting its responsibility and stoutheartedly recognizing the legal issue in this case, the Majority attempts to bolster an archaic doctrine with cases which have no resemblance to the fact situation before us. It says, for instance, that the decision in the case of *Ex parte Peru*, 318 U.S. 578, 63 S.Ct. 793, 87 L.Ed. 1014, is "controlling." It is not controlling. To begin with, the *Peru* case preceded the Tate Proclamation which announced the restricted sovereign immunity rule, and, more importantly, it antedated the decision of the Supreme Court in the *Republic of China* case, which affirmed the restrictive sovereign doctrine. Moreover, the facts in *Peru* are wholly different from the facts in the case at bar. The Peruvian vessel "Ucayli" had been seized and was being detained at the time of the lawsuit. The ship in the instant case, the "Cuidad de Valencia," although originally attached, was released two days later and the proceedings here are *in personam* and not *in rem*. The plaintiff is not seeking execution on a judgment, it is not holding property belonging to the defendant, it is not embarrassing foreign relations between Venezuela and the United States. It is merely seeking an adjudication in an American court of its legal rights. Even if it obtains judgment the question as to whether the judgment can be collected is something to be decided later but certainly it has the legal and constitutional prerogative to have its rights determined in a court of law.

*   *   *

Another reason why *Peru* is not controlling is that the vessel which was there involved, the "Ucayali," was seized while the United States was at war. At the time of its arrest the vessel was "under engagement to transport materials for the United States Army."

The Majority Opinion says that the case of *F. W. Stone Engineering Co.* v. *Petroleos Mexicanos*, 352 Pa. 12, 42 A.2d 57, is "likewise pertinent and controlling," but since *Stone Engineering* is built on *Peru* and we have seen that *Peru* is no longer authority for the proposition urged by the defendant, *a fortiori, Stone Engineering* would not be authoritative in the case at bar. In addition, it is to be noted that in *Stone Engineering* our Court specifically stated that we accepted the Department of State's suggestion of immunity because it was a "determination with respect to political matters" concerning foreign relations. Exercising the most fertile imaginative creative faculty, it cannot be said that the litigation here involved, that is, the ascertainment of damages due to a breach of a business contract, constitutes a determination of "*political* matters concerning foreign relations."

The case of *Rich* v. *Naviera Vacuba, S.A.*, 4 Cir., 295 F.2d 24, also cited by the Majority Opinion, is also not controlling or relevant because there, again, there was a detained vessel and, in addition, the Suggestion of Immunity filed by the State Department specifically declared: "This is to inform you that it has been determined that the release of this vessel would avoid further disturbance to our international relations in the premises." No such precarious situation is presented or even hinted at in the case at bar, and it is particularly to be noted that in the *Rich* v. *Naviera* case the litigation was permitted to *go to judgment* in spite of the international relationship phase, the judgment entered in favor of the plaintiff amounting to $80,517.61. It was only when execution was attempted that the question of sovereign immunity arose. And I repeat that no execution or detention is involved in the instant case. The plaintiffs are seeking merely to have their case *adjudicated* as was done in *Rich* v. *Naviera.*

*   *   *

. . . It is a mystery to me how and why the Majority reached the conclusion that Venezuela, engaged in a commercial undertaking as business-like as a purchase of stock on the exchange or the buying of a consignment of bananas at a plantation, should be awarded an immunity from judicial processes which every department of our government has now recognized as controlling in profit-inspired transactions. I cannot understand why the government of Venezuela is guaranteed an immunity which the United States does not claim in any other country in the world. It is impossible for me to escape the conviction that this kind of a decision on the part of the Majority contributes to international irresponsibility and international disrespect for law.

*   *   *

Commercial Activities

VICTORY TRANSPORT, INC., v. COMISARIA GENERAL de ABASTECIMIENTOS y TRASPORTES
United States Court of Appeals, 1964
336 F.2d, 354

J. Joseph Smith, Circuit Judge

This is an appeal from an order of the United States District Court for the Southern District of New York, Thomas F. Murphy, District Judge, granting appellee's motion to compel arbitration and denying appellant's cross motions to vacate service and dismiss the petition. . . .

The appellant, a branch of the Spanish Ministry of Commerce, voyage-chartered the *S.S. Hudson* from its owner, the appellee, to transport a cargo of surplus wheat, purchased pursuant to the Agricultural Trade Development and Assistance Act, 7 U.S.C. § 1691 et seq, from Mobile,

Alabama, to one or two safe Spanish ports. The charter agreement contained the New York Produce Arbitration Clause, providing for the arbitration of disputes before three commercial men in New York. The ship was delayed and sustained hull damage in discharging its cargo in Spanish ports that were allegedly unsafe for a ship of the Hudson's size. When the appellant failed to pay for the damages or submit the dispute to arbitration, the appellee instituted this proceeding under section 4 of the United States Arbitration Act, 9 U.S.C. § 4, to compel arbitration. On March 22, 1963, appellee secured an ex parte order from the district court permitting service of its petition by registered mail at appellant's Madrid office. Service pursuant to this order was effected on April 1, 1963.

On October 15, 1963, the appellant moved to vacate the extraterritorial service as authorized by statute. Appearing specially and supported by an affidavit of the Spanish Consul, who stated that the appellant was a branch of the Spanish Government and immune from suit, counsel of the appellant also moved to dismiss the petition to compel arbitration because of a lack of jurisdiction and sovereign immunity. Rejecting these cross-motions, Judge Murphy held that the court had *in personam* jurisdiction and granted the appellee's motion to compel arbitration.

Appellant's primary contention is that as an arm of the sovereign Government of Spain, it cannot be sued in the courts of the United States without its consent, which it declines to accord in this case. There is certainly a great deal of impressive precedent to support this contention, for the doctrine of the immunity of foreign sovereigns from the jurisdiction of our courts was early entrenched in our law by Chief Justice Marshall's historic decision in *The Schooner Exchange* v. *McFaddon*, 7 Cranch 116 (U.S. 1812). The doctrine originated in an era of personal sovereignty, when kings could theoretically do no wrong and when the exercise of authority by one sovereign over another indicated hostility or superiority. With the passing of that era, sovereign immunity has been retained by the courts chiefly to avoid possible embarrassment to those responsible for the conduct of the nation's foreign relations. . . . However, because of the dramatic changes in the nature and functioning of sovereigns, particularly in the last half century, the wisdom of retaining the doctrine has been cogently questioned. . . . Growing concern for individual rights and public morality, coupled with the increasing entry of governments into what had previously been regarded as private pursuits, has led a substantial number of nations to abandon the absolute theory of sovereign immunity in favor of a restrictive theory. . . .

Meeting in Brussels in 1926, representatives of twenty nations, including all the major powers except the United States and Russia, signed a convention limiting sovereign immunity in the area of maritime commerce to ships and cargoes employed exclusively for public and non-commercial purposes. After World War II the United States began to restrict immunity by negotiating treaties obligating each contracting party to waive its sovereign immunity for state-controlled enterprises engaged in business activities within the territory of the other party. Fourteen such treaties were negotiated by our State Department in the decade 1948 to 1958. . . . And in 1952 our State Department, in a widely publicized letter from Acting Legal Adviser Jack B. Tate to the Acting Attorney General Philip B. Perlman, announced that the Department would generally adhere to the restrictive theory of sovereign immunity, recognizing immunity for a foreign state's public or sovereign acts (*jure imperii*) but denying immunity to a foreign state's private or commercial acts (*jure gestionis*). . . .

In delineating the scope of a doctrine designed to avert possible embarrassment to the conduct of our foreign relations, the courts have quite naturally deferred to the policy pronouncements of the State Department. . . . The Supreme Court's dictum in *Mexico* v. *Hoffman*, 324 U.S. 30, 35 (1945)—"It is therefore not for the courts to deny an immunity which our government has seen fit to allow, or to allow an immunity on new grounds which the government has not seen fit to recognize"—has been variously construed, but we think it means at least that the courts should deny immunity where the State Department has indicated, either directly or indirectly, that immunity need not be accorded. It makes no sense for the Courts to deny a litigant his day in court and to permit the disregard of legal obligations to avoid embarrassing the State Department if that Agency indicates it will not be embarrassed. . . . Moreover, "recognition by the courts of an immunity upon principles which the political department of government has not sanctioned may be equally embarrassing to it in securing the protection of our national interests and their recognition by other nations." *Mexico* v. *Hoffman, supra*, 324 U.S. at 36.

This is not to say that the courts will never grant immunity unless the State Department specifically requests it. A claim of sovereign immunity may be presented to the court by either of two procedures. The foreign sovereign may request its claim of immunity be recognized by the State Department, which will normally present its suggestion to the court through the Attorney General or some law officer acting under his direction. Alternatively, the accredited and recognized representative of the foreign sovereign may present the claim of sovereign immunity directly to the court. . . . In some situations, the State Department may find it expedient to make no response to a request for immunity. Where, as here, the court has received no communication from the State Department concerning the immunity of the Comisaria General, the court must decide for itself whether it is the established policy of the State Department to recognize claims of immunity of this type. . . .

Through the "Tate letter" the State Department has made it clear that its policy is to decline immunity to friendly foreign sovereigns in suits arising from private or commercial activity. But the "Tate letter" offers no guide-lines or criteria for differentiating between a sovereign's private and public acts. Nor have the courts or commentators suggested any satisfactory test. Some have looked to the nature of the transaction, categorizing as sovereign acts only activity which could not be performed by individuals. While this criterion is relatively easy to apply, it ofttimes produces rather astonishing results such as the holdings of some European courts that purchases of bullets or shoes for the army, the erection of fortifications for defense, or the rental of a house for an embassy, are private acts. . . . Furthermore, this test merely postpones the difficulty, for particular contracts in some instances may be made only by states. Others have looked to the purpose of the transaction, categorizing as *jure imperii* all activities in which the object of performance is public in character. But this test is even more unsatisfactory, for conceptually the modern sovereign always acts for a public purpose. . . . Functionally the criterion is purely arbitrary and necessarily involves the court in projecting personal notions about the proper realm of state functioning. . . .

The conceptual difficulties involved in formulating a satisfactory method of differentiating between acts *jure imperii* and acts *jure gestionis* have led many commentators to declare that the distinction is unworkable. However, the Supreme Court has made it plain that when the State Department has been silent on the question of immunity in a particular case, it is the court's duty to determine for itself whether the foreign sovereign is entitled to immunity "in conformity to the principles accepted by the department of the government charged with the conduct of foreign relations." . . . And since the State Department has publicly pronounced its adherence to the distinction, we must apply it to the facts of this case.

The purpose of the restrictive theory of sovereign immunity is to try to accommodate the interest of individuals doing business with foreign governments in being free to perform certain political acts without undergoing the embarrassment or hindrance of defending the propriety of such acts before foreign courts. Sovereign immunity is a derogation from the normal exercise of jurisdiction by the courts and should be accorded only in clear cases. Since the State Department's failure or refusal to suggest immunity is significant, we are disposed to deny a claim of sovereign immunity that has not been "recognized and allowed" by the State Department unless it is plain that the activity in question falls within one of the categories of strictly political or public acts about which sovereigns have traditionally been quite sensitive. Such acts are generally limited to the following categories:

1. internal administrative acts, such as expulsion of an alien.
2. legislative acts, such as nationalization.
3. acts concerning the armed forces.
4. acts concerning diplomatic activity.
5. public loans.

We do not think that the restrictive theory adopted by the State Department requires sacrificing the interests of private litigants to international comity in other than these limited categories. Should diplomacy require enlargement of these categories, the State Department can file a suggestion of immunity with the court. Should diplomacy require contraction of these categories, the State Department can issue a new or clarifying policy pronouncement.

The Comisaria General's chartering of the appellee's ship to transport a purchase of wheat is not a strictly public or political act. Indeed, it partakes far more of the character of a private commercial act than a public or political act.

The charter party has all the earmarks of a typical commercial transaction. It was executed for the Comisaria General by "El Jefe del Servicio Commercial," the head of its commercial division. The wheat was consigned to and shipped by a private commercial concern. And one of the most significant indicators of the private commercial nature of this charter is the inclusion of the arbitration clause. . . .

* * *

Even if we take a broader view of the transaction to encompass the purchase of wheat pursuant to the Surplus Agricultural Commodities Agreement to help feed the people of Spain, the activity of the Comisaria General remains more in the commercial than political realm. Appellant does not claim that the wheat will be used for the public services of Spain; presumptively the wheat will be resold to Spanish nationals. Whether the Comisaria General loses money or makes a profit on the sale, this purchasing activity has been conducted through private channels of trade. Except for United States financing, permitting payment in pesetas, the Comisaria General acted much like any private purchaser of wheat.

Our conclusion that the Comisaria General's activity is more properly labelled an act *jure gestionis* than *jure imperii* is supported by the practice of those countries which have adopted the restrictive theory of sovereign immunity. Thus the Commercial Tribunal of Alexandria declined to grant immunity to this same Spanish instrumentality in a more difficult case—a suit arising from the Comisaria's purchase of rice to help feed the people of netural Spain during wartime.

* * *

Though there are a few inconsistencies, the courts in those countries which have adopted the restrictive theory have generally considered purchasing activity by a state instrumentality, particularly for resale to nationals, as commercial or private activity.

* * *

Though in most cases jurisdiction over a foreign sovereign is obtained in *in rem* proceeding, there is no bar to the assertion of *in personam* jurisdiction. . . .

We hold that the district court had *in personam* jurisdiction to enter the order compelling arbitration. By agreeing to arbitrate in New York, where the United States Arbitration Act makes such agreements specifically enforceable, the Comisaria General must be deemed to have consented to the jurisdiction of the court that could compel the arbitration proceeding in New York. To hold otherwise would be to render the arbitration clause a nullity. . . . Unless the arbitration clause in this charter differs significantly from the arbitration clauses specifically enforced in the *Farr* and *Orion* cases, it is clear that the court has *in personam* jurisdiction, for we see no reason to treat a commercial branch of a foreign sovereign differently from a foreign corporation. The arbitration clause construed in *Farr* provided: "This submission may be made a rule of court by either party." The corresponding language in the arbitration clause in the instant case provides: "[F]or the purpose of enforcing any award, this agreement may be made a rule of the Court." Appellant argues that this slight difference in wording requires a different result, for the appellee is seeking an appointment of an arbitrator, not enforcement of an award. We cannot agree. This fine distinction did not trouble this court in *Orion*, where the corresponding language of the arbitration clause provided: "For the purpose of enforcing awards this agreement shall be made a Rule of the Court." Implicit in the agreement to arbitrate is consent to enforcement of that agreement.

The suggestion by the appellant that the subject matter of the controversy is without the admiralty jurisdiction of the United States courts is utterly devoid of merit. It has long been settled that a charter-party is a maritime contract and that disputes arising therefrom are within the admiralty jurisdiction of the United States courts. *Morewood* v. *Enequist*, 64 U.S. 491 (1860).

*   *   *

The order of the district court is affirmed.

Counterclaims by Sovereigns

NATIONAL CITY BANK OF NEW YORK v. REPUBLIC OF CHINA
United States Supreme Court, 1954
348 U.S. 356

Mr. Justice Frankfurter delivered the opinion of the court.

*　　　*　　　*

The Shanghai-Nanking Railway Administration, an official agency of respondent Republic of China, established a $200,000 deposit account in 1948 with the New York head office of petitioner National City Bank of New York. Subsequently, respondent sought to withdraw the funds, but petitioner refused to pay, and respondent brought suit in Federal District Court under 48 Stat. 184, as amended, 12 U.S.C. section 632.

In addition to various defenses, petitioner interposed two counterclaims seeking an affirmative judgment for $1,634,432 on defaulted Treasury Notes of respondent owned by petitioner. After a plea of sovereign immunity, the District Court dismissed the counterclaims, 108 F. Supp. 766, and entered judgment on them pursuant to Rule 54(b), Federal Rules of Civil Procedure. Petitioner appealed, and while the appeal was pending sought leave from the District Court to amend the counterclaims by denominating them setoffs and including additional data. The District Court denied leave. 14 F.R.D. 186. The Court of Appeals for the Second Circuit affirmed the dismissal and the denial on the ground that the counterclaims were not based on the subject matter of respondent's suit (whether they be treated as requests for affirmative relief or as setoffs) and, therefore, it would be an invasion of respondent's sovereign immunity for our courts to permit them to be pursued. 208 F.2d 627. Because of the importance of the question and its first appearance in this Court, we granted certiorari. 347 U.S. 951.

The status of the Republic of China in our courts is a matter for determination by the Executive and is outside the competence of this court. Accordingly, we start with the fact that the Republic and its governmental agencies enjoy a foreign sovereign's immunities to the same extent as any other country duly recognized by the United States. . . .

The freedom of a foreign sovereign from being haled into court as a defendant has impressive title-deeds. Very early in our history this immunity was recognized . . . and it has since become part of the fabric of our law. It has become such solely through adjudications of this Court. Unlike the special position accorded our States as party defendants by the Eleventh Amendment, the privileged position of a foreign state is not an explicit command of the Constitution. It rests on considerations of policy given legal sanction by this Court. . . .

But even the immunity enjoyed by the United States as territorial sovereign is a legal doctrine which has not been favored by the test of time. It has increasingly been found to be in conflict with the growing subjection of governmental action to the moral judgment. A reflection of this steady shift in attitude toward the American sovereign's immunity is found in such observations in unanimous opinions of this Court as "Public opinion as to the peculiar rights and preferences due to the sovereign has changed," *Davis* v. *Pringle*, 268 U.S. 315, 318; "There is no doubt an intermittent tendency on the part of governments to be a little less grasping than they have been in the past . . . ," *White* v. *Mechanics Securities Corp.*, 269 U.S. 283, 301; ". . . the present climate of opinion . . . has brought governmental immunity from suit into disfavor . . . ," *Keifer & Keifer* v. *Reconstruction Finance Corp.*, 306 U.S. 381, 391. This chilly feeling against sovereign immunity began to reflect itself in federal legislation in 1797. At that early day Congress decided that when the United States sues an individual, the individual can set off all debts properly due him from the sovereign. And because of the objections to *ad hoc* legislative allowance of private claims, Congress a hundred years ago created the Court of Claims, where the United States, like any other obligor, may affirmatively be held to its undertakings. . . .

The outlook and feeling thus reflected are not merely relevant to our problem. They are important. The claims of dominant opinion rooted in sentiments of justice and public morality are among the most powerful shaping-forces in lawmaking by courts. Legislation and adjudication are interacting influences in the development of law. A steady legislative trend, presumably manifesting a strong social policy, properly makes demands on the judicial process. . . .

More immediately touching the evolution of legal doctrines regarding a foreign sovereign's immunity is the restrictive policy that our State Department has taken toward the claim of such immunity. As the responsible agency for the conduct of foreign affairs, the State Department is the normal means of suggesting to the courts that a sovereign be granted immunity from a particular suit. . . . Its failure or refusal to suggest such immunity has been accorded significant weight by this Court. . . .

And so we come to the immediate situation before us. The short of the matter is that we are not dealing with an attempt to bring a recognized foreign government into one of our courts as a defendant and subject it to the rule of law to which nongovernmental obligors must bow. We have a foreign government invoking our law but resisting a claim against it which fairly would curtail its recovery. It wants our law, like any other litigant, but it wants our law free from the claims of justice. It becomes vital, therefore, to examine the extent to which the considerations which led this Court to bar a suit against a sovereign in *The Schooner Exchange* are applicable here to foreclose a court from determining, according to prevailing law, whether the Republic of China's claim against the National City Bank would be unjustly enforced by disregarding legitimate claims against the Republic of China. As expounded in *The Schooner Exchange*, the doctrine is one of implied consent by the territorial sovereign to exempt the foreign sovereign from its "exclusive and absolute" jurisdiction, the implication deriving from standards of public morality, fair dealing, reciprocal self-interest, and respect for the "power and dignity" of the foreign sovereign.

(a) The Court of Claims is available to foreign nationals (or their governments) on a simple condition: that the foreign national's government can be sued in its courts on claims by our citizens. An American or a Chinese could sue in the Court of Claims for default on a United States bond, 28 U.S.C. section 1491 (4), or could counterclaim—to the extent of the Government's claim—in a suit by the United States in any court, . . . Thus it seems only fair to subject a foreign sovereign, coming into our courts by its own choice, to a liability substantially less than our own Government long ago willingly assumed.

(b) The Republic of China is apparently suable on contract claims in its own courts, and Americans have the same rights as Chinese in those courts. No parochial bias is manifest in our courts which would make it an affront to the "power and dignity" of the Republic of China for us to subject it to counterclaims in our courts when it entertains affirmative suits in its own. . . .

(c) Respondent urges that fiscal management falls within the category of immune operations of a foreign government as defined by the State Department's 1952 pronouncement. This is not to be denied, but it is beside the point. A sovereign has freely come as a suitor into our courts; our State Department neither has been asked nor has it given the slightest intimation that in its judgment allowance of counterclaims in such a situation would embarrass friendly relations with the Republic of China.

(d) It is recognized that a counterclaim based on the subject matter of a sovereign's suit is allowed to cut into the doctrine of immunity. This is proof positive that the doctrine is not absolute, and that considerations of fair play must be taken into account in its application. But the limitation of "based on the subject matter" is too indeterminate, indeed too capricious, to mark the bounds of the limitations on the doctrine of sovereign immunity. There is great diversity among courts on what is and what is not a claim "based on the subject matter of the suit" or "growing out of the same transaction.". . . No doubt the present counterclaims cannot fairly be deemed to be related to the Railway Agency's deposit of funds except insofar as the transactions between the Republic of China and the petitioner may be regarded as aspects of a continuous business relationship. The point is that the ultimate thrust of the consideration of fair dealing which allows a setoff or counterclaim based on the same subject matter reaches the present situation. . . .

The judgment of the Court of Appeals must be reversed and the case remanded to the District Court with directions to reinstate the counterclaims and for further proceedings not inconsistent with this opinion.

*   *   *

Mr. Justice Reed, with whom Mr. Justice Burton and Mr. Justice Clark join, dissenting.

Some data must be premised if discussion is to be confined to a reasonable space. We start with the postulate that the sovereign is released from the jurisdiction of its own courts except as it may specifically submit itself to their power.

That does not create a situation of irresponsibility. Satisfaction of sovereign liability may be had through the legislative organ which recognizes a moral obligation to pay the creditors of the government and to compensate those injured by it.

A sovereign's freedom from judicial control does not arise from or depend upon the will of the courts. As was said in *The Schooner Exchange* in speaking of the immunity of a foreign government, it depends upon "the will of the sovereign of the territory." ". . . all exemptions from territorial jurisdiction, must be derived from the consent of the sovereign". . .

The reason for the sovereign's consent to the exclusion of foreign sovereignties from the general jurisdiction of its courts was said by Chief Justice Marshall to rest on this proposition:

"The world being composed of distinct sovereignties, possessing equal rights and equal independence, whose mutual benefit is promoted by intercourse with each other, and by an interchange of those good offices which humanity dictates and its wants require, all sovereigns have consented to a relaxation in practice, in cases under certain peculiar circumstances, of that absolute and complete jurisdiction within their respective territories which sovereignty confers . . ." 7 Cranch, at 136.

*   *   *

An ancillary principle of law is that, in determining whether a defendant is a sovereign, the courts follow the guidance of the political branch. . . .

. . . In the present case, the Court evidently feels that, since the counterclaim is limited to the amount of the Republic of China's claim, there is jurisdiction to allow a setoff to that extent. But the mere fact that a judgment over is not sought should not be relied upon to avoid the jurisdictional immunity of a foreign sovereign. I find no justification for the Court's restricting that immunity in the absence of legislative or executive action.

*   *   *

. . . Our country allots power to the judiciary in the confidence that, in view of the separation of powers, judicial authority will not undertake determinations which are the primary concern of other branches of our Government. . . .

The Court determines, however, that the question of changing the limitation of the immunity of foreign sovereigns pertains to its functions. Even on the assumption that such is a proper matter for judicial concern, I would reach a different conclusion than does the Court. If a direct suit cannot be brought against a foreign sovereign (as is conceded), why should we allow the same claim to be used as an offset to destroy the sovereign's right to recover? Why should the City Bank be able to assert its notes against the Republic of China, even defensively, when other noteholders not obligated to the sovereign are prevented from collecting their notes? Here we have an entirely disconnected claim on overdue national notes brought forward as a defense to an action to recover a bank deposit. . . . The counterclaim here is of much the same character as a suit against a foreign sovereign. Deposits may be the lifeblood necessary for national existence. It is not wise for us to tell the nations of the world that any assets they may have in the United States, now or in the future, upon which suit must be brought, are subject to every counterclaim their debtors can acquire against them at par or at a discount. It is unfair to our foreign friends and detrimental to our own financial and mercantile interests. For fairness we need not go beyond the allowance of counterclaims arising out of transactions foreign sovereigns seek to enforce in our courts. It seems to me that the Court sanctions a circuitous evasion of the well-established rule prohibiting direct suits against foreign sovereigns.

I would affirm.

International Organization Immunities

Immunities from local jurisdiction for the property and officials of international organizations contribute a comparatively new but rapidly developing aspect of international law. A few efforts were made to secure protection for the personnel of such organizations as the European Commission of the Danube and the Central Commission for the Rhine in the 19th century, and for justices of the Permanent Court of Arbitration and the Central American Court of Justice early in the 20th. But not until establishment of the League of Nations in 1919 did states face the comprehensive issue of jurisdictional immunities for an international organization's premises and personnel.

Article 7, paragraphs 4 and 5 of the Covenant provided:

Representatives of the Members of the League and officials of the League when engaged on the business of the League shall enjoy diplomatic privileges and immunities. The buildings and other property occupied by the League or its officials or by Representatives attending its meetings shall be inviolable.

These statements of principle were not self-executing within states, and the immediate issue of jurisdiction lay with Switzerland, where the League was located. Through exchanges of notes between them, the League and the Political Department of the Swiss government reached a modus vivendi, or agreement, which among other things recognized two categories of officials: the first was accorded privileges and immunities resembling those given to diplomatic agents from foreign states; the second obtained immunity only for acts performed in an official capacity, and received fewer privileges with respect to fiscal and customs matters than did the first category. Swiss nationals employed by the League presented a more difficult problem for the Swiss government, and over the years a number of questions arose, both administratively and judicially, concerning their salaries, taxation, military service duties, and so forth.

At the same time, the Netherlands government had to deal with the Permanent Court of International Justice at the Hague by negotiating a special agreement on immunities with the League. Many of the provisions were similar to the Swiss–League understanding, although the Dutch were somewhat more generous in granting immunities from local law to their own nationals when employed by the League or the Court.

Like the Covenant of the League, the Charter of the United Nations was not self-executing with respect to privileges and immunities of the organization's property, the member states' representatives to the organization, and the officials of the United Nations.

Article 105 of the Charter stated:

1. The Organization shall enjoy in the territory of each of its Members such privileges and immunities as are necessary for the fulfillment of its purposes.

2. Representatives of the Members of the United Nations and officials of the Organization shall similarly enjoy such privileges and immunities as are necessary for the independent exercise of their functions in connection with the Organization.

3. The General Assembly may make recommendations with a view to determining the details of the application of paragraphs 1 and 2 of this Article or may propose conventions to the Members of the United Nations for this purpose.

Through its own municipal legislation, the 1945 International Organization Immunities Act, and by the 1947 Headquarters Agreement with the United Nations, the United States provided the organization's privileges and immunites for its premises and property, representatives, and officials. Significantly, Section 7(b) of the International Organization Immunities Act reads,

Representatives of foreign governments in or to international organizations and officers and employees of such organizations shall be immune from suit and legal process relating to acts performed by them in their official capacity and falling within their functions as such representatives, officers, or employees. . . .

The President of the United States determines the applicability of the act.

Meanwhile, in 1946 the General Convention on Privileges and Immunities of the United Nations was adopted by the General Assembly, and in 1947 a Convention on Privileges and Immunities was adopted for the specialized agencies. Under the General Convention, the personal immunities of states' representatives to international organizations, the United Nations Secretary-General, and assistant secretaries-general roughly parallel the traditional diplomatic immunities. Other officials of international organizations have a number of privileges with respect to local administration, but they are usually granted freedom from local jurisdiction only in connection with their official activities. Immunities for United Nations officials may be waived by the Secretary-General.

In recent years, states have made dozens of agreements, some multilateral and some bilateral, with a growing number of international organizations. These agreements have recognized the legal capacity and personality of the organization as well as providing for local immunities. Among such accords have been provisions for the Organization of American States, the Council of Europe, the Arab League, and the European Court of Human Rights. Of special interest have been the provisions for international banks and funds, which plainly must have greater legal freedom in local monetary and fiscal matters, yet should not entirely escape suit for financial policies that involve private creditors or debtors.

Finally, one of the more interesting developments of this expanding international legal field has been several agreements between the United Nations and host states that provide for certain immunities from local jurisdiction for the various United Nations peacekeeping forces, such as the U.N. Emergency Force in Egypt in 1957 and the U.N. Force in the Congo in 1960.[9]

In the documents that follow, certain provisions of the *Convention on the Privileges and Immunities of the United Nations* are cited; the *Melekh* case illustrates the status and immunities of a United Nations official; and the *Lutcher* case indicates the way in which a regional financial international organization may be amenable to suit.

CONVENTION ON THE PRIVILEGES AND IMMUNITIES OF THE UNITED NATIONS
Adopted by the General Assembly of the United Nations 13 February 1946*
1 U.N. Treaty Series 15

*   *   *

Article I
Juridical Personality

Section 1. The United Nations shall possess juridical personality. It shall have the capacity:
(a) To contract;
(b) To acquire and dispose of immovable and movable property;
(c) To institute legal proceedings.

Article II
Property, Funds and Assets

Section 2. The United Nations, its property and assets wherever located and by whomsoever held, shall enjoy immunity from every form of legal process except insofar as in any particular case it has expressly waived its immunity shall extend to any measure of execution.

Section 3. The premises of the United Nations shall be inviolable. The property and assets of the United Nations, wherever located and by

---

[9] Members and civilian components of U.S. Armed Forces stationed abroad under the North Atlantic Treaty Organization or the Treaty of Mutual Cooperation with Japan and other mutual security arrangements have generally been governed by a status of forces agreement with the host state, dividing jurisdiction over them according to the connection of the act with duty, the place and nature of the offense, and other special conditions.

* In force for each United Nations member on date of its accession to the convention. Except for about 20 states, including the United States, all the United Nations members have acceded to the convention.

whomsoever held, shall be immune from search, requisition, confiscation, expropriation and any other form of interference, whether by executive, administrative, judicial or legislative action.

Section 4. The archives of the United Nations, and in general all documents belonging to it or held by it, shall be inviolable wherever located.

Section 5. Without being restricted by financial controls, regulations or moratoria of any kind,

(a) The United Nations may hold funds, gold or currency of any kind and operate accounts in any currency;

(b) The United Nations shall be free to transfer its funds, gold or currency from one country to another or within any country and to convert any currency held by it into any other currency.

Section 6. In exercising its rights under Section 5 above, the United Nations shall pay due regard to any representations made by the Government of any Member insofar as it is considered that effect can be given to such representations without detriment to the interests of the United Nations.

Section 7. The United Nations, its assets, income and other property shall be:

(a) Exempt from all direct taxes; it is understood, however, that the United Nations will not claim exemption from taxes which are, in fact, no more than charges for public utility services;

(b) Exempt from customs duties and prohibitions and restrictions on imports and exports in respect of articles imported or exported by the United Nations for its official use. It is understood, however, that articles imported under such exemption will not be sold in the country into which they were imported except under conditions agreed with the Government of that country;

(c) Exempt from customs duties and prohibitions and restrictions on imports and exports in respect of its publications.

Section 8. While the United Nations will not, as a general rule, claim exemption from excise duties and from taxes on the sale of movable and immovable property which form part of the price to be paid, nevertheless when the United Nations is making important purchases for official use of property on which such duties and taxes have been charged or are chargeable, Members will, whenever possible, make appropriate administrative arrangements for the remission or return of the amount of duty or tax.

Article III
Facilities in Respect of Communications

Section 9. The United Nations shall enjoy in the territory of each Member for its official communications treatment not less favourable than that accorded by the Government of that Member to any other Government including its diplomatic mission in the matter of priorities, rates and taxes on mails, cables, telegrams, radiograms, telephotos, telephone and other communications; and press rates for information to the press and radio. No censorship shall be applied to the official correspondence and other official communications of the United Nations.

Section 10. The United Nations shall have the right to use codes and to despatch and receive its correspondence by courier or in bags, which shall have the same immunities and privileges as diplomatic couriers and bags.

Article IV
The Representatives of Members

Section 11. Representatives of Members to the principal and subsidiary organs of the United Nations and to conferences convened by the United Nations, shall, while exercising their functions and during the journey to and from the place of meeting, enjoy the following privileges and immunities:

(a) Immunity from personal arrest or detention and from seizure of their personal baggage, and, in respect of words spoken or written and all acts done by them in their capacity as representatives, immunity from legal process of every kind;

(b) Inviolability for all papers and documents;

(c) The right to use codes and to receive papers or correspondence by courier or in sealed bags;

(d) Exemption in respect of themselves and their spouses from immigration restrictions, aliens registration or national service obligations in the state they are visiting or through which they are passing in the exercise of their functions;

(e) The same facilities in respect of currency or exchange restrictions as are accorded to representatives of foreign governments on temporary official missions;

(f) The same immunities and facilities in respect of their personal baggage as are accorded to diplomatic envoys, and also;

(g) Such other privileges, immunities and facilities not inconsistent with the foregoing as diplomatic envoys enjoy, except that they shall have no right to claim exemption from customs duties on goods imported (otherwise than as part of their personal baggage) or from excise duties or sales taxes.

Section 12. In order to secure, for the representatives of Members to the principal and subsidiary organs of the United Nations and to conferences convened by the United Nations, complete freedom of speech and independence in the discharge of their duties, the immunity from legal process in respect of words spoken or written and all acts done by them in discharging their duties shall continue to be accorded, notwithstanding that the persons concerned are no longer the representatives of Members.

Section 13. Where the incidence of any form of taxation depends upon residence, periods during which the representatives of Members to the principal and subsidiary organs of the United Nations and to conferences convened by the United Nations are present in a state for the discharge of their duties shall not be considered as periods of residence.

Section 14. Privileges and immunities are accorded to the representatives of Members not for the personal benefit of the individuals themselves, but in order to safeguard the independent exercise of their functions in connection with the United Nations. Consequently a Member not only has the right but is under a duty to waive the immunity of its representative in any case where in the opinion of the Member the immunity would impede the course of justice, and it can be waived without prejudice to the purpose for which the immunity is accorded.

Section 15. The provisions of Sections 11, 12 and 13 are not applicable as between a representative and the authorities of the state of which he is a national or of which he is or has been the representative.

Section 16. In this article the expression "representatives" shall be deemed to include all delegates, deputy delegates, advisers, technical experts and secretaries of delegations.

Article V
Officials

Section 17. The Secretary-General will specify the categories of officials to which the provisions of this Article and Article VII shall apply. He shall submit these categories to the General Assembly. Thereafter these categories shall be communicated to the Governments of all Members. The names of the officials included in these categories shall from time to time be made known to the Governments of Members.

Section 18. Officials of the United Nations shall:

(a) Be immune from legal process in respect of words spoken or written and all acts performed by them in their official capacity;

(b) Be exempt from taxation on the salaries and emoluments paid to them by the United Nations;

(c) Be immune from national service obligations;

(d) Be immune, together with their spouses and relatives dependent on them, from immigration restrictions and alien registration;

(e) Be accorded the same privileges in respect of exchange facilities as are accorded to the officials of comparable ranks forming part of diplomatic missions to the Government concerned;

(f) Be given, together with their spouses and relatives dependent on them, the same repatriation facilities in time of international crisis as diplomatic envoys;

(g) Have the right to import free of duty their furniture and effects at the time of first taking up their post in the country in question.

Section 19. In addition to the immunities and privileges specified in Section 18, the Secretary-General and all Assistant Secretaries-General shall be accorded in respect of themselves, their spouses and minor children, the privileges and immunities, exemptions and facilities accorded to diplomatic envoys, in accordance with international law.

Section 20. Privileges and immunities are granted to officials in the interests of the United Nations and not for the personal benefit of the individuals themselves. The Secretary-General shall have the right and the duty to waive the immunity of any official in any case where, in his opinion, the immunity would impede the course of justice and can be waived without prejudice to the interests of the United Nations. In the case of the Secretary-General, the Security Council shall have the right to waive immunity.

Section 21. The United Nations shall co-operate at all times with the appropriate authorities of Members to facilitate the proper administration of justice, secure the observance of police regulations and prevent the occurrence of any abuse in connection with the privileges, immunities and facilities mentioned in this Article.

* * *

Article VII
United Nations Laissez-Passer

Section 24. The United Nations may issue United Nations laissez-passer to its officials. These laissez-passer shall be recognized and accepted as valid travel documents by the authorities of Members, taking into account the provisions of Section 25.

Section 25. Applications for visas (where required) from the holders of United Nations laissez-passer, when accompanied by a certificate that they are travelling on the business of the United Nations, shall be dealt with as speedily as possible. In addition, such persons shall be granted facilities for speedy travel.

Section 26. Similar facilities to those specified in Section 25 shall be accorded to experts and other persons who, though not the holders of United Nations laissez-passer, have a certificate that they are travelling on the business of the United Nations.

Section 27. The Secretary-General, Assistant Secretaries-General and Directors travelling on United Nations laissez-passer on the business of the United Nations shall be granted the same facilities as are accorded to diplomatic envoys.

Section 28. The provisions of this article may be applied to the comparable officials of specialized agencies if the agreements for relationship made under Article 63 of the Charter so provide.

Article VIII
Settlements of Disputes

Section 29. The United Nations shall make provisions for appropriate modes of settlement of:

(a) Disputes arising out of contracts or other disputes of a private law character to which the United Nations is a party;

(b) Disputes involving any official of the United Nations who by reason of his official position enjoys immunity, if immunity has not been waived by the Secretary-General.

Section 30. All differences arising out of the interpretation or application of the present convention shall be referred to the International Court of Justice, unless in any case it is agreed by the parties to have recourse to another mode of settlement. If a difference arises between the United Nations on the one hand and a Member on the other hand, a request shall be made for an advisory opinion on any legal question involved in accordance with Article 96 of the Charter and Article 65 of the Statute of the Court. The opinion given by the Court shall be accepted as decisive by the parties.

* * *

U.S. v. MELEKH
United States District Court, 1960
190 F. Supp. 67

Herlands, District Judge

* * *

These proceedings seek the removal of the defendants Igor Y. Melekh and Willie Hirsch to the United States District Court for the Northern District of Illinois, Eastern Division, there to answer a three-count indictment (No. 60 Cr. 529) filed against them on October 27, 1960.

The Indictment against the Defendants

The first count of the indictment, hereinafter referred to as "the Illinois indictment," charges a conspiracy to violate Title 18 U.S.C.A. section 793. Part of the alleged conspiracy was to obtain information respecting the national defense of the United States of America by receiving and obtaining documents, sketches, photographs, maps and information concerning various places and military installations connected with the national defense, for the delivery to the Union of Soviet Socialist Republics, with the knowledge and intent that those materials would be used to the advantage of that foreign nation.

* * *

The defendants do not dispute the fact, independently established by the evidence, that they are the persons named as defendants in the Illinois indictment.

However, the defendant Melekh, interposing the claim of diplomatic immunity, resists the removal proceedings. According to the defense, this claim of diplomatic immunity has a double thrust: first, that Melekh's immunity renders the Illinois indictment void; second, that Melekh's immunity deprives this Court of jurisdiction, in the sense of power, to order his removal.

*　　*　　*

A statement of the material facts will sharpen the focus on the controlling issues of law.

*　　*　　*

The following is the complete text of the Soviet Ambassador's letter:

"EMBASSY OF THE
UNION OF SOVIET SOCIALIST REPUBLICS
"Washington 6, D.C.

"November 8, 1960

"The Honorable
District Judges of the U.S.
District Court for the
Southern District of New York

"Honorable Sirs:

"I hereby have the honor to draw your attention to the fact that the Soviet citizen, Igor Y. Melekh, has a diplomatic rank of the Second Secretary of the Ministry of Foreign Affairs of the USSR conferred on him in accordance with the provisions based on the Decree of the Presidium of the USSR Supreme Soviet of May 28, 1943.

"The Secretary General of the United Nations requested the Government of the USSR to make available the services of Mr. Melekh for the post of the Chief of the Russian language section in the office of Conference Services of the Secretariat of the UN and Mr. Melekh accepted this post with the knowledge and consent of the Government of the USSR.

"Mr. Melekh arrived in the United States on June 10, 1955, having the Soviet Diplomatic passport N 06211 and since that time has been attached to the Secretariat of the United Nations.

"The Secretariat of the United Nations and the Department of State of the United States at all these times had knowledge of and accepted the fact that Mr. Melekh retained and retains at the present time his diplomatic rank of the Second Secretary of the Ministry of Foreign Affairs of the USSR.

"(Signed) M. Menshikov
"Mikhail A. Menshikov
"Ambassador Extraordinary
and Plenipotentiary of the
USSR to the USA"

"(Seal)

Significantly, the Soviet Ambassador's letter does not state that Melekh was or is duly designated by the U.S.S.R. to serve as one of its representatives to the United Nations or that Melekh was or is on the staff of the

U.S.S.R. delegation to the United Nations or that Melekh ever performed or was ever assigned to perform any diplomatic duties in behalf of the U.S.S.R. vis-à-vis the Government of the United States or any other government while he was here.

On the contrary, the letter makes it unmistakably plain that, ever since his arrival in the United States on June 10, 1955, Melekh "has been attached to the Secretariat of the United Nations" in the capacity of "Chief of the Russian language section in the office of Conference Services of the Secretariat of the UN."

Melekh's Passport and the American Visas Therein

Melekh's non-representative status with respect to the U.S.S.R. in relation to the United Nations and his non-diplomatic status with respect to the U.S.S.R. in relation to the United States are also evidenced by the terms of the American visas in his passport. . . .

* * *

To recapitulate each of the six American visas were, on their face, designated as "Nonimmigrant Visa G–4," pursuant to 22 C.F.R. 41.5; and three of said visas carried the notation that Melekh was an "employee of the U.N. Secretariat."

* * *

The "types and validity of diplomatic visas," both "regular" and "limited" are governed by the provisions of 22 C.F.R. section 40.3(a) and (b). The "classes of aliens eligible to apply for diplomatic visas" of the "regular" type are defined and enumerated in 22 C.F.R. section 40.4(a), while those who are eligible to apply for "limited diplomatic visas" are defined and enumerated in 22 C.F.R. section 40.4(b).

The latter provision expressly *excludes* from its coverage "subordinate members, including employees" of any "international organizations so designated by Executive order.". . .

* * *

The U.S.S.R. has, of course, the unrestricted sovereign right, for its own internal purposes, to confer any diplomatic rank on Melekh or to give him a diplomatic passport. But, in the context of the pending proceedings, there is no legal significance to the purely incidental circumstance that Melekh was a Second Secretary of the Ministry of Foreign Affairs of the U.S.S.R. or that he arrived in the United States with a Soviet Diplomatic passport.

The salient and uncontradicted facts are that, at all material times, Melekh came here in a nondiplomatic capacity and worked exclusively in a nondiplomatic capacity; that his official activities here were exclusively as a United Nations employee; that he is not a public minister of a foreign state, authorized and received as such by the President, nor a domestic or domestic servant of one (cf. 22 U.S.C.A. sections 252, 254); that he did not enter the United States as an emissary from the U.S.S.R. to the United States and he was never received as such; that he was never notified to the United States as attached to the Soviet Embassy; that he was never accredited as a foreign diplomatic officer to any other government or to any international conference; and that he was never a member of the Soviet Delegation to the United Nations.

*   *   *

The general diplomatic immunity statute, Title 22 U.S.C.A. section 252, reads in pertinent part as follows:

"Whenever any writ or process is sued out or prosecuted by any person in any court of the United States, . . . whereby the person of any ambassador or public minister of any foreign prince or State, authorized and received as such by the President, . . . is arrested or imprisoned, . . . such writ or process shall be deemed void."

The word "minister," as used in the above provision, is given a functional definition by Title 22 U.S.C.A. section 178, which expressly declares:

"The word 'minister,' when used in sections . . . 251–258, . . . of this title, . . . shall be understood to mean the person invested with, and exercising, the principal diplomatic functions . . ."

The State Department's duly authenticated certificate (Exh. 1) reads as follows:

*   *   *

"I have caused diligent search to be made of such records and have found no record to exist that Mr. Igor Y. Melekh, a Soviet national employed by the United Nations Secretariat, is, or ever has been, notified to and recognized by the Department of State in any capacity which would entitle him to diplomatic immunity pursuant to the above-mentioned Sections 252–254.

"I further certify that the only records ever received in the Office of Protocol regarding the said Mr. Melekh showed him to be an employee of the United Nations Secretariat, in which capacity he was entitled to immunity from suit and legal process only with respect to acts performed by him in his official capacity falling within his functions as an employee of the United Nations, as provided in Section 288d(b) of Title 22 of the United States Code.

"Signed this fourth day of November, 1960, at Washington, D.C.

"(Signed) *H. Charles Spruks*
"H. Charles Spruks
"Acting Chief of Protocol"

Melekh's attorney expressly disavows any claim of immunity under Title 22 U.S.C.A. sections 252–254. In his reply memorandum (pp. 2, 10) he states:

"The defendant does not claim that he is entitled to diplomatic immunity under this Statute. Nor is it necessary that he should do so. He is entitled to diplomatic immunity by virtue of the Law of Nations (International Law) which is also the Law of the United States. . . ."

*   *   *

This disclaimer of possible immunity under Title 22 U.S.C.A. section 252 is defendant's unavoidable concession to the manifest fact that he was not a Soviet diplomat accredited to and received by the Government of the United States. If he were, he would have received complete immunity.

*   *   *

In 1945, Congress enacted the International Organizations Immunities Act (Title 22 U.S.C.A. sections 288–288 f, Public Law 291, chapter 652, 79th Cong., 1st Session 1945). . . .

*   *   *

However, section 288d(b), relating to immunity from suit and legal process, provides that representatives, employees, and officers of international organizations have immunity only with respect to "acts performed by them in their official capacity and falling within their functions as such representatives, officers, or employees." This provision does not confer general diplomatic status or immunity. . . .

*   *   *

Defendant's attorney does not assert immunity under the International Organizations Immunities Act of 1945, which has been rendered applicable to United Nations officers and employees. In his reply brief (p. 10), referring to that statute, defendant's attorney states: ". . . we respectfully submit (1) That the defendant has not made an assertion of immunity on the ground of this Statute; . . ."

This disclaimer of possible immunity under the International Organizations Immunities Act can mean only that the defendant does not argue that the alleged criminal acts, as charged in the indictment, grew out of or were incidental to his official activities as a United Nations officer or employee. If the charged acts had been ancillary to his United Nations functions, the defendant would have received complete immunity under the International Organizations Immunities Act.

*   *   *

On June 26, 1947, the United States and the United Nations entered into an agreement commonly called "the Headquarters Agreement." This agreement, signed on June 26, 1947 and covered by a joint resolution of August 4, 1947, authorized the President to effectuate the agreement. The agreement was approved on August 4, 1947. . . .

*   *   *

Under the above provisions of the Headquarters Agreement, diplomatic immunity is granted to four categories of representatives of member nations of the United Nations. However, the defendant cannot avail himself of the Headquarters Agreement. He is not the principal resident representative of a member; nor is he a resident representative with the rank of ambassador or minister plenipotentiary; nor is he a resident member of the staff of one of the aforementioned emissaries; nor does defendant come within any of the other categories of individuals granted immunity under the Headquarters Agreement.

*   *   *

The Headquarters Agreement did not confer the immunities of accredited diplomatic envoys upon officers and employees of the United Nations, as they are not mentioned in the Headquarters Agreement. Consequently, the immunity enjoyed by officers and employees of the United Nations—as distinguished from the four categories of resident representatives to the United Nations—are those that are defined in the International Organizations Immunities Act. And, as noted, the immunity provisions of the International Organizations Immunities Act sets up a functional test of immunity.

*   *   *

The foregoing analysis reveals that the defendant's position embraces these negative features: (1) the defendant does not claim that he was or is a diplomatic officer accredited to the United States or to any other government; (2) the defendant does not claim that the acts charged against him in the indictment were, directly or remotely, related to the functions of his United Nations employment; and (3) the defendant does not claim that he was a representative of the U.S.S.R. to the United Nations or a member of the staff of a U.S.S.R. representative to the United Nations. What, then, does the defendant affirmatively offer as the sources of his claimed diplomatic immunity?

The two bases offered are: Article 105 of the United Nations Charter and the uncodified, general principles of international law.

*   *   *

Under Article 105(2) of the United Nations Charter, the United States has an obligation to provide the representatives of member nations and the officials of the United Nations with such privileges and immunities as are "necessary" for the independent exercise of their "functions in connection with the (United Nations) Organization."

*   *   *

The privileges and immunities to be enjoyed by representatives of the members of the United Nations and by officials of the United Nations itself are by the very terms of Article 105 qualified and conditioned. Their privileges and immunities are those that "are necessary for the independent exercise of their functions in connection with the Organization." As expressly formulated by the United Nations Charter, the immunity is limited and specifically functional in scope and character. It is not the unlimited and unqualified immunity traditionally given to diplomats.

* * *

Putting aside the federal statutes (i.e., the general diplomatic immunities statute, the International Organizations Immunities Act of 1945, and the Headquarters Agreement of 1947) and the United Nations Charter, Article 105—the defendant seeks to establish his right to immunity by virtue of the Law of Nations.

There can be no dispute about the proposition that American courts are bound to recognize and apply the Law of Nations as part of the law of the land. . . .

* * *

The certificate of the Department of State (Exh. 1) states "that the only records ever received in the Office of Protocol regarding the said Mr. Melekh showed him to be an employee of the United Nations Secretariat." But aside from that certificate, all the other evidence in the record (including the Soviet Ambassador's letter, the American visas in the defendant's passport, and factual oral and written statements made in behalf of the defendant) shows that the relationship between the defendant himself and the United Nations was only that of employee and employer, not that of a Member State's representative to the United Nations and not that of a functioning diplomatic officer.

The defendant's main memorandum of law (p. 3) states:

"The passport *and visa* under which Mr. Melekh entered the United States reflected his claim and the claim of his government that he enjoys diplomatic status. . . ." (Emphasis supplied.)

This statement is factually erroneous, as the visas themselves show.

It is neither the defendant's position with his own government, as such, nor the relationship of the defendant's government, as such, with the United Nations that is decisive. What counts is the actual position occupied by the defendant in the United Nations and his actual duties and functions in the United Nations. Regardless of the significance of the defendant's lack of accreditation to the United States or to any other nation, and judged by the criteria established by the Law of Nations, the defendant was not a diplomatic agent when he entered the United States.

* * *

Inasmuch as the defendant did not enter the United States in 1955 or thereafter to date as a diplomatic officer and he has not been performing diplomatic functions or activities *de facto* or *de jure* in the United States, he is not entitled to diplomatic immunity under the general principles of international law—even if it be assumed *arguendo* that the specific and limited immunities provisions of Article 105 of the United Nations Charter and of the federal statutes are not dispositive of the defendant's claim.

*   *   *

The problem of the privileges and immunities of international organizations and of their officials and employees is one phase of the modern Law of Nations. The immunities of the personnel of international organizations have evolved out of a two-fold interacting process. That process has operated by analogy to the traditional concepts of diplomatic and parliamentary immunities and by recognition of the vital importance of the independent functioning of international organizations and their personnel in order to achieve their objectives.

Article 105 of the United Nations Charter and the implementing statutes represented by the International Organizations Immunities Act of 1945 and the Headquarters Agreement of 1947 are the specific legal expression and concrete projection of that process in action.

The United Nations Charter, the federal statutes, the Common Law of Nations have been given a broad and liberal application by the Court in this case. . . .

Despite that latitudinarian interpretation, the Court must conclude that the applicable provisions of law do not confer immunity upon the defendant Melekh with respect to the acts charged in the indictment. His claim of immunity is overruled and rejected.

Jurisdiction over the defendant Melekh and the co-defendant Hirsch and the subject-matter of these proceedings is vested in this Court.

Both defendants are ordered removed to the Northern District of Illinois.*

*   *   *

---

* At the request of the Attorney General of the United States, to better U.S.–U.S.S.R. relations, the charges against Melekh were dropped by the Illinois Court on 24 March 1961, on condition that Melekh leave the country, which he did on 7 April 1961. Charges against Hirsch were also dismissed.

LUTCHER, S. A., v. INTER-AMERICAN DEVELOPMENT BANK
United States District Court for the District of Columbia, 1966
5 International Legal Materials 480

Gasch, Judge

This cause came on for hearing on plaintiffs' motion for preliminary injunction and defendant's motion to dismiss. Plaintiffs seek to enjoin the Inter-American Development Bank from augmenting a loan to one of plaintiffs' competitors. The loan would facilitate the development of a pulp mill in Brazil. Plaintiffs are engaged in a similar business and contend that the market will not support two mills. Plaintiffs further contend that the Bank has ignored certain alleged market conditions and that if consummated, the additional loan to plaintiffs' competitor would not be a prudent act.

Defendant's motion to dismiss is predicated upon two points: (1) the Bank is immune from suit, such as the one filed in the instant case; and (2) the complaint does not state a claim upon which relief can be granted. . . .

The International Organizations Immunities Act provides, in part:

International organizations, their property and their assets, wherever located, and by whomsoever held, shall enjoy the same immunity from suit in every form of judicial process as is enjoyed by foreign governments, except to the extent that such organizations may expressly waive their immunity for the purpose of any proceedings or by the terms of any contract.

An Executive Order of President Eisenhower dated April 8, 1960, designated the Inter-American Development Bank as a public international organization which would be entitled to the immunities and exemptions flowing from the above-quoted statute. A subsequent Executive Order promulgated by President Kennedy provided that the first Executive Order should not be construed as affecting a certain provision of the Bank's Charter, which provides:

Actions may be brought against the Bank only in a court of competent jurisdiction in the territories of a member in which the Bank has an office, has appointed an agent for the purpose of accepting service or notice of process, or has issued or guaranteed securities.

No action shall be brought against the Bank by members or persons acting for or deriving claims from members. However, member countries shall have recourse to such special procedures to settle controversies between the Bank and its members as may be prescribed in this Agreement, in the by-laws and regulations of the Bank or in contracts entered into with the Bank.

Property and assets of the Bank shall, wheresoever located and by whomsoever held, be immune from all forms of seizure, attachment or execution before the delivery of final judgment against the Bank.

These pronouncements of executive policy and the Bank's position on its amenability to suit should be considered as important factors relating to the existence of jurisdiction of this Court in the instant case.

. . . Plaintiff argues that the Bank has been sued in previous situations: where a customer fell on the floor, where there was an alleged breach of a contractual relationship with a coffee shop, and where workmen's compensation was involved. However, situations comparable to the one in which the Court is confronted are clearly distinguishable for the reason that cases involving the discretion and judgment of the Bank's governing board in matters of economic policy closely associated with consideration of international politics are vastly different from cases involving simple torts and contracts. Where delicate, complex issues of international economic policy are involved, jurisdiction should be denied.

Assuming *arguendo* that this Court does have jurisdiction, it is highly questionable whether even a domestic bank could properly be sued by one of two competing customers who alleged that the Bank had imprudently loaned money to the second customer and thereby made more difficult the customer's obligation to respond. Here, it is clear that the situation with which the Court is confronted in this complaint is even more lacking in merit in the judicial sense. Plaintiffs' standing to raise the issues on which they rely is by no means established irrespective of the foreign policy consideration. . . .

Plaintiffs have failed to demonstrate irreparable injury or the probability of ultimate success.

Although counsel for the Bank has not raised the question of an indispensable party, nevertheless, the Court notes that the competing customer (the Klabin group) is not before the Court. This familiar doctrine alone would preclude the taking of such action as is sought by the plaintiffs. . . .

For these reasons, plantiffs' motion for preliminary injunction should be and is denied, and defendant's motion to dismiss is granted.

FOR FURTHER STUDY

Kuljit Ahluwalia. *The Legal Status, Privileges and Immunities of the Specialized Agencies of the United Nations and Certain Other International Organizations.* The Hague: Martinus Nijhoff, 1964.

Joseph M. Sweeney. *The International Law of Sovereign Immunity.* Washington, D.C.: U.S. Government Printing Office, 1963.

C. Wilfred Jenks. *International Immunities.* London: Oceana Publications, 1961.

Sompong Sucharitkul. *State Immunities and Trading Activities.* New York: Frederick A. Praeger, Inc., 1959.

IX

International Claims: Personal Injuries and War Damages

I N every state of the world, aliens must obey the local laws. Reciprocally, every state is expected to provide security and justice, *compatible with those laws*, for the person and property of the alien. Additional rights may be due an alien either through treaties to which the state of his residence and the state of his nationality are parties, or under general principles of international law.

If a wrong (*tort*) is done to an alien by an individual in a state—his body harmed by negligence, his property damaged by trespass, or his reputation wounded by slander—then his recourse for obtaining compensation lies with the local administrative or judicial processes. This has nothing to do with international law. Administrative manners and judicial opinions in that state may be completely different from those the alien would expect in the state of his nationality. But so long as it *is* the local law being applied to all—to nationals and aliens alike, without distinction—he has no further complaint.

Suppose, however, that the police officials who arrest an alien manhandle him in a way contrary to the tenets of the local law, and his protests receive no hearing whatsoever. Suppose that a judge requires of an alien an exorbitant amount of bail and conducts his trial with manifest prejudice and disregard of all the procedural safeguards clearly provided by the local law, while all appeals to any higher administrative or judicial review are denied. In such instances, the state itself, through its agents, may be guilty of wrongful conduct toward the alien, which *is* a matter of international law. The state of the alien's nationality may then take up his case and claim compensation for the injury.

343

In 1924, the Permanent Court of International Justice held:

It is an elementary principle of international law that a state is entitled to protect its subjects, when injured by acts contrary to international law committed by another state, from whom they have been unable to obtain satisfaction through the ordinary channels. By taking up the case as one of its subjects and by resorting to diplomatic action or international judicial proceedings on his behalf, a state is in reality asserting its own rights—its right to ensure in the person of its subjects, respect for international law.[1]

This aspect of international law has frequently been referred to as the international responsibility of states. It rests on the premise that states are bound by customary international law, if not actual treaty obligations, to follow a minimum standard of justice toward an alien and his property. Under international law, a state maintains an interest in and a concern for its nationals, whether they are resident or nonresident. As a protection for its nationals, a state may espouse their claims against other states when a denial of justice is manifest.

Lack of Diligent Protection

Considerable numbers of international claims have arisen in the past over the wrongful conduct of one state toward the nationals of another state. Some of the charges have been violent and unwarranted acts by police officials, others have alleged mean and degrading imprisonment, still others have complained about a lack of justice by the state in prosecuting and adjudging the wrongdoers. In 1891, for illustration, 11 men of Italian birth who had been charged with involvement in the murder of the chief of police of New Orleans, Louisiana, were killed by a mob that attacked the jail. In protest, the Italian government withdrew its minister, demanded of the United States (not Louisiana) official assurance that the guilty parties would be brought to trial, and called for recognition that an indemnity was due the relatives. Eventually, Congress passed an act giving to the federal district courts original jurisdiction for civil action by aliens for torts committed in violation of international law or United States treaties, and the United States paid a $24,330.90 indemnity to Italy.

To be liable for a claim, a state must commit or omit with respect to an alien an action for which it has responsibility as a sovereign governmental entity. Thus, a state is not responsible for a private wrong inflicted by one of its nationals on a resident alien, but only for its duty to arrest, try, and punish wrongdoers. A state may be held responsible for the actions of its officials, especially for their abuse of power; states have sometimes dis-

---

[1] *Mavrommatis Palestine Concessions Case*, P.C.I.J., Series A, No. 2 (1924).

claimed legal liability for wrongful conduct against an individual, yet have indemnified the family of a deceased resident alien as an act of grace.

Moroever, in all matters of security for aliens a state normally cannot be expected to give greater protection to an alien than it gives to its own nationals; a state is merely required under international law to use "due diligence" in providing for the security of the person and property of the alien. For instance, when an American superintendent of a mine in Mexico was killed by a body of armed men, the General Claims Commission clearly felt that Mexico could have used better methods in apprehending and punishing the culprits; but the state's delinquency was not such that it amounted to

. . . outrage, bad faith, willful neglect of duty, or to an insufficiency of governmental action so far short of international standards that every reasonable and impartial man would readily recognize its insufficiency and, therefore, the Commission rejected the claim.[2]

Although case law and claims arbitration proceedings do not provide a very wide coverage of the subject of diligent protection for aliens by a host state, it is a lively issue, frequently involving diplomatic protests. For example, in 1966, in line with a change of government policy, many "demonstrations" against the resident Chinese took place in Indonesia. In a strong note of 25 April 1966, Peking alleged: that mobs armed with clubs, knives, and axes broke into Chinese homes, beating young and old, women and children, causing death and injury; that under a pretext of protection, the Chinese were transported forcibly to a prison and county assembly hall; that the evacuated Chinese homes and shops were systematically looted by both the local government and mobs. The Chinese Embassy, representing the People's Republic of China, demanded not only release of the detained Chinese but also punishment of the culprits and payment of indemnities for personal and property losses. Whatever the outcome, the Peking government, acting like other governments, was outraged by what it called a gross violation of principles of international relations.

The document that follows (the *Janes* case) illustrates a denial of justice to an alien by a state.

---

[2] Opinions of the Commissioners (1927), *United States (Neer Claim)* v. *Mexico*, p. 71.

UNITED STATES (LAURA B. JANES) v. MEXICO
General Claims Commission, 1926
1927 Opinions of Commissioners 108

*   *   *

Byron Everett Janes, for some time prior to and until the time of his death on July 10, 1918, was Superintendent of Mines for the El Tigre Mining Company at El Tigre. On or about July 10, 1918, he was deliberately shot and killed at this place by Pedro Carbajal, a former employee of the Mining Company who had been discharged. The killing took place in the view of many persons resident in the vicinity of the company's office. The local police *Comisario* was informed of Janes' death within five minutes of the commission of the crime and arrived soon thereafter at the place where the shooting occurred. He delayed for half an hour in assembling his policemen and insisted that they should be mounted. The El Tigre Mining Company furnished the necessary animals and the posse, after the lapse of more than an hour from the time of the shooting, started in pursuit of Carbajal, who had departed on foot. The posse failed to apprehend the fugitive. Carbajal remained at a ranch six miles south of El Tigre for a week following the shooting, and it was rumored at El Tigre that he came to that place on two occasions during his stay at the ranch. Subsequently information was received that Carbajal was at a mescal plant near Carrizal, about seventy-five miles south of El Tigre. This information was communicated to Mexican civil and military authorities, who failed to take any steps to apprehend Carbajal, until the El Tigre Mining Company offered a reward, whereupon a local military commander was induced to send a small detachment to Carrizal, which, upon its return, reported that Carbajal had been in this locality but had left before the arrival of the detachment, and that it was therefore impossible to apprehend him.

*   *   *

Carbajal, the person who killed Janes, was well known in the community where the killing took place. Numerous persons witnessed the deed. The slayer, after killing his victim, left on foot. There is evidence that a Mexican police magistrate was informed of the shooting within five minutes after it took place. The official records with regard to the action taken to apprehend and punish the slayer speak for themselves. Eight years have elapsed since the murder, and it does not appear from the records that Carbajal has been apprehended at this time. Our conclusions to the effect that the Mexican authorities did not take proper steps to apprehend and punish the slayer of Janes is based on the record before us consisting of evidence produced by both Governments. . . .

*   *   *

A reasoning based on presumed complicity may have some sound foundation in cases of nonprevention where a government knows of an *intended* injurious crime, might have averted it, but for some reason constituting its liability did not do so. The present case is different; it is one of nonrepression. Nobody contends either that the Mexican Government might have prevented the murder of Janes, or that it acted in any other form of connivance with the murderer. The international delinquency in this case is one of its own specific type, separate from the private delinquency of the culprit. The culprit is liable for having killed or murdered an American national; the Government is liable for not having measured up to its duty of diligently prosecuting and properly punishing the offender. The culprit has transgressed the penal code of his country; the State, so far from having transgressed its own penal code (which perhaps is not even applicable to it), has transgressed a provision of international law as to State duties. The culprit can not be sentenced in criminal or civil procedure unless his guilt or intention in causing the victim's death is proven; the Government can be sentenced once the nonperformance of its judicial duty is proven to amount to an international delinquency, the theories on guilt or intention in criminal and civil law not being applicable here. The damage caused by the culprit is the damage caused to Janes' relatives by Janes' death; the damage caused by the Government's negligence is the damage resulting from the nonpunishment of the murderer. . . .

*   *   *

. . . Denial of justice, in its broader sense, may cover even acts of the executive and the legislative; in cases of improper governmental action of this type, a nation is never held to be liable for anything else than the damage caused by what the executive or legislative committed or omitted itself. In cases of denial of justice in its narrower sense, Governments again are held responsible exclusively for what they commit or omit themselves. Only in the event of one type of denial of justice, the present one, a State would be liable not for what it committed or omitted itself, but for what an individual did. Such an exception to the general rule is not admissible but for convincing reasons. These reasons, as far as the Commission knows, never were given. One reason doubtless lies in the well-known tendency of Governments (Hyde, I, p. 515; Ralston, 1926, p. 267) to claim exaggerated reparations for nonpunishment of wrongdoers, a tendency which found its most promising help in a theory advocating that the negligent State had to make good all of the damage caused by the crime itself. . . .

. . . It would seem a fallacy to sustain that, if in case of nonpunishment by the Government it is not liable for the crime itself, then it can only be responsible, in a punitive way, to a sister Government, not to a claimant. There again, the solution in other cases of improper governmental action shows the way out. It shows that, apart from reparation or compensation for material losses, claimants always have been given substantial satisfaction for serious dereliction of duty on the part of a Government; and this world-wide international practice was before the Governments of the United States and Mexico when they framed the Convention concluded September 8, 1923. . . . The indignity done the relative of Janes by nonpunishment in the present case is, as that in other cases of improper governmental action, a damage directly caused to an individual by a Government. . . .

As to the measure of such a damage caused by the delinquency of a Government, the nonpunishment, it may be readily granted that its computation is more difficult and uncertain than that of the damage caused by the killing itself. The two delinquencies being different in their origin, character, and effect, the measure of damages for which the Government should be liable can not be computed by merely stating the damages caused by the private delinquency of Carbajal. But a computation of this character is not more difficult than computations in other cases of denial of justice such as illegal encroachment on one's liberty, harsh treatment in jail, insults and menaces of prisoners, or even nonpunishment of the perpetrator of a crime which is not an attack on one's property or one's earning capacity, for instance a dangerous assault or an attack on one's reputation and honor. Not only the individual grief of the claimants should be taken into account, but a reasonable and substantial redress should be made for the mistrust and lack of safety, resulting from the Government's attitude. . . .

Giving careful consideration to all elements involved, the Commission holds that an amount of $12,000, without interest, is not excessive as satisfaction for the personal damage caused the claimants by the nonapprehension and nonpunishment of the murderer of Janes.

War Damages

In a sense, the idea of war damages due from states under international law owes its origin to the concept of wrongful conduct. Before World War I, states were liable for "illegal" acts of war. Under the 1907 Hague Convention on Land War, distinctions were drawn between acts required by military necessity and acts by which a state violated the rules of land warfare, such as the confiscation of enemy private property not connected with military operations.

These distinctions have not been entirely lost in contemporary rules of warfare. But considering the ferocity of World War I and World War II, as well as modern strategic planning that contemplates the destruction of a population's will to fight by leveling its cities, its factories, its communications, and every other national energy, the distinctions between public and private, military necessity and "illegal" acts of war, even human and inhuman tactics, seem terribly blurred. International law on this subject has been overtaken by the problem of outlawing international war itself, a subject discussed more fully in Section XI. In short, however, international conflicts still take place even with the United Nations Charter, and civil wars also require legal guidance for adjusting claims after hostilities cease. Even if the violence of the future should lie between an international police force and a state, the legal problem of compensating individuals for their incidental and unjust losses must be met.

The World War I and World War II practice was to force the defeated states to accept responsibility for all losses or damages caused to the Allied Powers or their nationals. Article 231 of the Treaty of Versailles read,

The Allied and Associated Governments affirm and Germany accepts the responsibility of Germany and her allies for causing all the loss and damage to which the Allied and Associated Governments and their nationals have been subjected. . . .

By Article 439, the Allied and Associated governments made Germany renounce any pecuniary claim against them based upon events before the Treaty of Versailles. In 1922, an agreement between Germany and the United States (which did not ratify the Versailles Treaty) established a Mixed Claims Commission, composed of an American, a German, and a neutral in event of disagreement. The commission did not inquire into the legality or illegality of the war acts for which Germany had accepted responsibility. By 1941, something over $150 million had been awarded and paid to private American claimants.

The post-World War II treaties with Italy, the East European States, and Finland in 1947, and with Japan in 1951 continued the practice of having the vanquished state renounce all its claims incidental to the hostilities. Moreover, in the Allied Powers' assessment of reparations or indemnities against the defeated states little or no attention was paid to whether the damage was caused by essential military action or exceptional war measures. In their terms, the peace treaties fixed the responsibility for war claims and provided very broad guidelines for their definition and adjustment at the expense of the vanquished.

The 1947 treaties provided for "conciliation commissions"—essentially, three-man international arbitral boards—to deal with property claims, but such commissions functioned only between Italy and four Allied Powers, including the United States. In 1948, the United States created a national War Claims Commission to receive and decide American war claims against Germany and Japan, especially for military and civilian personnel who had been interned as prisoners or held in concentration camps. Funds to pay the approved claims came from German and Japanese property that had been held by the Alien Property Custodian in the United States. In 1960 and 1963, the United States signed agreements with Rumania and Bulgaria, respectively, on lump-sum settlements of outstanding American claims for war damages as well as for nationalization, compulsory liquidation, or other taking of property. The funds amounted to over $28 million; approximately $25 million came from Rumanian and Bulgarian blocked assets in the United States, and the balance was paid by the two states to the United States.

The following document, certain articles from the *Italian Peace Treaty* of 1947, deals with war damages.

ITALIAN PEACE TREATY
War Claims Settlement, 10 February 1947
T.I.A.S. No. 1648

*　　　*　　　*

Article 76

1. Italy waives all claims of any description against the Allied and Associated Powers on behalf of the Italian Government or Italian nationals arising directly out of the war or out of actions taken because of the existence of a state of war in Europe after September 1, 1939, whether or not the Allied or Associated Power was at war with Italy at the time, including the following:

(a) Claims for losses or damages sustained as a consequence of acts of forces or authorities of Allied or Associated Powers;

(b) Claims arising from the presence, operations, or actions of forces or authorities of Allied or Associated Powers in Italian territory;

(c) Claims with respect to the decrees or orders of Prize Courts of Allied or Associated Powers, Italy agreeing to accept as valid and binding all decrees and orders of such Prize Courts on or after September 1, 1939, concerning Italian ships or Italian goods or the payment of costs;

(d) Claims arising out of the exercise or purported exercise of belligerent rights.

2. The provisions of this Article shall bar, completely and finally, all claims of the nature referred to herein, which will be henceforward extinguished, whoever may be the parties in interest. The Italian Government agrees to make equitable compensation in lire to persons who furnished supplies or services on requisition to the forces of Allied or Associated Powers in Italian territory and in satisfaction of non-combat damage claims against the forces of Allied or Associated Powers arising in Italian territory. . . .

*   *   *

Article 78

1. In so far as Italy has not already done so, Italy shall restore all legal rights and interests in Italy of the United Nations and their nationals as they existed on June 10, 1940, and shall return all property in Italy of the United Nations and their nationals as it now exists. . . .

*   *   *

(4) (a) The Italian Government shall be responsible for the restoration to complete good order of the property returned to United Nations nationals under paragraph 1 of this Article. In cases where property cannot be returned or where, as a result of the war, a United Nations national has suffered a loss by reason of injury or damage to property in Italy, he shall receive from the Italian Government compensation in lire to the extent of two-thirds of the sum necessary, at the date of payment, to purchase similar property or to make good the loss suffered. In no event shall United Nations nationals receive less favourable treatment with respect to compensation than that accorded to Italian nationals.

(b) United Nations nationals who hold, directly or indirectly, ownership interests in corporations or associations which are not United Nations nationals within the meaning of paragraph 9(a) of this Article, but which have suffered a loss by reason of injury or damage to property in Italy, shall receive compensation in accordance with sub-paragraph (a) above. This compensation shall be calculated on the basis of the total loss or damage suffered by the corporation or association and shall bear the same proportion to such loss or damage as the beneficial interests of such nationals in the corporation or association bear to the total capital thereof. . . .

* * *

9. As used in this Article:

(a) "United Nations nationals" means individuals who are nationals of any of the United Nations, or corporations or associations organized under the laws of any of the United Nations, at the coming into force of the present Treaty, provided that the said individuals, corporations or associations also had this status on September 3, 1943, the date of the Armistice with Italy. The term "United Nations nationals" also includes all individuals, corporations or associations which, under the laws in force in Italy during the war, have been treated as enemy;

* * *

(c) "Property" means all movable or immovable property, whether tangible or intangible, including industrial, literary and artistic property, as well as all rights of interests of any kind in property. . . .

* * *

Article 79

1. Each of the Allied and Associated Powers shall have the right to seize, retain, liquidate, or take any other action with respect to all property, rights and interests which on the coming into force of the present Treaty are within its territory and belong to Italy or to Italian nationals, and to apply such property or the proceeds thereof to such purposes as it may desire, within the limits of its claims and those of its nationals against Italy or Italian nationals, including debts, other than claims fully satisfied under other Articles of the present Treaty. All Italian property, or the proceeds thereof, in excess of the amount of such claims, shall be returned.

* * *

Procedures on International Claims

Although an injury, in fact, is done by a state to the alien himself or to his property through wrongful conduct, breach of contract, war, or expropriation, when a state takes up the claim of its national the state itself becomes the party to the controversy, and the dispute falls under the principles and rules of international law.

Nothing, except its own public policy, requires a state to espouse the claims of its nationals abroad. Ordinarily, it will not rush in to protect its subjects in respect to alleged violations of international law by another state unless it is satisfied: (*a*) that the individual appealing for diplomatic protection is one of its nationals from the time of injury to the time of presenting a claim; (*b*) that the alleged grievance either involves some act or some omission on the part of the foreign state contrary to its own laws, or violates general principles of international law, or seems outrageous to the minimal standards of justice and humanity; (*c*) that all local remedies have been exhausted.

The requirement that all local remedies must be exhausted stems from the need to satisfy the condition under international law that there has been a denial of justice to the alien, which gives his state a right to protect him. So long as remedies under the local laws exist and have not been tried, such as an appeal to a higher court of the state or a request for executive interposition, the possibility of righting the wrong exists, and an international claim cannot be justified. As the Commission of Arbitration established by Great Britain and Greece declared:

> These "local remedies" include not only reference to the courts and tribunals, but also the use of the procedural facilities which municipal law makes available to litigants before such courts and tribunals. It is the whole system of legal protection, as provided by municipal law, which must have been put to the test before a State, as the protector of its nationals, can prosecute the claim on the International plane.[3]

The rule cannot be strained so that any omission of any local remedy would negate a claim, and the rule cannot be rigorously applied with all states, since the requirement of exhausting local remedies in certain communist or other totalitarian states would be useless.

The procedure for asserting and settling international claims has never been static. Rapidly changing political and economic conditions have influenced legal procedures. However, after more than a century of international claims by states on behalf of their nationals there still exists

---

[3] *Ambatielos Claim,* 12 Reports of International Arbitral Awards 120 (1951).

no international tribunal to which individuals have access for this purpose.

Traditionally, the alien's procedure in claiming damages has been a request to his state to espouse his claim, to represent his private grievance as a public international complaint. The multiplication of claims, coupled to the obvious awkwardness and delay of governmental intervention in private matters, led to a more sensible use of *mixed claims commissions*, composed of the nationals of two states with claims against each other and, very often, the national of a third, neutral, state.

In 1794, the United States inaugurated the procedure of establishing mixed claims commissions in the Jay Treaty with Great Britain, often referred to as the beginning of modern international arbitration. Many other mixed claims commissions have been established through special agreements and treaties of peace. Two are the already-mentioned Mixed Claims Commission for the United States and Germany to decide war damage claims of American nationals after World War I, and the Conciliation Commission established between Italy and the United States after World War II. Other illustrations are the General Claims Commission between Mexico and the United States, created under a convention signed in 1923, to settle any outstanding claims for injury to their nationals since 1868, and the United States–Japanese Property Commission established in 1952.

The many mixed claims commissions, boards, or tribunals over the past 150 years have helped to clarify and develop the international law of state responsibility and claims. But such mixed arbitral bodies have not been without drawbacks. Better than a diplomatic negotiation for each individual claim, they nevertheless suffer from the delays of mixed languages and mixed systems of law, as well as the often contentious nature of commissioners who represent a national viewpoint. Moreover, when an agreement on the damages has finally been reached by a mixed claims commission, board, or tribunal, the actual payment may have to wait for further diplomatic negotiation and enabling legislation of the national congress or assembly.

As early as 1803, the United States accepted a lump-sum payment from France to settle a group of claims. The money was distributed to Americans through a *national claims commission*. Such commissions, established by the state itself and consisting of its own officials, receive and decide the claims of its nationals. Payment is then made to the individuals or corporations by the state from the lump sum already granted to it by the foreign state as a final settlement for all outstanding claims. In recent years, most of these international claims have been for the expropriation of private property, which will be discussed in further detail in Section X.

National claims commissions are quasi-judicial bodies. In deciding claims put before them, they will consider the provisions of the applicable claims agreement between their own state and the foreign state, and they will generally endeavor to apply principles of international law, justice, and equity. The advantage of a prompt and final settlement for the claimant through his own national claims commission is manifest but not guaranteed, for he must be able to justify the damages he seeks.

The Foreign Claims Settlement Commission, consisting of three men appointed by the President with the advice and consent of the Senate, is the permanent national claims commission of the United States. Established in 1954 and consolidating the work of the previous International Claims Commission and War Claims Commission, the Foreign Claims Settlement Commission has dealt with hundreds of thousands of claims amounting to more than $500 million. Claims have arisen out of World War II and from the nationalization of American properties abroad by such countries as Yugoslavia, Bulgaria, Rumania, Poland, and Cuba.

The use of mixed commissions, which helps to create a sounder international legal order, has not been abandoned by the United States. In 1965, for example, jurisdiction for the settlement of claims between the United States and Canada for the construction and removal (50 years later) of the Gut Dam in the St. Lawrence River was taken from the Foreign Claims Settlement Commission and given to a three-man Lake Ontario Claims Tribunal created by an agreement between Canada and the United States. In any case, the problem for international law is to reach a fair and prompt settlement for injuries suffered by aliens where a state is responsible and a denial of justice has occurred. The device of direct diplomatic espousal, mixed commissions, or national commissions with lump-sum settlements will probably be dictated by political exigencies.

In the documents that follow, (*a*) *American Claims Arising Out of World War II* contains a detailed statement by the chairman of the Foreign Settlement Claims Commission on war claims legislation; (*b*) the *Memorandum on Claims* shows actual procedure in submitting claims; and (*c*) the *Interhandel Case* deals with "exhaustion of local remedies" as a rule of international law.

War Claims

AMERICAN CLAIMS ARISING OUT OF WORLD WAR II
Hearings, War Claims and Enemy Property Legislation, 2–3 August 1961
Interstate and Foreign Commerce Committee
House of Representatives, 87th Congress

Statement of the Chairman of the Foreign Claims Settlement Commission.

*   *   *

In its supplementary report to the Congress on "War Claims Arising out of World War II" (H. Doc. 67, 83d Cong., 1st sess.), the former War Claims Commission observed that "The burdens of war do not fall equally on the people who are exposed to its hazards." The Commission also pointed out that all war claims legislation is an effort by the Government to alleviate the burdens of war.

Our own Government, in a series of enactments, has authorized recoveries on various types of American war claims upon which payments of roughly $700 million have been made. For the most part these payments have been made for deaths, injuries, disabilities, and personal sufferings of individuals occurring largely in the Philippines. The beneficiaries have been, almost exclusively, former American military prisoners of war in various war theaters, and American civilian internees in the Philippines, Guam, Wake, and Midway Islands or former U.S. nationals who became Philippine nationals, July 4, 1946. These same classes of individuals, with the exception of millions of military veterans or their survivors, who have received numerous various veterans benefits, very largely predominated the group which benefited from the enactment of laws authorizing substantial compensation for certain property losses occurring in the Philippines. There were, of course, a great many recoveries under war risk insurance programs. These are distinguishable, however, from the strictly war claims programs which provided for recoveries that were in the nature of gratuities.

Notwithstanding these efforts to ease the burdens of war, there remains a large segment of American war sufferers who have, to date, been bypassed in our Government's war claims programs. There are still more than 35,000 Americans whose investments abroad were taken or destroyed who have received nothing by way of compensation or restitution for their losses. In one way or another, prior to World War II, they were encouraged by our own Government to make these investments or to acquire such properties. Once acquired they could not, in all cases, be removed from areas of military operations or protected against military attack. Just as many American civilians were trapped in the Philippines, Guam, Wake, and Midway Islands, so the property of other Americans was engulfed in the tides of war. So far as these Americans are concerned, therefore, not only have the burdens of war not been lifted, but they have not even been partially relieved.

* * *

Utilization of the Liquidated Proceeds of Vested Assets, World War II

After the termination of the war questions concerning Germany's reparations were settled by the Paris reparation agreement of 1946. Under this agreement the United States, as well as other Allied Nations (excluding the Soviet Union and Poland), limited their individual demands against Germany largely to the assets located in their respective countries and agreed to hold or dispose of them in such a way as to preclude their return to German ownership or control. This was, of course, in lieu of reparations which the signatory nations did not favor in light of the Allied experience after World War I.

The signatory governments agreed that their respective shares of reparations "as determined by the . . . agreement, shall be regarded by each of them as covering all of its claims and those of its nationals against the former German Government and its agencies, of a governmental or private nature arising out of the war (which are not otherwise provided for). . . ."

Congress thereafter enacted the War Claims Act of 1948, which implemented the policy of retaining vested German and Japanese assets for war claims purposes and, more particularly, devoted these assets to the relief of American military and civilian personnel who had suffered in enemy prisoner of war and concentration camps. The policy of the Allied retention of vested assets was subsequently recognized in the Japanese Peace Treaty and was carried one step further in the Bonn Convention of 1952 between the Federal Republic of Germany and the United States, Britain, and France. In that convention, Germany agreed to compensate its own nationals for their loss of property through the vesting action of the Allied Powers. The latter, in turn, committed themselves to forego any claim for reparation against Germany's current production. These provisions for the Bonn Convention were reaffirmed in the Paris protocol of 1954, which brought about the sovereignty of the Federal Republic of

Germany. The Paris protocol was approved in the Senate on April 1, 1955, and became effective on May 5, 1955. The final action in this field is found in the 1956 Treaty of Friendship, Commerce, and Navigation between the United States and Germany. This reaffirmed the provisions of the Bonn Convention and added to them further agreement of complete cooperation.

*   *   *

The Administration Bill

The bill, H.R. 7479, is designed to amend the War Claims Act of 1948, as amended (62 Stat. 1240; 50 U.S.C. App. 2001–2016), to provide for the payment of claims by U.S. nationals based on physical damage to, destruction or loss of, American-owned property as the result of military operations or special measures directed against such property located in Albania, Austria, Czechoslovakia, Free Territory of Danzig, Estonia, Germany, Greece, Latvia, Lithuania, Poland, Yugoslavia, and portions of Hungary and Rumania, or in territory occupied or attacked by the armed forces of the Imperial Japanese Government, during World War II, not heretofore compensated in whole or in part. The bill also authorizes the adjudication of claims with respect to damage to or loss or destruction of ships or ship cargoes as a result of military action; net losses of maritime insurance underwriters incurred in the settlement of claims of insured losses on American-owned ships (excluding cargoes) lost, damaged, or destroyed by military action during World War II; death, injury, and disability claims sustained by American civilian passengers as a result of German and Japanese military action during the period September 11, 1939, and ending December 11, 1941; and losses resulting from the removal of industrial or capital equipment in Germany for reparation purposes, owned by Americans on the date of taking.*

*   *   *

Recoveries for American War Losses throughout the World

This Commission, and its predecessor, the War Claims Commission, have examined into the extent of recoveries for American war losses throughout the world. The absence of records showing the nationalities of the payees under these laws makes it impossible to determine the number or amount of awards to nationals of the United States. It appears, however, that recoveries were relatively small.

Under German laws, for example, although certain U.S. nationals are eligible for recoveries on a restricted basis, only a nominal number, probably less than 50 American nationals, are recorded as having received compensation for their losses under these laws. French authorities have

---

* H.R. 7283 was reported from the Committee in lieu of H.R. 7479, and became Public Law 87–846 in October, 1962, with substantially similar provisions.

reported that while some Americans may have been paid, it would be almost impossible to ascertain the exact number without examining the many thousands of claims processed.

Thirty-three countries have enacted war claims legislation in the decade following World War II. Of these, only 13 were found which afforded relief, or possible relief, to American claimants for property losses. . . .

* * *

In addition to the domestic laws of the 13 countries which may extend eligibility for war loss recoveries to nationals of the United States, the treaties of peace with Japan and Italy also make provision for American war claimants, many of whom have received fairly substantial compensation thereunder for losses and damages occurring in Italian territory.

* * *

Procedures

MEMORANDUM ON CLAIMS
United States Department of State, 1961
56 A.J.I.L. 166

Since 1959, the Cuban Government and authorities have nationalized, intervened and otherwise taken millions of dollars' worth of property of American nationals. The United States Government has vigorously protested such takings and urged the Cuban Government either to return the property or pay prompt, adequate and effective compensation. Thus far, the Cuban Government has not returned properties or been willing to make an agreement for compensation.

The Department is unable to predict when and in what manner it will be possible to settle this problem. In the past the Department has settled similar problems (1) by submitting individual claims through the diplomatic channel to the foreign government concerned and obtaining restitution or compensation; (2) by obtaining a lump sum in settlement of all claims, with the amount paid distributed by an agency of the United States Government; or (3) by an agreement submitting all claims to an international arbitral tribunal for adjudication.

Since the United States Government has not obtained agreement with Cuba for restitution, payment of a lump sum or for international arbitration, the only possibility at present would be for the United States Government formally to espouse through the diplomatic channel individual claims of American nationals. While the Department can give no assurance that claims it espouses would be paid by the Cuban Government, it is ready to receive and consider for presentation any claim which is properly prepared and documented and is valid from an international legal standpoint.

The Department does not use forms for claims against foreign governments but has memoranda explaining how such claims should be prepared and documented. Its memorandum of March 1, 1961, on the preparation of claims for loss of or damage to property is attached. In addition to the evidence which is mentioned in that memorandum, evidence should also be submitted showing that the American national exhausted such legal remedies as were available in Cuba and in the process sustained a denial of justice, as that term is understood in international law, or that the laws of Cuba do not provide a remedy or, if provided, that it would be futile to attempt to exhaust such remedy. The requirement for exhaustion of legal remedies is based upon the generally accepted rule of international law that international responsibility may not be invoked as regards reparation for losses or damages sustained by a foreigner until after exhaustion of the remedies available under local law. This, of course, does not mean that "legal remedies" must be exhausted if there are none to exhaust or if the procurement of justice would be impossible.

Each American national must decide whether to prepare a claim now, either with a view to its presentation through the diplomatic channel when ready, or in order that it will be ready in the event that a claims settlement with Cuba is effected at a later time. Each American national must also decide whether to "exhaust legal remedies" in Cuba, either with a view to obtaining restitution or adequate compensation or documentary evidence which could be used to show that justice could not be obtained by judicial proceedings. Generally, unsupported assertions to the effect that it would be useless to exhaust or attempt to exhaust legal remedies would, of course, have less evidentiary value than a court decree or other documentary evidence demonstrating the futility of exhausting or attempting to exhaust legal remedies.

*　　*　　*

INTERHANDEL CASE (SWITZERLAND v. UNITED STATES)
International Court of Justice, 1959
1959 I.C.J. Reports 6

On October 2, 1957, Switzerland instituted proceedings relating to the dispute with the United States regarding the Swiss claim to restitution by the United States of assets of *Société internationale pour participations industrielles et commerciales S.A.*, a Swiss company commonly known as "Interhandel." The Swiss application invoked the acceptance of compulsory jurisdiction under Article 36, paragraph 2, of the Court's Statute by the United States on August 26, 1946, and by Switzerland on July 28, 1948.

The United States raised the following preliminary objections:

* * *

(3) *Third Preliminary Objection*
that there is no jurisdiction in this Court to hear or determine the matters raised by the Swiss Application and Memorial, for the reason that Interhandel, whose case Switzerland is espousing, has not exhausted the local remedies available to it in the United States courts;

Although framed as an objection to the jurisdiction of the Court, this Objection must be regarded as directed against the admissibility of the Application of the Swiss Government. Indeed, by its nature it is to be regarded as a plea which would become devoid of object if the requirement of the prior exhaustion of local remedies were fulfilled.

The Court has indicated in what conditions the Swiss Government, basing itself on the idea that Interhandel's suit had been finally rejected in the United States courts, considered itself entitled to institute proceedings by its Application of October 2nd, 1957. However, the decision given by the Supreme Court of the United States on October 14th, 1957, on the application of Interhandel made on August 6th, 1957, granted a writ of *certiorari* and readmitted Interhandel into the suit. The judgment of that Court on June 16th, 1958, reversed the judgment of the Court of Appeals dismissing Interhandel's suit and remanded the case to the District Court. It was thenceforth open to Interhandel to avail itself again of the remedies available to it under the Trading with the Enemy Act, and to seek the restitution of its shares by proceedings in the United States courts. Its suit is still pending in the United States courts. The Court must have regard to the situation thus created.

The rule that local remedies must be exhausted before international proceedings may be instituted is a well-established rule of customary international law; the rule has been generally observed in cases in which a State has adopted the cause of its national whose rights are claimed to have been disregarded in another State in violation of international law. Before resort may be had to an international court in such a situation, it has been considered necessary that the State where the violation occurred should have an opportunity to redress it by its own means, within the framework of its own domestic legal system. *A fortiori* the rule must be observed when domestic proceedings are pending, as in the case of Interhandel, and when the two actions, that of the Swiss company in the United States courts and that of the Swiss Government in this Court, in its principal Submission, are designed to obtain the same result: the restitution of the assets of Interhandel vested in the United States.

The Swiss Government does not challenge the rule which requires that international judicial proceedings may only be instituted following the exhaustion of local remedies, but contends that the present case is one in which an exception to this rule is authorized by the rule itself.

The Court does not consider it necessary to dwell upon the assertion of the Swiss Government that "the United States itself has admitted that Interhandel had exhausted the remedies available in the United States courts." It is true that the representatives of the Government of the United States expressed this opinion on several occasions, in particular in the memorandum annexed to the Note of the Secretary of State of January 11th, 1957. This opinion was based upon a view which has proved unfounded. In fact, the proceedings which Interhandel had instituted before the courts of the United States were then in progress.

However, the Swiss Government has raised against the Third Objection other considerations which require examination.

In the first place, it is contended that the rule is not applicable for the reason that the measure taken against Interhandel and regarded as contrary to international law is a measure which was taken, not only by a subordinate authority but by the Government of the United States. However, the Court must attach decisive importance to the fact that the laws of the United States make available to interested persons who consider that they have been deprived of their rights by measures taken in pursuance of the Trading with the Enemy Act, adequate remedies for the defence of their rights against the Executive.

It has also been contended on behalf of the Swiss Government that in the proceedings based upon the Trading with the Enemy Act, the United States courts are not in a position to adjudicate in accordance with the rules of international law and that the Supreme Court, in its decision of June 16th, 1958, made no reference to the many questions of international law which, in the opinion of the Swiss Government, constitute the subject of the present dispute. But the decisions of the United States courts bear witness to the fact that United States courts are competent to apply international law in their decisions when necessary. In the present case, when the dispute was brought to this Court, the proceedings in the United States courts had not reached the merits, in which considerations of international law could have been profitably relied upon.

The Parties have argued the question of the binding force before the courts of the United States of international instruments which, according to the practice of the United States, fall within the category of Executive Agreements; the Washington Accord is said to belong to that category. At the present stage of the proceedings it is not necessary for the Court to express an opinion on the matter. Neither is it practicable, before the final decision of the domestic courts, to anticipate what basis they may adopt for their judgment.

Finally, the Swiss Government laid special stress on the argument that the character of the principal Submission of Switzerland is that of a claim for the implementation of the decision given on January 5th, 1948, by the Swiss Authority of Review and based on the Washington Accord, a decision which the Swiss Government regards as an international judicial decision. "When an international decision has not been executed, there are no local remedies to exhaust, for the injury has been caused directly to the injured States." It has therefore contended that the failure by the United States to implement the decision constitutes a direct breach of international law, causing immediate injury to the rights of Switzerland as the Applicant State. The Court notes in the first place that to implement a decision is to apply its operative part. In the operative part of its decision, however, the Swiss Authority of Review "Decrees: (1) that the Appeal is sustained and the decision subjecting the appellant to the blocking of German property in Switzerland is annulled. . . ." The decision of the Swiss Authority of Review relates to the unblocking of the assets of Interhandel in Switzerland; the Swiss claim is designed to secure the restitution of the assets of Interhandel in the United States. Without prejudging the validity of any arguments which the Swiss Government seeks or may seek to base upon that decision, the Court would confine itself to observing that such arguments do not deprive the dispute which has been referred to it of the character of a dispute in which the Swiss Government appears as having adopted the cause of its national, Interhandel, for the purpose of securing the restitution to that company of assets vested by the Government of the United States. This is one of the very cases which give rise to the application of the rule of the exhaustion of local remedies.

For all these reasons, the Court upholds the Third Preliminary Objection so far as the principal Submission of Switzerland is concerned.*

*   *   *

FOR FURTHER STUDY

RICHARD B. LILLICH. *International Claims, their Adjudication by National Commissions.* Syracuse, N.Y.: Syracuse University Press, 1962.

RICHARD B. LILLICH AND GORDON A. CHRISTENSON. *International Claims; Their Preparation and Presentation.* Syracuse, N.Y.: Syracuse University Press, 1962.

RENE WORMSER. *Collection of International War Damage Claims.* New York: Alexander Publishing Co., 1944.

A. V. FREEMAN. *The International Responsibility of States for Denial of Justice.* London: Longmans Green, 1938.

---

* In 1965, the claim on the part of Switzerland was finally settled by diplomatic negotiation and agreement. The chief asset of Interhandel in the United States—its interest in General Aniline and Film Corporation, held by the United States since World War II on allegations of German ownership—was sold to the public, and $123 million of the proceeds went to Interhandel.

X

International Claims: Breach of Contract and Expropriation of Property

INTERNATIONAL claims for the wrongful acts of states toward aliens present many difficulties under international law. The conduct of some states toward their own nationals has often been arbitrary, ruthless, and despoiling: when practiced on aliens who are nationals of the United Kingdom, France, the United States, and other states accustomed to a greater governmental respect for individual life, liberty, and property, there have been complaints about the lack of "a minimum standard of justice," even though in its laws or decrees or acts the state may have shown no discrimination between the treatment of its own nationals and aliens.

Some of the difficulties in arriving at agreement on the international responsibility of states toward aliens has been evident in the failure thus far, under both the League of Nations and United Nations, to formulate an international convention. As early as 1953, the General Assembly requested the United Nations International Law Commission to undertake codification of the principles of international law in this field; yet, despite years of efforts, in 1967 the commission had not arrived at a draft suitable for consideration as a convention. A Harvard Law School draft convention on the Responsibility of States for Damage Done in their Territory to the Person or Property of Foreigners, originally prepared in 1929 and revised several times after 1957 as a part of the International Law Commission's preparation, has received considerable criticism.

In breaches of contract—especially the expropriation of property—that lead to international claims, two points of view are reflected by states in the modern world. Those governments of Asia, Africa, and Latin America that have been intent on rapid national economic reforms with an appeal to social justice have inevitably collided with property and income interests secured by the foreign nationals of Western Europe and the United States through purchase, contract, or concession.

Breaches of Contract

Breaches of contract do not fall into the same category of law as torts. The obligations under a contract are created by the parties to the contract, not by public law. The state enforces only the obligation to perform the contract. But what about a breach of contract between a state and a foreign national? Suppose a foreign state engages an American private contractor to build a dam and then fails to pay the costs agreed on? Can anyone enforce the performance obligation?

Ordinarily, such breaches of contract would not be considered violations of international law in themselves but, rather, part of the risk of an alien doing business in a foreign jurisdiction. Only in extraordinary situations when a rank denial of justice was attached to the breach of contract between a state and an alien, such as in the absence of all local administrative or judicial process, would the alien's state be likely to take up his claim.

In the great expansion of United States and European economic interests to Latin America, Asia, and Africa in the 19th and early 20th centuries, the powerful states sometimes backed their nationals' claims for contractual default by a show of force against the weaker states. Thus, in 1902 Germany, the United Kingdom, and Italy blockaded Venezuela, with the acquiescence of the United States, until Venezuela submitted the claims of the European nationals to international arbitration. In 1907, the United States forestalled the European powers' coercion of the Dominican Republic for defaults in foreign debts by means of a treaty with the Dominican Republic, allowing the United States to appoint a receiver general of customs.

Dr. Drago of Argentina formulated the Drago Doctrine that denied the right of any European state to intervene forcibly in order to settle or collect public debts in America. And in 1907, the Second Hague Peace Conference adopted a convention in which states renounced the right to use armed force to recover the contract debts claimed by one government against another as due their nationals. With the League of Nations and the

United Nations, in the modern environment of world politics, such crude tactics for the diplomatic protection of nationals in cases of contractual default are—or should be—out of date. But the issue of recovery for states' breaches of contract with aliens when a denial of justice is involved has not disappeared.

Little evidence of the rules of international law in this area can be garnered from the International Court of Justice. However, in many international arbitrations, such as the 1926 *North American Dredging Company Case* or the 1931 *International Fisheries Company Case* between the United States and Mexico, damages were sought for breach of contract but were rejected by the claims commission due to a lack of evidence of denial of justice, "an arbitrary act . . . which in itself might be considered as a violation of some rule or principle of international law."[1]

By legislative enactment, moreover, public bonds—obligations of a state to repay a loan—have been devaluated by governments, causing international controversy. On the intervention of France, the Permanent Court of International Justice in 1929 held that bonds issued by Serbia and purchased by French nationals, among others, must be redeemed by gold francs that were equal in value to those at the time of issue.[2] In 1957, France again intervened against Norway for suspending certain gold clauses in the repayment of state loans to French nationals; but the International Court of Justice found that Norway had not submitted to the jurisdiction of the Court with respect to France, and the Court did not hear the case on its merits.[3] The devaluation of public loans and bonds by legislative action plainly touches an aspect of denial of justice to the alien somewhat different from that in contracts or concessions in which performance is sought; devaluation of bonds entails a confiscation of property, a liquidation of debt owed to the alien by the state through sovereign legislative power.

Expropriation of Property

By far the most common lament of aliens in the 20th century has concerned the expropriation of their properties by the state. Land, minerals, industries, banks, and commercial enterprises have been nationalized in the wake of political revolution and new economic development plans. When compensation is paid to the owners or shareholders through some

---

[1] U.S.–Mexico Claims Commission 1930–31, *International Fisheries Company Case*, p. 218.

[2] *Serbian Loans Case (France v. Serbia)*, P.C.I.J., Series A, No. 20.

[3] *Case of Certain Norweigan Loans (France v. Norway)*, 1957 I.C.J. Reports 9.

administrative or judicial process, without discrimination between nationals and aliens, the state acts with sovereign rights under international law, and no issue arises with other states. But when compensation is denied, or is so partial that it amounts to little more than confiscation of the alien's property, he may repair to the diplomatic protection of his state.

Writing to the Mexican Ambassador in 1938 about the expropriation of American agrarian properties, the U.S. Secretary of State noted:

The Government of the United States merely adverts to a self-evident fact when it notes that the applicable precedents and recognized authorities on international law support its declaration that, under every rule of law and equity, no government is entitled to expropriate private property, for whatever purpose, without provision for prompt, adequate, and effective payment therefor.[4]

In 1953, protesting the expropriation of land that belonged to an American corporation in Guatemala, the State Department maintained that "The obligation of a state imposed by international law to pay just or fair compensation at the time of taking of property of foreigners cannot be abrogated from the international standpoint by local legislation."[5] In 1963, protesting Ceylon's decision to give the state-owned Ceylon Petroleum Corporation a monopoly of the internal distribution of petroleum products, the State Department said:

The Government of the United States does not question the right of a sovereign nation to nationalize property belonging to American citizens or companies provided adequate and effective compensation is promptly paid in accordance with international law.[6]

Despite these stern statements, the absolute necessity for "prompt, adequate, and effective" compensation remains unclear under international law. No cases dealing with the subject have been put before the International Court of Justice. In 1958, the Indonesian government nationalized Dutch-owned enterprises within its territory, and within the same act provided for compensation to be determined by a committee whose members would be entirely appointed by the government. In 1960, the Cuban government offered to compensate the expropriation of American properties with the issuance of long-term, low-interest bonds, to be redeemed by a special fund consisting of foreign exchange received from the sale of sugar to the United States.

Questions arise on the time and value of the compensation, but the fact is that in practically all instances of recent nationalizations the expropriating governments *have* paid or have offered to pay for the taking of private property. In 1938, after many years, Mexico and the United States agreed on the sum of $24 million to settle claims for the expropriation of

[4] Green H. Hackworth, *Digest of International Law* (Washington, D.C.: U.S. Government Printing Office, 1942), Vol. III, pp. 658–59.

[5] 29 Department of State Bulletin 357 (1953).

[6] 49 Department of State Bulletin 245 (1963).

the land and petroleum holdings of American nationals. An agreement for compensation was made between Iran, the Anglo-Iranian Oil Company, and an international consortium in 1954, after that oil company was nationalized. Between 1958 and 1963, Egypt paid about $82 million to the former shareholders of the nationalized Suez Canal Company.

In 1948 and again in 1964, Yugoslavia signed lump-sum claims settlement agreements with the United States for the nationalization and taking of property of American nationals. Agreements of this kind were also reached with Poland and Rumania in 1960, and with Bulgaria in 1963. Negotiations for similar post-World War II agreements have taken place with Czechoslovakia and Hungary, as well as with the Soviet Union for United States nationals' losses between 1918 and 1933. In 1965, for the expropriation of their properties the government of Ceylon agreed to pay the oil companies of Caltex Ceylon, Esso Standard Eastern, Inc., and Shell about $11.5 million over a 6-year period.

In any event, a state's international obligation under international law for the taking of alien property cannot be unilaterally repudiated, even though full and prompt compensation may not be obtained.

In the documents that follow, (*a*) the *Claim of Silberg and Mogilanski* illustrates the work of the United States Foreign Claims Settlement Commission; (*b*) *United States Claims Against Cuba* treats the issue of the vesting and sale of local assets of a state, not an enemy under international law, for claims proceedings; and (*c*) *Pons* v. *Republic of Cuba* presents some interesting questions on a counterclaim against Cuban funds in the United States, based on a taking of property by act of state in Cuba.

Nationalization of Property

CLAIM OF SILBERG AND MOGILANSKI
Foreign Claims Settlement Commission of the United States
Mimeographed Decisions Nos. PO 62 and 63, 1961
56 A.J.I.L. 544

These claims are based upon the asserted ownership and loss by the claimants, LENA SILBERG and MUSIA MOGILANSKI, of property situated in Nieswiez, Krzywoszyn, and Ostrow in which each claims a one-half interest. The loss was alleged to have occurred after World War II, when territory including these three communities was ceded to the U.S.S.R.

Under Section 4(a) of the International Claims Settlement Act of 1949, as amended, the Commission is given jurisdiction over claims of nationals of the United States included within the terms of the Polish Claims Agreement of 1960, Article 2 of which provides:

Claims to which reference is made in Article 1 and which are settled and discharged by this Agreement are claims of nationals of the United States for

 (a) the nationalization or other taking *by Poland* of property and of rights and interests in and with respect to property;
 (b) the appropriation or the loss of use or enjoyment of property under *Polish* laws, decrees or other measures limiting or restricting rights and interests in and with respect to property . . . ; and
 (c) debts owed by enterprises which have been nationalized or taken *by Poland* and debts which were a charge upon property which has been nationalized, appropriated or otherwise taken *by Poland*. (Underlining added.)

If an award is to be made on a claim filed under the Agreement, the Commission must find that the claim comes within the purview of the above-quoted Article. Hence, a claim may be compensable only if based upon a loss arising from a nationalization, appropriation, or other taking of property *by the Government of Poland.*

*   *   *

Except for a short-lived "Congress Poland" (1815–1832), there was no independent state of Poland from the time of the Third Partition in 1795 until the close of World War I. Although the Allied Governments agreed upon a reconstitution of Poland, the Paris Conference of 1919 was unable to settle the matter of its eastern boundary, and hostilities continued between Poland and Russia in 1919 and 1920. The Curzon Line, which approximates the present boundary, had its origin when the northern half of the present line was proposed on December 8, 1919 by the Supreme Council of the Allied and Associated Powers for purposes of an armistice. It was rejected by both belligerents. Polish forces drove deep into Russia in the spring of 1920, but by July 10, 1920 had retreated to the gates of Warsaw, and announced that they would accept an armistice along the proposed line. In a note to the Russians, Lord Curzon, the British Foreign Secretary, extended the line southward to its present length. Russia declined the proffered armistice, and the conflict continued with the Poles prevailing until the Treaty of Riga was signed on October 12, 1920, establishing a border well to the east of the Curzon Line, and embracing between the two lines the Eastern Territories of interest herein. Both Governments approved the treaty on March 18, 1921. It was recognized by the Council of the League of Nations on February 3, 1923, by the Conference of Ambassadors on March 15, 1923, and by the United States on April 5, 1923, and remained unchallenged until 1939. During this period, privately owned property in the Eastern Territories was located within Poland and might have been subjected to Polish nationalization measures had the Government of Poland embarked upon any such programs.

Shortly before the onslaught of World War II, the Ribbentrop-Molotov agreement was signed on August 23, 1939, binding Germany and the U.S.S.R. to mutual non-aggression. By a secret protocol to the agreement, spheres of interest were laid down for application "in the event of a territorial and political rearrangement." Such an event occurred when Germany invaded Poland on September 1, 1939, and Russia followed suit on September 17, at which time the Polish Government fled the country to operate in exile from Rumania, France, and finally London. Poland was occupied completely by German and Russian forces, meeting at the Ribbentrop-Molotov line, which corresponded partially with the Curzon Line and otherwise was more favorable to the Soviet Union. This line was formalized by German-Russian treaty on September 29, 1939. The Polish Government in Exile rallied Polish armed forces to Allied support, but was at no time able to enforce its will in Poland.

On June 22, 1941, Germany attacked Russia. The British then moved to reconcile its old and new allies, Poland and Russia. After a month of negotittions, during which the Russians insisted that their western frontier was not open to discussion, an agreement was signed in London on July 30, 1941 by representatives of Poland and the U.S.S.R., which stated, among other things, that earlier German-Russian agreements had lost their validity, but was silent as to where the Russo-Polish frontier should be fixed. The Poles had wanted more than mere dissolution of the Ribbentrop-Molotov line, and had striven for specific treaty recognition of the 1921 boundaries; but they signed the agreement in the knowledge that they could get nothing better.

In the meantime, however, the Eastern Territories had been incorporated formally into the Soviet Union, supposedly according to the will of the inhabitants as freely expressed in a "plebiscite" held shortly after the 1939 Russian invasion. Immediately upon occupation of Eastern Poland in 1939, Soviet authorities had removed all members of State and local government administrations from office, arresting most of them, and appointing so-called "temporary administrations" in their place, composed principally of Red Army officers and Soviet officials. On October 6, 1939 an election was scheduled for October 22, 1939 of National Assemblies for the Western Ukraine and Western White-Ruthenia, which between them would govern the Eastern Territories. On the latter date, elections were conducted by the Red Army, NKVD, and Communist organizers. The two National Assemblies convened in Lwow and Bialystok, and on October 27 and 29, enacted resolutions for incorporation of their territories into the U.S.S.R. Formal incorporation of Western Ukraine was accomplished by Decree of the Supreme Council of the U.S.S.R. on November 1, 1939, and of Western White-Ruthenia on November 2, 1939.

The Poles now hopefully interpreted the London Agreement of July 30, 1941 as Soviet recognition of the pre-1939 boundary, but the Soviet Government would not commit itself, and made no move to disincorporate the territories. At every opportunity, the London Poles expressed their claim to all territory within their pre-war boundaries, but were met with official silence. In any event, all of Poland and the Eastern Territories was now under German control, with the battle line well into Russian territory. As they had advanced, the Germans had incorporated Western Poland into the Reich in two Gaus—Danzig and Warthegau. The rest of Poland up to the Ribbentrop-Molotov line was given the name General Government. Lands east of the line were administered separately, as part of German-occupied Russia.

Friction arose between the London Poles and the Soviet Government over many things, not least over the citizenship status of Poles who had fled or been deported to Russia. On November 29, 1939, a Soviet Decree stated that all citizens of Western districts of the Ukrainian and White-Ruthenian Soviet Socialist Republics who were present in those districts on November 1 and 2, 1939, acquired Soviet citizenship. As evidence of "good will," the Soviet Government exempted persons of "Polish origin" from this automatic Soviet citizenship; but on January 16, 1943 they eliminated this exception.

On February 19, 1943 an article appeared in Radianska Ukraina, setting forth in print for the first time since the agreement of July 30, 1941, the Russian claim to retention of the Eastern Territories, and characterizing Polish pretensions as wholly unjustified. A stiff Polish note of February 25 elicited a Soviet reply on March 1, 1943 invoking the Atlantic Charter of August 14, 1941 as justification for the Curzon Line. Then, in April 1943, the Germans announced the discovery at Katyn of a mass grave of thousands of Polish officers who had been missing since taken as prisoners-of-war by the Russians. The Poles appealed to the International Red Cross for an investigation, whereupon the Soviet Union broke off diplomatic relations with the Polish Government in Exile, stating that the motive for the Katyn accusations was to wrest concessions from them regarding the Eastern Territories.

The British now began urging the London Poles to accept the inevitability of the Curzon Line. With the tide of battle running in its favor, the Soviet Government issued a statement on January 11, 1944 that the injustices of the 1921 Riga Treaty had been rectified by the 1939 incorporation of the Eastern Territories into the Soviet Union, and that Poland must be reformed by the acquisition of German lands in the west. The eastern boundary was to be the Curzon Line, but willingness to negotiate adjustments therein as warranted by population majorities was expressed. . . .

* * *

At the Yalta Conference in February 1945, Roosevelt, Churchill, and Stalin agreed formally on the Curzon Line, with slight modifications in Poland's favor, and decided that the Lublin Government must be reorganized to include democratic leaders from the West, and must then hold free elections. . . . On June 28, 1945 the new Polish Provisional Government of National Unity was installed, with a twenty-man Cabinet including sixteen Lublin members. British and United States recognition came on July 5, 1945. The new government and the Soviet Union formalized their mutual frontier by the treaty of August 16, 1945, since which time the Eastern Territories have been indisputably under Soviet sovereignty.

From the above historical narrative, it will be seen that at no time since September 17, 1939 could there have been a nationalization or other taking of property in the Eastern Territories by a Polish Government. During a six-month period from January 5, 1945 to July 5, 1945, there were two rival Governments of Poland—the Lublin group which was recognized by the Soviet Union, and the London group recognized by Britain, the United States, and other nations. The London Poles, who had held out for re-establishment of the 1921 eastern frontier, never regained power within the country from which they had been exiled. The Lublin group, the only one to which the claimants' allegations could refer, was the pro-Soviet group which had pledged its acceptance of the Curzon Line as the eastern boundary of Poland before any Polish territory was liberated. As the liberation progressed, it was this group which received civil authority over lands west of the Curzon Line, and evolved into the postwar Government of Poland. The claimants' allegations of circumstances under which Polish taking of property in the Eastern Territories might have been accomplished between July 1944 and August 1945 are without foundation and contrary to fact.

In the instant claims, there is no evidence that the property of the claimants was nationalized or otherwise taken by the Government of Poland or any other government at any time. True, there was a transfer of sovereignty, from Poland to the U.S.S.R., of the territory in which the property was located; but, whether this occurred on August 16, 1945 or earlier, the transfer of sovereignty did not constitute a taking of the private property of individuals within the territory, and in itself did not disturb the title of private individuals to property. A taking by the Government of Poland of property owned by United States nationals in the Eastern Territories, when that government had the sovereign right and the power to effectuate such a taking, might give rise to a compensable claim under the Agreement. The loss of sovereignty over the territory was not a taking of private property within the territory by the Government of Poland; and a later taking of such property by the new sovereign is not within the purview of the Polish Claims Agreement.

. . . Accordingly, the claims are denied.

Vesting and Sale of Assets

UNITED STATES CLAIMS AGAINST CUBA
Department of State Letter to House Committee on Foreign Affairs, 1965
Hearings, Subcommittee on Inter-American Affairs, 89th Congress, 1st Session, 8 June 1965

DEPARTMENT OF STATE
Washington, May 17, 1965

HON. THOMAS E. MORGAN,
Chairman, Committee on Foreign Affairs,
House of Representatives

DEAR MR. CHAIRMAN: This letter is in reply to your request of April 30, 1965, for the Department's comments on H.R. 7622, a bill to amend title V of the International Claims Settlement Act of 1949 relating to certain claims against the Government of Cuba.*

*   *   *

. . . The Department of State strongly favors repeal of provisions of section 511 for the vesting and sale of Cuban assets in the United States and the use of the proceeds thereof, to the extent necessary, to reimburse the Government of the United States for the expenses of the Foreign Claims Settlement Commission and the Department of the Treasury in processing claims against Cuba. The vesting and sale of such assets would in the judgment of the Department of State have no beneficial effect, would weaken the principle of international law regarding the sanctity of property, would be contrary to the traditional policies and practices of the U.S. Government and would set an unfortunate example for countries less dedicated than the United States to the preservation of property rights.

The vesting and sale of Cuban property in the United States would not produce any immediate benefits to those suffering losses in Cuba. Under section 511 of the act such assets are to be used to reimburse the Government of the United States for the expenses of the Foreign Claims Settlement Commission processing claims against Cuba. Thus, repeal of these accompanied by an appropriation from the general funds of the United States for processing claims, as envisaged by the bill, will not have

---

* The bill to amend title V was enacted 19 October 1965.

any adverse effect on American claimants. Use of general funds of the United States would be consistent with the practice followed in 1962 when the Congress approved the use of such funds to defray expenses of processing claims of U.S. citizens for damages caused by the construction and maintenance of Gut Dam on the St. Lawrence River by the Canadian Government (Public Law 87–587; 76 Stat. 387). Nor would the amount realized from the sale of the property substantially reduce the burden on the taxpayer. The Department of Justice is of the view that the net amount of assets subject to vesting and sale is in the neighborhood of $350,000, which would probably be insufficient to defray more than one-third of the estimated expenses of the Foreign Claims Settlement Commission and the Department of the Treasury. Finally, repeal of the vesting and sale provisions of section 511 would not be of advantage to the Castro regime. The assets are already blocked under the Treasury regulations of July 8, 1963.

The sanctity of property has deep roots in international law and practice. As a nation with strong respect for law and large property interests abroad the United States has consistently and traditionally maintained that the taking of property of aliens imposes an obligation to pay prompt, adequate, and effective compensation. If Cuban assets are vested and sold such action could be construed as a change in the traditional policy of the United States and thus endanger the international law principles which protect holdings abroad, both private and government.

The vesting and sale of Cuban assets in the United States would be an unwise and undesirable departure from the customary policies and practices of the Government of the United States. The vesting and sale of foreign assets traditionally has been limited to wartime enemies of the United States. The treaties of peace with Bulgaria, Hungary, and Rumania illustrate the reluctance of this Government to vest foreign assets in time of peace. In those treaties, the three countries expressly waived all claims of their respective governments and nationals to property in the United States. Despite this waiver the Congress authorized the use only of government and corporate assets in the payment of claims of U.S. nationals (Public Law 285, 84th Cong., 69 Stat. 562). The blocked assets of Rumanian and Bulgarian individuals were released pursuant to agreements with those countries, and if an agreement with Hungary, now being negotiated, is concluded, the assets of Hungarian citizens will also be released. In respect of German property, the Bonn Conventions provide that the German owners of property seized for reparations are to be compensated by the German Government. . . .

In conclusion, it is the Department's view that the vesting and sale of Cuban property could set an unfortunate example for countries less dedicated than the United States to the preservation of property rights. The Government of the United States, as a matter of policy, encourages the investment of American capital overseas and endeavors to protect such investments against nationalization, expropriation, intervention, and taking. To vest and sell Cuban assets could, therefore, be counterproductive. It would place the Government of the United States in the position of doing what Castro has done. It could cause other governments to question the sincerity of the U.S. Government in insisting upon respect for property rights. The result could be a reduction, in an immeasurable but real degree, of one of the protections enjoyed by American-owned property around the world. Should this protection be diminished, the task of economic development to which the United States is devoting a great part of its strength and resources could become more difficult because of an attendant decrease in such investment.

*   *   *

Sincerely yours,
DOUGLAS MACARTHUR II
Assistant Secretary
for Congressional Relations
(For the Acting Secretary of State)

Public Policy

PONS v. REPUBLIC OF CUBA
United States Court of Appeals, 1961
294 F. 2d 925

Edgerton, Circuit Judge

*   *   *

Cuba brought this suit against Pons, a Cuban national. Aside from his counterclaim, Pons does not dispute Cuba's claim to the money in the court's registry. The counterclaim is for the value of property in Cuba which Pons says the Cuban government took from him without compensation.

"Every sovereign State is bound to respect the independence of every other sovereign State, and the courts of one country will not sit in judgment on the acts of the government of another done within its own territory." *Underhill* v. *Hernandez*, 1897, 168 U.S. 250, 252, 18 S.Ct. 83, 42 L.Ed. 456; . . . Specifically, "What another country has done in the way of taking over property of its nationals . . . is not a matter for judicial consideration here." *United States* v. *Belmont*, 1937, 301 U.S. 324, 332, 57 S.Ct. 758, 81 L.Ed. 1134.

Pons says his property was seized "Without any legal justification and without due process of law. . . ." We cannot consider this question. "It should make no difference whether the foreign act is, under local law, partially or wholly, technically or fundamentally, illegal. No such distinction may be gleaned from the cases. So long as the act is the act of the foreign sovereign, it matters not how grossly the sovereign has transgressed its own laws." *Banco de Espana* v. *Federal Reserve Bank*, 2 Cir., 1940, 114 F. 2d 438, 444. The Court of Appeals for the Second Circuit, in an opinion by Judge Learned Hand, has applied the principle to an act that was outrageous. The Nazis had seized the plaintiff's property because he was a Jew. Judge Hand found it "consistent with the record that they may have forced the plaintiff to transfer the shares before December 1938, and it was only in that month that any laws were passed, legalizing the confiscation of the property of Jews became of their race or religion. However, even though we assume that a German court would have held the transfer unlawful at the time it was made, that would be irrelevant. We have repeatedly declared, for over a period of at least thirty years, that a court of the forum will not undertake to pass upon the validity under the municipal law of another state of the acts of officials of that state, purporting to act as such. We have held that this was a necessary corollary of decisions of the Supreme Court, and if we have been mistaken, the Supreme Court must correct it." *Bernstein* v. *Van Heyghen Frères Société Anonyme*, 2 Cir., 1947, 163 F. 2d 246, 249, certiorari denied 332 U.S. 772, 68 S.Ct. 88, 92 L.Ed. 357.

We think we cannot refuse to apply the Supreme Court's rule to a counterclaim. *National City Bank of New York* v. *Republic of China*, 1954, 348 U.S. 356, 75 S.Ct. 432, 99 L.Ed. 389, on which Pons relies, does not support his position. The Supreme Court there allowed the defendant Bank to set off, against China, claims based on defaulted notes of China. The Court said a "chilly feeling against sovereign immunity began to reflect itself in federal legislation in 1797. At that early day Congress decided that when the United States sues an individual, the individual can set off all debts properly due him from the sovereign." . . . All the Court did in that case was limit a foreign sovereign's immunity as the domestic sovereign's immunity had been limited for 150 years. In our opinion this does not affect the rule that a foreign sovereign's seizure of its own national's property in its own territory cannot be reviewed in our courts.

On April 13, 1961, we invited the Department of Justice and the Department of State to file briefs, if they should see fit, expressing their views on any issues or questions of interest to them in this case. No briefs have been filed.

Affirmed.

Circuit Judge Burger Dissenting

Our courts have consistently considered themselves bound to recognize the acts of other sovereign states within their own territories even when those acts violated our own concepts of basic fairness and due process. As the majority opinion points out we have gone so far as to recognize the obnoxious decrees of Nazi Germany expropriating property of German nationals on the basis of racial origins. . . .

But I do not think we should carry the act of state doctrine to the point where we permit a foreign state to come into our courts as a suitor and secure equitable relief on better or different terms than those available to an American litigant in the same courts.

Cuba here sought the extraordinary equitable relief of an injunction and an accounting from Pons who, as an agent of Cuba, held property of that country. Pons freely acknowledged the claims of Cuba and has paid the fund into the registry of the court, but he demands that Cuba account to him for his property in its possession. Relying on the act of state doctrine, Cuba insists that our courts accord to it the extraordinary equitable relief it seeks but denies our right to require Cuba to comply with doctrines of equity which would govern an American citizen suing in this court for an accounting.

. . . To allow Cuba to withdraw the impounded funds from the jurisdiction of this court without meeting the duty to account to Pons is to decide this case without trying it. At the very least appellant is entitled to require appellee to meet with the formal requirements of an accounting with all impounded funds held intact pending final outcome of the litigation.

*   *   *

I would remand the case for trial under equitable rules governing accounting suits and hold all funds in the registry of the court until an accounting is made by both litigants under the familiar rules of equity jurisprudence. If that delays indefinitely the settlement of the accounts between the parties that will be by the appellee's choice.

Act of State Doctrine

To obtain justice for torts, breaches of contract, or taking of property by the state, an alien should have recourse to the local courts. But such a resort may be denied to him by the arbitrary actions of the government, or even by a state's constitutional refusal to be sued in its own courts without its consent.

If, however, the assets of such a state or the assets of an individual who has benefited from the allegedly unjust action of that state happen to be present in the state of which the alien is a national, he may have recourse to his own national courts. One bar to such action for obtaining compensation has already been discussed in Section VIII, under the doctrine of sovereign immunity, and was illustrated there by the *Chemical Natural Resources* v. *Republic of Venezuela Case*. Another bar to such action may be the act of state doctrine.

In 1897, Chief Justice Fuller of the United States Supreme Court summarized a legal doctrine that has guided American judges for a long time:

> Every sovereign state is bound to respect the independence of every other sovereign state, and the courts of one country will not sit in judgment on the acts of the government of another done within its territory. Redress of grievances by reason of such acts must be obtained through the means open to be availed of by sovereign powers, as between themselves.[7]

Twenty-one years later, the following case presented itself to the same bench. The ownership of two large consignments of hides was contested. The defendant claimed title to the hides by virtue of his purchase from Finnegan-Brown, a Texas corporation, which in turn had purchased them from General Francisco Villa of Mexico. But the plaintiff argued that the claim to title by purchase from Villa was invalid, for the general had confiscated the hides contrary to the provisions of the Hague Convention of 1907 respecting the laws and customs of war. Moreover, at the time of the confiscation Villa had been commissioned by General Carranza, whose forces were *not* recognized by the United States as the government of Mexico. At the time of hearing this case before the Supreme Court, however, the United States *had* recognized the Carranza government. The Court then said:

> . . . when a government which originates in revolution or revolt is recognized by the political department of our government as the de jure government of the country in which it is established, such recognition is retroactive in

---

[7] *Underhill v. Hernandez,* 168 U.S. 250 (1897).

379

effect and validates all the actions and conduct of the government so recognized from the commencement of its existence. . . .

Plainly this was the action, in Mexico, of the legitimate Mexican government when dealing with a Mexican citizen . . . and upon repeated decisions of this court such action is not subject to re-examination and modification by the courts of this country.[8]

These are classical enunciations of the act of state doctrine in the United States, a restraint the courts have imposed on themselves following the logic: (*a*) that a foreign state can better determine the validity of its own acts under its law; (*b*) that such acts, if upset by a foreign court, would challenge the state's authority and threaten the finality of all its acts; (*c*) that the courts could seriously disturb the conduct of foreign relations by the executive branch by denying the legality of another sovereign's act.

This reasoning has carried tremendous legal force up to the present day. In 1947, a United States Circuit Court of Appeals heard a plaintiff who alleged that he had been taken forcibly into custody by Nazi officials in Germany. Under duress of threats of bodily harm and business ruin, he had been compelled to execute documents transferring shares of a ship line to a Nazi designee. The Court felt that there was no dispute about any of the facts, except as to the meaning of "Nazi officials," which recurred a number of times in the complaint.

Does that phrase in the context in which the plaintiff used it "clearly indicate" that the duress under which he acted was imposed by persons who were acting, or who purported to be acting, as officials of the Third Reich? Obviously these were accredited agents of the government.

. . . even though we assume that a German court would have held the transfer unlawful at the time it was made, that would be irrelevant. We have repeatedly declared, for over a period of at least thirty years, that a court of the forum will not undertake to pass upon the validity under the municipal law of another state of the acts of officials of that state, purporting to act as such. . . . no court will exercise its jurisdiction to adjudicate the validity of the official acts of another state.[9]

Thus, a United States court upheld the legality of German acts under the Nazi regime, even though America had raised armies to defeat the principles of the Third Reich.

Will the courts of the United States uphold the acts of state of a government that is not recognized by Washington? As indicated in Section II, a New York court in the *Salimoff* case accepted as lawful the confiscatory decree of the Soviet Union against the property of a Russian national, even though the government was not recognized by the United States. But American courts have consistently concluded that such decrees had no *extraterritorial* effect, that is, the decrees do not in themselves

---

[8] *Oetjen* v. *Central Leather Co.,* 246 U.S. 297 (1918).

[9] *Bernstein* v. *Van Heyghen Frères, S.A.,* 163 F. 2d 246 (1947).

change the status of property situated in the United States or temporarily outside the borders of the state, or located in a third state at the time of the decree.

In the *Latvian State Cargo* case, three vessels owned by citizens and residents of the Republic of Latvia were in New York at the time of that state's occupation by the Soviet Union in 1940 and the subsequent nationalization decrees by the new socialist government of Latvia in 1941. The new Latvian government was not recognized by the United States. In its opinion, the U.S. Circuit Court of Appeals held that in the absence of recognition of a foreign government the courts could deny effect to an act of that government which "purports to change the ownership of a chattel absent from its borders. . . ."[10]

Moreover, courts will not always and invariably give recognition to acts of state, even of a recognized government, if they do some violence to the public policy of the *forum*—the place where the case is being heard. In 1921, a plaintiff in the United Kingdom seeking recovery of property that had been nationalized by the Soviet Union alleged that the act had been "pure robbery" and "is in its nature so immoral and so contrary to the principles of justice as recognized by this country, that the Courts of this country ought not to pay any attention to it."[11] In this case, the British Court did not agree.

But the French Court of Cassation held in 1928 that although the courts of a state, faced with a juridical situation governed by foreign law, should apply foreign law, the rule was obligatory only so far as application of foreign law and respect for the rights acquired thereby were not incompatible with those principles and provisions of their own law regarded as essential from the point of view of public policy.[12] In 1965, a United States district court held that recognition of a foreign government in and of itself was not a sufficient manifestation of federal policy to require the court to give extraterritorial effect to its confiscatory decrees.[13]

American courts have generally hesitated to use the public policy of the forum as a contradiction to foreign acts of state, fearing the easy entry of personal or local prejudice.

The courts are not free to refuse to enforce a foreign right at the pleasure of the judges, to suit the individual notion of expediency or fairness. They do not close their doors unless help would violate some fundamental principle of justice, some prevalent conception of good morals, some deep-rooted tradition of the common weal.[14]

---

[10] *Latvian State Cargo and Passenger S.S. Line* v. *McGrath*, 188 F. 2d 1000 (1957).

[11] *Luther* v. *James Sagor & Co.*, 3 Kings Bench 522 (Court of Appeals) (1921).

[12] *Russian State* v. *Ropit*, 55 Clunet 674 (1928), Annual Digest 1927–1928, Case No. 43.

[13] *Republic of Iraq* v. *First National City Bank*, 241 F.Supp. 567, affirmed by Court of Appeals, 353 F. 2d 47 (1965), "all questions relating to an act of state are questions of federal law."

[14] *Loucks* v. *Standard Oil Co. of New York*, 224 N.Y. 98 (1918).

Admittedly, the line is difficult to draw. Principles of justice and good morals tend to be relative matters.

Another uncertain ground for the refusal of national courts to enforce foreign acts of state is the violation of international law. If international law is acknowledged as part of the law of the land, then, in effect, the court may be defending the public policy of the forum, too. But a violation of international law may provide a judge with a more objective concept than does the slippery notion of public policy.

This recent method of approach by courts to the act of state doctrine does not lack pitfalls, for the international law relative to acts of state most likely to come before tribunals will owe its formulation to custom or general principles of law recognized by civilized nations rather than to clear-cut, multilateral treaties. Moreover, it may tend to limit the flexibility of diplomatic negotiations by the Executive. Nevertheless, such judgments could reinforce the idea of the transcendence of international law in a world of sovereign states, could promise relief from the narrow principle that virtually any act of state must be acknowledged in foreign courts, and could strengthen the argument for constantly redefining and clarifying international law through multilateral conventions and munici-pal judgments.

In 1962, in the *Banco Nacional de Cuba* v. *Sabbatino* case a United States Court of Appeals held that since a Cuban decree of expropriation not only failed to provide adequate compensation, but also was punitive in purpose and discriminated against United States nationals, it was in viola-tion of international law.[15] On appeal in 1964, the Supreme Court reversed the decision and held that in the absence of a treaty or other agreement American courts would not question the taking of property within its own territory by a sovereign government recognized by the United States.[16] This led to remand of the case to the district court, to congres-sional legislation, and to a new decision in 1965.

The Supreme Court decision in *Banco Nacional de Cuba* v. *Sabbatino*, with remand of the case as *Banco Nacional de Cuba* v. *Farr* to the U.S. district court, presents a fascinating case study of the application of the act of state doctrine, as well as of the United States intent to limit its use in cases on the expropriation of property by foreign sovereigns when such acts are contrary to international law.

---

[15] 307 F. 2d 845.
[16] 376 U.S. 398.

BANCO NACIONAL DE CUBA v. SABBATINO
United States Supreme Court, 1964
376 U.S. 398

Mr. Justice Harlan delivered the opinion of the Court.

The question which brought this case here, and is now found to be the dispositive issue, is whether the so-called act of state doctrine serves to sustain petitioner's claims in this litigation. Such claims are ultimately founded on a decree of the Government of Cuba expropriating certain property, the right to the proceeds of which is here in controversy. The act of state doctrine in its traditional formulation precludes the courts of this country from inquiring into the validity of the public acts a recognized foreign sovereign power committed within its own territory.

I

In February and July of 1960, respondent Farr, Whitlock & Co., an American commodity broker, contracted to purchase Cuban sugar, free alongside the steamer, from a wholly owned subsidiary of Compania Azucarera Vertientes-Camaguey de Cuba (C.A.V.), a corporation organized under Cuban law whose capital stock was owned principally by United States residents. Farr, Whitlock agreed to pay for the sugar in New York upon presentation of the shipping documents and a sight draft.

On July 6, 1960, the Congress of the United States amended the Sugar Act of 1948 to permit a presidentially directed reduction of the sugar quota for Cuba. On the succeeding day President Eisenhower exercised the granted power. The day of the congressional enactment, the Cuban Council of Ministers adopted "Law No. 851," which characterized this reduction in the Cuban sugar quota as an act of "aggression, for political purposes" on the part of the United States, justifying the taking of counter measures by Cuba. The law gave the Cuban President and Prime Minister discretionary power to nationalize by forced expropriation property or enterprises in which American nationals had an interest. Although a system of compensation was formally provided, the possibility of payment under it may well be deemed illusory. Our State Department has described the Cuban law as "manifestly in violation of those principles of international law which have long been accepted by the free countries of the West. It is in its essence discriminatory, arbitrary, and confiscatory."

Between August 6 and August 9, 1960, the sugar covered by the contract between Farr, Whitlock and C.A.V. was loaded, destined for

Morocco, onto the S.S. *Hornfels,* which was standing offshore at the Cuban port of Jucaro (Santa Maria). On the day loading commenced, the Cuban President and Prime Minister, acting pursuant to Law No. 851, issued Executive Power Resolution No. 1. It provided for the compulsory expropriation of all property and enterprises, and of rights and interests arising therefrom, of certain listed companies, including C.A.V., wholly or principally owned by American nationals. The preamble reiterated the alleged injustice of the American reduction of the Cuban sugar quota and emphasized the importance of Cuba serving as an example for other countries to follow "in their struggle to free themselves from the brutal claws of Imperialism." In consequence of the resolution, the consent of the Cuban Government was necessary before a ship carrying sugar of a named company could leave Cuban waters. In order to obtain this consent, Farr, Whitlock, on August 11, entered into contracts, identical to those it had made with C.A.V., with the Banco Para el Comercio Exterior de Cuba, an instrumentality of the Cuban Government. The S.S. *Hornfels* sailed for Morocco on August 12.

Banco Exterior assigned the bills of lading to petitioner, also an instrumentality of the Cuban Government, which instructed its agent in New York, Societe Generale, to deliver the bills and a sight draft in the sum of $175,250.69 to Farr, Whitlock in return for payment. Societe Generale's initial tender of the documents was refused by Farr, Whitlock, which on the same day was notified of C.A.V.'s claim that as rightful owner of the sugar it was entitled to the proceeds. In return for a promise not to turn the funds over to petitioner or its agent, C.A.V. agreed to indemnify Farr, Whitlock for any loss. Farr, Whitlock subsequently accepted the shipping documents, negotiated the bills of lading to its customer, and received payment for the sugar. It refused, however, to hand over the proceeds to Societe Generale. Shortly thereafter, Farr, Whitlock was served with an order of the New York Supreme Court which had appointed Sabbatino as Temporary Receiver of C.A.V.'s New York assets, enjoining it from taking any action in regard to the money claimed by C.A.V. that might result in its removal from the State. Following this, Farr, Whitlock, pursuant to court order, transferred the funds to Sabbatino, to abide the event of a judicial determination as to their ownership.

Petitioner then instituted this action in the Federal District Court for the Southern District of New York. Alleging conversion of the bills of lading, it sought to recover the proceeds thereof from Farr, Whitlock and to enjoin the receiver from exercising any dominion over such proceeds. Upon motions to dismiss and for summary judgment, the District Court, 193 F. Supp. 375, sustained federal *in personam* jurisdiction despite state control of funds. It found that the sugar was located within Cuban territory at the time of expropriation and determined that under merchant law common to civilized countries Farr, Whitlock could not have asserted ownership of the sugar against C.A.V. before making payment. It concluded that C.A.V. had a property interest in the sugar subject to the territorial jurisdiction of Cuba. The court then dealt with the question of Cuba's title to the sugar, on which rested petitioner's claim of conversion. While acknowledging the continuing validity of the act of state doctrine, the court believed it inapplicable when the questioned foreign act is in violation of international law. Proceeding on the basis that a taking invalid under international law does not convey good title, the District Court found the Cuban expropriation decree to violate such law in three separate respects: it was motivated by a retaliatory and not a public purpose; it discriminated against American nationals; and it failed to provide adequate compensation. Summary judgment against petitioner was accordingly granted.

The Court of Appeals, 307 F. 2d 845, affirming the decision on similar grounds, relied on two letters (not before the District Court) written by State Department officers which it took as evidence that the Executive Branch had no objection to a judicial testing of the Cuban decree's validity. The court was unwilling to declare that any one of the infirmities found by the District Court rendered the taking invalid under international law, but was satisfied that in combination they had that effect. We granted certiorari because the issues involved bear importantly on the conduct of the country's foreign relations and more particularly on the proper role of the Judicial Branch in this sensitive area. . . . For reasons to follow we decide that the judgment below must be reversed.

*　　　*　　　*

II

It is first contended that this petitioner, an instrumentality of the Cuban Government, should be denied access to American courts because Cuba is an unfriendly power and does not permit nationals of this country to obtain relief in its courts. Even though the respondents did not raise this point in the lower courts we think it should be considered here. If the courts of this country should be closed to the government of a foreign state, the underlying reason is one of national policy transcending the interests of the parties to the action, and this Court should give effect to that policy *sua sponte* even at this stage of the litigation.

Under principles of comity governing this country's relations with other nations, sovereign states are allowed to sue in the courts of the United States. . . . This Court has called "comity" in the legal sense "neither a matter of absolute obligation, on the one hand, nor of mere courtesy and good will, upon the other." *Hilton* v. *Guyot*, 159 U.S. 113, 163–164. Although comity is often associated with the existence of friendly relations between states . . . prior to some recent lower court cases which have questioned the right of instrumentalities of the Cuban Government to sue in our courts, the privilege of suit has been denied only to governments at war with the United States. . . .

Respondents, pointing to the severance of diplomatic relations, commercial embargo, and freezing of Cuban assets in this country, contend that relations between the United States and Cuba manifest such animosity that unfriendliness is clear, and that the courts should be closed to the Cuban Government. We do not agree. This Court would hardly be competent to undertake assessments of varying degrees of friendliness or its absence, and lacking some definite touchstone for determination, we are constrained to consider any relationship, short of war, with a recognized sovereign power as embracing the privilege of resorting to United States courts. . . .

*   *   *

We hold that this petitioner is not barred from access to the federal courts.

*   *   *

III

Respondents claimed in the lower courts that Cuba had expropriated merely contractual rights the situs of which was in New York, and that the propriety of the taking was, therefore, governed by New York law. . . .

*   *   *

Respondents' limited view of the expropriation must be rejected.

*   *   *

IV

The classic American statement of the act of state doctrine, which appears to have taken root in England as early as 1674, *Blad* v. *Bamfield*, 3 Swans. 604, 36 Eng.Rep. 992, and began to emerge in the jurisprudence of this country in the late eighteenth and early nineteenth centuries, see, e.g., *Ware* v. *Hylton*, 3 Dall. 199, 230; *Hudson* v. *Guestier*, 4 Cranch 293, 294; *The Schooner Exchange* v. *M'Faddon*, 7 Cranch 116, 135, 136; *L'Invincible*, 1 Wheat, 238, 253; *The Santissima Trinidad*, 7 Wheat. 283, 336 is found in *Underhill* v. *Hernandez*, 168 U.S. 250, where Chief Justice Fuller said for a unanimous Court (p. 252):

> Every sovereign state, is bound to respect the independence of every other sovereign state, and the courts of one country will not sit in judgment on the acts of the government of another done within its own territory. Redress of grievances by reason of such acts must be obtained through the means open to be availed of by sovereign powers as between themselves.

Following this precept the Court in that case refused to inquire into acts of Hernandez, a revolutionary Venezuelan military commander whose government had been later recognized by the United States, which were made the basis of a damage action in this country by Underhill, an American citizen, who claimed that he had been unlawfully assaulted, coerced, and detained in Venezuela by Hernandez.

None of this Court's subsequent cases in which the act of state doctrine was directly or peripherally involved manifest any retreat from *Underhill*.

*   *   *

Oetjen involved a seizure of hides from a Mexican citizen as a military levy by General Villa, acting for the forces of General Carranza, whose government was recognized by this country subsequent to the trial but prior to decision by this Court. The hides were sold to a Texas corporation which shipped them to the United States and assigned them to defendant. As assignee of the original owner, plaintiff replevied the hides, claiming that they had been seized in violation of the Hague Conventions. In affirming a judgment for defendant, the Court suggested that the rules of the Conventions did not apply to civil war and that, even if they did, the relevant seizure was not in violation of them. 246 U.S., at 301–302. Nevertheless, it chose to rest its decision on other grounds. It described the designation of the sovereign as a political question to be determined by the legislative and executive departments rather than judicial, invoked the established rule that such recognition operates retroactively to validate past acts. . . .

In *Ricaud* the facts were similar—another general of the Carranza forces seized lead bullion as a military levy—except that the property taken belonged to an American citizen. The Court found *Underhill*, *American Banana*, and *Oetjen* controlling. Commenting on the nature of the principle. . . .

*   *   *

To the same effect is the language of Mr. Justice Cardozo in the *Shapleigh* case, *supra*, where, in commenting on the validity of a Mexican land expropriation, he said (229 U.S., at 471): "The question is not here whether the proceeding was so conducted as to be a wrong to our nationals under the doctrines of international law, though valid under the law of the situs of the land. For wrongs of that order the remedy to be followed is along the channels of diplomacy."

In deciding the present case the Court of Appeals relied in part upon an exception to the unqualified teachings of *Underhill*, *Oetjen*, and *Ricaud* which that court had earlier indicated. In *Bernstein* v. *Van Heyghen Frères Société Anonyme*, 163 F. 2d 246, suit was brought to recover from an assignee property allegedly taken, in effect, by the Nazi Government because plaintiff was Jewish. Recognizing the odious nature of this act of state, the court, through Judge Learned Hand, nonetheless refused to consider it invalid on that ground. Rather, it looked to see if the Executive had acted in any manner that would indicate that United States

Courts should refuse to give effect to such a foreign decree. Finding no such evidence, the court sustained dismissal of the complaint. In a later case involving similar facts the same court again assumed examination of the German acts improper, *Bernstein* v. *N. V. Nederlandsche-Amerikaansche Stoomvaart-Maatschappij*, 173 F. 2d 71, but, quite evidently following the implications of Judge Hand's opinion in the earlier case, amended its mandate to permit evidence of alleged invalidity, 210 F. 2d 375, subsequent to receipt by plaintiff's attorney of a letter from the Acting Legal Adviser to the State Department written for the purpose of relieving the court from any constraint upon the exercise of its jurisdiction to pass on that question.

This Court has never had occasion to pass upon the so-called *Bernstein* exception, nor need it do so now.

*   *   *

V

Preliminarily, we discuss the foundations on which we deem the act of state doctrine to rest, and more particularly the question of whether state or federal law governs its application in a federal diversity case.

We do not believe that this doctrine is compelled either by the inherent nature of sovereign authority, as some of the earlier decisions seem to imply, see *Underhill, supra; American Banana Co.* v. *United Fruit Co.*, 213 U.S. 347; *Oetjen, supra*, at 303, or by some principle of international law. If a transaction takes place in one jurisdiction and the forum is in another, the forum does not by dismissing an action or by applying its own law purport to divest the first jurisdiction of its territorial sovereignty; it merely declines to adjudicate or makes applicable its own law to parties or property before it. The refusal of one country to enforce penal laws of another . . . is a typical example of an instance when a court will not entertain a cause of action arising in another jurisdiction. While historic notions of sovereign authority do bear upon the wisdom of employing the act of state doctrine, they do not dictate its existence.

That international law does not require application of the doctrine is evidenced by the practice of nations. Most of the countries rendering decisions on the subject fail to follow the rule rigidly. No international arbitral or judicial decision discovered suggests that international law prescribes recognition of sovereign acts of foreign governments . . . , and apparently no claim has ever been raised before an international tribunal that failure to apply the act of state doctrine constitutes a breach of international obligation. If international law does not prescribe use of the doctrine, neither does it forbid application of the rule even if it is claimed that the act of state in question violated international law. The traditional view of international law is that it establishes substantive principles for determining whether one country has wronged another. Because of its peculiar nation-to-nation character the usual method for an individual to seek relief is to exhaust local remedies and then repair to the executive authorities of his own state to persuade them to champion his claim in diplomacy or before an international tribunal.

*   *   *

The act of state doctrine, does, however, have "constitutional" under-pinnings. It arises out of the basic relationships between branches of government in a system of separation of powers. It concerns the compe-tency of dissimilar institutions to make and implement particular kinds of decisions in the area of international relations. The doctrine as formulated in past decisions expresses the strong sense of the Judicial Branch that its engagement in the task of passing on the validity of foreign acts of state may hinder rather than further this country's pursuit of goals both for itself and for the community of nations as a whole in the international sphere. Many commentators disagree with this view; they have striven by means of distinguishing and limiting past decisions and by advancing various considerations of policy to stimulate a narrowing of the apparent scope of the rule. Whatever considerations are thought to predominate, it is plain that the problems involved are uniquely federal in nature. If federal authority, in this instance this Court, orders the field of judicial competence in this area for the federal courts, and the state courts are left free to formulate their own rules, the purposes behind the doctrine could be as effectively undermined as if there had been no federal pronounce-ment on the subject.

*   *   *

However, we are constrained to make it clear that an issue concerned with a basic choice regarding the competence and function of the Judi-ciary and the National Executive in ordering our relationships with other members of the international community must be treated exclusively as an aspect of federal law. . . .

*   *   *

VI

If the act of state doctrine is a principle of decision binding on federal and state courts alike but compelled by neither international law nor the Constitution, its continuing vitality depends on its capacity to reflect the proper distribution of functions between the judicial and political branches of the Government on matters bearing upon foreign affairs. It should be apparent that the greater the degree of codification or consensus concerning a particular area of international law, the more appropriate it is for the judiciary to render decisions regarding it, since the courts can then focus on the application of an agreed principle to circumstances of fact rather than on the sensitive task of establishing a principle not inconsistent with the national interest or with international justice. It is also evident that some aspects of international law touch much more sharply on national nerves than do others; the less important the implications of an issue are for our foreign relations, the weaker the justification for exclusivity in the political branches. The balance of relevant considerations may also be shifted if the government which perpetrated the challenged act of state is no longer in existence, as in the *Bernstein* case, for the political interest of this country may, as a result, be measurably altered. Therefore, rather than laying down or reaffirming an inflexible and all-encompassing rule in this case, we decide only that the Judicial Branch will not examine the validity of a taking of property within its own territory by a foreign sovereign government, extant and recognized by this country at the time of suit, in the absence of a treaty or other unambiguous agreement regarding controlling legal principles, even if the complaint alleges that the taking violates customary international law.

There are few if any issues in international law today on which opinion seems to be so divided as the limitations on a State's power to expropriate the property of aliens. There is, of course, authority, in international judicial and arbitral decisions, in the expressions of national governments, and among commentators for the view that a taking is improper under international law if it is not for a public purpose, is discriminatory, or is without provision for prompt, adequate, and effective compensation. However, Communist countries, although they have in fact provided a degree of compensation after diplomatic efforts, commonly recognize no obligation on the part of the taking country. Certain representatives of the newly independent and underdeveloped countries have questioned whether rules of state responsibility toward aliens can bind nations that have not consented to them and it is argued that the traditionally articulated standards governing expropriation of property reflect "imperialist" interests and are inappropriate to the circumstances of emergent states.

*   *   *

When we consider the prospect of the courts characterizing foreign expropriations, however justifiably, as invalid under international law and ineffective to pass title, the wisdom of the precedents is confirmed. While each of the leading cases in this Court may be argued to be distinguishable on its facts from this one—*Underhill* because sovereign immunity provided an independent ground and *Oetjen*, *Ricaud*, and *Shapleigh* because there was actually no violation of international law—the plain implication of all these opinions, and the import of express statements in *Oetjen . . .* and *Shapleigh . . .* is that the act of state doctrine is applicable even if international law has been violated.

*   *   *

The possible adverse consequences of a conclusion to the contrary of that implicit in these cases is highlighted by contrasting the practices of the political branch with the limitations of the judicial process in matters of this kind. Following an expropriation of any significance, the Executive engages in diplomacy aimed to assure that United States citizens who are harmed are compensated fairly. Representing all claimants of this country, it will often be able, either by bilateral or multilateral talks, by submission to the United Nations, or by the employment of economic and political sanctions, to achieve some degree of general redress. Judicial determinations of invalidity of title can, on the other hand, have only an occasional impact, since they depend on the fortuitous circumstance of the property in question being brought into this country. Such decisions would, if the acts involved were declared invalid, often be likely to give offense to the expropriating country; since the concept of territorial sovereignty is so deep seated, any state may resent the refusal of the courts of another sovereign to accord validity to acts within its territorial borders. Piecemeal dispositions of this sort involving the probability of affront to another state could seriously interfere with negotiations being carried on by the Executive Branch and might prevent or render less favorable the terms of an agreement that could otherwise be reached. Relations with third countries who have engaged in similar expropriations would not be immune from effect.

*   *   *

Even if the State Department has proclaimed the impropriety of the expropriation, the stamp of approval of its view by a judicial tribunal, however impartial, might increase any affront and the judicial decision might occur at a time, almost always well after the taking, when such an impact would be contrary to our national interest. Considerably more serious and far-reaching consequences would flow from a judicial finding that international law standards had been met if that determination flew in the face of a State Department proclamation to the contrary. When articulating principles of international law in its relations with other states, the Executive Branch speaks not only as an interpreter of generally accepted and traditional rules, as would the courts, but also as an advocate of standards it believes desirable for the community of nations and protective of national concerns. In short, whatever way the matter is cut, the possibility of conflict between the Judicial and Executive Branches could hardly be avoided.

*   *   *

Another serious consequence of the exception pressed by respondents would be to render uncertain titles in foreign commerce, with the possible consequence of altering the flow of international trade. If the attitude of the United States courts were unclear, one buying expropriated goods would not know if he could safely import them into his country. Even were takings known to be invalid, one would have difficulty determining after goods had changed hands several times whether the particular articles in question were the product of an ineffective state act.

Against the force of such considerations, we find respondents' countervailing arguments quite unpersuasive. Their basic contention is that United States courts could make a significant contribution to the growth of international law, a contribution whose importance, it is said, would be magnified by the relative paucity of decisional law by international bodies. But given the fluidity of present world conditions, the effectiveness of such a patchwork approach toward the formulation of an acceptable body of law concerning state responsibility for expropriations is, to say the least, highly conjectural. Moreover, it rests upon the sanguine presupposition that the decisions of the courts of the world's major capital exporting country and principal exponent of the free enterprise system would be accepted as disinterested expressions of sound legal principle by those adhering to widely different ideologies.

*   *   *

It is suggested that if the act of state doctrine is applicable to violations of international law, it should only be so when the Executive Branch expressly stipulates that it does not wish the courts to pass on the question of validity. See Association of the Bar of the City of New York, Committee on International Law, A Reconsideration of the Act of State Doctrine in United States Courts (1959). We should be slow to reject the representations of the Government that such a reversal of the *Bernstein* principle would work serious inroads on the maximum effectiveness of United States diplomacy. Often the State Department will wish to refrain from taking an official position, particularly at a moment that would be dictated by the development of private litigation but might be inopportune diplomatically. . . . Of course, a relevant consideration for the State Department would be the position contemplated in the court to hear the case. It is highly questionable whether the examination of validity by the judiciary should depend on an educated guess by the Executive as to probable result and, at any rate, should a prediction be wrong, the Executive might be embarrassed in its dealings with other countries. We do not now pass on the *Bernstein* exception, but even if it were deemed valid, its suggested extension is unwarranted.

However offensive to the public policy of this country and its constituent States an expropriation of this kind may be, we conclude that both the national interest and progress toward the goal of establishing the rule of law among nations are best served by maintaining intact the act of state doctrine in this realm of its application.

*   *   *

The judgment of the Court of Appeals is reversed and the case is remanded to the District Court for proceedings consistent with this opinion.

IT IS SO ORDERED.

Mr. Justice White, dissenting

I am dismayed that the Court has, with one broad stroke, declared the ascertainment and application of international law beyond the competence of the courts of the United States in a large and important category of cases. I am also disappointed in the Court's declaration that the acts of a sovereign state with regard to the property of aliens within its borders are beyond the reach of international law in the courts of this country. However clearly established that law may be, a sovereign may violate it with impunity, except insofar as the political branches of the government may provide a remedy. This backward looking doctrine, never before declared in this Court, is carried a disconcerting step further: not only are the courts powerless to question acts of state proscribed by international law but they are likewise powerless to refuse to adjudicate the claim founded upon a foreign law; they must render judgment and thereby validate the lawless act. Since the Court expressly extends its ruling to all acts of state expropriating property, however clearly inconsistent with the international community, all discriminatory expropriations of the property of aliens, as for example the taking of properties of persons belonging to certain races, religions or nationalities, are entitled to automatic validation in the courts of the United States. No other civilized country has found such a rigid rule necessary for the survival of the executive branch of its government; the executive of no other government seems to require such insulation from international law adjudications in its courts; and no other judiciary is apparently so incompetent to ascertain and apply international law.

I do not believe that the act of state doctrine, as judicially fashioned in this Court, and the reasons underlying it, require American courts to decide cases in disregard of international law and of the rights of litigants to a full determination on the merits.

I

Prior decisions of this Court in which the act of state doctrine was deemed controlling do not support the assertion that foreign acts of state must be enforced or recognized or applied in American courts when they violate the law of nations. These cases do hold that a foreign act of state applied to persons or property within its borders may not be denied effect in our courts on the ground that it violates the public policy of the forum. Also the broad language in some of these cases does evince an attitude of caution and self-imposed restraint in dealing with the laws of a foreign nation. But violations of international law were either not presented in these cases, because the parties or predecessors in title were nationals of the acting state, or the claimed violation was insubstantial in light of the facts presented to the Court and the principles of international law applicable at the time. These cases do not strongly imply or even suggest that the Court would woodenly apply the act of state doctrine and grant enforcement to a foreign act where the act was a clear and flagrant violation of international law, as the District Court and the Court of Appeals have found in respect to the Cuban law challenged herein. 193 F. Supp. 375, aff'd, 307 F. 2d 845.

II

Though not a principle of international law, the doctrine of restraint, as formulated by this Court, has its roots in sound policy reasons, and it is to these we must turn to decide whether the act of state doctrine should be extended to cover wrongs cognizable under international law.

*   *   *

The reasons that underlie the deference afforded to foreign acts affecting property in the acting country are several; such deference reflects an effort to maintain a certain stability and predictability in transnational transactions, to avoid friction between nations, to encourage settlement of these disputes through diplomatic means and to avoid interference with the executive control of foreign relations. But to adduce sound reasons for a policy of nonreview is not to resolve the problem at hand but to delineate some of the considerations that are pertinent to its resolution.

Contrary to the assumption underlying the Court's opinion, these considerations are relative, their strength varies from case to case, and they are by no means controlling in all litigation involving the public acts of a foreign government. This is made abundantly clear by numerous cases in which the validity of a foreign act of state is drawn in question and in which these identical considerations are present in the same or a greater degree. American courts have denied recognition or effect to foreign law, otherwise applicable under the conflicts rules of the forum, to many foreign laws where these laws are deeply inconsistent with the policy of the forum, notwithstanding that these laws were of obvious political and social importance to the acting country. For example, foreign confiscatory decrees purporting to divest nationals and corporations of the foreign sovereign of property located in the United States uniformly have been denied effect in our courts, including this Court; courts continued to recognize private property rights of Russian corporations owning property within the United States long after the Russian Government, recognized by the United States, confiscated all such property and had rescinded the laws on which corporate identity depended. Furthermore, our courts customarily refuse to enforce the revenue and penal laws of a foreign state, since no country has an obligation to further the governmental interests of a foreign sovereign. And the judgments of foreign courts are denied conclusive or *prima facie* effect where the judgment is based on a statute unenforceable in the forum, where the procedures of the rendering court markedly depart from our notions of fair procedure, and generally where enforcement would be contrary to the public policy of the forum. These cases demonstrate that our courts have never been bound to pay unlimited deference to foreign acts of state, defined as an act or law in which the sovereign's governmental interest is involved; they simultaneously cast doubt on the proposition that the additional element in the case at bar, that the property may have been within the territorial confines of Cuba when the expropriation decree was promulgated, requires automatic deference to the decree, regardless of whether the foreign act violates international law.

* * *

The relevance of international law to a just resolution of this case is apparent from the impact of international law on other aspects of this controversy. Indeed it is only because of the application of international rules to resolve other issues that the act of state doctrine becomes the determinative issue in this case. The basic rule of the law of the situs of property is the proper law to be applied in determining title in other forums, whether styled a rule of private international law or domestic conflict of law, is rooted in concepts firmly embedded in a consensus of nations on territorial sovereignty. Without such a consensus and the conflicts rule derived therefrom, the question of whether Cuba's decree can be measured against the norms of international law would never arise in this litigation, since then a court presumably would be free to apply its own rules governing the acquisition of title to property. Furthermore, the contention that the sugar in question was within the territorial confines of Cuba when the Cuban decree was enacted itself rests on widely accepted principles of international law, namely, that the bays or inlets contiguous to a country are within its boundaries and that territorial jurisdiction extends at least three miles beyond these boundaries. See Oppenheim, International Law, Secs. 186, 190–191 (Lauterpacht, 8th Ed., ed. 1955). Without these rules derived from international law, this confiscation could be characterized as extraterritorial and therefore—unless the Court also intends to change this rule—subject to the public policy test traditionally applied to extraterritorial takings of property, even though embarrassing to foreign affairs. . . .

* * *

The Court accepts the application of rules of international law to other aspects of this litigation, accepts the relevance of international law in other cases and announces that when there is an appropriate degree of "consensus concerning a particular area of international law, the more appropriate it is for the judiciary to render decisions regarding it, since the courts can then focus on the application of an agreed principle to circumstances of fact rather than on the sensitive task of establishing a principle, not inconsistent with the national interest or with international justice.". . . The Court then, rather lightly in my view, dispenses with its obligation to resolve controversies in accordance with "international justice" and the "national interest" by assuming and declaring that there are no areas of agreement between nations in respect to expropriations. . . . I would not declare that even if there were a clear consensus in the international community, the courts must close their eyes to a lawless act and validate the transgression by rendering judgment for the foreign state at its own request. This is an unfortunate declaration for this Court to make. It is, of course, wholly inconsistent with the premise from which the Court starts, and under it, banishment of international law from the courts is complete and final in cases like this. . . .

IV

The reasons for nonreview, based as they are on traditional concepts of territorial sovereignty, lose much of their force when the foreign act of state is shown to be a violation of international law. All legitimate exercises of sovereign power, whether territorial or otherwise, should be exercised consistent with rules of international law, including those rules which mark the bounds of lawful state action against aliens or their property located within the territorial confines of the foreign state. . . .

*   *   *

Of course, there are many unsettled areas of international law as there are with domestic law, and these areas present sensitive problems of accommodating the interests of nations that subscribe to divergent economic and political systems. It may be that certain nationalizations of property for a public purpose fall within this area. Also, it may be that domestic courts, as compared to international tribunals, or arbitral commissions, have a different and less active role to play in formulating new rules of international law or in choosing between rules not yet adhered to by any substantial group of nations. Where a clear violation of international law is not demonstrated, I would agree that principles of comity underlying the act of state doctrine warrant recognition and enforcement of the foreign act. But none of these considerations relieve a court of the obligation to make an inquiry into the validity of the foreign act, none of them warrant a flat rule of no inquiry at all. . . .

V

There remains for consideration the relationship between the act of state doctrine and the power of the executive over matters touching upon the foreign affairs of the nation. . . .

Without doubt political matters in the realm of foreign affairs are within the exclusive domain of the Executive Branch, as, for example, issues for which there are no available standards or which are textually committed by the Constitution to the executive. But this is far from saying that the Constitution vests in the executive exclusive absolute control of foreign affairs or that the validity of a foreign act of state is necessarily a political question. International law, as well as a treaty or executive agreement, see *United States v. Pink*, 315 U.S. 203, provides an ascertainable standard for adjudicating the validity of some foreign acts, and courts are competent to apply this body of law, notwithstanding that there may be some cases where comity dictates giving effect to the foreign act because it is not clearly condemned under generally accepted principles of international law. And it cannot be contended that the Constitution allocates this area to the exclusive jurisdiction of the executive, for the judicial power is expressly extended by that document to controversies between aliens and citizens or States, aliens and aliens, and foreign states and American citizens or States.

A valid statute, treaty or executive agreement could, I assume, confine the power of federal courts to review or award relief in respect of foreign acts or otherwise displace international law as the rule of decision. I would not disregard a declaration by the Secretary of State or the President that an adjudication in the courts of the validity of a foreign expropriation would impede relations between the United States and the foreign government or the settlement of the controversy through diplomatic channels. But I reject the presumption that these undesirable consequences would follow from adjudication in every case, regardless of the circumstances.

*   *   *

There is a further possibility of embarrassment to the executive from the blanket presumption of validity applicable to all foreign expropriations, which the Court chooses to ignore, and which, in my view is far more self-evident than those adduced by the Court. . . .

*   *   *

Obviously there are cases where an examination of the foreign act and declaration of invalidity or validity might undermine the foreign policy of the Executive Branch and its attempts at negotiating a settlement for a nationalization of the property of Americans. The respect ordinarily due to a foreign state, as reflected in the decisions of this Court, rests upon a desire not to disturb the relations between countries and on a view that other means, more effective than piecemeal adjudication of claims arising out of a large-scale nationalization program of settling the dispute, may be available. Precisely because these considerations are more or less present, or absent, in any given situation and because the Department of our Government primarily responsible for the formulation of foreign policy and settling these matters on a state-to-state basis is more competent than courts to determine the extent to which they are involved, a blanket presumption of nonreview in each case is inappropriate and a requirement that in each case is necessary. . . .

*   *   *

This is precisely the procedure that the Department of State adopted voluntarily in the situation where a foreign government seeks to invoke the defense of immunity in our courts. . . .

Where the courts are requested to apply the act of state doctrine at the behest of the State Department, it does not follow that the courts are to proceed to adjudicate the action without examining the validity of the foreign act under international law. The foreign relations considerations and potential of embarrassment to the executive inhere in examination of the foreign act and in the result following from such an examination, not in the matter of who wins. Thus, all the Department of State can legitimately request is nonexamination of the foreign act. . . .

*   *   *

The position of the Executive Branch of the Government charged with foreign affairs with respect to this case is not entirely clear. As I see it no specific objection by the Secretary of State to examination of the validity of Cuba's law has been interposed at any stage in these proceedings, which would ordinarily lead to an adjudication on the merits. Disclaiming, rightfully, I think, any interest in the outcome of the case, the United States has simply argued for a rule of nonexamination in every case, which literally, I suppose, includes this one. If my view had prevailed, I would have stayed further resolution of the issues in this Court to afford the Department of State reasonable time to clarify its views in light of the opinion. In the absence of specific objection to an examination of the validity of Cuba's law under international law, I would have proceeded to determine the issue and resolve this litigation on the merits.

Act of State Doctrine—U.S. Hickenlooper Amendment

BANCO NACIONAL DE CUBA v. FARR
United States District Court, 1965
243 F. Supp. 957

Bryan, District Judge

This case is before me on remand from the Supreme Court of the United States [*Banco Nacional de Cuba* v. *Sabbatino et al.*, 376 U.S. 398 (1964)], which reversed summary judgment in favor of defendants granted by the District Court [193 F. Supp. 375 (1961)] and affirmed by the Court of Appeals [2 Cir., 307 F. 2d 845 (1962)]. . . .

The case involves the proceeds of the sale of a cargo of sugar which was expropriated by the Castro government while in Cuban territorial waters from Compania Azucarera Vertientes-Camaguey de Cuba (C.A.V.), a corporation organized under Cuban law whose capital stock was owned principally by United States citizens.

The sugar was sold to Farr, Whitlock & Co. (Farr), New York sugar brokers, and the proceeds of the sale came to the United States.

The claim of plaintiff Banco Nacional de Cuba (Banco), an instrumentality of the Cuban government, to the proceeds of the expropriated sugar is founded on the Cuban expropriation. Defendant Farr and defendant *Sabbatino*,* a State Court Receiver for C.A.V. who held the proceeds, took the position that the Cuban government was not entitled thereto but that the proceeds were the property of C.A.V. from whom the sugar was expropriated.

Judgment for the defendants below was granted on the ground that the expropriation of the sugar violated international law, was therefore invalid and unenforcable in our courts, and was ineffective to deprive C.A.V. of its rights in the sugar and its proceeds.

The Supreme Court held that the "act of state doctrine" proscribed a challenge to the validity of the Cuban expropriation law in this case even if it violated international law. It reversed and remanded the case to the District Court for further proceedings.

On October 7, 1964, subsequent to the decision of the Supreme Court

---

* Subsequent to the decision of the Court of Appeals and before the decision of the Supreme Court, Sabbatino was discharged as receiver of C.A.V., and the funds in dispute were placed in escrow pending the outcome of this suit. After remand, pursuant to stipulation of the parties, the action was discontinued as against Sabbatino, and the title was amended to name as defendants only the co-partners doing business as Farr, Whitlock & Co.

and before judgment was entered on remand, the President signed the Foreign Assistance Act of 1964 containing an amendment sponsored by Senators Hickenlooper and Sparkman, which precipitated the present phase of this litigation. (Section 301 (d) (4) of Public Law 88–633, 78 Stat. 1009, 1013, hereafter referred to as the Hickenlooper Amendment.) The Amendment provided:

Notwithstanding any other provision of law, no court in the United States shall decline on the ground of the federal act of state doctrine to make a determination on the merits giving effect to the principles of international law in a case in which a claim of title or other right is asserted by any party including a foreign state (or a party claiming through such state) based upon (or traced through) a confiscation or other taking after January 1, 1959, by an act of that state in violation of the principles of international law, including the principles of compensation and the other standards set out in this subsection: *Provided,* That this sub-paragraph shall not be applicable (1) in any case in which an act of a foreign state is not contrary to international law or with respect to a claim of title or other right acquired pursuant to an irrevocable letter of credit of not more than 180 days duration issued in good faith prior to the time of the confiscation or other taking, or (2) in any case with respect to which the President determines that application of the act of state doctrine is required in that particular case by the foreign policy interests of the United States and a suggestion to this effect is filed on his behalf in that case with the court, or (3) in any case in which the proceedings are commenced after January 1, 1966.*

*   *   *

The defendants . . . contend (1) that the Hickenlooper Amendment removed the bar interposed by the act of state doctrine to a determination of the validity of the Cuban expropriation under international law; (2) that under the Amendment this court is now required to adjudicate that issue; and (3) that in making such an adjudication this court is bound by the determination of the Court of Appeals in this case and defendants were therefore entitled to judgment dismissing the complaint.

Plaintiff, on the other hand, maintains (1) that the Hickenlooper Amendment is not applicable to this case, and (2) that if it is it is unconstitutional in its application to this case.

*   *   *

The questions posed here then are:

1. Does the Hickenlooper Amendment apply to pending cases generally?

2. Does it apply to the case at Bar?

3. Is it unconstitutional in any respect?

4. What is the effect of the Amendment on this case?

*   *   *

---

* The Foreign Assistance Act of 1965 (P.L. 89–171, 79 Stat. 653) struck out provision (3).

The Amendment does not deal with confiscations and transactions in the abstract. It deals with "cases" and the action which courts are to take upon such cases. It consistently uses the word "case" throughout its text. Nowhere does it distinguish between cases pending at the time of its enactment and cases which were commenced prior thereto. There is certainly no language which could be remotely said to exclude the case at bar.

* * *

The direction to the courts is mandatory. It is provided that "no court in the United States *shall decline* on the ground of the federal act of state doctrine to make a determination" *in a case* which it describes. These words are not prospective as has been urged. They are mandatory in their intention and effect and require the courts to give retroactive effect to the directions of the Amendment.

* * *

Congress was particularly concerned with the Cuban confiscations which had taken place on such a large scale. It was for this reason, as Senator Hickenlooper made clear, that the date of January 1, 1959 was used as the operative date. A prime concern was to prevent the Castro government from reaping the fruits of what Congress considered to be illegal and unconscionable acts in violation of international law. It can scarcely be assumed that Congress intended to exclude a substantial portion of the Cuban confiscations at which the statute was directed from the benefits of the statute in the absence of specific language to that effect.

* * *

It is urged that the Amendment should be construed so as to apply only to cases filed after its enactment because to do otherwise would not further these broad congressional purposes. It is difficult to see, however, how such purposes would be furthered by a construction which excluded from the deterrent effect of the Amendment a substantial number of confiscations which had already occurred and on which suits were presently pending. On the contrary, bold and immediate action with respect to all confiscations, including those already in litigation, would serve firm notice that as far as the United States was concerned no benefits would be permitted to accrue from such takings.

Congress was concerned not only with the assertion of claims to expropriated property but with permitting one who had suffered expropriation to resist a suit in our courts by the expropriating government to obtain the fruits of expropriation. . . .

* * *

It is urged that the Amendment does not apply to this case at least, even if it applies to other pending cases and that Congress so intended. I find nothing to sustain that view.

*   *   *

. . . In the light of its strongly expressed views concerning the iniquities of the Castro regime and its confiscations, it is most unlikely that Congress intended to exclude the *Sabbatino* case from the Amendment if this court has power to apply it. Due to no fault of the defendants *Sabbatino* was the bell-wether case on Cuban confiscation. Some forty pending cases were delayed to await its determination by the Supreme Court. Thus, by a purely fortuitous circumstance the defendants in *Sabbatino* would be the only victims of the confiscations among the litigants who would be denied the benefits of a determination on the merits under the principles of international law.

Moreover, the Cuban government would receive a windfall. It would avoid a determination on the merits as to whether the taking had been in violation of international law.

Against the background of the fulsome record of Congressional attitude with respect to the Castro government and its confiscations, no intention to permit such a result can be ascribed to Congress.

*   *   *

I hold (1) that this is a case within the purview of the Hickenlooper Amendment; (2) that the Amendment is supervening law which must be applied here despite the opinion of the Supreme Court in *Sabbatino;* and (3) that I am therefore required to make a determination on the merits giving effect to the principles of international law as the Amendment provides.

*   *   *

The power granted to Congress by Art. 1, No. 8, cl. 3, of the Constitution "to regulate Commerce with foreign Nations, and among the several States" is broad and plenary. . . .

It cannot be seriously disputed that the Foreign Assistance Act is a valid exercise of congressional power under the commerce clause. . . .

*   *   *

Congress sought to encourage foreign investment by removing the bar of the act of state doctrine to determination on the merits of suits arising out of foreign confiscations in violation of international law.

Whether the act of state doctrine is applied or withheld by the courts may profoundly affect foreign investments and the flow of international trade and commerce as the Supreme Court recognized in *Sabbatino.* . . .

Congress determined that the national interests in the areas of foreign investment and international trade and commerce require the elimination of the act of state doctrine except where the President determines otherwise. It so provided in the Hickenlooper Amendment. This, like the Foreign Assistance Act itself, was plainly within the powers of Congress under the commerce clause.

*　　　*　　　*

The suggestion is made that the Amendment impinges upon the power of the President over foreign relations and thus violates the doctrine of separation of powers. I see no merit in this suggestion.

This Amendment did not become law by the action of Congress alone. It was part of an act signed into law by the President. While the Executive Branch opposed the Amendment before the Senate committee, the President did not choose to exercise his veto power when it came before him for signature. He certainly had the power to do so had he felt that the Amendment seriously impinged upon his executive functions.

Indeed, the act cannot be said to impinge on such functions. It does not preclude the President from exercising his role in foreign relations. On the contrary, the exception written into the act expressly provides that the courts shall apply the act of state doctrine whenever the President determines that the foreign policy interests of the nation require its application and makes such a suggestion. . . .

*　　　*　　　*

Application of the act of state doctrine is not required by the Constitution as the Supreme Court made plain in *Sabbatino*.

*　　　*　　　*

While the act of state doctrine is not of constitutional dimensions, and there is no constitutional requirement that it be applied by the courts, this does not resolve the question of whether there is a constitutional impediment to a legislative direction that the courts abstain from applying it. Plaintiff urges that there is such an impediment, and that the legislative direction to the courts in the Amendment not to apply the doctrine is an unconstitutional interference with the judicial power. I do not agree.

There is no doubt that issues concerning international law as they may affect confiscations by foreign governments are within the constitutional jurisdiction and judicial competence of the courts, as *Sabbatino* makes clear. By applying the act of state doctrine the courts have merely declined as a matter of judicial policy to decide such issues where a decision may affect our foreign relations. . . .

*　　　*　　　*

When a determination is made by the political branches charged with the responsibility for foreign relations as to where the interests of the

United States lie, it is not for the courts to say them nay. The basic reason for the application of the act of state doctrine disappears. To require that the doctrine be applied despite the express directions of the political branches on the subject would be to place the court in the position of having the last word in matters affecting foreign affairs, the determination of which is committed to other branches of the Government. This would be wholly inconsistent with the doctrine of separation of powers and with the very rationale of the act of state doctrine.

*   *   *

It seems clear that when Congress, dealing with subject matter within the powers delegated to it by the Constitution, speaks with respect to a voluntary judicial policy of self-limitation, the courts are bound to follow its directions unless compelled not to do so by the Constitution. There is no constitutional compulsion to disregard the directions of Congress as to the elimination of the self-imposed limitation of the act of state doctrine as provided in the Amendment.

*   *   *

Finally, it is urged that the Amendment may not be constitutionally applied in the case at bar. The thrust of this contention is that application of the Amendment would retroactively deprive plaintiff of vested property rights without due process of law in violation of the Fifth Amendment.

*   *   *

Here . . . plaintiff acquired no vested rights. Whatever rights it may have had arose entirely from expropriation by the Cuban government. If the expropriation is wrongful under international law now it was wrongful then. No judgment has been entered in plaintiff's favor. The expropriation was plainly not made in reliance upon the protections afforded by the act of state doctrine. But even had it been, that doctrine creates no property rights. The Hickenlooper Amendment creates no new liabilities.

Here Congress has merely lifted a bar to consideration of pre-existing questions of substantive rights and liabilities. . . .

*   *   *

The Cuban government could acquire no vested right by virtue of the expropriation if it was wrongful and certainly not a vested right to be protected against liability for such wrongful act by the bar of the act of state doctrine.

*   *   *

The plaintiff here has received all the due process to which it was entitled. I hold that the application of the Amendment to the case at bar does not deprive the plaintiff of any vested rights in violation of the due process clause of the Fifth Amendment.

* * *

Defendants contend that since I have held the act of state doctrine as enunciated by the Supreme Court in *Sabbatino* to be inapplicable to this case under the Hickenlooper Amendment, this court is bound by the prior decision of the Court of Appeals, and without further inquiry on the merits, must give judgment for the defendants dismissing the complaint. Plainly I am bound by the decision of the Court of Appeals that the expropriation by the Cuban government violated international law. The opinion of the Supreme Court does not impair that holding. Its discussion of international law was limited to the question of compensation and did not relate to questions of discrimination and retaliation.

But defendants' position fails to take into account one vitally important factor. The Amendment provides that it shall not be applicable,

. . . in any case with respect to which the President determines that application of the act of state doctrine is required in that particular case by the foreign policy interests of the United States and a suggestion to this effect is filed on his behalf in that case with the court.

That exception is an integral and essential part of the Amendment. It must be given effect.

* * *

It is plain to me that proper respect and consideration for the Executive Arm requires that the court give full opportunity to the President to make the determination provided for by the Amendment and, if in his wisdom he sees fit, to have a suggestion filed on his behalf that in this case application of the act of state doctrine is required by the foreign policy interests of the United States.

* * *

For these reasons determination of the question as to whether final judgment dismissing the complaint should be entered in this case will be withheld for a period of sixty (60) days for the purposes I have indicated.

* * *

Memorandum Opinion of November 15, 1965*

District Judge Bryan

In my opinion dated July 30, 1965, I held that the Hickenlooper Amendment included in the Foreign Assistance Act of 1964 [Section 301

---

* 5 International Legal Materials 1209.

(d) (4) of the Public Law 88–633, 78 Stat. 1009, 1013, 22 U.S.C. sec. 2370 (e) (2)] applied to the case at bar, now before me on remand from the Supreme Court of the United States.

* * *

Up to the time when the opinion of July 30, 1965, was filed there had been no determination by the President that the application of the act of state doctrine to this case was required by the foreign policy interests of the United States, and no suggestion to that effect had been filed with the court. However, the record was incomplete and unclear as to the position which the President might desire to take on this question.

In order to afford the executive arm full opportunity to make such a determination and to express its view to the court if it so desired, I withheld decision for a period of sixty (60) days as to whether final judgment dismissing the complaint in this action should be entered. Prior to the expiration of that period the court received a letter from the United States Attorney for the Southern District of New York dated September 29, 1965, reading as follows:

In its decision of July 30, 1965 this Court afforded the Executive Branch the opportunity to file a suggestion indicating whether the application of the act of state doctrine is required by the foreign policy interests of the United States, as provided for in Section 620 (e) (2) of the Foreign Assistance Act of 1961, as amended (22 U.S.C. 2370 [e] [2]). I am instructed to inform the Court that no determination has been made that application of the act of state doctrine is required in this case by the foreign policy interests of the United States.

So that there will be no ambiguity, the Court is advised that no such determination is contemplated.

This letter makes it clear that the President will make no suggestion to the court in this case as to the application of the act of state doctrine pursuant to the Hickenlooper Amendment. . . .

The moving defendants urge the entry of final judgment in their favor is now required by the prior decision of the Court of Appeals in this case, 307 F. 2d 845 (1964). In that decision the Court of Appeals affirmed the judgment of the district court dismissing the complaint granted on the defendants' motion for summary judgment. It held that the act of state doctrine did not bar determination on the merits in this case and that the Cuban decree of confiscation on which plaintiff's claim was founded violated international law. It stated (p. 868):

Since the Cuban decree of expropriation not only failed to provide adequate compensation but also involved a retaliatory purpose and a discrimination against United States nationals, we hold that the decree was in violation of international law.

The court concluded (p. 869):

Since the Cuban decree violated international law, the appellant's [plaintiff's] title is invalid and the district court was correct in dismissing the complaint.

The reversal of the Court of Appeals decision by the Supreme Court in *Banco Nacional de Cuba* v. *Sabbatino* (*supra*) was on the sole ground that the act of state doctrine proscribed a challenge to the validity of the Cuban expropriation decree even if it violated international law. The Supreme Court did not reach the question of violation of international law passed upon by the Court of Appeals and, indeed, such discussion of international law as there was in its opinion concerned only adequate compensation and not discrimination and retaliation. . . .

As I have held, application of the act of state doctrine to this case is now barred by the Hickenlooper Amendment since there will be no presidential suggestion to the contrary. The holding of the Supreme Court that the act of state doctrine bars determination on the merits no longer applies.

The Court of Appeals has already determined that absent the bar of the act of state doctrine the Cuban decree in this case on which plaintiff's claim is founded violated international law, that plaintiff's title, therefore, is invalid, and that defendants are entitled to judgment dismissing the complaint. I am plainly bound by that determination which is decisive of the issue now before me.

Defendants' motion to dismiss the complaint is therefore granted. . . .

* * *

Recovery for Expropriations

Many obstacles and delays await a person seeking recovery for expropriated property either through diplomatic espousal of claims by his own state or through local suit in the expropriating state, or through an action in his own national courts when the act of state doctrine may come into play. As indicated earlier, the United States has negotiated a number of lump-sum claims settlement agreements with other states for the nationalization or other taking of the property of American nationals, and legislation has provided that the Foreign Settlement Claims Commission may receive, decide, and award claims out of the funds available.

The funds rarely have covered the amount of the awards, but they have offered a measure of justice. Moreover, from 1954 to 1959, on claims against Bulgaria, and again from 1965 to 1967, on claims against Cuba, applications were received and awards made even before the funds were available in order to minimize delays in settlement and the attendant difficulties of gathering evidence as the years go by.

In general, nationalization and debt claims have been allowed only if the property alleged to have been taken was owned directly or indirectly by a United States national on the date of the loss, and if the claim has been held continuously by one or more United States nationals until the date of filing with the Foreign Claims Settlement Commission. "National" has been defined to mean (*a*) a natural person who is a United States citizen or (*b*) a corporation, organized under the laws of the United States, any state of the Union, the District of Columbia, or the Commonwealth of Puerto Rico, in which at least 50 percent of the capital stock or other beneficial interest is owned by citizens of the United States.

Another protection to American contractors and investors abroad has been the United States investment guaranties program. In 1948, under the Marshall Plan, American business was offered the first investment guaranties against the risk of inconvertibility of currency in 15 European states. Since then, through legislation under the several foreign assistance acts, the United States has offered to insure new American investments in friendly, economically underdeveloped states that have agreed to participate in the investment guaranty program against losses through: (*a*) inconvertibility; (*b*) expropriation, including abrogation, repudiation, or a foreign government's impairment of its own contract; (*c*) war, revolution, and insurrection; (*d*) extended risk, which have mainly been limited to housing projects. In 1966, one or more of these guaranties were available to American businessmen, for a fee, in about 35 states of the world.

However, such bilateral or unilateral remedies indicated above for aliens' claims against states still fall short of a permanent international institution for the prompt and decisive arbitration of issues in this delicate area of international relations. Since 1922, the International Chamber of Commerce in Paris, a private organization, has provided a Court of Arbitration to handle disputes over international contracts. States as well as private firms have had recourse to arbitration before this body as a result of contracts between state authorities and private enterprise; states have appeared as defendants in three quarters of the arbitration proceedings, and they have, with only one exception, invariably accepted the arbital award.

A new and promising step toward the conciliation and arbitration of investment disputes began with the 1962 study by the International Bank for Reconstruction and Development on the desirability and utility of an international facility for this purpose, to be sponsored by the Bank. In 1965, the Bank submitted to governments a Convention on the Settlement of Investment Disputes between States and Nationals of Other States. It provided for an International Centre for the Settlement of Investment Disputes, an autonomous international institution, with a secretary general and an administrative council of the contracting states.

Facilities through conciliation and arbitration panels, chosen from a large list of qualified persons designated by contracting states and the chairman of the administrative council, are used to settle investment disputes. Jurisdiction is obtained by written consent of the parties and is limited to "any legal dispute arising directly out of an investment" between a contracting state and a national of another contracting state. The convention's provisions seem to offer a fresh and salutory approach to the urgent problems of claims under investment disputes in a world that requires full and fair cooperation between the rich and poor nations for their mutual advantage.

In the following document, key provisions of the *Convention on the Settlement of Investment Disputes between States and Nationals of Other States* indicate the scope and thrust of a new public international institution to settle claims arising from investment disputes.

Arbitration of Investment Disputes

CONVENTION ON THE SETTLEMENT OF INVESTMENT DISPUTES BETWEEN STATES AND NATIONALS OF OTHER STATES, 1965*
International Bank for Reconstruction and Development
18 March 1965

Article 1

1. There is hereby established the International Centre for Settlement of Investment Disputes (hereinafter called the Centre).

2. The purpose of the Centre shall be to provide facilities for conciliation and arbitration of investment disputes between Contracting States and nationals of other Contracting States in accordance with the provisions of this Convention.

Article 2

The seat of the Centre shall be at the principal office of the International Bank for Reconstruction and Development (hereinafter called the Bank). The seat may be moved to another place by decision of the Administrative Council adopted by a majority of two-thirds of its members.

Article 3

The Centre shall have an Administrative Council and a Secretariat and shall maintain a Panel of Conciliators and a Panel of Arbitrators.

Article 4

1. The Administrative Council shall be composed of one representative of each Contracting State. An alternate may act as representative in case of his principal's absence from a meeting or inability to act.

2. In the absence of a contrary designation, each governor and alternate governor of the Bank appointed by a Contracting State shall be *ex officio* its representative and its alternate respectively.

Article 5

The President of the Bank shall be *ex officio* Chairman of the Administrative Council (hereinafter called the Chairman) but shall have no vote. During his absence or inability to act and during any vacancy in the office

---

* In force 14 October 1966.

of President of the Bank, the person for the time being acting as President shall act as Chairman of the Administrative Council.

Article 6

1. Without prejudice to the powers and functions vested in it by other provisions of this Convention, the Administrative Council shall:
   a. adopt the administrative and financial regulations of the Centre;
   b. adopt the rules of procedure for the institution of conciliation and arbitration proceedings;
   c. adopt the rules of procedure for conciliation and arbitration proceedings (hereinafter called the Conciliation Rules and the Arbitration Rules);
   d. approve arrangements with the Bank for the use of the Bank's administrative facilities and services;
   e. determine the conditions of service of the Secretary-General and of any Deputy Secretary-General;
   f. adopt the annual budget of revenues and expenditures of the Centre;
   g. approve the annual report on the operation of the Centre.

*   *   *

Article 9

The Secretariat shall consist of a Secretary-General, one or more Deputy Secretaries-General and staff.

Article 10

1. The Secretary-General and any Deputy Secretary-General shall be elected by the Administrative Council by a majority of two-thirds of its members upon the nomination of the Chairman for a term of service not exceeding six years and shall be eligible for re-election. After consulting the members of the Administrative Council, the Chairman shall propose one or more candidates for each such office.

*   *   *

Article 12

The Panel of Conciliators and the Panel of Arbitrators shall each consist of qualified persons, designated as hereinafter provided, who are willing to serve thereon.

Article 13

1. Each Contracting State may designate to each Panel four persons who may but need not be its nationals.
2. The Chairman may designate ten persons to each Panel. The persons so designated to a Panel shall each have a different nationality.

*   *   *

Article 18

The Centre shall have full international legal personality. The legal capacity of the Centre shall include the capacity:
   a. to contract;
   b. to acquire and dispose of movable and immovable property;
   c. to institute legal proceedings.

Article 19

To enable the Centre to fulfill its functions, it shall enjoy in the territories of each Contracting State the immunities and privileges set forth. . . .

*   *   *

Article 25

1. The jurisdiction of the Centre shall extend to any legal dispute arising directly out of an investment, between a Contracting State (or any constituent subdivision or agency of a Contracting State designated to the Centre by that State) and a national of another Contracting State, which the parties to the disputes consent in writing to submit to the Centre. When the parties have given their consent, no party may withdraw its consent unilaterally.

2. "National of another Contracting State" means:
   a. any natural person who had the nationality of a Contracting State other than the State party to the dispute on the date on which the parties consented to submit such dispute to conciliation or arbitration as well as on the date on which the request was registered . . . but does not include any person who on either date also had the nationality of the Contracting State party to the dispute; and
   b. any juridical person which had the nationality of a Contracting State other than the State party to the dispute on the date on which the parties consented to submit such dispute to conciliation or arbitration and any juridical person which had the nationality of the Contracting State party to the dispute on that date and which, because of foreign control, the parties have agreed should be treated as a national of another Contracting State for the purposes of this Convention.

*   *   *

Article 26

Consent of the parties to arbitration under this Convention shall, unless otherwise stated, be deemed consent to such arbitration to the exclusion of any other remedy. A Contracting State may require the exhaustion of local administrative or judicial remedies as a condition of its consent to arbitration under this Convention.

Article 27

1. No Contracting State shall give diplomatic protection, or bring an international claim, in respect of a dispute which one of its nationals and another Contracting State shall have consented to submit or shall have submitted to arbitration under this Convention, unless such other Contracting State shall have failed to abide by and comply with the award rendered in such dispute.

*   *   *

Article 28

1. Any Contracting State or any national of a Contracting State wishing to institute conciliation proceedings shall address a request to that effect in writing to the Secretary-General who shall send a copy of the request to the other party.

*   *   *

Article 29

1. The Conciliation Commission (hereinafter called the Commission) shall be constituted as soon as possible after registration of a request pursuant to Article 28.

    2. a. The Commission shall consist of a sole conciliator or any uneven number of conciliators appointed as the parties shall agree.

      b. Where the parties do not agree upon the number of conciliators and the method of their appointment, the Commission shall consist of three conciliators, one conciliator appointed by each party and the third, who shall be the president of the Commission, appointed by agreement of the parties.

*   *   *

Article 34

1. It shall be the duty of the Commission to clarify the issues in dispute between the parties and to endeavor to bring about agreement between them upon mutually acceptable terms. To that end, the Commission may at any stage of the proceedings and from time to time recommend terms of settlement to the parties. The parties shall cooperate in good faith with the Commission in order to enable the Commission to carry out its functions, and shall give their most serious consideration to its recommendations.

*   *   *

Article 36

1. Any Contracting State or any national of a Contracting State wishing to institute arbitration proceedings shall address a request to that

effect in writing to the Secretary-General who shall send a copy of the request to the other party.

Article 37

1. The Arbitral Tribunal (hereinafter called the Tribunal) shall be constituted as soon as possible after registration of a request pursuant to Article 36.

     2. a. The Tribunal shall consist of a sole arbitrator or any uneven number of arbitrators appointed as the parties shall agree.

         b. Where the parties do not agree upon the number of arbitrators and the method of their appointment, the Tribunal shall consist of three arbitrators, one arbitrator appointed by each party and the third, who shall be the president of the Tribunal, appointed by agreement of the parties.

Article 38

If the Tribunal shall not have been constituted within 90 days after notice of registration of the request has been dispatched by the Secretary-General in accordance with paragraph (3) of Article 36, or such other period as the parties may agree, the Chairman shall, at the request of either party and after consulting both parties as far as possible, appoint the arbitrator or arbitrators not yet appointed. Arbitrators appointed by the Chairman pursuant to the Article shall not be nationals of the Contracting State party to the dispute or of the Contracting State whose national is a party to the dispute.

Article 39

The majority of the arbitrators shall be nationals of States other than the Contracting State party to the dispute and the Contracting State whose national is a party to the dispute; provided, however, that the foregoing provisions of this Article shall not apply if the sole arbitrator or each individual member of the Tribunal has been appointed by agreement of the parties.

*   *   *

Article 42

1. The Tribunal shall decide a dispute in accordance with such rules of law as may be agreed by the parties. In the absence of such agreement, the Tribunal shall apply the law of the Contracting State party to the dispute (including its rules on the conflict of laws) and such rules of international law as may be applicable.

2. The Tribunal may not bring in a finding of *non liquet* on the ground of silence or obscurity of the law.

3. The provisions of paragraphs (1) and (2) shall not prejudice the power of the Tribunal to decide a dispute *ex aequo et bono* if the parties so agree.

*   *   *

Article 48

1. The Tribunal shall decide questions by a majority of the votes of all its members.

*   *   *

Article 52

1. Either party may request annulment of the award by an application in writing addressed to the Secretary-General on one or more of the following grounds:
   a. that the Tribunal was not properly constituted;
   b. that the Tribunal has manifestly exceeded its powers; . . .
   c. . . . .

*   *   *

. . . the Chairman shall forthwith appoint from the Panel of Arbitrators an *ad hoc* Committee of three persons. None of the members of the Committee shall have been a member of the Tribunal which rendered the award, shall be of the same nationality as any such member, shall be a national of the State party to the dispute or of the State whose national is a party to the dispute. . . . The Committee shall have the authority to annul the award or any part thereof on any of the grounds set forth in paragraph (1).

*   *   *

Article 54

1. Each Contracting State shall recognize an award rendered pursuant to this Convention as binding and enforce the pecuniary obligations imposed by that award within its territories as if it were final judgment of a court in that State. A Contracting State with a federal constitution may enforce such an award in or through its federal courts and may provide that such courts shall treat the award as if it were a final judgment of the courts of a constituent state.

*   *   *

Article 64

Any dispute arising between Contracting States concerning the interpretation or application of this Convention which is not settled by negotiation shall be referred to the International Court of Justice by the application of any party to such dispute, unless the States concerned agree to another method of settlement.

*   *   *

FOR FURTHER STUDY

RICHARD B. LILLICH. *The Protection of Foreign Investment: Six Procedural Studies.* Syracuse, N.Y.: Syracuse University Press, 1965.

B. A. WORTLEY. *Expropriation in Public International Law.* New York: Cambridge University Press, 1959.

XI

The Legal Regulation of International Force

I n his introduction to *On the Law of War and Peace*, published in 1625, the first man to systematically approach the whole subject of international law, Hugo Grotius, wrote that there were "laws for the community which are valid both in respect of war and during war." More than three centuries later, men are still hopefully grasping for ways and means to avoid or limit the violence that too frequently characterizes the relations between states and often explodes into international war.

Throughout the social history of man, ideological, economic, and cultural conflicts have incited rabid and hostile passions between families and between nations. Even within states, municipal law has not prevented outbursts of group violence. National headlines are filled with labor strife, cultural linguistic battles, race riots, sporadic rebellions, and mass insurrections. But *war* as a term of international law is applied to a certain kind of hostility between states; war affects the legal relations between states— states that are parties to the conflict and "at war" with each other as well as neutral states.

War may include violence; however, not all violence between states can be called war. Throughout the course of history, states have used many punitive measures against other states, including blockades, seizure of ships, bombardments, and landing of troops, without being in a "state of war." Terms like reprisal, embargo, pacific blockade, and intervention have been used under international law to reflect the employment of force by one state against another without resorting to war. From 1931 to 1941, although Japan had violently seized Manchuria and later launched an all-out attack on China, the two states were not "at war." By contrast, although the World War II hostilities officially ceased for the United

States on 31 December 1946 the state of war with Germany was not terminated until 19 October 1951.

Moreover, neither the fighting in Southeast Asia between the French and the North Vietnamese from 1947 to 1954, nor that between the United States, South Vietnam, and other states and the North Vietnamese from 1965 onward was called war. When Chinese and Indian forces fought on the borders of India in 1962, and when Pakistan and Indian forces went into battle in 1965, war was not declared. None of the United Nations actions in Korea in 1950, in Egypt in 1956, or in the Congo in 1960 bore the legal title of war, although soldiers were killed, wounded, and captured in fierce and destructive combat under public flags.

However, the legal distinction between the exercise of organized public force under the authority of a state—or, in recent times, an international organization—and *war* cannot be disregarded. Under international law, both rights and obligations for states come into play if and when belligerency actually begins, not before. For example, a belligerent or war-waging state has the right to stop and search neutral vessels on the high seas when they are suspected of carrying contraband; a neutral state has the right to intern belligerent forces fleeing or falling into its territory; and when war begins, the word "enemy" takes on a special legal meaning for application under both municipal and international law. Finally, all the relevant treaties applying to the conduct or rules of war must be applied by the contracting parties when war is declared or acknowledged by states.

Because a declaration of war may (*a*) breach treaty pledges, (*b*) invite neutrality and neutrality regulations from other states, (*c*) awaken domestic constitutional and political problems in the conflicting states, or (*d*) widen rather than localize violence, states have frequently engaged in armed conflict without giving such actions the legal status of war.

The first two documents that follow, Convention (V) and Convention (XIII) on the *Rights and Duties of Neutral Powers*, adopted with several other conventions at the Hague Peace Conference of 1907, show some of the attitudes and practices crystallized by 19th century experience with respect to belligerent operations. Although the conventions had little legal effect as positive law, since they applied to the contracting parties only when *all* the belligerents were also contracting parties, the agreements did, and to some extent still do, represent the customary international law of war. In the third and fourth documents that follow, the *Shneiderman Case* elaborates the legal definition of war with facts drawn from the conflict between Israel, Britain, France, and Egypt in 1956, showing a disagreement on when war or acts of war legally terminate; and the *Effects of a Formal Declaration of War*, in a statement by the Department of Defense, illustrates United States reasoning with respect to its use of force in Vietnam.

Laws of War

CONVENTION (NO. V) RESPECTING THE RIGHTS AND DUTIES OF NEUTRAL POWERS AND PERSONS IN WAR ON LAND
Signed at The Hague, 18 October 1907
36 U.S. Statutes at Large 2310
CHAPTER I. THE RIGHTS AND DUTIES OF NEUTRAL POWERS

Article 1

The territory of neutral Powers is inviolable.

Article 2

Belligerents are forbidden to move troops or convoys of either munitions of war or supplies across the territory of a neutral Power.

Article 3

Belligerents are likewise forbidden to:

(a) Erect on the territory of a neutral Power a wireless telegraphy station or other apparatus for the purpose of communicating with belligerent forces on land or sea:

(b) Use any installation of this kind established by them before the war on the territory of a neutral Power for purely military purposes, and which has not been opened for the service of public messages.

Article 4

Corps of combatants cannot be formed nor recruiting agencies opened on the territory of a neutral Power to assist the belligerents.

Article 5

A neutral Power must not allow any of the acts referred to in Articles 2 to 4 to occur on its territory.

It is not called upon to punish acts in violation of its neutrality unless the said acts have been committed on its own territory.

Article 6

The responsibility of a neutral Power is not engaged by the fact of persons crossing the frontier separating (*sic*) to offer their services to one of the belligerents.

Article 7

A neutral Power is not called upon to prevent the export or transport, on behalf of one or other of the belligerents, of arms, munitions of war, or, in general, of anything which can be of use to an army or a fleet.

Article 8

A neutral Power is not called upon to forbid or restrict the use on behalf of the belligerents of telegraph or telephone cables or of wireless telegraphy apparatus belonging to it or to companies or private individuals.

Article 9

Every measure of restriction or prohibition taken by a neutral Power in regard to the matters referred to in Articles 7 and 8 must be impartially applied by it to both belligerents.

A neutral Power must see to the same obligation being observed by companies or private individuals owning telegraph or telephone cables or wireless telegraphy apparatus.

Article 10

The fact of a neutral Power resisting, even by force, attempts to violate its neutrality cannot be regarded as a hostile act.

CHAPTER II. BELLIGERENTS INTERNED AND WOUNDED TENDED IN NEUTRAL TERRITORY

Article 11

A neutral Power which receives on its territory troops belonging to the belligerent armies shall intern them, as far as possible, at a distance from the theatre of war.

*   *   *

CONVENTION (NO. XIII) CONCERNING THE RIGHTS AND DUTIES OF NEUTRAL POWERS IN NAVAL WAR
Signed at The Hague, 18 October 1907
36 U.S. Statutes at Large 2415

Article 1

Belligerents are bound to respect the sovereign rights of neutral Powers and to abstain, in neutral territory or neutral waters, from any act which would, if knowingly permitted by any Power, constitute a violation of neutrality.

Article 2

Any act of hostility, including capture and the exercise of the right of search, committed by belligerent war-ships in the territorial waters of a neutral Power, constitutes a violation of neutrality and is strictly forbidden.

Article 3

When a ship has been captured in the territorial waters of a neutral Power, this Power must employ, if the prize is still within its jurisdiction, the means at its disposal to release the prize with its officers and crew, and to intern the prize crew.

If the prize is not in the jurisdiction of the neutral Power, the captor Government, on the demand of that Power, must liberate the prize with its offices and crew.

Article 4

A Prize Court cannot be set up by a belligerent on neutral territory or on a vessel in neutral waters.

Article 5

Belligerents are forbidden to use neutral ports and waters as a base of naval operations against their adversaries, and in particular to erect wireless telegraphy stations or any apparatus for the purpose of communicating with the belligerent forces on land or sea.

Article 6

The supply, in any manner, directly or indirectly, by a neutral Power to a belligerent Power, of war-ships, ammunition, or war material of any kind whatever, is forbidden.

Article 7

A neutral Power is not bound to prevent the export or transit, for the use of either belligerent, of arms, ammunitions, or, in general, or anything which could be of use to any army or fleet.

Article 8

A neutral Government is bound to employ the means at its disposal to prevent the fitting out or arming of any vessel within its jurisdiction which it has reason to believe is intended to cruise, or engage in hostile operations, against a Power with which that Government is at peace. It is also bound to display the same vigilance to prevent the departure from its jurisdiction of any vessel intended to cruise, or engage in hostile operations, which had been adapted entirely or partly within the said jurisdiction for use in war.

Article 9

A neutral Power must apply impartially to the two belligerents the conditions, restrictions, or prohibitions made by it in regard to the admission into its ports, roadsteads, or territorial waters, of belligerent warships or of their prizes.

Nevertheless, a neutral Power may forbid a belligerent vessel which has failed to conform to the orders and regulations made by it, or which has violated neutrality, to enter its ports or roadsteads.

Article 10

The neutrality of a Power is not affected by the mere passage through its territorial waters of war-ships or prizes belonging to belligerents.

*   *   *

The Meaning of War

SHNEIDERMAN v. METROPOLITAN CASUALTY COMPANY OF NEW YORK
Supreme Court, Appellate Division, New York, 1961
220 N.Y.S. 2d 947

Eager, Justice

This is a submission of a controversy on agreed statement of facts pursuant to paragraphs 546 to 548 of the Civil Practice Act. Involved is the right of the plaintiff to recover the death benefit under a special disability insurance policy issued by defendant to David Seymour on February 1, 1953. The policy provided *inter alia* for payment of the principal sum of $5,000 to plaintiff, as the designated beneficiary, for loss of life of the insured resulting from accidental bodily injury. The policy, however, contained the express exclusory provision that "This insurance does not cover death . . . caused by war or any act of war or sustained by the Insured while in the military or naval service of any country at war, and in the latter event the pro rata unearned premium will be returned to the Insured."

At the time of the issuance of the said policy, the insured, David Seymour, was by occupation a photographer-journalist and he continued in such occupation until time of death. He was killed on November 10, 1956 at El Quantara in the Suez Canal zone while engaged on a photographic journalistic assignment.

In October, 1956, prior to the death of the insured, war, with extensive military and naval action, had been commenced by the British, Israeli and French governments against the Egyptian government to seize control of the Suez Canal. Following the hostilities between the British, Israeli and French governments on the one hand and the Egyptian government on the other hand, an agreement to cease fire effective November 6, 1956, was entered into by these nations.

The insured's death on November 10, 1956, occurred following the agreement to cease fire. The insured, at time of death, was attempting to cross from the British-French lines to the Egyptian side with a party exchanging wounded. The insured and a French photographer were traveling with the party in a jeep. They were killed when they were fired upon by the Egyptians and their jeep plunged into a nearby canal. Upon the foregoing facts, which are agreed, the question is, was the death of the insured "caused by war or any act of war" within the meaning of the exclusory provisions of the policy.

The position of the defendant insurance company is that, at the time of the insured's death, war or a state of war existed between Great Britain, France and Israel on the one side and Egypt on the other side. If this be so, it would follow that the insured's death was an incident thereof and, therefore, not covered by the policy. On the other hand, if the war, within the meaning of the term as used in the policy, had ended, then, for reasons hereinafter set out, it would appear that there was coverage.

By the statement of facts, the parties have stipulated that "An agreement to cease fire, effective November 6, 1956, was entered into by the parties." This was in pursuance of arrangements under a resolution of the General Assembly of the United Nations. It is significant that, following this cease fire on November 6, 1956, the warring nations did not thereafter engage in maneuvers of hostilities for the purpose of gaining military or naval advantage. Such incidents of violence or minor fighting as did thereafter occur were not in the furtherance of the prosecution of the war as such.

That a war may be terminated by the actual cessation of hostilities is recognized by authorities in international law and by judicial decision. While it is written in text books that a regular or normal way of ending a war is by a treaty of peace or by conquest and annexation, it is conceded by the authors that actual cessation of hostilities pending peace preliminaries may mark the ending of a war. Wheaton's *International Law*, "War" (7th Ed.), p. 615; Oppenheim's *International Law*, "Disputes, War and Neutrality" (7th Ed.), Ch. VII, paragraph 262, p. 597. Where, as here, the agreement by warring nations to cease fire was with the view toward the final termination of hostilities, it was an agreement to end a war. Thereupon, there was a termination in fact of overt and organized hostilities in furtherance of the war. The period following was a period for settlement of disputes by negotiation as distinguished from a period of war. The war in fact was then ended and the absence of a formal peace treaty is of no significance. In truth, the resolution of the United Nations is to be considered here as having the same effect of terminating the war and restoring peace as a traditional treaty of peace.

The defendant, however, points particularly to the continuance of sporadic raids and miscellaneous fighting along the Israeli border occurring from time to time, and argues that, in reality Israel and Egypt were at war or in a state of war continuing from the time of the declaration of independence by Israel in 1948 to the present time. The insured's death, however, was not an incident of any such alleged state of war. As a matter of fact, his death did not occur in the Israeli- Egyptian zone but rather in the Anglo-French-Egyptian zone. Immaterial here, therefore, are the incidents of violence between Israel and Egypt which were unconnected with the war in the Suez Canal zone and which, in any event, did not cause the death of the insured.

Of course, our ultimate aim here is to find and give effect to the intention of the parties in contracting for exclusion from coverage for death "caused by war or any act of war." The words used are to be taken and read in their plain and ordinary sense. "Such meaning must be given to the terms used as would be ascribed to them by the average man in applying for insurance and reading the language of the policy at the time it was written. . . .

"War, in the practical and realistic sense in which it is commonly used, refers to the period of hostilities and not to a technical state of war which may exist after the fighting has ended. *New York Life. Ins. Co.* v. *Durham*, 10 Cir., 166 F. 2d 874, 876 [1948]; . . . the plain, ordinary and generally accepted meaning of the word 'war' is war in fact." *Wilkinson* v. *Equitable Life Assur. Soc.*, 2 Misc. 2d 249, 252, 151 N.Y.S. 2d 1018, 1022 [1956]. In the mind of the ordinary or average man, a war is considered at an end on the final cessation of hostilities following an armistice or cease fire looking toward complete peace. For example, a common expression when the fighting stops, heard in the street or seen in the headlines, is the "War is over."

Consequently, in connection with the interpretation of private contracts, the courts have treated the actual cessation of hostilities as synonymous with the cessation of war. . . . Therefore, the term war when used in an exclusory clause of an insurance policy is generally construed as referring to the period of actual hostilities, that is, in the absence of context plainly having the effect of broadening the term beyond such limits. . . .

Moreover, in limiting the meaning of the terms "war" and "act of war" as used in the exclusory clause of the meaning of war in its real and practical sense, we are giving effect to the apparent intention of the parties. The usual purpose of exclusory clauses, such as the one here, is to protect the insurance company from extraordinarily hazardous risks; and from the insurance company's standpoint, the risk of loss of life incident to actual warfare is the risk that it must guard against. . . . Loss of life as a war hazard from the insurance company's view does not exist at all or exists to a very limited extent from the time when the parties have agreed to end hostilities. So, reasonably, an insured, in the absence of plain provision to the contrary, would expect to be covered for death occurring while engaged in his normal occupation after the termination of the war as such. . . .

In any event, we are bound to consider the policy as a whole and, on such consideration, construe it liberally to give effect to the purpose for which it was written. It is, therefore, of particular significance that we have here a special disability policy and that the defendant wrote it with the understanding that the insured's occupation was that of photographer-journalist and a member of the American Society of Magazine Photographers, Inc. It was written under the particular premium classification for such occupation and contained provision (paragraph 12) for adjustment of premium if the insured should change his occupation to a less hazardous one. As written, therefore, it was generally intended to include indemnity for disability and loss of life caused by any accidental bodily injury resulting from any hazard incident to the insured's occupation. In order to limit such generally intended coverage, the company was bound to use "clear and unmistakable terms, so that no one could be misled" (see *Birnbaum* v. *Jamestown Mut. Ins. Co.*, 298 NY 305, 313, 83 N.E. 2d 128, 132) [1948]. . . .

Here, the company used ambiguous terms. In generally excluding from coverage death "caused by war or any act of war," it used terms which are incapable of exact definition and wording which is susceptible to different meanings (see *Thomas* v. *Metropolitan Life Ins. Co.*, 388 Pa. 499, 131 A. 2d 600, 605 [1957]; *N.Y. Life Ins. Co.* v. *Bennion*, 158 F. 2d pp. 265, 267 [1946]). The uncertainty in the language used is chargeable to the company, and any doubt in the construction to be adopted must be resolved against it. Thus, reasonably, the exclusory clause should be limited in its application to a death occurring as a direct consequence of war. Here the direct cause of death *was not the war or an act of war* but an *unexplained act of violence* following the ending of the war.

The spasmodic incidents of violence in the war area following the cease fire agreed upon by all the warring nations were nothing more than in the nature of the turbulence, disruption and disorder which many times follow a war. The insured's death, occurring during such an incident, was merely related to the war in the sense that it resulted from the aftermath thereof. Had defendant company desired to exclude from coverage a death from acts of violence which might follow warfare, it should have spelled this out clearly rather than to generally circumscribe its risk to the point of war and acts of war.

* * *

In view of the foregoing, we conclude that the plaintiff should have judgment against the defendant for $5,000 with interest from December 1, 1956, and with costs.

* * *

All concur except Justice Steuer.

I dissent from the opinion of the majority. I am constrained to this conclusion not by any marked disagreement with the principles of law stated in the opinion but with their applicability to the facts likewise stated with accuracy, which I find unexceptionable. It is a correct statement of the law that the continuance of war as defined in the policy is not dependent upon the diplomatic or political arrangements made between the belligerent nations and that what is to be understood by the term is the period of actual hostilities. This period may be greater or less than the formal state of war originated by a declaration and terminated by a treaty or an armistice. Thus, it would be indisputable that a condition or an act of war existed at Pearl Harbor prior to any formal declaration, and the same is true if organized hostilities continue beyond the time that either or both of the belligerents have signified their intention to desist from such activities. The question is whether in fact they do so desist.

While it is doubtless true that sporadic acts of individuals, even though induced by the disruptive conditions following a war, do not constitute a prolongation of the war or an act of war, the same is not true of organized military actions conducted by one of the belligerents. The facts here show that the deceased was killed as a result of gunfire from a position regularly maintained by one of the belligerents as his jeep was approaching that position. There is nothing to show that any motive personal to the soldiers who fired the barrage motivated their act. This distinguishes the *post bellum* cases cited in the majority opinion. Nor is there any showing that the act was the result of unauthorized or disorganized pillage or rioting. The only inference that can be drawn from the meager statement of facts presumably embracing all that can be ascertained of the incident is that the Egyptian forces were engaged in the continuation of hostilities despite their equivocal acceptance of the United Nations recommendation for a cease fire.

No explanation is forthcoming as to why the plaintiff's jeep was fired upon by regular troops from a regularly maintained position. This could only mean that an act of war was being perpetrated by one of the belligerents contrary to its declared intention. As we have already seen, the declared intention is not the criterion. It is what is actually done.

The controversy should be determined in favor of the defendant.

EFFECTS OF FORMAL DECLARATION OF WAR
Statement by U.S. Department of Defense, 1966
Hearings, Committee on Armed Service, Military
Procurement Authorizations, Fiscal Year 1967
U.S. Senate, 89th Congress, 2d Session

*   *   *

From the international standpoint it seems undesirable to request a declaration of war for the following reasons:

1. The policy of the United States in Vietnam is to assist the Government of the Republic of Vietnam, at the latter's request, in thwarting an armed aggression from North Vietnam and to achieve a workable settlement of the dispute among the principal parties involved. This policy is pursued with limited aims, seeking to end the aggression against South Vietnam without threatening the destruction of North Vietnam, allowing a miscalculation by the enemy as to our intentions, or unnecessarily enlarging the scope of the conflict. The United States believes that the struggle must be won primarily in South Vietnam and is in that context a defensive military effort.

2. To declare war would add a new psychological element to the international situation, since in this century declarations of war have come to imply dedication to the total destruction of the enemy. It would increase the danger of misunderstanding of our true objectives in the conflict by the various Communist states, and increase the chances of their expanded involvement in it. Such a declaration would question the continued validity of the President's statements concerning his desire for a peaceful settlement allowing the various nations of the area, including North Vietnam, to live together in economic cooperation, and his reiteration that we do not threaten the existence of North Vietnam.

3. On balance, a declaration of war—which would be the first since the signing of the United Nations Charter—would significantly reduce the flexibility of the United States to seek a solution among extremely complex factors and reduce the chances that our adversary will take a reasoned approach to a solution, when U.S. policy from the beginning has attempted to avoid closing off any possible avenue of resolution and to make the North Vietnamese more rather than less rational in the situation.

4. There is nothing in modern international law which requires a state to declare war before engaging in hostilities against another state; nor would a formal declaration of war impose any obligations on an enemy by which he would not otherwise be bound.

5. Absence of a formal declaration of war is not a factor which makes

an international use of force unlawful. The only relevant legal question is whether the use of force is justified. Examples of hostilities begun without prior declaration of war abound in recent history. The fighting in Korea from 1950 to 1953, that in Indochina from 1947 to 1954, that in and around the Suez Canal in 1956, and that in West New Guinea between the Dutch and Indonesians in the spring and summer of 1962 all took place without benefit of declarations of war. We are not aware that the absence of declarations of war in these cases has been alleged to constitute a violation of international law.

6. The legal rules of international law concerning the conduct of armed conflicts apply to all armed conflicts without regard to the presence or absence of declarations of war. All that is required is armed conflict between two or more international entities. The 1949 Geneva Conventions for the Protection of War Victims were specifically made applicable to any "armed conflict of an international character" between two or more of the parties. The rules of war embodied in the Hague conventions formulated in the early years of this century are considered, in general, to be part of customary international law binding on all states, and their applicability is unrelated to declarations of war.

Domestic Considerations

From the point of view of U.S. law it would be undesirable for the President to seek a declaration of war for the following reasons:

1. A declaration of war is not necessary either to authorize the actions that have been taken by the United States in Vietnam or to provide an expression of congressional intent on the Vietnamese situation. The President has power under Article III, section 2, of the Constitution as Commander in Chief to deploy U.S. military forces to Vietnam for the purpose of assisting South Vietnam to defend itself from armed aggression by North Vietnam. Since the Constitution was adopted, there have been at least 125 instances in which the President, without congressional authority and in the absence of a declaration of war, has ordered the Armed Forces to take actions or to maintain positions abroad. Some of these historical instances have involved the use of U.S. forces in combat. Congressional intent is expressed by the joint resolution of Congress of August 10, 1964, passed by a combined vote of 504 to 2, explicitly approving all necessary steps, including the use of armed force, in the defense of freedom in southeast Asia. . . .

2. A declaration of war does not seem necessary in order to provide emergency authority to the executive branch. Many laws become operative in time of national emergency or in time of war. Most of these are operative today by virtue of the state of emergency proclaimed by President Truman in December 1950. These laws give the executive branch increased power to deal with the problems in Vietnam as well as other areas of the world. For example, they include special authority with

respect to the movement of aliens in and out of the United States, the Armed Forces, Reserves, and the National Guard; procurement of material for the services; transactions in foreign exchange, Government contracts, security, and the protection of defense information; and defense transportation. . . .

The International Maintenance of Peace

War has a legal status, but are all wars made by states legal? And when are armed actions taken by states, such as reprisals, interventions, interdictions, or military support, short of war, justified under contemporary international law?

Since ancient times, men have tried to deal with the problem of war between peoples. Plato felt that war should be waged only for the benefit of the state and that war against non-Greeks did not countervene natural law; Aristotle justified war (*a*) in self-defense, (*b*) to establish hegemony over others for their benefit, or (*c*) to control nations that deserved to be enslaved. The Romans also had "just" causes for war, declared so by a college of priests. Early Christianity rejected all wars as unjust until it became a religion of the state; then the church fathers reasoned that war was just when preceded by an injury. Later, St. Thomas Aquinas stated that to be just, a war must be waged under the authority of a prince (public authority) for a cause that would advance good rather than evil.

Well-publicized studies of theologians, lawyers, and military men from the 14th to the 17th century dealt at length with the problem of defining a just war, and expressed objections to the cruelties that were commonplace in fighting, sacking, and slaying during those centuries of Christian combat.[1] After the Peace of Westphalia in 1648 and the emergence of a number of foreign states in Western Europe that recognized no legal superior in either the Pope or the Holy Roman Emperor, the philosophical arguments about a just war gradually yielded to the rationalization of war as a right of all states. In a community of several independent sovereigns, where ambitions were pursued and security maintained by shifting balances of power, war, no matter how unpleasant, was considered neither just nor unjust.

Belligerency, then, became an instrument of national policy. In 1758, the diplomat Emerich de Vattel, whose volume on international law was extensively quoted by judges across two centuries, aptly wrote that war is "that state in which a nation prosecutes its right by force."[2]

With the right to *make* war universally acknowledged in the 19th century, the states of Europe and America limited their attention to the

---

[1] Among others, see Giovanni da Legnano, *Tractatus de bello, de represalius et de duello* (1360); Francisco Vitoria, *De jure belli Hispanorum in barbaros* (1532); Pierino Belli, *De re militari et bello tractatus* (1561); Balthasar Ayala, *De jure et officiis bellicis et disciplina militari* (1582); Alberico Gentili, *De jure belli libri tres* (1598); as well as Hugo Grotius, *De jure belli ac pacis* (1625).

[2] *Droit des Gens*, Book III, chap. 1.

conduct of war; to the legal rights and duties of states during a war, as epitomized in the Hague Peace Conferences of 1899 and 1907 with their conventions; and to the mitigation of human suffering under conditions of war. But the new destructive weapons and mass violence of World War I fell on whole populations, especially in Europe, affecting belligerents and neutrals with the worst ravages of unlicensed battle. Out of that holocaust came the first international effort to limit states in their right to make war, and to distinguish essentially between legal and illegal wars under international law.

The League of Nations Peace-Keeping System

The Covenant of the League of Nations, subject of so many high hopes and grave disillusionments about international peace, marks one of the great historical departures into new legal doctrine. War was not outlawed in 1919 by the Covenant to which 45 original member states subscribed. But war—any war or threat of war, whether immediately affecting any of the members of the League or not—was declared "a matter of concern to the whole League." Moreover, every member state pledged *not* to go to war in the event of an international dispute until, first, it had submitted the matter to either arbitration or a judicial settlement or an inquiry by the Council of the League, and second, until it had waited for three months after the award or decision or report.

Thus, states for the first time agreed to certain *procedures* before exercising their right to make war; failure to follow such procedures was a violation of the Covenant, a breach of international law. Moreover, the League members accepted the obligation to carry out any arbitral or judicial settlement. However, with respect to "political" quarrels that could be placed before the Council (or referred to the Assembly) the disputant states were only bound to wait until three months after the Council's report. Having done so, their procedural obligations under the Covenant were discharged, and they might resort to war.

If the Council's report was unanimous, all members of the League pledged not to take up arms against a state that carried out the recommendations of such a report; if the report was not unanimous (not counting the parties to the dispute), the League members could take whatever action they felt necessary. If any League member resorted to war without regard to these obligations and procedures, the League members promised to sever diplomatic relations and impose various economic sanctions. The Council could also "recommend" that member states contribute to armed forces to protect the covenants of the League.

At a minimum, neutrality as a theory of international war and law began to be challenged by the principles of collective security and a permanent international organization, which had been developed to maintain international peace. The sovereign right of states to make war in pursuance of national interests could at least be questioned under their own pledges to follow certain procedures before an international forum. In sum, the Covenant required that states on the verge of conflict should attempt a peaceful means of settlement or, as a minimum, delay any forcible action until the Council heard arguments and reported, with at least a 90-day wait to stave off war. But the legal use of violence by a state was admitted in the last resort.

The United States remained morosely aloof from the bold Geneva beginning toward the condemnation of all international war; America failed to ratify the Versailles Treaty, of which the Covenant was a part. From 1920 to 1940 many member states either reinterpreted their obligations under the Covenant or violated their pledges. Moreover, the strong political interests of Britain and France, pillars of the League, often tended to outweigh the new international rules.

In 1931, Japan began an aggression against China which the League was powerless to delay, let alone stop. In 1935, Italy blatantly and arrogantly defied the Covenant by its invasion of Ethiopia. Many members of the League on that occasion condemned Italy, severed diplomatic relations with Rome, and organized economic sanctions to restrain Italy's war effort. But no military actions were taken, and the oil embargo was thwarted, partly because Germany and the United States, not members of the League, supplied Italy with oil and other commodities.

Italy's triumph over Ethiopia was followed by General Francisco Franco's victory over the Spanish government with the aid of Germany and Italy (1937), Japan's full-scale attack on China (1937), and, under Adolf Hitler, Germany's precipitation of World War II through seizure of Austria (1938), dismemberment of Czechoslovakia (1938), and attack on Poland (1939).

In this period the League did very little. Its last convulsive action in the international security field was to condemn the Soviet Union for its attacks on Finland in 1939, expel the Soviet Union from the League, and instruct the Secretary General to organize and coordinate such material aid as might be offered by member states to Finland—actions that were virtually futile in view of a world already dividing into the enemy camps of World War II.

Efforts to "outlaw" war prior to 1939 were not limited to the League of Nations, but the root of the problem lay, as always, in defining just and unjust war—in modern parlance, condemning "aggression" while allowing states their rights of self-defense and self-preservation. In a resolution unanimously adopted by the Eighth Assembly of the League of Nations on 24 September 1927, wars of "aggression" were branded as international crimes, to be renounced and prohibited.

Eleven months later, the United States joined France and other great powers, together with Belgium, Czechoslovakia, and Poland, in signing the General Act for the Renunciation of War (Briand-Kellogg Pact), a multipartite instrument eventually adhered to by most of the states of the world. The parties condemned a recourse to war for the solution of international controversies, and renounced war as an instrument of national policy in their relations with one another. Nevertheless, wars of "self-defense" were tacitly excluded; definition of that delicate phrase was left to the state itself. As the United States Secretary of State interpreted the agreement,

Every nation is free at all times and regardless of treaty provisions to defend its territory from attack or invasion and it alone is competent to decide whether circumstances require recourse to war in self-defense.[3]

The London Disarmament Conference of 1933 tried to go further. It actually listed five signs of aggression: a declaration of war; an invasion; an attack on the territory, vessels, or aircraft of another state; a naval blockade; and support to armed bands invading a state from the territory of another state. But on examination these criteria had about as many legal loopholes as any other and were not the official basis for the League's recourse to condemnation for violation of the Covenant and the imposition of sanctions.

Law exists only in a political context. Post-World War I expectations that the drafting of procedural rules for great states would chasten their ambition and bridle all the powers that had been accumulated over centuries were legalistic folly. In consequence of the calculated and stunning aggressions of Japan, Italy, and Germany prior to World War II, cynicism about regulating international force and war through international organization and law was rampant.

However, despite the chagrin of the pioneers of world order the League of Nations did develop and clarify the postulates that all states should refrain from war, settle their differences amicably, and abide by the decisions of an international council or the judgments of an international court. In this way, the League began to make a distinction between unjust (aggressive) wars and just (defensive) wars, while it generated in a widening world community a new consensus about the illegality of war itself.

Excerpted in the document that follows are key articles of the *Covenant of the League of Nations* in 1919.

---

[3] Quoted in James T. Shotwell, *War as an Instrument of National Policy* (New York: Harcourt, Brace & Co., 1929), p. 297.

Legal and Illegal War

COVENANT OF THE LEAGUE OF NATIONS, 1919
The League Yearbook, 1932, pp. 3–16

*   *   *

Article 10

The Members of the League undertake to respect and preserve as against external aggression the territorial integrity and existing political independence of all Members of the League. In case of any such aggression or in case of any threat or danger of such aggression, the Council shall advise upon the means by which this obligation shall be fulfilled.

Article 11

1. Any war or threat of war, whether immediately affecting any of the Members of the League or not, is hereby declared a matter of concern to the whole League, and the League shall take any action that may be deemed wise and effectual to safeguard the peace of nations. In case any such emergency should arise, the Secretary-General shall, on the request of any Member of the League, forthwith summon a meeting of the Council.

2. It is also declared to be the friendly right of each Member of the League to bring to the attention of the Assembly or of the Council any circumstance whatever affecting international relations which threatens to disturb international peace or the good understanding between nations upon which peace depends.

Article 12

1. The Members of the League agree that if there should arise between them any dispute likely to lead to a rupture they will submit the matter either to arbitration *or judicial settlement* or to enquiry by the Council,

and they agree in no case to resort to war until three months after the award by the arbitrators *or the judicial decision* or the report by the Council.

2. In any case under this article the award of the arbitrators *or the judicial decision* shall be made within a reasonable time, and the report of the Council shall be made within six months after the submission of the dispute.

Article 13

1. The Members of the League agree that whenever any dispute shall arise between them which they recognise to be suitable for submission to arbitration *or judicial settlement*, and which cannot be satisfactorily settled by diplomacy, they will submit the whole subject-matter to arbitration *or judicial settlement*.

2. Disputes as to the interpretation of a treaty, as to any question of international law, as to the existence of any fact which, if established, would constitute a breach of any international obligation, or as to the extent and nature of the reparation to be made for any such breach, are declared to be among those which are generally suitable for submission to arbitration *or judicial settlement*.

3. *For the consideration of any such dispute, the court to which the case is referred shall be the Permanent Court of International Justice, established in accordance with Article 14, or any tribunal agreed on by the parties to the dispute or stipulated in any Convention existing between them.*

4. The Members of the League agree that they will carry out in full good faith any award *or decision* that may be rendered, and that they will not resort to war against a Member of the League which complies therewith. In the event of any failure to carry out such an award *or decision*, the Council shall propose what steps should be taken to give effect thereto.

Article 14

The Council shall formulate and submit to the Members of the League for adoption plans for the establishment of a Permanent Court of International Justice. The Court shall be competent to hear and determine any dispute of an international character which the parties thereto submit to it. The Court may also give an advisory opinion upon any dispute or question referred to it by the Council or by the Assembly.

Article 15

1. If there should arise between Members of the League any dispute likely to lead to a rupture, which is not submitted to arbitration *or judicial settlement* in accordance with Article 13, the Members of the League agree that they will submit the matter to the Council. Any party to the

dispute may effect such submission by giving notice of the existence of the dispute to the Secretary-General, who will make all necessary arrangements for a full investigation and consideration thereof.

2. For this purpose, the parties to the dispute will communicate to the Secretary-General, as promptly as possible, statements of their case with all the relevant facts and papers, and the Council may forthwith direct the publication thereof.

3. The Council shall endeavour to effect a settlement of the dispute, and if such efforts are successful, a statement shall be made public giving such facts and explanations regarding the dispute and the terms of settlement thereof as the Council may deem appropriate.

4. If the dispute is not thus settled, the Council either unanimously or by a majority vote shall make and publish a report containing a statement of the facts of the dispute and the recommendations which are deemed just and proper in regard thereto.

5. Any Member of the League represented on the Council may make public a statement of the facts of the dispute and of its conclusions regarding the same.

6. If a report by the Council is unanimously agreed to by the members thereof other than the Representatives of one or more of the parties to the dispute, the Members of the League agree that they will not go to war with any party to the dispute which complies with the recommendations of the report.

7. If the Council fails to reach a report which is unanimously agreed to by the members thereof, other than the Representatives of one or more of the parties to the dispute, the Members of the League reserve to themselves the right to take such action as they shall consider necessary for the maintenance of right and justice.

8. If the dispute between the parties is claimed by one of them, and is found by the Council, to arise out of a matter which by international law is solely within the domestic jurisdiction of that party, the Council shall so report, and shall make no recommendations as to its settlement.

9. The Council may in any case under this article refer the dispute to the Assembly. The dispute shall be so referred at the request of either party to the dispute provided that such request be made within fourteen days after the submission of the dispute to the Council.

*   *   *

Article 16

1. Should any Member of the League resort to war in disregard of its covenants under Articles 12, 13 or 15, it shall, *ipso facto*, be deemed to have committed an act of war against all other Members of the League, which hereby undertake immediately to subject it to the severance of all trade or financial relations, the prohibition of all intercourse between their

nationals and the nationals of the Covenant-breaking State, and the prevention of all financial, commercial or personal intercourse between the nationals of the Covenant-breaking State and the nationals of any other State, whether a Member of the League or not.

2. It shall be the duty of the Council in such case to recommend to the several Governments concerned what effective military, naval or air force the Members of the League shall severally contribute to the armed forces to be used to protect the covenants of the League.

*   *   *

The United Nations Peace-Keeping System

From the very beginning of World War II, a few scholars and diplomats began addressing themselves to the problem of maintaining international peace in the postwar world through legal standards enforced by a permanent international organization. Therefore, as it emerged from the Dumbarton Oaks proposals of the great victorious powers and from the discussions of the San Francisco Conference of 1945, the United Nations Charter attempted to narrow further the right of states to make war—indeed, to eliminate that right under international law and to substitute the force of the United Nations itself to moderate disputes and curb international aggression.

First, United Nations members reiterated the League members' pledges to refrain from violent settlement of their disputes and to resort to negotiation, arbitration, or judicial settlements. Second, the Charter specifically forbade the use of force to settle international disputes, except (*a*) for individual or collective self-defense against armed attack and (*b*) for collective measures authorized by Security Council decisions or General Assembly recommendations. Thus, the legal use of armed force by individual states under the Charter remains possible, but narrowly circumscribed.

The one vital condition for the denial of force to individual states in pursuing their national interests is that the United Nations itself take action in the event of a threat to or a breach of international peace. For the first five years of United Nations history, such collective action depended entirely on decisions of the Security Council, which require the unanimity of the five permanent members—the United States, the Union of Soviet Socialist Republics, the United Kingdom, France, and China. But since 1950, it has been argued—particularly by the United States—that under the Uniting for Peace Resolution the General Assembly may make recommendations to member states to carry out collective measures for maintaining or restoring international peace if the Security Council is unable to act because of the permanent members' failure or inability to agree on a course of action.

This argument has run into considerable difficulty with the Soviet Union and other states, especially after the 1956 United Nations peace-keeping operations in Egypt were initiated by the General Assembly and organized by the Secretary-General. The Soviet Union has regarded decisions about the use of armed forces to restore international peace as a prerogative of the Security Council under Section VII of the Charter, and has deplored efforts to shift this responsibility to the General Assembly under the guise of "recommendations" as a violation of the Charter's provisions.

Another issue that has bedeviled the role of the Security Council in international peace-keeping has been the availability of military forces. The Charter intended peace-keeping forces to be available to the United Nations from states by agreement with the Security Council. When required, such forces would be under the strategic direction of a Military Staff Committee. However, since 1945 no amount of talking has prevailed on the Great Powers to establish an international force directed by the Military Staff Committee under the Security Council. Although it has met every two weeks for more than 16 years, after 1947 the Military Staff Committee never considered a matter of substance. Indeed, one of the few remembered decisions was a unanimous agreement in 1947 to accept an invitation from the Chamber of Commerce in Minot, North Dakota, to fly out for a pheasant hunt.[4]

In consequence of the political divisions between the permanent members of the Security Council, with their power to veto decisions on peace-keeping, and of the failure to establish international forces under the direction of the Military Staff Committee, whatever enforcement measures have been taken by the United Nations to maintain the peace-keeping standards of the Charter have been due to the cooperative action of individual states. In practice, at the request of either the Security Council or the General Assembly or both, some states have supplied to the United Nations the men and materials for peace-keeping forces; the Secretary-General has acted as the organizer and coordinator of the international operation.

Moreover, each peace-keeping operation of the United Nations since the 1950 defense of South Korea has been different, and it is far too early to generalize about the organization's legal basis and effectiveness in eliminating war from the lexicon of international relations. No war has been "declared" since the United Nations was established. But in Hungary and Egypt in 1956, in Goa in 1961, in Borneo and Malaysia in 1964, and elsewhere, members of the United Nations have resorted to violence outside the provisions of the Charter. In addition, international legal definitions have been shattered by the use of subversion or indirect aggression that undermines the traditional doctrines that once divided the domestic from the international affairs of a state. The United States, for example, has been accused of violating the Charter by landing marines in Lebanon in 1958 and in the Dominican Republic in 1965, as well as by its bombardment and attack on North Vietnam since 1965. In each of those military actions, however, the issues were the subversion and collapse of the local government, with long-run effects on United States interests, rather than the overt and direct international aggression contemplated by the Charter.

---

[4] *New York Times*, 9 August 1964.

The following documents include excerpted key articles from the *Charter of the United Nations* in 1945 and the *Uniting for Peace Resolution* in 1950, which relate to the use of force in international relations.

CHARTER OF THE UNITED NATIONS, 1945
United States Department of State Treaty Series, No. 933

CHAPTER I. PURPOSES AND PRINCIPLES

Article 1

The Purposes of the United Nations are:

1. To maintain international peace and security, and to that end: to take effective collective measures for the prevention and removal of threats to the peace, and for the suppression of acts of aggression or other breaches of the peace, and to bring about by peaceful means, and in conformity with the principles of justice and international law, adjustment or settlement of international disputes or situations which might lead to a breach of the peace;

* * *

Article 2

The Organization and its Members, in pursuit of the Purposes stated in Article 1, shall act in accordance with the following Principles.

1. The Organization is based on the principle of the sovereign equality of all its Members.

2. All Members, in order to ensure to all of them the rights and benefits resulting from membership, shall fulfill in good faith the obligations assumed by them in accordance with the present Charter.

3. All Members shall settle their international disputes by peaceful means in such a manner that international peace and security, and justice, are not endangered.

4. All Members shall refrain in their international relations from the threat or use of force against the territorial integrity or political independence of any state, or in any other manner inconsistent with the Purposes of the United Nations.

5. All Members shall give the United Nations every assistance in any action it takes in accordance with the present Charter, and shall refrain from giving assistance to any state against which the United Nations is taking preventive or enforcement action.

6. The Organization shall ensure that states which are not Members of the United Nations act in accordance with these Principles so far as may be necessary for the maintenance of international peace and security.

7. Nothing contained in the present Charter shall authorize the United Nations to intervene in matters which are essentially within the domestic jurisdiction of any state or shall require the Members to submit such matters to settlement under the present Charter; but this principle shall not prejudice the application of enforcement measures under Chapter VII.

*   *   *

CHAPTER VI. PACIFIC SETTLEMENT OF DISPUTES

Article 33

1. The parties to any dispute, the continuance of which is likely to endanger the maintenance of international peace and security, shall, first of all, seek a solution by negotiation, enquiry, mediation, conciliation, arbitration, judicial settlement, resort to regional agencies or arrangements, or other peaceful means of their own choice.

2. The Security Council shall, when it deems necessary, call upon the parties to settle their dispute by such means.

Article 34

The Security Council may investigate any dispute, or any situation which might lead to international friction or give rise to a dispute, in order to determine whether the continuance of the dispute or situation is likely to endanger the maintenance of international peace and security.

Article 35

1. Any Member of the United Nations may bring any dispute, or any situation of the nature referred to in Article 34, to the attention of the Security Council or of the General Assembly.

2. A state which is not a Member of the United Nations may bring to the attention of the Security Council or of the General Assembly any dispute to which it is a party if it accepts in advance, for purposes of the dispute, the obligations of pacific settlement provided in the present Charter.

3. The proceedings of the General Assembly in respect of matters brought to its attention under this Article will be subject to the provisions of Articles 11 and 12.

Article 36

1. The Security Council may, at any state of a dispute of the nature referred to in Article 33 or a situation of like nature, recommend appropriate procedures or methods of adjustment.

2. The Security Council should take into consideration any procedures for the settlement of the dispute which have already been adopted by the parties.

3. In making recommendations under this Article the Security Council should also take into consideration that legal disputes should as a general rule be referred by the parties to the International Court of Justice in accordance with the provisions of the Statute of the Court.

Article 37

1. Should the parties to a dispute of the nature referred to in Article 33 fail to settle it by the means indicated in that Article, they shall refer it to the Security Council.

2. If the Security Council deems that the continuance of the dispute is in fact likely to endanger the maintenance of international peace and security, it shall decide whether to take action under Article 36 or to recommend such terms of settlement as it may consider appropriate.

Article 38

Without prejudice to the provisions of Articles 33 to 37, the Security Council may, if all the parties to any dispute so request, make recommendations to the parties with a view to a pacific settlement of the dispute.

CHAPTER VII. ACTION WITH RESPECT TO THREATS TO THE PEACE, BREACHES OF THE PEACE, AND ACTS OF AGGRESSION

Article 39

The Security Council shall determine the existence of any threat to the peace, breach of the peace, or act of aggression and shall make recommendations, or decide what measures shall be taken in accordance with Articles 41 and 42, to maintain or restore international peace and security.

Article 40

In order to prevent an aggravation of the situation, the Security Council may, before making the recommendations or deciding upon the measures provided for in Article 39, call upon the parties concerned to comply with such provisional measures as it deems necessary or desirable. Such provisional measures shall be without prejudice to the rights, claims, or position of the parties concerned. The Security Council shall duly take account of failure to comply with such provisional measures.

Article 41

The Security Council may decide what measures not involving the use of armed force are to be employed to give effect to its decisions, and it may call upon the Members of the United Nations to apply such measures. These may include complete or partial interruption of economic relations and of rail, sea, air, postal, telegraphic, radio, and other means of communication, and the severance of diplomatic relations.

Article 42

Should the Security Council consider that measures provided for in Article 41 would be inadequate or have proved to be inadequate, it may take such action by air, sea, or land forces as may be necessary to maintain or restore international peace and security. Such action may include demonstrations, blockade, and other operations by air, sea, or land forces of Members of the United Nations.

Article 43

1. All Members of the United Nations, in order to contribute to the maintenance of international peace and security, undertake to make available to the Security Council, on its call and in accordance with a special agreement or agreements, armed forces, assistance, and facilities, including rights of passage, necessary for the purpose of maintaining international peace and security.

2. Such agreement or agreements shall govern the numbers and types of forces, their degree of readiness and general location, and the nature of the facilities and assistance to be provided.

3. The agreement or agreements shall be negotiated as soon as possible on the initiative of the Security Council. They shall be concluded between the Security Council and Members or between the Security Council and groups of Members and shall be subject to ratification by the signatory states in accordance with their respective constitutional processes.

Article 44

When the Security Council has decided to use force it shall, before calling upon a Member not represented on it to provide armed forces in fulfillment of the obligations assumed under Article 43, invite that Member, if the Member so desires, to participate in the decisions of the Security Council concerning the employment of contingents of that Member's armed forces.

Article 45

In order to enable the United Nations to take urgent military measures, Members shall hold immediately available national airforce contingents for combined international enforcement action. The strength and degree of readiness of these contingents and plans for their combined action shall be determined, within the limits laid down in the special agreement or agreements referred to in Article 43, by the Security Council with the assistance of the Military Staff Committee.

Article 46

Plans for the application of armed force shall be made by the Security Council with the assistance of the Military Staff Committee.

Article 47

1. There shall be established a Military Staff Committee to advise and assist the Security Council on all questions relating to the Security Council's military requirements for the maintenance of international peace and security, the employment and command of forces placed at its disposal, the regulation of armaments, and possible disarmament.

2. The Military Staff Committee shall consist of the Chiefs of Staff of the permanent members of the Security Council or their representatives. Any Member of the United Nations not permanently represented on the Committee shall be invited by the Committee to be associated with it when the efficient discharge of the Committee's responsibilities requires the participation of that Member in its work.

3. The Military Staff Committee shall be responsible under the Security Council for the strategic direction of any armed forces placed at the disposal of the Security Council. Questions relating to the command of such forces shall be worked out subsequently.

4. The Military Staff Committee, with the authorization of the Security Council and after consultation with appropriate regional agencies, may establish regional subcommittees.

Article 48

1. The action required to carry out the decisions of the Security Council for the maintenance of international peace and security shall be taken by all the Members of the United Nations or by some of them, as the Security Council may determine.

2. Such decisions shall be carried out by the Members of the United Nations directly and through their action in the appropriate international agencies of which they are members.

Article 49

The Members of the United Nations shall join in affording mutual assistance in carrying out the measures decided upon by the Security Council.

Article 50

If preventive or enforcement measures against any state are taken by the Security Council, any other state, whether a Member of the United Nations or not, which finds itself confronted with special economic problems arising from the carrying out of those measures shall have the right to consult the Security Council with regard to a solution of those problems.

Article 51

Nothing in the present Charter shall impair the inherent right of individual or collective self-defense if an armed attack occurs against a

Member of the United Nations, until the Security Council has taken the measures necessary to maintain international peace and security. Measures taken by Members in the exercise of this right of self-defense shall be immediately reported to the Security Council and shall not in any way affect the authority and responsibility of the Security Council under the present Charter to take at any time such action as it deems necessary in order to maintain or restore international peace and security.

UNITING FOR PEACE RESOLUTION
General Assembly, United Nations, 1950
United Nations Bulletin, Vol. 9, No. 10, pp. 508–9.

The General Assembly,

* * *

1. *Resolves* that if the Security Council, because of lack of unanimity of the permanent members, fails to exercise its primary responsibility for the maintenance of international peace and security in any case where there appears to be a threat to the peace, breach of the peace, or act of aggression, the General Assembly shall consider the matter immediately with a view to making appropriate recommendations to Members for collective measures, including in the case of a breach of the peace or act of aggression the use of armed force when necessary, to maintain or restore international peace and security. If not in session at the time, the General Assembly may meet in emergency special session within 24 hours of the request therefor. Such emergency special session shall be called if requested by the Security Council on the vote of any seven members, or by a majority of the Members of the United Nations; . . .

* * *

Regional Peace-Keeping

The Charter of the United Nations plainly encouraged attempts at settling international disputes at a regional level before raising them to worldwide issues in the Security Council. Inter-American experience, in particular, influenced Chapter VIII of the Charter, which provides for regional peace-keeping arrangements. The Inter-American Treaty of Reciprocal Assistance (Rio Pact) of 1947 and the institution of the Organization of American States (OAS) in 1948 has provided the most relevant ways and means for helping to maintain international peace in the Western hemisphere. Between 1948 and 1965, the OAS formally intervened 11 times in hemispheric disputes, virtually all involving the Central American–Caribbean area. Consultation, fact-finding, a call for cease-fire, and conciliation have generally been used by the Organ of Consultation to avoid conflict and restore a peaceful environment; but in 1964, sanctions were approved against Cuba for its subversive activities against Venezuela.

The tension within the United Nations peace-keeping system, with its possibility of either Security Council–General Assembly action, regional arrangements, or both, was highlighted in the Dominican Republic in 1965. On April 28, 1965, the United States unilaterally landed troops in the Dominican Republic to protect American citizens from civil strife. On April 30, the OAS passed its first resolution on the situation, and on May 3 the Security Council began considering the issue. Eventually, *both* a committee for the OAS and representatives of the Secretary-General were sent to the Dominican Republic to help restore peace between the local factions, while an inter-American Force—the first in history—was authorized by the OAS on May 6.

Article 53 of the U.N. Charter requires that any enforcement action taken by any regional organization must first be authorized by the Security Council, but OAS practice, under the leadership of the United States, has been to try to keep hemispheric disputes within the regional arrangement and, under Article 54, to keep the Security Council "fully informed."

The first document that follows, the *OAS Application of Measures to Cuba*, shows the inter-American peace-keeping system at work; while *the Legality of United States Participation in the Defense of Vietnam*, relates the American justification under international law for its use of force in Vietnam.

446

OAS APPLICATION OF MEASURES TO CUBA, 1964
9th Meeting of Consultation of Ministers of Foreign Affairs*
Organization of American States Doc. 48, Rev. 2 Corr., 26 July 1964.

The Ninth Meeting of Consultation of Ministers of Foreign Affairs, Serving as Organ of Consultation in Application of the Inter-American Treaty of Reciprocal Assistance.

HAVING SEEN the report of the Investigating Committee designated on December 3, 1963, by the Council of the Organization of American States, acting provisionally as Organ of Consultation, and

CONSIDERING:

That the said report establishes among its conclusions that "the Republic of Venezuela has been the target of a series of actions sponsored and directed by the Government of Cuba, openly intended to subvert Venezuelan institutions and to overthrow the domestic Government of Venezuela through terrorism, sabotage, assault, and guerrilla warfare," and

That the aforementioned acts, like all acts of intervention and aggression, conflict with the principles and aims of the inter-American system,

RESOLVES:

1. To declare that the acts verified by the Investigating Committee constitute an aggression and an intervention on the part of the Government of Cuba in the internal affairs of Venezuela, which affects all of the member states.

2. To condemn emphatically the present Government of Cuba for its acts of aggression and of intervention against the territorial inviolability, the sovereignty, and the political independence of Venezuela.

3. To apply, in accordance with the provisions of Articles 6 and 8 of the Inter-American Treaty of Reciprocal Assistance, the following measures:

   a. That the governments of the American states not maintain diplomatic or consular relations with the Government of Cuba;

   b. That the governments of the American states suspend all their trade,

---

* Adopted July 26, 1964, by a vote of 15 to 4 (Bolivia, Chile, Mexico, and Uruguay). Venezuela was not eligible to vote.

whether direct or indirect, with Cuba, except in foodstuffs, medicines, and medical equipment that may be sent to Cuba for humanitarian reasons; and

c. That the governments of the American states suspend all sea transportation between their countries and Cuba, except for such transportation as may be necessary for reasons of a humanitarian nature.

4. To authorize the Council of the Organization of American States, by an affirmative vote of two thirds of its members, to discontinue the measures adopted in the present resolution at such time as the Government of Cuba shall have ceased to constitute a danger to the peace and security of the hemisphere.

5. To warn the Government of Cuba that if it should persist in carrying out acts that possess characteristics of aggression and intervention against one or more of the member states of the Organization, the member states shall preserve their essential rights as sovereign states by the use of self-defense in either individual or collective form, which could go so far as resort to armed force, until such time as the Organ of Consultation takes measures to guarantee the peace and security of the hemisphere.

6. To urge those states not members of the Organization of American States that are animated by the same ideals as the inter-American system to examine the possibility of effectively demonstrating their solidarity in achieving the purposes of this resolution.

7. To instruct the Secretary General of the Organization of American States to transmit to the United Nations Security Council the text of the present resolution, in accordance with the provisions of Article 54 of the United Nations Charter.

Self-Defense

LEGALITY OF UNITED STATES PARTICIPATION IN DEFENSE OF VIETNAM
Memorandum of Legal Adviser of the Department of State, 4 March 1966
54 Department of State Bulletin 474–489 (1966)

In response to requests from the Government of South Vietnam, the United States has been assisting that country in defending itself against armed attack from the Communist North. This attack has taken the forms of externally supported subversion, clandestine supply of arms, infiltration of armed personnel, and most recently the sending of regular units of the North Vietnamese army into the South.

*   *   *

International law has traditionally recognized the right of self-defense against armed attack. This proposition has been asserted by writers on international law through the several centuries in which the modern law of nations has developed. The proposition has been acted on numerous times by governments throughout modern history. Today the principle of self-defense against armed attack is universally recognized and accepted.

The Charter of the United Nations, concluded at the end of World War II, imposed an important limitation on the use of force by United Nations members. Article 2, paragraph 4, provides:

All Members shall refrain in their international relations from the threat or use of force against the territorial integrity or political independence of any state, or in any other manner inconsistent with the Purposes of the United Nations.

In addition, the charter embodied a system of international peace-keeping through the organs of the United Nations. Article 24 summarizes these structural arrangements in stating that the United Nations members:

. . . confer on the Security Council primary responsibility for the mainte-nance of international peace and security, and agree that in carrying out its duties under this responsibility the Security Council acts on their behalf.

However, the charter expressly states in article 51 that the remaining provisions of the charter—including the limitation of article 2, paragraph 4, and the creation of United Nations machinery to keep the peace—in no way diminish the inherent right of self-defense against armed attack. Article 51 provides:

Nothing in the present Charter shall impair the inherent right of individual or collective self-defense if an armed attack occurs against a Member of the United Nations, until the Security Council has taken the measures necessary to maintain international peace and security. Measures taken by Members in the exercise of this right of self-defense shall be immediately reported to the Security Council and shall not in any way effect the authority and responsibil-ity of the Security Council under the present Charter to take at any time such action as it deems necessary in order to maintain or restore international peace and security.

Thus, article 51 restates and preserves, for member states in the situa-tions covered by the article, a long-recognized principle of international law. The article is a "saving clause" designed to make clear that no other provision in the charter shall be interpreted to impair the inherent right of self-defense referred to in article 51.

Three principal objections have been raised against the availability of the right of individual and collective self-defense in the case of Vietnam: (1) that this right applies only in the case of an armed attack on a United Nations member; (2) that it does not apply in the case of South Vietnam because the latter is not an independent sovereign state; and (3) that collective self-defense may be undertaken only by a regional organization operating under chapter VIII of the United Nations Charter. These objections will now be considered in turn.

     *   *   *

The argument that the right of self-defense is available only to members of the United Nations mistakes the nature of the right of self-defense and the relationship of the United Nations Charter to international law in this respect. As already shown, the right of self-defense against armed attack is an inherent right under international law. The right is not conferred by the charter, and indeed, article 51 expressly recognizes that the right is inherent.

The charter nowhere contains any provision designed to deprive nonmembers of the right of self-defense against armed attack. Article 2, paragraph 6, does charge the United Nations with responsibility for insuring that nonmember states act in accordance with United Nations "Principles so far as may be necessary for the maintenance of international peace and security." Protection against aggression and self-defense against armed attack are important elements in the whole charter scheme for the maintenance of international peace and security. To deprive nonmembers of their inherent right of self-defense would not accord with the principles of the organization, but would instead be prejudicial to the maintenance of peace. Thus article 2, paragraph 6—and, indeed, the rest of the charter—should certainly not be construed to nullify or diminish the inherent defensive rights of nonmembers.

The United States has the right to assist in the defense of South Vietnam although the latter is not a United Nations member.

The cooperation of two or more international entities in the defense of one or both against armed attack is generally referred to as collective self-defense. United States participation in the defense of South Vietnam at the latter's request is an example of collective self-defense.

The United States is entitled to exercise the right of individual or collective self-defense against armed attack, as that right exists in international law, subject only to treaty limitations and obligations undertaken by this country.

It has been urged that the United States has no right to participate in the collective defense of South Vietnam because article 51 of the United Nations Charter speaks only of the situation "if an armed attack occurs against a Member of the United Nations." This argument is without substance.

In the first place, article 51 does not impose restrictions or cut down the otherwise available rights of United Nations. By its own terms, the article preserves an inherent right. It is, therefore, necessary to look elsewhere in the charter for any obligation of members restricting their participation in collective defense of an entity that is not a United Nations member.

Article 2 paragraph 4, is the principal provision of the charter imposing limitations on the use of force by members. It states that they:

. . . shall refrain in their international relations from the threat or use of force against the territorial integrity or political independence of any state, or in any other manner inconsistent with the Purposes of the United Nations.

Action taken in defense against armed attack cannot be characterized as falling within this proscription. The record of the San Francisco conference makes clear that article 2, paragraph 4, was not intended to restrict the right of self-defense against armed attack.

One will search in vain for any other provision in the charter that would preclude United States participation in the collective defense of a nonmember. The fact that article 51 refers only to armed attack "against a Member of the United Nations" implies no intention to preclude members from participating in the defense of nonmembers. . . .

*   *   *

It has been asserted that the conflict in Vietnam is "civil strife" in which foreign intervention is forbidden. Those who make this assertion have gone so far as to compare Ho Chi Minh's actions in Vietnam with the efforts of President Lincoln to preserve the Union during the American Civil War. Any such characterization is an entire fiction disregarding the actual situation in Vietnam. The Hanoi regime is anything but the legitimate government of a unified country in which the South is rebelling against lawful national authority.

The Geneva accords of 1954 provided for a division of Vietnam into two zones at the 17th parallel. Although this line of demarcation was intended to be temporary, it was established by international agreement, which specifically forbade aggression by one zone against the other.

The Republic of Vietnam in the South has been recognized as a separate international entity by approximately 60 governments the world over. It has been admitted as a member of a number of the specialized agencies of the United Nations. The United Nations General Assembly in 1957 voted to recommend South Vietnam for membership in the organization, and its admission was frustrated only by the veto of the Soviet Union in the Security Council.

In any event there is no warrant for the suggestion that one zone of a temporarily divided state—whether it be Germany, Korea, or Vietnam—can be legally overrun by armed forces from the other zone, crossing the internationally recognized line of demarcation between the two. Any such doctrine would subvert the international agreement establishing the line of demarcation, and would pose grave dangers to international peace.

*   *   *

There is nothing in the charter to suggest that United Nations members are precluded from participating in the defense of a recognized international entity against armed attack merely because the entity may lack some of the attributes of an independent sovereign state. Any such result would have a destructive effect on the stability of international engagements such as the Geneva accords of 1954 and on internationally agreed lines of demarcation. Such a result, far from being in accord with the charter and the purposes of the United Nations, would undermine them and would create new dangers to international peace and security.

*   *   *

Some have argued that collective self-defense may be undertaken only by a regional arrangement or agency operating under chapter VIII of the United Nations Charter. Such an assertion ignores the structure of the charter and the practice followed in the more than 20 years since the founding of the United Nations.

The basic proposition that rights of self-defense are not impaired by the charter—as expressly stated in article 51—is not conditioned by any charter provision limiting the application of this proposition to collective defense by a regional arrangement or agency. The structure of the charter reinforces this conclusion. Article 51 appears in chapter VII of the charter, entitled "Action With Respect to Threats to the Peace, Breaches of the Peace, and Acts of Aggression," whereas chapter VIII, entitled "Regional Arrangements," begins with article 52 and embraces the two following articles. The records of the San Francisco conference show that article 51 was deliberately placed in chapter VII rather than chapter VIII, "where it would only have a bearing on the regional system."

Under article 51, the right of self-defense is available against any armed attack, whether or not the country attacked is a member of a regional arrangement and regardless of the source of the attack. Chapter VIII, on the other hand, deals with relations among members of a regional arrangement or agency, and authorizes regional action as appropriate for dealing with "local disputes." This distinction has been recognized ever since the founding of the United Nations in 1945.

For example, the North Atlantic Treaty has operated as a collective security arrangement, designed to take common measures in preparation against the eventuality of an armed attack for which collective defense under article 51 would be required. Similarly, the Southeast Asia Treaty Organization was designed as a collective defense arrangement under article 51. . . .

By contrast, article 1 of the Charter of Bogota (1948), establishing the Organization of American States, expressly declares that the organization is a regional agency within the United Nations. Indeed, chapter VIII of the United Nations Charter was included primarily to take account of the functioning of the inter-American system.

In sum, there is no basis in the United Nations Charter for contending that the right of self-defense against armed attack is limited to collective defense by a regional organization.

*　　*　　*

A further argument has been made that the members of the United Nations have conferred on United Nations organs—and, in particular, on the Security Council—exclusive power to act against aggression. Again, the express language of article 51 contradicts that assertion. A victim of armed attack is not required to forego individual or collective defense of its territory until such time as the United Nations organizes collective action and takes appropriate measures. To the contrary, article 51 clearly states that the right of self-defense may be exercised "until the Security Council has taken the measures necessary to maintain international peace and security."

As indicated earlier, article 51 is not literally applicable to the Vietnam situation since South Vietnam is not a member. However, reasoning by analogy from article 51 and adopting its provisions as an appropriate guide for the conduct of members in a case like Vietnam, one can only conclude that United States actions are fully in accord with this country's obligations as a member of the United Nations.

Article 51 requires that:

Measures taken by Members in the exercise of this right of self-defense shall be immediately reported to the Security Council and shall not in any way affect the authority and responsibility of the Security Council under the present Charter to take at any time such action as it deems necessary in order to maintain or restore international peace and security.

The United States has reported to the Security Council on measures it has taken in countering the Communist aggression in Vietnam. In August, 1964, the United States asked the Council to consider the situation created by North Vietnamese attacks on United States destroyers in the Tonkin Gulf. The Council thereafter met to debate the question, but adopted no resolutions. Twice in February, 1965, the United States sent additional reports to the Security Council on the conflict in Vietnam and on the additional measures taken by the United States in the collective defense of South Vietnam. In January, 1966, the United States formally submitted the Vietnam question to the Security Council for its consideration and introduced a draft resolution calling for discussions looking toward a peaceful settlement on the basis of the Geneva accords.

At no time has the Council taken any action to restore peace and security in Southeast Asia. The Council has not expressed criticism of United States actions. Indeed, since the United States submission of January, 1966, members of the Council have been notably reluctant to proceed with any consideration of the Vietnam question.

The conclusion is clear that the United States has in no way acted to interfere with United Nations consideration of the conflict in Vietnam. On the contrary, the United States has requested United Nations consideration, and the Council has not seen fit to act.

The existence or absence of a formal declaration of war is not a factor in determining whether an international use of force is lawful as a manner of international law. The United Nations Charter's restrictions focus on the manner and purpose of its use and not on any formalities of announcement.

It should also be noted that a formal declaration of war would not place any obligations on either side in the conflict by which that side would not be bound in any event. The rules of international law concerning the conduct of hostilities in an international armed conflict apply regardless of any declaration of war.

*   *   *

United Nations Peace-Keeping Operations

The actual United Nations peace-keeping operations in the Middle East (UNEF, 1956), in the Congo (ONUC, 1960), in West New Guinea (UNTEA, 1962), and in Cyprus (UNFICYP, 1964) have been essentially diplomatic attempts to interpose forces between combatants and to assist in dampening belligerency by standing impartially between contending parties until a peaceful atmosphere can be restored. The extremely complex Congo operation undoubtedly went beyond mere United Nations interposition. United Nations belligerent action there against domestic secessionist forces was partly rationalized as self-defense, but the political, legal, and fiscal questions left in the wake of ONUC hardly suggest that the operation will be regarded as a legal precedent.

Finally, in every case the United Nations peace-keeping forces were introduced with the general consent of the contending parties and with the specific consent of the state in which the United Nations forces were stationed. All this may seem a far cry from the formal intentions of the men who drafted the Charter at San Francisco in 1945, and from the legal niceties of Chapters VI and VII, but what counts eventually must be the spirit in implementing the purposes of the organization.

The United Nations is a political organization that reflects the wills of states to join in a common cause of maintaining international peace and security: where national interests diverge sharply, where the strongly disparate views of states divide the United Nations councils, clearly law will be strained, if not violated. Nevertheless, the obligations under the Charter laid on all member states are unmistakably the dictates of international law.

As the common sense of the world community in permanent diplomatic session, the United Nations declares, interprets, and applies international law to the most crucial issues of the day, including the use of force in international relations. Small powers cannot ignore the United Nations, and great powers have found it increasingly difficult to do so. To avoid a formal declaration of war and to rationalize their interventions or other armed activities as self-defense, collective security, or domestic insurrection may be the modern hypocrisies of states in exercising their power. But such euphemisms also betray a subservience to international opinion and a self-restraint by states in their foreign policy, which improve the hopes of international law for the regulation and control of international violence.

The Mitigation of War

Armed conflict between states, with all the cruel, devastating, and dismembering attributes of war, has not been eliminated by the United Nations Charter, despite all the pleas for peace. The bloody battles in Greece, Korea, Egypt, Vietnam, and elsewhere from 1945 to the present speak for themselves as political facts. But legally: (a) the United Nations itself may take action against a state by air, land, or sea forces; (b) wars can be fought by states as individual or collective "defensive" measures under the Charter, continuing until the United Nations intervenes, which may or may not happen; and (c) civil wars, essentially within the domestic jursidiction of a state, when not threatening international peace, may fall outside the purview of the Charter.

Mass violence, whether under the name of war, police action, aggression, civil conflict, or armed subversion, can still be expected in any part of the world. Despite the desire of all right-thinking men to eliminate the *causes* of international conflict, the time has not come to abandon the rules of war and the principles of international law that have been so carefully nurtured over the last century in order to reduce human suffering in the conduct of those hostilities that do occur.

To mitigate war, states have engaged in various kinds of international commitments in order to avoid injury to noncombatants; to improve the treatment of combatants who are captured, sick, or wounded in the course of war; to eliminate the weapons that cause cruel and wholesale killing and maiming in belligerent activities.

Some of the most terrible battles of the 19th century were fought during the Civil War in America from 1861 to 1865. When hostilities began, President Abraham Lincoln asked the jurist Francis Lieber to draft a code on the laws of land warfare which was published in 1863 as *Instructions for the Government of the Armies of the United States in the Field*. This was the first written code of conduct used by military commanders in a campaign, and it had considerable influence in shaping the rules of war eventually acknowledged by many states of the world.

In 1864, 12 states met in Geneva to draw up the first multilateral convention in history on the relief of those wounded in battle and the safeguarding of noncombatants who, under a Red Cross emblem, cared for them. The Geneva Convention for the Relief of the Wounded and Sick of Armies in the Field was revised in 1906, again in 1929, and, as World War II revealed its abuse or deficiency, was reformulated in 1949

456

into a new Geneva Convention for the Amelioration of the Condition of the Wounded and Sick in Armed Forces.

Prisoners of war in ancient times were slain or enslaved, and as late as the 19th century were ransomed with personal profit for the captors. Prisoners have always been vulnerable to the most atrocious abuse by their captors. The problem of improving the treatment of prisoners of war by a belligerent power in times of national crisis and enmity without compromising the loyalty of the prisoners themselves has severely challenged international law.

The first international declaration on the condition and treatment of prisoners of war was drafted at the Brussels Conference of 1874. This declaration was followed by regulations that were included in the Hague Convention on the Laws and Customs of War on Land in 1907. A new detailed convention on the subject of prisoners of war, adopted at Geneva in 1929, introduced the practice of entrusting to a neutral state a "protective" power to observe any abuses by a belligerent against the convention. In 1949, following World War II, the 1929 convention was replaced by the Geneva Convention Relative to the Treatment of Prisoners of War. Two other conventions applying to the wounded, sick, and shipwrecked members of the armed forces at sea and to the protection of civilian persons in time of war were also signed at Geneva in 1949. These conventions are now in force as international law for a very large number of contracting states.

The cruelties of battle and captivity revealed in 1966 in Vietnam only make more urgent the present and future application of international law through the Geneva conventions. If governments cannot yet submerge their aims and ambitions to peaceful international settlements, they can at least endeavor to restrain the brutality of their troops against the helpless sick, wounded, or captive.

Another approach to reducing the horrors of battle, both on combatant and noncombatant, has been international agreement on the use of weapons. The poisoning of wells was deemed unlawful by the ancient Greeks, and the crossbow at one time was regarded as illegal by the medieval papacy. In 1868, the St. Petersburg Declaration of 17 states decried the use in war of dumdum bullets—bullets with soft noses allowing the iron projectile to shred within a man's body. The 1899 and 1907 Hague Convention Respecting the Laws and Customs of War on Land provided the most fundamental and acceptable international rules of warfare at the beginning of the 20th century. Among its many provisions that have been outdated, commanders were required to notify defenders in advance of bombardments that might injure noncombatant civilians. The first use of gas warfare in World War I led to the 1925 Geneva Gas and Bacteriological Warfare Protocol which condemned poison gas as a tactic of battle.

Today, the use of nuclear weapons, demonstrated in a small way by the

United States in 1945 in its devastating bombardments of Nagasaki and Hiroshima in Japan, offers a horrendous and appalling vision of any future war. By 1967, the United States, the Soviet Union, Great Britain, France, and the People's Republic of China could already manufacture and detonate atomic bombs, while other states did not lack the potentiality for fabricating such weapons of mass destruction.

Once again, states are trying to limit or avoid the use of terrible weapons that can obliterate all distinctions between soldiers and civilians, adults and children, the healthy and the helpless. In 1961, the General Assembly of the United Nations passed a Declaration on the Prohibition of the Use of Nuclear or Thermo-Nuclear Weapons, which stated that the use of such weapons was a violation of the Charter and contrary to the rules of international law. But the majority vote was strongly opposed by some 20 states, including the United States. More cogent legally was the Nuclear Test Ban Treaty in force between the United States and the Soviet Union in 1963, which prohibited nuclear weapon test explosions in the atmosphere, in outer space, and under water (but not under ground). This treaty is open to all states for signature or accession. Another approach has been to limit by treaty the areas for nuclear weapons testing or nuclear arsenals, such as the Antarctic Treaty, discussed in Section IV. Bans on use of outer space and celestial bodies for these purposes were finally being realized in 1967.

Still confronting the cynic is the problem of maintaining a pacific community in which states must continue to jostle one another on a shrinking planet filled with dreadful weapons for human extermination. Political accommodation must be diligently sought through bilateral, regional, and universal negotiations, despite the evangelical idealist who wants nothing but total disarmament and total peace. Law must also play a part. International law on the conduct of warfare should yield to the changing technologies of combat, and should be gradually amended by negotiation and consent to meet the needs of a modern world community. But norms are imperative in order to set the optimum standards of human relationships under the most abrasive conditions of international change. International law, in the final analysis, affects people, and those individuals who may be caught up in the blind and angry maelstrom of international conflict deserve every protection that the law of nations can provide.

Contemporary rules for the mitigation of war are shown by the Geneva Conventions (a) *For the Amelioration of the Condition of the Wounded and Sick in Armed Forces in the Field* and (b) *Relative to the Treatment of Prisoners of War*, which follow; (c) the *Law of Land Warfare* document illustrates the guidance given by the United States in this field to its military personnel; (d) the *Treaty Banning Nuclear Weapon Tests* document provides the main article for limiting the United States, the Soviet Union, and other adhering states in their development of nuclear weapons, and (e) the resolution of the United Nations General Assembly on the *Immunization of Outer Space from Nuclear Weapons* represents an international effort to avoid the arms race in outer space.

GENEVA CONVENTION FOR THE AMELIORATION OF THE CONDITION OF THE WOUNDED AND SICK IN ARMED FORCES IN THE FIELD, 1949
United States Department of State T.I.A.S. 3362

Article 1

The High Contracting Parties undertake to respect and to ensure respect for the present Convention in all circumstances.

Article 2

In addition to the provisions which shall be implemented in peacetime, the present Convention shall apply to all cases of declared war or of any other armed conflict which may arise between two or more of the High Contracting Parties, even if the state of war is not recognized by one of them.

The Convention shall also apply to all cases of partial or total occupation of the territory of a High Contracting Party, even if the said occupation meets with no armed resistance.

Although one of the Powers in conflict may not be a party to the present Convention, the Powers who are parties thereto shall remain bound by it in their mutual relations. They shall furthermore be bound by the Convention in relation to the said Power, if the latter accepts and applies the provisions thereof.

Article 3

In the case of armed conflict not of an international character occurring in the territory of one of the High Contracting Parties, each Party to the conflict shall be bound to apply, as a minimum, the following provisions:

(1) Persons taking no active part in the hostilities, including members of armed forces who have laid down their arms and those placed *hors de combat* by sickness, wounds, detention, or any other cause, shall in all circumstances be treated humanely, without any adverse distinction founded on race, colour, religion or faith, sex, birth or wealth, or any other similar criteria.

To this end, the following acts are and shall remain prohibited at any time and in any place whatsoever with respect to the above-mentioned persons:

   (a) violence to life and person, in particular murder of all kinds, mutilation, cruel treatment and torture;
   (b) taking of hostages;

(c) outrages upon personal dignity, in particular humiliating and de-
    grading treatment;

(d) the passing of sentences and the carrying out of executions without
    previous judgment pronounced by a regularly constituted court,
    affording all the judicial guarantees which are recognized as indis-
    pensable by civilized peoples.

(2) The wounded and sick shall be collected and cared for.

An impartial humanitarian body, such as the International Committee
of the Red Cross, may offer its services to the Parties to the conflict.

The Parties to the conflict should further endeavour to bring into
force, by means of special agreements, all or part of the other provisions
of the present Convention.

The application of the preceding provisions shall not affect the legal
status of the Parties of the conflict.

*   *   *

Article 8

The present Convention shall be applied with the cooperation and
under the scrutiny of the Protecting Powers whose duty it is to safeguard
the interests of the Parties to the conflict. For this purpose, the Protecting
Powers may appoint, apart from their diplomatic or consular staff, delegates from amongst their own nationals or the nationals of other neutral
Powers. The said delegates shall be subject to the approval of the Power
with which they are to carry out their duties.

The Parties to the conflict shall facilitate, to the greatest extent possible,
the task of the representatives or delegates of the Protecting Powers.

The representatives or delegates of the Protecting Powers shall not in
any case exceed their mission under the present Convention. They shall, in
particular, take account of the imperative necessities of security of the
State wherein they carry out their duties. Their activities shall only be
restricted as an exceptional and temporary measure when this is rendered
necessary by imperative military necessities.

*   *   *

Article 12

Members of the armed forces and other persons mentioned in the
following Article, who are wounded or sick, shall be respected and
protected in all circumstances.

They shall be treated humanely and cared for by the Party to the
conflict in whose power they may be, without any adverse distinction
founded on sex, race, nationality, religion, political opinions, or any other
similar criteria. Any attempts upon their lives, or violence to their persons,
shall be strictly prohibited; in particular, they shall not be murdered or

exterminated, subjected to torture or to biological experiments; they shall not wilfully be left without medical assistance and care, nor shall conditions exposing them to contagion or infection be created.

Only urgent medical reasons will authorize priority in the order of treatment to be administered.

Woman shall be treated with all consideration due to their sex.

The Party to the conflict which is compelled to abandon wounded or sick to the enemy shall, as far as military considerations permit, leave with them a part of its medical personnel and material to assist in their care.

Article 13

The present Convention shall apply to the wounded and sick belonging to the following categories:

(1) Members of the armed forces of a Party to the conflict, as well as members of militias or volunteer corps forming part of such armed forces.

(2) Members of other militias and members of other volunteer corps, including those of organized resistance movements, belonging to a Party to the conflict and operating in or outside their own territory, even if this territory is occupied, provided that such militias or volunteer corps, including such organized resistance movements, fulfil the following conditions:

(a) that of being commanded by a person responsible for his subordinates;

(b) that of having a fixed distinctive sign recognizable at a distance;

(c) that of carrying arms openly;

(d) that of conducting their operations in accordance with the laws and customs of war.

(3) Members of regular armed forces who profess allegiance to a Government or an authority not recognized by the Detaining Power.

(4) Persons who accompany the armed forces without actually being members thereof, such a civil members of military aircraft crews, war correspondents, supply contractors, members of labour units or of services responsible for the welfare of the armed forces, provided that they have received authorization from the armed forces which they accompany.

(5) Members of crews, including masters, pilots and apprentices, of the merchant marine and the crews of civil aircraft of the Parties to the conflict, who do not benefit by more favourable treatment under any other provisions in international law.

(6) Inhabitants of a non-occupied territory who, on the approach of the enemy, spontaneously take up arms to resist the invading forces, without having had time to form themselves into regular armed units, provided they carry arms openly and respect the laws and customs of war.

*   *   *

Article 49

The High Contracting Parties undertake to enact any legislation necessary to provide effective penal sanctions for persons committing, or ordering to be committed, any of the grave breaches of the present Convention defined in the following Article.

Each High Contracting Party shall be under the obligation to search for persons alleged to have committed, or to have ordered to be committed, such grave breaches, and shall bring such persons regardless of their nationality, before its own courts. It may also, if it prefers, and in accordance with the provisions of its own legislation, hand such persons over for trial to another High Contracting Party concerned, provided such High Contracting Party has made out a *prima facie* case.

Each High Contracting Party shall take measures necessary for the suppression of all acts contrary to the provisions of the present Convention other than the grave breaches defined in the following Article.

In all circumstances, the accused persons shall benefit by safeguards of proper trial and defence, which shall not be less favourable than those provided by Article 105 and those following of the Geneva Convention relative to the Treatment of Prisoners of War of August 12, 1949.

Article 50

Grave breaches to which the preceding Article relates shall be those involving any of the following acts, if committed against persons or property protected by the Convention: wilful killing, torture or inhuman treatment, including biological experiments, wilfully causing great suffering or serious injury to body or health, and extensive destruction and appropriation of property, not justified by military necessity and carried out unlawfully and wantonly.

Article 51

No High Contracting Party shall be allowed to absolve itself or any other High Contracting Party of any liability incurred by itself or by another High Contracting Party in respect of breaches referred to in the preceding Article.

*　　*　　*

GENEVA CONVENTION RELATIVE TO THE TREATMENT OF PRISONERS OF WAR, 1949
United States Department of State T.I.A.S. 3364

* * *

Article 12

Prisoners of war are in the hands of the enemy Power, but not of the individuals or military units who have captured them. Irrespective of the individual responsibilities that may exist, the Detaining Power is responsible for the treatment given them.

* * *

Article 13

Prisoners of war must at all times be humanely treated. Any unlawful act or omission by the Detaining Power causing death or seriously endangering the health of a prisoner of war in its custody is prohibited, and will be regarded as a serious breach of the present Convention. In particular, no prisoner of war may be subjected to physical mutilation or to medical or scientific experiments of any kind which are not justified by the medical, dental or hospital treatment of the prisoner concerned and carried out in his interest.

Likewise, prisoners of war must at all times be protected, particularly against acts of violence or intimidation and against insults and public curiosity.

Measures of reprisal against prisoners of war are prohibited.

Article 14

Prisoners of war are entitled in all circumstances to respect for their persons and their honour.

Women shall be treated with all regard due to their sex and shall in all cases benefit by treatment as favourable as that granted to men.

Prisoners of war shall retain the full civil capacity which they enjoyed at the time of their capture. The Detaining Power may not restrict the exercise, either within or without its own territory, of the rights such capacity confers except in so far as the captivity requires.

Article 15

The Power detaining prisoners of war shall be bound to provide free of charge for their maintenance and for the medical attention required by their state of health.

Article 16

Taking into consideration the provisions of the present Convention relating to rank and sex, and subject to any privileged treatment which may be accorded to them by reason of their state of health, age or professional qualifications, all prisoners of war shall be treated alike by the Detaining Power, without any adverse distinction based on race, nationality, religious belief or political opinions, or any other distinction founded on similar criteria.

Article 17

Every prisoner of war, when questioned on the subject, is bound to give only his surname, first names and rank, date of birth, and army, regimental, personal or serial number, or failing this, equivalent information.

If he wilfully infringes this rule, he may render himself liable to a restriction of the privileges accorded to his rank or status.

Each Party to a conflict is required to furnish the persons under its jurisdiction who are liable to become prisoners of war, with an identity card. . . .

No physical or mental torture, nor any other form of coercion, may be inflicted on prisoners of war to secure from them information of any kind whatever. Prisoners of war who refuse to answer may not be threatened, insulted, or exposed to unpleasant or disadvantageous treatment of any kind.

*   *   *

THE LAW OF LAND WARFARE
United States Department of the Army, July 1956
Basic Field Manual 27–10

1. Purpose and Scope

The purpose of this Manual is to provide authoritative guidance to military personnnel on the customary and treaty law applicable to the conduct of warfare on land and to relationships between belligerents and neutral States. Although certain of the legal principles set forth herein have application to warfare at sea and in the air as well as to hostilities on land, this Manual otherwise concerns itself with the rules peculiar to naval and aerial warfare only to the extent that such rules have some direct bearing on the activities of land forces.

This Manual is an official publication of the United States Army. However, those provisions of the Manual which are neither statutes nor the text of treaties to which the United States is a party should not be considered binding upon courts and tribunals applying the law of war. However, such provisions are of evidentiary value insofar as they bear upon questions of custom and practice.

2. Purposes of the Law of War

The conduct of armed hostilities on land is regulated by the law of land warfare which is both written and unwritten. It is inspired by the desire to diminish the evils of war by:

a. Protecting both combatants and noncombatants from unnecessary suffering;

b. Safeguarding certain fundamental human rights of persons who fall into the hands of the enemy, particularly prisoners of war, the wounded and sick, and civilians; and

c. Facilitating the restoration of peace.

3. Basic Principles

a. *Prohibitory Effect.* The law of war places limits on the exercise of a belligerent's power in the interests mentioned in paragraph 2 and requires that belligerents refrain from employing any kind or degree of violence which is not actually necessary for military purposes and that they conduct hostilities with regard for the principles of humanity and chivalry.

The prohibitory effect of the law of war is not minimized by "military necessity" which has been defined as that principle which justifies those measures not forbidden by international law which are indispensable for securing the complete submission of the enemy as soon as possible. Military necessity has been generally rejected as a defense for acts forbidden by the customary and conventional laws of war inasmuch as the latter have been developed and framed with consideration for the concept of military necessity.

b. *Binding on States and Individuals.* The law of war is binding not only upon States as such but also upon individuals and, in particular, the members of their armed forces.

4. Sources

The law of war is derived from two principal sources:

a. *Lawmaking Treaties (or Conventions),* such as the Hague and Geneva Conventions.

b. *Custom.* Although some of the law of war has not been incorporated in any treaty or convention to which the United States is a party, this body of unwritten or customary law is firmly established by the custom of nations and well defined by recognized authorities on international law.

Lawmaking treaties may be compared with legislative enactments in the national law of the United States and the customary law of war with the unwritten Anglo-American common law.

5. Lawmaking Treaties

a. *Treaties to Which the United States Is a Party.* The United States is a party to the following conventions pertinent to warfare on land:

(1) Hague Convention No. III of 18 October 1907, Relative to the Opening of Hostilities, cited herein as H. III.

(2) Hague Convention No. IV of 18 October 1907, Respecting the Laws and Customs of War on Land, cited herein as H. IV, and the Annex thereto, embodying the Regulations Respecting the Laws and Customs of War on Land, cited herein as HR.

(3) Hague Convention No. V of 18 October 1907, Respecting the Rights and Duties of Neutral Powers and Persons in Case of War on Land, cited herein as H.V.

(4) Hague Convention No. IX of 18 October 1907, Concerning Bombardment by Naval Forces in Time of War, cited herein as H. IX.

(5) Hague Convention No. X of 18 October 1907 for the Adaptation to Maritime Warfare of the Principles of the Geneva Convention, cited herein as H. X.

(6) Geneva Convention Relative to the Treatment of Prisoners of War of 27 July 1929, cited herein as GPW 1929.

(7) Geneva Convention for the Amelioration of the Condition of the Wounded and Sick of Armies in the Field of 27 July 1929, cited herein as GWS 1929.

(8) Treaty on the Protection of Artistic and Scientific Institutions and Historic Monuments of 15 April 1935, cited herein as the Roerich Pact. Only the United States and a number of the American Republics are parties to this treaty.

(9) Geneva Convention for the Amelioration of the Condition of the Wounded and Sick in Armed Forces in the Field of 12 August 1949, cited herein as GWS.

(10) Geneva Convention for the Amelioration of the Condition of Wounded, Sick and Shipwrecked Members of Armed Forces at Sea of 12 August 1949, cited herein as GWS Sea.

(11) Geneva Convention Relative to the Treatment of Prisoners of War of 12 August 1949, cited herein as GPW.

(12) Geneva Convention Relative to the Protection of Civilian Persons in Time of War of 12 August 1949, cited herein as GC.

*   *   *

TREATY BANNING NUCLEAR WEAPON TESTS IN THE ATMOSPHERE IN OUTER SPACE AND UNDER WATER, 1963*
49 State Department Bulletin 239

*   *   *

Article 1

1. Each of the Parties to this Treaty undertakes to prohibit, to prevent, and not to carry out any nuclear weapon test explosion, or any other nuclear explosion, at any place under its jurisdiction or control:
   (a) in the atmosphere; beyond its limits, including outer space; or under water, including territorial waters or high seas; or
   (b) in any other environment if such explosion causes radioactive debris to be present outside the territorial limits of the state under whose jurisdiction or control such explosion is conducted. It is understood in this connection that the provisions of this subparagraph are without prejudice to the conclusion of a treaty resulting in the permanent banning of all nuclear test explosions, including all such explosions under ground, the conclusion of which, as the Parties have stated in the Preamble to this Treaty, they seek to achieve.

2. Each of the Parties to this Treaty undertakes furthermore to refrain from causing, encouraging, or in any way participating in, the carrying out of any nuclear weapon test explosion, or any other nuclear explosion, anywhere which would take place in any of the environments described, or have the effect referred to, in paragraph 1 of this article.

Article 2

1. Any Party may propose amendments to this Treaty. The text of any proposed amendment shall be submitted to the Depositary Governments which shall circulate it to all Parties to this Treaty. Thereafter, if requested to do so by one-third or more of the Parties, the Depositary Governments shall convene a conference, to which they shall invite all the Parties, to consider such amendment.

2. Any amendment to this Treaty must be approved by a majority of the votes of all the Parties to this Treaty, including the votes of all of the Original Parties. The amendment shall enter into force for all Parties upon the deposit of instruments of ratification by a majority of all the Parties, including the instruments of ratification of all of the Original Parties.

---

* In force 10 October 1963.

Article 3

1. This Treaty shall be open to all states for signature. . . .

2. This Treaty shall be subject to ratification by signatory states. Instruments of ratification and instruments of accession shall be deposited with the Governments of the Original Parties—the United States of America, the United Kingdom of Great Britain and Northern Ireland, and the Union of Soviet Socialist Republics—which are hereby designated the Depositary Governments.

3. This Treaty shall enter into force after its ratification by all the Original Parties and the deposit of their instruments of ratification.

*   *   *

6. This Treaty shall be registered by the Depositary Governments pursuant to Article 102 of the Charter of the United Nations.

Article 4

This Treaty shall be of unlimited duration.

Each Party shall in exercising its national sovereignty have the right to withdraw from the Treaty if it decides that extraordinary events, related to the subject matter of this Treaty, have jeopardized the supreme interests of its country. It shall give notice of such withdrawal to all other Parties to the Treaty three months in advance.

*   *   *

IMMUNIZATION OF OUTER SPACE FROM NUCLEAR WEAPONS
United Nations General Assembly Resolution*
1884 (XVIII), 17 October 1963

The General Assembly,

Recalling its resolution 1721 A (XVI) of 20 December 1961, in which it expressed the belief that the exploration and use of outer space should be only for the betterment of mankind,

Determined to take steps to prevent the spread of the arms race to outer space,

1. *Welcomes* the expressions by the Union of Soviet Socialist Republics and the United States of America of their intention not to station

---

* See also p. 196 and the outer space treaty open for signature in 1967 prohibiting nuclear weapons on celestial bodies or in space.

in outer space any objects carrying nuclear weapons or other kinds of weapons of mass destruction;

2. *Solemnly calls upon* all States:
   (a) To refrain from placing in orbit around the earth any objects carrying nuclear weapons or any other kinds of weapons of mass destruction, installing such weapons on celestial bodies, or stationing such weapons in outer space in any other manner;
   (b) To refrain from causing, encouraging or in any way participating in the conduct of the foregoing activities.

FOR FURTHER STUDY

MYRES S. McDOUGAL AND FLORENTINO P. FELICIANO. *Law and Minimum World Public Order.* New Haven, Conn.: Yale University Press, 1961.

MORRIS GREENSPAN. *The Modern Law of Land Warfare.* Berkeley: University of California Press, 1959.

D. W. BOWETT. *Self-Defense in International Law.* New York: Frederick A. Praeger, Inc., 1958.

JULIUS STONE. *Aggression and World Order.* Berkeley: University of California Press, 1958.

XII

The Development of
International Law

THE greatest excitement of international law lies not in its past, but in its future growth and development as a means for maintaining world peace, prosperity, and human dignity. Among the most provocative questions for modern international relations are: What new law is needed and how can it be fashioned? At what frontiers, political or judicial, can statesmen and judges forge ahead in clarifying the existing international legal norms applicable to the states of the world and their peoples?

The law of nations, as indicated in all the preceding sections, stems, first, from the customary behavior of states, sanctioned by such long and universal experience that it comes to be regarded as a legal norm, not merely etiquette; second, from obligations specifically undertaken by states through international agreements. Furthermore, interpretations of the application of those fundamental legal norms supplied by custom and positive agreement emanate from judicial decisions. In cases presented for an opinion or a decision, courts clarify the rules of international law by filling in details and by providing cogent meaning for the pertinent norms.

Therefore, the advocate of strengthening international law, who frankly acknowledges the many gaps in both its definition and application, must look to improved means for (*a*) ascertaining customary law among nations, (*b*) reaching additional international agreements, and (*c*) making judicial interpretations more frequent and constructive.

United Nations Practice:
Customary Law

Until recently, the task of ascertaining customary international law posed inordinate difficulties. First, a lawyer or a court called on to declare the prevailing rule has had to gather separately the practices of many states by examining their statutes and procedures. Second, advocates and judges have attempted to say whether enough states over a sufficiently long time had followed a rule that had consequently become an international rule, legally binding. For example, the United States Supreme Court in 1871 found that certain rules of navigation accepted into their national laws by the United States, Great Britain, and more than 30 other commercial states had become through common consent international maritime law applicable to British and United States vessels that collided on the high seas.[1] In the *Asylum* case, discussed in Section I, the Court was compelled to look into various Latin-American conventions and national practices only to find a reasonable doubt that any custom, legally binding, obtained between certain Latin-American states. It decided that Peru had assumed no obligation, either explicitly or implicitly, on the institution of asylum as a rule of international law.

To ascertain customary international law still requires a search of the legal practice of states, but since the establishment of the United Nations the opinions and usages of virtually all states of the world on some subjects can be witnessed in one place and at one time. Through the declarations and resolutions of the General Assembly some 120 states can now express their views on any international practice or rule.

The General Assembly has not been endowed with legislative powers under the Charter: it is a forum of mankind with specific powers to create structures, elect members, and budget expenses for the United Nations organization itself, and with general powers to study, discuss, declare, resolve, and recommend on almost any public international issue. However, when either the General Assembly or the Security Council makes rules for the internal organization and procedure of the United Nations with respect to such subjects as statehood, recognition, treaties, domestic jurisdiction, or the settlement of disputes, they not only fill out the meaning of the great multilateral treaty, the Charter, that binds all the member states, but they also obviously affect interpretations of these subjects of international law by foreign offices, national courts, international courts, and other international organizations. The records of the General Assembly and the Security Council, as well as other organs of the United Nations,

---

[1] *The Scotia*, 14 Wallace 170.

are filled with discussions and votes that register legal views, whether the subject be the admission of Mongolia to the United Nations, the disabilities of the African peoples in Portuguese Angola, or the power of the General Assembly to assess members for peace-keeping activities.

Furthermore, as the General Assembly declares, resolves, or recommends through unanimous or overwhelming votes its views of proper international practice or sound international rules, while not creating international law it nevertheless provides substantial evidence of the customary practices of states and their willingness to regard such declarations, resolutions, or recommendations as *potentially* binding in law on them. When resolutions deliberately recommend norms of international law, as did the General Assembly resolutions on principles of international law applying to outer space in 1961 and 1963, the evidence of rules that states tend to accept as legally binding becomes even clearer.

International Conventions:
Positive Law

For positive legal obligations, however, international law looks to bilateral and multilateral treaties or conventions as well as unilateral acts by states signifying adhesion to or acceptance of such conventions. But here, too, the United Nations has proved an invaluable instrument in developing international law through the draft conventions or codes of its International Law Commission, with occasional recommendations for their submission to individual states or an international conference.

At San Francisco in 1945, the delegates were overwhelmingly opposed to conferring legislative power on the United Nations or allowing the General Assembly any power to impose international conventions on the member states by majority voting, but they did agree on studies and recommendations for "encouraging the progressive development of international law and its codification" under Article 13 of the Charter. In consequence, the International Law Commission was established in 1947.[2] It held its first session in 1949, with a selection of 14 topics of public international law suitable for codification.

Since then, acting on its own choice of subjects for study or responding to priority requests of the General Assembly to deal with certain

---

[2] Members are persons of recognized competence in international law elected from a list of candidates nominated by the governments of member states of the United Nations. The term of office since 1955 has been five years. Originally, there were 15 members, then 21 (1956), and since 1961, 25.

questions, the International Law Commission has produced a large number of reports, considering that its members meet only a few months of the year. Some reports have been merely submitted to the General Assembly, some carry recommendations for further action, and some, like the drafts on the law of the sea, statelessness, diplomatic intercourse and immunities, and consular intercourse and immunities, have led to actual international conventions.

An excellent illustration of the "lawmaking" process of the United Nations system was the 1961 Vienna Convention on Diplomatic Relations.

At its first meeting *in 1949,* the International Law Commission of the United Nations had provisionally selected as one of the topics suitable for codification "diplomatic intercourse and immunities." *In 1952,* the General Assembly resolved that all states ought to observe the existing principles of international law with respect to diplomatic intercourse and immunities. *In 1954,* the International Law Commission began work on this subject of international law, and *in 1957* it provisionally adopted 37 draft articles for transmittal through the Secretary-General of the United Nations to member states for their observations.

In 1958, the International Law Commission finished a draft text of 45 articles, taking into account the views of the United Nations member states, and in December of that year the General Assembly put the item of diplomatic intercourse and immunities on its agenda for its next session. *In 1959,* the General Assembly adopted the resolution that convened the *1961* Vienna Conference, which considered, approved, and opened the convention for ratification by the states. After 22 ratifications, the convention entered into force *in 1964.*

International lawmaking through a study by the International Law Commission, followed by draft articles, a General Assembly resolution, an international conference, individual state signatures, individual state ratifications, and finally deposit with the Secretary-General of the United Nations, suffers from procedural awkwardness and talkative delay. Ten years elapsed between the time the International Law Commission began working on diplomatic intercourse and immunities, one of the oldest and best defined subjects of international law, and the date a convention went into legal force.

Yet, this "legislative" system, cumbersome as it may be, represents great progress over the past, and its success is due to the continuous presence and interest of the United Nations and all its agencies. Not only can the General Assembly state its views by recommendations on the principles of international law that ought to be observed by states, but it also has available a commission of experts in annual session devoted to the development of international law. The General Assembly also can take the initiative in submitting draft rules to states for review and comment, as well as in convening almost all the states of the world to approve a legal convention.

Parenthetically, like the United Nations, the constitutions of the several specialized agencies provide the organizations with rule-making powers that apply to all the member states. While the legal framework of such international organizations as the World Health Organization, the International Labour Organization, or the Food and Agriculture Organization is a multilateral treaty, with an ultimate right of withdrawal for each state, in many matters of minor political sensitivity the member states have shown a willingness to accept regulations made by a qualified majority vote. For example, the Assembly of the International Civil Aviation Organization can adopt by majority action rules of air and air traffic control practices, and the Assembly of the World Health Organization can adopt rules on international sanitary codes that are binding on all members of those organizations, except if they positively request an exemption. The Universal Postal Union and the International Labour Organization pass regulations through qualified majority voting.

Moreover, expenditures—the key to political power that girds the law—have been assessed on members of international organizations by weighted voting (International Bank for Reconstruction and Development), by a simple majority (Food and Agriculture Organization, UNESCO), and by a two-thirds majority (United Nations General Assembly). Such rules, almost universally applied, give detail to the legal obligations of states participating in the several organizations.

The Judicial Process:
Interpretation and Application

Because no world legislature exists, courts can contribute enormously to the development of international law. Nearly all cases that have international legal aspects still come before municipal courts; some of the most interesting interpretations of international law can be found in the judgments of American, British, French, Dutch, Italian, Indian, Japanese, and other national courts. But judgments based upon different cultures, traditions, and values in different courts, as well as an unequal jurisprudence and a national political bias, are bound to stunt the growth of any universal legal system.

On the other hand, states have been notoriously reluctant to submit their controversies with other states to the International Court of Justice and, like the United States, have often vitiated their acceptance of the Court's compulsory jurisdiction on strictly legal issues by ultraconservative reservations. Their fears, in part, stem from their own blatant nationalism, developed over decades of history, which creates internal political difficulties for any government offering to be judged by an international body. And, in part, fears stem from a genuine doubt and wariness about a 15-man court of 15 different nationals that, without the guidance of a legislature or a fully acceptable legal code, may create new law even as it presumably interprets the existing law.

Reciprocally, the International Court of Justice has been diffident in exercising its jurisdiction over international litigation, being reluctant to awaken either national charges of political bias or accusations that the Court is usurping legislative powers. In the contentious cases before it, the Court has stuck rather narrowly to clarifying the law, and its opinions have hardly been marked by any bold judicial innovation to develop international law. Indeed, no fault lies with the individual judges, who have been men of extraordinary wisdom and probity; it lies, rather, with the judicial system created by states out of a 19th-century background of international law. Until states demonstrate a greater trust in the Court to solve their disputes by litigation, which may require amendments in the Court's membership, organization, procedure, and jurisdiction, not much progress can be made through judicial interpretation in developing international law.

Plainly enough, the Court has made greater advances in interpreting international law through its advisory opinions than in its judgments of contentious cases. Advisory opinions, under the Court's statute, may be solicited by the General Assembly or other organs of the United Nations authorized by the General Assembly. The *Reparations for Injuries Suffered in the Service of the United Nations Opinion* (1949), *International Status of South West Africa Opinion* (1950), and *Certain Expenses of the United Nations Opinion* (1954), respectively, have taken bold stands on the legal competence of the United Nations to institute international claims, on the transfer of an international obligation from the League of Nations to the United Nations, and on the General Assembly's capacity to assess the member states for its authorization of peace-keeping expenses. In other advisory opinions, the Court has given legal weight to a more liberal approach of regarding reservations to multilateral treaties as not *per se* nullifying the obligation of the reserving state or other states under the treaty;[3] and it has strengthened the independence of an international judicial institution, the United Nations Administrative Tribunal, against the political influence of the General Assembly in declaring that expenditures rightfully authorized by one organ of the United Nations must be honored by the whole international organization.[4]

The advisory opinions, of course, have been mainly concerned with the internal regulations of the United Nations system or with the relationship of the United Nations system to the states of the world. Less troubled by the questions of court jurisdiction that often close out litigation, and received only as "advisory" opinions, the Court's pronouncements escape some of the political rebuffs suffered in contentious cases. Yet, gaps in the international judicial system are still wide.

In the *Certain Expenses of the United Nations Opinion*, which follows, the deep political cleavages of the leading states over the conduct of United Nations peace-keeping activities in Egypt and the Congo and the very nature of the United Nations organization itself cannot be escaped. A majority opinion has thus far failed to induce the Soviet Union, France, and other states to pay for certain expenses of peace-keeping, because those states hold that the General Assembly's authorization was *ultra vires* and itself illegal under the multilateral treaty of the United Nations Charter.

In the *South West Africa Cases*, which follow, certain events must be recalled. In 1947, South Africa submitted its first and last report to the United Nations on the League of Nations mandated territory of South-West Africa. This led in 1950 to an International Court of Justice Advisory Opinion that held that South Africa still had an international obligation to submit to the supervision of the General Assembly for its administration of South-West Africa. Further opinions in 1955 and 1956 dealt

---

[3] *Reservations to the Convention on Genocide*, 1951 I.C.J. Reports 15.
[4] *Effect of Awards of Compensation Made by The United Nations Administrative Tribunal*, 1954 I.C.J. Reports 47.

with voting procedures in the General Assembly with respect to the mandate, and with the right to hear oral petitions from the territory.

In 1960, Ethiopia and Liberia instituted proceedings against South Africa for violating its obligations under the mandate by imposing on the native people of South-West Africa an extreme form of racial discrimination known as *apartheid*. Overriding four objections of South Africa, the Court found: that the mandate still existed[5]; that Liberia and Ethiopia, as members of the League of Nations when it was dissolved, had the right to invoke the Court's jurisdiction; that the present dispute fell under disputes envisaged in Article 7 of the Mandate; and that there was no probability that negotiation beween the parties outside the Court could lead to a settlement. By a vote of eight to seven, the Court found that it had jurisdiction to adjudicate on the merits of the dispute. Four years later, however, as will be seen in the *South West Africa Cases* (1966), the Court found that Liberia and Ethiopia did *not* have any legal right or interest in the subject matter of their claims.

CERTAIN EXPENSES OF THE UNITED NATIONS
International Court of Justice (Advisory Opinion), 1962
1962 I.C.J. Reports 151

The request which laid the matter before the Court was formulated in a letter dated 21 December 1961 from the Acting Secretary-General of the United Nations to the President of the Court, received in the Registry on 27 December. In that letter the Acting Secretary-General informed the President of the Court that the General Assembly, by a resolution adopted on 20 December 1961, had decided to request the International Court of Justice to give an advisory opinion on the following question:

Do the expenditures authorized in General Assembly resolutions 1583 (XV) and 1590 (XV) of 20 December 1960 [etc.] . . . relating to the United Nations operations in the Congo undertaken in pursuance of the Security Council resolutions of 14 July, 22 July and 9 August 1960, and 21 February and 24 November 1961, and General Assembly resolutions 1474 (ES–IV) of 20 September 1960 and 1599 (XV) [etc.] . . . and the expenditures authorized in General Assembly resolutions 1122 (XI) of 26 November 1956, [etc.] . . . relating to the operations of the United Nations Emergency Force undertaken in pursuance of General Assembly resolutions 997 (ES–I) of 2 November 1956, etc. . . . . constitute 'expenses of the Organization' within the meaning of Article 17, paragraph 2, of the Charter of the United Nations?

*   *   *

---

[5] See Section III, *South West Africa Cases* (Preliminary Objections), 1962.

Before proceeding to give its opinion on the question put to it, the Court considers it necessary to make the following preliminary remarks:

The power of the Court to give an advisory opinion is derived from Article 65 of the Statute. The power granted is of a discretionary character. . . . in accordance with Article 65 of its Statute, the Court can give an advisory opinion only on a legal question. If a question is not a legal one, the Court has no discretion in the matter; it must decline to give the opinion requested. But even if the question is a legal one, which the Court is undoubtedly competent to answer, it may nonetheless decline to do so. . . .

*   *   *

The Court finds no "compelling reason" why it should not give the advisory opinion which the General Assembly requested by its resolution 1731 (XVI). It has been argued that the question put to the Court is intertwined with political questions, and that for this reason the Court should refuse to give an opinion. It is true that most interpretations of the Charter of the United Nations will have political significance, great or small. In the nature of things it could not be otherwise. The Court, however, cannot attribute a political character to a request which invites it to undertake an essentially judicial task, namely, the interpretation of a treaty provision.

In the preamble to the resolution requesting this opinion, the General Assembly expressed its recognition of "its need for authoritative legal guidance." In its search for such guidance it has put to the Court a legal question—a question of the interpretation of Article 17, paragraph 2, of the Charter of the United Nations.

*   *   *

The question on which the Court is asked to give its opinions is whether certain expenditures which were authorized by the General Assembly to cover the costs of the United Nations operations in the Congo (hereinafter referred to as ONUC) and of the operations of the United Nations Emergency Force in the Middle East (hereinafter referred to as UNEF), "constitute 'expenses of the Organization' within the meaning of Article 17, paragraph 2, of the Charter of the United Nations."

Before entering upon the detailed aspects of this question, the Court will examine the view that it should take into consideration the circumstance that at the 1086th Plenary Meeting of the General Assembly on 20 December 1961, an amendment was proposed, by the representative of France, to the draft resolution requesting the advisory opinion, and that this amendment was rejected. The amendment would have asked the Court to give an opinion on the question whether the expenditures relating to the indicated operations were "decided on in conformity with the provisions of the Charter;" if that question were answered in the affirmative, the Court would have been asked to proceed to answer the question which the resolution as adopted actually poses.

If the amendment had been adopted, the Court would have been asked to consider whether the resolutions *authorizing the expenditures* were decided on in conformity with the Charter; the French amendment did not propose to ask the Court whether the resolutions *in pursuance of which the operations in the Middle East and in the Congo* were undertaken, were adopted in conformity with the Charter.

* * *

The rejection of the French amendment does not constitute a directive to the Court to exclude from its consideration the question whether certain expenditures were "decided on in conformity with the Charter," if the Court finds such consideration appropriate.

* * *

Turning to the question which has been posed, the Court observes that it involves an interpretation of Article 17, paragraph 2, of the Charter. On the previous occasions when the Court has had to interpret the Charter of the United Nations, it has followed the principles and rules applicable in general to the interpretation of treaties, since it has recognized that the Charter is a multilateral treaty, albeit a treaty having certain special characteristics.

* * *

The text of Article 17 is in part as follows:

1. The General Assembly shall consider and approve the budget of the Organization.
2. The expenses of the Organization shall be borne by the Members as apportioned by the General Assembly.

Although the Court will examine Article 17 in itself and in its relation to the rest of the Charter, it should be noted that at least three separate questions might arise in the interpretation of paragraph 2 of this Article. One question is that of identifying what are "the expenses of the Organization;" a second question might concern apportionment by the General Assembly; while a third question might involve the interpretation of the phrase "shall be borne by the Members." It is the second and third questions which directly involve "the financial obligations of the Members," but it is only the first question which is posed by the request for the advisory opinion. The question put to the Court has to do with a moment logically anterior to apportionment, just as a question of apportionment would be anterior to a question of Members' obligation to pay.

* * *

The text of Article 17, paragraph 2, refers to "the expenses of the Organization" without any further explicit definition of such expenses. It would be possible to begin with a general proposition to the effect that the "expenses" of any organization are the amounts paid out to defray the costs of carrying out its purposes, in this case, the political, economic, social, humanitarian and other purposes of the United Nations. The next step would be to examine, as the Court will, whether the resolutions authorizing the operations here in question were intended to carry out the purposes of the United Nations and whether the expenditures were incurred in furthering these operations. Or, it might simply be said that the "expenses" of an organization are those which are provided for in its budget. But the Court has not been asked to give an abstract definition of the words "expenses of the Organization." It has been asked to answer a specific question related to certain identified expenditures which have actually been made, but the Court would not adequately discharge the obligation incumbent on it unless it examined in some detail various problems raised by the question which the General Assembly has asked.

It is perhaps the simple identification of "expenses" with the items included in a budget, which has led certain arguments to link the interpretation of the word "expenses" in paragraph 2 of Article 17, with the word "budget" in paragraph 1 of that Article; in both cases, it is contended, the qualifying adjective "regular" or "administrative" should be understood to be implied. Since no such qualification is expressed in the text of the Charter, it could be read in, only if such qualification must necessarily be implied from the provisions of the Charter considered as a whole, or from some particular provision thereof which makes it unavoidable to do so in order to give effect to the Charter.

*   *   *

It is a consistent practice of the General Assembly to include in the annual budget resolutions, provision for expenses relating to the maintenance of international peace and security. Annually, since 1947, the General Assembly has made anticipatory provision for "unforeseen and extraordinary expenses" arising in relation to the "maintenance of peace and security." In a Note submitted to the Court by the Controller on the budgetary and financial practices of the United Nations, "extraordinary expenses" are defined as "obligations and expenditures arising as a result of the approval by a council, commission or other competent United Nations body of new programmes and activities not contemplated when the budget appropriations were approved."

The annual resolution designed to provide for extraordinary expenses authorizes the Secretary-General to enter into commitments to meet such expenses with the prior concurrence of the Advisory Committee on Administrative and Budgetary Questions, except that such concurrence is not necessary if the Secretary-General certifies that such commitments relate to the subjects mentioned and the amount does not exceed $2 million. At its fifteenth and sixteenth sessions, the General Assembly resolved "that if, as a result of a decision of the Security Council, commitments relating to the maintenance of peace and security should arise in an estimated total exceeding $10 million" before the General Assembly was due to meet again, a special session should be convened by the Secretary-General to consider the matter. The Secretary-General is regularly authorized to draw on the Working Capital Fund for such expenses but is required to submit supplementary budget estimates to cover amounts so advanced. These annual resolutions on unforeseen and extraordinary expenses were adopted without a dissenting vote in every year from 1947 through 1959, except for 1952, 1953, and 1954, when the adverse votes are attributable to the fact that the resolution included the specification of a controversial item—United Nations Korean War decorations.

*   *   *

Turning to paragraph 2 of Article 17, the Court observes that, on its face, the term "expenses of the Organization" means all the expenses and not just certain types of expenses which might be referred to as "regular expenses." An examination of other parts of the Charter shows the variety of expenses which must inevitably be included with the "expenses of the Organization" just as much as the salaries of staff or the maintenance of buildings.

*   *   *

Article 17 is the only article in the Charter which refers to budgetary authority or to the power to apportion expenses, or otherwise to raise revenue, except for Articles 33 and 35, paragraph 3, of the Statute of the Court which have no bearing on the point here under discussion. Nevertheless, it has been argued before the Court that one type of expenses, namely those resulting from operations for the maintenance of international peace and security, are not "expenses of the Organization" within the meaning of Article 17, paragraph 2, of the Charter, inasmuch as they exclusively stem from the Security Council, and more especially through agreements negotiated in accordance with Article 43 of the Charter.

The argument rests in part upon the view that when the maintenance of international peace and security is involved, it is only the Security Council which is authorized to decide on any action relative thereto. It is argued further that since the General Assembly's power is limited to discussing, considering, studying and recommending, it cannot impose an obligation to pay the expenses which result from the implementation of its recommendations. . . .

*   *   *

Article 24 of the Charter provides:

In order to ensure prompt and effective action by the United Nations, its Members confer on the Security Council primary responsibility for the maintenance of international peace and security. . . .

The responsibility conferred is "primary," not exclusive. This primary responsibility is conferred upon the Security Council, as stated in Article 24, "in order to ensure prompt and effective action." To this end, it is the Security Council which is given a power to impose an explicit obligation of compliance if for example it issues an order or command to an aggressor under Chapter VII. It is only the Security Council which can require enforcement by coercive action against an aggressor.

The Charter makes it abundantly clear, however, that the General Assembly is also to be concerned with international peace and security. Article 14 authorizes the General Assembly to "recommend measures for the peaceful adjustment of any situation, regardless of origin, which it deems likely to impair the general welfare or friendly relations among nations including situations resulting from a violation of the provisions of the present Charter setting forth the purposes and principles of the United Nations." The word "measures" implies some kind of action, and the only limitation which Article 14 imposes on the General Assembly is the restriction found in Article 12, namely, that the Assembly should not recommend measures while the Security Council is dealing with the same matter unless the Council requests it to do so. . . .

*   *   *

By Article 17, paragraph 1, the General Assembly is given the power not only to "consider" the budget of the Organization, but also to "approve" it. The decision to "approve" the budget has a close connection with paragraph 2 of Article 17, since thereunder the General Assembly is also given the power to apportion the expenses among the Members and the exercise of the power of apportionment creates the obligation, specifically stated in Article 17, paragraph 2, of each Member to bear that part of the expenses which is apportioned to it by the General Assembly. When those expenses include expenditures for the maintenance of peace and security, which are not otherwise provided for, it is the General Assembly which has the authority to apportion the latter amounts among the Members. The provisions of the Charter which distribute functions and powers to the Security Council and to the General Assembly give no support to the view that such distribution excludes from the powers of the General Assembly the power to provide for the financing of measures designed to maintain peace and security.

*   *   *

The practice of the Organization throughout its history bears out the foregoing elucidation of the term "action" in the last sentence of Article 11, paragraph 2. Whether the General Assembly proceeds under Article 11 or under Article 14, the implementation of its recommendations for setting up commissions or other bodies involves organizational activity—action—in connection with the maintenance of international peace and security. Such implementation is a normal feature of the functioning of the United Nations. Such committees, commissions or other bodies or individuals, constitute, in some cases, subsidiary organs established under the authority of Article 22 of the Charter. The functions of the General Assembly for which it may establish such subsidiary organs include, for example, investigation, observation and supervision, but the way in which such subsidiary organs are utilized depends on the consent of the State or States concerned. The Court accordingly finds that the argument which seeks, by reference to Article 11, paragraph 2, to limit the budgetary authority of the General Assembly in respect of the maintenance of international peace and security, is unfounded.

*　　　*　　　*

The Court has considered the general problem of the interpretation of Article 17, paragraph 2, in the light of the general structure of the Charter and of the respective functions assigned by the Charter to the General Assembly and to the Security Council, with a view to determining the meaning of the phrase "the expenses of the Organization." The Court does not find it necessary to go further in giving a more detailed definition of such expenses. The Court will, therefore, proceed to examine the expenditures enumerated in the request for the advisory opinion. In determining whether the actual expenditures authorized constitute "expenses of the Organization within the meaning of Article 17, paragraph 2, of the Charter," the Court agrees that such expenditures must be tested by their relationship to the purposes of the United Nations in the sense that if an expenditure were made for a purpose which is not one of the purposes of the United Nations, it could not be considered an "expense of the Organization."

The purposes of the United Nations are set forth in Article 1 of the Charter. The first two purposes as stated in paragraphs 1 and 2, may be summarily described as pointing to the goal of international peace and security and friendly relations. The third purpose is the achievement of economic, social, cultural and humanitarian goals and respect for human rights. The fourth and last purpose is: "To be a center for harmonizing the actions of nations in the attainment of these common ends."

The primary place ascribed to international peace and security is natural, since the fulfillment of the other purposes will be dependent upon the attainment of that basic condition. These purposes are broad indeed, but neither they nor the powers conferred to effectuate them are unlimited. Save as they have entrusted the Organization with the attainment of these common ends, the Member States retain their freedom of action. But when the Organization takes action which warrants the assertion that it was appropriate for the fulfillment of one of the stated purposes of the United Nations, the presumption is that such action is not *ultra vires* [of] the Organization.

*   *   *

In the legal systems of States, there is often some procedure for determining the validity of even a legislative or governmental act, but no analogous procedure is to be found in the structure of the United Nations. Proposals made during the drafting of the Charter to place the ultimate authority to interpret the Charter in the International Court of Justice were not accepted; the opinion which the Court is in course of rendering is an *advisory* opinion. As anticipated in 1945, therefore, each organ must, in the first place at least, determine its own jurisdiction. If the Security Council, for example, adopts a resolution purportedly for the maintenance of international peace and security and if, in accordance with a mandate or authorization in such resolution, the Secretary-General incurs financial obligations, these amounts must be presumed to constitute "expenses of the Organization."

*   *   *

Similarly, obligations of the Organization may be incurred by the Secretary-General, acting on the authority of the Security Council or of the General Assembly, and the General Assembly "has no alternative but to honour these engagements."

The obligation is one thing: the way in which the obligation is met— that is from what source the funds are secured—is another. The General Assembly may follow any one of several alternatives: it may apportion the cost of the item according to the ordinary scale of assessment; it may apportion the cost according to some special scale of assessment; it may utilize funds which are voluntarily contributed to the Organization; or it may find some other method or combination of methods for providing the necessary funds. In this context, it is of no legal significance whether, as a matter of book-keeping or accounting, the General Assembly, chooses to have the item in question included under one of the standard established sections of the "regular" budget or whether it is separately listed in some special account or fund. The significant fact is that the item is an expense of the Organization and under Article 17, paragraph 2, the General Assembly therefore has authority to apportion it.

*   *   *

In his first report on the plan for an emergency international Force the Secretary-General used the language of resolution 998 (ES–I) in submitting his proposals. The same terms are used in General Assembly resolution 1000 (ES–I) of 5 November in which operative paragraph 1 reads:

Establishes a United Nations Command for an emergency international force to secure and supervise the cessation of hostilities in accordance with all the terms of General Assembly resolution 997 (ES–I) of 2 November 1956.

This resolution was adopted without a dissenting vote. In his second and final report on the plan for an emergency international Force of 6 November, the Secretary-General, in paragraphs 9 and 10, stated:

While the General Assembly is enabled to *establish* the Force with the consent of those parties which contribute units to the Force, it could not request the Force to be *stationed* or *operate* on the territory of a given country without the consent of the Government of that country. This does not exclude the possibility that the Security Council could use such a Force within the wider margins provided under Chapter VII of the United Nations Charter. I would not for the present consider it necessary to elaborate this point further, since no use of the Force under Chapter VII, with the rights in relation to Member States that this would entail, has been envisaged.

The point just made permits the conclusion that the setting up of the Force should not be guided by the needs which would have existed had the measure been considered as part of an enforcement action directed against a Member country. There is an obvious difference between establishing the Force in order to secure the cessation of hostilities, with a withdrawal of forces, and establishing such a Force with a view to enforcing a withdrawal of forces.

Paragraph 12 of the Report is particularly important because in resolution 1001 (ES–I) the General Assembly, again without a dissenting vote, "*Concurs* in the definition of the functions of the Force as stated in paragraph 12 of the Secretary-General's report." Paragraph 12 reads in part as follows:

. . . the functions of the United Nations Force would be, when a cease-fire is being established, to enter Egyptian territory with the consent of the Egyptian Government, in order to help maintain quiet during and after the withdrawal of non-Egyptian troops, and to secure compliance with the other terms established in the resolution of 2 November 1956. The Force obviously should have no rights other than those necessary for the execution of its functions, in cooperation with local authorities. It would be more than an observers' corps, but in no way a military force temporarily controlling the territory in which it is stationed; nor, moreover, should the Force have military functions exceeding those necessary to secure peaceful conditions on the assumption that the parties to the conflict take all necessary steps for compliance with the recommendations of the General Assembly.

It is not possible to find in this description of the functions of UNEF, as outlined by the Secretary-General and concurred in by the General Assembly without a dissenting vote, any evidence that the Force was to be used for purposes of enforcement. Nor can such evidence be found in the subsequent operations of the Force, operations which did not exceed the scope of the functions ascribed to it.

*   *   *

The financing of UNEF presented perplexing problems and the debates on these problems have even led to the view that the General

Assembly never, either directly or indirectly, regarded the expenses of UNEF as "expenses of the Organization within the meaning of Article 17, paragraph 2, of the Charter." With this interpretation the Court cannot agree. In paragraph 15 of his second and final report on the plan for an emergency international Force of 6 November 1956, the Secretary-General said that this problem required further study. Provisionally, certain costs might be absorbed by a nation providing a unit, "while all other costs should be financed outside the normal budget of the United Nations." Since it was "obviously impossible to make any estimate of the costs without a knowledge of the size of the corps and the length of its assignment," the "only practical course . . . would be for the General Assembly to vote a general authorization for the cost of the Force on the basis of general principles such as those here suggested."

Paragraph 5 of resolution 1001 (ES–I) of 7 November 1956 states that the General Assembly "*Approves provisionally* the basic rule concerning the financing of the Force laid down in paragraph 15 of the Secretary-General's report."

In an oral statement to the plenary meeting of the General Assembly on 26 November 1956, the Secretary-General said:

. . . I wish to make it equally clear that while funds received and payments made with respect to the Force are to be considered as coming outside the regular budget of the Organization, the operation is essentially a United Nations responsibility, and the Special Account to be established must, there-fore, be construed as coming within the meaning of Article 17 of the Charter.

At this same meeting, after hearing this statement, the General Assembly in resolution 1122 (XI) noted that it had "*provisionally approved* the recommendations made by the Secretary-General concerning the financing of the Force." It then authorized the Secretary-General "to establish a United Nations Emergency Force Special Account to which funds received by the United Nations, outside the regular budget, for the purpose of meeting the expenses of the Force shall be credited and from which payments for this purpose shall be made." The resolution then provided that the initial amount in the Special Account should be $10 million and authorized the Secretary-General "pending the receipt of funds for the Special Account, to advance from the Working Capital Fund such sums as the Special Account may require to meet any expenses chargeable to it." The establishment of a Special Account does not necessarily mean that the funds in it are not to be derived from contributions of Members as apportioned by the General Assembly.

The next of the resolutions of the General Assembly to be considered is 1089 (XI) of 21 December 1956, which reflects the uncertainties and the conflicting views about financing UNEF. The divergencies are duly noted and there is ample reservation concerning possible future action, but operative paragraph 1 follows the recommendation of the Secretary-

General "that the expenses relating to the Force should be apportioned in the same manner as the expenses of the Organization." The language of this paragraph is clearly drawn from Article 17:

1. *Decides* that the expenses of the United Nations Emergency Force, other than for such pay, equipment, supplies and services as may be furnished without charge by Governments of Member States, shall be borne by the United Nations and shall be apportioned among the Member States, to the extent of $10 million, in accordance with the scale of assessments adopted by the General Assembly for contributions to the annual budget of the Organization for the financial year 1957.

This resolution, which was adopted by the requisite two-thirds majority, must have rested upon the conclusion that the expenses of UNEF were "expenses of the Organization" since otherwise the General Assembly would have had no authority to decide that they "shall be borne by the United Nations" or to apportion them among the Members. It is further significant that paragraph 3 of this resolution, which established a study committee, charges this committee with the task of examining "the question of the *apportionment* of the expenses of the Force in excess of $10 million . . . and the principle or the formulation of *scales of contributions different from the scale of contributions* by Member States to the ordinary budget for 1957." The italicized words show that it was not contemplated that the Committee would consider any method of meeting these expenses except through some form of apportionment although it was understood that a different *scale* might be suggested.

* * *

Resolution 1151 (XII) of 22 November 1957, while contemplating the receipt of more voluntary contributions, decided in paragraph 4 that the expenses authorized "shall be borne by the Members of the United Nations in accordance with the scales of assessments adopted by the General Assembly for the financial years 1957 and 1958, respectively."

Almost a year later, on 14 November 1958, in resolution 1263 (XIII) the General Assembly, while "*Noting with satisfaction* the effective way in which the Force continues to carry out its function," requested the Fifth Committee "to recommend such action as may be necessary to finance this continuing operation of the United Nations Emergency Force."

* * *

The Court concludes that, from year to year, the expenses of UNEF have been treated by the General Assembly as expenses of the Organization within the meaning of Article 17, paragraph 2, of the Charter.

The operations in the Congo were initially authorized by the Security Council in the resolution of 14 July 1960 which was adopted without a dissenting vote. The resolution, in the light of the appeal from the

Government of the Congo, the report of the Secretary-General and the debate in the Security Council, was clearly adopted with a view to maintaining international peace and security. However, it is argued that the resolution has been implemented in violation of provisions of the Charter inasmuch as under the Charter it is the Security Council that determines which States are to participate in carrying out decisions involving the maintenance of international peace and security, whereas in the case of the Congo the Secretary-General himself determined which States were to participate with their armed forces or otherwise.

By paragraph 2, of the resolution of 14 July 1960 the Security Council "*Decides* to authorize the Secretary-General to take the necessary steps, in consultation with the Government of the Republic of the Congo, to provide the Government with such military assistance as may be necessary." Paragraph 3 requested the Secretary-General "to report to the Security Council as appropriate." The Secretary-General made his first report on 18 July and in it informed the Security Council which States he had asked to contribute forces or material, which ones had complied, the size of the units which had already arrived in the Congo (a total of some 3,500 troops), and some detail about further units expected.

On 22 July the Security Council by unanimous vote adopted a further resolution in which the preamble states that it had considered this report of the Secretary-General and appreciated "the work of the Secretary-General and the support so readily and so speedily given to him by all Member States invited by him to give assistance." In operative paragraph 3, the Security Council "*Commends* the Secretary-General for the prompt action he has taken to carry out resolution S/4387 of the Security Council, and for his first report."

On 9 August the Security Council adopted a further resolution without a dissenting vote in which it took note of the second report and of an oral statement of the Secretary-General and in operative paragraph 1: "*Confirms* the authority given to the Secretary-General by the Security Council resolutions of 14 July and 22 July 1960 and requests him to continue to carry out the responsibility placed on him thereby." This emphatic ratification is further supported by operative paragraphs 5 and 6 by which all Member States were called upon "to afford mutual assistance" and the Secretary-General was requested to "implement this resolution and to report further to the Council as appropriate."

The Security Council resolutions of 14 July, 22 July and 9 August, 1960 were noted by the General Assembly in its resolution 1474 (ES–IV) of 20 September adopted without a dissenting vote, in which it "fully supports" these resolutions. Again without a dissenting vote, on 21 February 1961 the Security Council reaffirmed its three previous resolutions and the General Assembly Resolution 1474 (ES–IV) of 20 September 1960 and reminded "all States of their obligations under these resolutions."

Again without a dissenting vote on 24 November 1961, the Security

Council, once more recalling the previous resolutions, reaffirmed "the policies and purposes of the United Nations with respect to the Congo (Leopoldville) as set out" in those resolutions. Operative paragraphs 4 and 5 of this resolution renew the authority to the Secretary-General to continue the activities in the Congo.

In the light of such a record of reiterated consideration, confirmation, approval and ratification by the Security Council and by the General Assembly of the actions of the Secretary-General in implementing the resolution of 14 July 1960, it is impossible to reach the conclusion that the operations in question usurped or impinged upon the prerogatives conferred by the Charter on the Security Council.

*   *   *

For the reasons stated, financial obligations which, in accordance with the clear and reiterated authority of both the Security Council and the General Assembly, the Secretary-General incurred on behalf of the United Nations, constitute obligations of the Organization for which the General Assembly was entitled to make provision under the authority of Article 17.

In relation to ONUC, the first action concerning the financing of the operation was taken by the General Assembly on 20 December 1960, after the Security Council had adopted its resolutions of 14 July, 22 July and 9 August, and the General Assembly had adopted its supporting resolution of 20 September. This resolution 1583 (XV) of 20 December referred to the report of the Secretary-General on the estimated cost of the Congo operations from 14 July to 31 December 1960, and to the recommendations. It decided to establish an *ad hoc* account for the expenses of the United Nations in the Congo. It also took note of certain waivers of cost claims and then decided to apportion the sum of $48.5 million among the Member States "on the basis of the regular scale of assessment" subject to certain exceptions. It made this decision because in the preamble it had already recognized:

. . . that the expenses involved in the United Nations operations in the Congo for 1960 constitute 'expenses of the Organization' within the meaning of Article 17, paragraph 2, of the Charter of the United Nations and that the assessment thereof against Member States creates binding legal obligations on such States to pay their assessed shares.

By its further resolution 1590 (XV) of the same day, the General Assembly authorized the Secretary-General "to incur commitments in 1961 for the United Nations operations in the Congo up to the total of $24 million for the period from 1 January to 31 March 1961." On 3 April 1961, the General Assembly authorized the Secretary-General to continue until 21 April "to incur commitments for the United Nations operations in the Congo at a level not to exceed $8 million per month."

Importance has been attached to the statement included in the preamble of General Assembly resolution 1619 (XV) of 21 April 1961 which reads:

Bearing in mind that the extraordinary expenses for the United Nations operations in the Congo are essentially different in nature from the expenses of the Organization under the regular budget and that therefore a procedure different from that applied in the case of the regular budget is required for meeting these extraordinary expenses,

However, the same resolution in operative paragraph 4:

Decides further to apportion as expenses of the Organization the amount of $100 million among the Member States in accordance with the scale of assessment for the regular budget subject to the provisions of paragraph 8 below [paragraph 8 makes certain adjustments for Member States assessed at the lowest rates or who receive certain designated technical assistance], pending the establishment of a different scale of assessment to defray the extraordinary expenses of the Organization resulting from these operations.

*   *   *

The conclusion to be drawn from these paragraphs is that the General Assembly has twice decided that even though certain expenses are "extraordinary" and "essentially different" from those under the "regular budget," they are none the less "expenses of the Organization" to be apportioned in accordance with the power granted to the General Assembly by Article 17, paragraph 2. This conclusion is strengthened by the concluding clause of paragraph 4 of the two resolutions just cited which states that the decision therein to use the scale of assessment already adopted for the regular budget is made "pending the establishment of a *different scale of assessment* to defray the extraordinary expenses." The only alternative—and that means the "different procedure"—contemplated was another *scale* of assessment and not some method other than assessment. "Apportionment" and "assessment" are terms which relate only to the General Assembly's authority under Article 17.

*   *   *

For these reasons,

The Court is of the opinion,

by nine votes to five,

that the expenditures authorized in General Assembly resolutions 1583 (XV) [etc.] relating to the United Nations operations in the Congo undertaken in pursuance of the Security Council resolutions of 14 July [etc.] . . . relating to the operations of the United Nations Emergency Force undertaken in pursuance of General Assembly . . . constitute "expenses of the Organization" within the meaning of Article 17, paragraph 2, of the Charter of the United Nations.

Judge Spiropoulos makes the following declaration:

While accepting the Court's conclusion, I cannot agree with all the views put forward in the Advisory Opinion. In particular, I consider that the affirmative reply to the request for an opinion is justified by the argument that the resolutions of the General Assembly authorizing the financing of the United Nations operations in the Congo and the Middle East, being resolutions designed to meet expenditure concerned with the fulfillment of the purposes of the United Nations, which were adopted by two-thirds of the Members of the General Assembly present and voting, create obligations for the Members of the United Nations.

*   *   *

The French delegation had proposed to the General Assembly the acceptance of an amendment to the text . . . according to which amendment the question put to the Court would have become: "Were the expenditures authorized, etc. . . . decided on in conformity with the provisions of the Charter, and if so, do they constitute 'expenses of the Organization' within the meaning of Article 17, paragraph 2, of the Charter of the United Nations?"

On December 20, 1961, in the course of the meeting of the General Assembly . . . the French delegation . . . said:

In the opinion of the French delegation, the question put to the Court does not enable the latter to give a clear-cut opinion on the juridical basis for the financial obligations of Member States. The Court cannot, in fact, appraise the scope of those resolutions without determining what obligations they may create for Member States under the Charter.

It is for this reason that the French delegation is submitting to the Assembly an amendment [A/L.378] the adoption of which would enable the Court to determine whether or not the Assembly resolutions concerning the financial implications of the United Nations operations in the Congo and the Middle East are in conformity with the Charter. Only thus, if the matter is referred to the Court, will it be done in such a way as to take into account the scope and nature of the problems raised in the proposal to request an opinion.

The French amendment was rejected.

The rejection of the French amendment by the General Assembly seems to me to show the desire of the Assembly that the conformity or non-conformity of the decisions of the Assembly and of the Security Council concerning the United Nations operations in the Congo and the Middle East should not be examined by the Court. It seems natural, indeed, that the General Assembly should not have wished that the Court should pronounce on the validity of resolutions which have been applied for several years. In these circumstances, I have felt bound to refrain from pronouncing on the conformity with the Charter of the resolutions relating to the United Nations operations in the Congo and the Middle East.

*   *   *

Separate Opinion of Judge Sir Percy Spender

I agree that the question should be answered in the affirmative.

*   *   *

In the proceedings on this Advisory Opinion practice and usage within the United Nations has been greatly relied upon by certain States, which have availed themselves of the opportunity to present their views to the Court, as establishing a criterion of interpretation of relevant Charter provisions.

It was for example contended by one State that usages developed in the practice of the United Nations have dealt with certain items of expenditure as expenses of the Organization within the meaning of Article 17 (2) and that such usages whether or not they could be said to have attained the character of customary legal principle are relevant for the purposes of interpreting the meaning and scope of resolutions adopted by the General Assembly concerning specific questions. So usage within the United Nations, it was urged, has sanctioned the inclusion in the budget expenses of the Organization of items which related to other than the ordinary administrative and routine duties of the Organization as, for example, those connected with special peace-keeping operations and operations of a similar character initiated by either the General Assembly or the Security Council.

. . . The proposition advanced was that it is a general principle that a treaty provision should be interpreted in the light of the subsequent conduct of the contracting parties . . . and that the uniform practice pursued by the organs of the United Nations should be equated with the "subsequent conduct of contracting *parties* as in the case of a bilateral treaty."

Similar contentions were made by other States. The practice of the parties in interpreting a constituitive instrument, it was submitted, was a guide to that instrument's true meaning. The practice of the Security Council, as well as that of the General Assembly, demonstrated, it was said, that the power to approve and apportion the budget of the United Nations was recognized to be the province of the General Assembly alone. . . .

The contention of one State went further. The claim was made that any interpretation of the Charter by a United Nations organ should be upheld so long as it is an interpretation which is not expressly inconsistent with the Charter and that since any such interpretation would reflect the support of the majority of the Member States, and considering the interpretation of the Charter which has been applied by the Assembly in regard to financing the operation of the UNOC and UNEF, the Court should give its advisory opinion in this case in the affirmative.

These contentions raise questions of importance which should not, I think, be passed over in silence, particularly having regard to the extent to which the Court itself has had recourse to practice within the United Nations from which to draw sustenance for its interpretation of Charter provisions.

It is of course a general principle of international law that the subsequent conduct of the parties to a bilateral—or a multilateral—instrument may throw light on the intention of the parties at the time the instrument was entered into and thus may provide a legitimate criterion of interpretation.

*   *   *

I find difficulty in accepting the proposition that a practice pursued by an *organ* of the United Nations may be equated with the subsequent conduct of *parties* to a bilateral agreement and thus afford evidence of intention of the parties to the Charter (who have constantly been added to since it came into force) and in that way or otherwise provide a criterion of interpretation. Nor can I agree with a view sometimes advanced that a common practice pursued by an organ of the United Nations, though *ultra vires* and in point of fact having the result of amending the Charter, may nonetheless be effective as a criterion of interpretation.

It is not I think permissible to move the principle of subsequent conduct of parties to a bilateral or multilateral treaty into another field and seek to apply it, not to the *parties* to the treaty, but to an *organ* established under the treaty.

*   *   *

The Charter establishes an Organization. The Organization must function through its constituted organs. The functions and authorities of those organs are set out in the Charter. However the Charter is otherwise described the essential fact is that it is a multilateral treaty. It cannot be altered at the will of the majority of the Member States, no matter how often that will is expressed or asserted against a protesting minority and no matter how large be the majority of Member States which assert its will in this manner or how small the minority.

*   *   *

Each organ of the United Nations, of course, has an inherent right to interpret the Charter in relation to its authority and functions. But the rule that they may do so is not in any case applicable without qualification. Their interpretation of their respective authorities under the Charter may conceivably conflict one with the other. They may agree. They may, after following a certain interpretation for many years, change it. In any case, their right to interpret the Charter gives them no power to alter it.

The question of constitutionality of action taken by the General Assembly or the Security Council will rarely call for consideration except within the United Nations itself, where a majority rule prevails. In practice, this may enable action to be taken which is beyond power. When, however, the Court is called upon to pronounce upon a question whether certain authority exercised by an organ of the Organization is within the power of that organ, only legal considerations may be invoked and *de facto* extension of the Charter must be disregarded.

* * *

Separate Opinion of Judge Sir Gerald Fitzmaurice

I have not written this separate opinion because I disagree with the operative conclusion of the Opinion of the Court.

* * *

The real question however, in my view (and the Court does not deal with it), is whether such a ruling would have to be regarded as final. In the course of the oral proceedings, the Court was in effect invited to take the view that this would be the case. It was suggested, for example, that the mere fact that certain expenditures had been actually apportioned by the Assembly, was conclusive as to their validity. Apportionment would certainly be conclusive as to the majority view of the Assembly, but this merely begs the question. It amounts to saying that even if, on an objective and impartial assessment, given expenditures had in fact been invalidly and improperly incurred or authorized, they would nevertheless stand automatically validated by the act of the Assembly in either apportioning them among Member States or, in the event of a challenge, subsequently resolving that the apportionment was good.

This is a view which I am unable to accept. It is too extreme.

* * *

The core of the difficulty is how to reconcile the obligatory character of the liability to meet the expenses of the Organization with the non-obligatory character of many, indeed most, of the resolutions under which these expenses are incurred. To me, it has not seemed self-evident that Article 17, paragraph 2, on its actual wording, necessarily or automatically disposes of this difficulty; and unless it can be disposed of satisfactorily, the affirmative reply given to the question addressed to the Court must be less convincing than it ought to be.

There is clearly no problem in the case of *decisions* of the Security Council which, under Article 25 of the Charter, are binding on Member States, even on those Members of the Council which voted against them, and equally on those Members of the Assembly which, not being Members of the Council, *ex hypothesi* did not vote at all.

*   *   *

Similar considerations can hardly apply to the case of a vote which does go to the length of being cast against the resolution concerned—a resolution which is in any case purely recommendatory. Certainly it would seem at first sight an odd position that a Member State which is not itself bound to carry out such a resolution, and which has manifested disapproval of its being carried out at all by anyone, should nevertheless be legally obliged to contribute to the expenses of executing it.

*   *   *

Dissenting Opinion of Judge Basdevant

In accordance with Article 65, paragraph 2, of the Statute of the Court, the request asking the Court to give an advisory opinion must contain "an exact statement of the question upon which an opinion is required." It is in these circumstances and on that basis that, under Article 65, paragraph 1, the Court "may give an advisory opinion."

This provision has not been complied with.

The request for an opinion starts from a given factual element, namely the existence of "expenditures authorized in General Assembly resolutions." As stated the request for an opinion does not determine whether the Court should purely and simply start from the existence of "expenditures authorized" or whether it should first of all ascertain whether those expenditures were properly authorized by the General Assembly. If the Court is purely and simply to start from the existence of "expenditures authorized" the reply to the question put would appear to be fairly simple: the expenditures were an element of the activity of the United Nations as such, they were incurred and made under its responsibility, and they thereby become expenses of the Organization.

*   *   *

But the factual element set forth in the request for opinion may also be construed as including a legal question, namely: were the authorized expenditures referred to authorized in a proper manner? This question occupied a substantial place in the oral proceedings before the Court and, consequently, in the Opinion. In noting this I am by that very fact compelled also to note that the request for opinion did not, on this essential point, comply with Article 65, paragraph 2, of the Statute which requires "an exact statement of the question upon which an opinion is required."

*   *   *

I regret to have to express my conviction that the request for an opinion has not been presented in a proper fashion. It is for this reason that I consider myself unable to concur in the Opinion by which the Court replies to the request submitted to it.

*   *   *

Dissenting Opinion of Judge Moreno Quintana

It would have been for me a matter of great satisfaction to contribute in the exercise of my judicial function to the most effective realization of the essential purpose of the Organization. But I cannot depart from certain legal concepts which to my mind are of cardinal importance for the interpretation of the Charter; they are those which, in the present case, preclude the Court from giving the opinion requested of it.

*   *   *

The Court has received twenty-one written statements by Member States of the United Nations on the question referred to it, in addition to the ample account which the Secretary-General has given in his Introductory Note for the Court. It has also heard oral statements by the representatives of nine States which confirmed the position set forth in their written statements. A further indication of the various positions taken up is also given by the views more than once expressed by the Secretary-General in the Fifth Committee and the Advisory Committee, in his reports to the General Assembly, in the opinions expressed by various delegations at the meetings of the competent organs, and in the legal tone itself of the resolutions of the General Assembly.

All this material could be simplistically classified by establishing whether the answer to the question is *yes* or *no*. But such a method would be quite inadequate for the purposes which must be sought.

*   *   *

(1) The Charter of the United Nations gave the Organization the financial independence required for the fulfillment of its purposes, but this does not mean that all the Members are under the obligation to contribute to all the expenses which may result;

(2) The question of the legal nature of the resolutions by which the General Assembly and the Security Council undertook the operations in the Middle East and in the Congo constitutes the decisive element in the present case;

(3) The budgetary procedures and practices of the organs of the United Nations, which are of a technical and not of a legal character, do not on that account prevent a clear separation being made between two categories of expenses;

(4) The preparatory work of the San Francisco Conference does not indicate in any precise fashion which of the Members of the United

Nations are required to contribute to the financing of specific operations, but they enable the reply to the question raised to be inferred *a contrario sensu;*

(5) The exegesis of Article 17, paragraph 2, leads to giving to its words the legal construction which seems to proceed from it, in the sense that the expenses it refers to are the administrative expenses of the Organization and not those expenses which, by their nature, are the exclusive responsibility of the Members of the Security Council;

(6) The circumstances in which the question put to the Court in the request for an advisory opinion as worded do not, in view of the resulting limitation of its competence, permit the Court conscientiously to accomplish its task in the present case.

*   *   *

Dissenting Opinion by Judge Koretsky

I regret that I cannot agree with the Opinion of the Court both (a) as I do not consider that the Court would and should give an opinion on the given question posed to it by the General Assembly of the United Nations, and (b) as the Court, to my mind, did not come to the acceptable conclusion in relation to the question which in substance is a question of financial obligations of Member States in peace-keeping operations.

*   *   *

The whole history of financing the United Nations operations in the Middle East, mentioned above, shows that in no case could it have been carried out according to the regular scale of assessments, as those operations had an anti-Charter but at the same time a peace-keeping character. It is known that the financing of peace-keeping operations is not made within the regular budget. One should apply to Article 43 and not to Article 17. And though the Secretary-General and some of the delegations were forcing the General Assembly to refer to Article 17, the General Assembly makes no direct reference in its resolutions to Article 17 (2) of the Charter.

Coming to the operations in the Congo, the Opinion of the Court gives no detailed analysis: neither of the Security Council's resolutions nor those of the General Assembly. In its Opinion the Court limited itself to objecting to the statements, that the resolutions were implemented in violation of the Charter, stressing that the actions of the Secretary-General in implementing the resolution of 14 July 1960, and consequently other resolutions of the Security Council, were confirmed, approved, and ratified by the Security Council and the General Assembly.

*   *   *

To place the Security Council, as the Opinion does, beside the General Assembly, considering them as interchangeable in solving and implementing the tasks of maintaining international peace and security, would be objectively to replace the Security Council by the General Assembly, to put the Council aside and thereby undermine the very foundations of the Organization. It does not befit the Court to follow this line. It has been said that you cannot leave one word out of a song. The Charter represents one of the most important international multilateral treaties, from which it is impossible to leave out any of its provisions either directly or through an interpretation that is more artificial than skillful.

The Court's Opinion thus limits the powers of the Security Council and enlarges the sphere of the General Assembly. The Opinion achieves this by (a) converting the recommendations that the General Assembly may make into some kind of "action," and (b) reducing this action, for which the Security Council has the authority, to "enforcement or coercive action," particularly against aggression.

*   *   *

In February 1961 tragic events occurred. The Congolese national leaders, M. Lumumba and others, were killed. The Belgian troops were still not called back. The Security Council, having come to the conclusion that an immediate and impartial investigation should be carried out in order to ascertain the circumstances of the death of M. Lumumba and his colleagues and that the perpetrators of these crimes should be punished, approved a resolution on 21 February 1961 in which it urged "that the United Nations take immediately all appropriate measures to prevent the occurrence of civil war in the Congo, including arrangements for ceasefires, the halting of all military operations, the prevention of clashes, and the use of force, if necessary, in the last resort;" and "that measures be taken for the immediate withdrawal and evacuation from the Congo of all Belgian and other foreign military and paramilitary personnel and political advisers not under the United Nations Command, and mercenaries."

Inasmuch as the Opinion of the Court states that this resolution was also approved without a dissenting vote, a fact which is regarded as constituting approval of the Secretary-General's actions, I am obliged to quote the statement made by the Representative of the USSR in the Security Council while this resolution was being voted on. He said that the delegation of the Soviet Union decided not to prevent the adoption of this resolution despite its weakness and shortcomings, as it still contained an objective condemnation of the national leaders' murderers and a demand to take measures for the immediate withdrawal and evacuation from the Congo of all Belgian and other foreign military and paramilitary personnel and, also, because the delegation was taking into consideration the wish of the African and Asian countries.

But at the same time the representative of the USSR made an objection against entrusting the Secretary-General with the implementation of the suggested measures.

Therefore, any kind of vote on the resolution (and especially abstention from voting) does not mean that *all* the paragraphs of the resolution were approved by all those who did not cast a dissenting vote. Such reservations are often made, even while voting "for" a resolution.

* * *

The Assembly clearly acknowledged that "the extraordinary expenses for the United Nations operations in the Congo are essentially *different in nature* from the expenses of the Organization under the regular budget and that, therefore, a procedure different from that applied in the case of the regular budget is required for meeting these extraordinary expenses;" and decided "to open an *ad hoc* account for the expenses of the United Nations operations in the Congo for 1961" and to apportion as expenses of the Organization the amount of $100 million among the Member States in accordance with the scale of assessment for the regular budget. At the same time, there was fixed for some of the States a reduction up to 80 per cent of the corresponding assessment. This, however, was considered as a temporary measure. There was mentioned a year (1961) for which this sum was appropriated and the sum itself ($100 million) that was to be apportioned. Besides, it was stated that the aforementioned apportionment was effected "pending the establishment of a different scale of assessment to defray the extraordinary expenses of the Organization resulting from these operations."

In this last part of the phrase the Opinion finds confirmation of the fact that in this case reference is made only to *another scale of assessment* and not to some method other than assessment. But it is important to stress that the resolution states that the expenses for operations in the Congo are essentially *different in nature* from the expenses of the Organization under the regular budget.

* * *

The budget of the Organization provides for all the expenses necessary for its maintenance (in the narrow sense of this word). These are usually called common expenses, running expenses, and the budget itself is called a regular budget, budget proper, etc. . . . They are expenses for the sessions of the General Assembly, the councils, commissions and committees, for special conferences, investigations and inquiries, for Headquarters, the European Office, Information Centres, hospitality, advisory social welfare functions, etc. These expenses are contrasted with the so-called operational expenses for the various kinds of economic social and technical assistance programmes. Determined by the various interests of different countries they are usually financed through voluntary contributions, in any case outside the regular budget. In the document submitted by the Secretariat (Dossier No. 195) on the "Budgetary and Financial Practice of the United Nations" there is a division into two parts: (1) *Regular budget* (General Fund and Working Capital Fund), and (2) Trust Funds, Reserve Accounts and Special Accounts *outside the regular budget*. The document enumerates thirteen such Special Accounts among which it names: Special Account for UNEF and *ad hoc* Account for the United Nations operations in the Congo.

*   *   *

Even the fact that those expenses have never been included in the regular budget proves that it is impossible to argue that these expenses might be apportioned under Article 17, paragraph 2, of the Charter. It has been said more than once that peace-keeping operations should be financed another way.

*   *   *

One cannot consider that decisions of the Security Council regarding the participation of any Member State in concrete peace-keeping operations are not obligatory for a given Member. . . . The General Assembly may only *recommend* measures. Expenses which might arise from such recommendations should not lead to an obligatory apportionment of them among all Members of the United Nations. That would mean to convert a non-mandatory recommendation of the General Assembly into a mandatory decision; this would be to proceed against the Charter, against logic and even against common sense.

*   *   *

Dissenting Opinion of Judge Bustamante

I am among the Judges who held the view that the question of the *conformity or non-conformity with the Charter of the United Nations resolutions concerning the Middle East and the Congo should be examined as being a necessary means of appraisement in order to reply to the question put by the General Assembly in its request for an advisory opinion.*

*   *   *

It cannot be maintained that the resolutions of any organ of the United Nations are not subject to review; that would amount to declaring the pointlessness of the Charter or its absolute subordination to the judgment—always fallible—of the organs. . . . An advisory opinion, taking the place of judicial proceedings, is a method of voluntary recourse which, if only by way of elucidation, precedes the decision which the Organization is called upon to give with regard to legal objections raised by Member States.

*   *   *

. . . in principle, I am of opinion that expenditures validly authorized by the competent organ for the carrying out of an armed action with the purpose of maintaining international peace and security constitute "expenses of the Organization." But in the case of the expenditures authorized for the operations in the Middle East and the Congo, it is for the competent organ of the United Nations to pronounce on the legal objections put forward by certain States against the relevent resolutions. Only after this pronouncement on the legality or the non-legality of these resolutions would, in my opinion, a reply to the request be possible.

In consequence, I conclude that the expenditures referred to in the request for an advisory opinion would constitute expenses of the Organization if, after consideration of the legal objections raised by certain Member States, the competent organ of the United Nations succeeds in determining as *legal* and *valid* the resolutions by virtue of which the expenses in question were incurred.

*   *   *

Since this definition has not been given and having regard to the limitations of the request, the Court—in my view—cannot declare whether the expenditures in question are or are not expenses of the Organization within the meaning of Article 17, paragraph 2, of the Charter. But if the Court must in voting reply categorically "yes" or "no" to the question put in the request, my reply can only be negative for, according to the foregoing, I am not in a position to assume the responsibility for an affirmative characterization of the legality of the expenditures.

SOUTH WEST AFRICA CASES (ETHIOPIA v. SOUTH AFRICA; LIBERIA v. SOUTH AFRICA) Second Phase International Court of Justice, 1966 Mimeographed Text, Registry, I.C.J., 18 July 1966

In the present proceedings the two applicant States, the Empire of Ethiopia and the Republic of Liberia (whose cases are identical and will for present purposes be treated as one case), acting in the capacity of States which were members of the former League of Nations, put forward various allegations of contraventions of the League of Nations Mandate for South West Africa, said to have been committed by the respondent State, the Republic of South Africa, as the administering authority.

In an earlier phase of the case, which took place before the Court in 1962, four preliminary objections were advanced, based on Article 37 of the Court's Statute and the jurisdictional clause (Article 7, paragraph 2) of the Mandate for South West Africa, which were all of them argued by the Respondent and treated by the Court as objections to its jurisdiction. The Court, by its Judgment of 21 December 1962, rejected each of these objections, and thereupon found that it had "jurisdiction to adjudicate upon the merits of the dispute."

In the course of the proceedings on the merits, comprising the exchange of written pleadings, the oral arguments of the Parties and the hearing of a considerable number of witnesses, the Parties put forward various contentions on such matters as whether the Mandate for South West Africa was still in force,—and if so, whether the Mandatory's obligation under Article 6 of the Mandate to furnish annual reports to the Council of the former League of Nations concerning its administration of the mandated territory had become transformed by one means or another into an obligation to furnish such reports to the General Assembly of the United Nations, or had, on the other hand, lapsed entirely;—whether there had been any contravention by the Respondent of the second paragraph of Article 2 of the Mandate which required the Mandatory to "promote to the utmost the material and moral well-being and the social progress of the inhabitants of the territory." . . .

*   *   *

The Parties having dealt with all the elements involved, it became the Court's duty to begin by considering those questions which had such a character that a decision respecting any of them might render unnecessary an enquiry into other aspects of the matter. There are two questions in the present case which have this character. One is whether the Mandate still subsists at all, as the Applicants maintain that it does . . . for if it does not, then clearly the various allegations of contraventions of the Mandate by the Respondent fall automatically to the ground. But this contention . . . is itself part of the Applicants' whole claim as put forward in their final submissions, being so put forward solely in connection with the remaining parts of the claim, and as the necessary foundation for these. For this reason the other question, that of the Applicants' legal right or interest in the subject matter of their claim, is even more fundamental.

. . . it should be made clear that when, in the present Judgment, the Court considers what provisions of the Mandate for South West Africa involve a legal right or interest for the Applicants, and what not, it does so without pronouncing upon, and wholly without prejudice to, the question of whether that Mandate is still in force. The Court moreover thinks it necessary to state that its 1962 decision on the question of competence was equally given without prejudice to that of the survival of the Mandate, which is a question appertaining to the merits of the case. It was not in issue in 1962, except in the sense that survival had to be assumed for the purpose of determining the purely jurisdictional issue which was all that was then before the Court. It was made clear in the course of the 1962 proceedings that it was upon this assumption that the Respondent was arguing the jurisdictional issue; and the same view is reflected in the Applicants' final submissions (1) and (2) in the present proceedings, the effect of which is to ask the Court to declare (*inter alia*) that the Mandate still subsists, and that the Respondent is still subject to the obligations it provides for. It is, correspondingly, a principal part of the Respondent's case on the merits that since (as it contends) the Mandate no longer exists, the Respondent has no obligations under it, and therefore cannot be in breach of the Mandate. This is a matter which, for reasons to be given later in another connection, but equally applicable here, could not have been the subject of any final determination by a decision on a purely preliminary point of jurisdiction.

*   *   *

The Court now comes to the basis of its decision in the present proceedings. . . . it is necessary to stress that no true appreciation of the legal situation regarding any particular mandate, such as that for South West Africa, can be arrived at unless it is borne in mind that this Mandate was only one amongst a number of mandates . . . the salient features of the mandates system as a whole were, with exceptions to be noted where material, applicable indifferently to all the mandates. . . .

The mandates system, as is well known, was formally instituted by Article 22 of the Covenant of the League of Nations. As there indicated, there were to be three categories of mandates, designated as 'A,' 'B,' and 'C' mandates respectively, the Mandate for South West Africa being one of the 'C' category. . . . although it was by Article 22 of the League Covenant that the system as such was established, the precise terms of each mandate, covering the rights and obligations of the mandatory, of the League and its organs, and of the individual members of the League, in relation to each mandated territory, were set out in separate instruments of mandate which, with one exception to be noted later, took the form of resolutions of the Council of the League.

. . . there were the articles defining the mandatory's powers, and its obligations in respect of the inhabitants of the territory and towards the League and its organs. These provisions, relating to the carrying out of the mandates as mandates, will hereinafter be referred to as "conduct of the mandate," or simply "conduct" provisions. On the other hand, there were articles conferring in different degrees, according to the particular mandate or category of mandate, certain rights relative to the mandated territory, directly upon the members of the League as individual States, or in favour of their nationals. Many of these rights were of the same kind as are to be found in certain provisions of ordinary treaties of commerce, establishment and navigation concluded between States. Rights of this kind will hereinafter be referred to as "special interests" rights, embodied in the "special interests" provisions of the mandates. . . .

*   *   *

In addition to the classes of provisions so far noticed, every instrument of mandate contained a jurisdictional clause which, with a single exception to be noticed in due course, was in identical terms for each mandate, whether belonging to the 'A,' 'B' or 'C' category. The language and effect of this clause will be considered later; but it provided for a reference of disputes to the Permanent Court of International Justice and, so the Court found in the first phase of the case, as already mentioned, this reference was now, by virtue of Article 37 of the Court's Statute, to be construed as a reference to the present Court. Another feature of the mandates generally, was a provision according to which their terms could not be modified without the consent of the Council of the League. A further element, though peculiar to the 'C' mandates, may be noted: it was provided both by Article 22 of the Covenant of the League and by a provision of the instruments of 'C' mandate that, subject to certain conditions not here material, a 'C' mandatory was to administer the mandated territory "as an integral portion of its own territory."

Having regard to the situation thus outlined, and in particular to the distinction to be drawn between the "conduct" and the "special interests" provisions of the various instruments of mandate, the question which now arises for decision by the Court is whether any legal right or interest exists for the Applicants relative to the Mandate, apart from such as they may have in respect of the latter category of provisions—a matter on which the Court expresses no opinion, since this category is not in issue in the present case. In respect of the former category—the "conduct" provisions—the question which has to be decided is whether, according to the scheme of the mandates and of the mandates system as a whole, any legal right or interest (which is a different thing from a political interest) was vested in the members of the League of Nations, including the present Applicants, individually and each in its own separate right to call for the carrying out of the mandates as regards their "conduct" clauses—or whether this function must, rather, be regarded as having appertained exclusively to the League itself, and not to each and every member State, separately and independently. In other words, the question is whether the various mandatories had any direct obligation towards the other members of the League individually, as regards the carrying out of the "conduct" provisions of the mandates.

. . . If the Court finds that the Applicants do have such a right or interest, it would then be called upon to pronounce upon the first of the Applicants' final submissions—(continued existence of the Mandate), since if that one should be rejected, the rest would automatically fall to the ground. If on the other hand the Court should find that such a right or interest does not exist, it would obviously be inappropriate and misplaced to make any pronouncement on this first submission of the Applicants, or on the second, since in the context of the present case the question of the continued existence of the Mandate, and of the Respondent's obligations thereunder, would arise solely in connection with provisions concerning which the Court had found that the Applicants lacked any legal right or interest.

It is in their capacity as former members of the League of Nations that the Applicants appear before the Court; and the rights they claim are those that the members of the League are said to have been invested with in the time of the League. Accordingly, in order to determine what the rights and obligations of the Parties relative to the Mandate were and are (supposing it still to be in force, but without prejudice to that question); and in particular whether (as regards the Applicants) these include any right individually to call for the due execution of the "conduct" provisions, and (for the Respondent) an obligation to be answerable to the Applicants in respect of its administration of the Mandate, the Court must place itself at the point in time when the mandates system was being instituted, and when the instruments of mandate were being framed. . . .

*   *   *

The enquiry must pay no less attention to the juridical character and structure of the institution, the League of Nations, within the framework of which the mandates system was organized, and which inevitably determined how this system was to operate—recourses. One fundamental element of this juridical character and structure, which in a sense governed everything else, was that Article 2 of the Covenant provided that the "action of the League under this Covenant shall be effected through the instrumentality of an Assembly and of a Council, with a permanent Secretariat." If the action of the League as a whole was thus governed, it followed naturally that the individual member States could not themselves act differently relative to League matters, unless it was otherwise specially so provided by some article of the Covenant.

*   *   *

The type of régime specified by Article 22 of the Covenant as constituting the "best method of giving practical effect to this principle" was that "the tutelage of such peoples should be entrusted to advanced nations . . . who are willing to accept it,"—and here it was specifically added that it was to be "on behalf of the League" that "this tutelage should be exercised by those nations as Mandatories." It was not provided that the mandates should, either additionally or in the alternative, be exercised on behalf of the members of the League in their individual capacities. The mandatories were to be the agents of, or trustees for the League,—and not of, or for, each and every member of it individually.

The same basic idea was expressed again in the third paragraph of the preamble to the instrument of mandate for South West Africa, where it was recited that the Mandatory, in agreeing to accept the Mandate, had undertaken "to exercise it on behalf of the League of Nations." No other behalf was specified in which the Mandatory had undertaken, either actually or potentially, to exercise the Mandate. The effect of this recital, as the Court sees it, was to register an implied recognition (a) on the part of the Mandatory of the right of the League, acting as an entity through its appropriate organs, to require the due execution of the Mandate in respect of its "conduct" provisions; and (b) on the part of both the Mandatory and the Council of the League, of the character of the Mandate as a juridical régime set within the framework of the League as an institution. There was no similar recognition of any right as being additionally and independently vested in any other entity, such as a State, or as existing outside or independently of the League as an institution; nor was any undertaking at all given by the Mandatory in that regard.

. . . By paragraphs 7 and 9 respectively of Article 22, every mandatory was to "render to the Council [of the League—not to any other entity] an annual report in reference to the territory committed to its charge;" and a permanent commission, which came to be known as the Permanent Mandates Commission, was to be constituted "to receive and examine" these annual reports and "to advise the Council on all matters relating to the observance of the mandates." The Permanent Mandates Commission alone had this advisory role, just as the Council alone had the supervisory function. The Commission consisted of independent experts in their own right, appointed in their personal capacity as such, not as representing any individual member of the League or the member States generally.

The obligation to furnish annual reports was reproduced in the instruments of mandate themselves, where it was stated that they were to be rendered "to the satisfaction of the Council." Neither by the Covenant nor by the instruments of mandate, was any role reserved to individual League members in respect of these reports, furnishable to the Council, and referred by it to the Permanent Mandates Commission. It was the Council that had to be satisfied, not the individual League members. The part played by the latter, other than such as were members of the Council, was exclusively through their participation in the work of the Assembly of the League when, acting under Article 3 of the Covenant, that organ exercised in respect of mandates questions its power to deal with "any matter within the sphere of action of the League." It was as being within the sphere of the League as an institution that mandates questions were dealt with by its Assembly.

These then were the methods, and the only methods, contemplated by the Covenant as "securities" for the performance of the sacred trust, and it was in the Covenant that they were to be embodied. No security taking the form of a right for every member of the League separately and individually to require from the mandatories the due performance of their mandates, or creating a liability for each mandatory to be answerable to them individually—still less conferring a right of recourse to the Court in these regards—was provided by the Covenant.

*　　*　　*

On the other hand, this did not mean that the member States were mere helpless or impotent spectators of what went on, or that they lacked all means of recourse. On the contrary, as members of the League Assembly, or as members of the League Council, or both, as the case might be, they could raise any question relating to mandates generally, or to some one mandate in particular, for consideration by those organs, and could, by their participation, influence the outcome. The records both of the Assembly and of other League organs show that the members of the League in fact made considerable use of this faculty. But again, its exercise—always through the League—did not confer on them any separate right of direct intervention. Rather did it bear witness to the absence of it.

By paragraph 8 of Article 22 of the Covenant, it was provided that the "degree of authority, control or administration" which the various mandatories were to exercise, was to be "explicitly defined in each case by the Council" if these matters had not been "previously agreed upon by the Members of the League." . . .

*　　*　　*

. . . the Mandate contained a clause—paragraph 1 of Article 7 (and similarly in the other mandates)—providing that the consent of the Council of the League was required for any modification of the terms of the Mandate; but it was not stated that the consent of individual members of the League was additionally required. . . .

The real position of the individual members of the League relative to the various instruments of mandate was a different one. They were not parties to them; but they were, to a limited extent, and in certain respects only, in the position of deriving rights from these instruments. . . . The existence of such rights could not be presumed or merely inferred or postulated. But in Article 22 of the League Covenant, only the mandatories are mentioned in connection with the carrying out of the mandates in respect of the inhabitants of the mandated territories and as regards the League organs. Except in the procedural provisions of paragraph 8 (the "if not previously agreed upon" clause) the only mention of the members of the League in Article 22 is in quite another context, namely at the end of paragraph 5, where it is provided that the mandatories shall "also secure equal opportunities for the trade and commerce of other Members of the

League." It is the same in the instruments of mandate. Apart from the jurisdictional clause, which will be considered later, mention of the members of the League is made only in the "special interests" provisions of these instruments. It is in respect of these interests alone that any direct link is established between the mandatories and the members of the League individually. In the case of the "conduct" provisions, mention is made only of the mandatory and, where required, of the appropriate organ of the League. The link in respect of these provisions is with the League or League organs alone.

. . . the Court considers that even in the time of the League, even as members of the League when that organization still existed, the Applicants did not, in their individual capacity as States, possess any separate self-contained right which they could assert, independently of, or additionally to, the right of the League, in the pursuit of its collective, institutional activity, to require the due performance of the Mandate in discharge of the "sacred tust." . . . By their right to activate these organs (of which they made full use), they [states] could procure consideration of mandates questions, as of other matters within the sphere of action of the League. But no right was reserved to them, individually as States, and independently of their participation in the institutional activities of the League, as component parts of it, to claim in their own name,—still less as agents authorized to represent the League,—the right to invigilate the sacred trust,—to set themselves up as separate custodians of the various mandates. This was the role of the League organs.

To put this conclusion in another way, the position was that under the mandates system, and within the general framework of the League system, the various mandatories were responsible for their conduct of the mandates solely to the League—in particular to its Council—and were not additionally and separately responsible to each and every individual State member of the League. . . .

*   *   *

The Applicants, as part of their argument in favour of deeming the functions previously discharged by the Council of the League to have passed now to the General Assembly of the United Nations, insisted on the need for "informed" dealings with the Mandatory: only a body sufficiently endowed with the necessary knowledge, experience and expertise could, it was said, adequately discharge the supervisory role. Yet at the same time it was contended that individual members of the League,—not directly advised by the Permanent Mandates Commission,—not (unless members of the Council) in touch with the mandates questions except through their participation in the work of the League Assembly—nevertheless possessed a right independently to confront the various mandatories over their administration of the mandates, and a faculty to call upon them to alter their policies and adjust their courses accordingly. The two contentions are inconsistent, and the second affronts all the probabilities.

No less difficult than the position of a mandatory caught between a number of possible different expressions of view, would have been that of the League Council whose authority must have been undermined, and its action often frustrated, by the existence of some forty or fifty independent centres of invigilatory rights.

Equally inconsistent would the position claimed for individual League members have been with that of the mandatory as a member of the Council on mandates questions. As such, the mandatory, on the basis of the normal League voting rule, and by virtue of Article 4, paragraphs 5 and 6, and Article 5, paragraph 1, of the Covenant, possessed a vote necessary to the taking of any formal Council decision on a question of substance relative to its mandate (at least in the sense that, if cast, it must not be adversely cast); so that, in the last resort, the assent, or non-dissent, of the mandatory had to be negotiated.

In the opinion of the Court, those who intended the one system cannot simultaneously have intended the other: and if in the time of the League—if as members of the League—the Applicants did not possess the rights contended for—evidently they do not possess them now. There is no principle of law which, following upon the dissolution of the League, would operate to invest the Applicants with rights they did not have even when the League was still in being.

*   *   *

. . . it may be said that a legal right or interest need not necessarily relate to anything material or "tangible" and can be infringed even though no prejudice of a material kind has been suffered. In this connection, the provisions of certain treaties and other international instruments of a humanitarian character, and the terms of various arbitral and judicial decisions, are cited as indicating that, for instance, States may be entitled to uphold some general principle even though the particular contravention of it alleged has not affected their own material interests;—that again, States may have a legal interest in vindicating a principle of international law, even though they have, in the given case, suffered no material prejudice, or ask only for token damages. Without attempting to discuss how far, and in what particular circumstances, these things might be true, it suffices to point out that, in holding that the Applicants in the present case could only have had a legal right or interest in the "special interests" provisions of the Mandate, the Court does not in any way do so merely because these relate to a material or tangible object. Nor, in holding that no legal right or interest exists for the Applicants, individually as States, in respect of the "conduct" provisions, does the Court do so because any such right or interest would not have a material or tangible object. The Court simply holds that such rights or interests, in order to exist, must be clearly vested in those who claim them, by some text or instrument, or rule of law;—and that in the present case, none were ever vested in individual members of the League under any of the relevant instruments, or as a constituent part of the mandates system as a whole, or otherwise.

* * *

It is also asked whether, even supposing that the Applicants only had an interest on the political level respecting the conduct of the Mandate, this would not have sufficed to enable them to seek a declaration from the Court as to what the legal position was under the Mandate, so that, for instance, they could know whether they would be on good ground in bringing before the appropriate political organs, acts of the mandatory thought to involve a threat to peace or good international relations.

The Court is concerned in the present proceedings only with the rights which the Applicants had as former members of the League of Nations—for it is in that capacity alone that they are now appearing. If the contention above described is intended to mean that because, for example, the Applicants would, under paragraph 2 of Article 11 of the League Covenant, have had "the friendly right . . . to bring to the attention of the Assembly or of the Council any circumstance . . . which threatens to disturb international peace or the good understanding . . . upon which peace depends" they would therefore also—and on that account—have had the right to obtain a declaration from the Court as to what the mandatory's obligations were, and whether a violation of these had occurred;—if this is the contention, the Court can only reply to it in the negative. . . .

. . . Under the Court's Statute as it is at present framed, States cannot obtain mere "opinions" from the Court. This faculty is reserved to certain international organs empowered to exercise it by way of the process of requesting the Court for an advisory opinion. It was open to the Council of the League to make use of this process in case of any doubt as to the rights of the League or its members relative to mandates. But in their individual capacity, States can appear before the Court only as litigants in a dispute with another State, even if their object in so doing is only to obtain a declaratory judgment. The moment they so appear however, it is necessary for them, even for that limited purpose, to establish, in relation to the defendant party in the case, the existence of a legal right or interest in the subject matter of their claim, such as to entitle them to the declarations or pronouncements they seek: or in other words that they are parties to whom the defendant State is answerable under the relevant instrument or rule of law.

* * *

. . . Throughout this case it has been suggested, directly or indirectly, that humanitarian considerations are sufficient in themselves to generate legal rights and obligations, and that the Court can and should proceed accordingly. The Court does not think so. It is a court of law, and can take account of moral principles only insofar as these are given a sufficient expression in legal form. Law exists, it is said, to serve a social need; but precisely for that reason it can do so only through and within the limits of its own discipline. Otherwise, it is not a legal service that would be rendered.

Humanitarian considerations may constitute the inspirational basis for rules of law, just as, for instance, the preambular parts of the United Nations Charter constitute the moral and political basis for the specific legal provisions thereafter set out. Such considerations do not, however, in themselves amount to rules of law. . . .

It is in the light of these considerations that the Court must examine what is perhaps the most important contention of a general character that has been advanced in connection with this aspect of the case, namely the contention by which it is sought to derive a legal right or interest in the conduct of the mandate from the simple existence, or principle, of the "sacred trust." The sacred trust, it is said, is a "sacred trust of civilization." Hence all civilized nations have an interest in seeing that it is carried out. An interest, no doubt;—but in order that this interest may take on a specifically legal character, the sacred trust itself must be or become something more than a moral or humanitarian ideal. In order to generate legal rights and obligations, it must be given juridical expression and be clothed in legal form. . . .

Thus it is that paragraph 2 of Article 22 of the Covenant, in the same breath that it postulates the principle of the sacred trust, specifies in terms that, in order to give "effect to this principle," the tutelage of the peoples of the mandated territories should be entrusted to certain nations, "and that this tutelage should be exercised by them" as mandatories "on behalf of the League." It was from this that flowed all the legal consequences already noticed.

* * *

Next, it may be suggested that even if the legal position of the Applicants and of other individual members of the League of Nations was as the Court holds it to be, this was so only during the lifetime of the League, and that when the latter was dissolved, the rights previously resident in the League itself, or in its competent organs, devolved, so to speak, upon the individual States which were members of it at the date of its dissolution. There is, however, no principle of law which would warrant such a conclusion. Although the Court held in the earlier 1962 phase of the present case that the members of a dissolved international organization can be deemed, though no longer members of it, to retain rights which, as members, they individually possessed when the organization was in being, this could not extend to ascribing to them, upon and by reason of the dissolution, rights which, even previously as members, they never did individually possess . . .

* * *

Another argument which requires consideration is that insofar as the Court's view leads to the conclusion that there is now no entity entitled to claim the due performance of the Mandate, it must be unacceptable. Without attempting in any way to pronounce on the various implications involved in this argument, the Court thinks the inference sought to be drawn from it is inadmissible. If, on a correct legal reading of a given situation, certain alleged rights are found to be non-existent, the consequences of this must be accepted. The Court cannot properly postulate the existence of such rights in order to avert those consequences. This would be to engage in an essentially legislative task, in the service of political ends the promotion of which, however desirable in itself, lies outside the function of a court of law.

* * *

The Court comes now to a more specific category of contention arising out of the existence and terms of the jurisdictional clause of the Mandate, and of the effect of the Court's Judgment of 21 December 1962 in that regard.

. . . it is contended that the question of the Applicants' legal right or interest was settled by that Judgment and cannot now be reopened. As regards the issue of preclusion, the Court finds it unnecessary to pronounce on various issues which have been raised in this connection, such as whether a decision on a preliminary objection constitutes a *res judicata* in the proper sense of that term—whether it ranks as a "decision" for the purposes of Article 59 of the Court's Statute, or as "final" within the meaning of Article 60. The essential point is that a decision on a preliminary objection can never be preclusive of a matter appertaining to the merits, whether or not it has in fact been dealt with in connection with the preliminary objection. When preliminary objections are entered by the defendant party in a case, the proceedings on the merits are, by virtue of Article 62, paragraph 3, of the Court's Rules, suspended. Thereafter, and until the proceedings on the merits are resumed, the preliminary objections having been rejected, there can be no decision finally determining or pre-judging any issue of merits. . . .

* * *

It is however contended that, even if the Judgment of 1962 was, for the above-mentioned reasons, not preclusive of the issues of the Applicants' legal right or interest, it did in essence determine that issue because it decided that the Applicants were entitled to invoke the jurisdictional clause of the Mandate, and that if they had a sufficient interest to do that, they must also have a sufficient interest in the subject-matter of their claim. This view is not well-founded. The faculty of invoking a jurisdictional clause depends upon what tests or conditions of the right to do so are laid down by the clause itself. To hold that the parties in any given case belong to the category of State specified in the clause—that the dispute has the specified character—and that the forum is the one specified—is not the same thing as finding the existence of a legal right or interest relative to the merits of the claim. The jurisdictional clause of the Mandate for South West Africa (Article 7, paragraph 2), which appeared in all the mandates, reads as follows:

The Mandatory agrees that, if any dispute whatever should arise between the Mandatory and another Member of the League of Nations relating to the interpretation or the application of the provisions of the Mandate, such dispute, if it cannot be settled by negotiation, shall be submitted to the Permanent Court of International Justice provided for by Article 14 of the Covenant of the League of Nations.

*   *   *

It is next contended that this particular jurisdictional clause has an effect which is more extensive than if it is considered as a simple jurisdictional clause: that it is a clause conferring a substantive right,—that the substantive right it confers is precisely the right to claim from the Mandatory the carrying out of the "conduct of the Mandate" provisions of the instrument of mandate—and that in consequence, even if the right is derivable from no other source, it is derivable from and implicit in this clause.

. . . it would be remarkable . . . if so important a right, having such potentially far-reaching consequences—intended, so the Applicants contend, to play such an essential role in the scheme of the Mandate—of all the mandates, and of the system generally—had been created indirectly, and in so casual and almost incidental a fashion, by an ordinary jurisdictional clause. . . . The Court considers it highly unlikely that, given the far-reaching consequences involved and, according to the Applicants, intended, the framers of the mandates system, had they had any such intention, would have chosen this particular type of jurisdictional clause as the method of carrying it out.

In truth however, there is nothing about this particular jurisdictional clause to differentiate it from many others, or to make it an exception to the rule that, in principle, jurisdictional clauses are adjectival not substantive, in their nature and effect. . . .

. . . Jurisdictional clauses do not determine whether parties have substantive rights, but only whether, if they have them, they can vindicate them by recourse to a tribunal.

Such rights may be derived from participation in an international instrument by a State which has signed and ratified, or has acceded, or has in some other manner become a party to it; and which in consequence, and subject to any exceptions expressly indicated, is entitled to enjoy rights under all the provisions of the instrument concerned. Since the Applicants cannot bring themselves under this head, they must show that the "conduct" provisions of the mandates conferred rights in terms on members of the League as individual States, in the same way that the "special interests" provisions did. . . .

. . . The original drafts contained no jurisdictional clause. Such a clause was first introduced in connection with the 'B' mandates by one of the States participating in the drafting, and concurrently with proposals made by that State for a number of detailed provisions about commercial and other "special interests" rights (including missionary rights) for member States of the League. It was little discussed but, so far as it is possible to judge from what is only a summary record, what discussion there was centred mainly on the commercial aspects of the mandates and the possibility of disputes arising in that regard over the interests of nationals of members of the League . . . No corresponding clear connection emerges between the clause and possible disputes between mandatories and individual members of the League over the conduct of the mandates as mandates. That such disputes could arise does not seem to have been envisaged. In the same way, the original drafts of the 'C' mandates which, in a different form, contained broadly all that now appears in the first four articles of the Mandate for South West Africa, had no jurisdictional clause and no "missionary clause" either. The one appeared when the other did.

The inference to be drawn from this drafting history is confirmed by the very fact that the question of a right of recourse to the Court arose only at the stage of the drafting of the instruments of mandate, and that as already mentioned, no such right figured among the "securities" for the performance of the sacred trust embodied in the League Covenant.

* * *

The Court will not consider a final contention which has been advanced in support of the Applicants' claim of right, namely the so-called "necessity" argument. . . .

. . . The various mandatories did not deal with the individual members of the League over the "conduct" provisions of their mandates, but with the appropriate League organs. If any difficulty should arise over the interpretation of any mandate, or the character of the mandatory's obligations, which could not be cleared up by discussion or reference to an *ad hoc* committee of jurists—a frequent practice in the League—the Council could in the last resort request the Permanent Court for an advisory opinion. Such an opinion would not of course be binding on the mandatory—it was not intended that it should be—but would assist the work of the Council.

In the Council, which the mandatory was entitled to attend as a member for the purposes of any mandate entrusted to it, if not otherwise a member—(Article 4, paragraph 5, of the Covenant), the vote of the mandatory, if present at the meeting, was necessary for any actual "decision" of the Council, since unanimity of those attending was the basic voting rule on matters of substance in the main League organs—(Article 5, paragraph 1, of the Covenant). Thus there could never be any formal clash between the mandatory and the Council as such. In practice, the unanimity rule was frequently not insisted upon, or its impact was mitigated by a process of give-and-take, and by various procedural devices to which both the Council and the mandatories lent themselves. . . .

*   *   *

Under this system, viewed as a whole, the possibility of any serious complication was remote; nor did any arise. That possibility would have been introduced only if the individual members of the League had been held to have the rights the Applicants now contend for. In actual fact, in the twenty-seven years of the League, all questions were, by one means or another, resolved in the Council; no request was made to the Court for an advisory opinion; so far as is known, no member of the League attempted to settle direct with the mandatory any question that did not affect its own interests as a State or those of its nationals, and no cases were referred to the Permanent Court under the adjudication clause except the various phases of one single case (that of the *Mavrommatis Concessions*) coming under the head of "special interests." These facts may not be conclusive in themselves, but they have a significance which the Court cannot overlook, as suggesting that any divergences of view concerning the conduct of a mandate were regarded as being matters that had their place in the political field, the settlement of which lay between the mandatory and the competent organs of the League—not between the mandatory and individual members of the League.

*   *   *

Such then is the background against which the "necessity" argument has to be viewed. The gist of the argument is that since the Council had no means of imposing its views on the mandatory, and since no advisory opinion it might obtain from the Court would be binding on the latter, the mandate could have been flouted at will. Hence, so the contention goes, it was essential, as an ultimate safeguard or security for the performance of the sacred trust, that each member of the League should be deemed to have a legal right or interests in that matter and, in the last resort, be able to take direct action relative to it.

*   *   *

. . . The plain fact is that, in relation to the "conduct" provisions of the mandates, it was never the intention that the Council should be able to impose its views on the various mandatories—the system adopted was one which deliberately rendered this impossible. It was never intended that the views of the Court should be ascertained in a manner binding on mandatories, or that mandatories should be answerable to individual League members as such in respect of the "conduct" provisions of the mandates. It is scarcely likely that a system which, of set purpose, created a position such that, if a mandatory made use of its veto, it would thereby block what would otherwise be a decision of the Council, should simultaneously invest individual members of the League with, in effect, a legal right of complaint if this veto, to which the mandatory was entitled, was made use of. In this situation there was nothing at all unusual. In the international field, the existence of obligations that cannot in the last resort be enforced by any legal process, has always been the rule rather than the exception—and this was even more the case in 1920 than today.

*   *   *

The Court feels obliged in conclusion to point out that the whole "necessity" argument appears, in the final analysis, to be based on considerations of an extra-legal character, the product of a process of after-knowledge. Such a theory was never officially advanced during the period of the League, and probably never would have been but for the dissolution of that organization and the fact that it was then considered preferable to rely on the anticipation that mandated territories would be brought within the United Nations trusteeship system. It is these subsequent events alone, not anything inherent in the mandates system as it was originally conceived, and is correctly to be interpreted, that give rise to the alleged "necessity." But that necessity, if it exists, lies in the political field. It does not constitute necessity in the eyes of the law. If the Court, in order to parry the consequences of these events, were now to read into the mendates system, by way of, so to speak, remedial action, an element wholly foreign to its real character and structure as originally contemplated when the system was instituted, it would be engaging in an *ex post facto* process, exceeding its functions as a court of law. As is implied by the opening phrase of Article 38, paragraph, 1, of its Statute, the Court is not a legitimate body. Its duty is to apply the law as it finds it, not to make it.

*   *   *

It may be urged that the Court is entitled to engage in a process of "filling in the gaps," in the application of a teleological principal of interpretation, according to which instruments must be given their maximum effect in order to ensure the achievement of their underlying purposes. The Court need not here enquire into the scope of a principle the exact bearing of which is highly controversial, for it is clear that it can have no application in circumstances in which the Court would have to go beyond what can reasonably be regarded as being a process of interpretation, and would have to engage in a process of rectification or revision. Rights cannot be presumed to exist merely because it might seem desirable that they should. . . .

* * *

In the light of these various considerations, the Court finds that the Applicants cannot be considered to have established any legal right or interest appertaining to them in the subject-matter of the present claims, and that, accordingly, the Court must decline to give effect to them.

For these reasons,

The Court,

by the President's casting vote—the votes being equally divided,

decides to reject the claims of the Empire of Ethiopia and the Republic of Liberia.

* * *

Dissenting Opinion of Judge Koretsky

I can in no way concur in the present Judgment mainly because the Court reverts in essence to its Judgment of 21 December 1962 on the same cases and in fact revises it even without observing Article 61 of the Statute and without the procedure envisaged in Article 78 of the Rules of Court.

The Court has said in the operative part of its Judgment that "the Applicants cannot be considered to have established any legal right or interest appertaining to them in the subject-matter of the present claims. . . ."

But the question of the Applicants' "legal right or interest" (referred to in short as their "interest") in their claims as a ground for instituting proceedings against the Respondent as Mandatory for South West Africa was decided already in 1962 in the first phase (the jurisdictional phase) of these cases.

At that time, the Respondent, asserting in its third preliminary objection that the conflict between the parties "is by reason of its nature and content not a 'dispute' as envisaged in Article 7 of the Mandate for South West Africa," added, "More particularly in that *no material interests* of the Governments of Ethiopia and/or Liberia or of their nationals are involved therein or affected thereby" (underlining added). The adjective "material" (interests) was evidently used not in its narrow sense—as a property interest.

In dismissing the preliminary objection of the Respondent the Court then said that "the manifest scope and purport of the provisions of this Article (i.e., Article 7) indicate that the Members of the League were understood to have a *legal right or interest* in the observance by the Mandatory of its obligations both toward the inhabitants of the mandated territory, and toward the League of Nations and its Members." (Underlining added.) (p. 343.). And a little later the Court said: "Protection of the material interests of the Members or their nationals is of course included within its compass, but the well-being and development of the inhabitants of the mandated territory are not less important" (p. 344).

So the question of the Applicants' interests in their claims was decided as, one might say, it should have been decided, by the Court in 1962. The question of an applicant's interest" (as a question of a "*qualité*") even in national-law systems is considered as a jurisdictional question. For example, "*le défaut d'intérêt*" of an applicant is considered in the French law system as a ground for "*fin-de-non-recevoir-de-procédure.*"

The Rules of Court, and the practice of the Court, do not recognize any direct line of demarcation between questions of the merits and those of jurisdiction. The circumstances of the case and the formulation of the submissions of the parties are of guiding if not decisive significance.

The Respondent, as noted above, raised the question of the Applicant's interest. The Court decided this question at that time. It did not consider it necessary to join it to the merits as the character of the Applicants' interests in the subject-matter of their claims was evident. Both Parties dealt with this question in a sufficiently complete manner. The Applicants, as will be noted later, did not seek anything for themselves; they asserted only that they have a "legal interest to seeing to it through judicial process that the sacred truth of civilization created by the Mandate is not violated." To join the question of the Applicants' "interests" in their claims to the merits would not "reveal" anything new, as became evident at this stage of the cases. And it is worthy of note that in the dissenting opinion of President Winiarski (pp 455ff.), in the joint dissenting opinion of Judge Sir Percy Spender and Sir Gerald Fitzmaurice (pp. 548ff.) and in the dissenting opinion of Judge *ad hoc* van Wyk (pp. 660ff.), the question of the Applicants' interests was considered on a jurisdictional plane.

The Respondent did not raise this question in its final submissions at this stage of the merits. The Court itself has now raised the question which was resolved in 1962 and has thereby reverted from the stage of the merits to the stage of jurisdiction. And thus the "door" to the Court which was opened in 1962 to decide the dispute (as the function of the Court demands (Article 38 of the Statute), the decision of which would have been of vital importance for the peoples of South West Africa and to peoples of other countries where an official policy of racial discrimination still exists, was locked by the Court with the same key which had opened it in 1962.

Has the 1962 Judgement of the Court a binding force for the Court itself?

The Judgment has not only a binding force between the parties (Article 59 of the Statute), it is final (Article 60 of the Statute). Being final, it is—one may say—final for the Court itself unless revised by the Court under the conditions and in accordance with the procedure prescribed in Article 61 of the Statute and Article 78 of the Rules of Court.

Dissenting Opinion of Judge Tanaka

*   *   *

Although we do not deny the power of the Court to re-examine jurisdictional and other preliminary matters at any stage of proceedings *proprio motu,* we consider that there are not sufficient reasons to overrule on this point the 1962 Judgment and that the Court should proceed to decide the questions of the "ultimate" merits which have arisen from the Applicant's final submissions.

We are again confronted with the question whether the Applicants possess a legal right or interest in the proper discharge by the Respondent, as the Mandatory, of the obligations incumbent upon it by virtue of the "conduct clauses" in the Mandate agreement.

A negative conclusion is derived either from the nature of the interest, or from the capacity of the Applicants.

It is argued that the dispute brought before the Court by the Applicants does not affect any material interest of the Applicant States or their nationals and is not envisaged in Article 7, paragraph 2, of the Mandate.

*   *   *

The personal structure of the mandates system is very complicated and *sui generis;* besides the mandatory, the League and the inhabitants of the territories, there are persons who are connected with the mandate in some way, particularly those who collaborate in the establishment or in the proper functioning of this system, such as the Principal Allied and Associated Powers and the Members of the League.

The interests corresponding to the categories of persons mentioned are multiple. Here, only the interest of Members of the League is in question, since the question of the existence of a legal interest of the Applicants as former Members of the League has now to be determined.

The interests which may be possessed by the Member States of the League in connection with the mandates system, are usually classified in two categories. The first one is the so-called national interest which includes both the interest of the Member States as States and the interest of their nationals (Article 5 of the Mandate). The second one is the common or general interest, which the Member States possess in the proper performance by the Mandatory of the Mandate obligations.

Whether the adjudication clause, namely Article 7, paragraph 2 of the Mandate can cover both kinds of interests, or only the first one, namely national interest, is the question that has to be answered in the present cases.

*   *   *

The interest which the Member States of the League possess regarding the proper administration of the Mandated Territory by the Mandatory is possessed by Members of the League individually, but it is vested with a corporate character. Each Member of the League has this kind of interest as a Member of the League, that is to say, in the capacity of an organ of the League which is destined to carry out a function of the League.

The question is, whether this kind of interest can be called *"legal interest," and whether law recognizes it as such.*

The historical development of law demonstrates the continual process of the cultural enrichment of the legal order by taking into consideration values or interests which had previously been excluded from the sphere of law. In particular, the extension of the object of rights to cultural, and therefore intangible, matters and the legalization of social justice and of humanitarian ideas which cannot be separated from the gradual realization of world peace, are worthy of our attention.

*   *   *

Each member of a human society—whether domestic or international—is interested in the realization of social justice and humanitarian ideas. The State which belongs as a member to an international organization incorporating such ideas must necessarily be interested. . . .

*   *   *

The supreme objectives of the mandates system, namely, the promotion of the well-being and social progress of the inhabitants of the Territory mentioned in Article 2, paragraph 2, of the Mandate, in spite of their highly abstract nature, cannot be denied the nature of a legal interest in which all Members of the League participate.

*   *   *

There are two main reasonings upon which the Court's denial of the Applicant's legal right now appears to be based. The one is the juridical character and structure of the institution, the League of Nations, within the framework of which the mandates system is both created and enshrined. The League functions "through the instrumentality of an Assembly and a Council" and "no role was reserved either by the Covenant or the mandate instruments to individual members. . . ."

*   *   *

The other reasoning is, that, in the Court's opinion, the Applicants do not possess a legal right directly or by a clearly necessary implication, through a substantive and not merely adjectival provision of the Mandate in the same way as they possess it by virtue of Article 5 of the Mandate which is concerned with the so-called "national rights" of the Member States. But in this case, whether a substantive right is conferred on Member States by that provision or not, is highly doubtful.

* * *

Although Article 5 of the Mandate is partly concerned with the national interest of the Member States of the League, the nature of this provision is not fundamentally different from that of the rest of the provisions of the Mandate. It possesses the same nature as the "conduct" clause. It does not confer upon the Member States any substantive right. They receive only a certain benefit as a "reflective" effect of the Mandate instrument, but not any right as an independent juridical act which does not exist.

* * *

Accordingly, the distinction between the "conduct" clause and the "national" clause is not an essential one. The latter must be considered as an integral part of the Mandatory's obligations which are derived from the objectives of the mandates system, namely the promotion of material and moral well-being and social progress. Whether some of the obligations are related to the interest of some of the Member States of the League or not, is quite immaterial to the nature of Article 5 of the Mandate.

Therefore the classification of the Mandate provisions into two categories, namely the conduct clause and the national clause, is of secondary importance.

As to the argument that the substantive right of the Applicants must be found, not in the jurisdictional, adjectival provision but in the substantive provision, we feel we should point out that in the Mandate the substantive and procedural elements are inseparably intermingled and that Article 7, paragraph 2, can confer substantive rights on the individual Member States of the League. . . .

* * *

In sum, Article 7, paragraph 2, as the means of judicial protection of the Mandate cannot be interpreted in such a way that it ignores the most fundamental and essential obligations of the Mandatory to carry out the "sacred trust" and excludes the "conduct clauses" from the "provisions" to which Article 7, paragraph 2, shall be applied. . . .

. . . we are unable to concur in the Court's opinion that the Applicants' claims are, on the ground of the lack of any legal right or interest, to be rejected.

Dissenting Opinion of Judge Jessup

Having very great respect for the Court, it is for me a matter of profound regret to find it necessary to record the fact that I consider the Judgment which the Court has just rendered by the casting vote of the President in the South West Africa case, completely unfounded in law. In my opinion, the Court is not legally justified in stopping at the threshold of the case, avoiding a decision on the fundamental question whether the policy and practice of apartheid in the mandated Territory of South West Africa is compatible with the discharge of the "sacred trust" confided to the Republic of South Africa as Mandatory.

Since it is my finding that the Court has jurisdiction, that the Applicants, Ethiopia and Liberia, have standing to press their claims in the Court and to recover judgment, I consider it my judicial duty to examine the legal issues in this case which has been before the Court for six years and on the preliminary phases of which the Court passed judgment in 1962. This full examination is the more necessary because I dissent not only from the legal reasoning and factual interpretations in the Court's Judgment but also from its entire disposition of the case. . . .

* * *

This is the fifth time the Court has given consideration to legal matters arising out of the administration by the Republic of South Africa of the mandated territory of South West Africa. In the course of three Advisory Opinions rendered in 1950, 1955 and 1956, and in its Judgment of 21 December 1962, the Court never deviated from its conclusion that the Mandate survived the dissolution of the League of Nations and that South West Africa is still a territory subject to the Mandate. By its judgment of today, the Court in effect decides that Applicants have no standing to ask the Court even for a declaration that the territory is still subject to the Mandate.

* * *

In reaching that conclusion the court had to reject the four preliminary objections filed by the Respondent. It did reject the four objections and thereby substantially held:

1. that the Mandate for South West Africa is a "treaty or convention in force" within the meaning of Article 37 of the Statute of the Court;

2. that despite the dissolution of the League, Ethiopia and Liberia had *locus standi* under Article 7, paragraph 2, of the Mandate, to invoke the jurisdiction of the Court;

3. that the dispute between the Applicants and the Respondent was a "dispute" as envisaged in Article 7, paragraph 2, of the Mandate; and

4. that the prolonged exchanges of differing views in the General Assembly of the United Nations constituted a "negotiation" within the

meaning of Article 7, paragraph 2, of the Mandate and revealed that the dispute was one which could not be settled by negotiation within the meaning of that same provision of the Mandate.

* * *

The Court now in effect sweeps away this record of 16 years and, *on a theory not advanced by the Respondent in its final submissions of 5 November 1965*, decides that the claim must be rejected on the ground that the Applicants have no legal right or interest.

The Applicants have not asked for an award of damages or for any other material amend for their own individual benefit. They have in effect, and in part, asked for a declaratory judgment interpreting certain provisions of the Mandate for South West Africa. The Court having decided in 1962 that they had standing (*locus standi*) to bring the action, they are now entitled to a declaratory judgment without any further showing of interest.

* * *

Whether any further right, title or interest is requisite to support Applicants' requests in this case for orders by the Court directing Respondent to desist from certain conduct alleged to be violative of its legal obligations as Mandatory, may well be a separate question, but the Judgment of the Court denies them even the declaratory judgment. . . .

* * *

The Judgment of the Court today does not constitute a final binding judicial decision on the real merits of the controversy litigated in this case. In effect reversing its Judgment on 21 December 1962, it rejects the Applicants' claims *in limine* and precludes itself from passing on the real merits. The Court therefore has *not* decided, as Respondent submitted, "that the whole Mandate for South West Africa lapsed on the dissolution of the League of Nations and that Respondent is, in consequence thereof, no longer subject to any legal obligations thereunder."

Further, the Court has *not* decided, as submitted by the Respondent in the alternative, that the Mandatory's former obligations to report, to account and to submit to supervision had lapsed upon the dissolution of the League of Nations.

The Court has *not* rendered a decision contrary to the fundamental legal conclusions embodied in its Advisory Opinion of 1950 supplemented by its Advisory Opinions of 1955 and 1956 and substantially reaffirmed in its Judgment of 1962.

Even more important is the fact that the Court has *not* decided that the Applicants are in error in asserting that the Mandatory, the Republic of South Africa, has violated its obligations as stated in the Mandate and in Article 22 of the Covenant of the League of Nations. In other words, the charges by the Applicants of breaches of the sacred trust which the Mandate imposed on South Africa are not judicially refuted or rejected by the Court's decision.

*   *   *

The Judgment of the Court rests upon the assertion that even though—as the Court decided in 1962—the Applicants had *locus standi* to institute the actions in this case, this does not mean that they have the legal interest which would entitle them to a judgment on the merits. No authority is produced in support of this assertion which suggests a procedure of utter futility. Why should any State institute any proceeding if it lacked standing to have judgment rendered in its favour if it succeeded in establishing its legal or factual contentions on the merits? Why would the Court tolerate a situation in which the parties would be put to great trouble and expense to explore all the details of the merits, and only thereafter be told that the Court would pay no heed to all their arguments and evidence because the case was dismissed on a preliminary ground which precluded any investigation of the merits?

*   *   *

Since, as I have explained, I believe the judicial task of the Court in interpreting Article 2 of the Mandate, is to be performed by applying appropriate objective standards—as, in other contexts, courts both international and national have done—it is not necessary for me to enter here into the meaning of a legal "norm" either as the term appears to have been used in the pleadings in this case, or with one or more of the connotations to be found in jurisprudential literature. This section of the Opinion has shown that the standard to be applied by the Court must be one which takes account of the views and attitudes of the contemporary international community. This is not the same problem as proving the establishment of a rule of customary international law, and I have already explained that I do not accept Applicants' alternative plea which would test the apartheid policy against an assumed rule of international law ("norm"). It is therefore not necessary to discuss here whether unanimity is essential to the existence of *communis opinio juris*. It has also been plainly stated herein that my conclusion does not rest upon the thesis that resolutions of the General Assembly have a general legislative character and by themselves create new rules of law. But the accumulation of expressions of condemnation of apartheid as reproduced in the pleadings of Applicants in this case, especially as recorded in the resolutions of the General Assembly of the United Nations, are proof of the pertinent contemporary international community standard. Counsel for Respondent, in another connection, agreed that "the effect of obtaining the agreement of an organization like the United Nations would, for all practical purposes, be the same as obtaining the consent of all the members individually, and that would probably be of decisive practical value," for the United Nations "represents most of the civilized States of the world." It is equally true that obtaining the disagreement, the condemnation of the United Nations, is of decisive practical—and juridical—value in determining the applicable standard. This Court is bound to take account of such a concensus as providing the standard to be used in the interpretation of Article 2 of the Mandate. . . .

Accordingly, it must be concluded that the task of passing upon the Applicants' third submission which asserts that the practice of apartheid is in violation of the Mandatory's obligations as stated in Article 2 of the Mandate and Article 22 of the Covenant of the League of Nations, is a justifiable issue, not just a political question. Therefore, the legal interest of Applicants in the proper administration of the Mandate, as set forth in other parts of this Opinion, was properly invoked by the Applications filed on 4 November 1960, and the Court should, in my opinion, have given judgment on the real merits of the case.

Conclusion

In the *South West Africa Cases,* states were left without a legal remedy against an alleged breach of international obligation, while the United Nations General Assembly remained the real disputant with South Africa. Yet, the United Nations can obtain only an advisory opinion, not a declaratory judgment with respect to this legal issue. Here is one of the many lacunae in the development of international law. In this instance, an amendment of the Statute of the International Court of Justice to allow the United Nations organization to be a party before the Court in certain contentious cases may be a way of filling this gap. But it illustrates the need for political decisions to improve the international judicial process. On 27 October 1966 the General Assembly adopted a resolution by 114 votes to 2, with 3 abstentions, terminating the South African League of Nations Mandate on South West Africa and placing the territory under the direct responsibility of the United Nations. A committee was established to recommend practical measures to administer the territory and enable its people to achieve self-determination, while South Africa continued to assert and maintain its rights.

International law, now or in the future, cannot be substituted for international politics. Nevertheless, a substantial improvement in international lawmaking must be made soon if legal definitions, procedures, and judgments ever hope to bridle a few of the startling changes in international relations today that threaten to jar the universe. Lawmaking cannot proceed more rapidly than the shared values of a community, and these, in turn, depend on a rough harmony of economic, ideological, aesthetic, and other interests. International law can be no better than the international political system that nurtures it. But politics cannot escape the rule of law, for law prescribes the right use of power. By strengthening international law, the hope of world order with justice may someday be realized.

FOR FURTHER STUDY

HERBERT W. BRIGGS. *The International Law Commission.* Ithaca, N.Y.: Cornell University Press, 1965.

ROSALYN HIGGINS. *The Development of International Law Through the Political Organs of the United Nations.* London: Oxford University Press, 1963.

D. W. BOWETT. *The Law of International Institutions.* London: Stevens and Sons, 1963.

Index

*This book has been set in 10 point Janson,
leaded 2 points, and 9 point Janson, leaded 1
point. Chapter numbers are 36 point Bulmer,
and chapter titles are 30 point Bulmer italic.
The size of the type page is 27 by 47 picas.*